IRISH STUDIES

IRISH STUDIES

Irish Studies presents a wide range of books interpreting important aspects of Irish life and culture to scholarly and general audiences. The richness and complexity of the Irish experience, past and present, deserves broad understanding and careful analysis. For this reason an important purpose of the series is to offer a forum to scholars interested in Ireland, its history, and culture. Irish literature is a special concern in the series, but works from the perspectives of the fine arts, history, and the social sciences are also welcome, as are studies which take multidisciplinary approaches.

Irish Studies is a continuing project of Syracuse University Press and is under the general editorship of Richard Fallis, associate professor of English at Syracuse University.

Irish Studies, edited by Richard Fallis

Children's Lore in Finnegans Wake. Grace Eckley
The Drama of J. M. Synge. Mary C. King
Fionn mac Cumhaill: Celtic Myth in English Literature. James MacKillop
Great Hatred, Little Room: The Irish Historical Novel. James M. Cahalan
Hanna Sheehy-Skeffington: Irish Feminist. Leah Levenson and Jerry Natterstad
In Minor Keys: The Uncollected Short Stories of George Moore. Edited by David B. Eakin and Helmut E. Gerber
Ireland Sober, Ireland Free: Drink and Temperance in Nineteenth-Century Ireland. Elizabeth Malcolm
Irish Life and Traditions. Edited by Sharon Gmelch
The Irish Renaissance. Richard Fallis
The Literary Vision of Liam O'Flaherty. John N. Zneimer
Northern Ireland: The Background to the Conflict. Edited by John Darby
Peig: The Autobiography of Peig Sayers of the Great Blasket Island. Translated by Bryan MacMahon
Selected Short Stories of Padraic Colum. Edited by Sanford Sternlicht
Shadowy Heroes: Irish Literature of the 1890s. Wayne E. Hall
Ulster's Uncertain Defenders: Protestant Political, Paramilitary and Community Groups and the Northern Ireland Conflict. Sarah Nelson
Yeats. Douglas Archibald

ELIZABETH MALCOLM

'Ireland Sober, Ireland Free'

DRINK AND TEMPERANCE IN NINETEENTH-CENTURY IRELAND

Syracuse University Press
1986

Copyright © 1986 by Elizabeth Malcolm
Published in Dublin by Gill and Macmillan
Published in the United States of America
by Syracuse University Press
Syracuse, New York 13244-5160
All Rights Reserved
ISBN 0-8156-2366-6
Print origination in Ireland by Keywrite, Dublin
Printed in Great Britain
by Richard Clay (The Chaucer Press) Ltd, Bungay, Suffolk

For John Malcolm

Contents

Preface   ix

Acknowledgments   xi

Abbreviations   xiii

1 Drink and Temperance in Ireland
before 1830   1

*Drink and its Critics: Sixteenth and Seventeenth
   Centuries*   1
*Drink and its Critics: Eighteenth and Early
   Nineteenth Centuries*   21

2 Moderation *versus* Teetotalism,
1829-38   56

3 'Mathew the Martyr'   101

4 Realignments:
the 1850s and 1860s   151

Temperance and Ulster Revivalism   153
The Temperance Movement within the Catholic Church   181
The Legislative Campaigns of the 1860s   192

5 Temperance in Parliament,
1870-1900   206

The Licensing Laws   206
The Fight for Sunday Closing, 1870-78   217
Temperance and the Liberal Government, 1880-85   251
Temperance and the Home Rule Party   261
Temperance in Decline from 1885   266

6 Temperance and the Churches
  after 1870   276

  Temperance and the Protestant Churches   276
  Temperance and the Catholic Church   293
  Father James Cullen and the Pioneers   306

Conclusion   322

Notes   335

Bibliography   343

Index   356

Preface

THIS book is a history both of the temperance movement and of changing patterns of alcohol consumption in Ireland. Much has been written by historians in Britain, Europe, North America and Australasia on the activities of temperance societies during the nineteenth century, while doctors, sociologists, psychologists and anthropologists have examined current and past levels of drink consumption. Yet it has seemed to me that the two subjects, drink and temperance, are inseparable, in that to understand the preoccupations of the temperance movement in a particular country one needs to know something of that country's drinking pattern. Drinking patterns differ widely and are almost as characteristic of a nation as its language. To what extent temperance movements affected drinking habits is a controversial issue, and one on which scholars would disagree, but it is an issue that can only be addressed through an examination of both drink and temperance. This is not to say, however, that the temperance movement in Ireland or elsewhere was a simple or direct response to rising levels of alcohol consumption. Many complex factors were at work in the spread of temperance societies from the 1820s: changing attitudes to work and recreation, new concepts of socially acceptable behaviour, the rise of Evangelicalism and changes in the social structure were but some of the forces involved. If it does nothing else, this study should demonstrate that changes in drinking habits and the development of the temperance movement are extremely complicated phenomena.

This book begins with a survey of drink consumption in the seventeenth and eighteenth centuries and an examination of the views of some of the critics of Irish drinking habits. This survey particularly highlights the enormous increase in whiskey consumption that occurred in Ireland after 1780 and the alarm that it aroused among members of the gentry and middle classes, who were at the same time beginning to curb their notorious fondness for massive amounts of wine. Chapter 2 examines the anti-spirits movement from 1829 and the introduction of teetotalism to Ireland, while Chapter 3 describes Father Mathew's great temperance crusade which began in 1838. Though the elitist anti-spirits movement had important successes among Protestants, particularly in Ulster, it had little impact on drink consumption, which appears to have reached record levels in the middle to late 1830s. Father Mathew's mass crusade, on the other hand, did significantly diminish whiskey consumption and also for the first time allied the temperance movement with Catholicism and nationalism. This alliance, however, proved to be a difficult one, and its problems are explored in some detail during the 1840s and afterwards. The remaining three chapters examine the temperance movement and drinking patterns after the famine. Chapter 4 looks at new developments in the 1850s and 1860s, particularly at the growth of teetotalism in Ulster in conjunction with revivalism and Evangelicalism; at efforts by some members of the Catholic hierarchy to revive a temperance movement within the church; and finally at the beginning of a well-organised campaign to secure temperance legislation for Ireland. Chapters 5 and 6 extend this analysis to the end of the century and somewhat beyond, mainly examining the ultimate frustration of the campaign at Westminster and the rise of a new Catholic teetotal crusade in the form of the Pioneer Total Abstinence Association.

In conclusion I have argued that, despite the popular reputation that the Irish have gained as problem drinkers, the temperance movement has had some remarkable successes, so that today Ireland has a higher proportion of teetotallers in its population than almost any country outside the Islamic world. As well as throwing light on a number of previously obscure, though interesting, areas of Irish history, I hope that this study will demonstrate that the stereotype of the drunken 'Paddy' is but one side of the coin of Irish drinking habits; the other side features the teetotal 'Paddy' — an important figure who is too often ignored.

Acknowledgments

THIS work has been long in the making, and many more people contributed to it than I think my publishers would allow me space to record. There are, however, a number of institutions, colleagues and friends whose assistance and support I do very much want publicly to acknowledge. Firstly, I have to thank Professor Pat O'Farrell of the University of New South Wales, Sydney, whose superb teaching inspired my interest in Irish history and who suggested the subject of this book, and secondly, the late Professor T. W. Moody of Trinity College, Dublin, who supervised the thesis on which the present work is based; a meticulous scholar and a generous man, he is greatly missed. I would also particularly like to thank the Queen's University of Belfast, which provided me with fellowships that made the writing of this book possible. At Queen's Professor David Harkness of the Modern History Department and Dr Ronnie Buchanan, Director of the Institute of Irish Studies, were unstinting in their support during a very difficult period.

Libraries and archives in Ireland, both north and south, England, Australia and Norway have facilitated my work, but I would especially like to acknowledge the assistance given me in Dublin by the Friends' Library, Eustace Street; the Capuchin friaries at Raheny and in Church Street; the Pioneer office, Sherrard Street; the library of the Church of Ireland, Braemor Park; the Dublin Diocesan Archives, Holy Cross College, Clonliffe; the Folklore Department at University College; the library of the Royal Irish Academy; the State Paper Office, Dublin Castle; Trinity College Library; and the National Library of Ireland. In Belfast working in the Linenhall Library and in the Public Record Office of Northern Ireland has been, in admittedly very different ways, a pleasure. In Cork the late Pádraig Ó Maidín of the County Library was always ready to answer queries, while the staffs of the City Library and University College Library were generous in their assistance. I would also like to mention the efforts — unfortunately fruitless — made by Father Fergal McGrath, archivist of the Irish province of the Society of Jesus, to trace the papers of

Father James Cullen. Perhaps readers of this book may be able to throw light on their whereabouts.

Many colleagues and friends have contributed information and advice from their own specialist fields, and I want to thank in particular Dr Roger Blaney, Dr Vincent Comerford, Nancy Curtin, Professor Jim Donnelly, John Gamble of the Emerald Isle Bookshop, Belfast, Dr Jackie Hill, Jack Johnston, Dr Peter Jupp, Stephen Lalor, Dr Bill Lowe, Dr Brian Walker, Dr Dick Walsh and Dr Chris Woods. Other friends have provided equally essential encouragement and support during long years of research and writing. My debts to Jean Cathcart, Tonie van Marle, Dr Bob Mahony and Tina Mahony are many; to Dr Ruth Sherry, Kate O'Kelly and Dr Bill Vaughan my debts are beyond calculation. I only regret that my father, William David Johnston from Killymackin, Co. Fermanagh, did not live to see this book in print. Finally, the dedication redeems an old pledge and acknowledges, with undiminished affection, a moment that is now history.

Abbreviations

A.T.S.	American Temperance Society
B.T.A.A.	Belfast Total Abstinence Association
C.E.T.S.	Church of England Temperance Society
C.I.T.A.A.	Church of Ireland Total Abstinence Association
C.I.T.S.	Church of Ireland Temperance Society
C.M.S.	Church Missionary Society
C.T.A.S.	Cork Total Abstinence Society
D.M.P.	Dublin Metropolitan Police
D.T.A.S.	Dublin Total Abstinence Society
D.T.S.	Dublin Temperance Society
H.T.S.	Hibernian Temperance Society
I.A.P.I.	Irish Association for the Prevention of Intemperance
I.P.B.A.	Irish Permissive Bill Association
I.S.C.A.	Irish Sunday Closing Association
I.T.L.	Irish Temperance League
I.T.U.	Irish Temperance Union
L.G.V.A.	Licensed Grocers' and Vintners' Association
N.T.A.A.	National Total Abstinence Association
R.I.C.	Royal Irish Constabulary
U.K.A.	United Kingdom Alliance
U.T.S.	Ulster Temperance Society

Drink and Temperance in Ireland before 1830

Drink and its Critics:
Sixteenth and Seventeenth Centuries

WHEN exactly distilling was first introduced into Ireland remains somewhat obscure. References to 'aqua vitae' or 'usquebaugh' do not appear in Irish sources until the fourteenth century, though it is thought that the art of distilling was invented in the twelfth century, possibly in Spain or southern Italy. Fermented liquors such as ale and mead had, however, long been staple drinks among the Celtic peoples. The Irish sagas contain many references to beer drinking, often to great feats of drinking. Thus Conchobor, King of Ulster, had at Emain Macha a beer vat known as the 'iron-chasm' into which a hundred fillings went every evening, but which could satisfy all the warriors of Ulster at one sitting. (**298**, 61; **208**, 6) It is interesting in this context to note that the name of the Celtic goddess Medb, who appears as the Queen of Connacht in the *Táin Bó Cuailnge,* literally means 'she who intoxicates' — a clear indication of the significance of drink in Celtic culture. (**342**, 327, 340) Even after the coming of Christianity references to beer drinking in the literature of Celtic Ireland were common. In an eleventh-century poem St Bridget, in the course of describing heaven, remarks:

I would like to have a great lake of beer for Christ the King.
I'd like to be watching the heavenly family drinking it down
through all eternity.
(**269**, 40; **193**, 284)

There is no suggestion in these lines of any contradiction between Christianity and alcohol consumption. References to wine occur during this period as well, though they are less frequent. In the famous poem 'The Old Woman of Beare', which probably dates from the tenth century, the old woman laments:

I who had my days with kings
And drank deep of mead and wine
Drink wheywater with old hags
Sitting in their rags and pine.   (**264**, 37)

As this verse indicates, drinking was a noble pastime, suggestive of the wealth and hospitality of kings. Mead was regarded as a warrior's drink, while only rulers could have afforded imported wine.

The coming of distilled drink in the fourteenth century and of more centralised English government in the sixteenth produced attitudes to alcohol that were more complicated and in some cases more negative. Spirits were valued at first purely for their medicinal properties. The Red Book of Ossory, which largely dates from the fourteenth century, contains an interesting 'Treatise on Aqua Vitae' in Latin. The author, undoubtedly a cleric, describes various methods of distilling 'aqua vitae', but regards its use as solely medicinal, recommending it as an unfailing remedy for numerous diseases. (**38**, 254-6) In Europe generally the art of distilling was spread by monks and apothecaries. Spirit drinking became increasingly popular after the Black Death of the late 1340s, and spirits were frequently prescribed by doctors in cases of plague and other fevers. (**342**, 341) Yet, surprisingly, the first reference to the consumption of whiskey in the Irish annals is a decidedly negative one. Under the year 1405 the Annals of Clonmacnoise state that 'Richard Magranell, chieftain of Moyntyreolas, died at Christmas by taking a surfeit of aqua vitae, to him aqua mortis.' (**256**, 325; **268**, 785; **155**, 283-93) By 1556 whiskey had gained such a hold on the popular taste that the English government felt it necessary to impose legislative controls. The preamble to the statute (3 & 4 P. & M., c. 7) remarked that 'Aqua vitae, a drink nothing profitable to be daily drunken and used, is now universally throughout the realm of Ireland made.' The act went on to decree that all those making whiskey, except for peers, gentlemen and borough freemen making it for their own use, would henceforth require a licence from the Lord Deputy. (**17**, I, 251) Given the lawless state of the country and the limited resources of the administration, it is most unlikely, however, that this act was at all strictly enforced. In fact nearly thirty years later, in 1584, the Lord Deputy received a 'brief note . . . for the reformation of the realm of Ireland', one of the principal suggestions of which was that 'the statute for the making of aqua vitae be put in execution, which sets the Irish mad and breeds many mischiefs'. (**81**, II, 398)

Even at this early date whiskey drinking was regarded by those in authority as helping to foster a spirit of recklessness and rebelliousness among the Irish — an attitude which was to persist well into the nineteenth century. So dangerous was whiskey considered that its manufacture was banned in Munster in 1571. Sir John Perrot, Lord President of the province, decreed a fine of £4 for the making and selling of whiskey, which he described as 'no common drink profitable to be drunk or used, and thereby much corn consumed, spent and wasted'. (**81**, I, 411) In 1602 a government memorandum noted that some London merchants were shipping 'white aqua vitae', costing 2s 8d a gallon in London, to Carrickfergus, colouring it 'the same yellowish with little cost like the Irish usquebaugh', and selling it to the rebels at 10s a gallon. The Irish evidently preferred their own spirits, or in this case an imitation of it, to that produced in England. The memorandum went on to advise that the trade in whiskey should be restricted, as it was 'one of the principal provisions which the rebels accustom themselves to carry and doth give them more relief and comfort than any other liquor'. (**4**, 509-10) Nor apparently did the situation change much in the following thirty years, for a memorandum of 1632 warned that the drinking of 'usquebaugh' was 'continual and extraordinary and impoverishes the country' and moreover was indulged in excessively by the most rebellious part of the population. (**9**, 169)

Critical comments, such as those just quoted, were common in the writings of sixteenth- and seventeenth-century observers of the Irish scene. They were very much part of the general critique of Irish life put forward by the English conquerors and doubtless reflected the need felt by a colonising power to denigrate the people whom it was seeking to subdue and to 'civilise'. Yet these accounts should certainly not be dismissed merely as rationalisations for imperialism. That they may well have been, but there is still much useful information about Irish life contained in both official and unofficial English sources.

One aspect of Irish life that English soldiers and administrators displayed a marked interest in was the native alcohol. Fynes Moryson, Mountjoy's secretary, in his *Description of Ireland* published in 1617, declared that

> Irish aqua vitae, commonly called usquebaugh, is held the best in the world of that kind, which is made also in England, but nothing so good as that which is brought out of Ireland. And the usquebaugh is preferred before our aqua vitae, because of the mingling of raisins, fennel-seed, and other things mitigating the heat, and making the taste pleasant, makes it less inflame, and yet refresh the weak stomach with moderate heat and a good relish.

Having dwelt upon the peculiar attractions of Irish whiskey, Moryson was nevertheless severely critical of both the 'English-Irish' and the 'mere Irish' for being 'excessively given to drunkenness'. So while praising the drink, he condemned the drinker. A similar opinion came from Sir Josias Bodley, a soldier who spent nearly twenty years in Ireland. In an account of a visit in 1602-3 to Sir Richard Moryson, Fynes's brother, near Downpatrick, Bodley put forward his views on drink at some length. Of Irish whiskey in particular, he wrote:

> It was not without reason we drank usquebaugh for it was the best remedy against the cold of that night and good for dispersing the crude

vapours of the French wine; and pre-eminently wholesome in these regions, where the priests themselves ... and men and women of every rank — pour usquebaugh down their throats by day and by night, and that not for hilarity only which would be praiseworthy, but for constant drunkenness which is detestable.

Bodley's distinction between the pursuit of pleasure and the pursuit of drunkenness would not have carried much weight among later critics of drink, particularly as he thought 'the abstemious are self-conscious of some great crime, which they fear they would betray if drunk. For wine is the father of ebriety, but ebriety is the mother of truth.' (**151**, 226-7, 250, 338, 335)

As both these extracts suggest, whiskey was generally mixed with various herbs and spices and was still highly valued for its medicinal properties. Edmund Campion, writing in 1571, noted that both the inhabitants of the country and newcomers were much subject to 'distillations, rheums and fluxes', the remedy for which was an 'ordinary drink of aqua vitae, so qualified in the making that it dries more and inflames less than other hot confections'. (**335**, 15; **187**, 24) In 1589 Sir George Carew, attempting to recover cannon from the wrecks of the Armada off the coast of Co. Galway, wrote to his superiors in London that 'Our diver was nearly drowned, but Irish aqua vitae has such virtues as I hope of his recovery.' (**81**, III, 8) Naturally English visitors and settlers were anxious that their friends and patrons at home should have the opportunity of sampling this marvellous liquor. In 1632 the Earl of Cork sent a 'runlet of mild Irish usquebaugh' to Lord and Lady Coventry in London, advising that

If it please his lordship next his hart in the morning [before breakfast] to drink a little of this Irish usquebaugh as it is prepared and qualified, it will help to digest all raw humours, expel wind, and keep his inward parts warm all the day after without any offence to his stomach. (**7**, 674)

It was not only whiskey, 'qualified' with herbs and spices, that was used as a form of preventive medicine; beer and wine were used similarly. In 1602 Josias Bodley, after a night of drinking wine and whiskey with Richard Moryson, was brought while still in bed the next morning

a certain aromatic of strong ale compounded with sugar and eggs ... to comfort and strengthen the stomach; they also bring beer (if any prefer it) with toasted bread and nutmeg to allay thirst, steady the head and cool the liver.

It should also be noted that the wine which Bodley was offered the previous evening contained burnt sugar, nutmeg and ginger and was intended to warm him after his long, cold ride. Similarly, in 1635 another English soldier, Sir William Brereton, on a visit to Carrickfergus was given 'cinnamon in burnt wine claret' to drink as a means of warding off 'the flux'. (**151**, 339, 332, 371) As these examples demonstrate, it was not only the Irish rebels who gained 'relief and comfort' from the country's liquors, whether whiskey, beer or wine. But perhaps the most telling account of the comforts that drink afforded Ireland's rulers occurs much later in the century. In June 1670 Sir Ellis Leighton, secretary to the Lord Lieutenant, in a letter from Dublin Castle to an official in London, complained that he was ill, as 'the air of this country does not agree with me'. Eating and drinking were the only solaces of Ireland, Leighton went on, and 'we shall have much ado to find matter for letters except we tell you whose healths we drink'. Exactly what drink offered such solace was revealed in September in another letter to the same correspondent. Leighton remarked in passing that, having returned to Dublin from England, he had been drunk for days with 'plentifulness of "the creature" '. (**13**, 145-6, 275)

Nor were the Irish themselves slow to note English tastes. The poet Dáibhí Ó Bruadair, in an elegy on the death of the Earl of Clancarty composed about 1665, wrote with resentment referring to his country: 'Her heroes' ale by upstarts quaffed'. (**233**, I, 121) If Ó Bruadair had substituted 'whiskey' for 'ale', his line might have been closer to the truth. For, while Irish whiskey was almost universally praised by the English, opinions of Irish beer and ale were much more mixed. In 1635 Sir William Brereton was entertained at Clonmullen Castle in Co. Carlow by Sir Morgan Kavanagh, being offered 'good beer, sack and claret, whereof he was no niggard'. But later in his travels, in Wexford town, Brereton was invited to dinner by the mayor and given 'a kind of beer (which I durst not taste) called chanter beer, mighty thick, muddy stuff'. (**151**, 389, 397) Similarly, the anonymous English author of *Advertisements for Ireland*, a description of the country during the reign of James I, written about 1623, thought that

> Scarce anywhere out of Dublin and some few other towns will you meet with any good beer... for your money, only you may have some raw, muddy, unwholesome ale, made solely of oats, which they buy there for 5d the quarter at the dearest and commonly for 4d, and yet they sell their ale pots dearer than here [England] they do the best beer.

Despite the poor quality of the drink, the profit from ale selling was 'so sweet' ('more than six for one', according to this observer) that the 'very aldermen themselves set up half a dozen alehouses apiece sometimes'. (**260**, 34-5) Thus the monopoly of granting alehouse licences, held at the time by Sir Thomas Roper, later Viscount Baltinglass, was far more valuable than that of granting licences to retail wine and whiskey. Roper charged 3s 6d for each alehouse registered and in return paid the state £2,000 per annum. So it is probable that there were at least 12,000 registered houses, and doubtless numerous unregistered ones, serving a population of between 1.4 and 2.1 million. (**260**, 16; **127**, 389; **6**, 390) Some perspective on this figure can be gained by noting that in the late 1830s, during a period of high alcohol consumption, there were between 20,000 and 21,000 beer retailers in Ireland serving a population of nearly 8 million. (**343**, 403) Although none of these figures can be considered highly reliable, they do suggest that complaints about the excessive numbers of alehouses in the first half of the seventeenth century may have had some basis in fact.

The author of *Advertisements for Ireland* exempted Dublin from his criticism as to the quality of Irish beer, but not so Barnby Rich. Rich, an English soldier who had lived in Dublin for over fifty years (**135**), wrote in 1610 that the 'whole profit of the town stands upon alehouses and selling of ale'. According to Rich, there were 'whole streets of taverns', and it was 'as rare a thing, to find a house in Dublin without a tavern, as to find a tavern without a strumpet'. Most of the taverns were kept by women, but far from all were 'strumpets', Rich himself conceding that many were of the 'better sort, as the aldermen's wives'. Ale brewing was a domestic craft, for 'every householder's wife is a brewer', so it was logical that many women should move on from making ale to selling it as well. Beer, both strong and small, was produced by three or four large 'brew-houses'. Like the author of the *Advertisements*, Rich was very critical of both the quality and the cost of Irish beer and ale. For instance, he claimed that a barrel of small beer costing 6s in Dublin would have sold in London for 4s and been 'better by odds'. Yet these admitted drawbacks do not seem to have deterred Rich from indulging himself to the full, for he goes on:

> I have been so long amongst these filthy alehouses, that my head begins to grow idle, and it is no wonder, for the very remembrance of that hogswash which they use to sell for 2d the wine quart, is able to distemper any man's brains, and as it is neither good nor wholesome, so it is unfit for any man's drinking, but for common drunkards. (**293**, 70-3)

Rich was no 'common drunkard', and yet this is undoubtedly the voice of experience speaking. The poor quality of Irish beer was thoroughly attested by many a drinker and was to be a major factor retarding the growth of Irish brewing well into the nineteenth century.

In addition to whiskey and beer, wine was also consumed in large amounts in Ireland during this period. English observers spoke especially of French and Spanish wines: French claret and sack, a white wine from Spain or the Canary Islands. Fynes Moryson said that in Dublin French and Spanish wines were commonly sold by merchants in pints and quarts from their own cellars, though some were also sold in the city's alehouses.(**151**, 332-3, 371, 389, 226) During much of this period wine was in fact the most substantial Irish import, being exchanged for fish and hides. It was thus both plentiful and cheap. (**81**, I, 76) In 1569 an attempt was made to control imports and to increase revenue (11 Eliz., c. 1). The preamble to this act complained of the 'superfluous abundance of wines that are yearly discharged within this realm' and of the 'disordered trade of aliens, to creeks and unhaunted ports and places', whereby a 'grievous decay of tillage and husbandry, idleness the mother of all vices, rage and fury in the minds of the disordered people' had been created. (**17**, I, 353-6) The act attempted to rectify these problems by placing a duty of 40s per tun (252 gallons) on Spanish wines and 26s 8d on French and by designating sixteen ports through which wine could legally be imported. But the act was by no means a success. In 1580 Lord Justice Pelham, writing to Walsingham from Limerick, mentioned that Spanish wines were being landed by 'divers strange vessels . . . in all these western havens'. This, in the light of the naval threat posed by Spain, Pelham took 'to be a device to make many able pilots for this coast'. (**81**, II, 228) Given the subsequent fate of the Armada off the Irish coast, this device, if such it actually was, failed disastrously.

The concern shown by the English government regarding the state of the wine trade can be better appreciated when the substantial contribution that wine duties made to Irish revenue is realised. The collection of the impost of wine was better organised than any other aspect of the customs administration until the establishment in 1613 of a general customs farm. (**325**; **326**) The wine farm had been leased in 1584 to an Englishman, Henry Broncard, for £2,000 per annum. (**1**, 71; **81**, II, 375) He was succeeded in 1607 by James Hay, later Earl of Carlisle, and the farm remained in the hands of the Hay family until it was acquired by Lord Deputy Wentworth in the 1630s. (**199**, 402; **271**, I, 314) In 1580 Pelham had referred to the wine duties as the 'most certain revenue . . . here'. (**81**, II, 242) In 1611, for instance, out of a total revenue of nearly £25,000, the wine duties contributed nearly £1,900. Despite Pelham's claim, however, the money raised could vary considerably, particularly when embargoes were placed on trade with France or Spain, as they were after 1588. In 1602, for instance, when O'Neill was in rebellion with Spanish support, the wine duties were down to a mere £9 out of a total revenue of £9,000. This drastic decline is perhaps partly explained by Sir George Carew's claim in the previous year that O'Neill's agents and the Spaniards were deliberately attempting to destroy the trade because the 'queen's impost upon Spanish wines is a great means to enrich her to maintain her wars in Ireland'. (**81**, VI, 130, IV, 504-5, 62; **1**, 541-2) If true, this would represent the first attempt by an Irish rebel to undermine English government by cutting off its revenue from Irish drink.

The trade, however, quickly recovered from these vicissitudes. Among the few and scattered figures on the wine trade which survive from the seventeenth century is an account of wine imported into Ireland between September 1614 and September 1615. This shows imports running at 1,500 tuns or 378,000 gallons per annum, which, estimating a population of around 1.5 million, is a considerable figure. Eighteenth-century consumption would have generally exceeded it, but it is very substantial by nineteenth-century standards. Again, to take the late 1830s as a point of reference, with a population of around 8 million, wine imports were running at between 350,000 and 450,000 gallons per annum. (**321**, 190) The major part of the wine imported in 1614-15 came from France, with the three ports of Calais, Bordeaux and Saint-Malo accounting for 75 per cent of the total. Only 6.5 per cent came directly from Spain. But as nearly all the wine from Calais and Saint-Malo was described as sack, implying a Spanish origin, it would seem that most Spanish wine was shipped to Ireland through French ports. The Irish ports receiving most of the trade were, in order of importance, Cork, Limerick, Galway, Dublin and Waterford. (**199**, 404-7) Figures also survive for the year 1665, when imports were running at 991 tuns or nearly 250,000 gallons, 60 per cent of this being classed as French and 40 per cent as Spanish. But, given that the population had risen little, if not fallen, mainly as a result of the wars and famines of the 1640s and 1650s, the decline in consumption is not as dramatic as might at first be thought. Wine was still a substantial revenue earner, as out of a total import revenue of £387,000 wine duties accounted for £45,000, being exceeded only by the duties on tobacco. (**11**, 698) Another interesting feature of these figures is the appearance of brandy as a significant item: in 1665 256 tuns or 64,500 gallons of brandy were imported, yielding a customs revenue of over £10,000. Brandy was to be a popular drink in Ireland during the first half of the eighteenth century, but competing as it did with the native spirit, it was to be a particular target for criticism.

The wars, both internal and external, of the 1680s and 1690s, followed by the War of the Spanish Succession, disrupted the wine trade severely. According to figures available for the years 1693-7, wine imports varied from 86,000 to 224,000 gallons. No French wine at all is recorded as being imported in the years 1693-5, and only small amounts in 1696 and 1697. Imports of brandy were down to only 6,000 gallons in 1694, though they recovered rapidly to reach nearly 30,000 by 1697. Spanish wine continued to be imported in substantial amounts, though it is interesting to see Portuguese wine for the first time taking the major share of the Irish market, even if this was only to be a temporary phenomenon. The other main Irish item of import, tobacco, continued, however, to grow in significance. Imports rose from 1.8 million pounds in 1665 to 2.7 million in 1691 and had passed 3.0 million by 1697. (**18**, II, xcvi) The French wine trade did recover very rapidly when peace between England and France finally came in 1713. Within a year, probably for the first time, official Irish wine imports passed the one million gallon mark, and they were seldom to fall below this level during the next one hundred years.

It was not only English observers who had much to say about drink in

Ireland during the seventeenth century. Irish poets, in celebrating and lamenting their rapidly disintegrating culture, also had occasion to refer frequently to the subject. The poems of Dáibhí Ó Bruadair *(c.* 1625-98) from Co. Cork are full of interesting references to drink, some poems being wholly devoted to the subject. The slightly later poet, Aodhagán Ó Rathaille (1670-1726) of Kerry, is also significant in this regard. Ó Rathaille, famous for his fine traditional elegies on the deaths of friends and patrons, frequently celebrated their hospitality and generosity in food and drink. Thus Dermot O'Leary of Killeen, Co. Kerry, who died in 1696, is notable because 'Bacchus gave him power over drink', so that he could provide 'abundant wines in golden goblets'. John Blennerhassett of Ballyseedy, also in Kerry, who died in 1709, is lamented in similar fashion. At his table

> There was wine from beyond the sea, ales bursting,
> Brandy and sugar in the beginning of February,
> With the lords of Munster pleasantly about him.

References to wine, ale, brandy, and even punch can be found in these poems, but Ó Rathaille seems to have made only one significant reference to whiskey. This occurs in a lament for Donal O'Callaghan of Co. Clare, who died in 1724. Ó Rathaille describes O'Callaghan's feasts, with

> Wines, newly opened, being drunk, and jollity,
> Viands on spits, and usquebaugh on tables...
> Every moment fresh casks being opened for the multitude,
> With no ebb in the liquid coming to that drinking feast.

Yet Ó Rathaille was obviously sensitive to the charge of drunkenness, for at O'Callaghan's feasts, while the companies are 'discoursing uproariously' and 'falling down with feverish pulse', they are at the same time 'inebriate without offence to their neighbours'. (**139**, 129, 131, 205, 77) The same sensitivity can be seen in Ó Bruadair. For example, in an elegy of 1679 on the death of Maurice Fitzgerald of Castleisheen, Co. Cork, the poet praises the dead man's 'temperance ne'er by meads intoxicated'.

Poems celebrating the hospitality of noblemen are, of course, very traditional and highly stylised. The genre has a long history in Irish literature, to say nothing of European literature generally. But in the poems of Ó Bruadair in particular there is a much more personal note: personal in the sense of relating to a specific period and place, as well as to a specific man. In 1674 the town of Cork was notable to Ó Bruadair for its 'gaily lighted ale-shops', with their 'Many quarts and pints and many draughts of liquor... Heart's desire for tipplers'. And there can be no doubt that Ó Bruadair was a 'tippler', for later in the same poem, referring to himself, he says: 'from feats of drinking filled to waist am found then / Ear to wall reclining'. In another poem, written about the same time, he describes himself standing at the counter of an alehouse, with 'feeble pulse' and 'parched lips', longing for a 'naggin of cask-drawn ale'. But some of the less attractive sides of drinking were familiar to Ó Bruadair as well, and he did not hesitate to include them in his poems. He notes 'drink's delusive cunning' that 'set my brain absurdly rattling', and he devotes a whole poem to an apology for his bad behaviour after getting drunk on a friend's wine. Yet there can be no doubting where Ó Bruadair's preferences ultimately lay, as an undated though late poem clearly illustrates:

> My delight, I confess, hath been always, both last year and this
> year, to have
> A pipe of fine wine and a flagon with liquor filled up to the brim,
> To sit down in a state of half-folly and gaily to chatter away,
> And heed not the sneers of the man who aims at increasing
> his herds.
> (**233**, II, 179, 77, 91, 29, 42-7, III, 7)

From the writings of these two poets and of others of the seventeenth century the picture that generally emerges is of three main forms of drinking. Firstly, there was the heavy periodic drinking of wine, ale and whiskey at feasts given by the gentry for their friends and dependants. Drinking of this sort had an extremely long history in Irish society, though it is interesting to note that the poets praise equally the native Irish, the Old English and also the more recent planter gentry for their hospitality. Secondly, there are references to fairly regular wine drinking at meals by members of the small urban middle class, some doubtless being merchants actually involved in the wine trade. Finally, as Ó Bruadair's personal testimony graphically relates, there was substantial consumption of beer and ale in the many alehouses to be found in towns like Dublin and Cork. But outside the towns with their taverns and away from the gentry and merchants, who could afford drink with meals and feasts, the drinking pattern of the ordinary rural Irish is less clear from these poems. In fact perhaps the best description of the drinking habits of rural society comes from an English source already quoted, Fynes Moryson. Writing in the early years of the century, Moryson said:

> Neither have they any beer made of malt and hops, nor yet any ale — no, not the chief lords, except it be very rarely; but they drink milk like nectar, warmed with a stone first cast into the fire, or else beef-broth mingled with milk. But when they come to any market town to sell a cow or a horse they never return home till they have drunk the price in Spanish wine (which they call the King of Spain's daughter), or in Irish usquebaugh, and till they have outslept two or three days' drunkenness. And not only the common sort, but even the lords and their wives, the more they want this drink at home, the more they swallow it when they come to it, till they be as drunk as beggars. (**151**, 229)

Moryson is here describing the classic drinking pattern of an impoverished rural society: periodic drunken bouts associated with special occasions like markets, fairs, weddings and religious festivals, separated by long stretches of total sobriety. It was a pattern still evident in Irish rural society during the nineteenth century and described by temperance critics as 'circumstantial drinking'. (**37**, 354, 396)

There are indications that drink consumption may have declined in the latter half of the seventeenth century, compared with the levels it had reached earlier. Complaints about Irish drunkenness seem fewer. Thus, while Sir William Petty's comments in 1672 on the excessive number of alehouses in Dublin and other towns are often quoted, the fact that Petty makes no mention of drunkenness as a common vice is seldom noted. Of the rural poor, Petty says they drank small beer mainly, but claims that their most striking extravagance was tobacco. (**283**, 13-14, 80) John Dunton, a rather eccentric London bookseller travelling in the west in 1698, also noted beer drinking, but was careful to take a store of tobacco with him, it being a thing the Irish 'prefer to meat and drink, and which made me a welcome guest wherever I came'. (**237**, 329; **135**; **147**) These opinions are supported by the few statistics available. As already noted, while tobacco imports nearly doubled between the 1660s and 1690s, imports of wine declined from the levels reached at the beginning of the century. Apart from the impact of war, the actions of government probably also played a part in this decline. From the 1630s significant measures aimed at curbing and regulating the production and sale of drink in Ireland had been implemented.

Complaints about the excessive numbers of alehouses and the detrimental effects of whiskey consumption were frequent during the first third of the century. The fact that the rights to grant licences for the sale of beer and of whiskey and wine were farmed out to favoured individuals, who in turn sub-let these rights to others in prescribed areas, meant that the pursuit of profit rather than any consideration of need governed the granting of liquor licences. The alehouse farm was controlled by Viscount Baltinglass, while the wine and whiskey farm, originally granted by James I to Lady Arabella Stuart to help pay her debts, had by the 1620s passed to the Earl of Carlisle, who already farmed the import duties on wine. The appointment of trustees and sub-lessees further complicated an already complicated arrangement, as did the fact that many peers and boroughs claimed a right to grant licences in their own domains. The Old English were particularly critical of these monopolies, as they resented them being granted to English royal favourites or to recently arrived planters. (**5**, 71, 420, 373-81) In 1623 the Commissioners of Ireland for the Increase of Manufacture concluded that the licensing monoplies were 'proving beneficial only to some private persons', the king gaining 'small benefit', while the multiplication of alehouses was 'one occasion of the dearth of corn'. (**6**, 426) So great was discontent with the liquor monoplies that three of the Graces of 1628 referred specifically to the subject. In no. 5 the king agreed that no further action should be taken by the controllers of the wine and whiskey farm until the grant had been considered by the next parliament. In no. 6 he declared that the ale and beer monopoly had 'no ground of law' and discontinued it, ordering parliament to establish a new licensing system. In no. 14 the right of certain principal officials in Ireland to receive wine free of duty, established by the wine duties act of 1569, was confirmed and extended. (**105**, 239, 242)

Sir Thomas Wentworth, later Earl of Strafford, who arrived in 1633 as Lord Deputy with the task of implementing the Graces, was both an opponent of drunkenness and a champion of the royal revenues, and for both reasons he was opposed to the liquor monopolies. If this 'swinish vice', as he termed drunkenness, could be diminished, while at the same time revenue derived from it was augmented and diverted from private into royal pockets, all the better. (**210**, I, 486) Baltinglass was thus deprived of his monopoly of alehouse licences, though he was compensated with a levy on the clergy — much to the annoyance of the Archbishop of Armagh, who thought that those 'who enjoy alehouses should pay for them'. (**7**, 633) In 1635 parliament passed what amounted to Ireland's first licensing act (10 & 11 Chas I, c. 5). Part of the motivation behind the act can be gleaned from its preamble, which complained of the 'excessive number of ale-houses', many of them erected 'in woods, bogs, and other unfit places' and 'kept by unknown persons not undertaken for, whereby many times they become receptacles for rebels and other malefactors'. The act went on to empower the Lord Deputy to choose commissioners from among the justices of the peace, who were to grant licences for a fee of 5s 6d per annum, plus a £10 recognisance. The commisssioners, assembled at quarter sessions, in deciding whether or not to grant a licence were to consider the character of the applicant and the fitness and convenience of the house. Licensed houses were to provide 'provisions for travellers and strangers at reasonable rates', not to 'suffer any drunkenness... or any common dicing... nor willingly to harbour any suspected persons' and, moreover, were to be marked by 'some sign, stake, or bush' at the door. This act contained many of the cardinal provisions of liquor licensing even as it exists down to the present day. (**17**, II, 151)

Wentworth also moved to acquire the monopoly of wine duties and of wine and whiskey licensing, but as the licensee was reluctant to surrender his grants, this proved a slow process. It entailed protracted negotiations with the Earl of Carlisle and, after his death, with his widow and assignees. (**210**, II, 71, 76-7, 81, 89, 102) Peers and boroughs lost their licensing rights as well, though in some cases not before a good deal of resistance. Ever mindful of revenue, Wentworth accepted Grace no. 14, though inserting a limit of £375 worth of duty-free wine per year for each of the officials concerned. (**271**, I, 311; **41**, I, 101; **210**, I, 192, 317) In a memorandum to the king in July 1636 Wentworth estimated that the impost of wine would bring in an additional £2,000 per annum in government revenue, and the wine and whiskey licensing monopoly an additional £1,000, while the licensing of alehouses was already yielding £3,000. These are substantial sums, given that Irish customs revenue in 1636-7 amounted to less than £40,000. (**210**, II, 8)

The 1630s thus saw major steps taken by the government to control the drink industry, the licensing act of 1635 being of most lasting significance. In all cases, however, the government's efforts to recover monopolies granted by its predecessors were principally motivated by Charles I's need to provide himself with a substantial independent revenue. Concern at the amount of grain consumed by brewing and distilling and at the use of ale-houses by rebels were secondary considerations. Despite Wentworth's personal views on the 'infinite excess of drunkenness in this kingdom', there is no suggestion that the policies of this decade were motivated by a belief in the virtues of temperance. (**210**, I, 192)

If the early Stuarts sought to introduce a measure of control over the drink industry in Ireland in order to maximise revenue, the Cromwellians did the same, though accompanying their actions with fierce denun-ciations of drunkenness. A declaration of June 1653 indicated the govern-ment's intention of firmly enforcing the existing statutes against drunken-ness. Corporations and justices of the peace were urged to limit the numbers of alehouses and to prosecute drunkards, while in Cork in 1653 the sale of beer was banned altogether for a time. (**146**, II, 351; **61**, 40-1; **41**, 530) T. C. Barnard in his pioneering study *Cromwellian Ireland* sees such measures as part of the English government's campaign to reform Irish manners, 'particularly those of the native Irish, supposedly the main keepers of alehouses and the worst drunkards'. (**61**, 76) Thus, in government rhetoric, drunkards were lumped together with 'adulterers', 'fornicators' and 'gamesters' as social outcasts deserving of severe punish-ment. In fact, however, the Cromwellians did not launch the headlong assault on the drink industry that one might have expected of them, for the financial benefits to be derived from regulating, rather than suppressing, the industry were too attractive to be disregarded, particularly by a government desperately in need of revenue.

The commission established in 1650 for 'ordering and settling the affairs of Ireland' was instructed both to see to the collection of the customs and excise duties and to the punishment of drunkenness. The former instruction seems, however, to have been the more pressing concern. Having toured the main northern ports, the commission reported from Belfast in August 1651 that 'Concerning the customs and sequestrations little has been done here in a regular way, and in the excise nothing at all.' Back in Dublin in February 1652 the commission gave permission for the authorities in Belfast to farm out the excise, provided that the grants were made for a short period only. (**146**, I, 4, 16, 135) Generally, however, up until 1658 revenue collection was in the hands of local commissioners of revenue, who were appointed in each of the administrative districts into which the country had been divided. (**288**, 8) In 1655 duties on wine, beer and spirits were increased, largely to meet defence expenses, and in 1657 Henry Cromwell, the Lord Deputy, began seriously considering the desirability of farming both customs and excise on a large scale. Trade was poor, and much of the revenue generated was consumed by the employment of collectors; but, reasoned Cromwell, if farmers were appointed from among the merchants, they would 'improve trade considerably, and would possibly allow us twice as much as we can save clear, our officers being paid'. (**9**, 812; **146**, II, 677) The Protector and Council of State in London appear to have accepted this argument, for in May 1658 copies of a contract for the farm of Irish customs and excise, granted to Thomas Morrice and William Dodson, were forwarded to Henry Cromwell. (**9**, 858-9) Initially the new scheme seemed a great success, for whereas customs and excise had only yielded around £12,000 in 1657, they were farmed in 1658 for £70,000 per annum. Yet the farm was abruptly terminated with the Restoration, and the state papers for May 1666 contain an order by Charles II for an inquiry into the farm held under the 'late usurpers and until 24 June 1660', on the grounds that Morrice and Dodson had attempted to defraud the government of £10,000. Whether this order was an exercise in royalist revenge or whether the farm had really been mismanaged is unclear from the existing documentation. (**12**, 114; **288**, 6, 9)

After the Restoration the policies of the 1630s and 1650s were continued in various important ways. Duties on drink were increased and retail licensing extended, and despite the condemnation of the Cromwellian revenue farm, farming was renewed on an even larger scale. Four major acts were passed early in the 1660s aimed at remodelling the whole Irish system of customs and excise and of liquor licensing. By two measures of 1661-2 (14 & 15 Chas II, cc 8, 9) customs and excise duties were granted in perpetuity to the crown, becoming part of what was termed the hereditary revenue and thus replacing the old system of feudal dues. Customs duties were divided into two types called poundage and tunnage, the latter being paid by the merchant on each tun of wine imported. (**17**, II, 365-431; **288**, 2, 15-16) The excise was divided into import and inland excise: the former was paid on most imported products, including wine, by the retailer, while the latter consisted of duties on locally made beer, ale and spirits. Licence duties for the retailing of beer, wine and spirits were included in the inland excise and were regulated by acts passed in 1662 (14 & 15 Chas II, c. 18) and 1665 (17 & 18 Chas II, c. 19). (**17**, II, 511-15, III, 185-9)

The Act for the Settling of the Excise or New Impost upon His Majesty (14 & 15 Chas II, c. 8) was especially important as it introduced not only duties on beer and ale but a duty of 4d a gallon on locally made spirits (sections 2-4). Thus began a tax which was to become and remain a vital source of revenue in Ireland. The act also set out the framework of an excise administration charged with collecting these duties, modelled on the customs commissioners who had been operating since early in the century. An excise office was to be established in Dublin with five commissioners and a surveyor. Brewers and distillers were to make weekly reports of the amounts that they produced, and gaugers were to be appointed with power to enter houses and check returns (sections 30, 34, 42). This was certainly an important beginning, though it is doubtful that the system worked very well in practice. For instance, when the Revenue Commissioners made a tour through the country in 1683 examing the machinery of the collection system, they noted that inland excise was being avoided in many areas and was generally well in arrears. (**288**, 12-14) E. B. McGuire in his history of Irish whiskey sums up the problem well when he says:

> A new system of excise taxation and a new department began without experience except such as could be learned from the customs, without a trained staff and without any knowledge of the numbers needed to police and collect the duties efficiently. Staff of some kind would be necessary in a number of widely separated towns and not concentrated in a few places as in the customs. It was, in fact, the first attempt to set up a civil department where most of its members would be remote from immediate control. (**234**, 98)

Not until well into the nineteenth century was a reasonably effective system of assessing and collecting inland excise actually devised.

Licensing was also part of the inland excise, and it too underwent major reform in the 1660s. By the legislation of 1662 (14 & 15 Chas II, c. 18) the 1635 act licensing alehouses was reaffirmed, though with the fee for a licence raised to 20s per annum (section 1). This change is interesting because it seems to have been a deliberate attempt on the part of the Lord Lieutenant, the Duke of Ormond, to reduce the numbers of alehouses in the country, even at the cost of losing revenue. In a memorandum of 29 November 1662 outlining the state of Irish revenue, Ormond estimated that there were about 7,000 holders of alehouse licences. Most were 'very poor' and lived in 'remote places', and thus it was thought 'desirable to reduce their number'. (**10**, 637) In fact initially the fee proposed was 30s, but the committee examining the bill in the Irish parliament rejected this as 'excessive', suggesting instead 10s. The committee acknowledged that most keepers of alehouses were poor and would be unable to 'pay so great a fine for a licence at one entire payment, over the charge in travelling to obtain the same'. It did not, however, favour a reduction in the number of alehouses, arguing that any lessening in 'houses of entertainment will lessen the excise, will disappoint [travellers] of having of lodging, and soldiers of quarter and will be very prejudicial to the country in general, by bringing down the price of corn'. (**18**, I, 538) But, as already noted, Ormond did in fact propose to reduce the numbers of alehouses. The fee of 20s which eventually appeared in the act was presumably a compromise between the Lord Lieutenant and parliament.

In 1665 another important licensing act was passed (17 & 18 Chas II, c. 19) which in effect extended the licensing provisions already imposed on alehouses to the sellers of wine and spirits. These retailers had required licences under the old wine and whiskey licence farm, but it is significant that whereas alehouses had been licensed by statute from 1635, it was to be thirty years before other liquor sellers were similarly licensed. (**81**, VI, 99, 207) Such a time-lag would suggest that alehouses were more numerous and more of a problem to control. This is further implied by the relative cost of licences. Fees for wine and spirit licences were on a sliding scale: in the case of the former ranging from £2 to £40 per annum, and in the case of the latter from 10s to £10 (section 2). With costs like these, wine and whiskey sellers must have been more prosperous and therefore fewer in number than the 'very poor' alehouse keepers referred to by Ormond in 1662

Farming of the various sections of the Irish revenue continued after 1660, though between 1669 and 1682 one farm of the whole of the revenue was granted to a succession of syndicates. This policy, however, was not a success, and from 1683 the management of revenue was turned over completely to a number of government-appointed commissioners. (**261**, 200-3; **312**, 400-2; **288**, 6) In 1665 wine and spirit licences had been farmed for £4,000 per annum, but twenty years later, in 1685, they were yielding only £3,500, which suggests either an inefficient collection system or a decline in demand. Over the same period the revenue from ale licences jumped from £3,400 per annum to nearly £10,000. (**11**, 555, 598; **261**, 200) Admittedly one has to be wary in interpreting these figures, as their accuracy is by no means assured. They would seem, however, to point to a substantial increase in both the production and consumption of beer and ale during this period. The same cannot be said for wine and whiskey, the consumption of which may, if anything, have declined. In this context it is worth noting that in 1670 the brewers of Dublin were granted a royal charter, a clear indication of their growing economic importance. (**13**, 288-9)

This brief survey would suggest that throughout the turbulent period from the middle of the sixteenth century to the end of the seventeenth, government policy in Ireland towards the production, importation and retailing of drink was largely dictated by a desire to maximise revenue. Given the significant contribution that the various taxes on drink made to the exchequer, this preoccupation is understandable. In 1611, for instance, the farms of the wine impost, ale licences and wine and whiskey licences were contributing about one-fifth of the Irish revenue, and by 1685 this figure had jumped to about one-third. (**81**, VI, 81; **6**, 390) Taxes on drink, then as today, were a substantial and moreover a very reliable source of revenue. Yet there were secondary considerations influencing policy which should not be overlooked. It was widely believed that the numbers of ale-houses were excessive, many in isolated areas beyond government control being potential, if not actual, refuges for rebels and outlaws. The statutory licensing of alehouses as early as the 1630s therefore reflected not only the desire for revenue but also the need to limit the numbers of alehouses and guarantee the loyalty of their proprietors. The use of large quantities of grain by brewers and distillers, the problem of drunkenness, as well as the quality and price of drink, were other issues having a bearing upon government actions.

In turning from central to local government, these issues are even more evident. Corporations, for instance, had long set maximum prices for drink. Thus in 1544 the authorities in Kilkenny decreed 3d as the maximum price for a gallon of 'good wholesome ale'; in 1622 Galway corporation passed a statute prohibiting the making of whiskey and strong beer if grain prices exceeded certain prescribed levels; while in Youghal in 1610 tradesmen were forbidden to keep inns or sell drink, and in 1616 additional alehouses were banned altogether from the town. (**35**, 262; **38**, 470; **90**, 7, 41) In 1617 the Lord President and Council of Munster ordered the suppression of all alehouses along the western coast of the province as they had been giving shelter to pirates. In 1626 the same body issued a proclamation claiming that innkeepers

> do only allow their guests bread and meat, and a kind of poor miserable beer fit for nothing but to enforce their guests to call in for another kind of stronger and heady drink, fit to nourish drunkenness and to breed disorder.

The document went on to order innkeepers to provide a 'competent kind of table beer', as 'in former times', so that the 'beastly sin of drunkenness so much practised and the disorders that depend thereon may be the better avoided'. (**6**, 148; **90**, 123) Later in the century the corporation of Waterford was setting maximum wine prices and was much concerned with preventing drinking at funerals. In 1663 it declared that 'Henceforth no funeral shall be served with drinking of wine or any other liquor.' This was done 'to prevent unseemly tippling and expense of poor men's estates who commonly spend more on the funeral of a child than they have left for the maintenance of two living'. (**282**, 42)

Town and provincial authorities were obviously anxious to keep tight control of the drink trade. The financial benefits to be derived from encouraging drink consumption were well appreciated, but the numerous local and national statutes passed during this period to regulate consumption demonstrate a healthy awareness of the dangers posed, particularly of the danger to civil order in an already disordered country.

The seventeenth century also yields a number of interesting attacks on drink, some of which very much anticipate the arguments of nineteenth-century temperance advocates. There is, for example, an anonymous document in the state papers dating from the reign of Charles I and entitled 'Some reasons demonstrating the prejudice and nuisancy that the importation of French brandy occasions to Ireland'. The author argues against the importation of brandy mainly on economic grounds: that it discourages local brewing and distilling, which in turn retards grain growing, and that the need to pay for these imports drains the country of goods and money. Such arguments, directed mainly against the French, were to become increasingly common in the first half of the eighteenth century as imported brandy and spirits took a large share of the Irish drink market. The author goes on, however, to note that the 'raw moisture' of the Irish climate predisposes the population to spirit consumption. This he does not necessarily consider a bad thing; indeed, he argues on the grounds of health that it would be far better for the Irish to drink their own spirits rather than brandy:

> By brandy is a sickly constitution of body begot, the radical moisture dried up, the stomach and liver burnt so as that not only the present generation is weakened, but the next is likely to suffer; whereas though strong waters are made of spirits and therefore likewise hot, yet by the joycy [?], oily quality and cordial nature of the ingredients whereof they are made, the malignant disposition of the spirit is altered and (not taken to excess) become grateful and cordial to the body. (9, 326)

The distinction drawn between brandy and native spirits is an interesting one, though it was not to be of any lasting significance. The author's account of the physiological damage caused by brandy, however, anticipates the medical and pseudo-medical attacks on spirits which were to become common in the late eighteenth and early nineteenth centuries, even down to the claim that such damage could be passed on from one generation to the next.

Another interesting critique comes later in the century in Colonel Richard Lawrence's pamphlet *The Interest of Ireland in its Trade and Wealth*, published in Dublin in 1682. Lawrence was a Cromwellian planter, fiercely anti-papist, and even admitted himself that he was regarded by some as a 'fanatic' on the subject of drink. Yet his arguments are worth examining for their entertainment value as well as for the information contained therein. He too concentrated on the damage done to health and wealth by drink. But, in keeping with the period's fondness for 'political arithmetic', Lawrence set himself to calculate in precise monetary terms the cost of Irish 'wealth-wasting lusts'. According to him, these took four

main forms: profane swearing and cursing; gambling; adultery and forni-
cation; and 'chiefly drunkenness and tippling, which is the mother of all the
rest of this cursed brood'. Lawrence calculated that each year these vices
cost Ireland nearly £350,000, or slightly more than the whole revenue
generated by the country. This figure was arrived at in the following
manner:

Swearing	£20,000
Gambling	£52,000
Adultery and fornication	£67,000
Drunkenness	£210,000
Total	£349,000

The overall cost of drunkenness Lawrence calculated on various bases, in
particular money spent by drinkers, loss of income through drunkenness,
the cost of supporting families left destitute by drunkards, and loss of
wealth through labour and capital that could be better employed. This
overall cost fell into five main parts:

7,500 spirit and wine drinkers at £10 each	£75,000
12,500 ale drinkers at £4 each	£50,000
5,000 inn and alehouse employees at £8 each	£40,000
Families of 12,500 ale drinkers at £2 each	£25,000
Losses to trade through drunkenness	£20,000
Total	£210,000

(**214**, 61, 37, 42-56)

Lawrence was very much a forerunner of nineteenth-century temperance
advocates who, also in an effort to refute the charge of fanaticism, devoted
enormous energy to endeavouring to calculate 'scientifically' how much
drink cost the country. His arithmetic, though highly eccentric, is nevertheless valuable. It further confirms the impression that ale and beer were
the most popular forms of liquor in the latter part of the seventeenth
century: he estimates that in each of the 2,500 parishes of Ireland there
were five drunkards produced by beer for every three produced by wine
and spirits. Lawrence's overall figure of 20,000 drunkards, who today
would probably be classed as very heavy drinkers, is also interesting, for
despite his strictures on the prevalence of drunkenness, at about 1 per cent
of the total population it is in fact low by modern Irish standards. (**265**, 172;
279, 137) While not accepting Lawrence's calculations as wholly reliable,
one must nevertheless concede that they are at least consistent with
evidence from other sources suggesting that whiskey was considerably
more expensive and less popular than beer as an alcoholic drink and that
drunkenness may have been less widespread in the last third of the century
than it had been in the first.

But not all the seventeenth-century critics were laymen. The martyred Archbishop of Armagh, Oliver Plunkett, in his efforts to revitalise the persecuted Irish church, was particularly concerned by the number of clergy who had fallen victim to the vice of drunkenness. Writing to Rome from Carlingford, Co. Louth, in April 1671, Plunkett informed his superiors that he had given

> a great deal of attention to trying to eradicate this cursed vice, which is mother and nurse to all sorts of scandals and disputes. I ordered under pain of privation of benefices that priests refrain from frequenting taverns and from taking whiskey, and indeed the results were very gratifying; these past six months only two priests, and this was on one occasion only, were drunk. And since deeds speak louder than words, I never take a drink between meals. Let us remove this defect from an Irish priest and he will be a saint.

As this extract shows, Plunkett himself was by no means a teetotaller. It was excessive drinking in public places that he sought to root out. Nor was this vice restricted to the lower clergy only. Plunkett complained bitterly of several bishops, in particular of Daniel Mackay, the Bishop of Down and Connor, who 'in the matter of drink... exceeds gravely, and this is public knowledge'. On Mackay's death in December 1673 Plunkett wrote, with more than a little sarcasm:

> This good prelate was somewhat too fond of the taverns, where he eventually ended his days, not having a halfpenny more than thirty-five baiocchi, so that to give him even a very private funeral it was necessary to sell some of his few belongings.

Plunkett's concern was further expressed in the statutes of the Synod of Ardpatrick, which were drawn up in August 1678. Under these statutes priests were forbidden to drink whiskey in any inn or public place; if they had been drinking after midnight, they were forbidden to celebrate mass that morning; nor were they to attend fairs or public markets, where heavy drinking would have occurred, without written permission. (**169**, 180-1, 393, 517-18) The ban on whiskey drinking is interesting, suggesting that beer and wine consumption were not considered at odds with priestly duties. In the latter part of the nineteenth century Catholic teetotallers were to see the penal era as the period in which drink gained its grip on the Irish, and they were to attribute this to the demoralisation occasioned by the repression of the church and by the destruction of Gaelic culture. (**244**, 106-7) While rejecting this interpretation, one would have to admit, with regard to the clergy at least, that the persecution of the late seventeenth and early eighteenth centuries did severely undermine discipline and morality. A number of bishops during the eighteenth century were forced to follow Plunkett in mounting campaigns to curb drunkenness among their priests, and though they clearly had much success, the problem was by no means unknown in the first half of the nineteenth century. (**115**, 61, 66)

Apart from drinking among clerics, the other issue which seems to have particularly concerned the church during this period was drinking at wakes and funerals. A number of synods, beginning with one in Armagh in 1614 and including Tuam in 1660, Clones in 1670, Waterford and Lismore in 1676, Meath in 1686 and Armagh again in 1660, 1668 and 1670, all passed statutes banning drinking, dancing and games at wakes. (**275**, 19, 146-8) As has been noted in Waterford in 1663, corporations also attempted to stamp out this custom. The church shared the lay authorities' concern at the amount of money spent by the poor on funerals, but it also considered drunken merriment to be impious, an insult to God and a scandal to the community. There is little evidence, however, that these strictures had much of an impact before the nineteenth century. Wakes were an important part of the circumstantial drinking pattern which had long prevailed in rural Irish society, and only when that society had changed radically would heavy drinking at wakes disappear.

Drink and its Critics:
Eighteenth and Early Nineteenth Centuries

The temperance movement in Ireland is traditionally considered to have begun in 1829 with the establishment of the first anti-spirits societies in New Ross, Belfast and Dublin. Though these may have been the first significant temperance societies, there had nevertheless been a well-organised campaign to curb drinking long before 1829. The eighteenth century had witnessed a substantial increase in alcohol consumption, mainly in the form of spirits, and this trend was both widely recognised and widely condemned at the time. In fact many of the issues and arguments that preoccupied the nineteenth-century critics of drink had been thoroughly aired in the preceding century. It was also at this time that important developments occurred in the drink industry — developments that were profoundly to influence Irish drinking patterns for many decades to come.

Lack of information, especially of reliable statistics, makes it difficult to study the development of the drink industry before 1780 in any great detail. The general picture seems, however, to have been one of numerous small breweries and distilleries fairly widely scattered throughout the country. In 1781, for instance, there were some 870 licensed stills in Ireland, the vast majority having a capacity of between 200 and 500 gallons. About 80 per cent of these were in the north and east, the Armagh and Strabane excise districts being the main centres in the north, while in the east Maryborough, Naas and Dublin city were the most significant.

The brewing industry was rather differently distributed. In 1790 there were over 930 breweries in Ireland, but the majority of these were retail breweries, which in effect meant the publican producing his own supplies. Of the 290 commercial breweries, over 50 per cent were in Leinster, with another 10 per cent in Munster. Thus, unlike distilling, commercial brewing was relatively insignificant in the north, but concentrated in the east and south. Dublin city was in fact far and away the major brewing centre, producing more than half the country's commercial beer and ale in the early 1790s. Next in importance was Cork, which boasted 29 breweries in 1790, compared with Dublin's 47. But if the north and west lacked large-scale commercial breweries, they were served to some extent by publican-brewers, 60 per cent of whom were located in these areas. (18, XII, cxc-cxci, X, dxxiii-dxxxii, XVI, ccclxxviii) This distribution pattern would suggest that whiskey was particularly popular in Ulster and Leinster, especially in areas of Scottish and English settlement. It would seem plausible to assume that the many Scots who came to Ulster in the seventeenth century brought with them a taste for whiskey and so contributed to the growth of the distilling industry in the north. Commercially produced beer, on the other hand, would appear to have been the main drink in urban areas of the south.

Determining the actual production and consumption of drink during the eighteenth century — and also, for that matter, during the first third of the nineteenth century — is an impossible task. Official figures are available and certainly can be used to indicate major trends, but they fail, of course, to gauge the very substantial illegal industry then in operation. With regard to spirits, figures presented to parliament towards the end of the century show a massive increase in consumption, far outstripping even the substantial growth in population under way at the time. Beer production, on the other hand, was stagnating and in real terms declining. Wine imports, though running at impressive levels, fluctuated considerably, but with no clear trend until after the turn of the century, when a marked decline set in. To be more precise, during the 1720s, with a population of approximately 3 million, duty was paid on some 5.2 million gallons of spirits, 5.3 million barrels of beer and 12.4 million gallons of wine. In the 1790s, when the population had grown to around 4.5 million, these figures were 44 million gallons of spirits, 6.1 million barrels of beer and 15 million gallons of wine. (113, 4-5; 254, 726-8) So while population increased by 50 per cent, over the same period beer and wine consumption only increased by 15 per cent and 21 per cent respectively, but spirit consumption increased by a massive 746 per cent. Even admittedly unreliable figures cannot gainsay this striking trend, particularly when it is corroborated by a great deal of impressionistic contemporary comment.

Consumption of legally produced spirits had risen substantially in the 1750s, 1760s and 1770s, so that in the 1770s it was nearly four times what it had been in the 1740s. Then in the 1780s consumption suddenly fell slightly, before making another massive leap in the 1790s. This apparent pause in the 1780s is, however, deceptive. Up until 1780 home-produced whiskey had been far exceeded by imports, mainly of West Indian rum, French brandy and Dutch gin. In the year 1770, for example, spirits paying duty in Ireland were made up of 51 per cent rum, 25 per cent whiskey, 14 per cent brandy and 10 per cent gin. What happened in the 1780s was that Irish spirit production doubled, while imports fell by nearly half, thus giving the overall impression of a small fall in consumption during the decade. In 1790 therefore Irish spirit consumption was made up of 66 per cent whiskey, 26 per cent rum, 6 per cent brandy and 1 per cent gin. A veritable revolution had in fact taken place in the Irish distilling industry, the effects of which were to be felt for at least fifty years. Not only was Irish production boosted substantially during the 1780s, but at the same time the industry underwent a rapid concentration. In 1781, as already noted, there were nearly 900 distilleries in Ireland, mostly small or medium-sized, producing some 1.8 million gallons of whiskey per annum. By 1790, however, there were only 238 of these distilleries left, though in that year they produced nearly 3 million gallons of whiskey. Of the distilleries that had closed in the 1780s, the greatest number were in the north: from having 35 per cent of licensed stills in 1781, Ulster's share fell below 20 per cent in 1790 and by 1796 was down to 10 per cent. (**18**, XII, cxl-cxliv, XVI, ccclxxii-ccclxxvi)

What had happened was that an apparently minor alteration in the distilling regulations had had catastrophic results. In a long and complex revenue act passed in 1779 (19 & 20 Geo. III, c. 12) an attempt was made to limit evasion of spirit duty, which was known to be widespread among licensed distillers (section 20). The duty had been increased substantially in 1775 from 10d to 1s 2d per gallon, and the Government was anxious to ensure that it received the additional revenue to which it was now entitled. Fraud by licensed distillers was difficult to defeat, owing to the primitive equipment and unreliable personnel available to the Revenue Commissioners. Thus the 1779 act, which came into operation in 1780, prescribed a minimum duty for each still, based on the estimated number of times the still could be worked off in twenty-eight days. But this system had the effect of encouraging the distiller to work his still as fast as he could in order to produce as much spirit as possible within the set time period. The authorities responded by increasing the minimum charge, with the result that the distiller further speeded his production. The act also sought to encourage large-scale distillers, presumably on the assumption that they would be easier to police. In section 30 it continued the ban first imposed in 1757 on stills smaller than 200 gallons and offered incentives, in terms of greater rebates on the duty, for stills over 1,000 gallons. (**17**, XI, 461-503)

E. B. McGuire sums up the effects of the system introduced in 1780 when he says:

> It was to become an uncontrollable monster. It caused the number of legal distilleries to fall catastrophically. The design of stills, working methods and the quality of the spirit were all affected. Evasion in legal distilleries was not checked and the number of illicit distilleries greatly increased. This minimum still charge fostered official corruption to a point where a regular system of fees, indistinguishable from bribes, was openly condoned by the Revenue Commissioners. (**234**, 127-8)

So while the output of whiskey increased dramatically after 1780, the quality declined as a result of the rapid production techniques adopted by the distillers in their frantic efforts to outwit the excisemen. As for the small distillers driven out of business by their inability to keep pace with increases in the minimum duty, many simply moved from the legal into the illegal industry. Some 260 stills disappeared from the official figures for Ulster in the 1780s. This is not to say, however, that they ceased to operate. Small distillers found that they could produce a cheaper and better product outside the corrupt and oppressive government licensing system. Illicit distilling had long been a feature of Irish life, and in fact private stills for household use were legal as long as they did not exceed twelve gallons in capacity. But the 1779 act gave an unprecedented boost to the illegal industry. It was one example among many, albeit a particularly spectacular one, of government licensing legislation which created the very opposite effect from that intended.

Before going on to look in more detail at the illegal industry, the other parts of the legal industry need to be considered. Irish brewing was in a fairly sorry state in the last quarter of the eighteenth century. Home production rose gradually from the 1730s, reaching a peak of 5.7 million barrels in the 1760s. But then it slumped seriously, falling to 4.2 million barrels in the 1780s, before recovering somewhat in the 1790s to 5.3 million barrels. (**254**, 153) Considering the growth in population and in spirit consumption over the same period, it is clear that the brewing industry was in serious decline. The reasons for this decline are not hard to find. Probably the main factor was simply that Irish beer was of very poor quality. Though seventeenth-century English visitors had criticised its taste and price, it had remained the most popular alcoholic drink. But in the following century its quality appears to have deteriorated so badly that the Irish themselves were loath to drink it. During debates on the industry in the Irish parliament in 1791 and 1792 John Beresford, the Chief Revenue Commissioner, accused the brewers of 'making such a liquor as the people will not drink while they can get any other'. Beresford was admittedly no friend of the brewers, but there is a good deal of evidence to support his assessment of the quality of Irish beer. In the 1770s and 1780s parliament, prompted by complaints from some of the brewers themselves, had been forced to set minimum standards for the ingredients in a barrel of beer. The brewers were accused of engaging in an extensive system of bribes in order to win customers for their unpalatable product. To recover the costs of this practice they then diluted their beer, reducing the malt or hop content and mixing small beer with ale. (**19**, XII, 268, XI, 79-82)

Irish beer, however, also faced severe competition from English imports. As large-scale brewing developed in London from the 1740s so imports rose steadily: from less than 1 per cent of the Irish market in 1740, English imports had by 1790 risen to nearly 20 per cent. The wars with France, however, quickly devastated this trade, so that by 1805 imports of English beer were almost negligible. (**248**, 153) Yet the critics of brewing seem generally to have agreed that it was the poor quality of beer, and not imports, which was causing the decline in the Irish industry. Thus an anonymous revenue official writing in the late 1770s stated categorically that it was not imports or cheap spirits 'which drove and forced the people into the use and consumption of other liquors', as the brewers liked to claim, but the 'very bad quality of the beer and ale brewed in this kingdom'. (**50**, 38; **47**, iii) The beer drinker's complaints are, however, perhaps most vividly portrayed in Aindrias Mac Craith's well-known poem, 'Small Beer', which was addressed to a fellow-poet who happened also to be a publican:

> You are a man who trades in small beer
> Without body or substance, and brandy
> That gives your customers nightmares...
>
> Bad ale you purvey every day as good porter
> That your wife decants in scant quarts...
>
> When yourself you pour your scarce pints
> The glasses are half filled with froth...
>
> Your poems and rhymes have no class
> And your metres are clumsy.
> With too many measures unfilled in your glasses
> And ditch-water lacing your brandy.
>
> (**200**, 38)

Beer was also, when compared with whiskey, particularly illegal whiskey, an expensive drink. Not only was the beer itself taxed, but so, after 1786, was the malt that went into its production and the hops, which had to be imported from England. Commercial breweries were concentrated in the south and east, with Dublin being the main centre, producing in 1790 some 65 per cent of Irish beer and ale. Commercially produced beer was thus very much a town drink, and, being relatively expensive, it was restricted to the better-off classes in the towns. In 1823 Arthur Guinness described the market for beer in Ireland, and there is no reason to think that his remarks were not applicable to the late eighteenth century as well. According to Guinness, beer was drunk mainly in the towns and cities of Munster and Leinster and in some parts of Connacht. The urban working classes were the main consumers, the 'lowest order of people' preferring whiskey. (**23**, 405) The market for commercial beer was thus, by definition, a relatively small one.

The brewers by no means calmly accepted their deteriorating position in the last decades of the eighteenth century. They lobbied parliament repeatedly seeking remedial legislation of various kinds. Their basic argument, as stated in a petition from the Dublin Corporation of Brewers in March 1760, was that 'Spirits . . . are retailed at such low prices, that the lower class of our manufacturers are frequently intoxicated therewith, and are rendered dissolute and idle, and the brewing trade is greatly injured thereby.' (**18**, IV, 204; **42**, 32-48) In seeking to defend their industry, the brewers therefore evolved a strong case against spirits and also against drunkenness, which they saw as essentially the result of spirit drinking. This case will be examined in more detail later; suffice it to say at the moment that the brewers won a good deal of support for their view of beer as the 'temperance drink'. The Irish parliament was certainly alive to the problems of the industry. In 1773 a committee of the House of Commons described brewing as being in 'gradual decay', and various remedial measures were attempted in the 1770s and 1780s. But acts which spoke of the 'great frauds' perpetrated by brewers and sought to regulate price and quality were not calculated to win the support of the industry. (**18**, IX, cliv; **17**, XI, 53-72) The brewers did, however, find a number of powerful allies in parliament prepared to argue their case. The most notable were Sir Lucius O'Brien from Co. Clare, David La Touche of the Dublin banking family, and Henry Grattan. O'Brien, who was much interested in the economic development of the country, saw spirit consumption as an impediment to the creation of a reliable and hard-working labour force. He also seems to have been involved in the wine trade, which may have influenced his attitude to spirits. La Touche and Grattan, on the other hand, represented the powerful Dublin brewers, both being related by marriage to the Guinness family (**43**, 192; **225**, 71)

By the early 1790s the government itself was seriously concerned about the massive growth in whiskey consumption, which was quite apparent from its own figures. A number of petitions from grand juries and religious groups spoke in increasingly alarmed terms of the 'universal poverty and depravity' and of the 'enormous crimes' occasioned by the 'immoderate use of spirituous liquors'. (**18**, VI, 86) There were frequent comparisons made between the situation developing in Ireland with regard to whiskey and that which had existed in England in the 1730s and 1740s with regard to gin. It is therefore not surprising that when La Touche moved a motion in January 1791 to condemn the excessive consumption of spirits and to set up a committee to examine the problem, he met with little opposition. Grattan immediately rose to propose that the duty on spirits should be 'raised so high, if possible, as to put them out of the reach of the mechanic and labourer, taking care at the same time, to provide him with a cheap and wholesome beverage; in order to which . . . no tax on brewing should be suffered to remain, save only that paid on the malt'. The tax on malt, introduced in 1786, was paid by both distillers and brewers. To have removed the tax on beer and to have increased that on spirits and malt, as Grattan was proposing, would have given the brewers a significant advantage over the distillers. In 1791, however, the government was not as yet prepared to go this far, and when Grattan moved a motion embodying his proposals it was defeated by 57 votes to 11. (**19**, XI, 36, 154) Instead the Chancellor of the Exchequer announced that the duties would be revised so as to advantage brewing over distilling, though less drastically than Grattan was demanding. Lord Shannon commented in a letter that the government preferred revenue and had 'consented to such a small tax on spirits as will bring them considerable revenue but will not discourage the use of spirits'. (**180**, 18)

During this debate frequent complaints were heard about the large numbers of unlicensed spirit retailers who flourished throughout the country and the unsavoury characters of many of those who had gone to the trouble of taking out a licence. Grattan, probably exaggerating, though by how much is impossible to tell, estimated that there were 90,000 houses selling spirits in Ireland, while only 8,000 licences had been issued. Certainly the government recognised that there were serious shortcomings in the licensing procedures, and, as a result, acts were passed in 1791 and 1792 which significantly increased the cost of spirit licences and allowed more rigorous supervision of licence-holders and their premises. (**19**, XI, 68; **17**, XV, 560-70)

But Grattan and the brewers were by no means satisfied with these measures. They continued their campaign to eliminate the beer tax, and by 1795, with spirit consumption still rising despite the 1791-2 legislation, the government finally came round to their point of view. The tax on beer was abolished and that on malt increased substantially. Further licensing acts followed in 1796 and 1797 (36 Geo. III, c. 40; 37 Geo. III, c. 45). These continued the effort begun in 1791 to regulate the sale of spirits and, in the case of the latter act, to promote the sale of beer. Lynch and Vaizey in their history of Guinness's brewery termed the 1795 act 'the most decisive and important single event in the whole history of Irish brewing'. (**225**, 68) This would seem to be something of an overstatement, however, suggesting as it does a dramatic improvement in the fortunes of the brewing industry subsequent to 1795. Observers during the next ten years, like Thomas

Newenham and Sir John Carr, certainly did remark upon the increasing popularity of beer, particularly among the 'lower orders', compared with the situation twenty years previously. (**258**, 141, 198; **88**, 416-17) But the growth of the industry was still very slow. Beresford for one remained unconvinced that the abolition of the beer duty had promoted brewing at all, and in 1797 he was able to persuade the Lord Lieutenant of this view. (**180**, 19) Whiskey was in fact to remain the favourite drink of the majority of the population for many years to come, and it was not really until after 1850 that Irish brewing as a whole entered upon a sustained period of expansion.

Wine imports ran at consistently high levels throughout the eighteenth century and up to 1815, though there were marked fluctuations influenced primarily by changes in the excise duty and by outbreaks of warfare. High points in the trade were the 1760s, 1790s and 1800s, while the troughs were the 1740s and 1780s. Only after 1815 did a consistent decline set in. The War of the Austrian Succession (1740-48), the Seven Years' War (1756-63) and the War of American Independence (1776-83) disrupted the French and Spanish wine trades and produced significant falls in Irish imports. (**125**, 47, 87, 115) During the Revolutionary and Napoleonic Wars (1793-1815), though imports fluctuated wildly, they generally remained at very substantial levels. As for import duties, they rose substantially in the 1770s, 1780s and 1810s and undoubtedly contributed to a lessening in demand during these decades. Wine duties, however, were levied discriminately. For instance, in 1790 the duty on a tun of Portuguese or Spanish wine was approximately £23, but on German it was £29 and on French £36. (**17**, XV, 1-13, 84-93) Under the Methuen Treaty of 1703 Portuguese wine had been granted favoured treatment in the British market. This was part of a systematic attempt, which lasted throughout the century, to discourage the consumption of French wine. That this policy succeeded, at least with regard to the English market, is clear from the fact that of wine imported legally into England between 1704 and 1785, 65 per cent was from Portugal, 29 per cent from Spain, and only 4 per cent from France. (**343**, 34-5) The policy, however, did not succeed to nearly the same extent with regard to Ireland. Duties were lower in Ireland; nor were the differentials as great. Unlike the English, therefore, the Irish generally remained loyal to their claret. Thus Swift, writing to Stella from London between 1710 and 1713, referred on a number of occasions to the fact that he was drinking white Portuguese wine, while she in Dublin was drinking claret. After complaining at first, he seems to have developed a taste for the Portuguese product, though, doubtless in deference to Irish opinion, he felt obliged to apologise for his 'sad vulgar taste'. (**320**, 440; **313**, 145-9) By the mid-1770s French wine still held around 60 per cent of the Irish market, though Portuguese had risen substantially to be over 30 per cent. Imports from Germany were almost negligible, while Spanish wine held the remainder of the market. (**18**, X, lvii) The long war with France which broke out in

1793, however, dealt a severe blow to the wine trade between France and Ireland. French wine was still holding about 40 per cent of the Irish market in the early 1790s, but by 1815 its share had fallen to a mere 8 per cent. Massive increases in duty played a significant part in this decline: from approximately £36 in 1790, the duty on a tun of French wine had jumped to nearly £150 by 1814 when the English and Irish wine duties were assimilated. (**25**, 369-82; **21**, 315-18)

The Irish gentry were notorious at the time — and since — for their partiality for wine, and the import statistics do indeed bear out this picture. In the century between 1720 and 1820 wine imports ran at over one million gallons per annum in all except twenty-one years — and this takes no account of the substantial amount of smuggling going on at the same time. Yet the number of wine consumers in Ireland would have been limited. At its maximum, towards the end of the period, the wine market might perhaps have numbered around 220,000. This is the estimated number of borough and county electors in 1815, and one can probably assume that persons wealthy enough to have the right to vote would also have been able to indulge a taste for wine, which was, when compared with beer or whiskey, an expensive drink. If this was indeed approximately the size of the market at the end of the Napoleonic Wars, it would suggest a *per capita* consumption of five gallons per annum at the very least. Such calculations are, of course, highly speculative, and too much weight should not be given to them; for a start, they ignore female wine drinkers. But they do give some hint, over and above contemporary impressionistic accounts, of the substantial quantities of wine being consumed by the wealthier classes in Ireland before 1815. At the same time, however, it has to be said that, unlike whiskey consumption, wine consumption was not increasing dramatically during the course of the century. In fact, given the growth in population and prosperity, particularly after 1750, it was probably declining in real terms. A peak was reached in the decade 1800-9, when imports rose above 2 million gallons per annum on three occasions. But after the end of the Napoleonic Wars a long decline set in, so that between 1800 and 1840, while population rose by around 80 per cent, wine imports fell by almost 40 per cent. (**262**, 575) Not until the 1860s, when legislation was passed at Westminster specifically intended to promote the consumption of wine, did Irish imports again rise repeatedly over the one million gallons per annum mark. This decline was doubtless partly due to economic factors: Irish wine duties were raised to English levels and assimilated in 1814, while the severe problems of the post-1815 Irish economy would have tended to reduce demand. But this marked decline in wine consumption also reflected changing attitudes to drink among the gentry and the middle classes who were to provide many of the leaders of the early temperance movement in Ireland.

In considering drink production in the eighteenth and early nineteenth centuries, one has to take into account the illegal as well as the legal industry, for illegal production and importation were conducted on an enormous scale so as seriously to rival the legal industry. The illicit industry took three main forms: the smuggling of spirits and wine from abroad, the marketing of spirits for which duty was unpaid by licensed distillers, and the illicit distilling of spirits by unlicensed distillers.

The smuggling of drink, in particular of brandy and wine, reached a peak in the middle of the eighteenth century, largely between the 1730s and the 1770s. It was part of a widespread effort in both England and Ireland aimed to circumvent the Navigation Acts, and as such it found much popular support. In fact, as F. G. James in his examination of Irish smuggling has pointed out, sympathy for the smuggler in Ireland was evident even in parliament and the courts. Thus Irish legislation to curb smuggling was nowhere near as severe nor as rigorously enforced as that of England. (**194**, 313) Dublin was the main market for the smuggler's goods, and the north Co. Dublin coast around Swords and Balbriggan was the major landing point. But the west also offered numerous secluded harbours for the smuggler, and the Kerry coast, Galway Bay and Inishowen were favoured landfalls. Brandy, mainly from France but also from Spain, was the most popular cargo. Like tea and tobacco, which were also smuggled in large quantities, brandy was very heavily taxed. L. M. Cullen has estimated, conservatively, that smuggled brandy accounted for as much as one-third of the total consumption of spirits in Ireland between the 1730s and the early 1770s.

The amount of wine smuggled is more difficult to determine, though clearly it was not smuggled on as large a scale as brandy. Cullen in fact thinks that wine 'was never smuggled in quantity. It was unsuitable for that trade: it was shipped in bulky hogsheads; the duty, though high, was not prohibitive; and long credit and the necessity of carrying large stocks of maturing wine made it unattractive for the smuggler.' (**125**, 161-5, 168-9) Yet the Irish parliament felt called upon on several occasions to legislate specifically against wine smuggling, which may suggest that it was more substantial than Cullen's remarks would seem to allow. In 1774, for instance, the importation of wine in casks under thirty-one gallons, or twenty-eight gallons for some types, was banned (13 & 14 Geo. III, c. 38, sect. 1) So smugglers were obviously not using 'bulky hogsheads', but landing wine in casks less than thirty gallons. Moreover, as mentioned already, official wine imports fluctuated considerably, particularly during the numerous wars which occurred in eighteenth-century Europe. Thus during the War of the Austrian Succession in the 1740s official imports fell by 20 per cent compared with the 1730s. Given the Irish gentry's appetite for large amounts of wine, it is hard to imagine that the smuggler did not capitalise on such troughs.

The gentry of Kerry and Clare were well known for their involvement in wine smuggling, the O'Connells of Derrynane perhaps subsequently being most notorious. We have already seen that Sir Lucius O'Brien of Dromoland, Co. Clare, was one of the most vocal parliamentary opponents of spirit consumption. But this opposition by no means implied a general hostility to drink. Total abstinence does not seem to have commended itself to the eighteenth-century mind. On the contrary, Sir Lucius was himself involved in a scheme in the 1760s to import wine into Clare. Moreover, this was quite in keeping with the traditions of his family. His grandfather, also called Lucius, had died prematurely in 1717 as a result of gout, while his father, Sir Edward, exhibited that partiality for enormous quantities of wine which has never ceased to amaze succeeding generations. Not long before his death one correspondent, while sympathising with him over his 'nervous disorder', nevertheless warned Sir Edward against 'bumping away all night' with a gallon instead of stinting himself to three pints. In the 1740s Sir Edward was therefore, as might be expected, an eager customer of the west-coast smugglers. Writing to a friend in 1749, he announced that a small two-masted vessel, with a Mr Russell as supercargo, had just arrived from France, and

> In a tide or two, she will come to anchor or run ground *by chance* near Nick McInerhinys — she has choice old claret, some burgundy and champagne on board and Mr Russell will sell it to you or me cheaper than to the merchants in Limerick; or than we can buy it from any Irish merchant (but this is *entre nous*). (**43**, 162)

The massive increase in whiskey production that occurred after 1780 naturally made the smuggling of spirits a much less rewarding occupation, but at the same time the new system for assessing duty introduced in 1780 gave an enormous boost to other illegal practices. Licensed distillers, struggling to keep up with increases in duty and to compete with the illicit distiller, were driven to revenue defrauding on a vast scale. Just how substantial these frauds were is made clear in the evidence of a number of leading distillers before a parliamentary inquiry in 1805. George Roe of Dublin admitted that though he paid duty on about 5,000 gallons a week, his actual production was between 9,000 and 10,000 gallons. Several other distillers gave a similar evidence, and Robert Haig, also of Dublin, said it was his opinion that 'for some years past considerable quantities of spirit have been made which were more than double the quantity chargeable by law, or for which duty was paid'. (**234**, 150) This evidence would suggest that at the turn of the century whiskey production in Ireland, even without taking account of illicit distillation, was perhaps double that recorded in official statistics. The government attempted to stamp out fraud by legislating to tighten the policing of distilleries, but it was ultimately defeated by a combination of the ingenuity of the distiller and the corruptibility of the revenue official.

Finally in 1821 a major inquiry into Irish excise revenue was instituted. The report of this commission resulted in both a significant lowering of duty and the introduction of a new formula for assessing duty, which largely avoided the pitfalls of the old still-licence system. The success of these reforms was almost immediately obvious: in 1823, with duty at 5s 7d per gallon, there were only 36 licensed distilleries officially recorded as producing 3.6 million gallons of whiskey; in 1824, after the lower duty of 2s 5d and the new methods of assessment had come into operation, there were 86 distilleries recorded as producing 6.7 million gallons, and by 1825 output had jumped substantially again to 9.3 million gallons. (**27**, 66-7; **24**, 27-8) So although the duty had been cut by more than half, within two years more revenue was being collected than under the old level of duty. That output had nearly trebled between 1823 and 1825 was certainly not due to a real increase in consumption, though lower prices probably did stimulate demand to some degree. This increase is rather some indication of how much whiskey was avoiding duty under the old assessment system. The methods used by licensed distillers to evade duty were indeed ingenious. The final report of the excise inquiry commission in 1823 provides detailed and fascinating accounts of such practices. One of the most interesting witnesses was Aeneas Coffey (1780-1852), then an inspector-general of Irish excise, but later to become famous as the inventor of the patent or Coffey still, which revolutionised distilling in the second half of the nineteenth century. (**299**, 1824-6; **230**, 56-9) Coffey told colourful stories of his efforts to defeat the illicit distillers of Derry and Donegal, who had seriously assaulted him on at least one occasion. But he also described the methods resorted to by licensed distillers in order to avoid paying excise duty. According to Coffey,

> There is scarcely a distillery near a town of any consequence (and they generally are near towns) that have not a number of persons employed, men, women, and children, in conveying their spirits out constantly in such small quantities, less than a gallon, which do not require a permit, and therefore are not liable to seizure. There are men, women, and children employed in taking it out in gallons, in bottles and bladders. At night, and the latter part of the day, they send out larger quantities, with gangs of men guarding them, so that no officer can venture to attack them without military. Another way is, by using a permit twice over, sending out two parcels under one permit. (**23**, 72)

Coffey estimated that by such practices distillers were able to avoid duty on about 20 per cent of what they produced. This would seem, however, to be rather a conservative estimate. In 1825, in evidence presented to a House of Lords committee investigating the state of Ireland, T. F. Lewis, an M.P. and a member of the excise inquiry commission of 1821-3, estimated that three-quarters of the whiskey produced in Ireland had been 'clandestinely brought to market, either by the licensed or the private distillers'. (**24**, 28)

The illicit distilling industry, which it is probably fair to regard as a cottage industry, flourished between the 1780s and the 1840s. It had certainly existed before 1780 and continued in existence after 1850, but during this seventy-year period it reached its peak. It had been given an enormous fillip by the virtual destruction of small-scale distilling as a result of the still-charge system introduced in 1780. As McGuire says, 'It is probable that many a licensed distiller took his small still out of the town to a quiet spot and used his skill to make poteen.' (**234**, 393) As we have seen, under the still-charge system licensed distillers were forced to work as fast as they could, often using raw grain to avoid the heavy duty on malt. This, of course, resulted in an inferior spirit. Spirit duty was first imposed in Ireland in 1661; then it was 4d a gallon. It rose very slowly in the next hundred years, so that by 1761 it was only 10d. But in the following fifty years, partly in an effort to maximise revenue and partly to discourage excess consumption, the government raised the duty substantially: by 1813 it was 5s 7d per gallon, and it remained at this level until 1823, except for 1815, when it reached 6s 1d. (**27**, 66-7) So after 1780 the people were being offered a spirit that was declining in quality as it rose in price. Not surprisingly, they were loath to purchase it. Government policy thus had the opposite effect to that intended: it helped create an enormous illegal industry, which deprived the exchequer of revenue both in terms of lost duty and policing costs, and it boosted consumption. With small stills readily available, with abundant barley in many areas, with men often under-employed, with families desperate for additional income to make up their rents, with a population accustomed to cheap spirits and not over-concerned with respect for the law, the conditions were ideal for the growth of a huge illicit industry.

The centres of this industry were in the north and west. Writing in 1812, Edward Wakefield claimed that the mountains in these districts were 'covered with stills' and that poteen 'was sold as openly as if it had been gauged by the revenue officer'. (**336**, I, 729) In 1823 the main illicit distilling counties, in descending order of importance, were claimed to be Donegal, Cavan, Leitrim, Mayo, Clare, Sligo, Monaghan and Tyrone, all in the north or west. Commercial brewing had never made much headway in these areas, and the once substantial distilling industry of Ulster had been decimated after 1780: with a population of nearly 2 million in 1821, Ulster had only eight registered stills. So the field was very much open for the illicit distiller. The legal industry was concentrated in the south, Dublin and Cork cities being the major centres. Licensed distillers, even operating fraudulently, were simply unable to compete economically with their illicit colleagues under the existing revenue laws, and the two industries were largely separated geographically. (**23**, 117-18; **20**, 17; **112**, 31)

The poteen trade was an extremely well-organised commercial under-taking during this period. At the time that Wakefield was writing there was a regular market at Magilligan Point on the eastern shore of Lough Foyle, where the barley of Derry, which was better than that of Donegal, was bartered for Inishowen whiskey. Barley was even sent from as far away as Scotland in exchange for Donegal poteen, such was its reputation for excellence. (**209**, 75-7; **23**, 78-9; **20**, 9) The Inspector-General of Excise for Donegal and Tyrone estimated that in 1810-12 there were 700 illicit distillers in the barony of Inishowen. Some could even be seen at work from the walls of Derry, and revenue officers did not dare to venture into the suburbs of the town without an armed escort for fear of attack. This assess-ment of the prevalence of illicit distilling in Inishowen is borne out by the number of fines imposed on the area. In 1814, for instance, 3,554 fines for illicit distilling were levied in the whole of Ireland; 13 per cent of these fell on Inishowen alone. (**22**, 1)

The main attraction of poteen was its cheapness when compared with the legal or 'parliament' whiskey. In 1823, when legal whiskey was selling at between 8s 6d and 9s 0d a gallon, 5s 7d of this being excise duty, poteen prices were: in Derry 3s 9d to 6s 0d, in Dundalk 4s 3d to 4s 6d, in Limerick 6s 0d to 6s 6d, and in Dublin 6s 0d to 7s 6d. But in Belfast, where poteen was said to be popular among the 'better class', people were sometimes prepared to pay up to 10s 0d or 12s 0d a gallon. (**23**, 57, 75, 400) So price was not always the determining factor. In 1834 Dr John Edgar, founder and leader of the Ulster temperance movement, told a select committee on drunkenness that illicit whiskey was popular in the north among the 'higher classes' and was generally to be found in the homes of 'magistrates and gentry'. Though claiming that drinking had fallen off among this group, Edgar nevertheless labled them as the 'chief patrons of drunken-ness'. Taste he thought an important factor, acknowledging that Inishowen whiskey in particular was 'remarkably fine'. Another factor he thought calculated to encourage the consumption of poteen was the

> mere secrecy of transactions; the idea of secrecy (stolen water is sweet) sometimes gives a sale to privately distilled spirit, in spite of threatened heavy penalties. . . . It is considered to be a sort of feat to have a bottle or two of *good* Inishowen, or other privately distilled spirit. (**26**, 75)

Apart from these considerations, the consumption of poteen also seems to have had party significance, in some circles at least. Lockhart, the biographer of Sir Walter Scott, reports that when he accompanied the novelist on a visit to Ireland in 1825 they were entertained on one occasion at a country gentleman's house in a mixed company of Catholics and Protestants. After dinner when punch was called for two magnums of whiskey appeared, the one bearing on its label KING'S, the other QUEEN'S. We did not at first understand these inscriptions; but it was explained, *sotto voce*, that the King's had paid the duty, the Queen's was of contraband origin; and, in the choice of the liquors, we detected a new shibboleth of party. The jolly Protestants to a man stuck to the King's bottle — the equally radiant Papists paid their duty to the Queen's. (**222**, 70)

Yet, despite Lockhart's and Scott's experience, it is clear that Protestant landlords in some parts of the country not only consumed but encouraged the production of poteen. In giving evidence before numerous government inquiries into distilling, revenue officers complained bitterly of the attitudes of landlords and magistrates. In 1823 landlords were accused of having 'a great dislike to the revenue officers'. (**23**, 73; **20**, 19) Understandably so, for in barren areas like Donegal, where crops were poor, landlords could still extract 3 guineas an acre in rent, and this largely through illicit distillation. In a report to the Revenue Commissioners in 1834 two officers said that in very few instances had the landlords

> been known to interfere to prevent distillation on their estates, and that, in most cases, particularly in the west of Ireland, it is the principal means by which the tenants make up the extravagant demands for their rents. In every instance where a landlord has been known to set his face against illicit distillation it is discontinued. (**27**, 70)

By 'setting his face against distillation' they meant either dispossessing tenants caught distilling or inserting a clause in the lease forbidding distillation on pain of having the lease terminated. In Donegal only two landlords, Sir Samuel Hayes and the Marquis of Abercorn, were singled out in the 1820s as actively opposing illicit distillation in this manner. Generally magistrates were accused of giving 'no active assistance' to the revenue officers, while one official complained that he 'could not get a jury in Donegal, that were not for the most part smugglers'. (**23**, 81, 83) Government figures would seem to substantiate this particular complaint. In 1814 20 per cent of fines for illicit distilling were levied on Donegal — obviously a disproportionately large number. These fines were imposed directly by the revenue authorities. But when we come to convictions, imposed by magistrates and juries, the picture is rather different: in 1814 662 persons were convicted for illicit distilling in Ireland, but only 4 per cent of these convictions took place in Donegal. (**22**, 2) This discrepancy between fines and convictions suggests that in Donegal at least the enthusiasm of the revenue officers was not matched by that of the magistrates and landlords.

Lacking local support, the government adopted various strategies in order to stamp out illicit distillation. Revenue officers were empowered to call on the military for assistance when they were on still-hunting expeditions, and there is every indication that such assistance was essential. Stories of excisemen assaulted and even murdered by illicit distillers were not uncommon. Daniel Logue, Inspector-General of Excise for Donegal and Tyrone, who was stationed in Derry from 1810 to 1812, testified in 1823 that he had never attempted to make a seizure without the support of troops, and even then he was by no means safe:

> I was pelted in the streets of Derry with twenty dragoons at that period; and I could not go into the suburbs of Derry, on revenue duty, without a serjeant's guard. . . . I escaped myself; but on one occasion, Mr Coffey, who was with me, was severely injured; he had his skull fractured, and two bayonet wounds in his thigh; and four soldiers, that were with him, were disarmed, and severely beaten, on that occasion. (**23**, 78-9)

The excisemen were heartily detested by landlord and tenant alike, particularly in the north, and the military were not over-enthusiastic about assisting them. Frequently attacked for being both corrupt and brutal, revenue officers clearly had a far from enviable job in attempting to enforce the unpopular excise laws.

In addition to the military, revenue officers could also use the revenue police. This force was first sanctioned in 1787-8, when seven landlords in the counties of Fermanagh, Leitrim and Sligo were given permission by the Lord Lieutenant to establish parties of still-hunters. At least two of these parties appear to have continued to operate till 1824, but by then a new revenue police force had been organised. In 1817 the army authorities were considerably alarmed by the detrimental effect that still-hunting was having on the discipline of their troops, and in that year regulations were introduced severely curtailing military assistance in revenue operations. This prompted the Revenue Commissioners to begin the introduction of their own police force, the first parties of which were stationed in Ballina and Sligo in 1818. By 1825 this force had 500 officers and men and, exclusive of rewards, was costing the treasury £27,000 a year to operate; by 1835 numbers had doubled to a little over 1,000, while the cost had jumped to £40,000. Yet a report in the same year was exceedingly critical of the general effectiveness of the force, noting that illicit distillation was increasing in areas where the revenue police had been stationed for many years. (**28**, 26-7; **32**, 236; **132**, 282-94) As a result, in 1836 Colonel William Brereton, a tough English artillery officer with thirty years' service, was called in to reform the force. Later, describing his experiences in Ireland, he said he had found the revenue police

> without discipline, and without instruction of any sort or kind, and objectionable in every way: every man almost was married, with a tribe of children; they were wretchedly lodged, and miserably clothed: their arms were in the worst possible condition: I cast off two-thirds of them, the first thing I did. (**32**, 6)

Assuming that this assessment is accurate, the ineffectiveness of the revenue police is easily understood. Brereton remained in charge of the force until 1846, but, with illicit distilling on the increase in the early 1850s, it was decided that the Irish Constabulary should take over the functions of the revenue police. Thus both a more effective and a cheaper form of policing was achieved at the one stroke. (**34**, 28)

Perhaps, however, the most controversial of the measures employed to suppress illicit distilling was the system of townland fines. First introduced in 1783, the system lasted until 1831, though it was inoperative between 1811 and 1813 and no fines were imposed after 1820. It was an oppressive system, whereby communities were held collectively responsible and fined for illicit distilling detected in their townland. It was moreover much open to abuse both by revenue officers and illicit distillers. Excisemen, who were entitled to a proportion of the fine imposed, were accused of planting distilling equipment in order to gain the reward, while distillers were thought deliberately to keep their stills in other townlands to avoid fines. Planting stills could also easily be used as a form of revenge. The Rev. Edward Chichester, rector of Cloncha and Culdaff in Co. Donegal, both parishes notorious for illicit distilling, claimed in a widely read attack on the excisemen in 1818 that fines alienated communities from the authorities, whether they engaged in illicit distilling or not. The large number of fines imposed on Donegal, amounting according to Chichester to over £140,000 by 1818, the use of troops to collect fines by force and the generally arrogant and brutal behaviour of the excisemen were driving otherwise peaceful communities into rebellion. Referring specifically to the assault on Coffey in 1810, which had occurred near his own parish, Chichester attributed it to popular resentment at the oppressive methods used to enforce the revenue laws. Coffey, in a reply to Chichester's pamphlet, upheld the effectiveness of townland fines, and it would indeed seem that they did act as a check on illicit distilling. The threat of fines, according to Coffey, was one of the few things that encouraged landlords to act against distilling on their estates. (**97**, 33, 68-9; **106**, 7) But the expense of the system, both in terms of rewards and of the difficulties involved in actually collecting the fines, particularly during the post-1815 depression, as well as the disorder which frequently accompanied collection efforts, had finally convinced the government by 1819 that townland fines created more problems than they solved, and none were imposed thereafter. (**311**, 291-302; **234**, 413)

The level of illicit distillation in Ireland, especially when compared with England or Scotland, remained high throughout the nineteenth century. But there were notable peaks and troughs. The price of grain, rises and falls in excise duty and the effectiveness of policing appear to have been the major determining factors. (**112**, 42; **234**, 419-20) No complete or reliable figures for detections of illicit distillation exist before 1832, but it would seem from the partial statistics available and from the evidence of revenue officials before various inquiries that peaks were reached in 1812-14 and 1820-23. (**22**, 1; **23**, 73, 80; **28**, 113) These were years of high duties, when townland fines were not in operation. The next peak was the period 1832-5, when detections were running at over 5,000 a year, a level not reached again during the remainder of the century. Minor peaks, however, occurred in 1836-8, 1843 and 1850-51, when detections exceeded 3,000 a year. By way of comparison it should be noted that in the period from 1830 to 1869 detections never exceeded 600 in England or 800 in Scotland. (**34**, 12) The troughs are also interesting: only twice during this forty-year period did detections fall below 1,000 in Ireland. This occurred in 1841 and again in 1847: the first after a substantial cut in duty and when Father Mathew's teetotal crusade was at its height, and the second during the worst of the famine, when grain prices were unusually high.

It is clear, then, that despite the reforms of 1823, combined with the imposition of heavy fines on communities and the efforts of both the army and the revenue police, illicit distilling remained a major domestic industry in Ireland into the 1850s. In his excellent study of the subject Kenneth Connell notes that, with the mechanisation of spinning by the 1830s, illicit distilling was thereafter the most profitable cottage industry in the country. (**112**, 49) Heavy-handed attempts at regulation and punishment often appear to have only succeeded in creating more friends and customers for the illicit distiller. On this point one could venture so far as to argue that the actions of government itself, in the form of high malt and spirit duties, the banning of small stills and the failure to give sufficient encouragement to brewing, were among the main factors giving rise to this vast illicit industry.

In turning from the industry to its critics, we find that much of the debate in the Irish parliament derived from the brewers' concern at the decline of their industry; but outside parliament there was an even more wide-ranging discussion. No organised anti-drink movement, in the form of a temperance society, existed, but there was developing an increasingly detailed, coherent and convincing critique of the drinking habits of Irish society. In the first half of the eighteenth-century much of the criticism expressed centred on the importation of French wines and brandy and on the level of drink consumption among the gentry. Thus in *The Querist*, the first part of which was published in 1735, Bishop Berkeley asked:

119. Whether if drunkenness be a necessary evil, men may not as well get drunk with the growth of their own country?

159. How many gentlemen are there in England of a thousand pounds per annum, who never drink wine in their own houses? Whether the same may be said of any in Ireland who have even one hundred pounds per annum? (**67**, 24, 31).

And in other writings, particularly in *Siris*, he was to extol the virtues of tar water and to propose it as an alternative to alcohol. (**68**, 29, 31) Berkeley well appreciated that you could not successfully deprive people of drink without substituting something palatable in its place. Except, however, for a small body of enthusiasts, tar water failed to attract many consumers. Writing in 1738, the Rev. Samuel Madden showed concerns similar to those of Berkeley. He argued for a total ban on the importation of brandy, high taxes on French wines and the encouragement by government of both Portuguese imports and the local distilling industry. Given what was to happen later in the century, it is rather ironic to find Madden, while severely attacking Irish drinking habits, nevertheless declaring:

> Our distillers make excellent spirits, from our own grain of aqua vitae, which are as palatable and vastly cheaper, and wholesomer, and do also furnish us with an usquebaugh, which no nation can come up to.

Like Berkeley, Madden placed a good deal of the responsibility for the spread of drunkenness at the door of the landed gentry. Drinking had become so fashionable, he wrote, that gentlemen competed eagerly to 'have the largest cellar and spend the most on hogsheads every year'. And, like all fashions, this one was spreading down the social scale as the people sought the 'glory of drinking like their betters'. Thus tradesmen 'if they get a little substance are apt to show they are got above ale drinking, and have business enough to enable them to pay vintners for their wine'. (**239**, 65, 69-70, 203)

But some of the bitterest complaints about heavy drinking, especially among the gentry, in the 1730s and 1740s occur in the letters of Lord Orrery (1707-62) and Lord Chesterfield (1694-1773). Admittedly Orrery was an embittered man who loathed Ireland, but his complaint that he was unfit 'to live in such a place' as he did not have a 'constitution to be always drunk' would appear plausible. In a letter from Dublin written to a friend in England in May 1736 he observed:

> Drunkenness is the touchstone by which they try every man, and he that cannot or will not drink, has a mark set upon him. He is abused behind his back, he is hurt in his property, and he is persecuted as far as the power of malice and intemperance can go. A right jolly glorious-memory Hibernian never rolls into bed without having taken a sober gallon of claret to his own share. You wonder what this animal is? It is a Yahoo that toasts the glorious and immortal memory of King William in a bumper without any other joy in the revolution, than that it has given him a pretence to drink so many more daily quarts of wine. The person who refuses a goblet to this prevailing toast is deemed a Jacobite, a papist and a knave. (**274**, I, 235, 157)

Chesterfield, who was Lord Lieutenant in 1745-6, was far more sympathetic to the country than Orrery, though no less averse to Irish drinking habits. Writing to Samuel Madden in September 1748, he echoed Madden's complaint that, while claret was ruining the 'people of fashion', the 'ordinary people... imitate them... and in whiskey'. In a letter of June 1747 to Richard Chenevix, the Bishop of Waterford, who had been his chaplain in the embassy at The Hague nearly twenty years before, Chesterfield took the view that

> Drinking is a most beastly vice in every country, but it is really a ruinous one to Ireland: nine gentlemen in ten in Ireland are impoverished by the great quantity of claret, which, from mistaken notions of hospitality and dignity, they think it necessary should be drank in their houses; this expense leaves them no room to improve their estates, by proper indulgence upon proper conditions to their tenants, who must pay them to the full, and upon the very day, that they may pay their wine merchants.

And in a letter to the same correspondent in October 1756 he passed on the opinion of his friend George Faulkner, the printer, that in Ireland 'more bottles are bought in one week, than books in one year'. [6]**196**, I, 331, III, 319-20, 347)

That Chesterfield's complaints were well founded is clear not only from the official figures for wine imports, which were certainly a gross under-estimate, but also from surviving estate account books. To take just one example among many, the Shapland Carew family of Castleboro, Co. Wexford, were in the 1740s and 1750s purchasing vast amounts of brandy, wine and beer. In January 1757 Councillor Carew paid £3 11s 10½d for 18½ gallons of brandy, which presumably had been consumed during the festivities marking Christmas 1756; in 1761 his accounts record that he spent nearly £14 on drink for his tenants and supporters during the elections of that year. It is revealing in this context to compare the prices of the different beverages consumed by the family at Castleboro. While Carew paid about 4s for a gallon of brandy, 8d for a gallon of beer, 1s 4d for a bottle of Portuguese wine and 1s 3d for a bottle of port, tea cost him nearly 10s per pound. There is no mention at all of coffee in these particular accounts, but from other sources we know that in Dublin in the 1750s coffee was selling for 2s 6d per pound. (**223**, 110, 121, 94; **238**, 281) Many observers remarked on the cheapness of Irish alcohol compared with that available in England, but it was also very cheap when compared with non-alcoholic alternatives. Coffee, and tea even more so, were simply too expensive for general consumption, and even among the landed gentry they must, given their cost, have been regarded as luxury items.

When reading Chesterfield's complaints it would be wrong to conclude that he and his fellow-critics of Irish drinking were total abstainers, or even that they were personally temperate by modern standards. In June 1758

Chesterfield wrote another letter to Bishop Chenevix, but this time it was to thank him for sending over from Ireland 'nine dozen and six pints of usquebaugh'. Earlier, in the 1740s, Chesterfield had been treated for an unspecified illness by the famous physician Dr George Cheyne, whose descendant Dr John Cheyne was to be an early leader of the Irish temperance movement. (135) Cheyne's treatment entailed the regular consumption of substantial amounts of mercury and burgundy; my 'two most constant friends', Chesterfield called them. (196, III, 355, 307) Cheyne's well-known *Treatise on Health and Long Life*, first published in 1724 and reprinted many times in both England and Ireland, contained a lengthy attack on 'strong liquors'. He praised water as the 'primitive, original beverage . . . the only simple fluid . . . fitted for diluting, moistening and cooling; the ends of drink appointed by nature'. But Cheyne himself was not a water drinker — personally he suffered from obesity and as a result he became a vegetarian — nor did he demand that his patients should give up drink, as Chesterfield's case demonstrates. Regarding the medicinal uses of alcohol, he wrote that he allowed every man 'that has been accustomed to drink wine, or strong liquors, a pint in 24 hours: and I am well satisfied that quantity is sufficient for health'. Cheyne was also very prepared to concede the social significance of drink, recognising that 'the cheerful cup' was a means of 'enlivening conversation, promoting friendship, comforting the sorrowful heart, and raising the drooping spirits'. Clearly he himself was not immune from the delights of alcohol, for, as he wrote,

> Perhaps I may like the harmless frolic, the warm reception of a friend . . . more than I ought: persons sober in the main, will receive little prejudice from such a fillip, when the occasions happen but seldom. (**93,** 33, 36, 38)

Cheyne's views appear to have been shared by many doctors of the time. Dr John Armstrong in his popular poem *The Art of Preserving Health*, published in both London and Dublin in 1744, summed up his opinions in the line 'We curse not wine: The vile excess we blame.' Like Cheyne, Armstrong was prepared to see positive benefits in the 'rare debauch':

> I would not always dread the bowl,
> Nor every trespass shun. The feverish strife,
> Rous'd by the rare debauch, subdues, expells
> The loitering crudities, that burden life;
> And, like a torrent full and rapid, clears
> The obstructed tubes.

Thus Armstrong advised his readers to 'learn to revel', though only by 'slow degrees . . . and only with your friends', for there were 'sweet follies, frailties to be seen / By friends alone'. But the drunkard was another matter altogether. For Cheyne a 'sot' was the 'lowest character in life', and Armstrong warned potential drunkards:

> Your means, your health, your parts decay;
> Your friends avoid you; brutishly transform'd
> They hardly know you; or if one remains
> To wish you well, he wished you in heaven.
>
> (**53**, 31-2, 65; **93**, 38)

Eighteenth-century medical opinion was therefore by no means opposed to the consumption of alcohol. Even critics of drink conceded that it had important medicinal and social functions. But regular, very heavy drinking of the sort that characterised Irish society was to be condemned: whereas a pint of wine in a day could be considered as conducive to health and merriment, the 'sober gallon of claret' consumed by many Irish gentlemen was unpardonable excess.

But perhaps the most comprehensive critique of Irish drinking habits came from the pen of a clergyman, Dr William Henry. Though born in England, Henry seems to have passed much of his life in Ireland. He was educated at Trinity College, Dublin, and spent more than thirty years as rector of parishes in Counties Fermanagh and Tyrone, before being appointed Dean of Killaloe in 1761. A Fellow of the Royal Society, Henry was also, according to the *Dictionary of National Biography*, 'a popular preacher, a keen observer of natural history and phenomena, and an earnest advocate both for temperance and for civil and religious liberty'. (**135**, XXVI, 128-9) He published at least four pamphlets during the 1750s attacking spirit consumption and in them showed that he was well acquainted with the campaign against gin drinking then under way in England. Henry mentions correspondence between himself and Dr Stephen Hales, one of the leading lights of this campaign, and in 1762 he arranged for the publication in Dublin of Hales's most important tract, *A New-Years-Gift to Dram-Drinkers*. (**163**) This familiarity with the English campaign probably accounts for the sophistication of Henry's arguments; nevertheless, his writings do deal specifically with Ireland. He identified a great upsurge in spirit consumption, which he argued had only occurred in recent times. Previously spirits had largely been confined to the 'dregs of the people', living in 'woods, lakes, fens and bogs'. But now spirits,

> under the various names and kinds, of brandy, rum, gin, usquebaugh, and above all, of whiskey, has spread over all parts of Ireland; nor is there any place from Cape Clear in the county of Cork, to Fair Head, the northernmost promontory in Antrim, wherein it has not shed its poison.

And, moreover, it had spread to all classes: it had 'seized the manufacturers, the husbandmen, the women, the young children, and even the gentlemen'.

Many of Henry's arguments anticipated those used in the 1830s by the first organised temperance societies, which were also concerned solely with the consumption of spirits. Like them, Henry appealed principally to those 'who either have not tasted, or have not yet drunk deep of, the invenomed cup', for he thought it futile to appeal to 'old hardened drinkers of spirits', whose 'senses are grown callous'. Addressing the young, he painted a frightening picture of the physical degeneration of the drunkard:

> Cast your eyes on the habitual dram drinker, with his limbs decrepid by the gout; his veins and bladder tortured with the stone, the great glands full of putrifying sores; his schirrous liver swollen to an enormous load; his dropsical belly protuberant like a tun; his asthmatic lungs panting for breath; his shrivelled ghastly countenance discoloured into a blackish yellow by jaundice; his hollow eyes unable to bear the light; his drivelling looks and his wretched soul, incapable to endure its shattered habitation, yet trembling with horror at the thoughts of being dis-possessed. (**177**, 2, 3, 10)

Yet, even more serious than this, spirits threatened the survival of the whole human race, for they prevented procreation, drying up the 'radical moisture in men' and rendering women barren; and in support of this claim Henry pointed to the devastating effects of the introduction of spirits on the native peoples of North America and the West Indies. The increasing consumption of spirits by the young and by women particularly alarmed Henry: he noted that in 1750, during a smallpox epidemic in Ulster,

> Most of the children of the lower people, who were seized with it first, died; which was occasioned by an unhappy practice of giving the children whiskey in order to strike out the pox as they termed it.

Eighty years later, during the 1832 cholera epidemic, the anti-spirits movement in Ulster was arguing against exactly the same practice, and with equally little success. Henry also deplored the common practice of giving pregnant women and nursing mothers spirits, so that, if not 'shrivelled up' in the womb, the children were destroyed 'by the very milk that should nourish them'. Arguments against spirit consumption on health and medical grounds were to figure prominently in temperance literature during the late eighteenth and early nineteenth centuries, for the prevailing opinion, not least among doctors themselves, was that spirits had medicinal benefits. It was essential for the anti-spirits movement to overturn this opinion, and much effort was therefore devoted to the conversion of doctors.

From a political point of view, Henry argued that a wise state had three principal aims: to 'increase the number of its inhabitants; to keep them well employed, and so to make them rich; and to preserve them in good humour, in a temper amenable to the laws'. The consumption of spirits undermined all three. Apart from destroying health and vitality, spirits induced 'sloth and idle habits'; they thus contributed to high labour costs which made Irish goods expensive and difficult to sell. Moreover, spirit production used up vast amounts of grain which should have gone into the making of bread or beer. Henry, like the brewers, wanted to encourage beer production and consumption. He complained that so much grain went into spirits that 'scarce a drop of good ale is to be got even in our market towns but what is imported from England'. In most inns the traveller 'must either drink whiskey and water, or want'. Being an Englishman, Henry was thoroughly convinced of the good properties of beer and wanted to see Irish farmers drinking 'malt drink at home, as in England'. He conceded that a man could get drunk on ale, but argued that this was a different form of drunkenness from that induced by spirits:

> He that gets drunk from ale is a stupid inoffensive sot; but the man who has his brain inflamed with hot spirits, is above the laws, is a madman, a lion let loose, ready for every mischief.

Like Berkeley, Henry was acutely aware of the threat posed by the 'mighty neighbouring monarchy' and that the first people to suffer by the disuse of spirits in Ireland would be the French:

> With them, it must be owned, we derive a great trade. We send them yearly our money, and vast quantities of beef; and, I fear, some wool, to enrich them at home, and feed their sugar colonies, which are ruining ours; while our own poor natives are, for want of their native beef and manufacture, left to starve, in rags, on potatoes and buttermilk. In return for this, the French send us vast quantities of brandy. . . . It is a strong reach of policy, in this nation which has long aimed at universal monarchy, to make themselves great by enervating us; that when we are sufficiently reduced, we may fall the more easy prey to the conqueror. (**177**, 11-12, 20-2, 25, 31, 35)

Henry recommended that the government ban small stills of less than 200 gallons, suppress 'low retailers' by demanding a good-conduct certificate from the magistrates before issuing a licence, and encourage the export of such spirit as was produced in Ireland (**178**, 8-13) If the French were 'poisoning' their neighbours with brandy, Henry obviously felt that they should be paid in kind with Irish whiskey. All these measures, together with discriminatory taxes to encourage brewing, were put into practice before the end of the century, yet in spite of them (and in some cases because of them), whiskey consumption continued to increase dramatically.

Berkeley, Madden, Orrery, Chesterfield and Henry, all writing between 1720 and 1760, had attacked the gentry for their drunkenness and for encouraging drinking among the people by their example. Perhaps the most significant development in the latter part of the century with regard to Irish drinking habits, apart from the replacement of imported spirits by whiskey, was the decline in heavy drinking among the landed gentry. This was a gradual process extending over many decades, and the reasons for it are difficult to infer. The influence of changing English fashions, particularly after the Union, was significant; for instance, the growth of Protestant Evangelicalism with its puritanical moral code had a profound effect on social behaviour among the upper and middle classes. Irish Evangelicals were to be very prominent in the temperance movement of the 1820s and 1830s. But this decline in drinking also points to an increasing insecurity among the ranks of the Protestant ascendancy. With a soaring Catholic population and widespread agitation for political reform, the gentry from about the 1780s could no longer be complaisant about their pre-eminence; the long Irish 'crisis of the aristocracy' had begun. Drunkenness, gambling and duelling were considered at the time characteristic of the Irish upper classes. While their position was secure such activities could be shrugged off as nothing more than colourful foibles, but towards the end of the century, as the ascendancy seemed under increasing threat, such pastimes came to be viewed as vices inappropriate in a ruling class. The ascendancy was being called upon, not least by critics from within its own ranks, to prove that it deserved its position though its moral superiority as well as its political and economic power. And as Catholics increasingly sought a share of this power, Protestants were driven more and more to moral justifications in order to explain, and to maintain, their status.

As early as the 1770s observers were beginning to comment on improvements in Irish manners. In 1769 George Faulkner was informing Chesterfield, who remained deeply interested in the subject of Irish drinking habits, that 'drinking is a good deal lessened'. (**196**, I, 327) In 1775 Richard Twiss toured the country and in the following year produced a book full of highly critical observations; so unpopular did these views make him in Dublin that a chamber-pot with his portrait inside, mouth open, known as a 'Twiss pot', was all the rage for a time. Twiss remarked that he had expected to find the Irish addicted to drinking, duelling and gambling, but that this was not in fact the case:

> Hospitality and drinking went formerly hand in hand, but since the excesses of the table have been so judiciously abolished, hospitality is not so violently practised as heretofore, when it might have been imputed to them as a fault.

It was one of the few complimentary things Twiss had to say about the Irish. That the reality of drinking among the gentry in Ireland did not generally match its reputation became a frequent comment in travellers' books from this time onwards. Thus in 1780 Philip Luckombe remarked:

> With respect to drinking, I have been happily disappointed; the bottle is circulated freely, but not to that excess we have heard it was, and I of course dreaded to find. (**328**, 8; **224**, 40)

Arthur Young, a far more famous visitor to Ireland in the late 1770s, said much the same thing, though he did discriminate among the gentry. 'Hard drinking' was 'very rare among people of fortune', Young had found, but he acknowledged that this 'change of manners' was 'not generally known in England'. By 'people of fortune' Young appears to have meant the leaders of society, those who spent a good deal of time in Dublin or even in London, for he singled out middlemen or small country gentlemen as perhaps the heaviest-drinking group in the country. These comprised

> tenants, who drink their claret by means of profit rents; jobbers in farms; bucks; your fellows with round hats, edged with gold, who hunt in the day, get drunk in the evening, and fight the next morning . . . these are the men among whom drinking, wrangling, quarrelling, fighting, ravishing, etc. are found as in their native soil; once to a degree that made them the pest of society; they are growing better. . . . A new spirit; new fashions; new modes of politeness exhibited by the higher ranks are imitated by the lower, which will, it is to be hoped, put an end to this race of beings. . . . I repeat it from the intelligence I received, that even this class are very different from what they were twenty years ago, and improve so fast that the time will soon come when the national character will not be degraded by any set.

Young complained of the cheapness of spirits: rum, brandy, but especially whiskey, 'with which a man may get dead drunk for two pence'. Nevertheless, the lack of hard currency meant that an Irish farmer or labourer, unlike his landlord, could not 'go on Saturday night to the whiskey house, and drink out the week's support of himself, his wife and his children, not uncommon in the alehouse of the Englishman'; an Irishman could 'neither drink whiskey from his potatoes, nor milk it from his cow'. Before the explosive growth in the illegal distilling industry as a result of the 1779 revenue act, Young thus identified the lesser rural gentry, rather than the peasantry, as the major consumers of drink in Irish society. (**347**, II, 111, 113, 108, 177, 31; **128**, 23)

Sir Jonah Barrington, who in his youth had associated with the country gentry of whom Young complained, commented at some length in his memoirs, published in the 1820s, on the changes that had occurred in drinking habits during his lifetime. Barrington grew up on his grandfather's estate near Abbeyleix in the 1760s, when 'every estated gentleman in the Queen's County was honoured by the gout'. His grandfather eventually succumbed to the disorder; he had a copy of Berkeley's treatise on the virtues of tar water in his library, but presumably he had not read it, or at least had not taken its message to heart. Barrington described great feats of eating and drinking, especially at festivals like Christmas. But, turning to the time of writing, some fifty years later, he observed a totally different picture:

> When I compare with the foregoing the habits of the present day, and see the grandsons of those joyous and vigorous sportsmen mincing their fish and tit-bits at their favourite box in Bond Street, amalgamating their ounce of salad on a silver saucer, employing six sauces to coax one appetite, burning up the palate to make its enjoyments the more exquisite, sipping their acid claret, disguised by an olive or neutralised by a chestnut; lisping out for the scented waiter, and paying him the price of a feast for the modicum of a Lilliputian, and the pay of a captain for the attendance of a blackguard — it amuses me extremely and makes me speculate on what their forefathers would have done to those admirable Epicenes. (**63**, I, 3-5, 41)

These are more than the nostalgic ramblings of an old rogue. Though Barrington was certainly prone to exaggeration and misrepresentation, it is true that the drunkenness and gluttony, which were perfectly acceptable among the gentry of the Irish midlands in the 1760s, were not acceptable in the fashionable society of Dublin or London during the 1820s.

While Barrington lamented the disappearance of the old manners, some from his own class welcomed it. Among these were the Edgeworths of Co. Longford, who did much to encourage and promote more restrained social behaviour. In *Castle Rackrent*, first published in 1800, Maria Edgeworth presented a highly critical portrait of the eighteenth-century Irish gentry, notably of Sir Patrick Rackrent, who had 'lived and died a monument of old Irish hospitality'. (**149**, 23; **128**, 242-8) Her father, Richard Lovell Edgeworth, in his memoirs recorded that, as an undergraduate at Trinity College, Dublin, around 1760, he had indulged in the 'copious potations which were in fashion'. But later in life, particularly under the influence of his friend Dr Erasmus Darwin, he had become a severe critic of Irish drinking habits. Writing of Darwin's views, Maria Edgeworth said:

> During his lifetime, he almost banished wine from the tables of the rich of his acquaintance; and persuaded most of the gentry in his own and the neighbouring counties, to become water drinkers. Partly in jest and partly in earnest, he expressed his suspicions, and carried his inferences on this subject, to a preposterous excess. When he heard that my father was bilious, he suspected, that this must be the consequence of his having, since his residence in Ireland, and in compliance with the fashion of the country, indulged too freely in drinking. His letter, I

remember, concluded with — 'Farewell, my dear friend, God keep you from whiskey — if he can.' To any one who knew my father, this must seem a laughable suspicion, for he was famous, or in those days, I may say, infamous, in Ireland, for his temperance.

Edgeworth, however, did not follow his friend into 'preposterous excess': he was not a 'water drinker' and in fact continued to believe in the medicinal value of alcohol. Writing to Darwin in October 1786, during an illness, he observed: 'I shall, as soon as I am stronger, come down from three (rarely four) to one or two glasses of wine; indeed, when I am well, I seldom exceed two.'

Nor was Edgeworth's temperance restricted to his own personal habits; he sought to impose it both on his family and on his tenants. According to Maria, he did not seek to convince his tenants by 'any moral or rational argument', believing that drunkenness could not be annihilated by the 'mere power of conviction'. Instead he made it clear that 'if the master should once catch a man drunk, he would never forget or forgive it to him or his'. (**150**, I, 76, II, 40-1, 84) It was temperance imposed by threat and coercion. Such paternalistic and authoritarian tactics were to be very much to the fore in the temperance movement of the following century. With his own extraordinary family of four wives and twenty-two children, however, Edgeworth had considerable success in propagating his temperance principles. Maria was later to adopt the excessive standpoint that she had criticised in Darwin and to become a total abstainer. She was a great admirer of Father Mathew, as were her stepmother, Frances, and half-sister, Harriet. They invited him to conduct a mission at Edgeworthstown in March 1841 and later entertained him in their home. (**189**, 112-13) Another daughter, Anna, married Dr Thomas Beddoes, a philosopher and chemist and one of her father's closest friends. He was also a vigorous temperance advocate, and his popular tract *Hints to Husbandmen* was republished in Dublin in 1813 with an introduction by Charles Sneyd Edgeworth. While not disputing the 'propriety of drinking freely of some kind of liquor', Beddoes strongly warned against the practice of providing large quantities of alcohol to rural workers during harvest time; the labourer would 'get the rot completely ere harvest is over', wrote Beddoes. He was thinking primarily of the ale and cider supplied to English labourers; how much worse was the Irish situation, wrote Sneyd Edgeworth in his introduction, where whiskey was the drink most commonly provided. (**135**; **65**, 10, 17, 4)

In the writings of the Edgeworths the anxiety of the landed gentry at the increasing whiskey consumption among tenants and labourers is obvious. Their response was not so much to seek to reform their social inferiors as to reform themselves and their own class. Their response can be seen in the family's progress from temperance to total abstinence, and also, more generally, in their support for greater restraint, particularly sobriety, at social gatherings of their class. Maria Edgeworth provides much evidence on the change in manners that occurred among the gentry between the 1770s and 1820s. Writing about 1819, she testified strongly to the great improvement over the preceding thirty or forty years in the 'general mode of living', 'manners' and 'information' of the 'middle classes of gentry in this part of Ireland'. She particularly noted the disappearance of 'those desperately tiresome, long, formal dinners' at which guests consumed 'more than they could eat, and twenty times more than they should drink'. The separation of the sexes after dinner was also diminishing, which she thought was another decided improvement:

> The gentlemen and ladies are not separated from the time dinner ends, till the midnight hour, when the carriages came to the door to carry off the bodies of the dead; or, till just sense enough being left, to find their way straight to the tea-table, the gentlemen could only swallow a hasty cup of cold coffee or stewed tea, and be carried off by their sleepy wives, happy if the power of reproach were lost in fatigue. (**150**, II, 375-6)

In 1812 Edward Wakefield observed that gentlemen did not begin to drink until tea and coffee were served after a meal, and even then there was no compulsion for them to drink at all. But he also noted in passing that this was a relatively new social phenomenon. (**336**, II, 787)

These changing fashions, which closely paralleled developments in England (**161**, 236-8), were not, however, restricted to the rural gentry; a similar picture emerges among the urban middle class. The letters of Dr William Drennan, the Belfast United Irishman, provide much interesting information on the lifestyle of this group around the turn of the century. Writing from Newry, Co. Down, to his sister in Belfast in the early 1780s, Drennan had complained of all-male drinking parties which it was impossible to avoid if one desired to make acquaintances and to advance in one's profession. But in 1800, having recently married and moved to Dublin, Drennan's letters portray far more sober social gatherings. At one party in that year hosted by Drennan himself, some porter and Portuguese wine were served, but 'no punch' and much 'excellent tea and coffee' and 'real good lemonade'. But these gatherings were certainly not staid affairs: one party for fifty people, after a midnight supper of lamb, veal, chicken, ham, tongue, crab, blancmange, cheese-cake, custard, lemon cream, tarts, almonds, raisins, oranges, apples, figs and French plums, continued dancing until after 3 a.m. (**91**, 12, 299)

Among much of the poorer rural population the pattern of periodic circumstantial heavy drinking, described by Moryson early in the seventeenth century, seems to have remained the rule. Several of the eighteenth-century observers already quoted complained not of rural drinking habits in general, but rather of the amount of drinking that inevitably accompanied special occasions, like christenings, marriages, funerals, fairs, markets and patterns. (**239**, 47-8; **52**, 8) In 1805 Thomas Newenham endorsed this picture, while drawing a significant distinction between rural and urban drinking patterns. According to him,

> Much has been said on the subject of the drunkenness of the inferior orders of the Irish; and ... their peculiar and irresistible partiality to whiskey.... In large towns, where, by the way, the observations on the drunkenness of the Irish have generally been made, that fault is, no doubt, very prevalent among the common people. But in the country, it is far otherwise. Except at fairs, patrons, wakes and weddings, those who dwell in the single-hearth houses, such as agricultural labourers, cottier-tenants, small farmers, country artificers and weavers, are scarcely ever seen intoxicated, and never use spirits at their meals. (**258**, 232-3)

As Arthur Young had noted, the lack of hard currency among the rural poor prevented frequent and regular heavy drinking, such as was found among the English rural population. But during the 1780s and 1790s complaints about increased spirit consumption, particularly among the urban working population, became very frequent. A number of the pamphlets appearing and a good deal of the debate in the Irish parliament were, as we have already seen, inspired by the brewers and their political allies. But this was by no means the whole story. The misguided reforms of 1779 had led to a massive increase in whiskey production, both legal and illegal. The cheapness of spirits and increasing prosperity meant that more of the population could afford to drink more whiskey. But, at the same time that whiskey consumption was increasing among the general population, heavy drinking was becoming less fashionable and less respectable among the landed gentry and the middle class. Moreover, at a time of political threat and instability as in the 1790s, increasing spirit consumption could be seen as spreading discontent and irresponsibility and preparing the ground for rebellion.

The growing alarm is obvious from the late 1780s. Thus grand juries of both the county and city of Dublin petitioned parliament against the 'unrestrained use of spirituous liquors' four times between 1785 and 1788. In 1789 the high sheriff, grand jury and gentry of Co. Kildare petitioned against the indiscriminate issuing of licences, 'granted to obscure and disorderly houses', while in the same year a petition from the Quakers of Ireland spoke of the 'great injury occasioned, particularly to the lower class of people, by the immoderate use of spirituous liquors'. (**18**, XI, 346, XII, 85-6, 426, XIII, 74, 112) The alarm seems to have been especially strongly felt in Dublin. This is understandable when one looks at the figures for spirit production in the city, which was the major centre of the industry.

Between 1786 and 1795 production nearly quadrupled, from under 400,000 gallons to nearly 1.5 million, thus far outstripping production for the country as a whole, which approximately doubled over the same period. (**18**, XVI, ccclxxviii, XIV, xliii; **234**, 149-51) In April 1788 representatives of the Dublin parish vestries of St Werburgh, St Peter, St Catherine, St Nicholas Without, St James and St Mary formed a committee to petition the Lord Lieutenant against the 'alarming' number of 'dram-shops' in the city, which ranged from one-seventh of the houses in St Mary's parish up to one-quarter in St James's, the proportion being found to 'increase in the parishes principally inhabited by the manufacturing and working people'. The committee also resolved to do all in its power to help the magistrates, churchwardens and police to stamp out the unlicensed selling of spirits and trading on Sunday. Appeals were made to the archbishops, bishops and clergy of all denominations, and a sub-committee was established to meet regularly and monitor the situation. (**171**, v, viii, x) Amongst those active on this committee were Sir Lucius O'Brien and David La Touche, both of whom were to champion the brewers' case in parliament in the early 1790s. Whether their alarm over increasing spirit consumption drew them into the brewers' camp, or whether their connections with the brewers made them opponents of spirits is impossible to say. But many of those protesting at the level of spirit consumption certainly did not have a vested interest in the brewers' case. Their concern sprang from the massive increase in spirit production, particularly illegal production, which had begun after 1780 and which, as they saw it, threatened both the economic prosperity and the political stability of the country.

The legislation of the 1790s did have the effect of encouraging beer consumption, but, while the still-licence system remained in operation, it could not stem the rising tide of spirits. In the five-year period 1780-84 legal production amounted on average to 2.6 million gallons annually; in the following five years, 1785-9, it jumped to 3.5 million gallons; and in the period 1790-94 it leapt further to reach 4.4 million gallons per annum. Massive tax increases imposed after 1795 by a government desperate for revenue to finance its European wars appear to have succeeded in curbing legal production: for while the duty on a gallon of spirits soared from 1s 5d in 1795 to 4s 1d by 1804, annual average production in the periods 1795-9 and 1800-4 remained at around 4.4 million gallons. (**254**, 726-8; **27**, 66-7) Unquestionably, however, as the price of 'parliament' whiskey rose steeply and demand consequently declined, the illicit distiller found many more eager customers for his cheaper product.

The measures taken by the government in the 1790s to curb whiskey consumption were not only largely unsuccessful but also very unpopular. Lord Shannon reported in a letter to his son on 15 February 1791 that there was rioting among the 'common people' in Dublin when parliament discussed measures to curb whiskey consumption, for rumours had circulated that it was 'to be made felony to drink a dram'. People 'paraded through the streets carrying a figure hung upon a gibbet, with an empty bottle and glass, crying: "The last speech of Captain Whiskey!", and ballad-singers were in all corners of the streets singing dismal lamentations at his sudden and unhappy fate'. Spirit sellers were adversely affected by various new licensing acts passed in 1791, 1792, 1796 and 1797. Together these considerably tightened the licensing procedures, increased the cost of spirit licences and the penalties for breaching the law, and made the retailing of wine and beer more attractive than that of spirits. Meanwhile grain producers in countries like Wicklow and Wexford saw the barley market collapse after the malt tax was raised from 2s 6d a barrel in 1791 to 5s 3d in 1796. At a time of growing popular unrest harsh measures to curb drink consumption were perhaps politically unwise; and in fact all these groups, Dublin artisans and labourers, spirit sellers and grain producers, were to figure prominently on the rebel side in the rebellion of 1798. (**180**, 18; **234**, 144-5, 160-4; **280**, 158)

The rebellion was to loom large in the mythology of the temperance movement throughout the nineteenth century. To Protestant temperance advocates, especially in the 1830s and 1840s, the Wexford massacres of loyalist prisoners were the work of whiskey-crazed madmen: only minds disordered by drink, it was argued, could have been capable of such atrocities. This interpretation was reflected in George Cruikshank's well-known illustrations for W. H. Maxwell's *History of the Irish Rebellion in 1798* (1845), where the rebels are repeatedly shown as grinning, drunken simians. (**249**, 82, 99, 154, 384) Catholic temperance supporters of the 1880s and 1890s were to adopt a rather similar interpretation, though from a wholly different point of view. They lamented battles, like New Ross, Arklow and Vinegar Hill, lost, they believed, principally through the rebels' fondness for drink. But at the same time they believed that whiskey consumption had been fostered in Ireland by the British government so as to render the people submissive in the face of oppression. (**244**, 110-11)

This latter interpretation was abroad even during the 1790s: writing in 1796, William Drennan for one felt that

> Ireland must continue as she is, while her lower orders are kept in a state of intoxication, perhaps designedly, for this keeps them beasts of burden; not strong, however, as they appear generally feeble, withered animals. (**91**, 238)

Some of the United Irish leaders were very critical of drink consumption, both because it encouraged degradation and indiscipline among potential recruits to their cause and also because the taxes derived helped to bolster and perpetuate British government. In March 1798 the city of Dublin committee condemned 'government which draws its resources from vice (such as GAMBLING AND DRUNKENNESS)'. But other United Irishmen took a wholly different stance. John Sweetman, one of the leading lights in the Dublin Directory and a prominent champion of Catholic rights, was himself a brewer, while there is much evidence that drink sellers were a significant group at the grassroots level of the organisation: 'saucy and uncivil' and 'deeply disaffected' was how Maxwell later termed them. The government certainly seems to have thought so, for in its efforts to smash the movement in the midlands in the spring of 1798 drink sellers, along with blacksmiths and carpenters (who were thought responsible for the manufacture of pikes), were the main groups singled out for interrogation and torture. It was widely believed that alehouses were used for United Irish meetings and for the storage of weapons. (**280**, 49, 83-4; **249**, 86)

In their lifestyles many United Irish leaders demonstrated little concern for temperance. Samuel Neilson, one of the Dublin leaders, was 'a slave to drink', who managed to get himself arrested in May 1798 when, under the influence, he appeared outside Newgate prison and proceeded to abuse the governor. (**280**, 119-20) Even more colourful drunken escapades feature prominently in the journal of Wolfe Tone. He and his friend Thomas Russell, despite frequent resolutions to change their habits, seem to have conducted a goodly amount of their political activities in the early 1790s in a highly intoxicated state. In 1791 and 1792 especially, while the United Irish Societies were being formed in Belfast and Dublin, phrases like 'very drunk', 'generally drunk', 'wakened very sick', 'waken drunk', 'great deal of wine', 'generally very drunk — bed. God knows how' are very frequent in Tone's diary. His accounts of drunken political dinners and discussions are often very amusing, as for instance when at a dinner of the 'chief United Irishmen' in Dublin on 1 November 1792 Mr Hutton (as Tone styles himself in the diary) was

> very much surprised, on looking down to the table, to see two glasses before him; finds, on looking at Hamilton Rowan, that he has got four eyes; various other phenomena in optics equally curious. Mr Hutton, like the sun in the centre of the system, fixed, but every thing about him moving in a rapid rotation; perfectly sober, but perceives that every one else is getting very drunk; essays to walk across the room, but finds it impossible to move rectilineally, proceeding entirely from his having taken a sprig of watercresses with his bread at dinner. 'God bless every body.'

The next day's entry begins: 'Sick as Demogorgon; purpose to leave off watercresses with my bread.' Despite his jocular style, the exclamation 'Bad! Bad!' often follows such accounts of drunken evenings, and Tone on one occasion, albeit to no end, meditated 'leaving off the use of wine altogether'. Certainly by 1796, when he was living in France, his habits do seem to have undergone a significant reformation. He remarked frequently on the soberness of the French and in March of that year recorded: 'I live very soberly at present, having retrenched my quantity of wine one half.' In comparing the Irish with the French, Tone noted their differing attitudes to drink:

The devil of it is, that poor Pat is a little given to drink, and the French are very sober. We must rectify that as well as we can; he is a good man that has no fault, and I have a sort of sympathetic feeling which makes me the more indulgent on this score.

Remembering his own dissipated days in Ireland, Tone might well have felt some sympathy for the Irishman too much given to drink. (**345**, I, 141-8, 152, 160, 172, 197, II, 55, 78)

But, on the other side too, drink proved a significant problem. When Sir Ralph Abercromby, the Irish commander-in-chief, made the notorious remark in February 1798 that the Irish army was 'in a state of licentiousness which must render it formidable to everyone but the enemy', he undoubtedly had drunkenness very much in mind. (**280**, 59) The militia were certainly grave offenders in this regard. In May 1796, for instance, Major George Matthews was forced to write to the Marquis of Downshire explaining how a recruiting party of the Downshire militia attending a fair at Dromore had become involved in a riot in which a woman was killed and many people injured. 'I believe', wrote Matthews, 'drunkenness has been the occasion of all this misfortune. Whiskey is the curse of this country and in the recruiting business it is impossible to keep them from it.' Nor had the situation apparently improved much by the following year, when, with a French invasion threatened, Matthews wrote again to the marquis to express the opinion that 'If France ever beats us it will be by whiskey and not by force of arms.'[1]

In the actual rising of 1798 drink played a part on both sides. In such a murderous *jacquerie*, with an ill-disciplined militia on the one hand and an embittered peasantry on the other and with much drink available from looted cellers and shops, it is hardly surprising that complaints of drunkenness, and particularly of atrocities committed while the perpetrators were drunk, are common. Yet the role of drink in the fighting was complicated, for it appears to have both helped and hindered the opposing parties. Thus the North Cork militia's foolish headlong charge up Oulart Hill in Co. Wexford in which they were slaughtered by the rebels was partly the result of drunken bravado, the militia having shortly before looted and burnt a public house. On other occasions, such as the assaults on Enniscorthy and New Ross, the rebels displayed extraordinary courage and determination, which loyalists found hard to explain except in terms of drink. But there were numerous times, particularly after the capture of towns, when discipline on both sides dissolved altogether in an orgy of drunkenness and murder. (**280**, 173-5, 200, 213, 230) Overall, drink appears to have contributed substantially to both the unpredictability and the ferocity of the conflict. Perhaps both views expressed by nineteenth-century temperance advocates were correct: drink not only undermined the discipline of the rebels, it also fuelled their rage against loyalists. This is only half the picture, however: exactly the same judgment could be made of the militia and yeomanry.

By the 1820s there was considerable alarm in Ireland, among Protestant landlords, clergy, doctors, lawyers and merchants, at the level of spirit consumption, particularly of illicit spirit consumption. Despite the imposition of heavy fines and the establishment of a special police force, a vast illegal industry flourished in Connacht and north-west Ulster, often with the connivance of local landlords and magistrates. Among labourers and artisans in urban areas like Dublin, Belfast and Cork, where legal distilleries were largely based, heavy, regular spirit consumption was also rampant. The still-licence reforms of 1823 had allowed 'parliament' whiskey to recapture a large share of the market from poteen, much to the government's satisfaction. But critics simply pointed to massive increases in the consumption of legal spirits, alongside a flourishing illegal industry. They cared little about improved government revenues; all they saw was an apparent trebling of consumption during a time of economic dislocation and political unrest. The parallel with the 1790s was obvious and highly disturbing. With memories of the 1798 massacres by drunken rebels still fresh in their minds, many Protestants were alarmed by Daniel O'Connell's appeal to the Catholic masses in support of Emancipation. Stated simply, their problem was how to bolster their own socio-economic position while at the same time reasserting their political influence over the people. Some put their faith in moderate reform and were prepared to accept measures like Emancipation; others championed the traditional Protestant supremacy by joining Brunswick Clubs or Orange lodges. But then, in 1829, came accounts from America of the operations of novel organisations called temperance societies.

2

Moderation versus Teetotalism, 1829-38

THE first large-scale temperance societies appeared in Ireland late in 1829, with Belfast and Dublin being the main centres of the movement. Their appearance was closely linked with contemporary religious, political and socio-economic developments. Almost wholly Protestant in composition, they reflected the rising tide of Evangelicalism in many of the Protestant churches; essentially middle-class in leadership, they showed the need for greater control of the Catholic masses felt in the wake of O'Connell's successful campaign for Emancipation; directed solely against spirit consumption, they indicated ascendancy alarm at increased whiskey drinking among farmers, labourers and artisans; strongly supported, in Belfast particularly, by merchants and mill owners, they demonstrated the capitalists' desire to create a sober and submissive workforce. But while factors peculiar to Ireland played a significant part in the emergence of temperance societies, it should not be forgotten that the Irish organisations were part of an international movement and that external influences were therefore also of vital importance. It was news of the successes of the American Temperance Society, founded in 1826 in Boston, that acted as a major spur to Irish temperance advocates, and the American experience was to remain an important model. The Irish movement in turn encouraged the establishment of societies, first in Scotland and then in England. If anything these overseas links were to become stronger as time passed, particularly in the 1840s when Father Mathew travelled in person to Scotland, England and the United States in the cause of total abstinence.

In evidence presented in 1825 to the House of Lords select committee on the state of Ireland, Thomas Frankland Lewis, an M.P. who had sat on commissions investigating Irish revenue and education, acknowledged the disastrous impact that the distillery laws had had upon the country. They had, he claimed, 'contributed materially to the unquiet state of many parts', tending to produce 'in large classes of persons a habit of insubordination'; such persons had 'abandoned all settled habits of industry' in favour of depravity and dissipation. More precisely, he defined those most deeply involved in illicit distillation as 'cottagers, persons of the lowest description, persons who had nothing to lose', mostly living in the north and west of the country. In general Lewis felt that 'A population which had been habituated to illegal distillation would be the most likely to forward . . . disturbances.'(**24**, 27-8) One could hardly wish for a clearer statement of the threat perceived to both political stability and economic prosperity by illicit distillation and consumption. Nine years later in 1834 Dr John Edgar, a Presbyterian clergyman from Belfast, told a select committee on drunkenness that drinking was mainly confined to the 'lower classes' and to some extent to the 'middle classes', but that 'a great improvement has taken place in that class peculiarly denominated the "higher"'. Yet he felt that 'At the present time, private distilling has seldom, if ever, been worse.' And, like Lewis, he drew the committee's attention to both the political and economic consequences of this state of affairs. After referring to atrocities committed in Co. Down in 1798 by drunken rebels, Edgar went on: 'There is a strong temptation for persons to unite themselves with political societies, on account of the spirit drinking which frequently takes place in the lodges of these societies.' As for the employer's viewpoint, Edgar quoted one who had told him that in ten years in trade 'he never had a man in his employment by whom he did not lose money on account of their drunkenness', except for one who did not drink whiskey at all. (**26**, 65-6) Despite the similarities between Lewis's and Edgar's evidence, there are several crucial differences: Lewis was chiefly condemning illicit distillation, while Edgar was condemning all forms of spirit production and consumption; also Lewis argued strongly that the distillery law reforms of 1823 had led to a considerable diminution in the problem, whereas Edgar, on the other hand, was convinced that only with the appearance of temperance societies in 1829 had any significant advance occurred.

During the first five years of the temperance campaign, from 1829 to 1834, it was Belfast which provided much of the dynamism, and in Belfast John Edgar was the acknowledged leader of the cause. Edgar was born in 1798 at Ballynahinch, Co. Down, into a Presbyterian family with strong connections with the Secession church; his father, great-uncle, brother, maternal uncle and two brothers-in-law were all Presbyterian clergymen. The Rev. Samuel Edgar, his father, was minister at Ballynahinch from 1793 until his death in 1826; a noted preacher and author of sermons, he was also a professor of divinity in the Belfast Academical Institution from 1815 to 1826 and clerk of the Secession Synod from 1819 until 1826. After study in Glasgow and at the Academical Institution, the younger Edgar was ordained in 1820 and immediately received a call from the second Seceding congregation in Belfast. This congregation, formed in 1814 and consisting of only about twenty families 'in humble circumstances', still did not have a permanent place of worship when Edgar was appointed six years later. But with characteristic energy he immediately set about raising the money to build a church. In January 1822, as a result of his endeavours, a small church was opened in Alfred Place, and this remained in use until 1837, when the congregation moved to a much grander building erected in Alfred Street. Even at this early stage of his career, however, Edgar's energy and single-mindedness stirred up opposition, most notably from within his own church. Thus he was not granted the *regium donum*, the government's stipend to Presbyterian clergy, mainly because of opposition from the other Seceding congregation in Belfast, which resented the establishment of a rival church in the town. (**317**, 272-4, 284, 286) Edgar's biographer, W. D. Killen, perhaps conveyed something of the impact of the man when he described his appearance and manner. He was, wrote Killen,

> little indebted for any degree of popularity he enjoyed to his personal appearance. He was robust and well proportioned, and somewhat above the middle size; but his complexion was swarthy, his features strongly marked, and his general aspect might have betokened a descent from one of the sable sons of Africa. His manner also was abrupt; and his voice, though good and strong, wanted those silver tones by which some speakers are so greatly recommended. But, though his gestures were not unfrequently grotesque, he had carefully studied the principles of elocution; he knew well how to put his arguments; and a critic might have found it difficult to detect anything amiss in the language of the rough orator. His observations were always striking and sensible; and, though cautious men often thought him rather rash, the candid portion of the public began to give him credit for honesty and manliness. (**206**, 16-17)

All in all, it was the portrait of a forceful and determined character, though one likely to give offence to others.

Edgar, like his father before him, was ordained into the Secession church. The Seceders in Scotland and Ulster had broken with the main body of the Presbyterian church in the 1730s and 1740s over the specific issue of patronage. But, in general terms, the Seceders tended to be more strictly orthodox and more Evangelically inclined than their fellow-Presbyterians in the Synod of Ulster. By the 1820s, however, orthodoxy and Evangelicalism were making rapid headway in the Synod of Ulster as well. This was the era of the great struggle between orthodoxy and Unitarianism, championed respectively by Henry Cooke and Henry Montgomery. Although Edgar, as a Seceder, was not directly involved in the struggle, his sympathies were clearly on the side of Cooke. Killen described him as a 'Calvinistic Presbyterian to the core'. Certainly he opposed Arianism, particularly in the Academical Institution, where he had followed his father as a professor in 1826. A close friend and colleague in the temperance movement was the Rev. James Morgan of Fisherwick Place church; Morgan was in turn a strong supporter and friend of Cooke's and the editor of the *Orthodox Presbyterian*, the mouthpiece for Cooke's party. (**255**, 67) Edgar's Evangelical bent was also obvious from an early stage. He was active in the Religious Tract Society, founded in 1815, and became its secretary in 1824. It was to provide an invaluable base from which to launch a pamphlet campaign in favour of temperance. He also joined the anti-Catholic Reformation Society during the Emancipation crisis and gave a series of controversial anti-Catholic lectures. Later in his life Edgar was to be closely engaged in mission work, especially in Connacht during the famine, but in the 1820s and 1930s his Evangelical endeavours were very much focused on his own town of Belfast.

The first Presbyterian congregation in Belfast had been formed in the year 1644, and by 1800 the town had five. In the next thirty years three more appeared: Edgar's in Alfred Place, Morgan's in Fisherwick Place, and Cooke's in May Street. But during the 1830s seven new congregations were formed. (**229**, 69) These creations reflected the rapid growth in the town's population: between 1821 and 1831 the population increased by 43 per cent, and between 1831 and 1841 by another 32 per cent. (**82**, 28) Edgar was acutely aware of the needs of this burgeoning population, much of it composed of country-bred poor attracted by the work opportunities offered in the new textile mills. The late 1820s and early 1830s were difficult years for the textile industry in Ulster. In Belfast they witnessed the replacement of cotton by linen as the main textile produced and the steady mechanisation of the industry. As we shall see, the temperance movement received considerable support from mill owners (in the English midlands and north, as well as in Ulster), for it held out prospects of increased worker efficiency and greater consumer demand. (**173**, 96) Edgar had many friends among the Presbyterian mill owners, and in 1828 he cemented his alliance with this group by marrying into the Grimshaw family.

In his early writings on temperance Edgar was particularly critical of the Presbyterian church and its ministers, as he felt that they had succumbed to the intemperate habits of the age. In 1829 he complained that the

> session-house of each congregation must have its cupboard and its bottle, and after the sermon, and perhaps before it, the ruling elder is ready with a dram for the minister. Wherever the minister goes in his visitations, the bottle is ready, and no matter how often he has drunk already, or how weak or hungry he may be, he must, in every house, take a drop of something.

Ordination dinners also came in for severe condemnation as occasions when drunkenness was considered permissible. (**207**, 4) Even before Edgar's strictures of 1829, however, there is evidence of concern about the level of spirit consumption, at least among the more orthodox branches of

Presbyterianism. James Morgan related that when he entered the ministry in 1820 he found that

> If I took punch after my dinner, as was then the custom, I was not so competent to pursue my studies as I would be without it, and therefore I did not use it. Thus, for the first eight or nine years of my ministry I very seldom tasted intoxicating drink, and never formed the habit of using it.

But Morgan's temperance extended beyond his own personal habits. In his memoirs he described his efforts to curb drinking in Lisburn, Co. Antrim, during the mid-1820s. At first he was offered spirits in almost every house he visited, as Edgar was later to complain, but Morgan immediately set about discouraging this practice. He found the butchers of the town particularly prone to drunkenness and

> endeavoured to change their habits by getting them under engagements to limit the quantity of intoxicants which they used. Abstinence was not then thought of. It will give some idea of the state of matters when I say that the smallest quantity I could induce them to promise to use was three glasses of spirits in the day. (**255**, 34-6)

Another Presbyterian who showed considerable concern over the issue of spirit consumption was that champion of orthodoxy, Henry Cooke. His evidence in 1825 before the select committee on the state of Ireland proved highly controversial, mainly because of his claims that the Academical Institution was 'a great seminary of Arianism' and that most ordinary Presbyterians opposed Catholic Emancipation. But in addition he presented his views on illicit distillation, on townland fines, on drink and party fights and on the suppression of shebeens, and in the process showed that drink was a subject which concerned him greatly and on which he had well-formed views. For instance, he thought that fighting between Orangemen and Ribbonmen was generally the result of drunkenness; that Orange processions were often organised by publicans in order to promote business; that the landed gentry were among the major patrons of illicit distillers; that spirits were too cheap and too easily obtained; and that magistrates should be given greater powers to collect evidence on and prosecute illicit sellers. (**24**, 209-19, 269-70) Most of Cooke's comments indicate a desire for governmental action to amend licensing and revenue laws, but he also envisaged a role for the clergy in curbing drunkenness. In February 1829 he wrote to the Rev. William Campbell of Islandmagee on the subject of wakes, advising:

> They are utterly to be discouraged; yet the work must be done gently, and prudently, and scripturally. As to your going and staying till twelve at night, it is such a thing as I would not do, nor advise you to do. Yet still if you find that your neighbouring ministers — I mean your co-

islanders — do it, you must in some degree conform to the old practice, till you can substitute a better. You know my plan. I generally refuse to go to houses of the dead, if spirits are given to the people. If I go to such houses, I taste not of their dainties. If any consent to give no spirits, I preach or lecture. Then I usually take the corpse into the meeting-house, read a chapter, comment, sing, and pray. (**285**, 138)

What is striking about this extract is the cautiousness of Cooke's actions. He obviously feared to offend local feeling by a forthright attack on wakes and their accompanying drunkenness. Like Morgan in Lisburn, he hoped 'gently' to bring about some diminution in consumption. Yet clearly both men were conscious of a serious problem. In an era of economic dislocation and political unrest, the Evangelically-minded focused their attention on the moral failings of society; with spirit consumption apparently at record levels, it was easy to make the connection between these failings and alcohol. Finding a strategy to solve the problem was, however, not nearly so easy.

In the event the strategy came from America. The American Temperance Society was established in 1826 and provided the model for societies in Ireland, especially for Edgar's Ulster Temperance Society. The American organisation was dominated by young Evangelical Presbyterians and Congregationalists from New England, products of the 'Second Great Awakening', the religious revival that swept the country between the 1790s and 1830s. The largest group of members were clergymen, though doctors and businessmen of various sorts were also well represented. Closely allied with mission and tract societies, the A.T.S. aimed its propaganda not at the drunkard, whom it considered beyond redemption, but at the affluent moderate drinker. If the leaders of society abstained from spirits and thus set an example to their subordinates, drinking would soon fall out of fashion. (**329**, 62-3, 71) Perhaps the most popular of the A.T.S.'s many tracts was the Rev. Lyman Beecher's *Six Sermons on Intemperance*, first published in Boston in 1826. Beecher was a leading Evangelical and one of the most influential Congregationalist ministers of his day, being president of his church's leading seminary between 1832 and 1850. His sermons presented a forcefully argued and comprehensive indictment of spirit drinking.

The Rev. Thomas Houston, a foundation member of the U.T.S., recalled in his memoirs that a 'cheap edition' of Beecher's work was circulating in Ulster in 1828 and early in 1829. He remembered extracts being read at a prayer meeting in Belfast and exciting a good deal of interest. (**310**, 9) But more decisive still seems to have been the visit of the Rev. Joseph Penney. Penney, a Seceder from Drumlee, Co. Down, had emigrated in 1819, becoming a minister in Rochester, New York. The Irish Seceders had had particularly close ties with American Presbyterianism, nearly forty ministers and probationers having emigrated between 1790 and 1823. (**317**, 180-1) Presbyterians were prominent in the A.T.S., and Penney had presumably been involved in the society's work. According to Killen,

> In the summer of 1829, he paid a visit to his native country; and, full of zeal for the extension of temperance societies, earnestly pressed their claims on the attention of many of his Irish brethren. Professor Edgar, who had formerly been his fellow-student, carefully weighed his arguments, and promptly determined to make the cause his own. He had just been appointed by a local committee to draw up an address to the public on the best means of discouraging the sale and consumption of ardent spirits on the Lord's Day; and he believed he had now discovered the true solution of the problem. He inaugurated his proceedings by opening his parlour window, and pouring out into the court before his house in Alfred Street, the remaining part of a gallon of old malt whiskey purchased, some time before, for family consumption. (**206**, 28-9)

The story of Edgar's emptying the family cellar out his parlour window sounds apocryphal, yet it is well authenticated. It certainly conveys his determination to take immediate and decisive action, which was very characteristic of the man.

Firstly he sought publicity: he wrote a letter, initially rejected by the *Belfast Guardian*, which was eventually published by the *Belfast Newsletter* on 14 August 1829. This letter is interesting, not only in that it is Edgar's first public statement on the subject of temperance, but also in that it indicates how his thought on the subject had evolved. He had, he wrote, originally been concerned about desecration of the sabbath, particularly about the selling of spirits on Sunday. But on further reflection (and presumably Penney's influence was important here) he had recognised that 'to have sanctity on the sabbath, there must be temperance all year round'. Nor was Edgar in any doubt as to how to achieve this goal: to 'promote a genuine, not an external, transient reformation, moral suasion must be employed ... there must be a general influencing of public feeling'. He saw the role of publicity in general and the press in particular as crucial. Edgar was also very clear as to whom he was appealing. It was certainly not to the 'present generation of drunkards', for, he wrote,

> It is impossible that the present system of drinking, and the manufacture and sale of spirituous liquor, can be supported by drunkards alone. If you that are temperate unite against them, they must go down, for by you they are maintained and made respectable.[1]

Where his ideas had originated Edgar was only too willing to acknowledge. His plan was 'not made in the spirit of idle speculation or of blind zeal'. He appealed to the 'facts', he said, and went on to record that his views rested on accounts of the successes of the temperance societies in the United States. Certainly his emphasis on the role of the temperate, the hopelessness of the drunkard's plight and the importance of swaying educated public opinion through publicity was characteristic of the operations of the A.T.S. This society, says a recent historian of the American temperance movement, 'developed a peculiar and highly original concept of deviancy. The delinquent was not so much the hopeless confirmed drunkard as the respectable man who was indifferent to the cause of temperance reform.' (**329**, 71) It is no coincidence that one of Edgar's earliest and most widely circulated tracts was entitled *Address to the Temperate*. It was no use, Edgar argued, employers telling their workmen and servants not to get drunk, landlords telling their tenants and clergymen telling their congregations, if they themselves continued to consume spirits, even if only in moderate amounts. If the respectable and temperate members of society abandoned spirits totally, only then could they expect to have any influence over the heavy-drinking working classes.

This American strategy seemed in some regards appropriate in Ireland, where the Protestant middle and upper classes felt themselves, in the wake of Catholic Emancipation, under threat from the Catholic masses. The early temperance movement was designed to reform and strengthen the Protestant ascendancy, while abandoning large numbers of their social inferiors to a drunkard's grave.

The American example also dictated the need for an organisation to spread the temperance message by publishing tracts and promoting meetings. Thus on 24 September 1829 at a gathering in the Religious Tract Society's depository in Waring Street, Belfast, the Ulster Temperance Society was formed. Its pledge required members to 'abstain from the use of distilled spirits . . . to dissuade others from using them, and by all proper means to discountenance the causes and practices of intemperance'. (**207**, 23) There is some confusion as to who the first six signatories were, but the evidence suggests that they were all Protestant ministers of different denominations: Edgar, a Seceding Presbyterian; James Morgan, a Presbyterian; Thomas Hincks, curate of St Anne's cathedral; Thomas Houston of Knockbracken, a Reformed Presbyterian; Hugh Hunter, a New Connexion Methodist; and Matthew Tobias, a Methodist. (**206**, 43; **310**, 10; **85**, I, 32) The executive of the new society was made up of Edgar and Hunter as secretaries, with Hincks as treasurer. The religious affiliations of the first signatories to the U.T.S.'s pledge are a fair reflection of the composition of the movement in Ulster: it was strongest among the more orthodox branches of Presbyterianism, among Methodists and among Evangelically inclined members of the Established Church. When Edgar preached the first sermon on temperance in Belfast in October it was in Tobias's Methodist chapel in Donegall Square, as his own church was considered too small. The second temperance sermon was preached by

Cooke's friend, James Morgan, in his Fisherwick Place church, a bastion of orthodox and Evangelical Presbyterianism.

The spread of the movement was rapid both within and without Ireland during the next six months. Edgar paid a visit to Glasgow in September and encouraged John Dunlop to establish the first Scottish society. He also arranged for the publication in Edinburgh of Beecher's tract, with a long introduction by himself. A Belfast edition of 3,000 copies soon followed. A Scottish merchant, influenced by the example of Glasgow, started the first English society at Bradford in February 1830, while a Dublin Quaker, G. H. Birkett, took a leading role in establishing the second and third English societies at Warrington and Manchester. (**206**, 42-4, **173**, 104-5)

The first society established in Ireland in 1829 was not in fact Edgar's U.T.S., but the New Ross Temperance Society, formed on 20 August by the Rev. George Whitmore Carr. Carr was something of an oddity. An ancestor of the playwright George Bernard Shaw, he was born in 1780 and educated at Trinity College, Dublin. He served with such distinction at the defence of New Ross during the 1798 rebellion that he was made a burgess of the town in the following year. He was ordained in 1800 in the Established Church and took control of his father's parish and endowed school two years later. Carr was an energetic Evangelical, being active in both the Bible Society and the Church Missionary Society. But, as the historian of the C.M.S. in Ireland remarks, he was a 'man of strong, original, and independent turn of mind. His views in many directions cut across the usual lines of demarcation.' In 1811, after a vigorous ministry of ten years, he abruptly left the church and set up an independent chapel, apparently taking most of his congregation with him. His reasons for this step are somewhat obscure, though he seems to have developed objections to the church establishment, or 'state churchism' as he sneeringly termed it, and to the baptismal and burial rites. (**71**, 67; **89**, 41-7; **221**, 224-5) Carr's Evangelical views doubtless go a long way towards explaining his strong support for temperance, though in his case there seems to have been a personal element involved as well. At a hearing of the 1834 select committee on drunkenness, when asked to state the reasons for his interest, he replied:

> I have the common experience of every Irish, perhaps I might add, of every British family; for where is the family that has not mourned over some member, a victim to drunkenness? (**26**, 228)

Carr appears to have been in the north early in August 1829, to have read Edgar's first letter in the newspapers, and to have discussed the subject with him personally. While Edgar waited for over a month before setting up a temperance society, Carr acted immediately, as he explained in a later letter:

> On the 20th of August last, within a few hours after my return from the

north, the New Ross Temperance Society was established at a full meeting held in the Quakers' or Friends' meeting-house. On this occasion I submitted an account of the American Temperance Society and the fundamental rules with which you furnished me — also your first appeal on the subject.... We have been joined by four private gentlemen, five respectable merchants, two medical gentlemen, one attorney, and eighteen tradesmen and farmers. (**206**, 38)

In the New Ross society we can already see features that were to characterise temperance societies in the south and set them off from those in the north; in particular, the important role played by Quakers, the largely non-clerical nature of the membership, and the significant representation of professional groups such as doctors and lawyers. Carr was important in another respect as well. Perhaps surprisingly for so convinced an Evangelical, he was on good terms with the local Catholic clergy, and in particular with the Bishop of Kildare and Leighlin, James Doyle, the celebrated pamphleteer 'J.K.L.'. Carr wrote to Doyle soon after the establishment of the New Ross society, enclosing copies of temperance literature, and seeking his endorsement of the movement. With reservations, this support was forthcoming. We shall examine Doyle's views in more detail later, but before the advent of Father Mathew in 1838 Doyle's letters to Carr represented the most substantial support given to the anti-spirits movement by a member of the Catholic hierarchy.

Temperance societies were also established in Dublin in 1829. Edgar's example was an important stimulus, but a movement against spirit consumption had been in evidence in the city for some time. This movement began not among clergy, but among doctors. It originated in a correspondence between Dr Joshua Harvey (1790-1871), a Quaker from Youghal, Co. Cork, and Dr John Cheyne (1777-1836), a Scotsman and physician-general to the army in Ireland. Harvey had apparently been urging upon Cheyne for some time the need to begin a 'crusade against intemperance'. In a reply dated 15 August 1829, which was subsequently published as a tract, Cheyne with heavy-handed irony pointed out that 'If an end were put to the drinking of port, punch, and porter, there would be an end to my worldly prosperity.... Nay, the whole profession, if we except the accoucheurs, would suffer.' (**94**, 2) Temperance would ruin the medical professional, Cheyne argued, because numerous diseases, from rheumatism to insanity, were either brought on or considerably worsened by drinking. Harvey was presumably anxious to enlist Cheyne on the side of temperance because of his eminent position: he was a Fellow of the College of Physicians, as well as being a physician to the Meath Hospital and the workhouse, and he had also made significant contributions to medical literature in the fields of paediatrics and epidemiology. (**135**) Harvey circulated the letter quoted above and encouraged Cheyne to write others.

The letter appeared, for example, in the *Belfast Newsletter* on 16 October, and Doyle in his letter to Carr of 29 December referred to tracts written by doctors that had been sent to him. The pro-temperance views of a famous physician, presumably based on sound medical grounds, were obviously significant to a movement considered by many to be ill-founded and fanatical.

The fact that Harvey was a Quaker and that other Quakers, like the printer R. D. Webb and the drapers Richard Allen and G. H. Birkett, were leaders of the temperance movement in Dublin reflected a tradition of temperance activity within the Quaker community. From the 1780s in both Britain and America Quakers had banned their members from making or selling spirits, and their staunch opposition to the slave trade often took the form of boycotts of rum. (**329**, 18; **173**, 93) As early as 1815 and 1818 the tract association established by the Dublin group in 1814 published pamphlets dealing with the subject of temperance. The first, *Temperance and Chastity Inculcated*, was an extract from Henry Tuke's influential work, *The Duties of Religion and Morality*, first published in York about 1807. In this Tuke put the classic biblical case for moderation, rejecting by implication total abstinence:

> We are not called upon to deny ourselves of the moderate, and what is, in the event, the most pleasurable, gratification of those appetites, which our all-wise creator has made necessary for our existence. We know, that 'every creature of God is good, and nothing to be refused, if it be received with thanksgiving'. But to this, and to all other knowledge, we are required to add temperance; and so to regulate our conduct as to fulfil the apostolic precept: 'Whether ye eat or drink; or whatsoever ye do; do all to the glory of God.' (**327**, 3)

The second tract, published in 1818 and reprinted twice in the 1820s, was entitled *The Importance of Sobriety, Illustrated by the Evils of Intemperance*, and it also, as the title implies, was an attack on excessive drinking. It in fact contained a sophisticated and remarkably comprehensive critique of intemperance, and one is left speculating if it was actually composed by one of the Dublin Quaker group, as it does not appear among the works emanating from tract associations in other Quaker centres. In this work drunkenness was claimed to destroy industry and health, to produce poverty, gambling, lying, swearing and fighting, to impair reason, and ultimately to bring about a miserable death. The author was familiar with the major English and American works on the subject and quoted extensively from Dr Thomas Trotter's *Essay on Drunkenness*, published in 1804, and from Dr Benjamin Rush's influential *An Inquiry into the Effects of Ardent Spirits*, which first appeared in Philadelphia in 1784. The work was aimed at both the intemperate and the temperate,

> for the former, that they may take warning and refrain — for the latter

that they may use the means of Christian reproof and persuasion, wherever their influence may avail, to arrest the progress, and remove from civilised society, the reproach of this destroying evil.

The author, relying on Rush, recognised the insidiously addictive power of drink and also that there 'may be excess, where there is no discovery of it'. Some fell under the control of drink by frequenting public houses, but for others the process was more subtle: drinking with meals or using spirits as a medicine could lead on to drunkenness. The young were particularly susceptible, and parents thus had a special duty to safeguard them. (**48**, 2, 4-5, 10-11) In publishing these tracts, the Dublin Quakers were in advance of their co-religionists in other countries: thus, while tract associations were established in London in 1813 and in New York and Philadelphia in 1817, the earliest temperance tracts published by these organisations were in 1819, 1822 and 1818 respectively. (**315**, II, 759, 807-8, 813) So when Dublin Quakers like Harvey, Webb and Allen became active in temperance societies from 1829 they already had a well-thought-out approach on which to base their actions.

But concern about intemperance in Dublin was not limited to the Quakers, though before 1829 their literature was far and away the most sophisticated. We have already had occasion to mention *Hints to Husbandmen*, published in 1813 under the auspices of the Edgeworth family. In 1823 another attack on whiskey appeared. It was a curious work, entitled *The Woe of Whiskey*, which presented its views in appalling doggerel and seems, interestingly, to have been aimed largely at a working-class audience. The author, William Kertland, a chemist of Lower Ormond Quay, addressing his readers as 'ye poor', warned them that whiskey 'marr'd the fortunes, killed the mind / Of Carolan and bonnie Burns'. He particularly condemned idle habits created by drunkenness, though perhaps the most forceful verse in this definitely woeful collection dealt with women and drink:

> A drunken man's a brute at best,
>   Prepar'd and prim'd for ev'ry evil,
> But woman drunk! — we scorn, detest —
>   And whiskey makes a wife, a devil!
> (**205**, 14)

Kertland may have been writing from personal experience, though the view that drunkenness among women was a significantly greater evil, given their role in rearing children, than among men was a common one in nineteenth-century temperance literature. Men who idealised women as angels in the home and guardians of the domestic virtues were naturally appalled at the prospect of these paragons taking to drink. Drunken wives were, as Kertland exemplifies, portrayed as harridans, while drunken single women were invariably equated with prostitutes. If whiskey produced brutish rebels among men, among women it destroyed all feminine modesty, producing viragos and sluts.

But a more concerted campaign against drink in the 1820s in Dublin than these scattered tracts would suggest was evident among the Catholic clergy of some of the city parishes. Father Henry Young and Dr Michael Blake, later Bishop of Dromore, of the parish of SS Michael and John established the Purgatorian Society of St John in 1817. Members of the society were to attend the sick and dying, to read religious literature to them, and to prepare them for the last sacraments. They were also to prevent wakes being marred by drinking — something the church had been attempting to do since at least the seventeenth century. However, the Purgatorian Society, which soon spread to other Dublin parishes, went further than this. In a booklet of rules, published in 1821, rule 17 stated that

> No member of this society shall sit down in a public house in the parish, on a Sunday or pay-day, without leave of the president, under the penalty of 10d, and if any member be seen drunk, he must pay 2s 6d for the first offence, and 5s 0d for the second; if he be drunk a third time, he shall be expelled from the society, and his name erased from the books.

Young's biographer believes that he was responsible for this rule; certainly he took a special interest in the problem of intemperance, publishing an interesting tract on the subject in 1823 entitled *Short Essay on the Grievous Crime of Drunkenness.* (**295**, 138-9, 142, 149)

This pamphlet, according to his biographer, was aimed at the 'poor and ignorant'. Like Kertland, Young addressed his audience in crude verse, at least in the first part of the work; in the second his arguments were elaborated in prose, presumably for a more sophisticated audience. Both parts, however, consisted of a blunt and strongly worded condemnation of drunkenness and of spirit drinking in particular. Drunkenness, according to Young, was 'a witch to the senses, a demon to the soul, a thief to the purse, the wife's woe, the husband's misery, the parent's disgrace, the children's sorrow, and the beggar's companion'. He was particularly severe on publicans, who would, he warned, 'have a most dreadful account to render at the divine tribunal of our Sovereign Judge after death, for their porter and punch, spirit and liquor business'. Employers who paid their workers in public houses, and respectable societies, particularly pious societies, which met there, also came in for sharp rebukes. Nor did Young mince his words regarding the ultimate fate of the drunkard:

> Almighty God in his justice and anger cuts the thread of life by a sudden death, in the midst of their drunkenness, rioting, perjuries, curses, blasphemies, impurities, and other heinous crimes; he then summons these drunken souls, thus stocked with treasures of iniquity, before his

awful and rigorous tribunal, and there fulminates against them the most dreadful sentence of reprobation and condemnation to the eternal torments of hell, which are intensely great, in proportion to the measure of their manifold crimes. The devils immediately seize on their black, hideous, and defiled souls, which they drag down into the lowest abyss of this infernal region.

With Young's rhetoric we are a long way from the 'gentle' approach being pursued in the north at the time by Cooke and Morgan. Although Young thought 'the most wholesome beverage is pure good water', he was prepared to concede that 'the moderate use of beer' and 'a little punch or wine after dinner ... may be accounted also wholesome'. (**348**, 7, 16, 28, 33, 14)

In 1827 Father Young began a series of missions in Co. Wicklow that lasted until 1840. During these he tried to eliminate drinking, particularly at wakes and fairs. He anticipated the tactics of the temperance movement by seeking to provide counter-attractions to drink. Thus at fairs and patterns he set up stalls selling coffee and buttermilk, but these were not an economic success and he was forced to discontinue them. In addition, he established purgatorian societies in Wicklow and, in the 1830s, temperance societies. Young was not alone in his temperance work in the 1820s and 1830s: he was assisted and supported by his brothers, Father James Young, parish priest at Howth and later Finglas, and Father William Young, parish priest at Baldoyle, who in the 1840s conducted temperance missions in Cornwall. (**295**, 248-9) Dr Blake, before his translation to Dromore in 1833, and Dr Yore, the priest of St Paul's in Dublin, also encouraged Young's work. Yore and Father Andrew O'Connell, who was Blake's successor at SS Michael and John's were later to join the Carmelite Dr John Spratt in leading the Dublin section of Father Mathew's crusade. Young, who lived until 1869, was working with Yore at St Paul's during this period, and though his name does not figure in reports of temperance activities, he presumably shared in Yore's work. Young's hardline approach and his campaigns during the 1820s and 1830s are a salutary reminder that there were individuals promoting temperance within the Catholic church at this time, even if the better-known temperance societies were Protestant-dominated.

The Dublin Temperance Society, the first substantial temperance society in the south of Ireland, was established in October 1829, mainly as a result of the efforts of Harvey and inspired by Edgar's actions in Belfast. The first members were Harvey, Cheyne, Webb, Dr William Urwick of York Street Congregational church, a leading Evangelical, and Philip Cecil Crampton, a prominent lawyer and aspiring Whig M.P., who was later Irish Solicitor-General. Like Edgar, the Dublin temperance advocates immediately began the publication of a series of tracts. These were in the main printed by Webb, and his printing works in William Street became the society's depository. Yet right from the beginning there were important differences between the Dublin and Belfast groups. As we have seen, the society in Belfast was dominated by clerics, mainly by Evangelical Presbyterians, and thus it had a strongly religious character. This was much less true in the south. Here the laity predominated, whether doctors, lawyers, merchants or landlords. Moreover, religious affiliations were more varied, with Quakers like Harvey and Webb playing a prominent role alongside members of the Established Church like Crampton. The Dublin group also showed a greater readiness to appeal to both the drunkard and the working classes and, closely related to this, a greater willingness to adopt total abstinence in place of mere abstinence from spirits.

The first and second tracts printed by Webb for the Dublin Temperance Society in October 1829 were two letters by Cheyne 'on the effects of wine and spirits'. The lumping together of wine and spirits in the titles is an important indication of the line pursued by Cheyne in the text. In the first letter he stated categorically that 'Ardent spirits ought to be relinquished by all persons in health,' and he went on to suggest that 'Not one in fifty, who's entitled to be considered healthy, required wine.' (95, 18) In the second letter he went even further, arguing that 'Ardent spirits and wine ought to be discontinued by all who are in the habit of drinking them,' and that those who did not drink fermented liquor should continue not to do so, 'unless under the direction of their medical adviser, he not being given to wine'. In treating wine in much the same way as spirits, Cheyne was well on the way to teetotalism. Unlike many of his fellow temperance advocates, Cheyne also held out some hope for the drunkard. Admitting that he had 'not seen many persons who have acquired a taste for ardent spirits, voluntarily relinquish their use; it is scarcely in human nature to do so', nevertheless he saw circumstances in which a reformation might be effected. Cheyne felt that the drunkard 'labours, as it were, under a disease of the stomach, the principal symptom of which is a thirst for strong liquors; and which nothing but the supervention of some other disease is likely to displace'. For example, drinking might be given up following an attack of palsy or gout. But if it was given up, then the denial needed to be total. 'In truth,' wrote Cheyne, 'his safest attitude is that of Christian in the *Pilgrim's Progress*; he ought to put his fingers in his ears, and having done so, run for his life, not looking behind him.' (96, 19, 11, 16) This strategy for combating what in modern terminology would be called alcoholism is one which many twentieth-century medical practitioners would endorse.

Nor was Cheyne the only leader of the D.T.S. inclining towards total abstinence. In 1830 Harvey disclosed that he had been a teetotaller for two years, though he was at pains to stress that the movement was one of temperance and did not seek 'to abridge any of the indulgences of the

humbler classes, except such as prove hurtful to them'. (**176**, 2; **181**, 11)
The fourth tract issued by the society and dated 9 November 1829 was
entitled *Remarks on the Evils, Occasions, and Cure of Intemperance*. Its author,
William Urwick, noting, presumably in reference to Cheyne, that it was
the 'opinion of eminent physicians that the habitual use of neither wine nor
spirits is generally necessary', attacked moderate drinkers: 'they who take
their glass or tumbler daily "in moderation", i.e. just sufficient to produce
a glow of pleasurable excitement'. Some had proposed to 'change the kind
or to diminish the quantity, or lessen the frequency' of consumption, but
Urwick rejected such half-measures. The prescription he offered was,
according to him, 'simple': 'it is the total, prompt, and persevering
abstinence from all intoxicating liquors'. (**332**, 19) Here, at the very
beginning of the Dublin temperance movement, was an unqualified call
for total abstinence. Urwick was an Englishman, born in 1791 into a
staunch Shrewsbury family of Dissenters. He came to Ireland first in 1815
as a missionary to Sligo and subsequently undertook much proselytising
work in Connacht. In 1826 he was called to be minister at the York Street
chapel, erected in 1808 by supporters of the Countess of Huntingdon's
Evangelical group. Urwick was active in various missionary enterprises,
such as the Bible Society, the Irish Evangelical Society and the Sunday
School Society. Like Harvey, he was also a teetotaller, as he was later to
reveal in his memoirs. In these he named himself, Cheyne, Harvey,
Crampton and John Mackay, a barrister, as the motivating forces in the
Dublin Temperance Society. The distress he had witnessed, particularly
among weavers, during the economic slump and severe winter of 1829
seems to have contributed to his hardline approach to the drink question.
(**331**, 44-5, 102-4, 115-16; 170-1)

The societies in Dublin and Belfast that appeared late in 1829 certainly
shared many similar concerns. The Evangelical clergy and mill owners of
Belfast, like the doctors and lawyers of Dublin, were alarmed by the
increasing spirit consumption of the 1820s, occurring, so it seemed to them,
in conjunction with increased popular unrest, economic decline, and a
resurgence of Catholic claims in the Emancipation campaign. The
temperance pamphlets pouring out of both centres frequently emphasised
the economic and political dangers of excessive spirit consumption. In the
tract quoted above, for instance, Urwick warned that

> A population addicted to intemperance is ready to obey the call of every
> political incendiary who addresses their passions, while they are
> backward to regard reasoning and expostulation; nor will they be
> deterred from advancing in the career of rebellion though the gibbet or
> the scaffold be in view.

Harvey in the third tract produced by the D.T.S. dwelt at some length on
the economic benefits to be derived from temperance:

Can it be supposed that a drunken population, living in a most degraded state, and clothed only with a covering of dirty rags, the results of drunkenness...can yield that revenue and profit to any state, which would readily be yielded by a sober, healthy, industrious, well-clad population, seeking and enjoying a number of rational luxuries, besides the necessities of life — 'consumers', themselves, of the grain and cattle which their country exports so abundantly, and customers for a hundred articles demanded by improved and civilised life, each of which articles would afford its suitable tax or revenue? (**175**, 5-6)

Harvey's tract was in fact entitled the *Political Evils of Intemperance*, for the political and economic arguments went hand in hand: a 'sober, healthy, industrious' population, as well as providing an expanded market for home industry and a steady revenue for the state, was unlikely to embark on a 'career of rebellion'.

If, however, the concerns of the societies in Dublin and Belfast were similar, their tactics, as already suggested, diverged right from the beginning. The Belfast group, under Edgar's leadership, insisted on adhering more strictly to the American model. Thus its attack was directed solely against spirits, and not other forms of alcohol, and its appeal was to the relatively prosperous moderate drinker, who, in the Ulster context, was almost invariably a Protestant. In Dublin the American model was less influential, partly perhaps because there was less direct contact with the American societies. The Dublin Quakers were certainly in touch with American reform movements, as their strong support for the abolition of slavery demonstrates; but much more information on American temperance activity appears in Ulster temperance publications than in those produced in the south, suggesting that the Presbyterian connection was a closer one. But an additional factor was that circumstances were different in important ways in the south. Spirits, particularly illicit spirits, were the dominant form of alcohol in the north. In Dublin, with its large breweries, beer was also a popular drink among tradesmen and labourers, while wine remained the principal drink of the commercial and professional classes and of 'society'. So it was perhaps less easy in Dublin to single out whiskey as the sole culprit for drunkenness. And while Edgar in Belfast, basing his argument on scripture, could separate spirits from other forms of alcohol because it lacked biblical sanction, the doctors in Dublin, working from medical evidence, came increasingly to the conclusion that all forms of alcohol had much the same deleterious effects and all tended to be addictive. The Dublin group also faced the problem that if its appeal was to be at all successful it needed to win Catholic support. Denying the lower orders whiskey, while reserving the right to drink wine themselves, was, as Bishop Doyle warned, not the way to win a mass following.

John Edgar was quick to see that the movement in Dublin was adopting significantly different tactics from his own, and, characteristically, he attacked the trend vigorously. At the inaugural meeting of the Hibernian Temperance Society in Dublin in April 1830 Edgar began his speech by saying:

> As I came into this room today, I observed that the word abstinence, and not temperance, was whispered from the various circles of conversation. This confirmed the opinion which articles in some of the Dublin journals had led me to form, that here, as elsewhere, objections had been raised against the society by the magic of a word.

Taking as his text St Paul's 'All things are lawful for me, but all things are not expedient; and it is good neither to drink wine, nor anything whereby thy brother stumbleth, or is offended, or is made weak', Edgar argued that

> The use of wine is permitted in scripture... but we trust it will be granted to us, in consistency with truth, that the use of wine which in general is lawful, in particular circumstances ceases to be expedient. ... We avoid, however, all appearance of abstemious rigour; our constitution only forbids the ordinary use of distilled spirits, and leaves every man full of liberty of conscience either to use moderately wine, and other fermented liquor, or to abstain from them, as he pleases. (**207**, 77, 79-80)

Because wine drinking was apparently condoned in the Bible, Edgar concluded that total abstinence was unscriptural, in fact that it was a form of Manicheism. Yet he could not deny that wine, like spirits, caused drunkenness and the numerous social problems that went with drunkenness. But, resorting to scripture again, he concluded that moderate wine consumption was permissible so long as it caused no harm to others. However, many Dublin temperance advocates, less concerned than Edgar with the finer points of biblical exegesis and more aware of the detrimental effects of both wine and beer consumption, were not particularly impressed by his arguments.

Edgar's chagrin at the April 1830 meeting may also have arisen partly from the fact that the Dublin group had taken the initiative from him by moving to establish a national organisation, to be called the Hibernian Temperance Society. The first public meeting of the society vividly illustrated the basic concerns of the movement, adopting an almost apocalyptic tone at times. P. C. Crampton, the chairman of the meeting, who was a close ally of Edgar's, sought to induce in his audience a sense of crisis. He warned that an 'overwhelming flood of intemperance' threatened 'to lay waste our land, and to bury in one common ruin the institutions, morals and character of our people'. Resorting to a disease analogy, he warned that the country was plagued with a 'dangerous disorder, a malady' which was undermining its constitution and which now threatened its very existence. His kinsman, Sir Philip Crampton, the Surgeon-General, developed this disease analogy even further in his speech. Portraying the Irish as a morbidly excitable people, he noted that the effects of spirits on the brain were to paralyse the moral properties while at the same time stimulating the 'animal', and thus to further accentuate the Irish tendency to reckless and desperate acts. This tendency would, moreover,

> be transmitted to the offspring, until the brute nature . . . prevailing over the human, the whole race scarcely exhibit any of the attributes of humanity except in the outward form, and are only to be governed — if indeed they can be governed — by the force of arms instead of the force of opinion.

The leaders of the Irish temperance movement thus saw themselves as defending their country — or at least the landowning, merchant, professional and 'respectable' working class of their country — against attack by spirit-crazed brutes, whose atrocities, whether committed in '98 or in more recent Ribbon outrages, amply demonstrated their animal nature.

It was indeed a terrifying vision. Little wonder that P. C. Crampton rejected the 'desperate purpose of preaching temperance to the confirmed sot'. But, as mentioned, not all members of the Dublin temperance group held such apocalyptic views. The Quakers certainly did not. And the differences were well illustrated in the address given to the same H.T.S. gathering by G. W. Carr of New Ross. He stressed how much more difficult it was for the poor to reform their habits than for the rich. But rather than using this fact as an excuse for abandoning the poor to their fate, Carr argued that, on the contrary, the 'poor man's example and influence are to be prized, and will be felt. Nothing can more encourage the friends of this cause than to see the poor come forward.' (**184**, 4-5, 23, 58)

Although established in 1830, it is not until the mid-1830s, when a temperance newspaper began publication in Dublin, that the activities of the H.T.S. can be examined in any great detail. Before then the Dublin group appears to have concentrated on producing tracts, setting up auxiliary societies and gathering support. In 1830 a declaration signed by forty-eight prominent doctors, including eleven Fellows of the College of Physicians and eighteen members of the College of Surgeons, advising against the use of spirits on the grounds of the disease and poverty created among the working classes, was circulated by the H.T.S. Another declaration, stressing the role of drink in causing crime, was signed by the Lord Mayor, two high sheriffs, the Recorder, Frederick Shaw, and the senior police magistrate, Henry Charles Sirr (notorious for his capture of Lord Edward Fitzgerald in 1798). (**144**, 11-13) Such endorsements by supposed experts were clearly intended to establish the credentials of the temperance movement among the educated classes.

Between 1829 and 1832 R. D. Webb issued some thirty tracts for the
D.T.S. and its successor, the H.T.S. Referring to the first six of these works,
the H.T.S. made it plain that they were 'intended for the richer classes
rather than the humbler orders'. (**182**, 3) It was only with the fourteenth
tract, written 'by a lady' and entitled *Philip and his Friends: or, Cottage
Dialogues on Temperance Societies and Intemperance*, that works directed to
servants and labourers, the 'mechanic and industrious classes', began to
appear. These mainly sought to prove that servants, farm labourers and
small farmers could be materially comfortable, whatever their wages or
circumstances, just so long as they gave up drinking spirits. Such
pamphlets were largely, if not solely, the work of Quakers. The 'lady', who
wrote three or four more 'cottage dialogues', was Betsy Shackleton, a
member of a well-known Quaker family; Joshua Harvey wrote at least two
tracts containing 'observations and advice' and 'hints to the poor'; while
two further dialogues, between 'Darby and Paddy', came from the pen of
George Downes, who was secretary of the Quaker-dominated Ballitore
Temperance Society. (**306; 140**) Clearly the Quakers were a leading force
in that section of the Dublin temperance movement concerned to reform
working-class drinking habits.

As for auxiliary societies, the H.T.S. issued a paper on the subject about
the middle of 1830. It outlined steps to be taken in establishing such
societies and gave examples of the groups operating in Dublin in 1830
under the aegis of the H.T.S. Members were instructed to

> generally fix on a convenient time and place for meeting, which is for the
> most part weekly; . . . invite their neighbours, both rich and poor; read
> some extracts from the publications of the parent society, and other
> sources; agree on such rules and regulations as may best suit them; and
> otherwise endeavour to give interest and stability to the branch
> association.

These were not exactly detailed or stimulating directions. Nevertheless, the
paper went on to report that an association consisting of 200 members,
'including 11 females', and called the St Peter's District Temperance
Association, was meeting every Wednesday in the Hatch Street schoolhouse. Its members, ranging in age from twelve to 103, comprised both
'mechanics' and 'gentry', and a 'savings bank system' had been 'blended in
the regulations'. The society's secretary was Dr Neason Adams, an
Edinburgh-educated Dublin physician, who was later to become notable
for his proselytising work in the west of Ireland. Three other societies were
mentioned by name: St Kevin's District, meeting in Little Digges Street
schoolhouse every Tuesday, with P. C. Crampton as treasurer; the
Mechanics', meeting in Tailors' Hall in Back Lane every Thursday, with
Charles Marchant, an ironmonger, as secretary; and St George's District,
meeting in the Dispensary Lane schoolhouse every Friday, with Dr James

Pope as secretary. Although 'mechanics' figured as members of these societies, all had 'gentry' from the committee of the H.T.S. in positions of authority, and they presumably constituted the directing force. The paper virtually acknowledged this situation when it remarked in passing that 'men of independence and influence' were 'happily uniting with well-disposed persons in humbler stations, and all acting harmoniously together for both public and private good'. Employers were particularly called upon to establish temperance societies in their factories and shops. But the fact, recorded in the final paragraph, that Ulster had between fifty and sixty societies, containing about 3,000 members, was clearly a cause for concern. The whole tone of the tract (the mention of only four societies, and these only sustained by direct H.T.S. participation) suggests that the temperance achievement in Dublin was not an impressive one; it certainly looked very shabby in comparison with the many flourishing societies of Ulster. (**183**, 1-2)

The composition of the H.T.S. remained fairly consistent throughout the 1830s. In 1832 the executive consisted of a president, five vice-presidents, four secretaries and a committee of thirteen. The president was P. C. Crampton, a Whig lawyer; the vice-presidents included a Whig land-lord, Lord Cloncurry, a Catholic bishop, James Doyle, a doctor, John Cheyne, and two military men, General Sir James Douglas and Admiral R. D. Oliver; the secretaries were two barristers and two doctors; and of the committee, four were doctors, three were barristers, three were clergymen (two Protestant and one Catholic), one was an alderman, one a retailer, and one has proved impossible to identify in terms of occupation. (**143**, 215) The majority of the executive was composed therefore of doctors and lawyers, with some clerical support, but with feeble landed and business representation. As the society looked particularly to employers and land-lords to set an example to their dependants, its failure to attract such people was a serious weakness. But by 1840 the society had gone some way towards rectifying this imbalance: Crampton remained president and the four secretaries consisted of three barristers and a Protestant clergyman, but the eighteen vice-presidents now included ten landlords (four of them peers) and two senior Protestant clerics, though only one mill owner; of the twenty-one committee members, a third were Protestant clergy and another third were barristers, five were businessmen (two of them book-sellers), one was a doctor, and one the governor of Richmond Bridewell. (**142**, 284-5) So within eight years the society had succeeded in attracting more landlords and more Protestant clergy (the majority being of the Established Church), while interest among merchants and traders had increased marginally. But Catholic clerical influence had disappeared altogether. The Dublin legal fraternity remained influential, however, while doctors were still significantly represented.

At the annual general meeting of the society in October 1836 interesting details of the extent of its operations and the nature of its support through-out the country emerged.[2] One of the honorary secretaries, A. E. Gayer, a barrister and unsuccessful Tory candidate for Dublin University, in his report singled out Ulster and Co. Cork as the areas in which the greatest progress had been made. In Ulster he considered the support of many Presbyterian and Methodist clergymen as decisive, while in Cork he remarked upon the sympathetic attitude of the landed gentry.

Influential Cork landlords, such as W. H. W. Newenham of Carrigaline and W. L. Shuldham of Dunmanway, were vice-presidents of the society, while James Redmond Barry and Henry Townsend of Glandore were enthusiastic temperance advocates. Barry, a wealthy Catholic landowner and merchant, under the influence of Owen and Bentham, had tried from about 1823 to turn Glandore into a model community. He was visited by radicals like John Finch, who reported his activities in England, was probably in touch with the socialist William Thompson, who owned an estate a few miles north of Glandore, and was certainly aware of the Owenite community that operated at Ralahine in Co. Clare between 1831 and 1833. Barry limited the operation of public houses in Glandore, but owned a copy of the Ralahine rules, no. 31 of which stated that 'no spirituous liquor of any kind, tobacco or snuff be kept in the store'. A member who bought spirits could be fined, and repeated offences ultimately led to expulsion from the community. The diet at Ralahine, which John Finch praised highly, consisted primarily of milk and vegetables. But Barry did not go this far. According to Finch's evidence before the 1834 select committee on drunkenness,

> He shut up the dram-shops in the village except two, and those were placed in a conspicuous part of the village, and there was only one way into them, and that from the public street of the village, and no back way; the consequence was, that every person that went in was seen, and those places were deserted, and the whole place had become sober and industrious, and they are all doing well. (**281**, 8, 15; **118**, 18-22; **119**, 39; **26**, 649-50)

Another precocious flowering of temperance occurring in Co. Cork was at Skibbereen, not far away from Glandore. Brian Harrison in his invaluable history of the English temperance movement refers to the establishment of a temperance society at Skibbereen in 1817. He considers this society 'irrelevant' to the history of the temperance movement, however, because 'if it existed', it wielded 'no influence outside its locality'. Harrison is in fact paraphrasing the judgment of Dr Dawson Burns, who wrote one of the standard nineteenth-century histories of the temperance movement. The society certainly existed, and it may have had more general significance than either Burns or Harrison is willing to concede: Finch and Barry, for instance, were both aware of its operations. It was begun in June 1817 by

Jeffrey (or Geoffrey) Sedwards (1776-1861), a nailer, who convinced twelve friends, most of them heavy drinkers, to join. The organisation was referred to as an 'abstinence society', and its first rule stated that 'No person can take malt or spirituous liquors, or distilled water, except prescribed by a priest or doctor.' The reference to malt as well as spirituous liquors and the use of the word 'abstinence' rather than 'temperance' suggests that the society was in fact based on total abstinence. This has led to it being described as 'Europe's first total abstinence society'. (**173**, 103; **85**, I, 13-14; **117**, 52-7) It seems in fact to have operated as a benefit society, with members making small regular contributions to insure themselves against illness and death. Branches were established in neighbouring towns, firstly and notably in Glandore, then in Rosscarbery and Clonakilty.[3] The Skibbereen society appears to have acted as an inspiration to those like Barry, Finch and also G. W. Carr, who were keen to do away with the elitist nature of the anti-spirits movement and appeal directly to the working classes and to drunkards, such an appeal being based on tee-totalism rather than temperance. This was the significance of the Skibbereen society in the 1830s: it demonstrated clearly that working-class drunkards could be redeemed through total abstinence.

Yet the U.T.S. and significant elements in the H.T.S. were still in 1836 actively seeking the support of landlords and employers. In the midlands and the south-east there were a number of societies, and here, as in parts of Cork, landlord influence was crucial. In Co. Kildare the Duke of Leinster with his wife and sister-in-law, Lord Cloncurry and Lord Harberton promoted societies, and the latter two were vice-presidents of the H.T.S. In Queen's County Lord de Vesci, another vice-president, encouraged several societies; in King's County Lord Oxmantown, later the Earl of Rosse, was sympathetic; in Co. Wexford Sir Francis Le Hunte, another vice-president, was instrumental in setting up a number of societies; in Co. Kilkenny William Tighe of Inistioge established a society among his tenants; while in Co. Carlow Thomas Kavanagh and his wife, Lady Harriet Kavanagh, subscribed to the erection of temperance tents at fairs. Further afield the importance of landlord sympathy was even more obvious: there were active societies in Sligo and Westport supported by the Earl of Sligo; the Dingle society enjoyed the patronage of Lord Ventry; while on Achill Island Sir Richard O'Donel encouraged his tenants to join the society there. In Ulster too, several influential landlords rallied to the temperance cause: in Co. Down the Marquis of Londonderry, Lord Bangor and Lord Annesley were sympathetic; in Co. Armagh the flourishing society at Markethill was supported by the Earl of Gosford, while his kinsman, Lord Mandeville, encouraged that at Tandragee, and William Blacker was president of the County Armagh Temperance Association; in Co. Cavan Lord Farnham was active; while in Co. Fermanagh the society at Lisnaskea enjoyed the patronage of the Earl of

Erne and his nephew, John Creighton, who was another vice-president of the H.T.S.[4]

A number of the H.T.S.'s landlord patrons were Evangelical Protestants, supporters of the proselytising activities of the so-called 'Second Reformation'. This is true of Farnham, Gosford, de Vesci, Mandeville and O'Donel. Others on the society's executive of similar persuasion were Dr Urwick, the Rev. John Grant of Monkstown, one of the honorary secretaries, the Rev. Thomas Kingston of St James's parish, and members of the La Touche family, who were the society's bankers. The members of the societies in Achill and Dingle were mainly converts from Catholicism given sanctuary by O'Donel and Ventry, who both encouraged proselytising. The connection is also clear in the case of several of the H.T.S.'s titled female supporters. Lady Harriet Kavanagh, for instance, was a niece of Power le Poer Trench, Archbishop of Tuam, while Lady Harriet Daly of Delgany, Co. Wicklow, was a sister of the Rev. Robert Daly, rector of Powerscourt and later Bishop of Cashel, both of whom were leaders of the Evangelical wing of the Established Church. Daly himself was an active supporter of the H.T.S. and had helped to establish a temperance society at Bray, near Dublin.

While temperance was associated with Protestant proselytising in some parts of the country and with Owenite communities in Cork and Clare, in Ulster there are intriguing hints of close connections between temperance societies and the Orange Order, particularly in Co. Armagh. In 1836, as a result of the investigations of the 1835 select committee on the Orange Order, the society was dissolved. At that time Lord Mandeville was Grand Master of the Co. Armagh lodge, with the Rev. James Blacker as Grand Chaplain, and Dr Patton as Grand Secretary. (**29**, 119) In October 1836, at a meeting of the Markethill Temperance Society held in Armagh, it was resolved to form a county-wide temperance association to encourage and co-ordinate the activities of local societies. The president of this association was William Blacker, a well-known soldier and land agent, who had joined the Orange Order in the year that it was founded, 1795, when he was only eighteen years of age. Subsequently he had been Grand Master of Co. Armagh and Deputy Grand Master of Ireland. Among those subscribing to the new temperance association were Lord Mandeville, the Rev. James Blacker, who was William Blacker's brother, and Dr Patton, all members of the Armagh executive of the recently dissolved Orange Order. There is no doubting, however, the genuineness of William Blacker's commitment to temperance: he advocated it vigorously over many years, even welcoming Father Mathew to Lurgan in September 1841.[5] Blacker, in his evidence before the 1835 select committee, had claimed that the Orange Order discouraged drunkenness, pointing to the 'peculiar tranquillity, the dead silence I may say' on the night of the Twelfth of July. But the weight of evidence was against him. A number of witnesses hostile to the Order, including the Earl of Gosford, testified that lodge meetings were usually held in public houses, with publicans putting up a picture of King William at their doors in order to attract Orange business; that, as Cooke had charged ten years earlier, publicans frequently promoted Orange processions to drum up trade; that though publicans were not supposed to hold office in lodges, this rule was not enforced; and that generally Orange meetings and marches were accompanied by scenes of drunkenness and disorder. (**29**, 217; **30**, 288-9, 348, 384) Against this background the involvement of a number of prominent Orangemen in a temperance association could be interpreted either as a stratagem to perpetuate the Orange organisation under another name, or as an effort to improve the character and behaviour of former members, which had been so heavily censured.

It is, however, worth noting here that the Markethill society, which was by far the largest in the county and which had initiated the establishment of a county association, was patronised by the Earl of Gosford, a vocal opponent of Orangeism, and also by his son, Viscount Acheson. Given also Blacker's genuine commitment to temperance, it would appear more likely that the County Armagh Temperance Association was a true temperance society, though some members may have hoped to use it to detach former Orangemen from their old allies, the publicans, and thus give them a far more respectable image. Outside of Armagh several other landed patrons of the H.T.S. were also prominent Orangemen: this was true of Lord Farnham in Co. Cavan, who was an active Evangelical as well, and of Lord Annesley in south Co. Down. But in these areas too, while former Orangemen and temperance men may have overlapped to some degree, there is no evidence of a systematic effort to reconstitute Orange lodges as temperance societies.

Generally in Ulster the progress of the anti-spirits movement was very rapid, at least initially. In an article entitled 'A Retrospect of Temperance Societies', which appeared in the February 1833 issue of the *Belfast Temperance Advocate* over the names of John Edgar, James Morgan and Thomas Hincks, it was claimed that there were 150 societies in the province with a total membership of 15,000.[6] From a study of reports appearing in the *Advocate* between April 1832 and March 1833 it is possible to identify twenty-nine of these societies with a combined membership of nearly 5,000. The strongholds of the movement were around the northern shores of Lough Neagh and in the lower Bann valley, in north-east Down around Strangford Lough and in north and central Tyrone, particularly around Cookstown, Omagh and Newtownstewart. In 1838 the H.T.S. in Dublin conducted a survey of temperance societies. This listed thirty-nine in Ulster, which is certainly a gross underestimate: in May 1837 twenty-three societies were affiliated with the County Armagh Temperance Association alone, while in November of the same year twenty-five societies were returned for the barony of Dungannon. Clearly the Dublin movement was ill-formed and out of touch with activities in the north, as its journal openly admitted on several occasions. Nevertheless, the distribution of these thirty-nine societies does tend to confirm the pattern observed for 1832-3, though east Tyrone and north Armagh have become more significant centres. All these areas had large Presbyterian populations, and the reports in the *Advocate* in 1832-3 make it clear that Presbyterian clergy, particularly Seceders, were usually presidents or patrons of local temperance societies. In the case of nineteen of the societies reporting we can identify the religious affiliation of the ministers leading them: more than half were Presbyterian, with the rest being either Methodists or clergy of the Established Church.[7]

In Belfast at least the U.T.S. had some success in winning the support of businessmen, particularly mill owners and provision merchants. Robert Workman, a muslin manufacturer, John Herdman, the proprietor of a large flax mill, and John and Thomas Sinclair, provision dealers, were all active temperance advocates, Workman in particular being treasurer of the U.T.S. for a number of years. (**156**, 22; **206**, 61, 63) Some assistance was also forthcoming from landlords, notably Sir Robert Bateson, Tory M.P. for Co. Londonderry from 1830 to 1842, Samuel Thompson of Muckamore Abbey, Co. Antrim, Lord Bangor of Castle Ward, Co. Down, Lord Farnham of Co. Cavan, John Crombie of Portstewart, William Blacker in Co. Armagh, and Sir Francis Workman Macnaghton of Roe Park, Limavady, Co. Londonderry. Like the landed supporters of the H.T.S., with whom they overlapped (as in the cases of Farnham and Blacker), those identifying themselves with the temperance cause in Ulster were generally conservative, Evangelically-minded Protestants. Unlike the H.T.S., however, the U.T.S. did not go out of its way to solicit landed and business support, though naturally this was welcomed when forthcoming. Instead the society under Edgar's leadership showed far greater interest in winning over the clergy of the various Protestant churches. Edgar devoted much effort to convincing ministers to give up the consumption of spirits; ultimately he hoped to make the U.T.S.'s pledge compulsory for all candidates for the ministry. In 1833 the U.T.S. was able to claim 200 ministers as members. In Belfast fourteen had joined, while in Lisburn, Co. Antrim, Saintfield, Dromore, Bangor and the Ards in Co. Down and in Omagh in Co. Tyrone nearly all the Protestant clergy were members. The majority of Seceding Presbyterians, nearly all Primitive Methodists and significant numbers of Reformed Presbyterians, Wesleyans, Presbyterians and ministers of the Established Church had taken the U.T.S.'s pledge. Thus, as a result of the efforts of the U.T.S., a significant nucleus of temperance clergy was created in Ulster.[8]

Between 1830 and 1834 Edgar travelled tirelessly, not only in Ireland but in England and Scotland as well, on behalf of the temperance cause.

Killen, his biographer, says that he 'acted on the principle of going wherever invited'. At the same time he wrote prodigiously on the subject: as well as editing the *Belfast Temperance Advocate* and contributing extensively to it, he produced some ninety separate publications relating to temperance. (**206**, 52-3, 57) But the latter half of the 1830s were to be difficult years for the anti-spirits movement and for Edgar in particular. Ill-health curtailed his activities. At the same time the U.T.S. was short of funds and had difficulty in employing suitable agents. Most 'in a short time' found the 'responsibilities of the situation too heavy for them'. One of the society's many agents, a Mr Barclay, died in 1838 after contracting an illness in the slums of Belfast, where he had enrolled 2,000 new members in eight months. Mr Barclay was certainly a success, but his fate was hardly calculated to encourage others to follow in his footsteps.[9] More significantly, the first total abstinence society was established in Ulster in 1835, and, as we shall see, from 1837 teetotalism made rapid strides in Ireland. Given the success of temperance in Ulster under Edgar's leadership, teetotal missionaries from England were particularly attracted to the north. Edgar continued to set his face firmly against total abstinence on scriptural grounds, but he gradually saw nearly all his old colleagues go over to the new movement. Eventually in 1841 he abandoned the temperance cause altogether to concentrate on other mission work, though not before he had created much division and bitterness in the Ulster temperance movement by his opposition to teetotalism. Later teetotal historians, while acknowledging his great contribution to the anti-drink cause, were nevertheless severe in their assessments of his later career. According to Dawson Burns, for instance,

> Unhappily Dr Edgar not only failed to accept the larger principle [of total abstinence], but thought it his duty to oppose its advocacy . . . and while he was impotent to arrest the total abstinence reform, his name became an excuse for those who wished to refrain from all temperance work whatever. (**85**, I, 33)

On the other hand, however, Edgar doubtless considered the fact that Irish teetotalism quickly fell under the control of Catholic priests and nationalists a vindication of his uncompromising opposition to it.

In the south-east and midlands a number of temperance societies resulted from the labours of one man, G. W. Carr. He had been encouraging societies for some time when, in December 1836, he was appointed agent for the H.T.S. Immediately he began a series of lengthy tours, establishing societies in Counties Tipperary, King's, Queen's, Carlow and Wexford. In the depths of winter, with 'incessant rains, influenza in most every house, and the uneasiness of an approaching election', it was, as the *Irish Temperance and Literary Gazette* acknowledged, a very difficult task indeed.[10] But Carr was made of stouter stuff than the

U.T.S.'s agents, who so quickly abandoned their work; yet even he was fighting a losing battle. The emphasis that both the U.T.S. and the H.T.S. put upon the need for an effective agency reflected the fact that, by the middle of the 1830s, the enthusiasm that had led to the setting up of societies in the early years of the decade was very much on the wane. The pages of the *Gazette*, founded in 1836 as a mouthpiece for the H.T.S., were soon full of accounts of societies established by zealous individuals which collapsed after a year or two as the original members left the district, died or their interest waned. The difficulty of obtaining interesting speakers for meetings in order to enthuse members was frequently remarked upon. It was hoped that an agency would overcome this particular problem. A blunt, popular and independent man like Carr was ideal for the job, but unfortunately for the anti-spirits movement there were few of his sort ready to work for the cause. As we shall see, teetotalism was much more successful than temperance in producing popular preachers.

While Crampton, Gayer and others on the executive of the H.T.S. harped upon the need for gentry, business and clerical support — Crampton, for instance, told the 1836 annual general meeting that the 'example and influence of the respectable members of society' were essential to the success of their work — Carr continued, as in 1830, to look to the working classes and to Catholics for support. Addressing the same annual meeting, he singled out Sedwards's pioneering society in Skibbereen for praise and complimented Father Coppinger and Father Eager on their work with the society in Midleton, Co. Cork. In fact he concluded that the 'cause had taken root in towns, not so in rural districts, country gentlemen have not taken it up'. But, as we have already seen, this observation is not really true. Where landlords, employers and clergy had taken up the temperance cause, as in parts of Ulster, the midlands and Cork, societies did flourish, albeit frequently on a narrow and fragile basis. In large towns and cities like Dublin, Cork, Waterford and Limerick, all with substantial drink industries and far less manageable working populations, temperance had only very limited success. Thus in his 1836 report Gayer noted that there had been 'some progress' in Dublin, but 'very disproportionate... either to the magnitude of the field open, or the importance of the object in view'. In that year in fact there were only eight societies in the city affiliated to the H.T.S., and all these were connected with Protestant congregations. Cork city had only three societies; that in Waterford had a mere 160 members; while the society in Limerick had been split by charges of proselytism and as a consequence was reduced to only 100 members.[11] Nevertheless, in his remarks Carr was echoing the views of the teetotallers, whom he was later to join: they wanted to appeal directly to the Catholic working classes, particularly in the cities, and were not prepared to wait upon the grudging sympathy of the 'respectable members of society'.

In this context it is worth remembering that it was Carr who appealed for Catholic support as early as 1829 in his letters to Bishop Doyle of Kildare and Leighlin. Doyle wrote two letters in response to Carr on the subject of temperance societies and subsequently he became one of the vice-presidents of the H.T.S. Doyle's letters were reprinted a number of times and widely circulated by the H.T.S. as evidence of Catholic endorsement of the anti-spirits cause. Doyle, however, was the only member of the hierarchy to support the temperance cause publicly at this stage, and even his support was by no means wholehearted. In fact his views on the subject of temperance were characteristically individualistic. He did not, like many members of the H.T.S., have much sympathy for the drunkard, remarking in his first letter to Carr:

> I would be . . . glad to heal the drunkard; but if he were obstinate, and obstinately persevered in his vice, I would feel upon his death, as I would upon the death of the murderer dying on the scaffold — that he had paid the forfeit of his life to the offended justice of earth and heaven.

Yet Doyle was by no means sanguine about the prospects of temperance societies, for he went on to say that he did not feel 'such societies in this country, at this time, and with our present laws and social government, can be productive of any great, or extensive, or permanent good'. Rather sarcastically, he argued that gentlemen preaching 'a temperance which they themselves do not always practise' could not really expect to convince the people 'who have not before experienced their friendship and protection'. An even greater obstacle to the progress of temperance societies Doyle considered to be the revenue laws: since the exchequer gained vast sums from spirit duties, the government was in fact committed to promoting spirit consumption. The only chance of real success that Doyle could see lay in the expansion of brewing: 'If malting and brewing were exempted from tax, and the impost on whiskey raised,' he argued, 'drunkenness in a little time would almost disappear from the country.' In seeing beer as a 'temperance drink', Doyle was adopting a decidedly old-fashioned view, and one that was to command little sympathy as the 1830s advanced towards the triumph of teetotalism. Doyle, however, regarded even moderation as 'too perfect for the generality of men'; had he lived (he died in 1834), he certainly would have opposed the even more perfectionistic views of the teetotallers. (**141**, I, 4-7, II, 6)

Before the commencement of Father Mathew's crusade in 1838 several other Catholic clerics, more junior in rank than Doyle, did give aid to the temperance cause. We have already noted the work of Father Henry Young in Dublin and Wicklow; in the city he had a co-worker in the person of the Carmelite Dr John Spratt. Spratt was briefly on the executive of the H.T.S., but seems to have abandoned it because of its strongly Protestant and conservative character, though he continued his own temperance work in the slums around the Whitefriars church in Aungier Street.[12] In 1836 in Co. Cork Father Eager and Father Coppinger of Midleton, Father Scannell of Blackrock and Father Michael O'Sullivan of Bantry were all actively supporting local temperance societies. Clerical aid was also forthcoming in Galway, where in April 1837 Father John Kenyon of Ennis, later famous for his Young Ireland sympathies, called upon all 'patriotic' Irishmen to rid their country of intemperance. In Galway city a society, established in December 1836, had by June 1837 secured Bishop Browne as patron and Father Fahy as president, while in March 1838 the Parsonstown Temperance Society could boast Bishop Kennedy of Killaloe as its vice-president.[13] But such encouragement was scattered, intermittent and largely ineffectual. Thus in December 1839 Michael T. Finnerty, secretary of the Galway society, conceded that before the advent of Father Mathew progress had been very slow, even given the encouragement of the local bishop. Fear of temperance societies as instruments of proselytism seems to have been the more general reaction of the Catholic clergy. Reports from Strabane, Derry and Limerick in 1836 and from Tipperary in 1838 spoke of sectarian clashes within societies and of the indifference, if not outright opposition, of the priests.[14]

An examination of the spread of temperance societies in Ireland between 1829 and 1835 suggests that the movement was not a success, except in parts of Ulster and perhaps of Co. Cork. In his notes for the years 1832, 1833 and 1834 Dawson Burns remarks that temperance 'held its ground' and was 'steadily maintained' in Ulster; this description hardly suggests any significant advance. As for the rest of the country, Burns refers to 'much opposition' and to the fact that by 1834 only a 'very faint impression' had been made on the other three provinces. By 1835 the cause was 'rather stationary than progressive'. (**85**, I, 64, 74, 82-3, 96) A much more contemporary account than Burns's 1889 study confirms this general picture. In his history of the temperance movement, published in 1843, J. B. Sheil mentions the years 1832 and 1833 as marking a notable decline in activity. Certainly consumption of spirits, having fallen in the four years 1830-33, rose in the three years 1834-6, though this was probably due more to a substantial fall in duty in 1834 than to fluctuations in temperance work. Nevertheless, such a clear trend must have been discouraging to the anti-spirits movement and underlined its failure to achieve its objectives.

Of some significance in this regard also may have been the cholera epidemic of 1832. Many temperance advocates saw a close link between cholera and drunkenness, both in spiritual terms (that the epidemic was God's judgment upon the drunkard) and in physiological terms (that those with bodies ravaged by drink were more likely to succumb to the disease). Yet the popular view in Ireland, as in much of the rest of the British Isles, was the very reverse: it was widely believed that spirits helped ward off, and sometimes even cure, the illness. G. W. Carr told the 1834 select committee on drunkenness that the epidemic opened 'an additional door...for drunkenness', for

> Independent of the destructive effects of spirits on cholera patients, multitudes began for the first time to drink them as a preservative from infection, and have thereby become drunkards; and very many, who had totally renounced the drink, company and habits of drunkards, were induced to take a little spirits by way of precaution, and have been thereby again entangled in drunkenness. Some have died of the disease which they thus fed; and others have not yet been recovered from their second slavery and disgrace. (**26**, 232)

Thus, rather than checking spirit consumption, the 1832 cholera epidemic tended to promote it and also, according to Carr, to produce relapses among those who had already taken the temperance pledge.

Sheil in his history points as well to an almost inevitable lessening of enthusiasm within temperance ranks as the movement failed to make a substantial impression on the Irish population. Even some of the early leaders fell away or, as Sheil puts it, 'had occasion to stay at home and mind their business'. Cheyne had suffered a nervous collapse and retired to England in 1833, where he died in 1836; P. C. Crampton was busily pursuing a political career, standing unsuccessfully as a Whig candidate in the 1831, 1832 and 1834 elections, and this must have detracted from his temperance work; Harvey, while remaining on the executive of the H.T.S., had sunk into inactivity. (**309**, 39; **135**; **337**, 413) Edgar, of course, remained active in Ulster, where the larger numbers of Evangelical Protestants provided a surer basis for the movement than in the south. However, the split between temperance and teetotalism after 1835 was to be particularly bitter in the north, and, as we have seen, after a staunch rearguard action even the formidable Dr Edgar was forced to admit defeat. But by the time of Edgar's withdrawal in 1841 the anti-spirits movement had already been moribund for at least four years.

In more general terms the whole strategy of the anti-spirits movement can be seen as highly suspect. The idea of the 'better classes' setting an example and encouraging their 'inferiors' may have made some sense in the United States or Britain (though ultimately it was not especially successful in either country) (**173**, 113-16; **220**, 68-74), but in Ireland, given deep and bitter economic and sectarian divisions, it was wildly unrealistic. Bishop Doyle's scepticism was well founded: gentlemen, not remarkable for their 'friendship and protection' of their tenants and workers, were asking the people to abandon whiskey, while they themselves continued to consume wine. Contemporary critics who mocked the movement as hypocritical and impractical obviously had a strong case. Temperance in the early 1830s was part of an effort by conservative Protestants to bolster their socio-economic position during a period of considerable stress. They sought through reasoned argument to eliminate drunkenness from among the middle classes and the more respectable and educated elements of the working classes. The *Irish Temperance and Literary Gazette* in the leading article of its first issue declared the goals of temperance to be 'peace, order, industry and sobriety' — sobriety being the means to achieve the other three.[15] But while the movement was very ready to acknowledge its goals of political order and economic growth, it was a good deal less ready to acknowledge its Evangelical and proselytising aspects. Certainly not all temperance advocates supported proselytising, but temperance did appeal to Evangelicals, and many of the leading figures of the 'Second Reformation' were to be found as patrons of temperance societies. The colonies of converts encouraged by Farnham in Cavan, O'Donel on Achill and Ventry in Dingle all boasted vigorous temperance societies, and Edgar was later to achieve notoriety for his proselytising activities in Connacht during the famine.

Yet even at this period there were cross-currents suggestive of very different developments in the future. Influential priests with strong nationalist sympathies, such as John Kenyon and John Spratt, could be found advocating temperance, as could radical Quakers and Unitarians in the cities of Dublin and Cork. Even the Owenite community at Ralahine found a significant place for temperance in its regulations. Temperance up to 1835 had largely been a conservative, Protestant movement, but it was certainly not inherently so. However, the major development that occurred in the anti-drink movement in the latter 1830s, the triumph of teetotalism, was as much the result of events in England as in Ireland — a salutary reminder that temperance was an international movement and that the cause in Ireland was very much subject to outside influences.

We have seen that voices had been raised in Dublin in favour of total abstinence from all forms of alcohol as early as 1829, though a significant proportion of the movement led by Dr Edgar set itself against such perfectionism. But it was not until 1832-3 that an influential society specifically dedicated to teetotalism was formed in Preston in Lancashire. Apart from its advocacy of teetotalism, this society differed in other significant ways from the anti-spirits groups established over the preceding four years. Its members were mainly craftsmen and tradesmen, many in fact being reformed drunkards eager to bear personal witness to the material advantages of teetotalism. Many were radicals in political terms and Nonconformists in their religious affiliations. Unlike the anti-spirits advocates, or moderationists as they came to be called, the Preston teetotallers did not aim to convert the educated classes by carefully reasoned tracts; rather they wanted to reclaim the drunkard, and their methods were therefore frequently dramatic. The mass meeting, highly charged with emotional fervour, and with ex-drunkards recounting harrowing tales of their enslavement to drink, was a standard technique for spreading the teetotal message. Itinerant preachers, so-called 'kings of reformed drunkards', proved enormously popular, for the teetotallers appreciated the need to entertain as well as to instruct their largely working-class and illiterate audiences. In the English context of the 1830s and 1840s teetotalism had close links with Chartism and with the anti-slavery and anti-Corn Law campaigns. It was one among the numerous social reform movements which characterised these turbulent decades, and by no means the most influential. (**173**, 107-26) But in the less cluttered arena of Irish reform campaigns teetotalism was to assume a far more significant role.

While individuals had argued in favour of teetotalism in Ireland before 1835, it was the activities of English missionaries that were to prove crucial in the development of an organised total abstinence movement, just as American influences had been crucial in the introduction of the anti-spirits campaign. The earliest of these missionaries was John Finch, a Liverpool iron merchant, who made annual visits to Ireland on business between 1833 and 1836. Of working-class origins, Finch was a founder member of the Liverpool Temperance Society in 1830, but quickly developed teetotal sympathies and encouraged the establishment of the Preston society. His teetotalism went hand in hand with his political radicalism. He was an Owenite socialist and was involved in various utopian experiments in England, Ireland and America. He was a close friend of the socialist William Thompson, whom he visited at Glandore, strongly approving James Redmond Barry's efforts to promote temperance in the area at the same time.

Passing through Strabane on business in June 1835, Finch gave a lecture on teetotalism which resulted in the setting up of a teetotal society with an initial membership of twenty-five. When the society held its first anniversary meeting in 1836 it had 640 members in the town and another 426 in eight neighbouring societies. On another visit in March 1836 Finch assured the Strabane teetotallers, who were described as consisting largely of 'tradespeople, mechanics etc.', that 'nothing but total abstinence would ever prove of any avail in reclaiming the drunkard, or stemming the flood of intemperance that overflowed the land'. Finch seems to have introduced teetotalism to Derry as early as 1834, but, unlike the Strabane society, that in Derry was mixed, containing both teetotallers and moderationists. The rapid strides made by the teetotal group in Strabane, however, heartened their comrades in Derry. Another issue on which the societies differed was the use of prayer at temperance meetings. In Derry meetings began and concluded with prayers, normally said by a Protestant cleric, but in Strabane meetings had no religious trappings. At the Strabane society's first anniversary gathering Anthony Begley, a Catholic member of the Derry delegation, who described himself as an 'operative', argued that the greater success of teetotalism in Strabane was due to the non-religious character of meetings:

When Catholics entertain conscientious scruples with respect to prayer, as adopted by other sectarians, those should not be censured but respected. Therefore, I should wish, that prayer were abolished in the Derry Temperance Society, thereby flinging open its portals for the free admission of persons of all religious denominations.

While moderationist societies in Ulster were so frequently patronised or presided over by Protestant clergy, it is understandable that Catholics were loath to join, seeing them merely as fronts for proselytising.

Samuel Morton, the secretary of the Strabane society, while agreeing with Begley that prayers were undesirable since their meetings were not of a religious character, nevertheless pointed out that they had come under severe criticism for their secularism. Certainly the *Strabane Morning Post* published a string of letters in the latter half of 1836 condemning teetotalism as 'totally opposed to scripture'; its repudiation of prayer was viewed as a symptom of its unholy character. Meetings of working men with clergy present to supervise proceedings could be seen as safe religious gatherings, but wholly secular discussion groups raised the spectres of Ribbonism and rebellion. These attacks on the Strabane society largely originated with Protestant moderationists, followers of Dr Edgar, but the local Catholic clergy also proved hostile towards the new movement. Finch for one was surprised by this hostility, describing it as 'most unaccountable and unexpected', and he told the March 1836 meeting in Strabane that on a recent coach trip from Galway to Tuam he had discussed temperance with a Catholic clergyman who was a fellow-passenger. This priest 'expressed his decided approbation of the cause, and his wish that persons could be sent throughout Ireland to promote temperance societies'. On inquiry at the end of their journey, Finch discovered that his agreeable companion had been none other than John MacHale, Archbishop of Tuam.[16] But given that the anti-spirits movement had been identified with proselytism and that teetotalism was being championed by English radicals like Finch, it is hardly surprising that most priests were highly suspicious of the whole temperance cause. Despite his words to Finch (presumably he did not know to whom he was speaking either), John of Tuam was later to become one of the strongest opponents of the teetotal crusade in Ireland, and in this his views were probably more representative of the Irish church in general than were those of Father Mathew.

Finch went on to establish other societies in Galway and Limerick and in Westport, Co. Mayo, and Drogheda, Co. Louth, before the end of 1835; on another trip to Ireland late in 1836 he formed some thirteen further societies. Teetotalism was introduced into Cork in 1835 by William Martin, a Quaker merchant, and to Dublin in the same year by Robert G. White, an army supplier and long-time temperance worker, who had visited Preston and been much impressed by teetotal successes among the working classes there. (**297**, 169; **85**, I, 97) Many societies initially followed the Derry model of combining moderation and teetotalism; this was certainly true of the parish societies promoted in Cork by the Rev. Nicholas Dunscombe and in Dublin of the influential Port of Dublin and Juvenile Temperance Societies. But a letter from Cork, published in the *Irish Temperance and Literary Gazette* early in 1838 and probably written by Dunscombe, summed up the experience of this dual system when it declared that

> The pledge of entire abstinence is better understood, and more easily kept by the working classes, than the pledge which binds to abstinence from distilled spirit alone.

A report from the Tandragee society in Co. Armagh confirmed this view, noting that one 'humble member' had declared:

> There is nothing like teetotalism. I say it from experience, for when I touch not and taste not the unclean thing, I have no hankering after it at all.[17]

Clearly once the temperance movement had set itself the aim of converting large numbers of the working classes, including drunkards, teetotalism became the only workable strategy.

After spreading only slowly in 1835 and 1836, teetotalism began to grow rapidly in 1837 and 1838. Here again English missionaries played an important role. Many, like Finch, were connected with societies in the English north and midlands; many were also ex-drunkards of working-class origins. A Mr McCurdy, an Irishman, secretary of the Halifax Temperance Society, addressed meetings in Belfast, Coleraine, Strabane, Derry, Tandragee and Dublin late in 1836 and early in 1837. Ralph Holker of Birmingham, a former soldier and agent for the first national teetotal society in England, helped to establish a society in Ballinasloe, Co. Galway, in February 1837 and was back in Ireland in August and September of the same year lecturing to societies in Dublin. In December 1837 George Pilkington spoke to the Dublin Juvenile Temperance Society on the subject of teetotalism, after which sixteen people came forward to take the total abstinence pledge. In 1838 James Clarke of Bristol, Edward Grubb of Preston, James McKenna of Liverpool, a Mr R. Winters of Staffordshire and John Clune, 'the Cumberland weaver', all conducted teetotal meetings in different parts of the country.[18] But by far the most influential of the English teetotal lecturers was John Hockings, popularly known as 'the Birmingham blacksmith'. By his own account, Hockings paid three visits to Ireland in 1838, spending altogether forty-one weeks in the country and travelling between three and four thousand miles. A former sailor and blacksmith, Hockings was one of the most colourful and most successful of the ex-drunkard itinerant lecturers. He did much to promote teetotalism in Belfast, Dublin and the south, supporting his activities by charging for admission to his meetings and by selling temperance medals. Although not the first to bring Birmingham-manufactured medals to Ireland — J. R. Barry was distributing them to the Glandore society in February 1837 after a trip to England — Hockings made them widely popular. According to J. F. Maguire, Father Mathew's biographer, he introduced medals to Cork, where Father Mathew was eventually to adopt their use. Hockings made a financial success of his temperance work, eventually buying his own home and ultimately emigrating to America. As we shall see, Father Mathew was not nearly so fortunate in his efforts to finance a temperance movement. (**240**, 199; **172**, 64)[19]

A total abstinence society had been established in Belfast in February 1837, but it needed all the resources that it could muster to counter the continuing opposition of Dr Edgar. Pamphlets were produced refuting his arguments in detail, but visiting English lecturers proved more effective with working-class audiences. (**116**) Hockings was on a tour of Ulster in February 1838, and it would appear that he had been invited over by the Belfast teetotallers specifically to counter Edgar. News of his successes reached Dublin, and in the same month he was invited to the city to address the Dublin Juvenile Temperance Society. This society was established as a junior branch of the H.T.S. in March 1837 by young tradesmen and clerks anxious to win over youth to the temperance cause. During 1838 a protracted debate occurred within the society over the issue of moderation *versus* teetotalism, with some members opting for one and some for the other. At a meeting in January 1838 Charles Corkran, one of the founding members, announced that he had become 'one of those singular things called teetotallers' because

> I wish to bring the temperance principles to bear on the neglected, degraded, and dissipated classes of society, and I think I could not go with clean hands to the poor wretched drunkard, who has nothing to preserve him from ruin but total abstinence, and call upon him to surrender one gratification while I am partaking of another of a similar kind.[20]

Here again was Doyle's and Carr's old argument for consistency. Eventually in 1839 the Juvenile Society did opt for total abstinence and changed its name to the Dublin Total Abstinence Society. The society's sponsoring of Hockings's visits to the capital in 1838 certainly did much to further the teetotal cause there.

Hockings's speech in the Adelphi Theatre in February 1838 created something of a sensation in Dublin, and when he returned in May to address the Juvenile Society again he drew an audience of over a thousand in the Rotunda. During these visits he succeeded in converting many moderationists to the virtues of total abstinence, most notably James Haughton, who was to be a leading figure in the Irish temperance movement for over thirty years. But the *Gazette*, the mouthpiece of the H.T.S., was far from impressed, commenting sourly after his first meeting that 'As an actor, we think him not inferior to many who have preceded him upon the boards of the Adelphi.' The paper particularly objected to Hockings's attacks on moderationists; as one correspondent wrote, 'Temperance... seems to be on his estimation one of the seven deadly sins.' But Hockings continued to attract substantial audiences on his journeys through the country: 400 in Youghal, Co. Cork, in June, and 500 at each of his two meetings in Wexford town in December. Most of these audiences, according to reports, were the 'middling and working classes', tradesmen and labourers particularly, and moreover Hockings went out of his way to appeal to Catholics. In various speeches he referred to the strong teetotal movement in Liverpool, composed of 3,000 members, 'all Roman Catholics, with the priests at their head'. Later in the same year tee-totalism's appeal to Catholics was reinforced when James McKenna of Liverpool, representing various English Catholic total abstinence societies, addressed a number of meetings, declaring his mission to be 'to speak to my Roman Catholic brethren in Ireland to remove all suspicion from their minds' regarding teetotalism.[21]

Although middle-class moderationists might sneer at Hockings's manner of address, it certainly had an impact on his largely working-class audiences. Brian Harrison aptly terms Hockings's style, the 'music-hall' approach, it being a 'strange combination of high-mindedness and sheer good fun'. (**173**, 129-30) The mixture proved as successful in Ireland as it had been in England. With disarming pride Hockings told his Rotunda audience in May:

> About four years ago, if any of you went to Birmingham, and saw me going down the street; if you enquired who I was, they would have pointed at me and said, 'that is drunken Jack'. But then I joined the tee-totallers since; and here I am tonight, and you might have heard some say 'that is *Mr* Hockings from Birmingham'.[22]

The simple lesson was that teetotalism brought respectability and by implication material prosperity. Colourful stories, either of the drunkard's pathetic fate or the teetotaller's successes, interwoven with jokes and rather appalling poetry were Hockings's stock-in-trade. He particularly amused his Irish audiences by attempting to imitate Irish accents in some of his stories; the results were outrageous. A comparison of Hockings's hilarious lectures with Dr Edgar's sober tracts provides a graphic illustration of just how far the temperance movement had travelled by 1838 from its origins in 1829. The message, the technique and the audience were all very different. Temperance had moved down the social scale, and in the Irish context this also meant that it had moved across the sectarian divide.

An examination of Hockings's travels shows that he concentrated his work in the south: beginning in Belfast, by February he was in Dublin; in May and June he held meetings in Celbridge, Parsonstown (Birr), Youghal and Cork; and in November and December he visited Parsonstown again, then Mountmellick, Mountrath, Roscrea, New Ross, Clonmel, Wexford, Enniscorthy and Waterford. In the latter city he became seriously ill, and this forced the termination of his Irish mission. The area that Hockings travelled through, south Leinster and east Munster, was soon to be the centre of Father Mathew's crusade. By early 1839 there were reports of large numbers flocking from here to Cork to take the pledge from Father Mathew, though he himself had as yet not visited the area. That Hockings's meetings helped to arouse popular, and particularly Catholic, interest in the teetotal cause is clear. In his valedictory letter to the Irish tee-totallers, published in December 1838, Hockings claimed that he

> never saw so pleasing a change in any country in the same time as there is in this; for go where I will — visit what town I may, the working class received me with pleasure, and appeared prepared to dash the poisonous cup from their lips.[23]

Even allowing for self-interested exaggeration on Hockings's part, there is doubtless truth in what he says. In retrospect the Birmingham blacksmith can best be seen as preparing the way for the Apostle of Temperance.

The year 1838 marked the definite victory of teetotalism over moderation in Ireland; Hockings's visits and the adherence in April of Father Mathew to the teetotal cause were the crucial events. In November the *Irish Temperance and Literary Gazette*, which had ceased publication at the end of September, reappeared as the *Dublin Weekly Herald*: 'A temperance, agricultural, commercial and mechanics' journal'. Not only had the paper widened its appeal in more practical directions, but its attitude to teetotalism had become far more sympathetic. Some clue to the nature of this transformation is provided by a letter which appeared in the paper in January 1842. The author, the Quaker draper Richard Allen, acknowledged that he had acted as editor for some time and had been 'one of those who was instrumental in bringing it over from the rotten and unsound principle of moderation to the safe and thorough going principles of total abstinence'.[24] Although both the H.T.S. and the U.T.S. lingered on into the early 1840s, this shift in the allegiance of the country's only temperance newspaper was a clear indication of what had happened throughout the country in 1838.

In February 1839 a new organisation, the Irish Temperance Union, was formed in Dublin to co-ordinate the activities of the many new teetotal societies that were springing up. Its founders were determined not to fall into the errors of the anti-spirits movement by leaving local societies to rely on their own limited resources. The I.T.U. aimed to establish a travelling agency, to open correspondence with all interested teetotal societies, to raise funds — initially £1,000 to employ agents and later £2,000 to build a temperance hall — to publicise and lobby on behalf of the cause, and to organise an annual delegate conference in Dublin. Although by no means all these plans were realised, they demonstrate a more realistic and practical approach to temperance than the old anti-spirits movement with its pleas to landlords, employers and clergymen. A list of the subscribers to the I.T.U. published in March revealed the principal basis of its support, in Dublin at least. Of the twenty-six subscribers, at least half were members of well-known Quaker and Unitarian families: the Allens, Webbs, Bewleys, Pims and Haughtons. The I.T.U.'s treasurer was R. D. Webb, a Quaker and former leading light in the anti-spirits movement; its secretary was Richard Allen, another Quaker; its assistant secretary was Charles Corkran, a Unitarian; while its headquarters were at 62 High Street, the site of Allen's drapery warehouse. A similar influence can be seen at work in the Juvenile Society, which became the Dublin Total Abstinence Society in May 1839 and which was a leading force promoting teetotalism in the city for many years. Its treasurer and most active spokesman was Charles Corkran; James Haughton, a Quaker who was influenced by Unitarianism, was one of its main financial supporters and later its president; while Richard Allen was for long periods on its executive. In Cork city the picture was somewhat similar. Of the three main temperance societies in operation before Father Mathew founded his own, one was headed by the Rev. Nicholas Dunscombe, a minister of the Established Church, who had been very active in the anti-spirits movement, but the other two were led by William Martin, a Quaker, and Richard Dowden, a Unitarian merchant, who was later mayor of the city. Both were staunch teetotallers, as were George Cox and George Gibbs, Quakers who worked closely with Martin and Dowden.[25] When Father Mathew later singled out Quakers as his most important early supporters, it is clear that he was only doing justice to their vital role in nurturing the Irish teetotal movement.

As well as inviting stirring lecturers from English teetotal societies, the Irish movement threw up its own colourful speakers. Perhaps the best-known Irish 'king of the ex-drunkards' was John Smith, a clerk in a Dublin coachmaker's business and later a bootmaker. Smith had been a drunkard for ten years and during that time had lost a number of jobs. By 1836 he was in Richmond Bridewell, having broken a street lamp while 'in a state of starvation'. The governor, Thomas Purdon, who was on the committee of the H.T.S., allowed the Rev. John Grant of Monkstown, one of the society's secretaries, to preach to the prisoners on the subject of temperance. Smith was deeply impressed by Grant's words, so much so that he took the teetotal pledge. After his release he began to speak of his experiences at temperance meetings and even accompanied Grant back to

Richmond Bridewell in March 1837 in order to convert his former colleagues. By September Smith was advertising himself in the *Gazette* as a 'reformed drunkard' and a bootmaker of 6 Bedford Row. His business must have been a success, for over a year later his advertisement was still appearing, and by the early 1840s he had moved his shop to the more salubrious location of Dawson Street. His career as a teetotal lecturer also prospered, for he was still speaking regularly in Dublin late in 1838 and early in 1839, styling himself 'king of the reformed drunkards of Dublin'.[26]

The very different slant that these working-class temperance advocates brought to the cause is well illustrated by Daniel Connolly, a 'labouring man' and ex-drunkard, who addressed a meeting at Athy, Co. Kildare, in April 1837.

> When he was an United Irishman, in the rebellion of '98 [Connolly told his audience], he was sent with a party of twelve men on some expedition. They went into a public house, and got something to drink, more like arsenic than whiskey; at all events it had the name and smell of whiskey, and that was enough; it left them so insensible that the enemy came upon them, and he alone escaped.[27]

While the respectable members of the H.T.S. saw whiskey as having motivated the rebels of 1798, Daniel Connolly from his personal experience could testify that it also at times inhibited them. Both were agreed in seeing the effects of drink as deleterious, though from wholly different political points of view. Connolly, however, represented the new political directions in which temperance was moving; teetotalism was not only more popular and more Catholic in its outlook, it was also more nationalistic.

As well as rousing meetings and lectures, the teetotallers found processions and music to be great aids to their cause. In 1835 temperance societies had been formed at Ravensdale and Leixlip, Co. Kildare, by Catholic working men, 'without any aid or influence from the higher classes'. In November 1836 these societies, led by a band and their banners, marched to Maynooth for a meeting organised by G. W. Carr and John Mackay, a Catholic barrister from Dublin and one of the H.T.S.'s secretaries. The *Gazette* recorded this event as the 'first temperance procession which has ever taken place in this country'.[28] Although these societies do not appear to have been teetotal, it is significant that they were working-class, for it was the new temperance men from the working class who were to be the main promoters of marches and music in later years.

St Patrick's Day, with its reputation for 'drowning the shamrock', became the main occasion for temperance processions; the teetotallers thereby hoped to counter the attraction of the public house. The first large-scale St Patrick's Day teetotal procession was held in Dublin in March 1839. It was mainly organised by the National Total Abstinence Association, a recently established Catholic working-class society based in

Denmark Street, though the Juvenile Society and the Mariners' Total Abstinence Society, which had grown out of the old Port of Dublin Society, also took an active part. The route was extensive, going from Denmark Street along Church Street, across the river to St Stephen's Green, down Grafton Street and around Trinity College, then back over the river via Parliament Street to Denmark Street again. The streets were thronged by 'an immense multitude', and in the evening the largest tea party ever held in Ireland took place in the Mansion House, with 2,000 sitting down to tea presided over by the Lord Mayor. The procession itself was headed by Patrick Thomas, president of the association, and John Smith, both on horseback. Behind them came a band playing national airs and the committee on foot, together with four members carrying the association's banner. This was made of green silk, nine feet by six, surmounted by a crown and harp; and it rewards detailed examination:

> On one side is presented a full-length figure of 'Hibernia', with an Irish wolf-dog reposing at her feet, and on either side is an aerial figure, proclaiming 'Good will to all classes and creeds'; underneath is a beehive, with the motto, 'Industry'. Various other mottos cover this side of the banner, such as — 'Erin go Bragh' — 'Obedience to the laws' — 'The secret of our strength is union' — 'For the prosperity of Ireland' — 'No political discussions' — 'No religious distinctions' — intimating the truly catholic principles on which the society is based. On the other side are three full-length figures; the centre being that of St Patrick, magnificently painted — the side figures are those of 'Hope' and 'Charity'; and underneath the motto 'Christian charity uniteth all men' — higher up is the name, and date of the foundation of the society. The whole is covered over with wreaths of golden shamrocks, gracefully intertwining the various devices.

The banner had been made by Mr Pakenham of Pill Lane, a painter and glazier and a member of the association.[29]

Just as the anti-spirits movement had relied heavily on tracts to influence its literate audience, so teetotalism relied on images, medals, music, entertaining lecturers and alternative recreations to reach its largely illiterate audience. In interpreting the nature and aims of teetotalism, the historian has thus both more diverse and more difficult sources to work with. This banner, for instance, presents rather contradictory impressions. Its mottoes reject religious and political involvement, emphasising the non-sectarian nature of the movement and its law-abiding methods; they suggest that teetotalism will promote industry and bring prosperity to the whole country. Yet the harp, wolfhound, shamrocks and the figures of St Patrick and Hibernia were all common nationalist symbols of the period, while the mottoes 'Erin go Bragh' and 'The secret of our strength is union' could easily be interpreted as having political overtones. (**308**, 8-13) It is interesting that in a leading article accompanying its report of this march the *Herald* felt called upon to defend the temperance movement's use of processions in the face of criticism from the Tory press. At the same time it did acknowledge that in the past in Ireland processions had frequently degenerated into violence and disorder. The sight of large numbers of working-class Dubliners marching in good order through the city must have been alarming to many conservative Protestants. St Patrick Day processions were to become a regular feature of the Irish teetotal movement, but they were to supply much ammunition to the movement's critics and to create considerable unease in Dublin Castle. Though permitting the March gatherings, the Castle was at times in the early 1840s to refuse permission for marches on other occasions as teetotalism became more and more identified with the Repeal movement.[30]

Reading-rooms, temperance hotels and coffee houses were another characteristic aspect of teetotalism. The anti-spirits movement had made gestures in this direction. Ulster typically led the way, with coffee houses in Belfast, Larne, Coleraine and Omagh by 1832 and an itinerant coffee seller in the streets of Lisburn. By 1836 the H.T.S. was acknowledging the establishment of coffee houses to be of 'paramount importance', but, except for movable temperance tents at some fairs and markets, mainly in the midlands, it appears to have done little. Given, however, that the anti-spirits advocates were essentially aiming to convert the gentry, middle class and most respectable elements of the working class, providing alternative drinks and recreation for the working class was not high on their list of priorities, despite the H.T.S.'s claim to the contrary. The teetotallers, on the other hand, considered such facilities as vital to their success, for without them the working man had little alternative but to patronise the public house. It is interesting to note, though, that Dublin lagged behind other centres in this regard. In September 1838 the Juvenile Society opened reading-rooms at 11 Eustace Street, but reports from Cork early in 1839 spoke of four temperance reading-rooms in that city. In March 1838 a leading article in the *Gazette* complained that Dublin had no temperance hotels or coffee houses, while Belfast, Cork and even some smaller towns had long supported them. But it was not until March 1839, a year later, that the capital's first coffee house and temperance hotel were opened at 4 Old Dominick Street. For, despite the publication of a temperance newspaper, the establishment of the Irish Temperance Union and the rapid growth of teetotal societies in the city in 1838 and 1839, Dublin was not the leading centre of the movement. The city depended too heavily on the drink industry in economic terms for its workers, businessmen or civic authorities wholeheartedly to embrace the teetotal cause. Just as Belfast had led the way in the anti-spirits campaign of the late 1820s and early 1830s, so Cork was to lead the way in the teetotal crusade of the late 1830s and early 1840s.[31]

Teetotalism argued its case on fairly simplistic materialist grounds: that sobriety would bring economic prosperity both to the individual and to the country. Ex-drunkards like Hockings and Smith offered living proof of this argument, and in the difficult economic circumstances of the late 1830s their example must have carried considerable weight among many struggling tenants and workers. But as well as convincing workers to abstain, it was also necessary to convince employers and landlords that teetotal employees and tenants were more reliable than non-abstainers. So the teetotal message was not restricted solely to the working classes. Some individual teetotallers took matters into their own hands by advertising for work in the newspapers and stressing their sobriety. Some societies, like the N.T.A.A. of Denmark Street, established registries of 'sober and honest workmen' which employers were urged to consult. The I.T.U., on the other hand, solicited funds from 'English as well as Irish capitalists', arguing that teetotalism would boost consumer demand for non-alcoholic products and thus encourage trade. The response of employers to moderation had generally been poor; teetotallers argued that employers could not expect their workers to abstain while they continued to drink themselves. But up to 1838 the response to teetotalism had also been patchy at best. The two most responsive groups were Quaker merchants, particularly in Dublin and Cork, and textile mill owners, mainly located in Ulster. The Quaker Nicolsons encouraged teetotalism in their linen mills at Bessbrook, Co. Down, as did the Malcolmsons in their large cotton mill at Portlaw, Co. Waterford. In 1839 the *Herald* reported that a group of Cork butter merchants had got together to provide a temperance reading-room for their employees.[32] Drink, however, was associated with many aspects of work, from harvest festivities in the country to the payment of workers in public houses in the towns. So it was perhaps only where the employer had a distinctive religious commitment to temperance, as in the case of the Quakers, or where the industry was new and required greater discipline, as with the rapidly mechanising textile industry, that the traditional drinking customs could be seriously undermined. (**173**, 55-8)

Despite repeated claims to the contrary by the temperance movement, there is little evidence that it had much impact on Irish spirit consumption between 1829 and 1839. Officially recorded production certainly dropped significantly between 1829 and 1833: from nearly 10 million gallons per annum in 1828 to just over 8 million in 1833. Substantial increases in spirit duty in 1826 and 1830 probably go a long way towards explaining this trend. But one should not conclude, as some in the anti-spirits movement did, that consumption was in fact falling. As we have seen, Dr Edgar conceded in 1834 that illicit distillation had seldom been worse, and the figures certainly bear out his opinion. The admittedly incomplete figures available show that detections jumped from some 5,400 in 1832 to over 8,000 in 1834; the increase in prosecutions was evn more dramatic over the same period, from around 1,000 to over 2,700. The evidence points to a marked upsurge in illicit distillation to satisfy the vast demand for cheap whiskey. With the revenue from spirit duties falling sharply, the government acted in 1834 and cut the duty drastically, from 3s 4d per gallon to 2s 4d, the lowest level of duty for nearly forty years. The results were predictable. Official consumption soared between 1835 and 1839, consistently surpassing 10 million gallons per annum, the only period it was to do so during the whole of the century. Conversely, detections and prosecutions for illicit distilling fell dramatically, in the case of the latter from nearly 2,000 in 1835 to a mere 300 in 1839. This was also a period of higher agricultural prices, when there was less incentive for the farmer to turn his grain into poteen. Although the balance between legal and illegal consumption swung wildly in the 1830s, the overall picture is one of high, indeed record, levels of spirit consumption. In the first half of the decade illicit spirits surged ahead, while in the second half cheaper legal spirits made up much lost ground. But in either case the anti-drink movement was having little if any impact on patterns of consumption. (**27**, 66-7; **31**, 551; **343**, 336-7)

Up to 1838 the anti-drink movement in Ireland had closely paralleled that in England and, to a lesser extent, in the United States. Societies initially appeared, under American influence, directed against spirit consumption and led by clergy and professional men. In class terms these societies aimed to reform the drinking habits of the landed gentry, the urban middle class, skilled workers and relatively prosperous tenant farmers. The poor generally and drunkards in particular were considered beyond redemption. The basic goal was to bolster the 'respectable' elements in society by promoting their economic prosperity and political status. But by the mid-1830s a very different anti-drink campaign was on the rise: teetotalism, or the rejection of all forms of alcohol. It was introduced into Ireland by English itinerant lecturers, many of them working-class ex-drunkards themselves, and it found its strongest Irish supporters among the Quaker community, particularly in Dublin and Cork. In political and religious terms the two movements were also distinctively different. The anti-spirits campaign was conservative in its outlook and had close links with Protestant proselytisers who were particularly active at this time. Teetotalism, on the other hand, while its leadership up to 1838 was still largely Protestant, appealed openly to Catholics and particularly to drunkards with what it claimed was a simple formula for their economic betterment. Politically its sympathies inclined towards nationalism, though through the Quaker involvement it was also aligned with other radical reform campaigns, such as anti-slavery, the peace movement, the anti-Corn Law campaign, feminism and Chartism. The anti-spirits movement's successes were very limited, except perhaps in Ulster, where it won strong support among the province's Protestant clergy. Up to the end of 1838 teetotalism was certainly making some headway, but only in the face of formidable opposition, from conservative moderationists, especially in Ulster, on the one hand, and from many Catholic clerics on the other. After 1838, however, the Irish anti-drink movement diverged dramatically from its English and American counterparts. For, in the person of Father Theobald Mathew, it found a leader whose influence was to exceed all others and who was, for the first time, to put teetotalism to the forefront of Irish political and social life.

3

'Mathew the Martyr'

IT IS impossible to discuss either the successes or the failures of the great temperance crusade of the 1840s without focusing a good deal of attention on Father Mathew himself. Unlike the temperance movement of the 1830s, the crusade of the 1840s was not the product of the labours of groups of men or societies; it was not directed by a committee; it did not issue numerous tracts or support a newspaper. The crusade was largely the product of one man's labours; it was substantially an emotional mass response to one man's appeal. An understanding of the nature of this appeal and of the nature of this man is thus essential in any discussion of the temperance crusade.

The Mathews were originally landed Welsh Catholics, who came to Ireland early in the seventeenth century, when George Mathew of Llandaff in south Glamorgan married Elizabeth Butler, widow of Viscount Thurles and mother of the first Duke of Ormond. By this marriage and others into the Butler family, the Mathews gained extensive estates in the rich plains of Co. Tipperary, while retaining their Welsh lands. At Thomastown early in the eighteenth century they built a vast castle which became the family's main seat. But, like other landed Catholic families, they faced the problem of inheritance posed by the penal laws' preference for Protestant heirs. A judicious policy of adherence to the Established Church by the principal heir enabled the Mathews to preserve their estates through the eighteenth century, while largely retaining their Catholicism as well. The family's fortunes probably reached their height with Francis Mathew (1744-1806), who succeeded his father Thomas in 1774. He sat for Co. Tipperary in the Irish parliament from 1768 until 1783, when he was raised to the peerage as Baron Llandaff; in 1793 he was made a viscount, and in 1797 an earl, and at his death in 1806 he was vigorously lobbying for a marquisate. Bishop David Mathew, a descendant writing in the 1940s with access to family papers, described the first Earl of Llandaff as a 'man gifted with great charm, a fine host', but also as one who 'kept his sails trimmed to the wind of government and never lost the prudence of restrained endeavour'. After some hesitation he thus supported the Union and was rewarded by being made a representative Irish peer. A handsome and extremely ambitious man, the earl's main extravagances were politics and fashion. (**294**, xviii)

The earl married three times and by his first wife had three sons and a daughter: Francis James, M.P. for Co. Tipperary in 1790-92 and 1796-1800 and at Westminster from 1891 to 1806, when he succeeded to his father's title; Montague, a lieutenant-general and M.P. for Tipperary from 1806 to his death in 1819, when the family's political significance effectively ceased; George, who also seems to have pursued a military career, but who died insane in 1832; and Elizabeth, who died in 1841. Only Francis James married, into the wealthy Dublin banking family of La Touche, but the marriage produced no children. (**83**, 793-4; **110**, 419-21; **84**, 360-1) The three brothers followed in their father's footsteps with regard to fashion and high living, but they lacked his political pragmatism. All three were notorious rakes and gamblers and appeared on a number of occasions in James Gillray's caricatures highlighting the excesses of the Prince of Wales's set. (**346**, 386, 462, 472) Politically they were staunch Whigs, opponents of the Union and champions of Catholic Emancipation. Indeed, Francis James's opposition to the Union seems to have ruined his father's chances of further advancement in the peerage. Montague became notorious for his vigorous espousal of Catholic relief in parliament and his generally critical attitude to the government's Irish policy. This stance undoubtedly damaged both his political and military career. The family's attitude to drink and to illicit distillation in particular can be glimpsed in Montague Mathew's contribution to a debate in May 1816. He defended poteen as far superior to legal whiskey and told the house that it was preferred by the Irish gentry as 'the finest diuretic in the world'. The Mathews presumably were among those many landlords turning a blind eye to illicit distillation on their estates, if not becoming actual customers for the poteen-maker. Montague himself was to die suddenly at Thomastown in 1819 after a heavy bout of drinking.[1] The extravagance of the first earl and his sons, their numerous costly election contests, their clothes and gambling, their high living in London and frequent trips to France and Italy, had its inevitable effect upon their inheritance. In 1813 all their Welsh lands and much of their Irish estates had to be sold off, mainly to pay gambling debts. Bishop Mathew comments that the brothers 'broke down that hampered fortune which their father had broached before them'. When Francis James, the second earl, succumbed 'to his own galloping extravagance' in 1833 he not only left no heir, but no will either. (**294**, xix) The remains of the family fortune, which now largely consisted of Thomastown Castle and its surrounding lands, passed to his younger sister, Lady Elizabeth Mathew. Although by all accounts a rather difficult and eccentric woman, she had always taken a marked interest in the welfare of her young relative, Theobald Mathew. He eventually came to expect that he, perhaps with his brothers as well, would inherit the Thomastown estate upon her death.

Theobald Mathew was born at Thomastown in October 1790, the fourth son of James Mathew, who acted as agent for the first earl. Father Mathew's clerical biographers tell us that his father, having lost his parents when young, was adopted and educated by the earl and eventually made agent for the Thomastown estates. Given the family's hopeless extravagance, it must have been a difficult position to fill successfully. James lived at the castle until about 1795, when he built a substantial house of his own at Rathcloheen, less than a mile to the east. It is suggested by Bishop Mathew, among others, that James was a descendant of a junior branch of the Mathew family, which settled at Two-Mile-Borris early in the eighteenth century. But though the family's genealogy is generally clear, the precise connection between James and the Borris Mathews is not. James is said to have had two sisters, both of whom married Protestants, but his own religious affiliation is by no means clear. Bishop Mathew describes it as 'rather shadowy'. He married Anne Whyte of Cappawhyte, a distant relative, who certainly was a Catholic and who brought up all her children as Catholics. As a child, Theobald, or Toby as he was called by his family, spent a great deal of time at the castle, where he received the respect from servants that befitted a member of the earl's family. He was, as mentioned, a special favourite of Lady Elizabeth, who paid for his education, first at Thurles, then at St Canice's Academy in Kilkenny, and finally at Maynooth.

It is impossible to prove, but there seems to exist a good deal of circumstantial evidence suggesting that James Mathew may have been the illegitimate son of Thomas Mathew, father of Francis, the first earl. The obscurity of his family connection is puzzling, while his favoured treatment by the earl, as well as his children's expectations of inheritance, all point in this direction. Moreover, a work dealing with the genealogy of the Earls of Llandaff, published about 1898 by Arnold Harris Mathew, an English clergyman who repeatedly claimed that his grandfather had been the first earl's eldest son, born in 1765, three years before Francis James, refers specifically to James as the 'natural son' of Thomas. Arnold Harris Mathew did for many years style himself fourth Earl of Llandaff, though it is a claim rejected for lack of evidence by the *Complete Peerage*. (**246**, 45; **110**, 421) Nevertheless, as his book amply demonstrates, A. H. Mathew was an expert on the genealogy of the Mathew family, and as he seems to have had no vested interest in making his statement regarding James Mathew, it is unlikely that he would have made it unless he believed it to be true. Leaving aside the problem of his father's parentage, however, the fact remains that Theobald Mathew was brought up in intimate connection with the family at Thomastown Castle; he considered them his family and Thomastown his home; in later years he returned there as frequently as possible, and from at least 1833 to 1841 he confidently expected to inherit the estate.

The Mathews, perhaps because of the family's interdenominational character, had not contributed any members to the priesthood, but Theobald Mathew's mother determined upon this career for him. He rather upset his family's plans, however, when in his first year, 1808, he was forced to leave Maynooth in order to avoid being expelled for holding what appears to have been a drunken party for his fellow-students. Nothing is known of the next two years of his life, but presumably he returned to Thomastown under a cloud, while his family pondered what to do with him. His next move, however, seems to have been taken on his own initiative: he applied to and was accepted by the Capuchin order as a novice and went to Dublin to be trained. It was in some respects a curious choice, for the Capuchins were, as Maguire his biographer acknowledges, the 'lowliest and least influential of the regular orders in Ireland'. (**240**, 10) But perhaps a young man who had all but been expelled from Maynooth could aspire to nothing higher. His training completed successfully, he was ordained in 1814 by Daniel Murray, later Archbishop of Dublin, who was to become a close and valuable friend.

Father Mathew's first posting was to Kilkenny, a town he must have known well, having been at school there. But problems with his superiors recurred. He became involved in a dispute with the secular clergy over the administration of Easter communion, which, under diocesan regulations, was forbidden to the regular orders: one of a number of restrictions imposed upon them by their often hostile secular brethren. (**294**, 13-15) As a result, he was moved to Cork after less than a year in Kilkenny. It was not an auspicious beginning to his ministry. In Cork he came under the influence of Father Daniel Donovan, who had trained and worked in France for many years before being forced to flee by the Revolution. In 1816 Donovan was elected provincial of the Capuchin order in Ireland. A rather brusque but basically kind-hearted man, Donovan seems to have exercised a stabilising influence on his young colleague, to whom he became very attached. It was with Donovan's assistance that Father Mathew began the study of Irish. He was eventually to attain a reasonable speaking knowledge of the language, which was to stand him in good stead when his work took him among native speakers. Donovan's favour may have accounted for the surprising fact that Father Mathew succeeded him as provincial of the order after his death in 1821. Given that Father Mathew was only thirty-two at the time and had been ordained for less than eight years, it was a striking advancement. But he had proved a popular and hard-working cleric. As a preacher he was not naturally effective, having a rather thin voice and a hesitant manner. He was not widely read and was no theologian or controversialist, but his simple, unadorned talks soon began to attract large audiences. He also became very popular as a confessor. His gentle and sympathetic approach won over those used to more strict and censorious priests. Early in his ministry he showed a bent towards practical charity. He established schools for poor girls and boys in which household skills were taught in addition to elementary subjects, and he became a strong supporter of the Christian Brothers who began work in Cork in the late 1820s. In 1819 Father Mathew set up a Josephian Society composed of middle-class Catholic youths who were organised to visit the sick and teach at a night school for poor boys. His faith in education and his belief in the duty of the higher orders to help those less fortunate than themselves were also to be reflected later in his work on behalf of temperance. (**56**, 36-7, 44, 48, 74)

In his long ministry in Cork between 1814 and 1838 there were two major projects to which he devoted much time and energy and which reveal many of his strengths and, perhaps more importantly, his weaknesses. Maguire tells us that he was popular with the poor because of his kindly and unaffected manner; he was 'respectful and tender, indeed almost reverential' to them. But he also had close connections with the rising Catholic middle class of the city and with many Protestants. 'He was respectful to those who held a high position, and deferential to authority, whether ecclesiastical or civil.' (**240**, 34) We shall discuss in more detail later the issue of Father Mathew's social status; however, it needs to be noted that his connections with the rich enabled him to raise large sums of money. In the 1830s he used this facility to purchase a cemetery for the city's Catholics and to begin building a church. Catholics lacked their own burial ground and had to seek permission and pay for burial in Protestant churchyards. This led to tensions and disputes between Catholic and Protestant clergy. After Catholic Emancipation the increasingly wealthy and confident Catholic middle class in Cork was prepared to find the money for their own cemetery as well as for several new churches. In 1830 Father Mathew organised the purchase of the old botanic gardens from the Royal Cork Institution and their consecration by the Archbishop of Cashel as St Joseph's cemetery. He had to tread warily in this matter so as not to offend Protestants on one side and the Catholic secular clergy on the other. On this occasion he was singularly successful.

But his schemes were by no means always so untroubled; in fact St Joseph's was rather the exception than the rule. The chapel in which he ministered in Blackamoor Lane was small and unimposing, and by the early 1830s he was planning the building of a new church. The fact that two other new churches, St Patrick's and St Mary's, were being built at the same time did not deter him. The estimated cost was £10,000, and he contributed some £4,500 of this himself. According to J. B. Sheil, this sum was 'all his pecuniary savings and the proceeds of his patrimonial property'. (**309**, 3) The remainder of the money he had to raise from the community, but Father Mathew's ability to produce large sums of money was an important source of his influence. Charity sermons produced some; more came from his commercial and professional friends. Nor was he loath to seek funds in unlikely quarters. Preaching in Dunmanway, Co. Cork, in March 1841 in aid of the local church's building fund, he told his audience that he had approached the Protestant Bishop of Cork for a subscription to his own church. He received £5 and the comment 'Father Mathew, I know I cannot make Protestants of your people. . . . I will endeavour to make them good Catholics.'[2] Father Mathew was on remarkably good terms with Protestants, and thus in such situations he was able to draw upon them for support. This ability, however, did not save him from serious troubles, many of them being financial and very much of his own making.

For his new church, which came to be called Holy Trinity, he was offered a site on Sullivan's Quay opposite Grand Parade, an imposing location. Against advice, he rejected this in favour of Charlotte's Quay, now called Father Mathew Quay. The choice was disastrous. The site proved to be marshy, which necessitated expensive drainage and the laying of special foundations. Moreover, Father Mathew became involved in a dispute with the architect; this led to a lawsuit which he lost, having ultimately to pay over £300 in expenses. The cost of the project steadily increased, and in 1837 he was forced to borrow £1,000 from the Board of Works. By 1840 £14,000 had been expended, but the church was still not completed. Now deeply involved in the temperance crusade, which made even greater financial demands, Father Mathew was unable to provide the builder with more funds and fell behind in the interest payments to the Board of Works. Building thus ceased. Father Mathew told an audience in Cork in April 1841 that until the temperance work was concluded he would not turn his attention to the unfinished church. In 1850, while he was in America, the incomplete church was dedicated and opened, but it was not until 1890 that the spire and façade were added. Ironically, this was done as part of the celebrations marking Father Mathew's centenary. Even Maguire, a most sympathetic biographer, thought his actions regarding the church 'impetuous' and 'not a little self-willed'. (**56**, 80, 82) Father Mathew's pig-headed enthusiasm and utter inability to manage money, both of which were demonstrated in the building of Holy Trinity, were to be revealed even more graphically, and tragically, in the temperance crusade.

During the crusade commentators frequently noted the importance of Father Mathew's personal appearance and manner as contributing to the impact and appeal of his message. He did not win people to his cause solely by the rationality of his arguments; on the contrary, the success of the crusade has to be explained, to some extent at least, in emotional terms. Although Father Mathew had many influential supporters and several imitators, the crusade was very much a personal one, focused almost exclusively on himself. The question inevitably arises: what was the man's appeal? What, to use the modern term, was the nature of his charisma?

One of the most detailed contemporary accounts of the personal appearance and impact of Father Mathew was given by the German traveller J. G. Kohl, who witnessed a temperance meeting at Kilrush, Co. Clare, early in 1842. Kohl found Father Mathew

> a man of decidedly distinguished appearance, and at once compre-
> hended the influence which he cannot fail to have over the people. The
> public require, in the individual whom they are to obey, an imposing
> figure and appearance, and Father Mathew is really a handsome man.
> He is about the same height and figure as Napoleon, and is withal
> thoroughly well proportioned, and well built. Though not corpulent, his
> person is well rounded, and displays nothing of the meagre, pale,
> sunken-cheeked, deep-eyed Franciscan monk [*sic*]. His complexion is
> very healthy and fresh. His movements and manner are simple and
> without affectation. . . . His features are perfectly regular, well defined,
> and in the highest degree noble, with an expression of mildness
> accompanied by great decision of character, yet with more of the latter
> than of the former. His eyes are large, his glance calm, and he often keeps
> his eye steadily fixed for a long time on one object. His forehead is
> straight, high, and commanding; and his nose . . . is particularly
> handsome, though perhaps a little too much arched in the middle. His
> mouth is small and well proportioned; and his chin round, projecting,
> firm and large, like Napoleon's. . . . Father Mathew has a very pretty
> and delicate hand, and dresses well, almost elegantly. He usually wears
> a fine black great-coat, and his linen is dazzlingly white. There is
> something particularly distinguished and gentlemanlike in his entire
> person and appearance, which is the more remarkable, as he has ever
> been a man of the people, has laboured and spoken for the humble and
> poor alone, and is beloved by them especially. (**211**, 97, 104)

In fact, as we have seen, Father Mathew was not a 'man of the people'. If we recall what we know of his family, his 'almost elegant' appearance comes as no surprise. Drawings done of him in the 1840s show a strong likeness to his fashionable cousins caricatured by Gillray around the turn of the century.

Kohl's description (and there are many others which confirm its essential accuracy) presents us with a decidedly handsome man: strong and healthy, well dressed, mild and unaffected in manner, yet confident, obviously a gentleman. That Father Mathew was a gentleman and as such was entitled to respect is frequently emphasised in contemporary newspapers and memoirs; 'a gentleman of independent fortune' was how the *Dublin Evening Post* introduced him to its readers in October 1839.[3] Much more than his status as a cleric and a Capuchin friar, his status as a gentleman was singled out for comment. In this respect the parallel with

Daniel O'Connell is striking: both had enormous popular appeal, and both were products of the old landed Catholic gentry. Perhaps an element of deference entered into both men's appeal. At a time when the priesthood was being increasingly filled with the sons of farmers, small businessmen and clerks, Father Mathew stood out as more representative of the eighteenth century, when members of the Catholic gentry had entered the priesthood in significant numbers. Admittedly he had not been trained abroad, as was the eighteenth-century practice, but then he was not a product of the Maynooth educational system either. While his unusual background may have contributed to his popular appeal, it also had the effect of isolating him within his own church. He was the head of a small order, not a secular priest; he was not a product of the Maynooth system — on the contrary, he was a reject from it; his family background was landed and aristocratic at a time when the sons of tenant farmers and small businessmen were coming to dominate the Irish church; his family background was also to a degree Protestant at a time when hostility between the churches in Ireland was reaching new heights. (**115**, 37-42; **204**, 239, 246-8) So factors calculated to broaden his appeal were equally calculated to create suspicion, if not antagonism, within his own church.

His personality had similar contradictory implications. Kohl noted his 'mildness' combined with 'great decision of character' and astutely identified the latter as prevailing over the former. Subsequent, mainly clerical, biographers have drawn attention to his simplicity and humility and have predictably found parallels with St Francis. Father Mathew's speeches are certainly full of expressions of his own sense of inadequacy and his reluctance to assume a leading or public role. So frequently are these sentiments repeated that they become in fact a mechanical and rather tiresome formula. He was indeed subject to fits of depression and serious self-doubt, and such moods dominated his last years. But his grand-nephew, Frank J. Mathew, in an unexpectedly critical biography, perhaps presents us with a more plausible portrait when he writes:

At first glance it might seem that Father Mathew showed small trace of [the] family character; yet a true insight would show the likeness. To begin with, his chief trait was his love of giving, and his fault too lavish charity. . . . He was never so happy as when he was giving feasts; from the day when he broke the rules at Maynooth, to the day when, just before his death, he was detected disobeying his doctor by giving a stealthy feast to some poor boys. All his life he was self-willed, and, in spite of his self-control, was liable to sudden flashes of hot temper, though no man was quicker to forgive, or to ask pardon for his shortcomings. The pride was represented by a quiet and unfailing dignity of manner; no one ever took a liberty with him. . . . His devotion to his life-work might be traced to the hot blood of his passionate forefathers — strange fruit to be borne by the follies of the dead. His own words bear this out. He was asked once what first turned his thoughts to total abstinence. 'My dear,' he answered, 'I thought how terrible it would be if I myself ever became a drunkard.' (**247**, 98-9)

His rejection of drink is usually ascribed to his experience of working among the poor of Cork, but the example of his own extravagant and hard-drinking family may not have been without significance.

Father Mathew joined the total abstinence movement in Cork in April 1838. Up until that time the local leaders had been the Rev. Nicholas Dunscombe, rector of St Peter's church and a member of one of the city's wealthy Whig merchant families; William Martin, who actually introduced teetotalism to Cork, an elderly and somewhat eccentric Quaker merchant; and Richard Dowden, a Unitarian, a Repealer and in 1845 Mayor of Cork. The leaders give a clear guide to the character of the movement: it was largely Protestant, liberal in its political inclinations, and drew considerable support from the city's business community. In November 1836 the *Irish Temperance and Literary Gazette* had singled out Cork as the area, after Ulster, in which the temperance cause had most prospered. As well as the three societies in Cork city, there were groups in Blackrock, Douglas, Cove, Carrigaline, Carrigadrohid, Midleton, Kinsale, Dunmanway, Enniskean, Schull, Clonakilty, Goleen, Bantry, Castlemartyr, Mallow, Ballincollig, Youghal, Skibbereen, Glandore and Ballydehob. The *Gazette* also remarked upon the fact that 'gentlemen of property and influence' had shown a greater inclination to support the cause in Cork than in other parts of the country. Perhaps the fact that illicit distillation was little known in the county had something to do with the greater willingness of landlords to sympathise with temperance; their rents did not depend at all on poteen production. Two who were on the committee of the H.T.S. were W. H. W. Newenham and W. L. Shuldham. Newenham was a large landowner, with properties in and near the city. He was on the Evangelical wing of the Established Church. In 1830 and 1832 he stood unsuccessfully as M.P. for the city, firstly as a Whig and then as a Tory. Shuldham was also a large Protestant landowner, with estates near Dunmanway. Another important landed temperance supporter was Sir William Chatterton, from a family very active in the Liberal politics of the city. As already noted, some Catholic clergy, particularly in Midleton, Blackrock and Bantry, were induced to lend their support to temperance societies. But in the county, as in the city, the movement's main support up until 1838 had come from wealthy Liberal Protestants. (**45**, 24, 146-9, 161-2)

With the advent of teetotalism in Cork in 1835, however, efforts were increasingly made to involve Catholics, though with only limited success. Late in 1839 the *Dublin Evening Post* summed up what was doubtless the judgment of many Catholics on the pre-1838 temperance movement when it said:

> Efforts were made by temperance societies, and others, to arrest the spread of the evil — but with very indifferent success. We do not, by any means, desire to undervalue the zeal of those gentlemen who have taken a prominent station as champions of temperance. But there has been too much show — too much speechification — too strong a tendency in gentlemen to throw themselves forward as orators or preachers — and there was, perhaps there is still, mixed up in many of them a certain fanatical disposition — a certain methodistical cant — a certain lurking at proselytism, which was quite sufficient to disgust sensible men — and more than sufficient to scare away that great mass of the population, for whose benefit chiefly these societies purported to be instituted.[4]

In Cork it was to be this issue of proselytism that first brought Father Mathew into the movement.

William Martin, helped by James McKenna, a Catholic ex-soldier, was the driving force in the city's teetotal movement. McKenna was the secretary of St Nicholas's Society, the committee of which was dominated by the Quakers Martin, Cox and Gibbs. Martin, who knew Father Mathew as both were governors of the workhouse, was particularly anxious to win Catholic support, and he seems to have had some success with St Nicholas's Society. Charges of proselytism, however, inevitably followed, though these seem to have been levelled more against Dunscombe than Martin. (**309**, 3)[5] Dunscombe denied them, but in March 1838 a clergyman named Lombard severely undermined Martin's endeavours when he gave a distinctly anti-Catholic talk to a meeting organised by Martin. Led by McKenna, the Catholic members withdrew from the society and in the process of discussing what to do next they consulted Father Mathew. This consultation quickly developed into an appeal from the Catholic teetotallers, with Martin's strong support, for Father Mathew to join them and establish his own society. This he was at first reluctant to do, and he requested a month to think the matter over. His reservations can be easily imagined: teetotalism was a new movement, considered extremist and impractical by many; it was Protestant-dominated and suspected of being a front for proselytising; moreover, his own family was heavily involved in the drink industry, a brother and brother-in-law both being distillers. But at a meeting with McKenna, Martin and other teetotallers on 10 April 1838 he told them that he felt bound 'as a minister of the gospel, to throw all personal considerations aside'. He had always attempted 'to discourage drunkenness, not with the success I desired, it is true; but I yielded to no one in my wishes to see our working class sober and self-respecting'. Now, 'after much reflection on the subject', he had come to the conclusion that alcohol was not required by 'anyone in good health'. And with that he signed the register of the Cork Total Abstinence Society, exclaiming simply: 'Here goes, in the name of God.' (**56**, 97-8)

From the very beginning Father Mathew's endeavours yielded striking success. At the first meeting of the new C.T.A.S. in a schoolroom in Blackamoor Lane thirty-five took the pledge. But before the second meeting McKenna had large posters distributed throughout the city announcing the establishment of the new society with Father Mathew as president and himself as secretary. These aroused considerable interest, for at the second meeting 330 members were enrolled. McKenna admitted that many were initially motivated by curiosity.[6] But the crowds grew so great that Father Mathew was soon forced to move his meetings to the Horse Bazaar, a large building on Sullivan's Quay that could hold up to 4,000. Meetings were held there every Sunday throughout 1838. Between April and July 1,400 signed the pledge; by September membership had jumped to over 4,000. For these periods Maguire gives totals of 25,000 and 131,000 respectively, but these are wild exaggerations. (**240**, 75) By February 1839 Father Mathew had enrolled 9,000 teetotallers, while the city's older temperance societies had only about 2,000 members between them. As the *Gazette* readily acknowledged, such success was 'unprecedented in this country'; outside Ulster no society appears to have exceeded 1,000 members before 1838.[7]

But by no means all these new teetotallers were from Cork city. In May 1839 McKenna estimated that between 200 and 300 persons were enrolling each week, many coming '60 or 80 miles from Cork without any other business but enrolling themselves in this society'. Some at least of these travellers were sent by their employers. In September 1839 the *Waterford Chronicle* reported that Quakers in Clonmel were recommending their servants to go and that 'those who join the society, are preferred in the employment of some of the merchants of the town'. In October the same paper noted that Robert Shaw, manager of the Mayfield factory, had sent twelve troublesome workers to Cork to take the pledge from Father Mathew. A 'friend' in Cork wrote in the same month to the *Dublin Evening Post* informing it that many 'poor people' were being sent to Cork by the 'Protestant country gentry' in order that they might take the pledge. Bacon, corn and butter merchants like the Grubbs of Waterford and the Russells and Westropps of Limerick all sent groups of their workers to Father Mathew during the course of 1839. The *Post* expressed the hope that the temperance 'medal or card will be the honest and sober man's pass-port to work', thus entirely eradicating 'that curse to the mechanic — combination'. Earlier the same paper had announced excitedly that 'men and women from every part of the south of Ireland are flocking to Cork'. The 'happy contagion' had not yet crossed the Shannon, but the *Post* mentioned Killarney, Tralee, Limerick, Clonmel, Slievaradagh, Dungarvan and Waterford as all feeling its impact. In this ready response to teetotalism from the south-east we can doubtless see the flowering of some of the seeds sown by Hockings in 1838.[8]

It was not only, however, the pressure of landlords and employers that encouraged thousands from Munster to seek out Father Mathew in 1838 and 1839. Already a superstitious veneration for the man himself was spreading. A 'friend' in Limerick wrote to the *Post* in November 1839:

> Our Catholic clergymen give every encouragement to those inclined to join the society, but such seems to be the opinion of the people in regard to Father Mathew, that they all prefer receiving their medal from him, and his blessing; a strange notion has got amongst them, that amongst the very few instances of any of the members relapsing, some fatality, such as death, epilepsy or some other visitation has been the penalty of such relapsing.

The inquiry instituted by Dublin Castle into the temperance movement in March 1840 also produced many instances in which pledge-breaking was believed to result in divine displeasure in the form of blindness or insanity. Such beliefs had attached themselves to pledges administered by Father Mathew himself, not by other priests. The *Post*'s Limerick 'friend', however, also noted that people 'who never were addicted to intemperance' were also taking the pledge so as to be 'entitled to the benefits to be derived in a pecuniary point of view to themselves or their families'.[9] From these observations it would seem that the major motivation behind pledge-taking was a mixture of materialism (a desire to secure or maintain a livelihood by winning the favour of a landlord or employer) and superstition (a belief that Father Mathew's medal and his blessing would bestow peculiar spiritual benefits).

It is not clear exactly when Father Mathew began to issue temperance medals, possibly late in 1838 or early in 1839. The *Post*'s correspondent in Cork noted in October 1839 that at the 'commencement of this society Mr Mathew was against introducing any symbol or token, lest it might be turned to a bad or superstitious use'. It was well known that secret societies used ribbons or tokens to denote membership, and right from the outset Father Mathew was anxious that teetotalism should not be identified with such organisations. But, as large numbers arrived from outside Cork city, often sent by employers, 'it was found needful and indeed requisite, that they should have some token to take back of their adhesion'. This correspondent astutely recognised, however, that Father Mathew had 'thus involved himself in interminable labour and unceasing expenditure'. Others, less sympathetic, viewed the situation rather differently. The *London Morning Post* claimed on 20 October 1839 that Father Mathew was 'driving a profitable trade; he gets one shilling from each penitent ... and gives him or her his blessing, and a pewter medal value half a farthing'. This marked the beginning of a bitter controversy over the financing of the temperance crusade, which was to tarnish Father Mathew's reputation severely and cause him much personal anguish.

That the visit to Father Mathew was a form of pilgrimage, the medal being a relic thereof, seems to have been a popular view. A Limerick priest told the *Dublin Evening Post* that, while not seeking to 'imitate' Father Mathew, the clergy did not restrain those wishing to visit Cork, 'as it is supposed that the fatigue of the journey, the change of place and circumstances, have the effect of making a stronger impression on their minds'.[10] Batches of ten, twenty or even thirty pilgrims could be found waiting in Father Mathew's parlour in Cove Street at nearly all hours to take the pledge. According to Maguire, some came 'sober and penitent', but others were obviously under the influence of drink and needed the goading of wives or mothers. 'We doubt', wrote Maguire, 'if there was a tap-room in Cork in which a more decided odour of whiskey and porter...was apparent.' (**240**, 121-3) Father Mathew's willingness to administer the pledge to those in a state of drunkenness caused considerable unease within the temperance movement and led critics to ridicule the sincerity of many pledges.

For over eighteen months Father Mathew received all who came to the friary in Cove Street, as well as speaking regularly at meetings in the Horse Bazaar. But while news of his work spread by word of mouth through Munster, the rest of the country remained largely ignorant of what was occurring in Cork. Maguire says that the press was very much to the fore in promoting the crusade, but there is little evidence of this in 1838 or in the first half of 1839. Presumably Maguire's later role as proprietor of the *Cork Examiner* predisposed him to give undue weight to newspaper influence. Father Mathew did not involve himself with existing temperance societies, and, except for meeting of the C.T.A.S., he avoided public occasions. The *Irish Temperance and Literary Gazette* and its successor the *Dublin Weekly Herald*, though largely devoted to Irish temperance affairs, only referred to him twice in 1838. In February 1839 a large tea party was held by the movement in Cork. Dowden was in the chair, and McKenna spoke of Father Mathew's marvellous successes; but of the man himself there was no sign, Dowden explaining that he did 'not like the public bustle of such a meeting'. In reporting the occasion, the *Herald* complained that it knew little of what was occurring in Cork, and it urged the societies there to supply 'more timely and frequent accounts of their proceedings'. It was only in September and October 1839, when the steady stream of pilgrims to Cork had become a flood, that the public in Dublin began to be treated to detailed reports of what was happening in Munster. F. W. Conway, editor of the *Dublin Evening Post*, 'discovered' Father Mathew in September, and, convinced that a 'miracle is in the process of accomplishment' to which he 'felt it a solemn obligation to become a witness', he began publishing lengthy articles on the movement. Conway relied for his information mainly on correspondents in Cork and on the *Waterford Chronicle*, which had already been impressed by the power of Father Mathew's appeal.[11] Initially it was only by reproducing the reports of the *Post* and the *Chronicle* that the *Dublin Weekly Herald* was able to inform its temperance readership of the progress of the cause in Munster. Clearly by the late 1830s the temperance movement had become highly fragmented, with little contact between societies in the major cities of Dublin, Belfast and Cork.

As already remarked, in May 1839 in a letter to the *Herald* McKenna predicted that, with the summer approaching, it was expected that 200 to 300 would be taking the pledge from Father Mathew each week. In November of the same year in a letter to the Belfast Total Abstinence Society Father Mathew himself wrote that 500 had taken the pledge that day and that membership of his society was increasing on average by 4,000 per week. Clearly there had been a massive and apparently unforeseen jump in numbers taking the pledge over the summer and autumn of 1839. In the summer of 1838 the rate at which people were joining the Cork society had certainly increased; this might have been predicted, summer being the traditional pilgrimage season. From the scattered figures available it would seem that between April and July 1838 on average about 100 joined each week, but between July and September this figure leapt to 400, before falling back again to about 100 between September 1838 and February 1839. These figures are certainly impressive in comparison with the experience of other temperance societies, which after several years' labour could usually only at best claim a few hundred members. On the other hand, they are not very impressive in that the rate at which people were joining in February 1839 seems to have been much the same as when Father Mathew began his work eleven months previously. But in the summer and autumn of 1839 the rate of joining soared dramatically. In October both the *Waterford Chronicle* and the *Nenagh Chronicle* agreed that membership had reached approximately 50,000. On 28 November the *Dublin Evening Post* reported that membership of Father Mathew's society on 14 November was 66,360 and that 14,360 people had taken the pledge in the three weeks between 22 October and 14 November: in other words, almost 4,800 a week, or somewhat more than Father Mathew's estimate of 4,000 in his letter to the Belfast teetotallers.[12] These were astounding figures, and it is easy to understand why the press outside Munster suddenly became alive to the crusade in the autumn of 1839. The most likely explanation for this sudden upsurge in pilgrims to Cork during the summer and autumn of 1839 is the severe and widespread failure of the potato crop which occurred during this period. It is against this background that we need to see the economic and superstitious motives already identified. With such a failure, the desire to please landlords or employers in order to mitigate rents or maintain employment must have been acute. Moreover,

Father Mathew's blessing and his medal could easily be seen as talismans to ward off such disasters in the future, if not to bring good fortune in the immediate struggle for survival.

By late 1839 Father Mathew was being pressed by numerous temperance societies to visit their towns. Many, as in the case of Belfast, he refused, pleading that it was impossible for him to leave Cork for any length of time given the large numbers arriving there to take the pledge from him personally. Some requests, however, he found it impossible to reject; these came from close at hand and from the hierarchy of his own church. A branch of the Cork society had been established in Limerick in July 1839, though many still travelled from the city to take the pledge from Father Mathew himself. In September the mayor, Alderman Garrett Fitzgerald, wrote inviting Father Mathew to visit, and this request was seconded by Bishop Ryan, an old friend. With some hesitation, Father Mathew agreed to preach a charity sermon in Limerick on behalf of the schools conducted by the Presentation nuns. The choice was significant: Nano Nagle, who had founded the order in the 1770s, was a connection of the Mathew family; moreover, Father Mathew himself had long been interested in the education of poor Catholic children. A visit to Limerick also afforded an opportunity to see one of his sisters, married to be a merchant called Dunbar. Given his commitments in Cork, however, he could only spend from Saturday 30 November to Tuesday 3 December in Limerick. He wanted no 'invitations, addresses and such like', for, as he wrote to the organisers, 'I am resolved not to make a spectacle of myself, except in the pulpit'; and for the whole of Monday he was determined to put himself at the disposal of Bishop Ryan, to do as the bishop desired. His anxiety to involve the local clergy in his visit and thus not give offence is obvious. McKenna, his secretary, was to accompany him, bringing some 2,000 medals and cards for distribution. If 4,000 were joining each week in Cork, then an estimate of 2,000 for the three days in Limerick doubtless seemed reasonable. (**56**, 111-12)

What happened during his three days in Limerick astounded even his most ardent supporters. By Friday, according to the *Limerick Reporter*, the city was packed with people and 5,000 were without a bed. Fortunately, though it was winter, the weather was relatively mild and many slept out of doors. On Saturday the road to Cork was lined with people for two or three miles outside the city, as Father Mathew's arrival was anxiously awaited. When he finally appeared late in the afternoon the crowds were such that he had great difficulty in getting from the coach to his brother-in-law's house in Upper Mallow Street. The next afternoon he preached the planned sermon at St Michael's and then proceeded to the county court-house, near the present Mathew Bridge, where he began to administer the pledge from the steps. The *Limerick Reporter* estimated that in the quarter of a mile from Denmark Street to the courthouse 30,000 people were gathered. To put such a figure in perspective we should perhaps note that, according to the 1841 census, the population of Limerick city was only 48,000. (**334**, 34)

He returned to his brother-in-law's house for a meal at about 5 o'clock, after which he continued to administer the pledge there until 9 p.m. On the Monday morning he resumed his labours at 5 a.m. But the crush around the house was so great that one woman was trampled to death, many others were injured, and substantial damage was done to the house itself. Father Mathew returned to the courthouse at 9 a.m. and continued uninterrupted there until 3 p.m. Again crowding became a serious problem, and a number of people were pushed into the river. Finally his friends, fearing for his safety, were forced to call for aid. A troop of Scots Greys cleared the way so he could return to Upper Mallow Street. There, according to the *Reporter*, 10,000 people knelt in the street to receive the pledge, while Father Mathew went among them with a military escort. On Tuesday he again spent most of the day in Mallow Street until 5 p.m. when, with difficulty, he boarded the coach for Cork. Later Father Mathew was to refer to this, his first mission outside Cork, as 'glorious' but 'awful'. According to the local paper, during these three days some 150,000 people took the pledge. The *Dublin Weekly Herald*, while reproducing the *Reporter*'s account, thought this figure 'greatly overstated'.[13] But Father Mathew's visit to Waterford a week later provides more reliable figures, and in so doing suggests that the *Reporter*'s estimate may not have been as exaggerated as the *Herald* claimed.

In Waterford the Christian Brothers, under Edmund Ignatius Rice and P. J. Murphy, had with the co-operation of Bishop Foran established tee-total societies in the summer of 1839 to cater for those unable to make the journey to Cork. Early in November Bishop Foran wrote to Father Mathew asking him to visit the city. (**51**, 3-10; **56**, 118-19) Father Mathew agreed to come on Wednesday 11 December, but arrived the preceding evening in order to avoid any demonstration. After conferring with Murphy, Rice and Foran, he began administering the pledge early the following morning from a platform erected at Ballybricken, on the out-skirts of the city. Anticipating trouble, two companies of troops and most of the city police had already occupied the site. Members of local temperance societies, with their medals prominently displayed, acted as stewards, trying to organise and control the crowds. But after the pledge had been administered to about 2,000 the platform was besieged, and the troops and police were unable to restrain the crowd. With some difficulty Father Mathew and his friends retreated to the courthouse. This proved a much better venue, for with troops occupying the steps, no more than about 200 were permitted to enter at a time. Having knelt and taken the pledge from Father Mathew, they were then ushered out by a different door, while another group immediately took their place. Nevertheless, the crowding in front of the courthouse caused numerous injuries, though unlike Limerick there appear to have been no deaths. By 12 o'clock the *Waterford Chronicle* estimated that 10,000 had taken the pledge in the courthouse and by 2 p.m. another 10,000 had been admitted. The process was now fairly well organised, for according to the *Chronicle*, 'each batch amounting, on an average, to 170 persons, is disposed of in about two minutes'. At 3.40 p.m. Father Mathew adjourned to the bishop's house, where he continued administering the pledge until nearly 10 p.m., breaking off only briefly for dinner. At 8 a.m. the next morning Father Mathew, accompanied by Bishop Foran, returned to the courthouse and resumed his work. Again troops had to struggle to keep the crowd from besieging the building. This time batches of 400 were admitted at a time, and the *Chronicle* estimated that it took Father Mathew three minutes to deal with each. At 4 p.m. Father Mathew returned to the bishop's house for a meal, protected all the way by soldiers from crowds endeavouring to touch him. He continued administering the pledge at the bishop's house until 8 p.m. when he boarded the coach for Cork.[14]

The *Waterford Chronicle* estimated that at least 90,000 people had taken the pledge during the two days. This figure is perhaps somewhat inflated, but not greatly so. Using the figures the *Chronicle* gives for the rate at which the pledge was administered in the courthouse, one arrives at a figure of 66,000. To this has to be added the 2,000 who took the pledge at Ballybricken and the many who received it on the Wednesday and Thursday evenings at the bishop's house. So the numbers joining must have been well over 70,000. Maguire estimated 80,000, which seems unusually accurate for him, but he was quoting Foran, who was in a good position to know, as his authority. So while it is impossible to verify the Limerick figure of 150,000, it would seem that contemporary estimates of 80,000 to 90,000 for Waterford are probably correct. Given that Limerick was a far bigger city — Waterford's population in 1841 was only 23,000 — and that Father Mathew spent longer there, the figure of 150,000 pledges does not seem as outrageous as at first sight. But the *Dublin Weekly Herald*'s scepticism regarding the number claimed at Limerick is understandable: if true, it meant that in three days he had gained more adherents for temperance than the Irish movement had been able to capture in the whole of the preceding ten years.

Newspaper reaction to these events was very mixed. In the *Dublin Evening Post*'s lengthy reports of both missions the words 'miracle', 'revolution' and 'glorious revolution' appeared frequently. The *Post* felt, moreover, that this 'revolution' would proceed despite the 'rabid ravings of the Orange press'. The Tory press was certainly hostile. In January 1840 the *Dublin Evening Mail* carried a report of Father Mathew's visit to Castlecomer in Co. Kilkenny. After describing the 'poor deluded peasantry' and the 'priest-ridden serfs for Rome' waiting in appalling weather to welcome Father

Mathew, it went on:

> Probably three or four thousand men, women and children have taken
> the mysterious pledge, scarcely any two of them agreeing as to its
> probable object. Some would have it as a means of uniting Irishmen,
> and as furnishing a common sign or pass by which, in supposed coming
> troublesome times, they might know each other; others, deeper versed in
> politics, regarded it as an effectual means of keeping out the Tories, by
> burking the excise ... and thus occasioning such a falling off in the
> revenue, as must oblige the [Tories] on resuming power to impose new
> taxes and thus render themselves unpopular — or else disbandon such a
> portion of the standing army, as will allow the Repealers to dissever the
> Union.

Whether the motives for pledge-taking were simple or complex, the paper
was convinced that at base they were aimed against the government. By
March, in a leader entitled 'Preparations for Insurrection', it was drawing
precise parallels between the temperance crusade and the spread of the
United Irish movement before the 1798 rebellion. In the same month,
referring to the St Patrick's Day temperance parades, the *Limerick Standard*
wrote:

> We have all along opposed the movement from a consciousness that it
> was not devised for any other purpose than to spread the most demor-
> alising and debasing superstitions among the people. We all along said
> that the plan would be converted into a mighty political engine for the
> attainment not merely of certain privileges in the state, but also for the
> ascendancy of the papal creed.

The processions had shown, according to the *Standard*, that 'Mr
O'Connell's legions were fully organised and in marching order, and that
the medal answered every purpose of mutual recognition and fraternity'.[15]
  The question of whether Father Mathew's crusade was really a 'mighty
moral miracle' or merely a stalking-horse for Repealers and Ribbonmen
was one that deeply troubled the established temperance movement. The
Dublin Weekly Herald was decidedly alarmed by the scenes enacted in
Limerick and Waterford: 'Something should be done to check the
irrational excitement of the people which leads them thus to rush forward
in blind admiration of an individual.' And it went on to warn that 'A
resolution adopted on the impulse of the moment, will not prove as lasting,
as strong, or as binding as one more duly and deliberately come to.' The
paper urged other Catholic clergy to take up the cause, to aid Father
Mathew and so to permit proper instruction of the people in the merits of
temperance, thus making the reformation secure. The *Herald* feared, quite
rightly as it transpired, that the disorder and hysteria occasioned by Father

Mathew's missions would be used by the enemies of temperance to discredit the whole movement.[16]

Unfortunately we do not have the space to trace Father Mathew's labours over the following three or four years in any detail. We can only sketch the general picture. This picture is one of almost ceaseless travelling. In the four years from 1840 to 1843 he conducted some 350 major temperance missions, to say nothing of numerous unrecorded minor ones. In 1841 he paid a brief visit to Birmingham; in 1842 to Glasgow; while in 1843 he conducted a major mission in England lasting two months. Only in 1843 did the pace slacken, and, for the first time since 1839, he actually spent a whole month in Cork. The geographical extent of the crusade is difficult to determine with any great accuracy. A study of Father Mathew's missions, however, suggests that it remained centred in Munster, where it had begun; not so much in Co. Cork itself, but in Tipperary, Limerick and Waterford. Co. Galway was another significant stronghold, as were Clare and Kerry. In Connacht Father Mathew conducted about forty missions between 1840 and 1843, but the vast majority of these were in either Counties Galway or Roscommon. Ulster also saw about forty missions, Cavan, Monaghan and Donegal being the main centres. Despite his early successes in cities like Limerick and Waterford, the crusade was more a rural than an urban phenomenon; many of those taking the pledge in Limerick and Waterford in December 1839 had travelled from the surrounding areas, just as many travelled to Cork in the earlier part of that year. The population of Cork city, as of Dublin city, was far less susceptible to Father Mathew's message. The *Dublin Evening Post* in 1839 and 1840 complained repeatedly of the failure of teetotalism in Dublin to match the achievements of Father Mathew in Munster. When he first visited the capital in March and April 1840 he enrolled about 70,000 in a week. (**56, 146**) But this was not particularly impressive compared with the numbers joining elsewhere. On his return in November he administered the pledge to 40,000 in three days: again, comparatively speaking, a poor performance. In May 1841 the *Dublin Weekly Herald* complained about the lack of support for the city's temperance societies; out of approximately 100,000 pledged teetotallers in Dublin, it estimated that only about 2,000 were active in the cause. In Cork, on the other hand, in February 1840 there were said to be nearly 30,000 teetotallers out of a population of around 80,000. But by September Father Mathew was complaining that the number of teetotallers in the city was declining, and in February 1841 at a meeting of the Cork society he again referred to the city's poor performance compared with gains elsewhere.[17] Father Mathew's limited appeal in the two cities, compared with country areas and small towns, was doubtless linked to the fact that they were major centres of the drink industry, employing many workers who might otherwise have inclined to teetotalism.

Father Mathew's message was basically the fairly straightforward teetotal doctrine that equated sobriety with material prosperity. In March 1840 he told audiences in Dublin that

> The man of temperance was always sure to better his own condition and infinitely more to advance the interests of his family. The money saved from the public house went to furnish his own — to clothe himself and his family, and supply them with the necessaries and comforts of life. He would after this be soon in a condition to lay by a little of his earnings in the savings' bank.... The teetotallers would be able to educate their children in such a manner as might raise them to the first order in the scale of society.

But teetotalism would not only bring socio-economic betterment for the working classes; in the Irish context he also saw it as bringing peace and an end to sectarian divisions:

> No employer will inquire of what creed the man is whom he is about to engage; no landlord, who may be going to let his land, will trouble himself to find out of what sect or party a person offering to take it may be. His only question will be, is he a teetotaller?

He urged an end to all 'bickering and contention', arguing that

> Teetotalism and charity would heal the wounds which were inflicted by political and religious dissension and bigotry. All creeds and classes will live together in unity and harmony, and, in a word, as Christians should live.

And, as an example to Dubliners, he pointed out that people, even in previously disturbed counties like Tipperary, 'where temperance prevailed appeared in general well clad, well fed, and well disposed to yield implicit obedience to the laws'. (**46**, 39-40, 21, 52, 38)

Father Mathew's hopes of ending religious and political strife proved wildly idealistic, and in fact his own crusade was to suffer deep divisions on these points. But his promise of economic prosperity and social advancement was obviously calculated to appeal to small tenant farmers, craftsmen, shopkeepers and clerks: the Catholic lower middle class and the higher ranks of the working class, the sort of people with aspirations to improve their position. The images displayed on the temperance card reinforced the crusade's materialist message. On the left-hand side, over the word 'Intemperance', was the picture of a squalid room in which a man, presumably the husband, grasps his wife by the hair and beats her with what looks like a hammer; a child clings to its father's leg in an effort to restrain him. Over this scene loom ominous images: a noose, a skull and a vulture, and further up a snake curls round a bottle, while a moth hovers over a candle. On the right-hand side of the card, over the word

'Temperance', we have a picture of a comfortably furnished living-room in which a well-dressed man, woman and child sit before a fire all reading books. Over the mantelpiece is a sign reading 'Savings Bank'. This scene is encircled by horns of plenty, and above it are the dove of peace and the beehive of industry.[18] For the illiterate particularly, the stark material differences between temperance and intemperance were graphically displayed on Father Mathew's temperance card.

But, in considering Father Mathew's arguments and appeal, one cannot ignore the irrational or superstitious aspects of his crusade. It is relatively easy to understand why an ambitious small farmer or shopkeeper might become a teetotaller in hopes of economic and social advancement for himself and his family. Observers are, however, agreed that in his travels through the country Father Mathew also attracted the very poor, labourers, impoverished cottiers, widows and beggars — those with little or no chance of material betterment. Sheil acknowledges that many attributed 'preternatural powers' to him, particularly the power to cure illness. Not very convincingly Sheil argues that this belief arose because those who took the pledge afterwards enjoyed better health. Father Mathew himself probably encouraged such beliefs by adopting a rather ambivalent attitude over the issue. While denying emphatically that he could perform miracles, he nevertheless, as Sheil puts it, 'feels persuaded that the Almighty, in regard to the extraordinary faith of some person, and in order to their entire conversion, may suspend in their favour the ordinary laws of nature'. (**309**, 49) Even the *Freeman's Journal* could describe Father Mathew as 'an angel from above, gifted with more supernatural powers — whose ministry was direct from God'. In similar vein, the *Waterford Chronicle*, under the heading 'A Miracle', described how a dumb and crippled man had been cured after taking the pledge from Father Mathew. Early in 1840 a handbill was circulating widely in the south, west and midlands claiming that Father Mathew had performed over 200 miracles between May and July 1839; details were given of sight, hearing and speech restored and of the crippled being enabled to walk. This item was produced in Cork, though who was responsible for its publication is unclear.[19] Such published 'evidence' of Father Mathew's powers must have fuelled popular superstitions. Mr and Mrs S. C. Hall, who were regular visitors to Ireland and spent from June to September 1840 in the country, summed up the issue when they wrote:

Beyond doubt, superstitious ideas are mixed up with it [the pledge] — a large proportion of those who have taken it conceiving that a breach of their promise would entail some fearful visitation. They go further than this: many of the pledged believe that Mr Mathew possesses the power to heal diseases, and preserve his followers from all spiritual and physical dangers — an error which Mr Mathew does not labour to remove,

although he is, certainly, not charged with having striven to introduce
or extend it. We cannot but lament the existence of this evil; yet all who
know the Irish peasantry know that an attempt to direct or control them
by mere appeals to reason must be utterly vain. It should also be borne in
mind, that it is by no means a new thing with them to connect superstitious notions with their clergy.

The last point is an important one: Father Mathew was by no means alone
at this period in having special power ascribed to him. A recent study has
shown that magical powers were fairly widely attributed to popular priests.
Yet, on the other hand, this belief was certainly important in the rapid
growth of the temperance crusade, particularly in rural areas. (**69**, 28-9;
164, I, 43; **115**, 117)

Also of crucial importance was the attitude of the local clergy. In Cork
Father Mathew's support in this quarter was rather limited. Bishop
Murphy was not an advocate of teetotalism, perhaps because of his lack of
interest in pastoral work, or more likely because he was a member of the
great Cork brewing family. Father Mathew's strongest supporters were
drawn from the city's rising Catholic middle class: wealthy laymen, like the
barrister J. F. Maguire, whose temperance newspaper the *Cork Total
Abstainer*, begun in February 1841, became in August the *Cork Examiner*;
Frank Walsh, another barrister and a leading Liberal; Thomas Lyons, a
wealthy merchant and in 1841 the first mayor under the new reformed
corporation; and William Fagan, Liberal mayor in 1843 and Repeal M.P.
for the city from 1847 to 1851. On the Protestant side, Dowden, mayor in
1845, and Martin remained loyal. It is worth noting that politically all
these men were Liberals and most became Repealers. (**204**, 11-12) In
Dublin Archbishop Murray, who had ordained Father Mathew and was
an old friend, publicly gave his blessing to the crusade, though he declined
to take the pledge himself. Several priests were very active in the city's
temperance societies, notably Dr Yore of St Paul's, Dr John Spratt of the
Carmelites, Dr Doyle of St Michan's, Father Andrew O'Connell of SS
Michael and John's and Father Patrick Mooney, curate of St James's.
Yet the exertions of zealous individuals could not hide the fact that in both
cities the majority of the Catholic clergy, as of the Protestant clergy, held
aloof from Father Mathew's crusade, despite many earnest appeals for
their support.[20]

The attitude of the local clergy, and particularly of the local bishop,
seems in fact to have largely determined where Father Mathew conducted
his missions. We have already seen that his first visits in December 1839
were to Limerick and Waterford, where Bishop Ryan and Bishop Foran
were strong supporters. He frequently returned to these dioceses over the
next four years, and the crusade accordingly flourished in them. But
equally he avoided dioceses where bishops were unsympathetic; some went

so far as to ask him not to come, and he always bowed to their wishes. Thus, while he conducted a number of missions in Counties Down and Armagh, these were all within the diocese of Dromore, where Bishop Blake was a long-standing temperance advocate. The dioceses of Armagh and Down and Connor he avoided, for both Archbishop Crolly and Bishop Denvir were hostile to the crusade and had asked him not to come.[21] A similar situation existed in Connacht. Co. Galway was a stronghold of the crusade, but Father Mathew's missions were largely restricted to the small diocese of Galway. He did visit the diocese of Tuam, but Archbishop MacHale's opposition limited his access. In September 1842, while in Moycullen with Bishop Browne of Galway, he received a delegation from the Tuam Temperance Society; they had come to him because it was felt unwise for him to attempt to conduct a mission in the town which was the archbishop's seat. (**204**, 10; **56**, 254)

In 1841 at a meeting addressed by Father Mathew in Cork it was estimated that eight bishops and 700 priests had taken the pledge. Given that there were twenty-seven bishops and nearly 2,200 priests in Ireland at the time, the fact that about one-third subscribed to Father Mathew's crusade appears at first sight impressive. (**115**, 33)[22] Yet Father Mathew, and his supporters even more so, frequently lamented the lack of support they received from the various churches and in particular the Catholic church. The eight bishops who had taken the pledge were not named, but one can assume that they at least included Ryan, Foran and Blake, as well as John Cantwell of Meath and John Browne of Kilmore, all of whom were zealous temperance advocates. Other members of the hierarchy welcoming Father Mathew to their dioceses were: in Tuam, Thomas Coen of Clonfert, George Browne of Galway and Thomas Feeny of Killala; all the bishops of the Dublin archdiocese, including Archbishop Murray, though James Keating of Ferns and William Kinsella of Ossory developed reservations about the crusade; in Cashel, aside from Ryan and Foran, only Cornelius Egan of Kerry actively promoted Father Mathew's cause; in Armagh, in addition to Blake, Browne and Cantwell, Edward Kernan of Clogher and Patrick MacGettigan of Raphoe were supporters, as was Edward Maginn, who became Coadjutor Bishop of Derry in 1845.

Counting Maginn, Father Mathew appears during the course of his crusade to have won the support of sixteen bishops, a clear majority of the hierarchy. But much of this support was only nominal, five or six at most being active and committed teetotallers. Also as the crusade progressed and controversies arose, particularly about the nature of the pledge, the movement's financing and its political affiliations, some bishops had second thoughts about their earlier support. As well as having advocates among the hierarchy, Father Mathew equally had his share of staunch opponents. Of the archbishops, only Murray was really sympathetic, though his support was largely passive. MacHale, on the other hand, was bitterly hostile. Archbishop Crolly of Armagh had asked Father Mathew not to visit his diocese, as he feared that the crusade would only increase sectarian strife in Ulster; and cetainly there were reports of Orange opposition to temperance processions.[23] Archbishop Slattery of Cashel put no obstacles in the way of Father Mathew's missions, but he was sceptical, and, as we shall see, his hostility emerged clearly in 1847 over the election of a new bishop for Cork. Among the bishops, Denvir, William Higgins of Ardagh and Patrick Kennedy of Killaloe were strong opponents. (**56**, 198-9) Higgins in particular, who was a close ally of both MacHale and O'Connell, refused Father Mathew admission to his diocese when they could not agree on how the proceeds of the mission should be used, and he announced in an abrupt letter that he planned to administer the pledge himself.[24]

As early as 1839 the *Dublin Evening Post* was urgently entreating priests to follow Father Mathew's example, as it was convinced that the crusade could not be sustained by the endeavours of one man alone.[25] But among the priesthood too, although many took the pledge, the numbers of active teetotallers were small. Dr Spratt in Dublin was seen by some as a rival to Father Mathew; Father John Foley of Youghal had established a flourishing temperance movement in south Co. Waterford before Father Mathew began his crusade; Father John Kenyon of Ennis was an early and vigorous supporter in Co. Clare; P. J. Murphy of the Christian Brothers in Waterford city was both a friend and an active teetotaller. Yet Dr Pise, a New York priest who visited Cork in September 1842, later wrote that the clergy of the city, while unanimous in their respect for Father Mathew, did not 'entertain very sanguine hopes with regard to the final result of this great movement, which all admit had done infinite good'. (**56**, 251) We shall look in more detail later at the criticisms of Father Mathew's crusade voiced from within his own church; suffice it to say for the moment that his ability to conduct temperance missions depended both on the goodwill of the hierarchy and the active co-operation of the local clergy — and increasingly after 1840 both goodwill and co-operation were lacking.

One of the most controversial aspects of the crusade then and since was the precise numbers joining and, related to this, the rate at which the crusade both grew and declined. Most writers on the subject see the movement as growing from 1840 to 1844, perhaps with a peak in 1842-3, and then a decline from 1845 occasioned by the famine. In this view, the history of the temperance crusade parallels that of O'Connell's Repeal campaign, and in fact the two movements are usually seen as complementary. But the situation was by no means this simple, nor this harmonious.

Ignoring Maguire's often wildly inaccurate statistics, it would appear from statements of Father Mathew quoted in the contemporary press that the crusade actually reached its numerical peak in the spring and summer of 1841. In November 1839, as already noted, the number of those having taken the pledge in Cork was estimated at 66,000; eighteen months later in May 1841 membership was claimed by Father Mathew to be 5.3 million. (**164**, I, 42) The accuracy of these figures, particularly of the latter one, can certainly be questioned, but the general impression of an astounding growth in the year 1840 would appear to be well founded. The figures given in the *Dublin Weekly Herald* are interesting: 1840, February 600,000, April 800,000, May 1.5 million, September 2.5 million, November 3.0 million; 1841, March 4.6 million, May 5.3 million. Again, as in 1839, the pattern suggests an enormous increase in membership during the summer and autumn of 1840, another period during which the potato crop failed badly. But after the spring of 1841 a stagnation set in: thus in April 1843 and again in December 1844 the membership figure was being given as approximately 5.5 million, though in March 1842 the *Freeman's Journal* put it as low as 4.3 million. The rise of the Repeal movement from 1841 doubtless detracted attention from teetotalism, while improved economic conditions, particularly in the countryside, removed some of the material motivation from pledge-taking. The growth of the temperance crusade was therefore even more spectacular than is usually supposed, and its decline more rapid; rather than paralleling Repeal it occurred before O'Connell's campaign had really got off the ground. Some contemporaries were aware of this situation. In May 1841, for instance, the *Herald* was expressing concern that a 'reaction' against teetotalism was starting, and in June the paper published an appeal by James Haughton to the clergy of Ireland for support. In this he noted the beginning of a decline which he attributed to the failure of the clergy, particularly the Catholic clergy, to give Father Mathew the assistance he desperately needed to ensure the permanency of the reformation.[26]

But what in practice, we may well ask, did these membership figures mean? One thing they did not indicate was the number of those taking the pledge. Right from the first mission in Limerick it had proved impossible for McKenna and Father Mathew's other secretaries to keep accurate records of all those taking the pledge. Father Mathew had been forced by the vast numbers involved to administer the pledge to hundreds and even thousands at a time. What the figures quoted by him referred to were the numbers of cards issued, for each card was numbered. But not all those taking the pledge received a card or even a medal. This led Father Mathew to claim that the figures he gave for membership were in fact a considerable underestimate. On the other hand, however, cards and medals were issued in a very indiscriminate manner. During or after a mission McKenna supplied cards and medals in bulk to local priests and temperance societies. It was then the task of the local organisers to issue these to the people who had taken the pledge, to collect money for the medals, and to return the money and any excess cards and medals to the headquarters in Cork. In practice, however, the grassroots organisation of the crusade was extremely inefficient. There were a number of cases of funds being misappropriated; in other instances local clergy simply wished 'to apply some small part of what we are at present receiving for medals to relieve some of the suffering poor': in other words, particularly during the difficult times of 1839-40, priests wished to keep monies raised in their own needy parishes.[27] Also thousands of cards and medals sent to patrons of societies simply disappeared, being neither issued to members nor returned to Cork. Thus the temperance cards held by the National Library of Ireland are numbered, dated and signed by Father Mathew, but no member's name appears on them. Presumably they were sent to Dublin to be issued to members and were never returned. Thus the two teetotallers for whom the cards numbered 4,000,233 and 5,222,611 were issued, though recorded in Cork as members, were in fact part of Father Mathew's considerable phantom army.[28] Apart from confusing efforts to establish accurate membership figures, the failure to distribute cards and medals efficiently involved Father Mathew in enormous financial losses and contributed significantly to his eventual bankruptcy.

In theory the basic organisational unit of the crusade was to be the local temperance society, preferably headed by a priest, who would report to Father Mathew and his secretaries in Cork. It was a very loose scheme, but this was deliberate. Father Mathew did not want to establish a highly structured national organisation like the Repeal Association, fearing that this would attract government opposition. When investigating the temperance movement in March 1840, one of the questions asked of police and magistrates by Dublin Castle was:

> Are those who take the pledge bound by any rules beyond the pledge itself — are they united as a society in which there are any thing like office bearers, who exercise a control over the members, etc., or have they any regular places or times of meeting, or do they wear any badge except the medal, and when is that worn?

The responses to this question indicated that in a great many instances societies of teetotallers had been formed so rapidly that, as yet, they had no rules or regular meetings, though the enthusiasm of the local priest was usually the key factor in determining the degree of organisation. In an undated letter to Edward Bullen, Father Mathew summed up his approach when he remarked: 'It was my constant care to prevent anything like organisation.'[29] So far did he take this policy that, though a list of membership cards issued was maintained in Cork, no register of societies was kept. With his missions Father Mathew sought to gain recruits for teetotalism, but, after that, as far as he was concerned, teetotallers were very much left to their own devices, or rather were subject to the attitude of their local priest. It is understandable therefore that Father Mathew's supporters became increasingly concerned when they felt by 1841, if not earlier, that he was not receiving the degree of enthusiastic backing from the priesthood that was essential if the crusade was to be maintained.

Father Mathew's teetotal movement is usually portrayed as facilitating the growth of O'Connell's Repeal Association, but the relationship between the two campaigns, as between the two men, was a complex one. O'Connell had long been a champion of the Irish drink industry. In 1833 he invested some £2,000 in a Dublin brewery run by his son Daniel and called O'Connell's brewery. The venture was not a success and collapsed in 1840, having produced no profits and with debts totalling £4,000. In a speech delivered in Dublin during the 1841 election campaign O'Connell claimed it was teetotalism that had ruined his son's business.[30] But the historians of Guinness's brewery have commented sarcastically that it 'would probably have failed even if Father Mathew had been a brewer's advocate'. They attribute the brewery's failure rather to lack of capital and poor management. (**225**, 91) The business did survive, however, and with the very appropriate name, Phoenix, rose to be one of the major Dublin breweries in the latter half of the century. O'Connell also had other important connections with the drink industry. The 1830s saw several efforts by the Liberals to control the issuing of publicans' licences, to limit the hours of sale, and to stamp out unlicensed selling; major acts were passed in 1833, 1836 and 1839.[31] O'Connell, representing Irish publicans and grocers, resisted these acts fiercely. In a letter of June 1836 he described the retailers as 'my most active, useful and valuable constituents' and himself as 'their chief manager and supporter'. Lord Morpeth, the Chief Secretary, later a friend of Father Mathew's, was, however, firmly convinced of the need for tighter control over the issuing of licences and over the operations of spirit grocers. Thus the legislation went through despite vigorous lobbying against it by O'Connell, who was left complaining: 'I never was so shocked in my life.' It is clear that at this stage O'Connell saw the vintners as useful political allies and financial backers and that he worked strenuously, if not very successfully, on their behalf at Westminster. He also took an interest in the industry as a whole, gathering information on its development since 1800. This was not only because of his family's connection with brewing, but because he believed the drink industry, like other Irish industries, had suffered under the Union. Thus in 1834 he was studying what he termed the 'wrongs of the Irish distillers' for inclusion in a speech on Repeal. (**152**, II, 61, 63, I, 425) Given O'Connell's personal involvement in brewing and his political links with the drink retailers, how, one may well ask, could he align himself with teetotalism? The answer is that his motivation was largely political expediency, and as a result, the alliance was a very uneasy one.

As early as October 1839 O'Connell had praised Father Mathew's work at a banquet in Cork. During a speech in Bandon on 5 December, a few days after Father Mathew's spectacular reception in Limerick, O'Connell again returned to the subject. Finding that about half his audience had taken the pledge from Father Mathew, he told them:

> The temperance societies are big with importance to the future welfare and independence of the country. In a moral and social point of view they are destined to produce vast amelioration amongst the people. Morality, comfort, cleanliness, and contentment, will take the place of recklessness, squalidness, filth and bickerings. . . . Nor is there a national or political right — one based upon the principle of equality — that will not be conceded — and that not a little by reason of the temperance societies.

Despite the confusing negatives, O'Connell in this speech was demonstrating the link he saw between temperance, material advancement and political change. Right from the outset, unlike Father Mathew, O'Connell perceived that temperance could make a contribution to the achievement of national rights. On this point the Tories were in agreement with him; they too saw Father Mathew's crusade as preparing the way for a political movement. Still in alliance with the Liberal government at the time, O'Connell was nevertheless increasingly disillusioned with his allies' failure to produce significant reform for Ireland. Father Mathew's success in rousing a mass movement in 1839 must have encouraged O'Connell in his decision early in 1840 to establish a popular association aimed at achieving repeal of the Union. Some of the teetotallers immediately welcomed O'Connell's endorsement. Thus James Haughton, president of the Dublin Total Abstinence Society, had 10,000 copies of the Bandon speech printed and circulated. (**56**, 107).[32] But others, notably Father Mathew himself, were anxious to prevent the temperance crusade being co-opted for political purposes.

O'Connell must have been aware of Father Mathew's desire that the crusade should be both non-sectarian and non-political, for it was a desire that he expressed at almost every opportunity. There were times even when O'Connell himself endorsed these sentiments. Thus, writing to the president of the Tralee Total Abstinence Society in September 1840, enclosing a subscription, O'Connell remarked that the temperance movement 'is too good to be tainted with sectarian differences; it is too useful to be distorted to political purposes'. But, struggling as he was to arouse support for his recently established Repeal Association, it was only to be expected that a politician as experienced as O'Connell should seek to exploit any worthwhile contemporary issue or campaign. In the letter just quoted, therefore, while declaring that temperance societies 'are not, nor shall they be, political societies', O'Connell nevertheless went on to say:

> However, political opinions will be the more patriotic by reason of the sober judgment of temperate men, and political exertions and the

struggles for the freedom of their fatherland will be the more discreet, the more safe, and the more persevering because of the effect of habits of temperance on each individual. (56, 164)

O'Connell saw teetotallers as providing committed and reliable Repeal advocates; the temperance movement was a secure foundation on which the edifice of the Repeal campaign could be built. At a Repeal meeting on the Curragh in March 1841 O'Connell in a striking reference 'compared the temperance movement to the appearance of a cross in the heavens before Constantine the Great, with the motto, "by this thou shalt conquer" '.[33] Leaving aside the interesting implications of O'Connell's comparison of himself with Constantine, his portrayal of temperance as both a sign of things to come and as a tool by which victory could be achieved is very revealing of his attitude. Clearly Father Mathew's success in 1839 and 1840 encouraged O'Connell in his decision to revive the Repeal agitation in what seemed at the time discouraging circumstances. But the temperance movement was not merely an inspiration; with its bands, reading-rooms and societies, it could also be of great practical use to Repealers.

During the hard-fought general election of July 1841 temperance bands provided music at Repeal meetings, while Repealers used temperance reading-rooms for their own gatherings. On 24 June Father Mathew wrote to supporters in Dublin and Cork instructing them that their bands were 'not to attend any political meetings or play in public until the general election will have terminated. The vital interests of the temperance society demand this strict neutrality.' But Father Mathew knew that his control was very limited. In a private letter he bemoaned the fact that if the parochial clergy who headed the teetotal societies were Repealers, he could not prevent bands playing at Repeal meetings. The loose structure of the crusade and Father Mathew's lack of a firm grip on local societies thus made it easy for determined and better-organised Repealers to take control and exploit the resources of teetotal societies, in particular their bands and meeting-rooms. At this stage, with Repeal winning only very limited popular support, the greater public acceptability of temperance was a considerable asset to O'Connell. If he could identify himself with tee-totalism, or more precisely identify Repeal with teetotalism, he had a chance of winning over many of the millions of teetotallers to his cause. He took the pledge himself about October 1840 and was at pains to assure audiences that it had done wonders for his health. He told one temperance society in May 1841 that 'He slept sounder, and got up more refreshed, and with a better appetite for his breakfast than at any period of his life.' And he went on in the same speech to take what amounted to a hardline teetotal stance, declaring that 'Temperate men have every chance of becoming intemperate.' At a temperance festival in the Mansion House in January

1842 he announced, to the delight of his audience, that he was more proud of being a teetotaller than of being Lord Mayor of Dublin. (**56**, 196)[34]

During the 1841 general election O'Connell had repeatedly expressed his support for teetotalism, but in Dublin at least he had not forgotten his old allies in the drink trade. In one speech he recalled his efforts on their behalf in parliament and praised them as 'one of the very best classes of our fellow-citizens'. It was in this context that he alluded to the collapse of his son's brewery, casting himself in the role of a 'common sufferer with the vintners'. He, like they, had suffered financially because of the temperance crusade, and thus he understood their grievances. In championing tee-totalism, O'Connell thus did not want to sacrifice the support he had long received from the drink industry; it was a highly precarious balancing act. From 1840 to 1842 he continued to appeal strongly to teetotallers, but as the crusade waned and Repeal became more securely established, O'Connell began to adopt a much more critical attitude towards the anti-drink movement. Despite his early endorsement of the physical benefits to be derived from abstinence, he eventually withdrew from his pledge on medical grounds. And in January 1843 he told a Dublin meeting called to honour Father Mathew that the temperance movement had passed 'too heavy a censure... on the former condition of the country' by suggesting that the Irish were a 'drunken people'. Using parliamentary figures, O'Connell argued that whiskey consumption was not excessive in Ireland and in fact that the Scots drank considerably more. By 1843 O'Connell no longer needed to pander to the views of the teetotallers. He was careful not to criticise Father Mathew personally, but this speech made plain that the support of the drink industry was now more important to him than that of the teetotal crusade. He had captured teetotalism and securely harnessed it to the chariot of Repeal.[35]

From 1840 O'Connell and Father Mathew were rivals for the basic allegiance of Irish teetotallers. Father Mathew wished to keep them out of politics, while O'Connell wished to win them for Repeal. Equal loyalty to both movements were not really practicable. From a financial point of view, for instance, the two causes were in direct competition: poor parishes could not afford both to buy medals and pay the 'Repeal rent'. Concerning meetings, Father Mathew was very much on the defensive, seeking to avoid clashes between his missions and O'Connell's Repeal gatherings; such clashes O'Connell, on the other hand, welcomed. In March 1840, for instance, both were in Galway city, Father Mathew on a mission and O'Connell for the spring assizes. A public dinner was given to honour O'Connell, attended by Bishop Browne among many prominent citizens. Several speakers, including O'Connell, praised Father Mathew's work, but of the man himself there was no sign. Lamely pleading pressure of work, he had declined the invitation. (**56**, 133) O'Connell's insistence as

Lord Mayor of Dublin on participating in the temperance procession in Cork at Easter 1842 angered Father Mathew, but there was nothing he could do to prevent it, nor on this occasion could he himself stay away. Similarly, it is no coincidence that between March and October 1843, while O'Connell was holding his monster meetings up and down the country, Father Mathew spent two months on mission in England and much of the rest of the time in Cork.

But despite Father Mathew's best efforts, O'Connell was largely successful in capturing the teetotal crusade. As early as March 1840 police inspectors in Counties Cork, Tipperary, Kilkenny and Wexford were reporting that 'Ribbonmen' were joining teetotal societies in large numbers and that nationalist newspapers were being read in temperance meeting-rooms. However, we should not take the term 'Ribbonmen' too literally in this context; recent studies have shown that true Ribbonism was centred in Dublin and Ulster during this period, and moreover that publicans were among its most significant supporters. (**157**, 138-42, 149; **64**, 129-31, 141) The police were inclined to use the term very loosely to describe those with nationalist sympathies. From both Cork and Wexford it was reported that those joining Father Mathew's crusade had expressed the view that '98 had been lost through drunkenness, but 'we are more secure and united now when the battle comes'. The police generally agreed that Father Mathew himself was not seeking to organise a political movement, but certainly some of those taking the pledge looked upon it as promoting discipline and unity in preparation for political struggles ahead.[36] So, even before O'Connell's Repeal Association had begun its work, the teetotal crusade had an identifiable nationalist aspect. Over the next three years this aspect increased markedly. By 1843 reports of Repeal wardens forwarded to Dublin from different parts of the country spoke of a close connection between the two movements, despite Father Mathew's strictures.[37] Dublin Castle was receiving similar information. A questionnaire sent to county inspectors in May 1843 concerning the Repeal campaign elicited the general view that members of teetotal societies were almost invariably Repealers. (**204**, 85)

Not unnaturally, many teetotallers simply failed to understand Father Mathew's opposition to Repeal; pro-Repeal newspapers also consistently identified the two causes. Perhaps, however, it was the Young Irelanders, and Thomas Davis in particular, who made the connection most strongly. Writing in the *Nation* in January 1843, Davis described Irish drunkenness as 'the luxury of despair — the saturnalia of slaves'; Irish temperance, on the other hand, was 'the first fruit of deep-sown hope, the offering of incipient freedom'.[38] While O'Connell's support for teetotalism can be seen as essentially the product of political expediency, the Young Irelanders far more genuinely expressed the ideals and hopes of the teetotal/repeal alliance: that a people which had proved itself sober, disciplined and prosperous could not be denied self-government. (**244**, 80-3) As the *Cork Examiner* declared in October 1841,

> A nation of sober men, with clear heads, with firm and erect forms, with the proud strength of moral independence about them, shall and *must* have the full completion of their liberty.[39]

In the face of such strongly argued and widely held views, Father Mathew's opposition to the teetotal/Repeal alliance was utterly futile.

Yet, as he had anticipated, the alliance did damage teetotalism in many quarters. Apart from depriving him of much-needed financial aid, the identification of teetotalism with Repeal drove moderate Protestants and Tories out of the anti-drink movement. His idealistic hopes of uniting Catholics and Protestants, nationalists and conservatives behind the temperance banner were frustrated. Attacks on teetotalism in the Tory press became increasingly bitter as O'Connell's Repeal campaign gained momentum. The *Dublin Evening Mail* had from the outset been highly suspicious of the crusade, but on the occasion of Father Mathew's first visit to Dublin in March 1840 it had, it said, 'honestly distinguished between the agent and the system'. Father Mathew it described as a 'warm-hearted, enthusiastic person, benevolently disposed and laborious'. Two years later, however, in March 1842 the paper was far more hostile and totally convinced of the essentially political nature of teetotalism. In an article dealing with St Patrick's Day temperance processions it identified teetotalism with Ribbonism as 'one under two names' and claimed that Ribbonmen used temperance festivities 'to encourage recruits and intimidate opponents'. Such festivals, said the paper, were

> demonstrations of a treasonable conspiracy, under the guise of a confederacy for moral purposes. . . . There can be no doubt that the teetotal association is a branch of a political movement, the object of which is the dissolution . . . of the legislative union.

Later that same year the *Mail* began using the term 'Repeal-teetotal' to describe Repeal meetings, underlining the total identification of the two in the Tory mind. As the *Mail*'s comments suggest, Tories were particularly alarmed by teetotal processions, especially the vast ones held on 17 March, which were conducted with military precision. The March 1842 procession in Cork, for instance, in which O'Connell participated, comprised some fifty-two societies from the city and county, forty-one bands, many in uniform, and in all nearly 8,000 marchers. To the *Mail* this amounted to an 'open and ostentatious display' of Ribbonism with an 'insulting exhibition' of its 'party badges and distinctions'.[40]

The government too had become increasingly hostile. Long suspicious of the potential dangers of teetotal bands and processions, by 1843 the staunchly Tory Lord Lieutenant, Earl de Grey, was informing Peel that the temperance movement had been captured by O'Connell and converted into an instrument of agitation to further the Repeal cause. Peel personally viewed Father Mathew 'with suspicion and distrust', though the more liberal Chief Secretary, Lord Eliot, assured him that Father Mathew did not sanction the political views of many teetotallers. Yet he was forced to concede that 'They love Father Mathew but obey O'Connell.' Lord Stanley, a member of the cabinet and a shrewd observer, recognised that one of the 'most formidable features' of the Repeal campaign was its 'religious character', which he attributed both to widespread clerical support and to 'the skill with which O'Connell has enlisted among his Repealers the temperance bands'. (**227**, 23, 143; **204**, 87) Music, provided by temperance bands, certainly became a characteristic feature of Repeal gatherings and probably contributed to recruitment. Ironically, however, the cost of instruments and the often elaborate uniforms for the hundreds of bands that sprang up proved a significant drain on Father Mathew's financial resources. Repealers reaped the benefit free of charge.

Father Mathew did retain a certain amount of Protestant support, however, his staunchest advocates continuing to be either Quakers or Unitarians. But this support was overwhelmingly lay. In Dublin, for example only the Congregationalist clergyman Dr William Urwick was prominent in Father Mathew's cause. This led the city's Conservative Society to lament in March 1841 that Urwick had 'mingled with priests' and been 'cajoled into joining a popish procession on Patrick's Day'. In fact in Dublin, Belfast and Cork the various temperance societies largely split along sectarian lines, many being based on either Catholic or Protestant parishes. There were some non-denominational societies, like the Dublin Total Abstinence Society, but even these were not immune from sectarian strains. Thus in 1841 the large Liverpool society split into Catholic and Protestant sections. And perhaps we should note in passing that Urwick, despite his willingness to associate with priests in the St Patrick's Day processions, was head of a society called the Protestant Total Abstinence Society. Many Protestants who supported Father Mathew's endeavours were still unwilling to take the pledge from him personally or to enrol themselves in societies led by Catholic clergy. In September 1840 Dr Spratt claimed that he had administered the pledge to fifteen Presbyterians, but this event attracted some publicity precisely because it was an exceptional case. Kneeling before a Catholic priest and receiving his blessing, particularly in public, was an act that few Protestants were prepared to undertake. Some resolved to practise teetotalism and accepted medals from Father Mathew, but were at pains to make clear that they had not taken the pledge from him.[41] The question of whether music should be played and processions held on Sunday was another divisive sectarian issue. Writing in 1842 to Richard Allen on this subject, Father Mathew said:

I respect the religious feelings which disapprove of music and processions on the Lord's Day — I would not, on any account, offer violence to tender consciences; but we Roman Catholics, after in general devoting the afternoon of Saturday and the forenoon of Sunday to religious observances, do not deem it a desecration of the sabbath for such as have been earning their bread by the sweat of their brows during the week to recreate themselves innocently during the remainder of the day.... It is my religious conviction that one sin of drunkenness, or one of the black deeds to which men are prompted when inflamed by intoxicating drink, outrages more the sanctity of a jealous God than all the music of the three hundred temperance bands on the sabbath day. (**341**, 45-6)

Such a view of the sabbath was, of course, anathema to Protestant Evangelicals.

But even with his most devoted Protestant supporters Father Mathew experienced conflicts. William Martin and Richard Dowden in Cork, James Haughton, Richard Allen and R. D. Webb in Dublin, all viewed temperance as part, and not always the most important part, of a humanitarian reformist programme. They thus campaigned against war, capital punishment, child labour, the opium trade, the East India Company monopoly and, above all, against slavery. Most, though not all, were Repealers, some were Chartists, and a few even were champions of women's rights. Father Mathew, on the other hand, was committed wholeheartedly to temperance and was most reluctant to become embroiled in other issues. Naively he seemed to believe that temperance should and could be totally isolated from other reform campaigns, whether social, economic or political. The Quakers, like the nationalists, took a very different view. They were particularly active in the abolitionist movement. Haughton, Allen and Webb attended the World Anti-Slavery Convention in London in 1840, where they met many of the leading American campaigners. As a result, W. L Garrison, with James and Lucretia Mott, visited Dublin. In the context of abolitionism the Irish Quakers joined the Garrison or extreme wing of the movement. Thus Haughton, who was a Repealer, fell out with O'Connell, who was also an abolitionist, but of a much more moderate variety. (**80**, 144-7; **292**) The Irish abolitionists, who supported teetotalism, were therefore extremely disappointed when Father Mathew refused to become involved in the issue. To them drunkenness was merely another form of slavery. R. D. Webb, who had been very active in the temperance movement since 1829, was, according to his son Alfred, so disillusioned with Father Mathew's failure to champion abolition that he largely abandoned temperance to devote all his energies to the anti-slavery cause.[42] When Father Mathew on his lengthy mission to the United States between 1849 and 1851 refused to take any stance on the slavery issue and visited slave states he discredited himself totally in the eyes of his remaining radical Protestant supporters. As we shall see also, their efforts to help him with his financial troubles led to further disputes and recriminations. Haughton, perhaps the most deeply committed temperance advocate in this group, summed up his view of Father Mathew before a temperance convention in London in 1862:

> By education, and by the previous habits of his life, Father Mathew was peculiarly well fitted to succeed in the great work he had undertaken.... His easy address made him acceptable to the educated and higher classes of society; his genial smile and warm greeting, when he mingled with the poor, made him the very idol of their affections.... [But] there were a few dark passages in Father Mathew's life which serve to show us that even the best men have serious imperfections of character. He was unkind to Father Spratt, of Dublin, of whom he appeared to entertain an unworthy jealousy.... Father Mathew's thoughtlessness about money was almost childlike, and this led him into many difficulties, from which some of our noblest and best sought to relieve him, and they would have done so effectually, but for insuperable bars placed in their way by Father Mathew himself.... When he proposed accepting the invitation to America, I entreated him not to go, for I knew the danger, and he fell beneath the wiles of the slaveholder. (**319**, 68-9)

These reflections exhibit the very mixed feelings that Father Mathew inspired in even his strongest supporters.

If conservative Protestants were hostile both on political and religious grounds and the small group of urban radical Dissenters who supported Father Mathew found him difficult to work with, his relations with the clergy of his own church were even more problematical. He built up, as we have seen, a substantial group of at least nominal clerical supporters in 1840. But many of these were subsequently to be confused and disillusioned by him, while some Catholic clergy were as fierce in their opposition to the crusade as any 'rabid' Tory.

In a letter to Dr Paul Cullen in Rome in September 1841 Father Mathew described Archbishop MacHale as an 'implacable enemy', who had in the preceding month, 'after a long tirade in Irish against the society', denounced him personally from the altar as a 'vagabond friar'. Although MacHale's language was excessively, if characteristically, harsh, there is little doubt that his attitude reflected a substantial body of opinion among Catholic clergy. One might have expected that Repeal priests would have been more disposed to support Father Mathew, but, as regards the bishops at least, this was not the case. Apart from being Father Mathew's most vocal clerical opponent, MacHale was probably one of the most committed Repealers among the bishops. In fact of the sixteen bishops who expressed some degree of support for the teetotal crusade, eight were Repealers; of the seven bishops who expressed opposition, four were Repealers. (**56**, 209; **204**, 75-7, 84-5, 330-1; **231**, 47-8) So their political sentiments did not determine the bishops' attitude to teetotalism, as they did in the case of many of the laity, most notably O'Connell himself. The bishops judged Father Mathew's crusade on other criteria.

MacHale felt that Father Mathew associated too much with Protestants, and even Cullen warned him against entertaining 'sentiments too liberal towards Protestants in matters of religion'. Both MacHale and Higgins of Ardagh, who distributed their own temperance medals and cards, were careful to use specifically Catholic ones, so that Protestant members of teetotal societies could not accept them. Father Mathew, on the other hand, frequently singled out Protestants, and especially Quakers, as his 'best and most efficient supporters', while early versions of his temperance card carried a line from the King James version of the Bible: 'He reasoned of righteousness, temperance and judgment to come' (Acts, 24:25). (**76**, 80-2; **56**, 210)[43] Such facts seemed to point to a continuing Protestant influence on the temperance crusade. MacHale's epithet 'vagabond friar' is a clue to other criticisms. Rivalry between the secular and regular clergy had long been a feature of the Irish church. The bishops particularly resented the independent ways of the friars, though there were only about 200 of them in the country in 1845. This is why Father Mathew was generally so scrupulous about seeking an invitation from local clergy, if not from the bishop himself, before he conducted a temperance mission in any diocese. His missions usually involved charity sermons in aid of church building or schools — another means of placating local feeling. Yet his critics, like MacHale, still claimed that he took 'great sums of money... out of the country to the serious injury of the people' by his missions, and, as we have seen, some priests were certainly reluctant to part with money for medals. (**204**, 52, 188)[44] In addition to this, Father Mathew's journeys through the length and breadth of the country indicated an independence that was obviously resented by some secular clerics. Although he himself was prepared to bow to the wishes of the hierarchy, many of his supporters were not. Dr Spratt, a Carmelite, conducted missions in Dundalk and Belfast without seeking the approval of the local clergy. For this he was reprimanded on more than one occasion by Father Mathew. In a letter of October 1846 to a supporter, which subsequently became public, Father Mathew wrote:

The Very Rev. Dr Spratt was well aware of the strictness with which I adhere to the rule of not holding a temperance meeting in any parish, unless expressly invited by the parish priest. He also knew that it was this motive of propriety that prevented me, during the last nine years, from going to Dundalk, Belfast, Londonderry, Armagh... (**56**, 408)

Writing to Haughton on the same subject, he stressed the need not to alienate his own church:

It is not for me, for the sake of a paltry triumph over the prejudices of a few ecclesiastics, and which are fast disappearing, to expose the temperance movement to the hostility of, in Ireland, an all powerful body. For however they may differ in opinion they will all unite in what they consider the maintenance of ecclesiastical discipline.[45]

An even more divisive issue as far as the church was concerned was the teetotal pledge itself. MacHale did not believe in lifelong total abstinence pledges; he felt it was far better to administer pledges for a shorter period, as then there was a better chance that people would be able to fulfil their promise. He also considered the pledge merely to be a promise; Father Mathew, on the other hand, was prepared to look upon the pledge as a sacred vow. His first pledge, 'I promise to abstain from all intoxicating drinks except used medicinally and by order of a medical man and to discountenance the cause and practice of intemperance,' was eventually replaced by the much stricter 'I promise with the divine assistance to abstain from all intoxicating liquors, and to prevent as much as possible by advice and example intemperance in others.' But Father Mathew's view of the pledge created serious opposition among some clergy. Catholics by their baptismal vows were required to practise temperance, but total abstinence was not an obligation placed upon them by their church. Frederick Lucas, editor of the influential Catholic journal the *Tablet*, on investigating attitudes to the pledge in Ireland in 1843, found that many teetotal priests did consider it a vow and refused absolution to those who broke it until they had sought Father Mathew's personal forgiveness. Nor would Father Mathew disavow this attitude. In October 1843 in Cork he was reported as saying:

It altogether depended on the disposition and mind of those who took the pledge whether they engaged in a vow or not. It was entirely a matter for their own consideration. And, surely, inasmuch as the national character of a people was concerned, it did not matter much whether the pledge were a vow or a promise, as long as the people adhered to an engagement which had drawn them out of incalculable misery, conferred happiness on themselves and their families, elevated them in the estimation of the world, and reflected on their country every honour that it could enjoy. He was surprised that persons with these facts before them could trouble themselves about the nature of the pledge. (**56**, 324)

But for many theologically-minded laymen like Lucas, to say nothing of many priests, the nature of the pledge was a vital issue, and Father Mathew's pragmatic approach was utterly unsatisfactory. Lucas, who had initially been sympathetic to the crusade, turned against it as a result of this disagreement.

From the latter part of 1841 the crusade began to lose momentum. Increasingly in 1842, and even more so in 1843, the popular mind was dominated by the issue of Repeal. Father Mathew curtailed the extent of his travels in 1842, concentrating his efforts in Munster, and in 1843 the number of his missions in Ireland was less than half what it had been in the preceding year. But it was not only the growth of the Repeal movement that restricted Father Mathew's work; after 1841 he was slipping deeper and deeper into financial chaos.

At the commencement of the crusade Father Mathew gave temperance medals away to those taking the pledge. But as numbers increased he became obliged to sell them. In March 1840 he told a Dublin meeting that he had given away 60,000 medals before beginning to charge for them. The medals were of burnished pewter and were made in Birmingham. They cost Father Mathew $3\frac{1}{2}$d each, and he sold them for a shilling. His critics were quick to attack this commercialism: in February 1840 the *Dublin Evening Mail* was estimating that if he had sold a million medals he would have received £50,000 and, even after paying the medal manufacturers, this would have left a substantial profit. (**56**, 363)[46] However, such calculations failed to take into account Father Mathew's total inability to manage money wisely.

His expenses in connection with the crusade were considerable. For example, Maguire says that in the six years between mid-1838 and mid-1844 he spent from £8 to £10 per week on printing, which amounts to nearly £3,000. In 1841 he was employing three secretaries at a cost of £200 per annum in salaries. In addition, he provided considerable financial aid to temperance bands and reading-rooms: in Cork city alone there were thirty-six bands, and between 1838 and 1841 Father Mathew spent some £1,600, mainly on instruments and elaborate uniforms. Travel was another substantial expense, though Charles Bianconi and Peter Purcell, both active supporters of the crusade, eventually provided him with free passes for travel on their cars. Moreover, at most towns and villages he visited Father Mathew donated money personally to the poor, to local charities and churches. During 1840 it was not unusual for him to distribute up to £100 in the course of a visit lasting two or three days. (**240**, 199; **56**, 364-5)[47] He was in fact constantly solicited for aid by numerous individuals: priests seeking help because of crop failures; publicans, whose businesses had been ruined, demanding compensation; societies wanting money for bands; intending emigrants requesting assistance, particularly good-character testimonials; others were in need of jobs or loans or simply desired his autograph. One of the most common requests, however, was for a free medal. Thus in August 1841 John Browne, a 'poor servant' from Templemore, Co. Tipperary, 'six months out of service' and with a 'mother and sister to support', who had been a teetotaller for over two years, wrote asking Father Mathew 'to take into consideration a poor labourer that has nothing and send me a meddle [*sic*] to comfort me'.[48] In the early years at least he seems to have responded positively to many of these requests.

Yet his expenses were not covered, as in theory they should have been, by the sale of medals, simply because he continued to give medals away. Maguire estimates that only about one in ten who took the pledge actually paid for a medal. Father Mathew donated 100,000 medals for school-children; all priests taking the pledge received a silver medal, and all bishops a gold one. By 1844 he had given away £1,500 worth of silver medals alone. He thus fell more and more into debt. According to Maguire, his debts amounted to £1,500 before he left Cork in December 1839 on his first mission; by the end of 1841 they were well over £5,000. (**240**, 197, 199; **56**, 362)

The obvious question that arises is: given his vow of poverty, where did the money come from? As provincial of the Capuchin order in Ireland and spiritual director of several convents, he did handle large sums of money. Letters from him to bankers in Paris survive in which sums of £1,000 and £1,500, belonging to the nuns of the South Presentation Convent in Cork, are referred to. One writer has recently speculated that he may have mis-appropriated some of this money, which would account for his reluctance to allow supporters access to details of his financial problems. (**80**, 261)[49] There is no real evidence, however, on which to base such an accusation, and in fact in many speeches and letters he unequivocally named his own family as his chief source of money. Ironically, his brothers seem to have made a good deal of money from the drink industry: his brother Tom had a distillery near Cashel, while his brother Charles and one of his sisters had both married into the Hackett family, owners of one of Cork's largest distilleries. Certainly the family had considerable economic resources: one brother farmed the family land at Rathcloheen, while others were involved in milling and the provision trade. (Strangely, there is no evidence that his brothers subscribed to teetotalism in the sense of having taken the pledge, though at least one of his nephews did.) It is therefore quite conceivable that he could have borrowed substantial sums of money from his own family.[50]

But he looked to one particular member of his family for even more substantial aid. As noted already, Lady Elizabeth Mathew had inherited the family estates, or what remained of them, when her brother, the second earl, died intestate in 1833. She was not married, and Father Mathew expected that on her death he and his brothers would inherit. Up until the end of 1841 he spent money extravagantly in the belief that this inheritance would ultimately be his. As he later wrote to a correspondent in Belfast,

In the first years of the great temperance movement vast unavoidable, yet unforeseen, expenses were incurred, and before I was aware of it I was deeply involved in debt. Having a well-grounded hope of being enabled by a rich relation to extricate myself, I concealed my difficulties from the world. My expectations were blighted by a sudden death, and every effort of mine made only increased my difficulties.[51]

This account is a trifle misleading, however. When Lady Elizabeth died in December 1841 it was found that she had left sums of money to two of Father Mathew's sisters and appointed him one of the executors of her will, but the bulk of the estate had gone to Viscount de Chabot, a French cousin with whom she frequently stayed. Father Mathew's expectations were well known: there was newspaper comment on them at the time of Lady Elizabeth's death. He remained convinced that she would have altered her will in his favour had she lived. But she was a difficult and eccentric woman, and he clearly had been foolish to rely so heavily upon her favour.[52] Other unexpected family deaths compounded his problems: two of his brothers died, Frank in May 1843 and Tom in September 1844, leaving in all twelve children to be cared for. The family's resources must have been stretched to their limit.

Father Mathew's financial situation was so serious by 1844 that he contemplated abandoning the crusade altogether, and certainly his travels continued to be much curtailed. Reports of his difficulties became public in October, and supporters in Ireland and England organised fund-raising committees. Some, like James Haughton, were appalled by Father Mathew's financial incompetence and proffered advice. This was curtly rejected. In a letter of November 1844 to Dr Spratt, Father Mathew complained of being treated superciliously by Haughton, who had criticised him before some of his strongest supporters. 'Nothing could induce me to place myself under his control and to have him for a ... paymaster,' Father Mathew concluded. At about the same time he was writing to Charles Gavan Duffy:

I would rather take a staff in my hand, and walk to the temperance meetings [than surrender] myself into the hands of a self-elected committee to unfold to them my most private affairs, allow them to arrange with my creditors, and receive from them whatever pittance they may deem sufficient to supply my daily wants. To this I will never submit.

His acute, and decidedly unco-operative, sensitivity over his debts is clear from such letters. Over a period of about six months some £8,000 was raised by his supporters, and this seems to have covered his most pressing debts, particularly those to the medal manufacturers. Yet he himself was disappointed at the response, complaining to Haughton: 'The teetotallers of Ireland have not upheld me, have not contributed for my relief half of what I expended for their happiness.' Much of the money was in fact raised in England. And he went on to inform Haughton that it was 'absolutely necessary' for him to revisit the 'scenes of my early labours' in order to revitalise the movement. He was at a loss, however, to know where he would find the money for further missions. Most unrealistically he concluded: 'I do not well see my way, but you may rest assured dear Mr Haughton, that I shall not involve myself in debt.'[53]

His financial solvency was relatively brief. By early 1846, with the added burden of famine relief, he was again in serious difficulty. A committee of supporters was formed in England to aid him, but after ten months' effort they were only able to raise £900 of their projected target of £7,000. Father Mathew described himself as 'much dispirited' by this result and as confined to Cork by lack of money.[54] In July 1846 Lord John Russell was prevailed upon by some of Father Mathew's English supporters to propose to the queen a civil list pension for him. The queen consented to £100 per annum, though with some reluctance, commenting: 'It is quite true that he has done much by preaching temperance, but by the aid of superstition, which can hardly be patronised by the crown.' Father Mathew, despite his pressing need, declined the offer. In letters to supporters he gave two main reasons for this action: firstly, 'I feared it would injure the cause to have me paid by the government,' and secondly, 'I was humbled beyond expression at finding my services so lowly estimated.' In other words, £100 was so paltry a sum as to be insulting. The man's pride and sensitivity behind his mask of humility are very clear in such a remark. But his pride had to be swallowed in the end. By June 1847 his situation was so desperate that he could not even afford to pay the premium on his life insurance, taken out to cover his debts to his family. One of his biographers has justly called this insurance the 'sole instance in his career when he displayed something resembling worldly prudence'. (**56**, 438, 440; **294**, 99) At about this time one poor petitioner, writing from a Dublin prison, was told that Father Mathew could not help him financially as 'I have not a single pound in my possession, and every resource is exhausted. There was a time when I would most cheerfully and immediately have responded to your call; but I was too lavish, and must now deny myself the pleasure of assisting my friends.'[55] In June 1847 he wrote a rather pathetic letter to Russell personally soliciting a pension. Two weeks later Russell replied that the queen had graciously granted him £300 a year.

It was not simply that Father Mathew was impractical regarding money. He could and did at times manage large sums without criticism, as in the case of the Presentation sisters of Cork. But when his motives or competence were called in question, then offended pride could lead him into an almost pathological extravagance. Writing to a friend in October 1844 about his debts, he said:

I was never during my life, influenced by a love of money . . . and always deemed it more blessed to give than to receive. Yet I was reviled as mercenary: I was charged with amassing wealth by the sale of medals. I was not content with my own conviction of the falsehood; I refused all pecuniary aid; I defrayed all the expenses attendant on public meetings. I distributed money and medals with both hands, and never refused calls for assistance from multitudinous associations until every resource was exhausted, even the affectionate liberality of my own family. I still clung to hope, and when everything else failed, having my life insured to the full amount of my debts, I hope to die soon, that they might be paid. (**56**, 368)

Reading an admission like this, one can only conclude that his financial problems were very much of his own making and were as much the product of pride as of incompetence.

As well as severely limiting his temperance work and causing him great personal anguish, his well-publicised debts had another damaging side-effect. In April 1847 John Murphy, the Bishop of Cork, died. Early in May at a meeting of the parish priests of the diocese to nominate a successor Father Mathew headed the list as *dignissimus*, most worthy. Coming as it did in the midst of the horrors of the famine, of his deepest financial difficulties and of the waning of his crusade, this nomination was obviously a great source of satisfaction to him. He knew, however, that his candidature would meet opposition from within the hierarchy, for, only five days after the priests' meeting, he was writing to Cullen in Rome: 'It is a case of life and death for me and the temperance cause in Ireland. After being honoured with the unsolicited suffrages of my very rev. and rev. brethren, the pastors of this diocese, it would degrade me in the eyes of the whole world if I were set aside.' (**56**, 427, 429) To strengthen his cause he sent a priest to Rome with an introduction to Cullen and instructions to argue his case.

But early in July news reached Cork that Father William Delany of Bandon, second after Father Mathew on the priests' list, had been chosen as bishop. Father Mathew attributed his defeat primarily to the opposition of Archbishop Slattery of Cashel, whom he bitterly accused of 'pretending the warmest friendship, dining at my table . . . and then stabbing me in the dark'. He also accused Kennedy of Killaloe of 'breathing vengeance against me' and Walsh of Cloyne of being a 'bitter enemy'. He believed that the 'unwillingness of the prelates to pronounce in favour of the temperance movement' was the main motive behind his rejection.[56] Given, however, his close Protestant connections, his opposition to O'Connell, his support for Peel's educational reforms, his friendships with many English Liberals and his recent government pension, it is understandable that in Rome he was looked upon with some suspicion, not least by Cullen himself.

In fact it is likely that Cullen's hostility, rather than Slattery's, was crucial in his rejection for the see of Cork. Independent, broad-minded and strong-willed clerics like Father Mathew were exactly the sort of people that Cullen was anxious to eliminate from positions of influence in the Irish church. Slattery's letters certainly show that he did oppose the appointment: in one to Cullen, dated 27 July, he complained of government and lay efforts to force Father Mathew's appointment upon the hierarchy. Higgins of Ardagh, an old enemy, in a far more scathing letter written at about the same time, accused Father Mathew of 'notorious latitud-inarianism', of 'lying' and 'hypocrisy', of ignoring episcopal authority, and of being the 'hired tool of a heretical government'. The latter accusation presumably referred to his pension. In fact, during the deliberations in Rome, only Bishop Ryan of Limerick seems to have pleaded Father Mathew's cause, arguing with his fellow-bishops for three hours. But it was to no avail. In September 1847 Father Mathew wrote to Dr Grant, Rector of the English College in Rome: 'All conclude that His Holiness would not have concurred in the act of the archbishop and his suffragans, with the noble exception of the Bishop of Limerick, unless something grievous had been proved against me.' (**56**, 443-5; **76**, 82-3) In the eyes of the leaders of his own church, he had certainly committed many 'grievous' errors; and in overturning the popular feeling in his favour, they had censured him accordingly.

In April 1848 Father Mathew suffered a stroke, which marked the beginning of a number of years of poor health. In August in the wake of the rising, in which a number of his friends and supporters had been impli-cated, and another failure of the potato crop, he wrote to a friend in England: 'With regard to myself, I have only to say that my health is improving, and if I were free, I would gladly abandon this land of horrors and misery.' In May 1849 he did abandon it, leaving for the United States, where he remained for two and a half years, still preaching temperance. However, his last five years, up until his death in December 1856, were spent in Ireland in failing health and increasing depression. Frank Mathew, his grand-nephew, later wrote of this period: 'He looked on his past with great humility and bitter self-reproach.' (**56**, 474; **247**, 217)

There exists much contemporary impressionistic evidence suggesting a marked decline in whiskey consumption in Ireland between about 1839 and 1842. Writing in 1840 Mr and Mrs S. C. Hall, who knew the country well, remarked that during a three-month visit from June to September they had seen only six people drunk. 'We can have no hesitation', they concluded, 'in describing sobriety to be almost universal throughout Ireland.' (**164**, I, 37-8) But in attempting to assess somewhat more objectively the impact of Father Mathew's crusade, it is necessary to ask two questions. Do the statistics measuring alcohol consumption reveal a marked decline during these years? And if they do, could this decline have been caused by factors other than the temperance movement?

The late 1830s were years of unprecedently high consumption of legally produced whiskey. In the four years from 1835 to 1838, with the duty at 2s 4d per gallon, spirits charged ranged from 11 to 12 million gallons per annum. The year 1839, however, witnessed a fall to slightly below 11 million gallons, a fall which became very striking in the following three years. Gallons charged with duty in 1840 were approximately 7.4 million; in 1841 they were 6.5 million; while in 1842 they were down to around 5.3 million. Thus in four years consumption of legal whiskey had been more than halved. Not since the excise reforms of the early 1820s had there been such a dramatic upheaval in the distilling industry. A cursory examination of the statistics would therefore suggest that Father Mathew was indeed remarkably successful in curbing whiskey consumption. On closer examination, however, the situation appears rather more complicated.

In 1840, the year of the most marked fall in consumption, the duty had been raised to 2s 8d per gallon; in 1842 it was raised again to the relatively high level of 3s 8d per gallon. On past performance one would have expected legal consumption to fall with a rise in duty, particularly a substantial one. On this evidence the fall need not be ascribed solely to Father Mathew's endeavours. But the fall had begun in 1839, before the duty revision. The years 1839 and 1840 were, as we have already noted, ones of crop failure and famine, in which grain prices were accordingly high. At such a time grain was more likely to be consumed as food than as drink. This is supported by the figures for detections of illicit distilling. These had been running at over 3,000 per annum between 1836 and 1838, but by 1840 they were down to around 1,000, and in 1841 to an unprecedentedly low 881. Normally falls in legal consumption, such as occurred between 1839 and 1841, would have provided opportunities for illicit distillers. But illicit distilling seems to have declined markedly in these years as well.

Thus the overall consumption of spirits, both legal and illegal, fell between 1839 and 1841. Another year in which a similar picture emerges is 1847: legal consumption fell by a quarter, detections again dipped below 1,000, while grain prices reached astronomical levels. The year 1847 was, of course, the worst year of the great famine. This raises the question: could the crop failures of 1839 and 1840 account for the marked fall in overall spirit consumption that occurred in the early 1840s? If we look at earlier crop failures such as in 1816-17, 1821-2, 1825-6 and 1829-31 and examine legal consumption figures for those years, the pattern that emerges is generally one of decline. Unfortunately the figures for detections of illicit distilling are not complete enough to produce a clear picture. But it would seem that a failure of the potato crop, producing famine and high grain prices, could have a significant impact on the consumption of legal whiskey and probably the consumption of poteen as well. Yet even in 1847, the worst year of the famine, legal consumption fell by only about a quarter, from approximately 8 to 6 million gallons; in the other famine years of 1845, 1846 and 1848 gallons charged with excise duty actually rose. Between 1838 and 1842, however, with only a partial famine in 1839 and 1840, legal consumption fell by more than half. Famine probably had an impact on overall consumption, but, like the increase in duty, it is clearly not sufficient to explain such a drastic fall. Only the success of the temperance crusade would appear to offer an adequate reason for the marked alteration in drinking habits that occurred after 1838.

The waning of Father Mathew's campaign can also be illustrated by the drink statistics. In 1842 detections for illicit distilling jumped notably to nearly 1,900, and in 1843 they were up again to nearly 3,500. In 1842, with legal consumption and revenue still falling, the government increased the duty dramatically to 3s 8d per gallon. This led to a modest increase in revenue in 1842, despite a further fall in legal consumption. But the up-surge in the illicit industry quickly produced second thoughts, and the duty was restored to 2s 8d in 1843, after which detections subsided again. From 1843 also legal consumption began to recover: in the four years to 1846 it rose steadily from 5.5 million gallons to nearly 8 million.

So, on the whole, the statistics agree with the evidence from other sources suggesting that the temperance crusade did indeed have a substantial impact on spirit consumption between 1839 and 1842; the fall that occurred during those years cannot be adequately explained in terms of economic factors. As might be expected with a total abstinence movement, it was not only spirit consumption which was affected. Beer too felt the impact of the crusade. After fluctuating at around 900,000 barrels per annum between 1837 and 1839, production fell dramatically in 1840 and 1841. It remained at around 500,000 barrels between 1841 and 1843 before recovering somewhat in 1844 and 1845. Again economic factors seem inadequate to account for this drastic decline: even during the famine period production remained relatively stable at around 600,000 barrels per annum. (**343**, 336-7, 318, 369)

In a recent article entitled 'Father Mathew: Apostle of Modernisation' H. F. Kearney has denied that the temperance crusade was 'merely . . . a charismatic movement based upon Father Mathew's miracle working'. He sees it rather as essentially a well-organised, urban-based campaign for social betterment: a force for modernisation. Yet our examination has suggested that the crusade won most of its recruits in the countryside and small towns, not in the large urban centres. Figures for pledge-taking in cities like Cork, Limerick and Waterford are misleading in that vast numbers flocked in from the surrounding countryside to take the pledge when Father Mathew visited such centres. In fact disappointment was being expressed as early as 1840 and 1841 at the failure of the crusade to match its rural successes with those in urban areas. Professor Kearney further argues that the crusade had a significant 'administrative substructure', and he offers the example of a teetotal society in Limerick which boasted elaborate rules and had a savings bank associated with it. One could certainly find other examples of similar societies: they were obviously modelled upon, if not actually derived from, the temperance societies of the early and middle 1830s. But, overall, the impression is that Father Mathew's crusade was considerably less well organised than the previous temperance movement. Certainly Protestants such as James Haughton who had supported the earlier societies before switching to teetotalism were severely critical of Father Mathew for failing to construct any national framework of the type which the old Hibernian Temperance Society had attempted to provide. Father Mathew in fact specifically ruled out any organisation beyond local societies for fear of arousing governmental, and probably also church, hostility. Thus the crusade was very loosely organised: some societies had elaborate rules and structures; some had none. The degree of administrative sophistication depended wholly on the enthusiasm and resources of the local leadership.

Professor Kearney links temperance with other reform movements of the period, such as Chartism, Repeal and the anti-slavery campaign. Each he says, 'represented a shift from "local" to "cosmopolitan" values, an attempt by urban men to control and reform rural society'. Yet Father Mathew was staunchly opposed to all efforts to connect teetotalism with other social or political movements. In this, of course, he failed dismally, but his opposition to Repeal and his failure to support the abolitionist movement do rather call into question the title 'Apostle of Modernisation'. Politically Father Mathew was a Whig, a conservative Liberal, as one might have expected with the product of an old Catholic landed family. In this context it is interesting to note that many of his English supporters (for example, Lord Stourton, Sir Edward Vavasour, the Hon. Stafford Jeringham, Lady Bedingfield, and the Earl of Arundel and Surrey, heir to the Duke of Norfolk) came also from landed and often Catholic backgrounds. There is little indication that Father Mathew espoused any very sophisticated political philosophy: his Whiggism was in keeping with his class and his religion. As for teetotalism, he saw it as a panacea for social and economic problems. If people would stop drinking, they would have the money or resources to live comfortably, to educate their children, and to provide for their old age. One is constantly struck by the naivety of his analysis: he saw drunkenness as the root cause of most of Ireland's problems; even political animosities, he believed, would disappear in a teetotal society. Material prosperity, not self-government or independence, would solve Ireland's political dilemmas. Holding such a view, it is easy to see why he considered Repeal a threat: it seduced and misled teetotallers into following a false doctrine which would not ultimately better their country. There was nothing especially modern about Father Mathew's political views.

In religious terms too he appears as decidedly old-fashioned. We have already noted his isolation within the church, being the head of a small order and not a secular product of the Maynooth educational system. Like his friend Archbishop Murray of Dublin, he showed strong Gallican tendencies, and it is no coincidence that he was criticised by Cullen, who, as Murray's successor, was to spearhead the Roman reform of the Irish church. Obviously there were still many priests who respected his industry and his sincerity, as their endorsement of him for the see of Cork in 1847 reveals, but in his opposition to the views of Cullen and of the nationalist clergy he was flying in the face of the two major forces shaping Irish Catholicism. In the religious context, however attractive his ecumenism now appears, he was a reactionary.

The Young Irelanders took up and supported his call for self-discipline, thrift and education, but as only one part of a much broader movement. To them major political reform was essential; teetotalism of itself was not adequate to achieve the desired ends. Only when Irishmen substantially controlled their own government would the country's problems be solved. The Young Ireland programme for political reform and social advancement shows all the hallmarks of a modernising urban radicalism, but at the same time it highlights the very limited and simplistic nature of Father Mathew's philosophy.

Professor Kearney denies that the crusade rested solely on Father Mathew's personal appeal, or that this appeal was essentially irrational. Certainly in 1839 people were being sent to Cork by landlords and employers or were coming of their own accord in the hope that teetotalism would guarantee their economic security during a time of crop failure and famine. Yet there is also a great deal of evidence testifying to the superstitious awe in which Father Mathew was held: the vast excited crowds which besieged him wherever he went, the many people who took the pledge when drunk or took it several times, and the eagerly believed rumours of miraculous cures, all suggest that something more than rational economic calculation was at work. The astounding speed with which the crusade gathered momentum in 1839 and 1840 points in the same direction. One has only to compare this with O'Connell's struggle, during the same period, to organise a popular movement in favour of Repeal to appreciate the difference between a campaign based on rational argument and one based on irrational enthusiasm. O'Connell's appeal certainly contained irrational elements, as recent exploration of the folklore associated with him has demonstrated, but with Father Mathew the irrational seems to have been far more prominent. Kearney suggests that 'there must be something amiss with our interpretation of the pre-famine period' when a man and a movement, so significant in contemporary eyes, have been largely ignored by subsequent historians. But it is only recently that the popular religious context in which the teetotal crusade occurred has begun to be explored, and there is still much we do not know about the beliefs of rural society in the pre-famine period. (**198**, 170-2, 175, 164; **277**, 30-42)

The decades of the 1820s, 1830s and 1840s were troubled ones, with widespread economic distress, agrarian violence and political agitation; they were also years of heightened popular religious expectations. The prophecies of Pastorini and Colmcille circulated widely, both promising the overthrow of Protestantism. In 1832, in the midst of a severe cholera epidemic, there occurred the curious episode of the 'blessed turf': the rapid dissemination throughout large parts of the country of magical tokens, often ashes, intended to ward off the cholera. It appears that in just six days these tokens were carried some 300 miles by anonymous individuals and groups, thus reaching at least three-quarters of the counties of Ireland. As a recent study of this phenomenon concludes, 'It offers [evidence] of a widespread willingness to believe in an immediate and concrete divine intervention at a time of crisis.' (**115**, 109-10; **114**, 229-30) Patrick O'Farrell, in another recent article, found little genuine millennialism in Ireland, at least before the famine, but he did identify instances of what he termed utopianism and messianism: the belief in the imminence of a better society and the belief that a particular individual could affect almost miraculous change. It is in this often murky and obscure world of popular fantasies and expectations, rather than in the world of urban reform campaigns, that we must look for much of the motivation behind the rush to take the pledge from Father Mathew in 1839 and 1840.

On the subject of anti-drink movements Professor O'Farrell says that the millennial strand evident elsewhere was not marked in Ireland: 'The Irish were encouraged towards national and moral regeneration through temperance, not promised salvation through teetotalism and prohibition.' (**270**, 49) This is certainly true of the temperance movement of the 1830s, but it is not wholly true of Father Mathew's crusade. Father Mathew did preach teetotalism, and he did promise a total transformation of both the individual and society through teetotalism. In O'Farrell's terms the crusade was utopian and messianic. Itinerant lecturers, like John Hockings, distributing medals and promising well-nigh miraculous advantages to those who took the pledge, had already made an impression on popular audiences, particularly in the south, by 1838. The appearance of a saintly friar repeating these promises during a time of crop failure and famine was therefore likely to stir widespread enthusiasm. As we have seen, even observers normally as sceptical as newspaper reporters and editors were convinced by 1840 that divine intervention was indeed occurring. His followers may not have expected Father Mathew to herald the Second Coming, but they did not expect him, under God's guidance, to lead them into a new and better era. And, as evidence of his divinely inspired mission, they believed that he could perform miracles, in particular heal the sick. Urban radicals and reformers were also attracted to the crusade, but Father Mathew was never really one of them, and it was certainly not their arguments that won him such a massive popular following. James Haughton, who supported him, while criticising his lack of organisation, his financial irresponsibility, his failure to endorse Repeal or the anti-slavery cause, and his pandering to popular superstition, is indicative of the urban radicals' attitude to the temperance crusade. They recognised its potential for social reform, but at the same time deplored the hysteria and chaos that seemed invariably to accompany it. And in its rapid decline they saw their criticisms vindicated.

Up until 1838 developments in the Irish anti-drink movement had generally been influenced by events in England or America, and, as we shall see later, a similar pattern is again apparent from the 1850s. But with Father Mathew's crusade the Irish movement suddenly took the initiative, branching out in new directions which had a profound influence on societies in other countries. Father Mathew's visits to Britain and the United States did a great deal to arouse interest in teetotalism, particularly among working-class Catholics, who had not previously been noted for their sobriety. But the rapid waning of the crusade, after hopes had initially been raised so high, created an inevitable backlash. Later teetotal leaders and writers were to judge Father Mathew harshly. Temperance in the 1820s was looked upon as a partial beginning; the arrival of tee-totalism in the mid-1830s was hailed as the real commencement of the fight against drink; but Father Mathew's crusade was seen as a diversion and as a dead-end. The temperance movement learned the fickleness and unreliability of popular enthusiasm, and with this lesson something of its optimism and its faith in human nature were destroyed. Father Mathew had convinced the majority of the Irish population to give up drink and had effected a moral revolution. Yet within a few years it was as though the crusade had never occurred. Some blamed the famine or even O'Connell for this collapse, but many concluded that the whole principle upon which Father Mathew had based his work was faulty. Right from the beginning the survivors of the old temperance movement had expressed anxiety about a campaign focused so narrowly on one individual: Haughton had called on the clergy of Ireland to rally to Father Mathew's support and to create a well-organised national campaign, so that the enthusiasm of the numerous converts would not be dissipated. But Father Mathew's opposition to organisation, his failure to win over his church and his financial mismanagement seemed to Haughton and others to vindicate their early anxieties. Only a well-organised and well-financed anti-drink movement, preferably with strong church support, could possibly succeed. Also popular enthusiasm was obviously not to be relied upon. Teetotallers needed to be thoroughly convinced and carefully instructed regarding the anti-drink case.

At about the same time from the United States emerged the view that governments and their licensing laws were the main barriers to the success of teetotalism. While governments protected and encouraged the drink trade, from which they derived substantial revenue, there was little or no hope of rooting out drinking practices. Teetotallers therefore had to influence, or even capture, political parties and ensure the passing of anti-drink legislation. It was no longer a matter solely or even principally of convincing people to reform themselves, but one of convincing governments to enforce reform on behalf of their people. Moral suasion, as the method of the temperance advocates and of Father Mathew was termed, was rejected during the 1840s in favour of legislative coercion.

4

Realignments: the 1850s and 1860s

ALTHOUGH Father Mathew lived on until December 1856, his crusade in Ireland had been eclipsed long before, and the temperance issue was not to figure again significantly on the national scene until the 1870s. Yet the 1850s and the 1860s saw important developments both in popular drinking habits and in the tactics employed by temperance advocates. Events in America continued to influence Ireland, but increasingly the Irish temperance movement looked to England for its inspiration. This was partly a function of the movement's growing pre-occupation with legislative reform. The passing of a prohibitory law in the state of Maine in 1851 and the establishment of the United Kingdom Alliance in 1853 to campaign for prohibition were important stimuli, as was the introduction of Sunday closing, successfully, in Scotland in 1853 and, unsuccessfully, in England in 1854. The twin goals of Sunday closing and prohibition were to preoccupy the Irish temperance movement for the rest of the century, but the mutually exclusive nature of the two was at the same time to prove deeply divisive.

But there were other important divisions as well. Father Mathew had sought, admittedly with only limited success, to create a mass, non-sectarian, non-political anti-drink crusade. The temperance movement which emerged in the 1850s, however, was both highly sectarian and highly political. The Protestant wing, with its headquarters in Belfast and Dublin, came increasingly to look to parliament for coercive legislation aimed against the drink trade. The rationale behind this strategy was that, while government condoned and encouraged the sale of drink, no temperance movement could possibly succeed. The Catholic wing, on the other hand, though taking some interest in the legislative campaign, was increasingly brought under the control of the clergy and integrated within the church's growing framework of devotional organisations. Temperance, and total abstinence even more so, became the hallmark of militant Catholicism. From the sectarian division there inevitably arose a geographical one as well. Beginning in 1829 there had been a split between Ulster and the rest of the country. In the 1830s this had been underlined by

Dr Edgar's opposition to teetotalism, and in the 1840s by the religious animosity to Father Mathew evident in the north. If anything this split widened in the second half of the century. The main Ulster temperance society, the Irish Temperance League (established in Belfast in 1858), was dominated by Protestant clergy, in particular Presbyterians. The League diverged from societies further south over tactics as well. It took a staunchly prohibitionist line, while its counterpart in Dublin, the Irish Association for the Prevention of Intemperance (established in 1878), devoted much energy to campaigns for Sunday closing and licensing reform. But these largely Protestant organisations had by the 1860s at least agreed on the need for personal total abstinence; the Catholic temperance movement, on the other hand, even as late as the 1890s, was still split between moderationists and teetotallers.

Some idea of the state of the temperance movement in various parts of the country at the beginning of the 1850s can be derived from a book entitled *Memorandums of a Tour in Ireland*, published in 1853 by Sir John Forbes, an eminent English physician who was also an ardent supporter of temperance. In the south and west Forbes inquired into temperance activity in Skibbereen, Kenmare, Killarney, Limerick, Athlone, Galway, Westport and Castlebar. Generally he found the movement in marked decline: in Skibbereen, for instance, where Sedwards had begun his pioneering society as early as 1817, from 'a muster of many hundreds at one time, the professed teetotallers had sunk down, it was supposed, to two or three'; Athlone boasted only fourteen teetotallers; Castlebar perhaps twenty to thirty; and Westport forty to fifty. In the latter two towns Forbes heard that the temperance movement had been destroyed by Archbishop MacHale's hostility to Father Mathew. But the situation was somewhat better in Killarney, where there had been a revival in 1850-51 promoted by three local priests. The town had three temperance halls, one containing a library of nearly 400 books, and about 250 pledged teetotallers. Limerick, one of Father Mathew's earliest strongholds, still had four temperance halls in operation. One, 'lighted with gas, and adorned with paintings and prints', had around 300 members, though at one time membership had been well over a thousand. In Galway too there had been something of a revival in 1849-50, and a new temperance hall, called St Patrick's, had been established with 200 members. Despite the collapse of Father Mathew's crusade, Forbes felt that intemperance was still nowhere near as bad as it had been in the 1830s, though he conceded that, given the very depressed economic conditions, this was perhaps due to the 'general want of the means to purchase the indulgence'. (**153**, I, 90, 211, 281, 291, 150, 192-3, 224)

In Ulster Forbes reported on the state of temperance in Enniskillen, Derry, Limavady, Coleraine, Ballycastle, Cushendall, Larne, Antrim, Armagh and Newry. Again, in many places the signs of decline were marked, but in others something of a revival was clearly under way. Enniskillen presented a depressing picture: a movement once about 2,000 strong had been broken up by the fear of cholera and fever during the famine and by religious differences; the temperance hall had disappeared, and now there were probably only about twenty pledged teetotallers in the town. But, interestingly, Forbes felt that the movement had probably survived better in the surrounding countryside, though he made no attempt to measure its strength in rural areas. In Derry one temperance hall continued to function, but largely as a benevolent society with members paying 3d weekly towards sickness and funeral expenses. In Limavady, Larne, Armagh and Newry, however, Forbes found evidence of a marked revival. In Limavady the Presbyterian clergy of six neighbouring parishes had taken the pledge and established a temperance society which, at the time of Forbes's visit, had nearly 2,000 members; similarly in Larne the clergy had enrolled 500 new members. In Armagh and Newry Forbes found both Catholic and Protestant societies. The Catholic society in Armagh, with 200 members, was a benevolent organisation to which members paid 10d a month; the Protestant Armagh Temperance Society had about a hundred members, with an affiliated juvenile branch numbering fifty. In Newry the Protestant society was Presbyterian-dominated and had fifty members. (**153**, II, 97-8, 117, 121, 191, 220, 262)

Although Forbes's observations are admittedly sketchy, they suggest that in the south after the famine the old strongholds of Father Mathew's crusade, like Limerick and Galway, still boasted modest temperance societies; in the north, particularly among the Presbyterians in Counties Antrim, Down and Armagh, where Edgar had gained most support, signs of a revival were evident. Many urban societies of the 1830s and 1840s had had benevolent associations and savings banks linked with them, and clearly in some instances these institutions survived when the temperance aspect went into decline. From Forbes's observations it would seem that working men's benevolent societies took over some of the old temperance halls and reading-rooms. But unfortunately Forbes restricted himself to the towns, ignoring both the cities and the countryside, although he does hint at the survival of temperance sentiment in rural areas even with the disappearance of the external trappings of societies, reading-rooms and bands.

Temperance and Ulster Revivalism

Forbes was right in detecting evidence of a revival in Ulster, particularly east of the Bann. The late 1830s and the 1840s were, as already indicated, difficult years for the temperance cause in Ulster. Consequently many of the old leaders of the cause seem to have turned their attention to other evangelical enterprises, in particular to the promotion of church missions.

John Edgar and James Morgan became the principal forces in the Presbyterians' home and foreign missions which were given a major boost by the unification of the Synod of Ulster and Seceders in 1840 to form the Presbyterian Church in Ireland. Edgar was secretary of the Home Mission and, together with Morgan, joint secretary of the Foreign Mission. While proselytising, particularly in the Irish-speaking west, was a major feature of the Home Mission's work, its main aim was to support existing Presbyterians in the south and in isolated parts of the north and to prevent them from being lost to the church. In an interesting recent article examining the nature of Ulster Presbyterianism Dr David Miller has characterised it as 'evangelical fundamentalism'. He argues persuasively that Ulster Presbyterianism had assumed this form by 1860, having moved away from its eighteenth-century preoccupation with doctrine and polity to an emphasis on 'conversionist Evangelicalism'. In this process the Presbyterians of Ulster were moving closer to the experience of early nineteenth-century American popular Protestantism. We can see this trend towards orthodoxy and Evangelicalism in the Synod of Ulster from at least the 1820s. Henry Cooke's victory over the forces of liberal Unitarianism and the reunification of 1840 were both important steps in this process, as was the establishment of church missions. Temperance could also find a significant role for itself in the new united and evangelical church. Edgar's opposition to teetotalism remained a problem, but a revival of temperance within the Presbyterian church in the 1850s was almost predictable. (**286**; **252**; **77**, 31-4)

A good example of the young Evangelically-minded clergy appearing in the 1830s and 1840s can be found in the person of Jonathan Simpson, for many years minister at Portrush, Co. Antrim, and a brief examination of Simpson's career up to 1860 reveals something of the nature of Ulster Presbyterianism at this time. Born in 1817 near Coleraine, Simpson was the son of a poor, self-educated small tenant farmer. His father acted as a lay preacher and was a supporter of Edgar's temperance movement. In 1832, at the age of fifteen, Simpson took the moderationist pledge from his schoolmaster in Ballymoney, and at the tender age of sixteen he gave his first temperance lecture at Garvagh, Co. Londonderry. Caught up in the first wave of temperance enthusiasm in the early 1830s, Simpson was to remain a committed temperance advocate for the rest of his life, still promoting the cause in his memoirs, published in 1895. He was trained at the Academical Institution in Belfast and became a fervent admirer of Henry Cooke, attending Cooke's May Street church regularly. However, Simpson found much of the instruction at 'Inst' irrelevant to the work of the ministry as he conceived it. While still a student in 1834 he was conducting sabbath school classes at the Brown Street school, where he must have come into contact with Alexander Smith Mayne, a teacher at the school, who had helped Edgar found the Ulster Temperance Society in

1829 and who was to be prominent in the establishment of the Irish Temperance League in 1858. Simpson certainly continued his interest in temperance while in Belfast, and he remembered attending lectures given by Edgar and G. W. Carr in 1835. Even as a student, mission work attracted Simpson and he undertook visits in his own parish. In 1836-7 he studied at the University of Edinburgh, coming under the influence of the Evangelical Thomas Chalmers, whose teaching had a profound influence on many Ulster clergymen. (**314**, 16, 18, 23, 32, 40-1)

On completing his studies Simpson began work as an agent of the Home Mission. Much of his time between 1839 and his call to Portrush in 1842 was spent opening mission stations in the south and west of the country. It was an exhausting and dispiriting enterprise, which severely undermined Simpson's health. He was ultimately forced to consult the eminent Dublin physician, Sir Philip Crampton, who had been active in the Hibernian Temperance Society. Crampton had obviously retained his moderationist views, for he told Simpson, who was in fact by this stage a teetotaller, not to drink spirits but that wine and beer would do him no harm. Simpson, needless to say, rejected the eminent doctor's advice. But one thing his years in the south did give Simpson was an abiding loathing for 'popery' and the 'usual concomitants of popery — rags and wretchedness'. In 1840 his work took him to Wexford and New Ross, where he received encouragement from G. W. Carr. In New Ross too he attended one of Father Mathew's meetings and spoke with the Apostle of Temperance, then at the height of his crusade. Simpson was not very impressed with Father Mathew's lecture, which he felt northern Presbyterians would regard as 'very simple', and he was shocked at the numbers of sick people attempting to have Father Mathew touch them. Never backward, Simpson

> ventured to take exception to his touching the sick, and asked him 'Did he really believe his touch *cured* them?' He at once candidly, and with a bland smile, said, 'Well, I don't; but *if they think* it does them good, what harm can there be in my touching them?' It did not satisfy me all the while of the propriety of the proceeding. . . . It seemed to me to be largely connected with superstition, and if it began in superstition it would not end well, as I fear the result of his temperance movement too melancholy proved.

Like so many others, Simpson found Father Mathew's pragmatic approach to the superstitious awe that surrounded him unacceptable.

When he accepted the call to Portrush, Simpson's travels were by no means ended. The congregation was small and ill provided for. So in 1843-4 Simpson spent nine months on an extensive tour through the northern and southern United States, raising over £1,000 in order to build a church. He was initially reluctant to enter the slave states, though he ultimately raised money there more rapidly than in the north. While appalled to see Presbyterian clergy actually owning slaves, Simpson kept his opinions to himself, reasoning that arguing against slavery in the south was like attacking popery in Rome. Private approaches to wealthy Presbyterian merchants and businessmen, many of Ulster descent, together with fiery anti-popery sermons and lectures, were Simpson's main means of raising money; 'begging' was his own term for such work. A strong supporter of Edgar's famine relief and proselytising in Connacht, Simpson believed the famine to be God's judgment on popery and a heaven-sent opportunity for the conversion of Catholics. In 1848-9 he was in the United States again, this time sent with Dr Dill by the Home Mission to raise money for missions to Catholics. As an official church delegation Simpson and Dill felt themselves precluded from visiting slave states, but still within six months they had raised well over £5,000. It was during this visit that Simpson became acquainted with the agitation for prohibition, or the Maine Law as it came to be called. In 1850, soon after his return to Ulster, Simpson gave a series of lectures on the subject in Counties Londonderry, Antrim and Down, which were well covered by the *Belfast Newsletter* and the *Banner of Ulster*.

One of the most frequently expressed criticisms of the Maine Law was that it was tyrannical in restricting the individual's right to drink what he pleased: it was one thing for temperance advocates to try to convince people to abstain, but altogether another thing for governments to impose abstinence on all. As a liberal and utilitarian, Simpson argued that *salis populi suprema lex*, which he chose to translate as 'the greatest good of the greatest number is the object of government', and thus he felt government was justified in legislating to restrict individual freedom. Arguing from analogy, Simpson told his audiences:

> Gambling-houses, betting-houses are suppressed by law, because of the wreck of fortune, family, soul they induce. But what are their wrecks compared to those by strong drink? Sanitary regulations, factory regulations, quarantine laws are enforced, yet these interfere with private vested rights. Is not the sale of liquors interfered with already — places, time, hours regulated by law? Private individuals interfere to prevent licences, and the question comes to this — Shall the interference be so extended as to prohibit the sale and manufacture altogether? I say yea; what say you?

Simpson's lecture on the Maine Law appears to have been very popular, for he was still giving it in 1854. He was to undertake mission work in the south of Ireland and fund-raising in the United States again, but during most of the 1850s, except for visits to Scotland, he confined his evangelical enterprises to his home province. Tract distribution, open-air preaching, temperance lecturing and ultimately involvement with the 1859 revival gave plenty of scope for Simpson's evangelical bent within Ulster. (**314**, 96-7, 59, 71, 76, 214, 287-8, 306, 416-18)

As Simpson's career demonstrates, many Presbyterians who had joined Edgar's movement early in the 1830s remained committed to the anti-drink cause, though they were unable, mainly for sectarian reasons, to support Father Mathew. However, they provided a reservoir of support which the Presbyterian church was to begin to tap in the 1850s. Just as in the 1820s Edgar had been drawn into the temperance movement when attempting to improve sabbath observance, so sabbatarianism was to prove the catalyst for revival in the 1850s as well.

In 1841 at its second meeting the General Assembly of the newly reunited church set up a committee on sabbath observance. Both Edgar and Morgan were members. The Assembly was particularly concerned about the running of trains and the opening of post offices on the sabbath, two recent innovations. During the 1840s presbyteries were urged to take various steps to promote proper sabbath observance: in particular, to establish their own sabbath committees, to set aside one Sunday each year for a sermon on the subject and to organise petitions to the queen and parliament. When, in 1850, the collection and delivery of mail on Sunday was stopped the sabbath observance committee expressed itself highly satisfied. But if Sunday postal and rail operations were objectionable, how much more objectionable was the Sunday trade in liquor. In 1849 the General Assembly was presented with a memorial regarding the 'profanation of the sabbath by the sale of spirituous liquors on the Lord's Day'. This memorial was recommended to the 'serious attention' of the Assembly's sabbath observance committee. It obviously reflected a growing body of interest and concern over the temperance issue within the Presbyterian church. (**287**, I, 78, 139-40, 331, 493, 673, 778, 837-8)

During the course of the 1850 General Assembly held in Belfast some twenty ministers came together in the May Street schoolhouse to form a temperance association for Presbyterian clergy. The initiative for the establishment of this body came largely from ministers of the Belfast presbytery. By 1853 this presbytery had its own committee on intemperance, which was engaged in lobbying the town's magistrates against the granting of further publicans' licences. It was also active in seeking to discourage Presbyterian publicans from trading on Sunday. In 1854 the Belfast presbytery presented an overture to the Assembly requesting the establishment of a committee on temperance. The committee which resulted consisted of sixteen clergy and four elders. Edgar and Morgan were both members, while the convenor was William Johnston of Townshend Street church, who was also the convenor of the Belfast presbytery's committee. Other notable members were Thomas Sinclair, an elder of Morgan's church and a leading Belfast businessman, W. B. Kirkpatrick, minister of Mary's Abbey in Dublin, and S. J. Moore, a minister from Ballymena. Johnston, Kirkpatrick and Moore were each later to take a prominent role in the 1859 revival. The convenor of the Assembly's sabbath observance committee, J. Meneely, also joined the temperance committee, underlinging the close connection between the two. (**344**, III, 17; **310**, 62; **287**, II, 296-7)[1]

It is significant, however, that although Edgar sat on the Assembly's temperance committee, he was not a member of the clergy's temperance association. The reason for this apparent anomaly was that the association was staunchly teetotal, while the Assembly's committee sought to promote 'Christian temperance', which was Edgar's term for moderation. In a letter to the *Irish Presbyterian* in June 1853 Edgar lamented the 'evil day . . . when the friends of temperance became two bands', and he went on to call for a new beginning. But his use of the term 'Christian temperance', his attacks on the spirit trade and his call to the temperate not to lend respectability to the trade showed clearly that he had not basically changed his position. He had still not accepted teetotalism.[2] In July 1854 to coincide with the Assembly's debate on temperance there was a meeting in the town hall, presided over by the mayor and devoted specifically to Sunday closing. It was attended by Morgan and Edgar, as well as by Johnston and Meneely. Also present were a number of leading businessmen, like Thomas Sinclair, Thomas Lindsay, John Herdman, Robert Workman senior and Thomas McClure. The tenor of the meeting was distinctly moderate. A publican in the audience declared that he always kept his house closed on Sunday and claimed that most of those who traded in Belfast on a Sunday were disreputable spirit grocers. Morgan in his address argued that Sunday closing would 'protect' respectable publicans from the unfair competition offered by those who stayed open on the sabbath. Sabbatarian arguments were employed by most speakers, though William Johnston noted the prevalence of public houses in working-class areas of the town, most of which opened on Sunday, and he made a strong appeal for support to mill owners, 'whose property was committed to the honesty and character of workmen'. Generally during the 1850s the Assembly's committee contented itself with petitioning for Sunday closing,[3] and in fact it became so closely identified with sabbatarianism that it and the sabbath observance committee were formally united during the General Assembly of 1860. This concentration on Sunday closing had the effect of avoiding the whole controversy surrounding the issue of moderation *versus* teetotalism. (**287**, II, 536, 871)

The clerical temperance association was, on the other hand, far more wide-ranging and adventurous in its activities. In order to overcome the doctrinal objections to teetotalism that Edgar had made so much of, it adopted the principle of 'Christian expediency'. Its first rule stated: 'We believe it to be expedient to abstain from things in themselves lawful, when thereby we can more effectually promote our neighbours' welfare.'

Thus against Edgar's dictum of 'Christian temperance' these teetotal Presbyterians set up the principle of 'Christian expediency': that alcohol in itself was not unlawful for Christians, but that, given its widespread abuse, charity called for abstinence. The use of intoxicating liquors was so 'fearfully prevalent', being the chief cause of crime, poverty, disease and degradation and the major impediment to the spread of the gospel, that the 'circumstances of society' made abstinence expedient.[4]

If the moderationists were spurred on by the successful passage of a Sunday closing act for Scotland in 1853, then the teetotallers were greatly encouraged by the introduction of prohibition in the state of Maine in 1851 and by the establishment of the United Kingdom Alliance in 1853, aimed specifically at securing prohibition for Britain. In January 1854 an auxiliary branch of the U.K.A. was established in Belfast with William Johnston as secretary. But it was the example of Maine which was most influential, as indicated by the fact that press articles dealing with teetotalism, whether in Ireland, England or America, tended simply to be headed 'The Maine Law'. (**66** [1856], 414)[5] During the 1850s the teetotal and prohibitionist movement gathered considerable momentum in the United States. By the end of 1855 twelve states had joined Maine in passing prohibitionist laws, giving the impression to Irish observers that teetotalism was sweeping all before it in the north-eastern United States. We have seen, as in the case of Jonathan Simpson, that Ulster Presbyterians visiting the country were deeply impressed by the American movement. But visits by leading American, and also British, teetotallers did much to stimulate enthusiasm within Ulster. Thus in 1857 Neal Dow, the architect of the Maine law, and the Rev. William Reid, first president of the Scottish Temperance League, both lectured to enthusiastic audiences during visits to Belfast sponsored by local temperance groups. (**329**, 260)[6]

By December 1856, having been in existence for over six years, the clerical temperance association had 97 members out of some 550 ministers belonging to the Irish church, or about 18 per cent. This was not a particularly impressive performance, though growth was much more marked in the second half of the decade. By September 1857, for example, membership had jumped to 125. The association was particularly well represented in the presbyteries of Armagh, Belfast, Tyrone, Omagh, Letterkenny, Down and Dublin, where at least one-third of the ministers were members. Though the president was W. B. Kirkpatrick of Dublin and the secretary I. N. Harkness of Stewartstown, Belfast remained the stronghold of the organisation, with six of the nine-member executive being from there. In 1857 and 1858 the association was very active, sending out deputations to numerous churches and publishing its own temperance tracts. By July 1857 five tracts had appeared, written by Harkness, Morgan, Kirkpatrick, Johnston and the Rev. John Hall of Armagh. At the same time the association was distributing U.K.A. publications. Beginning in December 1856, meetings were held in Counties Down, Antrim, Tyrone and Londonderry in order to establish temperance societies and Bands of Hope in association with as many churches as possible. I. N. Harkness, John Hall, S. J. Moore, Jonathan Simpson, together with J. L Rentoul of Ballymoney, L. E. Berkeley of Faughanvale and John Maxwell of Brigh, were the principal speakers at these gatherings. Members of the association were requested to subscribe 2s 6d per annum towards the cost of this work (mainly printing and travelling expenses). The association welcomed the General Assembly's call for one Sunday each year to be given over to a sermon dealing with temperance, particularly as some presbyteries had decided to donate the proceeds to the association's work.[7]

This revival of temperance work within the Presbyterian church was very closely linked with the general religious revival under way in Ulster at the time — a revival which culminated in the *annus mirabilis* of 1859. Many of the leading temperance advocates, in particular the teetotallers, were to play an important role in the events of the revival. S. J. Moore of Ballymena, who was a member of both the General Assembly's temperance committee and the clerical association, was one of the first to proclaim the revival in mid-Antrim in 1858-9. In Belfast among the revival's strongest supporters were Hugh Hanna, William Johnston and Robert Knox, all members of the clerical temperance association. On the other hand, the moderationists in the persons of Edgar and Morgan, while generally supporting revivalism, showed considerable reservations. Temperance also became an integral part of the church's mission work; 'one of the handmaids of evangelism' was how the *Irish Presbyterian* described it in 1856. Thus, for example, the agents of the Belfast Town Mission, of which the ubiquitous Edgar and Morgan were secretaries, made the promotion of temperance one of their prime objectives. 'Until the people are weaned from the debasing habits of intemperance, little can be done to bring them even within the range of the means of grace,' said the *Irish Presbyterian*.[8] Temperance, which increasingly meant total abstinence, thus became an essential preliminary to evangelisation.

It was not, however, only Presbyterian clergy who were active in the 1850s in promoting temperance in conjunction with sabbatarianism, revivalism and evangelism. Devout Protestant laymen were also keen to play their part in the work of religious revival and social reform. The Belfast Total Abstinence Association, which had originally been established in 1836 to combat Edgar's moderationist stance, continued in existence as a largely lay organisation. But, like some temperance societies in the south, by 1850 it was describing itself as primarily a benevolent society. Clearly it also functioned as a social club, for its 'soiree' in June of 1850 was a lively affair, with music provided by the society's band and with dancing until the early hours of the morning.[9] But as the temperance cause revived during the 1850s the B.T.A.A. was spurred on to appoint its own agent and to begin the production of its own newspaper. Without doubt, however, the most influential layman involved in the temperance resurgence was Alexander Smith Mayne. Mayne had been closely associated with Edgar in the anti-spirits movement, being an elder of Edgar's church. In the 1830s he was a teacher at the Brown Street school and was active in the Sunday School Union, which aimed to foster religious instruction for children. He helped to produce Edgar's *Belfast Temperance Advocate*, as well as other religious periodicals, aimed at children in particular. Although Mayne subsequently broke with Edgar to become an ardent teetotaller (he seems, for instance, to have been responsible for inviting Hockings to Ireland in 1838), the two continued to work together in the Ulster Tract Society, of which, in the 1850s, Edgar was secretary and Mayne manager. The society's depository on the corner of Chichester Street and Donegall Square became a major centre for both the publishing and selling of religious literature. As proprietor of such an establishment, Mayne occupied an influential position within the Ulster Protestant community. (**66** [1856], 415)

In January 1856 Mayne published a letter in the *Belfast Newsletter* addressed to the friends of temperance in Ulster. Noting the poverty of the country and the vast sums of money spent each year on drink, he urged the need to 'revive the cause' of temperance in order to counter this glaring evil. In particular he suggested the setting up of a fund for the employment of a full-time temperance agent in the north of Ireland. He seems to have been well informed of the progress of the temperance movement in Scotland, for, while praising the Scottish Sunday closing act, he also drew attention to the work of temperance agents in that country. He thought it inconsistent for the Irish churches to be sending missionaries abroad, while not employing even one temperance agent at home. Mayne urged the friends of temperance in Ulster to subscribe one shilling a year to this cause and announced that Anne Jane Carlisle of Dublin, the originator of the Band of Hope children's temperance movement, had already promised at least £1 per annum. In this way Mayne said he hoped to revive temperance in Ulster and 'to prepare the way for getting a sabbath act or Maine Law'.[10] In referring to both acts, Mayne was directing his appeal to both moderationists and teetotallers.

In his reminiscences, published in 1879, Mayne described the next major development, the employment of an agent:

> Towards the end of the year 1856, an energetic but rather awkward and disconsolate-looking little man, having a good recommendation from Robert Charlton, Esq., of Bristol, appeared in Belfast, armed with a small carpet bag and concertina, and most anxious for an employment as a temperance, ragged school, reformatory, or Band of Hope agent. Messrs. Alex. Robb and Alex. Riddel, Joseph Burne, and others of the

Total Abstinence Association committee, were applied to by the strange traveller, but having no funds at their disposal, declined to make any engagement, telling him his only chance for an appointment would be at No. 1 Donegall Square [Mayne's tract depository], to which place he soon came. After a trial of his vocal powers in the Methodist chapel and Victoria Hall, an arrangement with Mr Revel (for such was the new agent's name) was made — the terms being 100 pounds per annum paid weekly; he to give strict attention to instructions, receive any subscriptions offered, and give weekly reports of progress. (**310**, 21)

Revel concentrated particularly on children and on the formation of Bands of Hope: in the press he was described as a Band of Hope lecturer. Given that Anne Jane Carlisle was involved in his employment and that Mayne had been active in teaching and Sunday school work, this slant towards children is understandable. In March 1857 Revel was lecturing in Ballymena with the co-operation of S. J. Moore. By April the *Irish Presbyterian* was reporting that he was having great success promoting temperance among the young in the north of Counties Antrim and Londonderry. By July he had addressed over 2,000 people in Counties Fermanagh and Donegal and administered nearly 400 pledges. In August further, large-scale meetings occurred in north and mid-Antrim. Like the itinerant teetotal lecturers of the 1830s, Revel sought to entertain as well as to instruct. Again Mayne provides the fullest account of his operations:

In Belfast, the agent selected a choir, or class, of the best voices, which he trained to assist at meetings, so that when he raised the note by voice or instrument on the platform, and gave out the first line, the boys sitting on one side of the hall could take it up; next the girls, on the other; then all-together. His speech, with numerous anecdotes, then followed, with announcement of next meeting, to which all were admitted by ticket — children free, others 1d. Essays by advanced boys and girls on the evils of smoking and drinking were sometimes requested. About fifty of these were written, and after adjudication, prizes of books were awarded at the next public meeting. Towards the end of the meeting young and old were exhorted and always invited to the platform, where names of new members were taken. . . . (**310**, 22)

The setting up of penny savings banks, one in connection with the Brown Street school, was another aspect of Revel's work. He also put together a cheap Band of Hope songbook, which proved extremely popular. Yet the financial basis of his work was obviously precarious, for by the end of 1857 there was a deficit of £11 in the funds.[11]

Another interesting feature of this lay temperance work in Ulster in the late 1850s was the employment of American blacks as both temperance and abolitionist lecturers. There was an active abolitionist movement in

Belfast, though it was by no means as significant as the movement among Quakers in Dublin. The General Assembly, while exchanging greetings each year with its American counterpart, had, however, made very clear its opposition to slavery, much to the annoyance of Presbyterians in the southern states. (**287**, I, 622-3) In June 1856 Joseph Woodhouse, a former slave sponsored by the B.T.A.A., lectured on temperance and on slavery in St Matthew's schoolroom, Shankill. Revel, who had visited New York in 1858, returned with Benjamin Benson, a former slave, described as a 'coloured evangelist, preacher and temperance agent', and in 1859 Benson was employed as the first itinerant agent of the Irish Temperance League, which had been established in Belfast in the previous year.[12]

The I.T.L. was set up in September 1858, with the object of suppressing drunkenness 'by moral suasion, legislative prohibition, and all other lawful means'. This sweeping statement of the methods to be employed indicated the organisation's desire to win support from as wide a spectrum of opinion as possible. The members, however, were to be teetotallers, and they were to contribute not less than 2s 6d per annum to the League's funds. The organisation envisaged itself as an umbrella group, following up the work of temperance agents by encouraging the establishment and growth of local societies. Such societies were urged to affiliate with the League; in return for a subscription of not less than £1 per annum they would receive visits from agents and temperance literature. It is interesting to note the effort made right from the outset to put the League on a well-organised and self-financing basis. Mayne and his friends were anxious not to repeat the mistakes of the 1830s and 1840s. The League's first president was William M. Scott, a chandler; he was followed in 1860 by John Coates, a solicitor; in 1862 by J. P. Corry, a timber merchant and shipowner, who was later a Conservative M.P. for Belfast (1874-85) and Co. Armagh (1886-91); and in 1866 by M. R. Dalway, Conservative M.P. for Carrickfergus (1868-80). The first secretary was Mayne, but he was replaced in 1860 by William Church, a printer, who worked for the *Belfast Newsletter* and had previously been secretary of the B.T.A.A. In 1866, in a discussion of its first years, the League's *Journal* admitted that it had had 'a small and, some would say, unpromising beginning', for 'difficulties were encountered at every step'. But, without doubt, the religious revival that swept Ulster in the 1850s, culminating in 1859, provided an important stimulus to the League and to temperance activities generally.[13]

Revivalism had been evident in Ulster since the early years of the decade. Thus Jonathan Simpson, with the encouragement of William Johnston, I. N. Harkness and John Hall, had begun outdoor preaching in the summer of 1853. It was, however, a hazardous enterprise, as Johnston's advice to Simpson revealed: 'Get into a central situation, against a wall, on a chair.... Do not go into any details, but the grand fundamentals, the A, B, C of religion. You will feel shy till your first prayer is up and over; then when once fairly into it you will like it.' In 1854 in Moville, Co. Donegal, Simpson found himself forced to preach in front of the revenue police barracks, the only place, according to the *Derry Sentinel*, 'where he could have secured safety from assault'. Even so, his audience of several hundred drowned out most of his sermon with a continuous round of 'Three cheers for Patrick's Day' and 'Three groans for the preacher'. As Simpson's experience indicates, the evangelical activities of the Presbyterians, particularly open-air preaching, heightened sectarian tension — the more so as many preachers found that the 'grand fundamentals... of religion' could not be conveyed without bitter attacks on the Catholic church. Catholic opposition to these activities reached a peak in Belfast in July and August 1857 with large-scale rioting in Sandy Row and the Pound, sparked off by attacks on preachers, in particular on Hugh Hanna, whose fiery sermons delivered from the Custom House steps had become a focus for Catholic hostility. (**58**, 108-9) Yet, despite fierce opposition, Simpson recorded that preaching was effective and that his own had led to a striking number of conversions. So when, in the autumn of 1858, he heard of many conversions occurring in the parish of Connor in mid-Antrim under the Rev. John H. Moore, Simpson decided to go and observe the situation for himself. He found vast attendances at services and a great eagerness for home visits. 'There was no excitement, no noise, the usual undemonstrative style of quiet, solemn Presbyterian service.' But Simpson was in no doubt that 'there was a great work of grace going on among that people'. The revival did not, however, remain quiet and undemonstrative for long. Simpson held his first large-scale prayer meeting, with the co-operation of the local rector, on a hill behind Portrush in June 1859. Some 2,000 people attended, though the town had a population of only about 900. Short addresses were delivered by the clergymen present and by several 'converts' from Ballymoney. Then 'a very remarkable scene took place':

> The first two 'stricken' ones were one a Presbyterian and the other an Episcopalian, as if God would honour the first union prayer meeting. Shortly several others became prostrated, varying from the ages of nine to about seventy, and till midnight the manse presented a remarkable scene, with souls weeping under a sense of sin, or rejoicing in an accepted saviour. A solemn awe crept over the entire populace, and many a house heard 'the voice of rejoicing and salvation' (Ps. cxviii, 15). ... The churches were crowded all summer. The Episcopal church has been enlarged, and the Presbyterian would require to be double its present capacity to contain the anxious applicants for accommodation. (**314**, 388, 397, 404-11, 436, 438-9)

The revival had begun in mid-Antrim late in 1858, as Simpson had noted, with its main centres being Kells, Connor, Ahoghill and Ballymena. By May and June 1859 it had spread north to Ballymoney, Portrush and

Ballycastle, east to Larne, Carrickfergus and Belfast, and into Co. Down. In June it was brought to Derry by revivalists from Ballymena, while later in the month and in July it appeared in Tyrone and Armagh. Fermanagh, with its substantial Episcopalian population, was little affected. Many contemporary accounts of the revival commented particularly on the decline in drinking and drunkenness which seemed to accompany it. Hugh Hanna reported from Belfast in September 1859: 'You rarely see a drunken man now; brawling and disorder are consequently rare; and our police hardly know what to do with themselves.' Of the revival in Derry, Rev. Richard Smyth wrote: 'Drunkards have become sober...some publicans have given up their unsanctified calling...our churches are crowded with eager worshippers.' (**273**, 46-53; **340**, 150) The Rev. William Gibson in his important study, *The Year of Grace*, published in 1860, quoted numerous reports attesting to the improvement in public morals. The Rev. Archibald Robinson of Broughshane, Co. Antrim, wrote in April 1860, for instance:

> There is a marked improvement in the public morals of the community. Men are ashamed of doings that formerly were considered things of course. Two public houses have been obliged to close. The owners of others have assured me their trade is gone, and two more intimated their intention not to renew the licence....Sabbath desecration, profane swearing, drunkenness, uncleanness, unseemly strife, and such like sins, are much abated and decreased. (**159**, 40)

Benjamin Scott, in another substantial study published in 1860, quoted the evidence of more than sixty witnesses, almost all of whom mentioned decreased drinking and drunkenness as one of the most obvious results of the revival. Newspapers at the time were struck by the sobriety evident at fairs and markets, traditionally occasions for heavy drinking. The *Londonderry Standard* reported in July 1859 that in Limavady on market days people 'transact business without lying and cursing [and] at an early hour they return to their homes in sobriety'. Similarly, the *Coleraine Chronicle* in December observed that, whereas fair-days in Larne had long been 'notorious for the scenes of drunkenness and turbulence...a correspondent informs us that on the last fair-day he saw only three drunken persons, and that long before the evening the great bulk of those who had been present had wended their way homeward'. (**304**, 400)

But, even at the time, there were those who challenged this rosy picture. The *Northern Whig*, which had supported the liberal wing of Presbyterianism in the 1820s and 1830s, was not at all sympathetic to the revival. It pointed out, for example, that arrests for drunkenness in Belfast in 1859 were more than 20 per cent higher than in the previous year. The Rev. Richard Oulton of Armagh, a Church of Ireland critic of the revival, in noting these figures, attacked revivalists for 'the most absurd extravagances and the most melancholy delusions' in claiming that 'drunkenness and vice had literally disappeared from some localities'. But the most ferocious attack on the revival and its supporters, Gibson in particular, came from the pen of another Presbyterian minister. This was the Rev. Isaac Nelson, later Home Rule M.P. for Co. Mayo (1880-85), who scorned revivalists and in fact Evangelicals in general. As the title of his book, *The Year of Delusion*, published in 1861, implied, Nelson thought the whole revival was a dangerous delusion, which actually encouraged rather than diminished immorality. As for the claim that the revival had swept away drunkenness, Nelson drew a damning analogy with Father Mathew's crusade:

> Priest Mathew, by the force of superstition over an ignorant people, did more than any other temperance reformer Ireland ever produced; and his work ended where it began, because it was not the true remedy. (**278**, 97, 143; **257**, 182)

Debate raged between supporters and opponents of the revival, particularly over the arrest statistics for drunkenness. According to Gibson, 'No person has, during the year in question, been before the police court of Belfast, on a charge of drunkenness, who has ever been brought under religious influences.' It was well known, he continued, that the 'majority of the "drunken" cases are persons who make no profession of any form of Protestantism.... The immense majority of them are nominally Roman Catholics.' Hugh Hanna also laid the responsibility for the increase in Belfast drunkenness at the door of the town's Catholic population. Benjamin Scott, during his investigation of the revival, personally visited prisons in Belfast to check on the religious affiliations of their inmates. He claimed that the Catholic third of Belfast's population supplied half of the committals in normal times, but nearly all of them since the revival. This debate rumbled on into 1861, with even the London *Times*, which was highly sceptical of the claims of revivalists, taking a stance on the issue. (**159**, 253-4; **340**, 190; **305**, 40)

Richard Oulton, however, had probably put his finger on the key to the question when he wrote in his 1859 pamphlet: 'The statistics of more flagrant crime have long shown a decrease in Ulster and other parts of the country to a very considerable extent. It is not easy to see why such a decrease should therefore, all at once, be ascribed to the revival.' There was a significant decline in convictions in Ulster in 1859, but these had been falling since at least 1855. Arrests for drunkenness in Belfast may have actually increased in 1859, but generally drunkenness was on the decline, and Oulton rightly attributed this to the dramatic increase in spirit duty that had taken place during the previous ten years. Anxious to equalise Irish and British duties and convinced that the famine had largely destroyed the illicit industry, the government raised the level of duty on seven occasions during the decade, so that from 2s 8d in 1850 it had reached

10s by 1860, where it remained for the next thirty years. As a result, spirit consumption in Ireland plummeted: gallons charged for home consumption fell from 8.1 million in 1855 to 6.8 million in 1857 to 5.4 million in 1859 and were down to 3.8 million in 1863, after which a modest recovery began. (**278**, 97; **273**, 179; **343**, 337) Nor apparently did the illicit distiller step in to fill the gap, for there was no dramatic increase in detections; if anything, they were tending to fall in the mid-1850s. In 1870 the Revenue Commissioners in their thirteenth report made some interesting comments on what had happened in the 1850s compared with what had occurred in the early 1840s when similar efforts had been made to raise the level of duty. In the former decade they thought that various causes had

> combined to give a fair chance to the experiment of imposing an additional duty, unsuccessfully attempted in the year 1842. The price of grain was high — the people improved in condition and less lawless in character, — communications with markets for the farmers' produce opened or improved, — and large numbers of those, who used to live chiefly by smuggling, removed either by the calamities which had swept off such a vast portion of the population, or by their voluntary emigration. But, whatever may be the explanation of the difference between the results of the similar measures of 1842 and 1853, the fact was established, that Ireland could bear a much higher duty on spirits than that which was in existence before 1853.... (**34**, 14)

So the revival of 1859 happened to occur at a time when spirit consumption, always heaviest in Ulster, was in marked decline, partly owing to massive increases in duty and partly to the decimation of illicit distilling by the famine. The revival may have contributed to this trend, but it certainly did not cause it.

If the revival was not largely responsible for the decrease in drunkenness evident in the late 1850s and early 1860s, revivalism generally did play a major role in the resurgence of the temperance movement under way at the same time. One of the most interesting witnesses to the relationship between temperance and revivalism is Dr John Edgar. He was by no means a wholehearted supporter of the revival, being deterred, like many, by the 'outbursts of animal feeling' which accompanied it. He felt that its effects had been exaggerated by its proponents, who often in fact had only encouraged 'heresy, folly or immorality' among 'talkative youths' and 'poor females'. But the boost it had given to the temperance movement he could not gainsay. He saw temperance both as a 'forerunner and follower' of the revival, arguing that temperance activities among the clergy had prepared the way for religious revival, while the revival in turn had stimulated temperance activity. There is doubtless much truth in this claim. (**148**, 1, 3, 11)

Drunkards 'saved' during the revival toured the province in the following years preaching against the evils of drink. And in fact Hugh Hanna considered that, as a result of the revival, temperance societies had lost their *raison d'être*:

> Our temperance societies were numerous and active, but they made small progress in reclaiming the masses. But the gospel has annihilated the temperance societies — not all, but many of them. A higher argument and influence than they can wield, has regenerated the masses. (**273**, 214; **340**, 150)

But Hanna's dismissal of temperance societies was a trifle premature: during 1859 and in the years immediately following they were, if anything, more rather than less active. The temperance committee's report to the General Assembly in 1859 was 'of an encouraging character'. The B.T.A.A. at its annual general meeting in July 1859 noted a large increase in members since the previous meeting. As for the I.T.L., Benjamin Benson, its agent, had taken full advantage of the revival to extend the organisation's work. At its first annual meeting in January 1860 he reported that in the previous year he had 'formed 18 auxiliaries, lectured in 40 towns and villages, held 224 public meetings, visited 1,400 families, distributed 7,000 tracts, and enrolled 5,400 members'. (**310**, 27)[14]

By the early 1860s the I.T.L. had won the support of a number of notable survivors of the anti-spirits movement of the 1830s, though Edgar, who died in 1866, was never active in its cause. However, James Morgan of Fisherwick Place church and Thomas Houston of Knockbracken were among its vice-presidents, as was James Haughton of Dublin. These three, together with William Urwick of York Street chapel in Dublin, had also volunteered their services as lecturers. An examination of the League's committee in 1863 shows that it was dominated by Belfast Presbyterian clergy, or at least that they were the largest single group represented. Of the thirty-five vice-presidents, eighteen were clerics; and of these, twelve were Presbyterian, including the influential Dr Hanna. J. L. Rentoul of Ballymoney, convenor of the General Assembly's temperance and sabbath observance committee, while not a vice-president, was listed as a voluntary lecturer. The lay vice-presidents seem also to have been mainly Presbyterians, though with a significant number of Methodists. Most were tradesmen and businessmen rather than professionals: shopkeepers and mill owners being strongly represented. But all the vice-presidents, with the exception of Haughton, were northerners, and sixteen, plus the three-member executive, were residents of Belfast. So in the early years the I.T.L. very much represented the views of the Belfast Presbyterian community, if not of the Belfast presbytery.[15]

In September 1863 the I.T.L. *Journal* League was 'lengthening its cords certainly during the 1860s the organisation grew steadily. In that year it already had a hundred affiliated societies.[16] Its own affiliation in the previous year with the United Kingdom Alliance was an important step in its development. The financial support which it thereby obtained enabled the League in 1863 to establish its own journal, to employ another agent, John Pyper, and to open central offices in Donegall Street. William Church, the League's secretary, had already produced twelve issues of a periodical, called the *Irish Temperance Standard,* in 1861. Its success encouraged the League to begin its own journal. This was planned for 1862, but in the event the first issue did not appear until February 1863. Until it ceased publication in 1903 the *Irish Temperance League Journal* was to provide an unequalled record of the activities of the Irish temperance movement. The League's finances were also beginning to appear decidedly healthy in the early 1860s: from a mere £101 in 1859, revenue had reached £309 by 1863 and £500 by 1864. Given that each agent alone cost £100 per annum, the League obviously needed a substantial income to finance its various activities. (**85**, I, 432, II, 27, 41)[17]

In return for the Alliance's support the League vigorously took up the causes of prohibition, the permissive bill and Sunday closing, all of which were being agitated for in England in 1863-4. Somes's Sunday closing bill was before parliament in 1863, while Sir Wilfrid Lawson had introduced his first permissive bill in 1864. The permissive bill gave ratepayers the right to ban the drink trade in their district if a two-thirds majority of them so desired it. It marked a retreat from the Maine Law, being local and permissive, where the latter was national and imperative. But the leaders of the U.K.A. had concluded that it was the most that could be won at Westminster, where the majority of M.P.s were hostile to prohibition. (**136**, 17-18) The I.T.L.'s constitution had stated its object to be the suppression of drunkenness, and, as we have seen, proposed various methods to achieve this end, including moral suasion and legislative coercion. But, in its connection with the U.K.A., the League was demonstrating a preference for the second agency, as prohibition was the Alliance's stated objective. Admittedly the permissive bill was a compromise, but for both the Alliance and the League national prohibition remained the real aim.

In 1860 the League had amalgamated with the Band of Hope Union, which had been established in Belfast in 1856 to organise children's temperance societies, and this name was added to the League's title. In 1862 the title was further lengthened with the addition of Permissive Bill Association, to signify the League's commitment to Lawson's cause. In March 1863 the *Journal* sought to clarify the League's methods by saying that 'It stops not at merely "moral suasion", but goes forward to seek for legal prohibition.' It 'would seek not only to make men sober, by inducing them to become total abstainers, [but] keep them from falling into the evil habit of partaking of strong drinks, by removing out of their way the tempting whiskey shops'. The League thus committed itself to both total abstinence and prohibition: the former to be achieved through the promotion of Bands of Hope and adult teetotal societies, and the latter through the agency of a permissive bill passed by parliament.[18]

As well as providing the League with a subsidy, which amounted to £200 per annum by the early 1870s, the U.K.A. also supplied visiting lecturers and delegations for League meetings. In the early part of 1863, for example, Dr F. R. Lees, one of the Alliance's leading spokesmen, toured Ireland to promote the permissive bill. But John Pyper, one of the League's own agents, was also extremely active. A teacher before he joined the League, Pyper was later to become a Congregationalist minister, but even then he remained deeply involved in the temperance movement, being an outspoken opponent of the use of alcoholic communion wine. His life as a temperance agent was obviously a hectic one, as his itinerary for July and August 1863, which is by no means untypical, illustrates:

July		August	
1	Strabane, Co. Tyrone	3	Pomeroy, Co. Tyrone
3	Omagh	4-7	Dungannon
7-10	Belfast, Co. Antrim	10	Bangor, Co. Down
15	Caledon, Co. Tyrone	11	Donaghadee
16	Glennan	12	Newtownards
24	Hyde Park	13	Comber
27	Coalisland	14	Killinchy
28	Stewartstown	17	Ballyclare, Co. Antrim
29	Lurgan, Co. Armagh	18	Glenarm
30	Moira, Co. Down	19-21	Ballycastle
31	Magheralin	24-26	Ballymena
		27	Coleraine, Co. Londonderry
		28	Portrush, Co. Antrim[19]

This itinerary also reveals in passing the areas in which the League had greatest support. In each town or village Pyper attended at least one meeting of the local temperance society and delivered a lecture. Privately he consulted with local leaders over strategy, supplied them with literature and examined their financial status. Typical of such meetings was one held at Caledon, Co. Tyrone, on the evening of Wednesday 15 July. To quote the report which appeared in the *Journal*:

> A meeting of the Caledon Temperance Society was held in the town hall. There was a numerous attendance, and the chair was occupied by the Rev. W. B. Armstrong. A logical and conclusive lecture having been delivered by Mr Pyper, Mr Joseph Worthington ably moved a resolution in favour of the permissive bill. The motion was seconded by Mr Robert Lindsay, and carried unanimously.[20]

Resolutions passed at these meetings could be sent to local M.P.s in order to convince them that there was a widespread popular demand for temperance legislation.

At the annual meeting of the League in April 1863 Pyper said that 'he did not see why they should not occupy a similar position in this country to that which the great Alliance did in England'. The League aimed to be an umbrella organisation, co-ordinating and assisting the work of local temperance societies, and, with the support of the popular movement thus created, lobbying parliament for prohibitive legislation. The so-called national conference on temperance, which followed the 1863 annual meeting, however, clearly revealed the sectional nature of the League. Delegates from twenty-four cities and towns attended, as well as a delegation from the Scottish Temperance League. But, with the exception of three delegates from Dublin, among them James Haughton, all the places represented were in the north of Ireland, most being in Counties Antrim, Down, Londonderry, east Tyrone and north Armagh. Yet, as Pyper had indicated, the League did aspire to be a national body. In March, therefore, before the Belfast meeting, Pyper had accompanied Dr Lees to Dublin, and, while Lees gave public lectures, Pyper addressed the city's main temperance societies, including the Dublin Total Abstinence Society' Dr Urwick's York Street group, and special meetings called by the Presbyterians and Quakers. He was anxious to extend the League's work to Dublin and felt that the temperance cause in the city needed to be revitalised. Finally a meeting, sponsored by the Dublin branch of the U.K.A., which had been established in 1858, was held. This meeting resolved that a branch of the I.T.L. should be established in Dublin and that it should supercede the Alliance branch. But it was not until the appointment of T. W. Russell in September 1864 as the I.T.L. agent for the south of Ireland, with his headquarters in Dublin, that this branch really became active.[21]

Perhaps the most energetic campaigner for temperance legislation in Ireland in the latter part of the century, Russell was born in 1841 at Cupar in Fife, the son of a stonemason. He came to Ulster in 1860 and was employed for nearly five years as a clerk in Brown's soap factory at Donaghmore near Dungannon, Co. Tyrone. There he began a long friendship with his fellow Sunday school teacher, Thomas A. Dickson, who held various seats as a Liberal M.P. between 1874 and 1892. Their friendship came to an abrupt end, however, when Russell, standing as a Liberal Unionist, narrowly defeated Dickson in Tyrone South in a bitter election contest in 1892. Russell had first been elected in Tyrone in 1886, and he was to sit continuously for the county, with one brief interruption, until 1918. But before his long political career he had spent over twenty years in the thick of temperance politics. His temperance career began in 1863 when, at the age of twenty-two, he was elected secretary of the Dungannon Temperance Society. In August of that year Pyper lectured to the society, and in his report he commended its 'energetic' young secretary. When therefore, late in 1864, it was decided to appoint a permanent agent in Dublin to reorganise the movement in the south, young Russell was the League's choice for the job. His task was 'to convert opponents into followers' and 'to instruct the illiterate without offending the taste of the well-informed'. In return for undertaking this formidable task he was to receive a 'large and, no doubt, progressive salary'. In examining the long lists of speeches given, meetings attended and articles written by Russell in subsequent years, one cannot doubt that he well earned his 'large' salary. (**300**, 56-7; **236**, II, 158-9; **87,** 263-4; **170,** 241).[22]

He was a man of great energy and determination, with, during the early years at least, an unwavering commitment to the cause of temperance. Soon after his appointment to Dublin he wrote an interesting article for the I.T.L. *Journal* entitled 'A False Stereoscope', which began:

> Although not belonging to, the writer of this paper is daily reminded of, the existence of a class, who in the sincerity of their hearts believe that the world is getting worse — who do not doubt that just as God was tempted of old by the wickedness of man to visit the world in judgment — so again the wrath of the Most High will be made manifest in these latter days.

Russell was decidedly not of this pessimistic frame of mind: 'Ascend the hilly crags of the past,' he advised, 'see what the Lord hath done, and return from the survey with renewed strength and invincible determination.' Russell had no time whatever for those who sighed after the 'simple manners and rude life' of the past. He did not see the path of mankind as leading inevitably downwards, away from the golden age — quite the contrary. Russell had an unshakable faith in progress, in the concept that human affairs were gradually evolving out of suffering and barbarism towards rationality and prosperity. But in Russell's view there was still 'one blot upon the present, a stain that should have been washed away long, long since had the church of Christ done its duty'. This blot was, of course, the consumption of alcohol. Although drunkenness was no longer as fashionable as it had been in the eighteenth century, drinking was still exceedingly popular. But, typically, Russell refused to be pessimistic about this state of affairs, and in fact he found much that was encouraging. Who, he asked, twenty years ago would have dreamed that temperance would be preached on the floor of the House of Commons? Who would have imagined that it would create a literature of its own, and that from the halls of science, from the bench and the bar men would flock to do battle on its behalf? Certainly organisations like the U.K.A. and the I.T.L., with their professional agents, paid parliamentary lobbyists, newspapers and journals and elaborate administrative systems, were a world away from the chaos and hysteria of Father Mathew's crusade.

Russell was no believer in mass temperance of the sort that Father Mathew had inspired. He envisaged the temperance campaign being prosecuted 'in many a town and in many a village' by 'a few earnest spirits... toiling amid much that is discouraging'. Russell's concept of the temperance movement was basically elitist rather than democratic, perhaps closer to the views of the early 1830s than of the 1840s. He made this perfectly clear in the second instalment of 'A False Stereoscope' in March 1865:

> I speak the truth when I say that nearly all the good that is done in the world is the work of a few. The great mass stand aloof. Should they catch the echo of a cheer they will give a brave hurrah, but on some pair of shoulders must fall the heat and burden of the day.

Russell clearly saw himself as having such a pair of shoulders, and indeed he was to carry much of the burden of the Irish temperance movement in the 1870s. And what was the ultimate goal of this great labour? Although he may have differed from Father Mathew with regard to tactics, Russell too was inspired by a utopian dream. He, like his contemporary disciples of progress, saw utopia in terms of a golden age of materialism here on earth. Through all ages there was an 'increasing purpose', he wrote, and that was the widening of the thoughts of man:

> As they widen, so will the time draw nigh when the war-drum shall cease to throb, when the battle-flag shall be furled 'in the parliament of man the federation of the world', and old king alcohol shall be driven from the throne where he has so long reigned and ruled at will.

Then would the 'weary workers' rest and 'forget the sorrows of a long night in the joy of a glorious morning'. Despite his rather turgid prose, there is no doubt that Russell was genuinely inspired by this vision of a better world, for he vigorously exerted his considerable talents in pursuit of it.[23]

In Russell's scheme of temperance reformation, parliament was to be the vital agency of change. It was through parliament that the temperance elite would ensure the triumph of their ideas at the national level. In 1866, writing with his fellow-editor J. A. Mowatt, an insurance agent, in the *Irish Temperance Star*, Russell put forward his views on the licensing laws and on the general question of legislative reform. If the liquor trade was good, they wrote, there was no reason why any and every man should not be able to engage in it. The very fact that parliament found it necessary to restrict the trade attested to its evils. Over 400 licensing acts had been passed since the reign of Queen Elizabeth, all with the avowed object of keeping the liquor traffic within bounds and of lessening if possible its injurious effects upon society. The failure of these measures was amply illustrated in police returns and crime statistics. Mowatt and Russell's solution to this dilemma was both extreme and simple:

If the trade be a useful and beneficial one, let it be wholly free; if it be an injurious trade, producing great evils and no counteracting good, let it be, not licensed, but prohibited.

Free trade and prohibition were the only viable alternatives; the middle ground of restrictive licensing was swept aside as a demonstrable failure. Free trade in liquor was so unthinkable that Mowatt and Russell did not take the time even to argue against it. For them prohibition was the simple answer to all the problems of liquor licensing; it would, in effect, legislatively abolish the problem. They admitted that prohibition was claimed to be unworkable in practice, but again their response to this objection was direct and simple, to the point of naivety in fact: 'Our ... laws against theft, burglaries, and even murder are violated. But that is not the fault of the law.' Addressing the I.T.L. in March 1865, Russell had outlined three main areas of activity for the temperance movement. The first was 'to reclaim the lost' — in other words, to convince drunkards to take the total abstinence pledge; the second was 'to win the young', to indoctrinate them as children so that they would never even start to drink; and the third, and main, area of activity was legislative prohibition. 'Sweep away not only the god they worship, but the altar at which so many bow with more than an eastern devotion,' advised Russell. Attempts to 'patch up some "amended" licensing law' would no doubt continue, but Russell was convinced that 'licensing must ultimately be abolished, and the entire liquor traffic ... be treated only as a public nuisance'.[24]

In a second article on licensing laws in the November 1866 issue of the *Star* Mowatt and Russell sought to explain why the drink trade could not 'be left to the stern laws of demand and supply' as other trades were. The temperance movement generally was at pains to dissociate drink from legitimate business and trade and to reassure its middle-class supporters that the attack on the drink industry could in no way be construed as part of a general assault on free-enterprise principles. Noting the addictive properties of alcohol, Mowatt and Russell argued that the supply of drink created the demand for it, thus 'reversing all the ordinary laws of trade and commerce which regulate all other businesses'. And if the demand were allowed to be satisfied without restraint, 'it would wholly ruin the people of these kingdoms'. To Russell, then, the drink trade was a positive public nuisance, and this justified the use of the most extreme legislative measures against it. Doctrines upholding individual rights or freedom of trade were totally inappropriate in such circumstances. As 'private rights must ever yield to social rights' and 'the state has a perfect right, in the interests of society at large, to restrict individual liberty', so practices harmful to the individual or the community were legislated against. Murder and suicide were forbidden, and increasingly there were laws against industrial nuisances, like smoke and foul smells. As Jonathan Simpson had argued fifteen years earlier, on the basis of consistency alone alcohol should be banned. Or, as Mowatt and Russell put it,

> We *prohibit* the smoke and the smell from the bakery, chandlery, and vitriol works, while we *license* the public house to deal out ruin and death. We cannot see upon what principle of law or equity this class of distinction is made.[25]

Russell, however, could not ignore the realities of the political situation at Westminster. And so, though his 1866 articles on licensing argued strongly for a 'full and perfect' prohibition as the only ultimate solution, in the short term he, like the rest of the movement, was forced to fall back on the expedient of local option or the permissive bill. Certainly a number of American states had passed prohibition laws with the most beneficial results, but whether 'we can in these lands carry through a parliament of brewers and distillers and landlords a bill to prohibit the sale of drinks, is questionable'. But with 'the growing feeling which exists against the present licensing system', Russell felt that there was a chance of carrying a permissive prohibitory liquor bill. Mowatt and Russell lauded the situation in the village of Bessbrook, Co. Armagh, where John Grubb Richardson, a Quaker mill owner, had banned public houses.(**49**). Why, they asked, should not the inhabitants of every village and town be able to do for themselves what had been done at Bessbrook? In this they overlooked the rather important fact that prohibition had been imposed on Bessbrook from above by the all-powerful proprietor; it had not been voted for from below by his employees. The tactical change from national prohibition to local option in fact led to a fundamental inconsistency in Russell's thinking. We have seen that his view of the temperance movement was basically elitist, in that he thought the most important activity, lobbying parliament for repressive legislation, should be conducted by a small and dedicated band of workers. But in being forced to support Lawson's permissive bill, he and the movement generally had to resort to campaigning for mass support. Russell himself knew that the public were not 'seriously alive to the evils which flow from the traffic' and that the 'entire country would not at once put such a permissive act in force'. But, ever the optimist, he chose not to regard this as an argument against local option. Districts might not act immediately against the drink trade, but eventually some 'startling homicide, or frightful scene' produced by drink would convince them, and then the unheeded permissive act would be 'taken down, dusted, and enforced against the fearful public house nuisance'. For a basically practical man, T. W. Russell was rather prone to wishful thinking, on the temperance issue at least.[26]

In January 1865, on Russell's initiative, the I.T.L. opened offices in Dublin at the Metropolitan Hall in Molesworth Street; like the offices in Belfast, these were made available, rent free, for the use of other temperance societies. This was, of course, intended to stimulate temperance activity in the capital. Thus the Dublin Temperance Tract and Visiting Association, established in July 1864, was able to commence operations in January 1865, using the League's offices. Home visiting and the distribution of tracts played a significant role in mission and temperance work in Ulster, and the new association sought to promote similar activities in Dublin. In its 1866 report it was able to announce that it had distributed over 10,000 English and Scottish temperance tracts and had visited some 5,500 persons, though, as regards pledges, the result was a disappointing 112. Five thousand copies of a tract entitled *Water*, written by the association's president, George Checketts, had been published, and the report looked forward to the creation of an indigenous temperance literature. In November 1865 the association had also begun the publication of a monthly journal, the *Irish Temperance Star*, with T. W. Russell and J. A. Mowatt as editors. There had been plans late in 1865 to publish the I.T.L. *Journal* in Dublin, but when this had proved impractical, Russell and the Tract Association got together to produce a periodical themselves. Yet the position of the *Star* remained slightly confusing. 'Although the *Star* has never appeared as the recognised organ of the southern branch of the League,' wrote Russell late in 1866, 'it will be easily understood from the position of the publisher and the editor that it really acts as such.' From the beginning of 1867, however, the *Star* did become the official organ of the southern branch of the League.

Russell involved himself in the activities of a number of Dublin temperance groups. He seems in fact to have been behind the formation of the Ladies' Metropolitan Temperance Union, which first met in the League's offices early in 1866. One of its honorary secretaries was Mrs Russell, formerly Harriet Agnew, whom Russell had married in the previous year. Generally the committee seems to have been made up of the wives and daughters of temperance activists: Mrs Mowatt and Miss Urwick, for example. On the whole, Irish women did not play an active independent role in the temperance movement, as was to be the case in the United States. Such female temperance organisations as existed in Ireland were usually firmly under male control. Russell also worked closely with the capital's Quaker and Presbyterian communities. Temperance meetings were held regularly at the Friends' Institute and at Mary's Abbey Presbyterian church. For the young the Presbyterians had organised a Band of Hope and a young men's association, the latter of which Russell addressed on a number of occasions. James Haughton was still active in the Dublin Total Abstinence Society, and the committee in the persons of Richard Allen, Adam Woods, Henry and J. R. Wigham was Quaker-dominated. The D.T.A.S. was connected with the Tract Association, for George Checketts was president of both. Haughton, with his friend Dr John Spratt, also ran a temperance hall in Cuffe Lane, near Spratt's Carmelite church in Aungier Street, where they held weekly meetings and aimed to attract working-class audiences. Russell gave lectures for them as well, and the League printed 5,000 copies of Spratt's pamphlet entitled *Appeal to the People on the Horrid Crime of Drunkenness* for distribution in Dublin. In his work Russell received some assistance from Benjamin Benson, the former slave and the League's first agent, who by 1865 was proprietor of the Prince Leopold Temperance Hotel in Lower Abbey Street.[27]

But Russell's work was by no means restricted to Dublin: he was officially the League's agent for the south of Ireland. In the year 1866 he addressed 152 meetings and formed a chain of societies throughout the south and west. In his 1865-6 report to the League, Russell noted that he 'had to travel very considerable distances, and that by methods not familiar to such a province as Ulster'. However, he felt that the extension of the railways into even the remotest parts was making travel easier and less expensive. During 1865 and 1866 Russell had 'opened up eighteen of the twenty-three counties committed to our care'; Galway, Kilkenny, Kerry, Carlow and Meath being those still without temperance societies affiliated with the I.T.L. Visits from leaders of the movement in Britain and America were also eagerly sought as a means of gaining publicity and sparking enthusiasm. James Raper, the United Kingdom Alliance's parliamentary agent, attended a conference on the permissive bill held in the Mansion House in December 1865, while during a ten-day period early in March 1866 Edward Grubb, also from the U.K.A., accompanied Russell on a trip from Limerick to Dungannon, giving lectures on the bill every evening. In June Neal Dow from Maine spoke before a large audience in the Friends' Institute, telling them that the American successes had been largely due to the support of the clergy and that if ministers of religion united to denounce drink 'the evils of the grog-shops . . . could be removed in almost one day'. Russell also joined the battle being waged by the existing temperance groups to diminish the number of liquor licences issued for Dublin. With Haughton, Spratt, Mowatt, Urwick, Henry Wigham and J. R. Wigham, he formed deputations to lobby the Recorder on the issue.[28] In November 1866 the Irish Sunday Closing Association was formed in Dublin to agitate for an Irish Sunday closing bill, and in January 1869 the Irish Permissive Bill Association also appeared. In both Russell was to be a driving force. That Dublin became the focus for much of the parliamentary agitation of the 1870s, despite the strength of the I.T.L. in the north, must in fact be largely attributed to the work of T. W. Russell in the city from 1864.

In Cork city too during the 1860s there was something of a revival in temperance acitivity. According to the I.T.L. *Journal*, in 1863 the movement in the city had been 'in rather a languishing state for some time'. In October 1859 and March 1860 J. B. Gough, an American reformed drunkard who had become a colourful and very effective temperance lecturer, addressed large audiences in Cork, and as a result of his visits, the

County and City of Cork Temperance Society was formed. Gough, however, was an opponent of prohibition and had clashed bitterly with the United Kingdom Alliance, successfully suing Dr Lees in 1858 when the latter questioned the sincerity of Gough's commitment to teetotalism. Gough, who worked for the London-based National Temperance League, believed in moral suasion and piecemeal legislation, such as licensing reform and Sunday closing. Given the I.T.L.'s links with the Alliance and its support for prohibition, its dismissal of Gough's endeavours is understandable. Late in 1862 Benjamin Benson had spent some weeks conducting meetings on the League's behalf in both the city and county.[29] But it was the erection of a statue of Father Mathew in Patrick Street in 1864 that spurred temperance advocates to greater efforts. (**173**, 212-14)

The statue, made by J. H. Foley, the leading Irish sculptor of the period, cost nearly £1,000. Its erection was the result of a campaign conducted in the *Cork Examiner* by its proprietor, J. F. Maguire, whose biography of Father Mathew had been published in 1863. Maguire was mayor of the city in 1864 — one of four occasions on which he filled the office — and Liberal M.P. for Dungarvan (1852-65) and then Cork city from 1865 until his death in 1872. However, the I.T.L. remained sceptical of both Maguire and the statue. In Dublin the *Star* remarked:

> It is sadly true, indeed — as true as that bronze [*sic*] statue, whilst it speaks eloquently, still fails to shed around the genial influence of him whose memory it is designed to perpetuate — that the old spirit is dead.

Generally the League looked upon Father Mathew as misguided, and Maguire's failure to support the permissive bill in parliament damned him in the eyes of the prohibitionists. But in Cork, where the Rev. Nicholas Dunscombe was still active and where Catholic clergy still took an interest in the temperance cause, the extreme measures advocated by northern Presbyterians were frowned upon. As Gough's visits indicate, moral suasion was still the preferred approach. This attitude was also reflected in the establishment in June 1865 of the Cork and South of Ireland Temperance League, which set itself the primary task of introducing alternative forms of refreshment and recreation.

Prohibitionists, with their aim of abolishing the drink trade legislatively, saw little need for seeking to entice the working class away from the public houses. But to more moderate temperance advocates, temperance hotels and coffee palaces were important weapons in the battle against the trade's monopoly of working-class recreation. And, as it became clear in the 1860s that parliament was not about to introduce prohibition, even prohibitionists began to see value in the promotion of alternative recreations, particularly if they could be made commercially successful, thus generating revenue for the temperance movement. In January 1866 the Cork Refreshment Rooms Company Ltd was established by the Cork and South of Ireland Temperance League, with among its directors J. F. Maguire, Robert Scott, a vice-president of the I.T.L., and Frederick Allman, a son-in-law of Richard Dowden, one of Cork's temperance pioneers. Shortly afterwards a refreshment house was opened on Lavitt's Quay by the mayor, Sir John Arnott, and in March T. W. Russell described it for his readers in Dublin:

> The ticket office confronts the visitor on entering, at which a card for dinner, breakfast or luncheon, as the case may be, must be received. The tables are placed in two long rows, and, along with the attendants, are scrupulously clean; the 'bar', where everything is served out, being at the extreme end of the commodious building. The fare is most excellent — the tea and coffee being infinitely superior to that often served up at a private hotel. Prices, too, are remarkably low. Imagine breakfast, including tea, bread, and egg for 3½d! Yet this is paying the shareholders; and the nine hundred men who daily throng the place attest that the labours of the directors are appreciated.

The first report of the company showed that tea, coffee, eggs, buns, soup and Irish stew were being served to between 500 and 700 customers each day, and after six months there was a profit of £124.[30]

In Dublin James Haughton and the Quakers were active in promoting alternative recreations. Haughton had long campaigned for the opening of parks and museums, particularly on Sunday, to allow workers recreation away from the temptations of drink. Up to the 1870s the city was very deficient in cafés and restaurants. R. D. Webb and his son Alfred, both teetotallers, who moved their printing works to Abbey Street in 1870, were forced to have meals in public houses. According to Alfred Webb's manuscript autobiography, only a few confectioners served tea at the time, and none of these were in the vicinity of Abbey Street. In 1875 the D.T.A.S. took a major step towards rectifying this deficiency by opening a temperance hall and coffee palace at 6 Townsend Street, near the Theatre Royal. On the ground floor was a bar-room ad behind it a lecture hall. The bar-room, measuring 32 feet by 19 feet, had a marble-topped bar in one corner, behind which were mirrors and glass shelves bearing vases of flowers and a tank of goldfish. There was a fireplace and six tables in the room, togehter with a reading-stand containing current issues of the Dublin newspapers; coloured glass and mirrors decorated the walls. Clearly, while banishing the drink, the D.T.A.S. sought to retain the atmosphere of a public house. In 1879 T. Wilson Fair, honorary secretary of the society, described the rest of the building in some detail:

> Leaving the ground floor, and passing the society's office, we enter the large reading-room, where are to be found all the principal papers, magazines, directories, such games as chess, draughts, etc. It is lofty, well

lighted and comfortable. Then there are the library, club-room and smoke-room, and the bar for refreshments beyond what are supplied below. On the next floor are the dining and billiard room, smaller room for committees, store room, etc. On each of these floors there are lavatories, etc. On the top floor there are another small room for private parties, the apartments for the domestics, and . . . the kitchen, whence no odours or heat ever reach the rooms below; a lift or hoist travels from this floor to every storey below. During the evening the dining and other rooms are occupied by various societies — loan society; also Rechabite, Good Templar and other organisations. This is regarded as an important item: for not only is it a source of revenue; but accommodation for building societies, working men's clubs and the like, away from drink influence, is very much needed.

The coffee palace was obviously a success, for when the society celebrated its diamond jubilee in 1897 it was still in operation. Moreover, the society established another at Kingstown and opened a number of coffee stalls in different parts of the city to cater particularly for travellers, porters and cab drivers. Even the prohibitionists eventually came to appreciate the value of hotels and cafés in influencing working-class tastes and in generating revenue. The I.T.L. made a great success of its coffee stalls and Lombard café in Belfast, while in the mid-1870s T. W. Russell and his wife opened their own hotel on the corner of Harcourt Street and St Stephen's Green in Dublin; before its demolition in the early 1970s it was to become one of the city's most famous hotels. (**310**, 74-6)[31]

The 1850s and 1860s thus saw the emergence in Ireland of a highly organised and professional temperance movement, closely linked to societies in England and Scotland. Yet this was not a period characterised by increasing drink consumption; on the contrary, in the case of whiskey particularly, the late 1850s and the early 1860s saw a marked fall in home consumption, mainly as a result of massive tax increases. The temperance movement was in fact responding to sectional pressures. It expressed the interests of urban, middle-class employers and was inspired by Protestant Evangelicalism. The growing demand for prohibition in both the United States and Britain was also influential. The movement was strongest in Ulster, where Presbyterian clergy and laymen, motivated by religious revivalism, had created the Irish Temperance League, modelled on and affiliated with the powerful United Kingdom Alliance. The League had quickly embraced prohibition as the only really effective means of combating the drink menace. When this strategy failed to win the political support in Britain that it had gained in the United States, the League, following the example of the Alliance, backed Sir Wilfrid Lawson's permissive prohibitory bill, seeing in it a gradual means of achieving a total ban. In the south the temperance movement was fragmented and poorly organised in the wake of the collapse of Father Mathew's crusade; some societies inspired by him survived, though much reduced in membership and often functioning mainly as clubs and benefit societies. In Dublin, however, the Quakers and Unitarians, with Presbyterian and Methodist support, continued to work through local church-based groups and through the old Dublin Total Abstinence Society. The arrival of T. W. Russell in the city late in 1864 as agent for the I.T.L. and the establishment soon after of central offices and a journal did much to stimulate temperance activity in the capital. Yet the southerners, possibly more sensitive to Catholic opposition, did not commit themselves wholly and solely to prohibition. Some, like James Haughton for instance, did support it, but at the same time they were prepared to promote more moderate reforms. They campaigned for the permissive bill, but increasingly in the late 1860s and 1870s attention came to focus on Sunday closing legislation. Aside from these legislative campaigns, there were many other areas in which temperance advocates were active: the running of local societies and Bands of Hope; the establishment of coffee stalls, cafés and restaurants; agitation for reform of the licensing laws; monitoring breaches of these laws by the drink trade; opposing applications for liquor licences in the courts; and electioneering on behalf of pro-temperance candidates, whether standing for Westminster or local councils and corporations. Efforts were made to win popular support through public meetings and lectures: in Belfast in the 1860s, for instance, the I.T.L. persuaded some mill owners to allow temperance agents to lecture to their workforces.[32] But generally the lay and Protestant temperance societies of the second half of the century focused their attention on the political arena. The leaders of the 1830s and 1840s naively declared that temperance was not a political issue. From the 1860s, however, lobbying and electioneering came to dominate the movement's activities. In England this eventually led the temperance cause into alliance with the Liberal party, but in the highly polarised atmosphere of Irish politics it was far more difficult for the temperance movement to establish a political base.

The Temperance Movement
within the Catholic Church

The controversy which had surrounded Father Mathew's crusade, together with the rapid decline of the movement, left the Catholic church with little enthusiasm for a new venture in the field of temperance reform. Thus the national synod of the church, held at Thurles in August 1850 and called by Archbishop Cullen to help restore unity among the bishops, particularly over the education question, made no reference whatsoever to temperance. In an examination of the Catholic temperance movement, written in 1889, Father Michael Kelly, later Archbishop of Sydney, recognised that other, apparently more pressing, problems preoccupied the hierarchy in 1850:

> Pestilence had prevailed; eviction was rampant; emigration was sweeping away the people. A difficult and dangerous conflict with the enemies of Catholic education overcharged the chief pastors. So the 'demon of drink' again gained ground. (**202**, 631)

Kelly, as a committed teetotaller, regretted the missed opportunity for action by the church. But temperance, and particularly teetotalism, was a divisive issue and not one calculated to restore the unity that Cullen sought.

During the course of his primacy it became clear that Cullen did not in fact consider temperance a vital issue, on a par with the many political, social and religious issues which confronted him. His Lenten pastorals usually contained a fairly conventional condemnation of the evils of drunkenness, and this altered little over the years. His 1865 pastoral is typical:

> As to drunkenness, dearly beloved, all we shall say is, that it is a most disgraceful and fatal sin. It deprives man of the use of his most noble faculty, and sinks him to the level of the brute; it entails disease and sickness on his shaken limbs, it shortens his unhappy days, and oftentimes brings on an unprovided and an untimely death. How many tradesmen have been reduced to the lowest state of destitution by indulging in drink! How often do they bring disgrace and infamy, and ruin on their wives and children! How many are now pining away in want, who, if they had been temperate, might have happy homes and cheerful families! How many other crimes have their origin in drunkennesss, such as illegal combination in secret societies, faction fights, public assaults, and scandalous immoralities! . . . And if [the drunkard's] fate be sad in this world, what will it be in the next, when his [fate] will be in burning fire, and when he shall have to suffer an unceasing thirst for having in the present time gratified the cravings of his corrupt appetite?

Cullen attacks drunkenness for the spiritual, physical, economic and political evils that it produces, but, beyond the threat of hell-fire, he has little to offer in the way of a remedy. He endorses moderation rather than total abstinence, but how the drunkard is to be made temperate is not at all clear. Only in 1857, following the death of Father Mathew, did a more urgent note enter into Cullen's pastoral, and again in 1867, when an Irish Sunday closing bill was before parliament. (**242**, 279-80)

In 1867 Cullen, with ten Catholic bishops, signed a declaration addressed to Irish M.P.s supporting legislation to prohibit Sunday trading. Dr Spratt and the Quaker Henry Wigham, the honorary secretaries of the Irish Sunday Closing Association, discussed the question with Cullen in letters and at two personal interviews, and apparently secured his support.

But in his evidence to a parliamentary select committee investigating Sunday closing in 1888 Dr P. J. Tynan, who had been Cullen's secretary from 1872 until his death in 1878, claimed that the cardinal had been deceived by the I.S.C.A. Tynan was himself strongly opposed to the closing of public houses on Sunday, believing that it would only lead to an increase in home drinking and in illegal drinking in shebeens and bogus clubs. Moreover, he considered the motivation behind the demand for Sunday closing was essentially Protestant-inspired sabbatarianism. Though Cullen had been a vice-preisdent of the I.S.C.A., Tynan claimed that he

> was not in favour of Sunday closing; he was in favour of earlier closing on Saturday evenings. . . . I remember on one occasion a deputation came asking Cardinal Cullen to support Sunday closing, and he refused to do so, unless early closing on Saturday evening was added. The deputation gave him a distinct promise (at least I had it from his own lips; I was not present) that they would add on early Saturday closing to Sunday closing. On that condition his name appeared as a promoter of what you call the Sunday Closing Association, but he was very bitterly disappointed when he saw afterwards that early Saturday closing was not added on according to the promise given him. He was in favour of Sunday closing; that is to say he would give in on that point if the Sunday Closing Association would give in upon the other.

T. W. Russell, who was a member of the select committee, questioned Tynan closely on this point, obviously feeling that his evidence was damaging to the Sunday closing cause. He also took up the matter with Henry Wigham, who was the next witness to appear. Wigham maintained stoutly that Cullen had indeed supported Sunday closing of itself, and quoted a letter to this effect written by the cardinal to the I.S.C.A. in October 1876. He conceded that Cullen was probably 'even more in favour of early Saturday closing than of total Sunday closing', but denied that he had made his support for Sunday closing conditional upon the association accepting early Saturday closing. Wigham concluded by claiming that Tynan was mistaken and had confused events in his mind. (**39**, 270, 283, 285) However, in a letter apologising for his inability to attend a conference organised by the association in December 1873, Cullen had said:

> In order to give greater efficacy to so laudable an object, I beg to say that it is necessary that steps should also be taken to secure the early closing of public houses on Saturday evenings. If this be not done the movement against the sale of liquors on Sunday will not produce the desired effect. Many of the working classes, having received their week's wages, forgetful of the necessities of their families too, spend on Saturday night in a few hours all, or a great part of what they had earned by hard labour and the sweat of their brow during the preceding days. Hence they often spend the Sunday without thinking of God or religion.[33]

This letter certainly supports Tynan's claim that Cullen considered early Saturday closing as important as Sunday closing. He must therefore have been rather disillusioned with the I.S.C.A. when it did not take up the former issue. As evidence presented to various select committees investigating Irish licensing laws showed that, in Dublin at least, Saturday night was the most popular drinking time, the association's rejection of Cullen's suggestion implied that it was motivated by sabbatarianism rather than by a genuine desire to reduce working-class drink consumption.

Tynan had also been secretary to Cardinal McCabe, who succeeded Cullen as Archbishop of Dublin and Primate of Ireland in 1878, and he went on in his evidence to state that McCabe too had been no friend of the Sunday closing movement. When Russell pointed out that McCabe had signed a declaration in favour of Sunday closing, Tynan replied that McCabe had been ill at the time and that 'his failing health made him approve certain things which afterwards he disapproved of, and amongst those was the declaration which he signed in favour of Sunday closing'. In the case of McCabe there is much evidence to support Tynan's account of events. For instance, while a parish priest at Kingstown, McCabe had given evidence before a select committee which in 1867-8 investigated Sunday closing. Then he had indeed opposed it and advocated early Saturday closing as likely to have a more beneficial effect. But, as Tynan suggests, by the early 1880s, perhaps as a result of illness, McCabe's views had become considerably less coherent. In February 1882 McCabe in a speech given in the Father Mathew Temperance Hall in Halston Street attacked teetotallers. He urged them not to 'put themselves forward as censor of those who might very likely be better than themselves' but who had not taken the pledge.

> He did not wish [he said] to convey to them that every bishop should be a teetotaller, and further, he did not wish to make them understand that every priest was bound to become a teetotaller. Some people could not get on without the use of spirituous drinks, and, indeed, those who could get on without them deserved little credit for abstaining.

This speech evidently provoked controversy. Father Mitchell, the Capuchin president of the society which operated the hall, preserved a copy of it in a private notebook together with a copy of a letter written by McCabe a week later in which he sought to moderate his harsh remarks. Yet McCabe was reflecting a genuine and widespread Catholic suspicion of the extremism of the teetotallers. In June 1884 Dr R. S. D. Lyons, Liberal M.P. for Dublin city, read a letter to the Commons on the subject of Sunday closing which McCabe had written in the previous February. In this McCabe said that the clergy of Dublin were divided on this issue, but that most wanted shorter hours on both Saturday and Sunday rather than total Sunday closing. Referring to the declaration in favour of Sunday closing that he had signed, he said: 'I feel now that I should not have been persuaded to sign the document in question.' And he went on to propose as a compromise Saturday closing at 10 p.m. and Sunday trading hours of 2 p.m. to 6 p.m. (**33**, 105-7)[34]

Both Cullen and McCabe were obviously reluctant to commit themselves to the temperance cause in any very decisive manner. Neither endorsed total abstinence, for the pledge remained suspect in Catholic eyes. By focusing so heavily on Sunday closing, the campaign for licensing reform raised for many Catholics the spectre of sabbatarianism. Tynan certainly believed that the preoccupation with Sunday and the tendency to consider Saturday less significant, though heavy drinking in cities and towns usually began on Saturday night, proved that the temperance movement was less interested in the drink problem and more in imposing 'certain pharisaical views regarding the observance of the sabbath'. (**39**, 267) In other words, despite Father Mathew's crusade, to many Catholics temperance remained a Protestant-inspired movement.

Yet, even given this fear of sabbatarianism, there was a trend within the hierarchy during the 1850s and 1860s in favour of Sunday closing. The Archbishop of Cashel and the Bishops of Ferns, Kilmore, Clogher, Ossory and Galway all introduced Sunday closing of public houses into their dioceses. The movement was begun by Bishop Thomas Furlong in Ferns in 1857, though its most vocal advocate was Patrick Leahy, a close ally of Cullen, who was Archbishop of Cashel from 1857 to 1875. Furlong and Leahy, unlike Cullen and McCabe, had to deal with the 'circumstantial' drinking pattern which characterised rural Ireland. In the towns most drinking occurred after workers were paid on Saturday evening, but in the countryside heavy drinking was associated with holydays and festivals. After mass on Sundays, at markets, on holydays, during weddings, these were the great occasions for drink consumption in rural areas. So in some ways Sunday closing, if combined with closing on holydays, made more sense in the countryside than in the towns. Furlong began his campaign in his cathedral town of Enniscorthy, with a temperance mission which culminated on the feast of SS Peter and Paul, 29 June, in 1857. He called on publicans not to sell drink on that day or on future Sundays and festivals of obligation. In the following autumn he issued a pastoral letter on temperance, ordering a novena for the conversion of drunkards and the suppression of intemperance to be celebrated before the feast of All Saints. Then he slowly extended his prohibition on the sale and purchase of drink on Sundays and holydays to the whole of the diocese. Various other devotional exercises were introduced associated with temperance, and Furlong went so far as to ban the holding of fairs on holydays. He also established temperance sodalities and was possibly the first bishop to make use of the teetotal pledge at confirmation. (**39**, 286; **202**, 632-3)[35] In

Furlong's temperance missions and devotions we can see the beginnings of an effort to integrate temperance into the church's religious practices.

Archbishop Leahy had been a great admirer of Father Mathew, and on his accession he resolved to promote a temperance crusade in Cashel. He spoke frequently on the subject in his travels through the diocese and encouraged pledge-taking. But at the same time he was concerned to avoid Father Mathew's mistake in imposing lifelong total abstinence pledges. In 1863 he said:

> A pledge for life, except in rare instances, or of total abstinence, except in the case of confirmed drunkards, I have seldom, if ever, administered, preferring easy temporary pledges as more likely to do good to the mass of the people.

Neither Leahy nor Furlong were teetotallers. However, in what he called his 'Sunday temperance law' Leahy thought he had found a new and important weapon in the struggle against drunkenness. This 'law' stated that

> Whosoever, unless in the case of necessity, of which the clergy in their respective parishes are the judges, buys or sells anything spirituous on a Sunday, in a licensed or unlicensed house, is hereby deprived of the use of the sacraments, by the withdrawal of faculties from the clergy until the person transgressing presents himself or herself to the bishop of the diocese.

Leahy in fact insisted on dealing with breaches himself, and he reproved priests who granted absolution on their own authority. He demanded that each transgressor come to him, 'even from the most distant parts of the diocese', and he induced Sunday drinkers to tell him where they had bought liquor. Having thus uncovered the offending publican, Leahy would instruct the local parish priest to visit the seller and remonstrate with him or her. Again probably influenced by Father Mathew's failure, Leahy was extremely cautious in introducing his 'Sunday temperance law'. He said that he

> introduced it first by degrees. . . . I tried it first in one parish, and then in another, until I had gone through the greater part of the diocese, and then I made it a general regulation. I had been trying it two or three years in that way, up to 1861, when I made it a rule for the entire diocese. (**33**, 20)[36]

Like Furlong, Leahy adopted other means in addition to Sunday closing to encourage temperance. He established a devotional temperance society, called the Pious Society for the Conversion of Poor Sinners Given to Drinking, which admitted two categories of members: the temperate, and drunkards who were anxious to reform. The aims of the society were to encourage moderation in drinking and to promote the 'Sunday law'; to achieve the latter members were to watch local public houses to ensure that they did not trade on Sundays. Drunkards wishing to join were required to abstain totally from drink for at least a year before they could be admitted as full members. Leahy also promoted temperance through other diocesan organisations like sodalities and young men's associations. He enforced the church's ban on drinking at wakes and funerals, which had been in operation for centuries but which was generally ignored. Leahy revived this ban in 1862 and ordered that it be read at mass once every quarter. (**242**, 289-90)

In his evidence given to the 1867-8 select committee on Irish Sunday closing, Leahy testified that, to his knowledge, the people of the diocese reckoned the 'Sunday temperance law' to be the 'greatest possible blessing'. Committals for drunkenness to the Cashel Bridewell had declined from 522 in 1858 to 184 in 1867, while over the same period committals for Sunday drunkenness had declined from 97 to none. Violations of the 'law', according to Leahy, were 'extremely venial, no more than a glass of beer, or something as small as that'. As to Protestant attitudes, Leahy stated that there were only two public houses in the diocese owned by Protestants. One of these had stayed open on Sunday, hoping thereby to attract extra business, but the owner then had great difficulty in getting his licence renewed by the magistrates, who were Protestants and who strongly supported Leahy's 'law'. The licence was finally renewed, but only on condition that the house stayed closed on Sunday. Leahy was certainly very conscientious in enforcing the 'Sunday law', throwing the full weight of his considerable authority behind it: he even threatened on one occasion to deny a church burial to breakers. The results of his endeavours, however, were not quite as impressive as he liked to claim. The 'law', for instance, did not apply to holydays, on which a great deal of drinking occurred, particularly at markets and fairs. Leahy tried to have markets prohibited on church holydays, but Sir Robert Peel, who introduced a bill to regulate markets and fairs in 1862, replied that this was 'hardly possible', and despite further efforts by Leahy, the 'law' was never extended to these days as it had been in Ferns. Reports from county inspectors, ordered by the Chief Secretary prior to the select committee, generally agreed that the ban worked well with regard to Sunday. But while Christopher de Gernon, who had been Resident Magistrate for Tipperary since 1863, praised the effects of the 'law' in lowering crime and disorder, he nevertheless pointed out that the people of Co. Tipperary 'were as much addicted to drinking ... as they are in any other place on weekdays'. Moreover, faction fighting, though much diminished, continued to be a problem and was frequently associated with drinking at fairs. In 1861 and 1862 and again between 1872 and 1874 there were upsurges of faction fighting in the diocese of Emly. Leahy organised retreats, issued pastorals and upheld the 'Sunday law' in the face of these outbreaks.[37]

Another problem for the archbishop was the attitude of his clergy to the temperance issue. Generally Leahy was not popular among them and thus found it difficult at times to enforce his wishes. 'It is evident', wrote one of them, Father O'Carroll, in his diary in December 1863, 'that he aspires to be a big man before the country, while in his own diocese he is the reverse.' The general elections of 1857, 1865 and 1868, for instance, produced deep political divisions among the clergy, with charges of riot, bribery, intimidation and pro-Fenianism being levelled against them. Even Leahy himself and one of his brothers were implicated in electoral bribery during an investigation into the 1868 election in Cashel, which recommended in 1870 that the borough be disfranchised and included for electoral purposes in the county of Tipperary. Many of his priests in fact disagreed with his very conservative political views, his hostility to Fenianism, his extravagant plans for the building of Thurles cathedral, and with the amount of time he insisted on devoting to temperance. O'Carroll sourly described the 'Sunday law' as Leahy's 'hobby-horse' and remarked that it was 'almost his never-failing theme of conversation among a gathering of priests'. (**242**, 292) Leahy's decision to take charge of the enforcement of the 'law' himself probably reflected not only his own enthusiasm but also the lack of it among his clergy. If he had difficulty in winning over his own priests, he was equally unsuccessful in convincing his fellow-bishops with regard to Sunday closing. In 1868 he acknowledged that the ban was extremely difficult to enforce and that 'what we have done was attended with a great deal of trouble'. Other bishops might not be prepared to go to the lengths that he had gone to. He also admitted that in cities such as Dublin, Cork and Limerick it was simply impractical for the clergy to hope to be able to enforce Sunday closing. Their authority was not sufficient to close all public houses, and if even only a few remained open, in a short time the ban would be undermined.

'Nothing', said Leahy, 'could arrest intemperance in large towns but an act of parliament.'

> Where the voice of the minister of religion would not be heeded either by the publican or by the man given to drink, the strong arm of the law would shut the door of the public house in spite of both the publican and the drunkard. If the secular and ecclesiastical authorities all through the country were to go hand-in-hand, each supplementing the work of the other, they would be irresistible.

As for the nature of the proposed legislation, Leahy would hear of nothing short of total compulsory Sunday closing. He rejected shorter hours, the permissive principle, the selling of liquor only with meals or only for consumption off the premises, as well as the selling of only beer on Sundays.

'I think', he said, 'every measure, short of the total closing of public houses on Sunday, would be altogether inefficacious, or at least to a great measure inefficacious.' This answer was elicited by a question from N. D. Murphy, Liberal and later Home Rule M.P. for Cork city, a member of a well-known brewing family and a staunch opponent in parliament of temperance legislation. The bill that the committee was examining aimed essentially to shorten Sunday hours and was sponsored by Myles O'Reilly, Liberal and later Home Rule M.P. for Co. Longford, a leading Catholic layman and a friend of Leahy. But by insisting on total Sunday closing, Leahy was playing into the hands of the bill's opponents and providing them with ammunition to use against it. The committee did not accept Leahy's views in favour of total Sunday closing; in fact it went in the opposite direction by moderating the bill even further. So Leahy's campaign for Sunday closing in Cashel, in the absence of real support from his own clergy, from his fellow-bishops and from parliament, only succeeded to the extent that it did through his own exertions. (**33**, 21, 25, 27) His successor, Archbishop Croke (1875-1902), was also a forceful advocate of temperance, but Croke did not maintain the 'Sunday law'. As with Father Mathew, Leahy's advocacy of temperance isolated him within his own church, and thus his work was not maintained.

The best known Catholic temperance advocate, after Father Mathew in the 1840s and Archbishop Leahy in the 1860s, was Dr John Spratt (1795-1871), provincial of the Carmelite order from 1863, who was also noted for his charitable work among the Dublin poor. He had joined the committee of the Hibernian Temperance Society in 1832, but, like his friend James Haughton, Spratt had gravitated to total abstinence in the late 1830s. He supported Father Mathew's crusade vigorously and was its acknowledged leader in Dublin. Unlike Father Mathew, however, Spratt was an active supporter of Repeal: money was collected for O'Connell at Dublin temperance meetings, and temperance processions in the city often carried Repeal banners. Later, with Haughton, Spratt also raised money for Young Ireland prisoners and agitated for their release. As we have seen, Spratt's temperance missions in Ulster, conducted without episcopal approval, also evoked bitter opposition from Father Mathew. The two were in fact seen by many as rivals for the leadership of the temperance movement. Spratt's biographer, writing in the 1890s, perpetuated this competition, noting with satisfaction that more of those taking the pledge from Spratt 'kept their promise, comparatively speaking, than did those of the great apostle himself'. Even Maguire, Father Mathew's biographer, admitted that the cause of temperance was upheld more staunchly in Dublin after the famine than in Cork, owing to Spratt's efforts. (**242**, 296; **240**, 546)[38]

Spratt continued to rely primarily on the total abstinence pledge, despite clerical opposition to it. He also supported the new legislative campaigns that emerged in the 1860s and was from 1866 until his death one of the honorary secretaries of the Irish Sunday Closing Association. Temperance was a vital element in Spratt's philanthropic work aimed at improving the lot of the Dublin poor. From the 1850s he and Haughton conducted weekly meetings at their temperance hall in Cuffe Lane, and in 1863 between five and six hundred people were attending each meeting. In addition, Spratt worked for nearly forty years on behalf of the Sick and Indigent Roomkeepers Society, one of the city's oldest charities; in 1860 he established a refuge for homeless women, St Joseph's Refuge in Brickfield Lane; St Mary's Catholic Asylum for the Industrious Blind, now on the Merrion Road, was another institution which resulted from his efforts. Like Haughton, Spratt regarded drink as the root cause of most of the poverty, disease and crime with which the city was afflicted. Tradesmen and labourers, he wrote in 1867, 'might be comfortable and happy; they are now poor and miserable; they might be virtuous and respectable; they are vicious and despised'. Teetotalism, he believed, would 'enable them to educate and clothe their children, who are now ignorant and in rags, and to lay up some subsistence for their helpless age; but the public house leaves their children destitute and sends themselves — through want of the necessities of life — to premature graves'.[39]

Spratt, as we have seen, helped induce Cardinal Cullen to support Sunday closing publicly. But Cullen was suspicious of the political connections of the Dublin temperance movement, as well as of its Protestant character. Just as he had worked to secure the release of Young Ireland prisoners after the 1848 rebellion, so Spratt joined the Fenian amnesty campaign after 1867. In September 1869 he and Haughton signed a memorial addressed to the queen, on behalf of the D.T.A.S., seeking clemency for the men 'whom erroneous patriotic feelings led astray'. The D.T.A.S. already had links with the Fenians, for it had regularly advertised in their paper, the *Irish People*, in 1864 and 1865. Cullen, who was trying to prevent priests from co-operating in fund-raising for the Fenian Amnesty Committee, would doubtless have deplored Spratt's political activities. In a letter to Archbishop Leahy in April 1869 Cullen complained particularly that temperance organisations had given money to the amnesty campaign. (**242**, 298)[40] Like Leahy, though for rather different reasons, Spratt was also an individual enthusiast who did not command a following within his church.

When in 1889 Father Michael Kelly came to review the history of the Catholic temperance movement, he saw the work of Furlong, Leahy and Spratt in the 1850s and 1860s, like that of Father Mathew in the 1840s, as having essentially failed. A firm believer in the total abstinence pledge, Kelly felt that the partial pledges employed by Furlong and Leahy were ineffective. Nor did Kelly have much faith in the reformist societies and legislation championed by Spratt. Like Father Mathew, the three did not create a permanent organisation which could carry on their work. James Haughton's son reported in his biography of his father that no priest could be found to replace Spratt in Cuffe Lane after his death in 1871 and that the society had begged Haughton to administer the pledge himself. Similarly, as already noted, though Archbishop Croke was sympathetic to the temperance cause, he did not maintain Leahy's 'Sunday law' in Cashel. Like Mathew too, Leahy and Spratt provoked controversy within the church by their methods and alienated many of the clergy. For Kelly the culmination of this work was to be found in the 'woeful declaration' issued by the national synod held at Maynooth in 1875 and signed by 'Dr Leahy's successor and Dr Furlong in person'. Said the bishops:

> With the deepest pain, and after the example of the apostle, weeping, we say, that the abominable vice of intemperance still continues to work the dreadful havoc among our people.... Is it not, dearly beloved, an intolerable scandal, that in the midst of a Catholic nation, like ours, there should be found so many slaves of intemperance, who habitually sacrifice to brutal excess in drinking not only their reason, but their substance, their health, their life, their souls and God himself?

Having deplored the vice, the bishops then went on to suggest how it could be combated:

> Against an evil so widespread and so pernicious, we implore all who have at heart the honour of God and the salvation of souls, to be filled with holy zeal.... The habit of daily prayer faithfully persevered in; frequent and worthy approach to the holy sacraments; the devout hearing of the word of God; and the avoiding of dangerous occasions, are the only sure means by which intemperance can be overcome.

In Kelly's eyes, however, this declaration admitted the failure of the Catholic temperance movement after nearly forty years of work, but offered no new remedies. The pastoral, he commented, 'doubtless in wisdom... employs... general phrases' and 'directs the earnest and fervent employment of the general means of grace'. But Kelly clearly did not consider these measures adequate, and he remarked on the lack of a 'suggestion regarding the special antidote of total abstinence'. Kelly was forced to turn outside Ireland, to England, the United States and Australia, to find Catholic clergy pursuing the 'traditions of Father Mathew' with good results. The only bright spot in Ireland in the 1870s was the diocese of Ferns, where the new bishop, Michael Warren, had expanded Furlong's work by launching a teetotal crusade. (**242**, 299; **202**, 632-6)

The Legislative Campaigns of the 1860s

From 1863, when an English Sunday closing bill was before parliament, and 1864, when the permissive bill was first introduced, the Irish temperance movement became largely preoccupied with campaigns to secure these two pieces of legislation. In this the movement worked closely with its English counterparts, especially the United Kingdom Alliance. The permissive bill was intended to apply to the whole of the United Kingdom, but after it became clear that Sunday closing was unlikely to be introduced in England the Irish movement began to work for a separate Irish Sunday closing bill.

Sunday liquor trading had been regulated in Ireland by Perrin's Act of 1833 (3 & 4 Will. IV, c. 68, sect. 14), which permitted sales to occur between 2 p.m. and 11 p.m. But, as a consequence of the report of a select committee on drunkenness in 1834, these hours were reduced in 1836 to between 2 p.m. and 9 p.m. (6 & 7 Will. IV, c. 38, sect. 3). Closing at 11 p.m. was, however, restored in the 1860s following legal interpretation of the Refreshment Houses Act of 1860 (23 & 24 Vict., c. 107, sect. 29). Efforts to secure total Sunday closing before the 1860s had been spasmodic and unco-ordinated. Interest in the issue in Ireland was stirred in 1853-4 by the introduction of acts in both England and Scotland for the closing of public houses on Sundays. The Scottish Forbes/Mackenzie Act was accepted without serious opposition, but the English Wilson/Patton Act led to rioting in Hyde Park in 1855. A shocked parliament severely modified the act; but, as a result, for the rest of the century proponents of Sunday closing had to face the objection that their measure would produce large-scale public disorder. This objection was particularly potent in a country as notoriously unsettled as Ireland. Voluntary Sunday closing had been imposed, as we have seen, by several Catholic bishops. And in Ulster too, no doubt reflecting Protestant sabbatarianism, voluntary Sunday closing appears to have been widespread. In Belfast in 1868, for example, police surveys showed that 146 out of 535 public houses in the town were closed on Sunday. (**242**, 57-8; **173**, 238-9)

The Irish Temperance League supported Sunday closing from the start, while at the same time regarding the permissive bill as more important and more likely to produce significant results. When Somes's English bill was defeated in 1863 by a majority of 175 the League in its comments began to stress the special situation of Ireland. There was no necessity for Sunday trading in Ireland, said the I.T.L. *Journal*, whatever might be the situation in England. 'Here the people are unanimously opposed to that mode of profaning the Christian's holy day. And it is the opinion of many of our friends, whose views are entitled to much weight, that we should agitate for a Sunday closing bill.' The League argued that Sunday drinking created particular problems in Ireland, problems which were not to be found in

England. 'When, and where,' it asked, 'are most of our red-handed Irish crimes concocted? In the public house on Sunday.' With money and leisure on that day and little open except the public house, people were tempted into drinking, gambling and, worst of all, conspiring against the government.

> It is notorious [the article went on] that illegal societies are got up by publicans to promote their business, and that the time of meeting is usually Sunday evening. It is well understood in Leitrim, that the real 'Molly Maguire' was a publican, who got up the organisation as a whiskey-selling speculation.

Similar charges were soon to be levelled against the Fenians, who did indeed make considerable use of public houses for their meeting and recruiting. The League claimed, inaccurately, that crime generally, and drunkenness especially, were more prevalent in Irish towns on Sunday than on any other day of the week. Thus it was absurd for parliament to go on making laws against secret societies and agrarian outrage on the one hand, 'while all the time fostering the system that nurtures them — the Sunday liquor trade!' Such arguments, the League felt, were more likely to appeal to English politicians than those based on religious principles. So Sunday drinking as the 'fountain of Irish crime' needed to be stressed, together with the unanimous opinion of the Irish people in favour of Sunday closing. English members, thought the League, 'will scarcely have the hardihood to deny us one of the few things about which we are agreed'. To what extent the League believed its own political arguments is difficult to determine, but the impression given is that sabbatarianism was the real driving force behind the Sunday closing campaign.[41]

In September 1864 a Sunday closing association was established in Belfast by leaders of the I.T.L. to agitate for an Irish bill. H. C. Knight, the new secretary of the League, told the inaugural meeting that although Somes's bill had been heavily defeated, more Irish members had voted for it than against it. In fact the majority in favour was only two, 20 having voted for and 18 against. But undeterred by this, the association resolved to seek funds and to find an M.P. who would be willing to introduce an Irish Sunday closing bill. In the latter task, however, the association made no headway. Somes himself, after his defeat, had concluded that it was impossible to carry 'so complete a measure' at present and had urged supporters of Sunday closing to be satisfied with agitating merely to shorten Sunday trading hours. But the Belfast association persisted in canvassing support for an Irish bill. In October 1864 a deputation, headed by the mayor and including Knight and Corry, the president of the League, called upon Sir Hugh Cairns, one of the Conservative M.P.s for the town, and asked him to sponsor such a measure. Cairns told them that he thought the opposition to Sunday closing in England was very strong and that even in Scotland support for the Forbes/Mackenzie Act had waned considerably since 1854. To get an Irish bill through would therefore require the wholehearted support of most of the Irish M.P.s. This he felt was lacking. Out of 105 Irish M.P.s, only 38 had bothered to vote in the division on Somes's bill, and the majority in favour had been very small. Moreover, 14 out of the 20 in favour of the bill were Protestants; only 6 Irish Catholic M.P.s had voted for it. Although some members of the hierarchy had spoken in favour of Sunday closing, Cairns said that he was not impressed by the support for the measure among Catholic M.P.s. He therefore refused to sponsor an Irish bill.[42]

The League fared little better in its efforts to win political support for the permissive bill. It lobbied the Belfast candidates on the subject before the 1865 general election. Cairns declared outright that he would not vote for it, as 'there was something tyrannical about it'. Lord John Hay, the Liberal candidate, refused to commit himself one way or the other. But S. G. Getty, the other Conservative M.P., declared that he would certainly vote for its first and second readings, though he would 'not pledge himself to endorse everything contained in it'. The League had to be satisfied with this far from total commitment, and in July it endorsed Getty and recommended the 'friends of temperance' to vote for him. When Cairns and Getty were re-elected the League expressed satisfaction at the result. It was hardly a great achievement, though admittedly in Dublin the situation was even worse. Deputations consisting of, among others, Haughton, Allen, Russell, Mowatt and the Wighams had called on the Conservative members for the county, Colonel Taylor and Ion Trant Hamilton, and also on two of the candidates for the city, John Vance, the Conservative member, and Jonathan Pim, the Liberal candidate. Benjamin Lee Guinness, the brewer and second Conservative candidate, had refused to receive a deputation. There had been a 'vigorous argument' with Taylor and Hamilton, who would only promise 'careful consideration' of the permissive bill. Vance received them 'favourably', and Pim, though also 'favourable', would not pledge himself to vote for the measure in the house. Taylor and Hamilton were elected, as were Guinness and Pim. The I.T.L. *Journal* commented sourly that the 'metropolis had been disgraced for the present by the return of Mr Benjamin Lee Guinness'. Haughton had written a public letter to Guinness after the latter had declined to receive a temperance delegation, enclosing with it a copy of the electoral address of the Dublin branch of the U.K.A. and informing him that he was 'unfitted' to be a member of parliament because of his brewing interests. Guinness clearly did not appreciate Haughton's opinion, and his reply was little short of insulting. He refused to read more than the first page of Haughton's letter.

> Such [he replied] has been my habit for many years with anything written by you, or reported as spoken by you. I return herewith the letter

alluded to, and as I have no respect for, and take no interest whatever in, your vagaries, I beg to decline any further communication with you.

Haughton commanded immense respect in temperance circles in both Ireland and England, even if his nationalist politics were not generally shared. The tone of Guinness's reply thus caused much annoyance. The *Journal* thought that the letter of the 'head beerseller of all Ireland' displayed

> an amount of gentlemanly bearing, intelligent appreciation of great public questions, and a desire to thoroughly understand all the topics of the day, such as could only be found among beersellers everywhere.

But the League's sarcasm was probably prompted as much by disappointment with the election results as by its anger at Guinness's behaviour. The results were no more encouraging in England, where both Somes and Lawson lost their seats. The temperance movement was not as yet a significant political force.[43]

The campaign for Sunday closing and the permissive bill nevertheless continued. As we have seen, a Sunday closing association linked to the I.T.L. had been formed in Belfast late in 1864. A national Sunday closing association had been set up in England in December 1863, centred on Hull, but with the defeat of Somes's bill and the failure to find a sponsor for an Irish one, both organisations collapsed. Just two years later, however, similar bodies appeared in England and the south of Ireland. In Manchester in October 1866 the Central Association for Stopping the Sale of Intoxicating Liquors on Sunday was formed, while in November in Dublin the Irish Association for Closing Public Houses on Sunday appeared. The Irish Sunday Closing Association, as it was generally known, was formed on 29 November at a meeting held in the Rotunda. The meeting was attended by most of the capital's temperance stalwarts, including Haughton, Spratt, Urwick, Allen and Henry and J. R. Wigham. Present as well were the Rev. Nicholas Dunscombe from Cork, Edward Alworthy from the I.T.L., Dr Lees from the U.K.A., and representatives of the recently formed English Sunday closing association, notably the Rev. Dr John Garrett, its secretary. The meeting referred to the work of Leahy and Furlong and to the establishment of the English association, and declared that an Irish association was needed to lobby to have Sunday closing made general by law throughout the country. The supporters of temperance, especially Dublin's Quaker businessmen, quickly subscribed £160 to the new association. Henry Bewley gave £50; six members of the Pim family gave £35 between them; Richard Allen gave £10; and the Wighams £15. It is interesting that T. W. Russell was not involved in the setting up of the association and that James Haughton gave only £1 towards its funds. Both were committed to prohibition at this stage and doubted the efficacy of partial measures like Sunday closing. The I.S.C.A. began by calling on the mayor to organise a public meeting on Sunday closing in the Mansion House. The *Irish Times* commented that the resolutions to be put to the meeting were intended to serve as the basis for future legislation. The meeting on 19 December passed, though not without some opposition from the floor, a series of resolutions in favour of Sunday closing and urged the Dublin M.P.s to support an Irish Sunday closing bill.[44]

The I.T.L. did not see the immediate need for a similar meeting in Belfast: 'As the voice of Ulster is already unanimously in favour of the God-honouring, man-loving cause, it would be a useless expenditure of time and money to do so.' Instead the League advised presbyteries, church conferences and committees of temperance societies to get up petitions in favour of Sunday closing. Petition forms were sent to clergy and temperence societies, who were told if they needed more to contact either Garrett in Manchester, Henry Wigham in Dublin or H. C. Knight in Belfast. Obviously the English and Irish Sunday closing associations and the I.T.L. were working together to have bills introduced. The League, however, remained firmly convinced that Ireland, which was 'much riper for the reform than England', should be dealt with in a separate bill. 'Were we', it said, 'to unite with England in asking a joint bill for both countries, there might be years of delay . . . .' It was also anxious to enlist all temperance sympathisers in the cause, whether they were teetotallers or not, and to have the campaign appear as widespread and representative as possible: 'While temperance friends and societies will have the greatest part of the work to do in getting up the petition, yet for obvious reasons it will be more prudent to do it, not in the name of their organisations, but as from the community generally.' The League advised teetotallers to work with others and 'for the time to hold their distinctive principles in abeyance'. Clearly the League felt it impolitic to parade teetotalism and prohibition in the Sunday closing campaign, yet its ultimate goal remained uncompromised. Sunday closing, said the *Journal* in March 1867, 'is the thin edge of the wedge which when properly driven home will yet utterly demolish the infernal traffic and custom together'.[45]

Once the temperance movement had compromised on prohibition and decided to support lesser measures, even if only as a means to prohibition, the question of where to draw the line then arose. The permissive bill and Sunday closing could be supported, but what of measures merely to shorten hours of trading? Disagreement within the movement on where to draw this line was in fact to destroy any small chance there was of getting an Irish Sunday closing act in the 1860s. In March 1867 a large public meeting was held in the Ulster Hall in Belfast, and a deputation was appointed to go to London and help organise the introduction of an Irish Sunday closing bill. A similar deputation went from Dublin, and they met with Dr Garrett to work out the details of the measure. Garrett, however, in the meantime had resigned as secretary of the English Sunday closing organisation because, like Somes, he had become convinced that it was impossible to obtain total Sunday closing at the present time. He and others were thus working towards the introduction of bills for England and Ireland that would merely limit the hours of trading on Sunday. J. A. Smith, Liberal M.P. for Chichester, and Major Myles O'Reilly, Liberal M.P. for Co. Longford, had agreed to introduce these bills. The Belfast deputation did not know of this change in Garrett's stance before they met him. The Dublin deputation was convinced by Garrett of the need for this compromise, but the men from Belfast would not commit themselves. On 26 March a meeting in Belfast rejected Garrett's proposal and appointed a committee, consisting of Corry, Knight, Alderman Robert Lindsay and the Rev. John Macnaughton, to go to London and uphold the principle of total Sunday closing. O'Reilly, however, refused to introduce such a measure; the Dublin movement supported him, and no other co-operative Irish M.P. could be found. The Belfast temperance societies were then faced with the unpleasant choice of either supporting or opposing the partial bill proposed. They chose to support it. 'It would be wrong', said the I.T.L., 'to oppose friends who were zealously and con-scientiously working in the direction of that which we aimed at.' But at the same time the I.T.L. 'felt disheartened by the mutilated form of the bill', and 'from that time forward little active support was given to the measure in the north of Ireland'. The League and its agents, such as Pyper and Russell, concentrated instead on the permissive bill. Sabbatarians were bitterly disappointed, regarding shorter hours as no improvement whatsoever, and the General Assembly's committee on sabbath observance severely criticised O'Reilly's bill.[46]

In Dublin the bill attracted little public attention. During 1867 the newspapers were preoccupied with the reform bill, with the Fenian threat and, later in the year, with the issue of Disestablishment. By May, however, the Licensed Grocers' and Vintners' Association, which represented most of the 784 publicans in the city of Dublin, had become concerned enough to resolve that they should petition against the bill and raise money to mount a campaign against it. They sent a delegation to London to see Lord Naas, the Chief Secretary, and to lobby Irish M.P.s. In this they were assisted by Sir John Gray, owner of the *Freeman's Journal* and Liberal M.P. for Kilkenny city, and by Sir Benjamin Lee Guinness, whose brewery con-tributed 10 guineas to the publicans' funds. But even the trade seemed rather apathetic and not wholly convinced of the need for vigorous opposition. In June at a special meeting of the L.G.V.A. there was much criticism of the lack of interest being shown in O'Reilly's bill. James Carey, a town councillor and Poor Law Guardian, who had been one of the London delegation, informed the meeting that Sunday closing was 'the beginning of the end', for behind it were 'canting hypocrites' and 'puritans', whose real aim was to introduce the permissive bill and ultimately the

Maine Law. Carey clearly felt that the way to rouse the trade was not to attack Sunday closing of itself, but to portray it as the first step on the road to prohibition. With regard to the aims of the I.T.L., his analysis was perfectly correct, though not all temperance advocates were prepared to go as far as the Belfast organisation. Carey also appealed to economic nationalism by claiming that the anti-drink movement sought to strike a blow 'at the last remnant of manufacture in this country by closing the breweries and distilleries'. This was an argument that O'Connell had used in defence of the drink industry; presumably it was intended to appeal to brewers like Guinness and nationalists like Gray, from whom the publicans expected most of their support to come.[47]

The bill introduced in 1867 was sponsored by three Irish Liberal M.P.s. As well as O'Reilly, who was a moderate nationalist and leading Catholic layman, they were Jonathan Pim, a Quaker, who sat for Dublin city from 1865 to 1874, and Lord Cremorne, of the wealthy landed Dawson family, who sat for Co. Monaghan from 1865 to 1868. The bill proposed that spirits, wine and beer should be sold for consumption off the premises on Sunday between 1 p.m. and 2.30 p.m. and between 8 p.m. and 9 p.m. and that keepers of eating-houses should sell liquor for consumption on the premises to purchasers of food. The bill aimed to do away with drinking in public houses on Sunday, while at the same time permitting drinking at home and with meals in cafés and restaurants. It was felt by the less extreme advocates of temperance that these latter forms of drinking were less likely to lead to drunkenness than public-house drinking. Both the English and Irish bills were read for the first time in March, though Smith subsequently withdrew his. The I.T.L. *Journal* believed this was because the bill had no chance of success, as Smith 'had not the cordial support of the temperance community'. O'Reilly, however, went ahead and on 5 June moved the second reading. The bill's opponents countered by urging the setting up of a select committee to investigate the desirability of the measure and its likely impact. Lord Naas, representing the government, did not oppose the second reading outright, but his speech was far from enthusiastic. He pointed out that drunkenness was not increasing greatly in Ireland at the time, and therefore there was 'no special evil to meet'. Police and local authorities were divided in their opinions: the Mayor of Cork was 'partially' in favour of the bill, but the Lord Mayor of Dublin was 'strongly opposed'; the police in Cork welcomed the bill, but the Dublin metropolitan force feared an increase in illicit drinking if it was passed. The second reading was deferred until July, and when the bill came up Lord Naas was definitely in favour of a select committee. O'Reilly correctly interpreted this as an effort to kill the bill. Naas's comments were far more hostile than they had been in June. 'If they attempted legislation in the sense of this measure,' he said, 'it would be necessary to review the whole licensing system in Ireland,' and he clearly had no intention of doing this.

On a motion moved by N. D. Murphy of Cork, the bill's chief opponent, it was referred to a select committee by 92 votes to 71. At the division most Irish M.P.s were absent, but the bill's promoters were able to secure a small majority in favour of the second reading: 25 voted for the second reading and 22 for the select committee. But even J. F. Maguire, Father Mathew's friend and biographer, was among those voting, in effect, against the bill. The division bore out Cairns's assertion in 1864, that the vast majority of Irish Catholic M.P.s were opposed to Sunday closing. The *Journal* was appalled at the committee proposed and suggested that it indicated O'Reilly's 'indifference'. For, of the seventeen members, seven had actually voted against the bill, only three for it, and the remainder had been absent during the division. However, this may merely have reflected O'Reilly's conviction that the committee would never sit. Such was in fact the case. It was too late in the session for a select committee to begin its operations, and so the order was discharged.[48]

O'Reilly introduced the bill again in the 1868 session and this time quickly agreed to a select committee in order to forestall opposition and delay. On 16 March the fifteen members of the committee were selected, with O'Reilly as chairman. O'Reilly exercised his right to nominate six members, but the nine-man majority was composed either of outright opponents, like Murphy, William Stacpoole, Liberal M.P. for Ennis, and N. P. Leader, Conservative M.P. for Co. Cork, or of sceptics, like the Earl of Mayo (formerly Lord Naas) and Chichester Fortescue, Liberal M.P. for Co. Louth. If the committee was not particularly sympathetic to the bill, neither were the witnesses. Well-known and influential advocates of Sunday closing, such as Archbishop Leahy, played into the hands of the bill's opponents by calling for total Sunday closing and denying that shorter hours would make any material difference. Even those who supported shorter Sunday hours generally wanted a two-hour reduction in the evening, from 11 p.m. to 9 p.m., rather than the complex arrangements proposed in the bill. Then there were witnesses opposed to any change at all. In fact, all in all, there was hardly anyone with a good word to say for the measure in its existing form. It suffered the fate of so many compromise schemes: it failed to satisfy either side. The committee therefore voted to amend the bill drastically. Hours of sale on Sunday were reduced, to between 2 p.m. and 9 p.m. in towns with more than 5,000 inhabitants, and to between 2 p.m. and 7 p.m. elsewhere. These were the hours later to be introduced by the Liberals in their 1872 Licensing Act. But in 1868, as a result of these drastic amendments, O'Reilly was forced to withdraw his bill.

The *Irish Times* considered the original bill to have been 'remarkably bad' and expressed itself pleased at its mutilation. In May 1868 a special correspondent wrote:

This bill, principally through the exertion of Mr Murphy, one of the members for Cork city, has been cut to pieces, and out of the very small remains of Mr O'Reilly's handiwork on a subject about which he knew very little, if anything, a new measure more in consonance with the spirit of the times and the equitable claim to protection of a large and respectable interest, has been prepared.

Certainly the amended bill found more support among the trade, though even less among the teetotallers. Carey, now president of the L.G.V.A., was prepared to consider it more sympathetically than the previous one. Some publicans even welcomed the proposed shorter hours. 'A Vintner', writing to the *Irish Times*, warned aginst 'having some unpopular, troublesome and impractical bill passed into law — the work of enthusiastic religionists of every denomination, and of utopian teetotallers'. But at the same time 'A Vintner' acknowledged that there was a public demand for shorter hours and sympathy for this measure from within the trade. He therefore advised the publicans to take action themselves 'to have prepared a well-digested substitute for every inadmissable proposal in this Sunday closing bill'.[49] The Grocers' Assistants' Association came out strongly in favour of Sunday closing, as they wanted their members to have one free day a week. Jonathan Pim identified himself with their cause and made sure that their case was heard in parliament and before the select committee. Others were less pleased, especially the total abstinence advocates. Mowatt assailed the select committee for being biased and for only taking evidence that supported its preconceived ideas. He claimed that it had accepted evidence from working men opposed to Sunday closing, but would not hear working men in favour of the measure who had been selected by the I.S.C.A. Nor would it hear him, although he was prepared to pay his own expenses in going to London. Despite its 'mutilation', however, the Irish bill had at least fared better than the English one. Smith had reintroduced his bill in 1868, and it too had been referred to a select committee; but in June, after examining 59 witnesses, the committee had voted by 7 to 6 to reject the bill entirely.[50]

O'Reilly persevered and introduced the amended bill in 1869, presumably hoping that the newly elected Liberal government would be more sympathetic than its Tory predecessor had been. During the second-reading debate the bill's supporters were at pains to stress its moderateness and how small a change it in fact involved. Chichester Fortescue, the new Chief Secretary, spoke on its behalf, and, as a result, Murphy and the bill's other opponents withdrew their objections. But in June, during the committee stage, Chichester Fortescue announced that the government was planning a major reform of the licensing laws. He hoped, he said, to introduce a measure next session to 'put an end to the anomalies and evils of the licensing system in Ireland', and Sunday trading hours would certainly be considered. Despite electoral and parliamentary failures, the temperance movement was clearly beginning to have an impact on the Liberal party: both Gladstone and H. A. Bruce, the new Home Secretary, had spoken in terms viewed as sympathetic to temperance. With these assurances, O'Reilly agreed to withdraw his bill, saying that he believed the government's proposed measure would restict Sunday trading hours along the lines suggested in his own bill. (**136**, 30-1; **173**, 259-61)[51]

At the time the L.G.V.A. were meeting in Dublin. They received a telegram from Carey, who was with their delegation in London, announcing the withdrawal of O'Reilly's bill. The telegram stated that the bill had been withdrawn, 'thanks to the efforts of Mr Murphy, M.P. for Cork, many other members of parliament, and the good sense of the government'. The announcement was received with applause. The publicans had been given assistance by English trade associations in their campaign against O'Reilly's bills, but by March 1869 their efforts had cost them over £300. Understandably they were happy at their victory, though the Chief Secretary's promise of sweeping reform in the near future showed that they had won only one battle and not the whole war. The Spirit Grocers' Association, on the other hand, welcomed Chichester Fortescue's pledge. They took it as an endorsement of their complaints against the publicans' favoured position and hoped that he would very soon bring in a bill 'to equalise the licensing system, and place all in the trade on the same footing'.[52] As for the I.T.L., it had long before written its own epitaph for O'Reilly's bills. In August 1867, after his first bill had been referred to a select committee, the *Journal* declared:

> No Sunday closing measure of any value can ever be got for Ireland unless it be based upon some principle that will command the confidence and secure the co-operation of the friends of both the sabbath and of temperance. Major O'Reilly's bill was minus the former element, and had but little of the latter; and we trust its fate, which, as a publican triumph, we sincerely deplore, will teach a useful lesson in the future.[53]

O'Reilly's failure to get either of his bills through was not perhaps such a 'publican triumph' as the League believed. The Irish trade was divided over the question of Sunday hours, with the publicans, spirit grocers and grocers' assistants, all taking up substantially different positions, and thus it had been slow to organise political lobbying. It had had to rely heavily on the English trade and English anti-temperance M.P.s, though obviously Murphy of Cork had served the Irish trade well. O'Reilly's failure was due more to divisions in the temperance movement, which considerably weakened the anti-drink campaign. Thus he had from the outset received little support from the powerful movement in Ulster. The conflict over these bills, however, had the effect of convincing both sides of the need for unity and for more effective lobbying. The temperance movement closed ranks on the issue: shorter hours were rejected, and total Sunday closing became the aim. The publicans and spirit grocers remained at odds, but in Michael Dwyer, a former journalist and election agent, the publicans found a formidalbe publicist and lobbyist on their behalf. Dwyer was secretary of the L.G.V.A. for most of the 1870s and became the *bête noire* of the Irish temperance movement.

The 1868 general election saw the I.T.L. much more politically active than it had been in 1865. With O'Reilly's bill before the house and, more importantly, another permissive bill proposed, it was essential to secure the election of sympathetic M.P.s. Pyper therefore travelled extensively through Ulster interviewing candidates and trying to persuade them to endorse both the permissive bill and Sunday closing. Temperance was not, however, a particularly significant issue in the campaigns, as the electorate was preoccupied with Disestablishment, land reform and denominational education. Licensing reform was part of the Liberals' substantial programme, but it came well down the list and was not spelt out in any great detail. Even M. R. Dalway, the League's president, campaigning against a Conservative landlord in Carrickfergus, did not raise the temperance issue. Moreover, less than half the Irish seats were contested: in Ulster there was only one contest in the counties, which were all held by landlords or their relatives, and only five in the boroughs. This situation made efforts to influence M.P.s particularly difficult. Yet the results were generally more encouraging than they had been in 1865. In Ulster the four Liberals returned, William Kirk in Newry, Richard Dowse in Derry, Thomas McClure in Belfast, and Captain Saunderson in Co. Cavan, were all publicly commited to support temperance legislation, to some degree at least. Among the Conservatives, some, like Sir Hervey H. Bruce in Coleraine, Colonel Knox in Dungannon and Colonel Cole in Co. Fermanagh, made it very clear that they would not vote for such legislation; but Dalway was elected in Carrickfergus, and in Belfast William Johnston of Ballykilbeg, a staunch temperance advocate, topped the poll. Benjamin Whitworth, a vice-president of the United Kingdom Alliance, was re-elected as Liberal M.P. for Drogheda, though he was later unseated on petition. In Dublin Jonathan Pim was returned with Sir Arthur Guinness. Guinness, however, was unseated on petition and replaced in 1870 by Sir Dominic Corrigan, a noted physician and a Liberal, who, though he did not support the permissive bill, was a strong believer in Sunday closing. In Longford O'Reilly was returned unopposed, while Maguire and Murphy were easily re-elected as Liberal M.P.s for Cork city. So although the temperance issue played no great part in the election, a number of Irish M.P.s sympathetic to temperance legislation had been sent to Westminster; most were Liberals, but some, mainly in Ulster, were Conservatives. (**338**, 186-216)[54]

Partly no doubt as a result of their disappointment with O'Reilly's Sunday closing bills, Irish teetotallers campaigned vigorously on behalf of the permissive bill. Sir Wilfrid Lawson had decided to reintroduce the measure in the 1869 session. In support of this, on 26 January 1869 the Irish Permissive Bill Association was formed in Dublin with T. W. Russell as secretary and A. M. Sullivan, the influential editor of the *Nation*, as chairman of the executive. The Dublin Quakers were well represented on the general council of the organisation; James Haughton also joined, as did J. G. Richardson of Bessbrook, who was later to be president of the I.T.L. In four months the association had raised £450 and collected 100,000 signatures on petitions in favour of the permissive bill. But when the bill was introduced the Home Secretary informed Lawson, as the Chief Secretary had informed O'Reilly, that the government was proposing a general reform of licensing laws in the next session and would thus oppose any piecemeal reforms at the present time. This statement, according to the I.T.L. *Journal*, took many votes from the bill, which was defeated by 200 to 94. The Irish vote, however, registered a small majority in favour, with 20 for and 15 against; Ulster M.P.s accounted for twelve of those in favour and only one of those against. Lord Hill-Trevor of Co. Down was the only M.P. to 'disgrace' Ulster, as the *Journal* described it. Given that the majority against had been over 250 in 1864, when the bill had first been voted upon, the 1869 vote, though still a defeat, marked a considerable advance as far as the temperance movement was concerned. Pressure on the Liberal government to take action over the licensing question thus mounted. The I.T.L. was particularly pleased with the Ulster vote, seeing in it the culmination of ten years' temperance agitation. Irish M.P.s outside Ulster voting for the bill included several well known for their temperance sympathies, such as J. A. Blake, Liberal M.P. for Waterford city, McCarthy Downing, Liberal M.P. for Co. Cork, W. P. Urquhart, Liberal M.P. for Co. Westmeath, and Thomas Whitworth, who had replaced his brother Benjamin as Liberal M.P. for Drogheda. The eight M.P.s supporting the bill outside Ulster were all Liberals, but the majority of those supporting it from Ulster were Conservatives. In backing temperance legislation from this time onwards, many Ulster Conservatives were to become increasingly at odds with their own party, which was more and more identified with the drink interest. But while the temperance movement was making progress among Ulster M.P.s, the overall picture with regard to Ireland was still fairly bleak. Only a third of the Irish members had bothered to vote in the division on the permissive bill, and over 40 per cent of these were opposed to it.[55]

The 1850s and 1860s were not decades of increasing drink consumption as the 1820s and 1830s appear to have been; on the contrary, in the late 1850s and early 1860s consumption fell markedly owing to massive tax increases. So the Irish temperance movement was not responding during these years to a direct challenge from the drink industry. What seems to have influenced it more were religious forces and developments in the United States and Britain. The revival of temperance in Ulster in the 1850s, culminating in the foundation of the Irish Temperance League in 1858, reflected the rising tide of Evangelicalism, particularly among Presbyterians. To Evangelicals alcohol was anathema as it represented a major barrier to conversion and to the pursuit of a morally pure life. The appearance of prohibitionist organisations in the United States and Britain, and particularly the successful passage of prohibitory laws in many American states, also acted as a major stimulus to the Irish temperance movement. After the depressing failure of Father Mathew's moral suasionist crusade, prohibition offered not only a new tactic but renewed hope to many of the survivors of the 1840s. Yet there were some who found it too extreme and were more ready to welcome the campaigns for Sunday closing and licensing reform that arose in Britain in the 1850s.

But, whatever the motivation behind it, the character of the temperance movement of the 1850s and 1860s was very different from that of the 1830s and 1840s. Appeals to the rationality of the ruling classes in the 1830s and to the emotions of the people in the 1840s had clearly failed. The new goal was coercive legislation, and it necessitated thorough organisation: the formation of enduring societies, the raising of large sums of money, the employment of professional agents, the production of a sophisticated literature, and the lobbying, if not election, of sympathetic M.P.s. Perhaps the key word here is professional, used both literally and loosely. The temperance advocates of the 1830s and 1840s had been mainly clergy, doctors, lawyers or reformed drunkards working on a part-time basis and sustained by little except their own personal enthusiasm. But from the 1850s there appeared professional temperance advocates: men like Benjamin Benson, John Pyper and T. W. Russell, whose full-time occupation was the promotion of the temperance cause. The movement also became much more professional in a looser sense, being far better organised and financed and not wholly dependent on the zeal of a few individuals for its success or failure.

After the famine the environment in Ireland was in many respects more favourable to the temperance cause: the illicit industry had been largely destroyed; the decline in traditional festivals limited opportunities for excessive drinking; improved education and better policing were generally producing a more tractable population; while the rapid spread of the railway network and the introduction of a cheap national postal service made places and people more easily accessible to temperance agents and their propaganda. But Ireland was predominantly a Catholic country, and thus the position adopted by the Catholic church was crucial to the success or failure of the temperance cause. Despite some staunch individual support for temperance among the clergy, the bulk of the church remained indifferent, if not openly suspicious. The link between temperance and

Protestantism was too strong and the memory of Father Mathew's controversial views too recent to allow the church in the 1850s and 1860s to embrace the anti-drink cause wholeheartedly. Lacking the support of the majority church, the temperance movement had little choice but to pin its hopes on parliament if any substantial change was to be effected.

Temperance in Parliament, 1870-1900

The Licensing Laws

IN 1877 a judge described the Irish licensing laws as 'so complex, uncertain, and contradictory, that it is difficult to carry them into effect, or to reach the meaning and intention of the legislature'. (**40**, 1) After 1872 in Ireland there were fourteen distinctly different types of licence permitting the sale of intoxicating liquors, each licence having attached to it a different set of qualifications and operating conditions. For our purposes, however, only four of these licences are significant: the public-house licence, the spirit-grocer licence, the wholesale beer dealer's licence, and the beer retailer's licence. These were the most commonly held licences, and they also occasioned the most criticism.

The public-house licence was granted to 'inns, alehouses, or victualling-houses' for the sale of beer and other intoxicating liquors in any quantity for consumption on or off the premises. By the mid-1870s there were four classes of publican's licence: the ordinary, or seven-day, licence, which was the most frequently held; the six-day licence, which up until 1878 usually entailed Sunday closing; the early-closing licence, introduced in 1874, which required the publican to close an hour earlier than the holder of an ordinary licence; and fourthly, the six-day early-closing licence, also introduced by the Licensing Act of 1874. The latter three types of licence, with their correspondingly lower fees, were all intended to encourage publicans to shorten their trading hours, particularly at night and on Sunday. But they were not a great success: out of 16,576 public-house licences held in 1877, only 3,159 were of these three varieties, the overwhelming majority of publicans having opted for the full seven-day licence. (**290**, xlvi-xlvii; **36**, 12)

All public-house licences were issued by the excise authorities upon production by the applicant of a certificate granted by the recorder or the magistrates at quarter sessions. This certificate attested to the good character of the applicant, the fitness of his proposed premises to be a public house, and the desirability of further licensed premises in the neighbourhood. The police could appear before the justices and object to the granting of such a certificate, but their objection had to be based on one of these three grounds. Licences had to be renewed each year, and this required the production of two certificates, both testifying to the good character of the publican and the orderly conduct of his house during the preceding twelve months; one certificate was to be signed by six householders of the parish and the other by two or more magistrates presiding at petty sessions. Licences could also be transferred by petty-session magistrates, to another person in the event of the publican's death or to another house in the event of the publican's removal to new premises. In 1878, however, in the case of *The Recorder of Dublin v. Clitheroe* it was decided that a 'transfer cannot be objected to on the grounds of the number of previously licensed houses'. This judgment had the effect of considerably diminishing the powers of the police and magistrates to suppress licences and virtually recognised the publican's vested interest in his or her licence. (**290**, xlvii-lii; **40**, 5)

Some magistrates, particularly the Recorders of Dublin and Belfast, had been endeavouring to reduce the numbers of licences in their cities. Sir Frederick Shaw, who was Recorder of Dublin for nearly forty years up until his death in 1876, had decided in the 1850s that the city had sufficient public houses for its needs, and thereafter he became most reluctant to grant certificates for new ones. His successor, F. R. Falkiner, followed a similar policy, as did Judge Fitzgibbon, who was Recorder of Belfast from 1888. This policy, as intended, did stabilise the numbers of public houses, but it also had the effect of increasing their value substantially and of forcing aspiring publicans to seek other types of liquor licence. A. M. Sullivan, former editor of the *Nation* and Home Rule M.P. for Co. Louth from 1874 to 1880, told the House of Lords select committee on intemperance in 1878 that over the previous twenty years the marketable value of public houses in Dublin had gone up over 500 per cent. In the same year public houses in Merrion Row and on Eden Quay were being sold for around £3,000 each. Although the tied house owned by a brewery or distillery, so common in England, was little known in Ireland, from the 1880s chains of public houses began to appear, for example the Mooney chain in Dublin. (**135**; **40**, 21; **37**, 347; **191** [1888], 11)[1]

Publicans were becoming an increasingly prosperous group in town and country and a group that wielded considerable political power. Even their temperance critics agreed that most publicans were 'respectable'. Samuel Lee Anderson, one of the law officers at Dublin Castle, who took a special interest in licensing questions, thought that publicans had become more law-abiding simply because their licences were too valuable to put at risk. Publicans expressed their political power particularly through town and city corporations. In 1888 Maurice Healy, Home Rule M.P. for Cork city (1885-1900), claimed that 'You have in Irish municipalities practically what I may call a publican franchise. . . . It is a franchise which is up to the level of the the average public house, which excludes persons who are below that level.' In most of the municipalities this level was a property rating valuation of £10, and it created a relatively small electorate. Thus in Dublin, where there were some 40,000 parliamentary voters, there were only 6,644 municipal voters in fifteen wards, ranging in size from 250 to 754 voters. Yet at the same time there were nearly a thousand licensed publicans in the city. Similarly in Cork there were about 14,000 parliamentary voters, but, according to Healy, only 2,059 municipal voters in seven wards, with the average in each being 250. Yet licensed publicans numbered more than 500. In these circumstances it is not surprising to find publicans disproportionately represented on corporations, nor that corporations frequently petitioned against temperance legislation. Healy claimed that Cork corporation was dominated by publicans, though he did not supply any figures to prove this. In 1898, however, a priest from the city, Father Patrick O'Leary, told a royal commission on licensing laws that the city council was 'greatly under the influence of the trade in many ways', with at least ten members being publicans. In 1888 Charles Dawson, twice Lord Mayor of Dublin, admitted that fourteen out of the sixty aldermen and councillors were publicans, though T. W. Russell countered by claiming that in fact twenty, or one-third, of the Dublin corporation were connected with the drink trade. Certainly by the 1890s publicans and grocers were the largest single interest group represented on Dublin corporation, and they did indeed hold one-third of the elected places. Of the eight mayors who appeared before the 1888 select committee on Irish Sunday closing, six were opposed to temperance legislation; two, the Mayors of Waterford and Clonmel, were publicans themselves, while the Mayor of Kilkenny, though having no connection with the trade, told the committee that eleven out of the twenty-four members of his corporation were publicans. (**37**, 407; **39**, 20, 418, 426, 432; **40**, 203; **129**, 205)

As they became more prosperous and politically influential the publicans also became more determined to establish their social respectability. Trade protection societies appeared in Dublin, Belfast and Cork in the 1860s and 1870s. In Dublin the publicans, represented by the Licensed Grocers' and Vintners' Association, regarded themselves as a thoroughly sober and law-abiding section of the community, proved by their flourishing businesses and their active role in civic and charitable affairs. Michael Dwyer, who was secretary of the association in the 1870s, drew attention to the publicans' social responsibilities when in 1877 he said:

> The publican is to be a person fit to be entrusted with a licence; fit, not from his ability to sell liquor, because any man can do that, but from his ability to protect what is much more important, namely good order and temperance. (**36,** 117)

The publicans thus deplored attempts by some temperance advocates to lump them together with what they considered low-class drink sellers, like spirit grocers and beer dealers.

The spirit-grocer licence, which was first introduced in the 1780s and was not dropped until 1910, was largely regulated by the Excise Licences Act of 1825 (6 Geo. IV, c. 81). Under this act a grocer was defined as 'any person dealing in or selling tea, cocoa-nuts, chocolate, or pepper', and once such a person had acquired a liquor licence by paying a fee to the excise, he could sell any quantity of spirits, not exceeding two quarts at a time, for consumption off the premises. This licence was therefore relatively easy to obtain, and persons wishing to sell drink, who were unable to acquire a publican's licence owing to the stringent requirements and the reluctance of magistrates in some areas to grant new ones, could without much difficulty set themselves up nominally as grocers in order to qualify for a spirit grocer's licence. Robert Lindsay, a Belfast merchant and magistrate, estimated in 1868 that only 5 per cent of the town's 102 spirit grocers were genuine grocers, selling tea, coffee and sugar in substantial amounts; the rest relied almost solely on the trade in spirits. The reluctance of the licensing authorities in both Dublin and Belfast to grant new public-house licences led to a substantial increase in spirit grocers in the two places: in 1877 of the 641 spirit grocers in Ireland, 231 were in the city of Dublin and 134 in the town of Belfast. James Kavanagh, secretary of the Dublin Spirit Grocers' Association, said in 1877 that, with the growth of the city and Shaw's refusal to grant publicans' licences, many new areas were left without drink outlets. Kavanagh was very critical of this state of affairs, as it meant that older parts of the city had numerous, if not too many, public houses, while newer parts had none. However, setting up spirit-grocer shops in areas without public houses only encouraged drinking on the premises in violation of the grocer's licence. (**33**, 45; **36**, 12-13, 225, 236, 339)

In other ways also the laws regulating spirit-grocer licences seemed merely to court abuse. In his evidence given to the 1867-8 select committee on Sunday closing, Michael Ralph, president of the Dublin spirit grocers' body, explained that although spirit grocers were permitted to sell up to two quarts at a time, the most frequently purchased amount was a 'noggin' or two glasses. The grocer would supply this in a bottle, though often the customer brought his own bottle and might even insist on pouring in the liquor himself. 'When he does that,' Ralph told the committee, 'he may drink it on the premises in spite of all I can do.' Richard Corr, a superintendent of the Dublin Metropolitan Police force, told the same committee that the 'majority of spirit grocers in Dublin violate the spirit of their licence', though at the same time he agreed when the committee's chairman, Myles O'Reilly, described some of the provisions of the spirit-grocer licence as 'absurd'. (**33**, 34, 82)

The 1872 Licensing Act attempted to improve the situation by bringing spirit grocers for the first time under the control of the magistrates, requiring for their licence a good-character certificate similar to the one needed by publicans, Moreover, the cost of licences, based on the rating valuation of houses, was such as to advantage the publican considerably over the spirit grocer. Thus a publican with a house rated under £10 could get a licence to sell beer and spirits on the premises for £3 6s 1½d, but a spirit grocer with a licence to sell only spirits for consumption off the premises had to pay £9 18s 5¼d per annum. Despite these reforms, however, in summing up his opinion of spirit grocers in 1877 Captain George Talbot, Assistant Commissioner of the D.M.P., declared that 'As long as a spirit grocer can sell a glass of whiskey it will be consumed on the premises.' In February of that year the D.M.P. had sent the Chief Secretary a report on the city's spirit grocers which estimated that about one-half of their shops were 'not well conducted'. At the same time Dublin temperance societies had been undertaking their own investigations of spirit grocers. T. W. Russell toured fifteen spirit-grocer shops one night and claimed to have been served for consumption on the premises in every single one of them. In most cases, he later testified,

> men were drinking at the counter. In other cases they were drinking in a room behind, separated from the shop by a partition, a check-string from behind the counter opening the door. We saw as many as a dozen people drinking in those places, with the police often standing on the pavement outside the shop. We saw people in other spirit grocers' shops from the windows drinking openly just the same as if they were public houses. . . .

The erection of partitions in grocer shops behind which drinking could take place was apparently a common practice, as was the stationing of boys at strategic locations outside the shop to give warning, usually by a whistle, of the approach of the police. (**290**, lxxiii-lxxiv; **36**, 21, 144-5, 124, 151)[2]

Relations between publicans and spirit grocers were generally far from amicable. The publicans felt that they were acquiring a bad name and having unnecessary restrictions imposed upon them because of the reckless and often illegal conduct of spirit grocers and beer dealers. They were, moreover, losing business to these traders who were more ready to stay open during prohibited hours, when law-abiding publicans were forced to close their houses. Michael Dwyer denied that the publicans wanted to see spirit grocers 'driven into the bankruptcy court or their livelihoods altogether taken away from them'. Nevertheless, in the 1860s and 1870s the publicans were frequently in agreement with the police and magistrates, and even with some temperance advocates, in seeking stricter regulation of other drink traders. They went so far as to send deputations to London in 1876 to lobby M.P.s in favour of a bill imposing minimum rating valuations on beerhouses. The spirit grocers for their part resented the fact that they had to pay a higher licence fee than the publicans, while at the same time their right to sell drink was more limited. Moreover, when they attempted to apply for publicans' licences they were invariably opposed in the courts, not so much by temperance men, but by the publicans themselves. Michael Ralph, who claimed to represent the majority of the 198 spirit grocers in Dublin city in 1868, said that they wanted one licence for all liquor retailers to sell for consumption on or off the premises, the cost of the licence being a function of the valuation of the house. He added that he wanted all beerhouses suppressed — and, on this point at least, the publicans and the spirit grocers were in agreement. (**36**, 117-18, 101, 241; **33**, 32)[3]

In an effort to encourage the consumption of liquors other than spirits and also to raise revenue, parliament passed two acts in 1863 and 1864 affecting Irish liquor licensing. The first, the Revenue Act of 1863 (26 & 27 Vict., c. 33), permitted wholesale beer dealers — that is, anyone having taken out an excise licence to sell not less than $4\frac{1}{2}$ gallons of beer at any one time for consumption off the premises — to take out an additional licence on payment of the excise duty of 1 guinea to sell beer in any quantity less than $4\frac{1}{2}$ gallons for consumption off the premises. This retail beer licence required no magistrate's certificate, the only qualification necessary being the possession of a wholesale beer licence. The second act, the Beerhouses Act of 1864 (27 & 28 Vict., c. 35), attempted to restrict eligibility for the retail licence by specifying that the excise authorities could not grant such a licence or its renewal without a certificate from the magistrates. But this 1864 act did not specifically withdraw the right conferred in 1863 of a wholesale beer dealer to obtain a retail licence simply on payment of a fee. People seeking a retail licence therefore found that they could circumvent the requirement for a magistrate's certificate by first acquiring a wholesale licence from the excise, which required no certificate, and then taking out a retail one. In these circumstances, under the 1863 act, no certificate was required for a retail beer licence. As a result of these provisions, by the end of 1864 there were over 300 retail beerhouses in Ireland, and within five years they had risen to nearly 900. (**34**, 421)[4]

Condemnation of the beerhouses, before they were substantially reformed in 1874 and 1877, was both widespread and severe, particularly in Dublin, where nearly one-third of them were concentrated. The *Freeman's Journal* editorialised against them frequently for over ten years, describing them on one occasion as an 'unmitigated evil', which 'generate and shelter . . . hideousness and abominations'. Charles Joseph O'Donel, a long-serving Dublin divisional magistrate, portrayed the beer dealers in 1877 as 'a miserable type of penniless paupers', and he claimed that the whole profit of their trade was on Sunday morning, their 'dens' being 'frequented by hundreds of the lower ranks of the labouring class'. However, it was a working man, Patrick Higgins, a master cooper at

Guinness's brewery and president of the Coopers' Society, who most graphically described the *modus operandi* of the beerhouses. He said that

> It was the system with the people in the lower parts of the city, if they had only a dozen of turf, to bring it into the shop or cellar, it did not matter which, and a few pipes, and some bottles with Guinness's label on them; and they would pick up an old label of Guinness's or Mander's, and would stick them in the window. There was sufficient guarantee for the person that owned the apartment to go and get out a licence to sell beer from six o'clock in the morning until six o'clock the following morning, night and day. (**36**, 123, 162)[5]

Pressure for reform of the beerhouses mounted. In the 1874 Licensing Act magistrates' certificates were introduced as requirements for wholesale beer dealers' licences, thus closing the major loophole left by the legislation of 1863-4. Furthermore, in 1877 Charles Meldon, Home Rule M.P. for Co. Kildare, had little difficulty in getting through parliament his Beer Licences Regulation (Ireland) Act (40 & 41 Vict., c. 4). This act specified rating valuations of £15 or upwards in cities and towns with populations exceeding 10,000 and £8 or upwards elsewhere, before a house could qualify for a wholesale or retail beer licence. In addition, such rated premises had to have been in the exclusive occupation of the applicant for at least three months preceding the date of the grant. This latter provision aimed to do away with the temporary use of cellars and rooms in tenements for the sale of beer, as described by Higgins. The effect of this legislation was dramatic. The number of wholesale beer dealers fell from 1,223 in 1873 to 635 in 1878-9, while the number of retail dealers fell over the same period from 939 to 466. (**343**, 403-5)

The story of the retail beer licence during the 1860s and 1870s provides a classic example of how well-intentioned licensing legislation only succeeded in creating rather than solving problems. Much of the criticism directed at beer dealers, spirit grocers and even publicans really concerned the regulations under which they were forced to operate, for these regulations were frequently inadequate, confusing, impossible to enforce properly and sometimes simply ridiculous. Sections of the Irish temperance movement therefore devoted much of their attention to the issue of licensing, believing that reform in this area would go a long way towards solving the problem of excessive drinking.

These complex licences by no means exhaust the forms of liquor retailing practised in Ireland in the last third of the nineteenth century. They merely cover the legal trade, sanctioned and administered by the government. The illegal trade, carried on in 'night-houses' and 'shebeens', was clearly a significant feature during the period. How it compared with the legal trade in numbers of houses or quantities of liquor sold is impossible to determine with any accuracy. Statistics of prosecutions for illegal selling are highly unreliable, being a function of the attitude of the police rather than a true reflection of the size of the industry. However, the continued existence of an obviously substantial illegal trade, as well as the contempt for the licensing laws frequently shown by spirit grocers and beer dealers, was attributed by many supporters of temperance reform to laxity on the part of the police. A. M. Sullivan claimed in 1878 that the 'police in Dublin could put their hands in a morning upon nearly every shebeen in the city; those places are very well known'. T. W. Russell, on his late-night tours of spirit-grocer shops, found constables standing on the pavement outside, making no effort to intervene in the illegal drinking going on within. When Captain Talbot, recently promoted to be Commissioner of the D.M.P., told the House of Lords select committee on intemperance in 1878 that Sunday drunkenness was not a great problem in Dublin, temperance supporters were out in force the following Sunday between 7 p.m. and 9 p.m., watching fifty public houses in the city. They counted 1,066 drunken persons emerging from these shops, whereas police arrests for drunkenness on that day amounted to only thirty-eight. (**37**, 351, 391)

Temperance advocates like Russell were convinced that the police did not properly enforce the licensing laws because too many had relatives in the drink trade or aspired to the status of publican themselves on retirement. It is certainly true that the Royal Irish Constabulary was forced to institute measures to prevent the wives of policemen from taking out liquor licences. But the situation was rather more complex than this. Nationalists, for instance, claimed that the problem was not that the police did not enforce the laws, but that they enforced them in a discriminatory fashion. Eugene Crean, president of the Cork United Trades Council, was a teetotaller, though his council strongly opposed temperance legislation. In 1888, acknowledging that the 'great majority' of Cork publicans were nationalists, Crean claimed that the police were much more ready to prosecute nationalist publicans for minor breaches of the licensing laws than they were to prosecute non-nationalist publicans. Father Robert Power, a parish priest in Waterford city for nearly twenty years and the head of a temperance society, agreed that similar discrimination occurred in Waterford. The police, however, did face genuine difficulties in their task of enforcing the licensing laws, difficulties arising both from public opinion and from the laws themselves. In 1877 F. R. Falkiner, the recently appointed Recorder of Dublin, summed up one of these problems well when he said:

It is fair for me to say with respect to the police, that I believe any supineness on their part which has been in the past, is to a large extent a reflection of the general apathy on the part of the public largely. I think that the police force can do anything in which they are supported by the public voice and by their own authorities; but it could not be expected that a policeman would wish to take the invidious position of summoning and having heavily fined, or having a man's livelihood taken away, by opposing at the renewal sessions a person who was not committing a police offence, as a policeman's idea would understand it, that is to say, who was not committing any breach of the peace, but who was quietly going in and getting a glass of whiskey.

A rather similar point was made twenty years later by Sir Andrew Reed, Inspector-General of the R.I.C., who was also a barrister and the author of a major work on Irish licensing laws. Referring to the limited influence that the clergy seemed able to exercise against drunkenness, he said the main problem was public opinion, which did not regard drunkenness as a 'moral offence'. (**40**, 37, 28; **39**, 352-3, 392; **36**, 64) So while the public chose to regard petty breaches of the licensing laws as no crime at all, policemen were understandably loath to pursue too vigorously those selling or consuming drink illegally.

But perhaps an even greater obstacle to the effective policing of the retail drink trade was to be found in some of the provisions of the laws themselves. We have already seen how shortcomings in the laws regulating spirit grocers and beer dealers opened the way for illegal trading. On this point it is only fair to note that senior police officers were very much to the fore in identifying these shortcomings and suggesting ways in which they could be overcome. In 1868 the then Commissioner of the D.M.P., John Lewis O'Ferrall, placed a comprehensive plan before the select committee on Irish Sunday closing for reforming the laws relating to spirit grocers and beer dealers, and many of these suggestions found their way into the Licensing Acts of 1872 and 1874. (**197**; **33**, 119) The police in fact repeatedly complained of unnecessary restrictions placed upon their power to enter suspected houses, of poorly defined offences, and of the lack of effective penalties.

Two examples will suffice to illustrate the sort of problems the police faced. The illicit trade was regulated by the Unlicensed Houses Acts of 1839 and 1854 (2 & 3 Vict., c. 79; 17 & 18 Vict., c. 89), which authorised magistrates to issue police with warrants to enter suspected houses and set a maximum fine of £2 for 'selling, keeping or exposing for sale' liquor without a licence. By the 1860s the police were complaining of the inadequacy of this penalty, and, as a result, in the 1872 Licensing Act the fine was raised substantially to a maximum of £50 for the first offence. But at the same time the definition of the offence was narrowed by the omission of the phrase 'keeping for sale'. This had the effect of making successful prosecutions of unlicensed traders far more difficult, for the police had now to prove that an actual sale had occurred, not merely that it was intended. Talbot admitted before the 1877 select committee that this was 'almost impossible'. The police therefore found themselves having to revert to the

1854 act, which had not been repealed, in order to ensure a conviction. As Talbot explained, 'We entered under the act of 1874, but were directed to proceed under the 17th and 18th of Victoria.' But the problem with invoking the old act was that the maximum penalty for the first offence then remained at a £2 fine. In other important respects also the 1872 and 1874 acts curtailed police powers. Previously it had been an offence to 'oppose, obstruct or delay to admit' a constable onto licensed premises at any time. Under sections 35 of the 1872 act and 23 of the 1874 act, however, the offence became 'refuses or fails to admit' a constable, and it carried a penalty of up to £5 for the first offence. Again Talbot explained the considerable practical implications of this apparently minor alteration of wording:

> The consequence is that when we go to the premises, and ask to go in, they may have drinking inside, but they delay to admit us; then, after they have cleared away everything from the police, and let the men out, perhaps by the back premises, they open the door and say 'we have not failed to admit you'.

Thus, although the 1872 and 1874 Licensing Acts facilitated the regulation of spirit grocers and beer dealers through the introduction of magistrates' certificates, they made policing of illicit traders more difficult through the omission of the offences of 'keeping for sale' and 'delaying to admit'. (**36**, 38; **37**, 336)

As well as legal impediments, police tactics, in Dublin at least, also probably contributed to problems in enforcing the licensing laws. In Belfast, Cork, Waterford and Limerick the police employed a small number of plain-clothes officers in order to detect illicit trading. In Belfast, for instance, at least two plain-clothes men were assigned to each of the town's four police districts. Such an officer was instructed not to act as an *agent provocateur*, encouraging illicit sales, but merely to observe sales and prosecute sellers. The various inspectors who reported on this system in 1877 expressed considerable satisfaction with its operation. The D.M.P., however, strongly resisted the suggestion that plain-clothes men should be used in this way. Talbot claimed that the magistrates were hostile to such tactics and that such men would be looked upon as 'common informers' by the people. (This consideration did not deter some of the city's temperance societies: they used informers to gather evidence upon which objections could be lodged in the courts to the renewals of many drink sellers' licences.) According to Talbot, the D.M.P. did not

> put a man to watch the public houses; he walks his beat, for instance, from King Street to Stephen Street, or to George Street, and he walks back again, and he watches the whole of the public houses on that beat, and if he detects an infringement of the law, he reports it to the serjeant, because

there is a serjeant armed with warrants, whose particular business it is to go through every district watching the public houses and entering them; and if they find breaches of the law, it is reported to the Commissioner of Police, who orders a summons to take place.

Here, then, is the explanation for the constables T. W. Russell saw standing outside spirit-grocer shops. Constables of the D.M.P. were considered too young and inexperienced to be allowed to enter and investigate licensed premises, unless specifically called in by the owner of the house to maintain order. Only specially selected sergeants were permitted to enter such dangerous territory, though doubtless in many instances by the time the sergeant had arrived illegal selling had ceased. In Belfast, on the other hand, every policeman was charged with enforcing the licensing laws. In his influential *Irish Constable's Guide* Sir Andrew Reed set out R.I.C. policy based on section 23 of the 1874 Licensing Act. This was that a constable was

authorised at all times to enter the licensed premises of a publican, beer retailer, or spirit grocer... but this right is subject to the qualification that his entry be for the purpose of preventing or detecting the violation of any of the provisions of either Licensing Act, 1872 or 1874.

In the case of the enforcement of some earlier licensing acts, the constable required a warrant from a magistrate before entry. (**36**, 226, 249, 271, 307, 37; **289**, 218-19)

In Dublin the failure to use plain-clothes men and the cautious use of uniformed constables undoubtedly diminished police effectiveness, particularly given the ingenuity of illicit traders. John Duignan, secretary of the city's Brassfounders' Society, in urging greater police vigilance in 1877, drew on his own experience to illustrate the problem:

I live at 17, Lower Gloucester-street, and there is in that street the Gloucester diamond. I generally go to prayers in the morning about 8 o'clock, or a little before, and in the centre of that diamond I see a boy, or a young lad perhaps, 16 or 18 years of age, or sometimes younger, and he can see up and down and crosswise. A policeman could not come within 300 or 400 yards before he would be seen, and I have heard some shrill whistle given by the lad putting his finger in his mouth, and I have seen men coming out of the houses immediately.

Criticisms of the D.M.P.'s tactics reached a peak in 1876. The Irish Permissive Bill Association led by Russell conducted its own investigation into illicit drinking in the city and laid its findings in the form of a twenty-page submission before the Chief Secretary, Sir Michael Hicks Beach. This document contained eleven specific charges against the police, and it elicited in response a fifty-page document from Sir Henry Lake, and

D.M.P. Commissioner, refuting each criticism in detail. After close questioning by Hicks Beach, however, Lake conceded that a 'departure, to some extent, from the ordinary system of supervision may now be adopted'. The result was the creation of a small staff of experienced men under Inspector Gorman to deal solely with licensed houses, supported by the issuing of warrants to one hundred first-class constables. This group came into operation in April 1877, and its effectiveness was warmly attested to by T. W. Russell, who said: 'We saw that where formerly there was one prosecution for illicit dealing there were thirty then, and the trade was astounded.' (**36,** 151; **37,** 394)[6]

Although the Irish temperance movement took an active interest in measures to reform and enforce the existing licensing laws, essentially it sought major changes in these laws, particularly in the form of Sunday closing and the permissive bill. So, while it monitored the actions of police, opposed licence applications before the magistrates and fought against publicans in local elections, most of its time and money in the 1870s and 1880s went into campaigns to promote legislation at Westminster.

The Fight for Sunday Closing, 1870-78

In 1869 the Liberal government had committed itself to a major reform of the licensing laws in the following session. A licensing bill was announced in the queen's speech in February 1870, but the government failed to introduce it, much to the disappointment of the temperance movement in both England and Ireland. The government, however, indicated that it would bring in such a bill in 1871. In the meantime both the Irish Permissive Bill and Sunday Closing Associations continued their agitation for their respective measures. Lawson's bill was introduced again in 1869 and 1870, but was defeated soundly in both cases — by 193 to 87 and 121 to 90 respectively. Lawson 'noted how in permissive bill debates the sound of the division bell caused members to rush out of the house instead of rushing in; in a division where public feeling ran high both for and against, members wanted to save their consciences and their seats'. (**173,** 261) Doubtless many Irish M.P.s found it expedient to be absent during divisions on Irish temperance legislation, for absenteeism proved a continuing problem for temperance lobbyists. During these years the Irish Sunday Closing Association held numerous meetings and petitioned the government to include total Sunday closing in their proposed bill, rather than a shortening of hours as O'Reilly's bill had envisaged. But when the government bill, drawn up by H. A. Bruce, the Home Secretary, finally appeared in April 1871 it infuriated the trade on the one hand, while failing to satisfy the various elements in the temperance movement on the other.

The bill was imaginative, far-reaching, and also very complicated, running to some ninety foolscap pages. It stated that all existing licence-holders were to be entitled to renew their licences for ten years at a small charge and that no reduction in the numbers of licences was to occur during this period. At the end of it, however, the licensing authorities were to decide, according to a prescribed formula, how many licences were to be issued for the next ten years, and these were to be sold to the highest bidder — the process to be repeated every ten years. The proportion of licences to population was to be 1 per 1,000 in urban areas and 1 per 60 in rural areas. If the magistrates proposed to grant more than the allotted quota, a poll of ratepayers was to be taken. A majority vote of 60 per cent against such an extension could prevent it. Thus the bill contained an element of local control. Bruce also proposed a sharp reduction in hours of opening and admitted another local control mechanism when he specified that 60 per cent of ratepayers could empower the magistrates to curtail weekday evening closing to 9 p.m. and to close public houses totally on Sunday. (**173**, 264-5; **343**, 106)

The English drink trade mounted a fierce campaign against this bill. In the wake of the Paris Commune, they called Bruce a 'communist', claiming that in effect the measure meant that after ten years their property would be confiscated. An increasing number of Conservatives came to support the vintners, and eventually, in the face of mounting opposition, the government decided to drop the bill. In April 1872 Bruce brought in a second licensing bill, far more moderate than the first, which became the Licensing Act of 1872. (**316,** 145-8, 166-9; **136,** 30-3) The United Kingdom Alliance had also condemned the 1871 bill, but, in its case, for not going far enough, and it devoted much of its attention to the permissive bill, which was introduced again in 1871 and 1872. Under this barrage of licensing legislation in the early 1870s, the political parties were becoming polarised, with the Liberals, influenced by the Nonconformist churches, tending to look more sympathetically upon bills aimed to restrict the drink trade, while the Conservatives began to appear as champions of the drink industry. This trend can be seen clearly in the division lists for the permissive bill. When the bill was first introduced in 1864 151 Liberals and 111 Conservatives had voted against it. Ten years later, however, in 1874, these figures were 78 and 192 respectively. Leaders of the U.K.A., such as Sir Wilfrid Lawson and G. O. Trevelyan, who were both also Liberal M.P.s, were beginning to speak of the Liberal party as the 'temperance party'. (**173**, 269-70)

The Irish temperance movement was also deeply involved in these developments. In 1870 and 1871 the Irish Permissive Bill Association was especially active, holding meetings throughout the country. Resolutions in favour of the permissive principle passed at such gatherings were forwarded to Dublin Castle and to Westminster. Bruce's gesture towards local option in his 1871 bill was welcomed, but generally regarded as not going far enough. In April 1871 a meeting in Ballymena passed a resolution expressing 'satisfaction' with Bruce's bill 'so far as it concedes the principle of a ratepayers' veto, and curtails limits the sale of intoxicating liquors'. But at the same time the meeting protested

> in the most emphatic manner against those clauses by which the ratepayers' veto is limited, by which new licences will be granted to present holders of licence certificates, and by which new licences will be granted for ten years instead of one as at present.

Other gatherings organised by the I.P.B.A. passed almost identical resolutions.[7] The association lobbied the members for Dublin city, Jonathan Pim and Sir Dominic Corrigan, but though both supported Sunday closing, neither would commit himself to the permissive principle. In that year, however, 33 Irish M.P.s did vote in favour of Lawson's bill, with 18 voting against it.[8] But abstentions remained high, while those in favour of the bill were overwhelmingly M.P.s representing Ulster constituencies. In January 1872 a deputation from the I.P.B.A. saw Lord Hartington, the Chief Secretary, who made it clear that the government had no intention of supporting their measure. They were followed on the same day by a deputation from the I.S.C.A. To them Hartington said that the government would limit Sunday trading hours in its proposed bill, but that it would not introduce total Sunday closing. Within a month Pim and Corrigan, who had accompanied both delegations, had, with the support of several Ulster M.P.s, introduced an Irish Sunday closing bill.[9]

There was clearly more support in Ireland for measures to limit hours and restrict licences than there was for the permissive bill. On 11 December 1871, in a editorial dealing with what it saw as the approaching crisis in the licensing question, the *Freeman's Journal* urged the vintners to take a more positive stance:

> We freely acknowledge, as we have often acknowledged before, that the vintners of Ireland constitute a body of staunch friends of the Liberal party, and of willing helps in every cause of charity that is put before them. But, in this matter of licensing they have seemed to fancy every man's hand was lifted against them, and it was needful to clothe themselves all over in an impenetrable panoply.

But the *Freeman's Journal* felt that 'to rest content with picking holes in the well-meant proposals of others, and to take no share in the suggestion of better', was a 'mistaken policy'. For it was 'beyond dispute' that reforms were called for. 'We have only to walk in our streets', the editorial went on, 'to be made sensible that drunkenness is not decreasing in our midst.' The *Freeman's Journal* suggested that Sunday opening be restricted to three or four hours, that weeknight closing be set at 10 p.m., and that trade societies be forbidden to meet in public houses. The response of the Licensed Grocers' and Vintners' Association, however, was to shift all the blame on to their competitors, the spirit grocers and the beer dealers. A deputation from the association saw the Chief Secretary on 12 January 1872 and told him that these other drink traders should be more strictly controlled and that illicit selling should be stamped out. The *Freeman's Journal* professed itself disappointed, for 'nothing was proposed — nothing was suggested', and it went on to charge that 'Whilst vintners and spirit grocers are warring about points of trade our people are being ruined and slain by the demon evil that is amongst us.' But the paper took up some of the publicans' suggestions and added to its earlier list of reforms the suppression of beerhouses and good-conduct certificates for spirit grocers. However, it opposed total Sunday closing, believing that this would cause great inconvenience to the public and that it would lead inevitably to an increase in illicit drinking.[10]

But on 28 February Sir Dominic Corrigan introduced just such a bill. In moving the second reading in June, Corrigan stressed that the bill only aimed to introduce in Ireland the system that had been in existence in Scotland for many years. He stated categorically that the bill was not in any way connected with the permissive bill agitation. Corrigan personally did not support local option, but, as we have already seen, both the Irish Temperance League and the vintners regarded Sunday closing as merely a step on the road to prohibition. The second-reading debate was adjourned at the dinner recess and never resumed. The *Times*, in commenting on the bill, admired Corrigan's courage in introducing such a measure, for he had aroused the 'fierce hostility of the vintners', who exercised great political influence in Ireland and especially in Dublin. The Dublin vintners were certainly infuriated. They claimed not to have been informed of Corrigan's intention to move such a bill, and they immediately sent representatives to London, both to see Corrigan and also to organise opposition with the help of the English trade. As a result, W. St J. Wheelhouse, M.P. for Leeds, who was one of the English trade's staunchest parliamentary supporters, gave notice of a question concerning the undue haste with which the bill was being proceeded. The vintners believed that this quick action on their part, with English help, led to the delaying of the second reading until June and ultimately to the demise of the bill.[11]

On 15 March the Dublin vintners' association held a general meeting at which Corrigan was present. Michael Dwyer, their hard-working secretary, attacked the bill savagely, labelling it a 'penal law' which was aimed against Corrigan's own constituents. He claimed that it was 'vexatious' to raise the question of Sunday closing just when the government was proposing comprehensive legislation. Corrigan, in reply, denied that he had rushed the bill, arguing that there would be plenty of time to discuss it during the committee stage. He also said that support for such a measure was widespread, instancing the various religious and political allegiances of its movers. He referred to the Catholic dioceses in which Sunday closing had been operating for more than ten years, without increases in illicit drinking or protests from the inhabitants. Laurence Byrne, chairman of the meeting, responded by regretting that Corrigan had allowed himself to become 'an instrument' of the 'platform patriots, and the sham philanthropists of the permissive society'. The meeting thereupon passed a resolution calling for the withdrawal of the bill. At their regular meeting the following week Byrne answered Corrigan's remarks further by pointing out that in 1870 most of them had voted for him rather than for Guinness, whom they might have been expected to support out of trade interests. They thus now felt betrayed by one whom they had expected to act as their champion. Byrne went on to deplore the fact that William Johnston of Ballykilbeg, who was notorious for his sectarian views, was one of the bill's sponsors. Byrne argued that voluntary Sunday closing carried out by the clergy, traders and people co-operating together was a very different matter from a 'coercion bill smuggled through parliament'.[12]

The Irish vintners found themselves working closely with the English trade to fight temperance legislation, for the English trade already had well-organised defence associations and a strong parliamentary presence. But this drew the Irish vintners, who were generally Liberals, closer to the Conservatives. In April 1872, for instance, the vintners received urgent requests from trade societies in London, Manchester, Birmingham and Liverpool, asking them to rally Irish M.P.s to support the Conservatives' licensing bill proposed by Sir Henry Selwin Ibbetson. (**316**, 167-8) The Dublin association, however, waited until the last minute hoping for the government's proposed measure to appear, as they were most reluctant to support a Conservative bill. Finally they did ask Irish M.P.s to attend and support the bill. Sir John Gray, for instance, wrote that he had attended at their request, but the bill had been talked out.[13]

At a special conference on licensing organised by the Dublin vintners in June the problems faced by the trade were made clearer. Byrne said that

> With regard to Sir Dominic Corrigan's Sunday closing bill, their society opposed it, and would continue to oppose it, firstly because it originated with the agents of the Permissive Bill Association, who merely used it as a weapon to strike at the trade, and who, if they succeeded with Sunday closing, would simply regard it as a first step towards carrying their pet scheme, viz., the total closing of licensed houses on weekdays as well as Sunday. But they opposed it still more because of the disastrous effect their adhesion to such a scheme would have on their relations with the English trade, to whom they were under many obligations and whose interests they would be sacrificing by going in for Sunday closing.[14]

So Byrne was not arguing that the Irish trade was against Sunday closing *per se*, but that opposition was necessary for tactical reasons. He feared that Sunday closing, if conceded, would strengthen the hand of the prohibitionists. Moreover, the Irish needed to remain on good terms with the

English trade, which was not prepared to make any concession on the issue of trading hours. These pressing considerations doubtless accounted for the vintners' negative attitude, of which the *Freeman's Journal* had complained. But they were under pressure from the other direction as well. They were sensitive to criticism, particularly from sympathetic sources like the *Freeman's Journal*. The support given by Cardinal Cullen and a number of the bishops to Sunday closing was an embarrassment, while they found themselves in the invidious position, for an Irish organisation, of being dependent on the English trade and increasingly committed to supporting Conservative policies. From this political impasse the Irish vintners were ultimately saved by the emergence of the Home Rule party. Support for it allowed them to reconcile their political principles with their material interests.

The Liberals' Licensing Act of 1872 did not satisfy the Irish temperance movement, as it did not contain any local option mechanism and merely shortened Sunday trading hours along the lines proposed in O'Reilly's 1869 bill. Other matters arising from the act also created concern. In September a deputation from the I.P.B.A. saw Colonel Henry Lake, the Commissioner of the Dublin Metropolitan Police, and presented him with various questions regarding the operation of the act, particularly concerning the definition of a town under the act and after-hours sales in hotels and taverns. At the same time the I.T.L. wrote to Hartington pointing out confusions in the act with regard to trading hours. This forced the vintners into the position of defenders of the act. Certainly it was less unacceptable to them than the 1871 bill or the measures proposed by the temperance movement. Writing to Hartington in May 1873, Dwyer conceded that there had been 'some petty misunderstandings in its administration by the magistrates', but that, despite these, the act had 'already effected a very great amount of public good'. Several drafts of bills to amend the 1872 act with regard to Ireland were prepared by Dublin Castle early in 1873. On 31 July Colonel Lake wrote to the Under-Secretary at the Castle, T. H. Burke, urging the 'expediency of passing, if at all practicable, before the session closes, the bill prepared to amend the Licensing Act, 1872'. However, on 2 August Hartington noted on this letter: 'I found that it was useless to introduce this bill, as any amendment of the Licensing Act would be made use of for the purpose of reopening the discussion on the whole question.'[15] Doubtless Hartington was correct. The temperance movement had numerous objections to the act, while one of the first actions of the new Tory government in the following year was to introduce a major licensing bill.

As well as criticising the Liberals' Licensing Act, the Irish temperance movement during 1873 continued its campaign for Sunday closing. Corrigan reintroduced his bill, though, as in the previous year, he had great difficulty in getting time for a second-reading debate. He did not secure this until July, which meant that the bill had little chance of getting through. In his speech he urged the house to complete what the Licensing Act had begun.

> I do not want [he said] to interfere with England — give us what they have in Scotland. . . . I appeal now to English members. If drunkenness, with its train of vice, fighting, and murder — has become a national disgrace in Ireland, who inflicted it on us? Not an Irish, but an English parliament.

Although personally opposed to Home Rule, Corrigan was here demonstrating that the licensing question could easily be turned into an argument in favour of an Irish parliament. The ensuing debate showed the Irish members to be deeply divided over the question. Philip Callan, Liberal M.P. for Dundalk, opposed the bill as coercive, discriminatory legislation which would only promote the growth of shebeens, though at the same time he upheld the permissive principle. Henry Bruen, Conservative M.P. for Carlow, criticised the bill as too extreme, but as he had received a petition from his constituents in its favour and none against, he felt obliged to support the second reading at least. Sir Frederick Heygate, Conservative M.P. for Co. Londonderry, took a similar line for the same reason. But Sir Patrick O'Brien, Liberal M.P. for King's County, who also opposed the measure personally and had received petitions in its favour, decided to abstain. Sir Hervey Bruce, Conservative M.P. for Coleraine, opposed the bill as discriminatory, as did Serjeant Sherlock, Liberal M.P. for King's County. McCarthy Downing, Liberal M.P. for Co. Cork, like Callan, supported local option but felt that Sunday closing would discriminate against the poor and so was opposed to it. On the other hand, John Martin, elected for Meath in 1871 as an Independent Nationalist, supported the bill, believing it was what the Irish people wanted. With more genuine commitment than Corrigan, he also evoked the spectre of Home Rule, adding that if an Irish parliament was sitting in College Green the wishes of the people would certainly be observed. Ironically, the nationalist Martin found a supporter in Colonel Stuart Knox, Conservative M.P. for Dungannon, though Knox argued in favour of Sunday closing from a very different premise. According to him, Fenians used public houses on Sundays to hold meetings and seek recruits, and thus Sunday closing would be an important blow against them. As this example shows, the debates in parliament on Irish temperance legislation produced curious political alignments, sometimes throwing Home Rulers and Conservatives together and sometimes driving Home Rulers and Liberals apart. In this particular debate Hartington replied for the government by arguing that the new Licensing Act was adequate to handle all the problems that existed. The government therefore opposed any further legislation. Wheelhouse, who also spoke, contented himself with the simple but powerful warning to English members, that if Sunday closing was passed for Ireland, England would be next. That this argument carried much weight was shown by the division which followed. Callan's amendment that the bill be read three months hence was carried by 140 to 83. The majority in favour was largely composed of English M.P.s.[16]

The defeats of 1872 and 1873 forced upon the Sunday closing movement the need for reorganisation. English M.P.s had to be shown that there was a strong popular demand for Sunday closing in Ireland. On 9 December 1873 a national conference organised by the I.S.C.A. was held in Dublin with the aim of revitalising the campaign. It was attended by leaders of the Dublin temperance movement, clergy, magistrates and aldermen. T. W. Russell was present and agreed to become secretary of the association, while retaining the same position with the I.P.B.A. An important step was thus taken towards uniting the two organisations. Corrigan became president, with thirty-six vice-presidents. Twenty of these were clerics, including Archbishop Leahy of Cashel, Archbishop Trench of Dublin, seven Catholic and three Church of Ireland bishops, the Presbyterian Moderator, and the leaders of the Wesleyan and Primitive Methodist Conferences. The executive committee consisted of twenty-four members, with the names Allen, Webb, Wigham and Pim being prominent. P. P. McSwiney, the future Lord Mayor of Dublin, and A. M. Sullivan, the future Home Rule M.P., were also members. The conference appointed agents, both to lobby M.P.s and to publicise the cause in Ireland, and resolved to raise a fighting fund of £1,000. (55)

The unexpected general election of February 1874 set both the reorganised Sunday closing movement and the publicans' associations campaigning vigorously. With more temperance legislation pending, both were anxious to increase their support in parliament. The Dublin vintners' association sought to avoid the problem of its divided political loyalties by declaring itself politically neutral but determined to prevent the election of persons hostile to trade interests. In an election manifesto it reiterated its argument that Sunday closing was merely a front for the prohibitionists:

> Those who, from religious motives, would be favourable to Sunday closing, if it were possible to enforce it without vastly increasing the illicit drinking in beerhouses and unlicensed premises, now so extensively prevalent throughout the city and suburbs, are respectfully reminded that the present attack is mainly supported by the paid agents of the United Kingdom Alliance for the Total Suppression of the Liquor Traffic, whose avowed object is to injure the licensed traders as much as they can, and who, if they succeed in closing licensed houses on one day of the week, will be encouraged to make redoubled efforts to shut them up during the other six days also.

The vintners' tone was injured and a trifle bewildered, but at the same time they were careful to emphasise their political power. James Mooney, the new president of the association, noted that they had 'borne very calmly the insults which had been freely heaped upon them by people from whom they did not deserve them', while the former president, Laurence Byrne, remarked that they were 'as respectable as any other class of traders, had as much ideas of right and wrong', and were merely trying to protect their vested interests and their good name. But he followed this by warning that there were 800 licensed traders in Dublin, with quite enough votes between them to determine the election in the city. That this was no exaggerated claim was clearly demonstrated by the election result. Corrigan did not even stand, concluding that his opposition to Home Rule, combined with the hostility of the vintners towards him, 'made his candidature hopeless'. Pim was soundly defeated. He had been in Florence when the election was announced and did not get back to Dublin until 31 January. But his opposition to Home Rule and denominational education, together with his support for Sunday closing, were probably the main reasons for his defeat. (**259**, 275-322)[17]

Both the I.P.B.A. and the I.S.C.A. lobbied candidates and issued addresses urging voters only to support those who had pledged themselves to vote for temperance legislation. The I.S.C.A. issued a special address in Dublin supporting Pim, but the influential *Freeman's Journal* supported Maurice Brooks, the Lord Mayor, and rejected both Pim and Sir Arthur Guinness because they were hostile to Home Rule. In Dublin Guinness topped the poll with 5,213 votes, followed by Brooks with 4,838, and with Pim a distant third, receiving only 1,937 votes. The *Freeman's Journal* attributed Guinness's victory in large measure to his having won the votes of Liberal vintners and to Pim splitting the rest of the Liberal vote by standing against Brooks as an anti-Home Rule candidate. 'But for the vote of Liberal vintners,' said the paper, 'which naturally went to their trade champion, the Lord Mayor would have been at the head of the poll.'[18]

The 1874 election was a disaster for the Liberals, and nowhere more so than in Ireland. In 1868 66 Liberals had been elected for Irish constituencies; in 1874 the figure was 10. The Conservatives fell from 37 to 33, while 60 M.P.s committed in varying degrees to Home Rule were elected. Although Corrigan, Pim, Lord Claud Hamilton and Thomas McClure, all sponsors of the 1872-3 Sunday closing bill, were defeated, the overall results were rather pleasing to the Irish temperance movement. It was estimated that, as a result of the election, between 60 and 70 Irish M.P.s supported the principle of Sunday closing, about 15 were definitely hostile, and the rest were uncommitted. Temperance had not been a particularly prominent issue in the south, where Home Rule and the education question occupied most attention. However, the loss of Corrigan and Pim, the parliamentary leaders of the Sunday closing campaign, was a salutary reminder of the political power of the drink trade, especially in Dublin. (**54** [1873-4], 6; **337**, 193, 272)[19]

In Ulster the temperance issue, particularly the permissive bill, was considerably more significant, largely as a result of the vigorous campaign mounted on its behalf by the I.T.L. The League was much better organised than the Dublin-based I.S.C.A. and began its work early. In July and August 1872, with the co-operation of the Good Templars (a teetotal friendly society which began in the United States in the 1850s and was introduced into Ireland in 1870), it had established a temperance electoral association to work at parochial, municipal and parliamentary level. At the same time a vacancy occurred in Londonderry city, owing to the appointment of Richard Dowse, the Liberal member, as baron of exchequer. The executive committee of the League estimated that between 400 and 500 out of 1,600 electors in the city would be prepared to vote for a permissive bill candidate and contemplated standing its own candidate. The League's local contacts advised against this, and agents were sent to lobby the existing candidates. Ultimately C. E. Lewis, a Conservative, was returned over Christopher Palles, the Liberal candidate. The League was pleased with this result, for Lewis was strongly committed to temperance legislation, and he was in fact to lead the Ulster Conservatives in supporting the Sunday closing bill. It is a measure, however, of the temperance movement's growing disenchantment with the existing parties that it should, at this early stage, have already been thinking about putting forward its own candidates. Future events served only to deepen this disenchantment. (**338**, 234-8)[20]

Like the United Kingdom Alliance, the League had begun to give serious and detailed thought to the criteria on which it should endorse candidates. Publicly the League stated it would support those who pledged themselves to vote for the second reading of the permissive bill, but privately it fully realised that the situation would seldom be as simple as this. What if there were several candidates prepared to pledge different degrees of support? In December 1873 this issue was discussed at the League's general council meeting. There it was suggested that the League should work not only on the principle of getting supporters of the permissive bill elected, but also on the principle of attempting to prevent opponents of the bill getting in. Thus, if there was no candidate in favour of the bill, the League should encourage voters to support a candidate who at least would not oppose it, over one who would. 'When we cannot gain a vote for the bill, let us try to prevent the publicans gaining a vote against it.' (**136**, 26-7; **167**, 211-13)[21]

The general election in the following month put such principles to the test. The biggest problem occurred in Belfast, where the sitting members were William Johnston, a Conservative, and Thomas McClure, a Liberal, both of whom had sponsored the Sunday closing bill and voted for the permissive bill since their election in 1868. Now, however, McClure refused to renew his pledge to vote for the second reading of the bill. His main opponent was the Conservative, J. P. Corry, the former president of the I.T.L. and a staunch supporter of local option. In this case, despite strong representations from McClure's supporters, the League urged voters to return Johnston and Corry. Corry topped the poll, with Johnston a close second and McClure a distant third. McClure had been elected in 1868 on a pro-Disestablishment platform with both Catholic and Presbyterian support, but his endorsement of denominational education and his refusal to commit himself to local option alienated many of his Presbyterian supporters. The temperance issue was prominent in several contests, notably in Armagh, Coleraine and Newry, but nowhere more decisively than in Belfast. (**338**, 278-81; **322**, 178-220; **236**, I, 290-3)[22]

On the whole, the League was very pleased with the Ulster results. Of the 29 M.P.s returned, 20 had pledged themselves to vote for the permissive bill, 3 were definitely opposed to it, and 6 were unclear in their views. The League estimated it had lost one vote, that of Lord Claud Hamilton in Tyrone, but had gained six, including William Whitworth in Newry, T. A Dickson in Dungannon, and Richard Smyth in Co. Londonderry, all Liberals. M. R. Dalway, the I.T.L. president, had been returned for Carrickfergus, while a former president had been elected in Belfast. But three declared opponents of the bill, all Conservatives, had been re-elected: Thomas Conolly in Donegal, H. A. Cole in Fermanagh, and John Vance in Armagh city. Also it is clear that some supporters of the League, particularly Liberals, began to have doubts about the organisation's electoral strategy as a result of the election. The policy of endorsing candidates solely on the basis of their personal attitude to the permissive bill had meant, as in Belfast, that the League sometimes supported Conservatives and opposed Liberals. Yet in England the Tories were being increasingly identified with the drink interest, while the Liberals showed much greater sympathy to temperance. Would it thus be wiser for the I.T.L. to support the Liberal party and all Liberal candidates, regardless of their individual views? Writing in April 1874 in the I.T.L. *Journal*, 'A.J.C. of Londonderry' acknowledged that 'Some of our friends... say our principles are right when they help to gain a seat for a Liberal candidate, but wrong when they throw our votes into the Conservative scale.' 'A.J.C.' criticised such 'friends' for caring more about the 'party cry of political faction' than about the drink problem and went on to attack the previous Liberal government for its failure to pass temperance legislation:

A Liberal government, unparalleled in power, swayed our legislature during the past five years. With an overwhelming majority it carried almost impossible measures, but it quailed before the liquor traffic, and, in its failure, we read the lesson that from no party, merely in virtue of either its Conservatism or its Liberalism, can we expect true temperance legislation, while we fail to compel attention to our claims, by having our parliamentary representatives pledged to support them.[23]

Perhaps the real truth was that, with the decimation of the Liberal party in Ireland, the Irish temperance movement had little choice but to do the best it could with the Conservatives in the north and later with the Home Rulers in the south. But in the long run, as we shall see, the fact that the political party which was most strongly committed to temperance was also the weakest in Ireland was to handicap the Irish temperance movement severely.

The reorganised I.S.C.A. was anxious to introduce its bill into the new parliament, but with the defeat of four of its previous seven sponsors, new ones had first to be found. The association invited Richard Smyth, a Presbyterian clergyman and Liberal M.P. for Co. Londonderry, to be the bill's leading sponsor. He accepted, as did another seven M.P.s, representing, so the association claimed, 'every political and religious party in the country'. (**54** [1873-4], 6; **236**, I, 138, 353-4) Of the previous seven sponsors, three had been Liberals and four Conservatives, three had been from the south and four from Ulster. Of the eight selected in 1874, two were Liberals, three Conservatives and three Home Rulers, while three were from the south and five from Ulster. The relative decline in the number of Liberals sponsoring the bill and the relative increase in the number of Ulster M.P.s reflect significant changes in support for temperance legislation among Irish M.P.s as a result of the 1874 general election.

Smyth introduced the bill in March 1874, and its second reading was set for May. But without government assistance, he was not able to get a night for the debate, so he withdrew the bill and introduced instead a resolution in favour of Sunday closing for Ireland. In his first major parliamentary speech on the subject Smyth was careful not to offend the Irish drink trade. He 'emphatically disclaimed making the motion a basis of attack upon a trade which has the sanction of the legislature, and which is meeting what is still regarded as a want of the community'. Instead he attacked the English trade, claiming that the main opponent of the Irish bill was the National Licensed Victuallers' Defence League of England:

> I am quite willing that Ireland should be ruled by the Queen, Lords and Commons of this United Kingdom... but I am not willing that the licensed victuallers of Birmingham should constitute themselves a parliament for Ireland.

Smyth argued that Sunday closing was a local Irish question and thus had to be considered purely in terms of Irish conditions. The Irish, for instance, did not drink beer as part of their ordinary diet as the English did. The Irish workers and farmers drank whiskey 'at fairs, and markets, and for good companionship'. Such drinking was particularly prevalent on Sundays. Irish legislation needed therefore to be adapted to Irish conditions and treated quite separately from English legislation. Like his predecessor Corrigan, Smyth, although a staunch Unionist, was not above parading the threat of Home Rule before English M.P.s in order to add weight to his arguments:

> I am among those who have thought that the interests of Ireland would be best maintained by an unimpaired union with the sister countries; but when we find the members of parliament, to whose counsels we cling, coming down to this house to overbear the Irish vote on a question which concerns only the social habits of the people, and has no political significance whatever, there will be secret reflections whether we are much wiser than many of our fellow-countrymen who have disavowed all confidence in the present government of their country. Even to carry this resolution I do not want an Irish parliament; but I must add that if we had an Irish parliament, it is among the first that would be carried.

Smyth's mixture of cajolery and threat was to no avail, however. The new Tory government, elected with the support of the English drink trade, was strongly opposed to the resolution. Sir Michael Hicks Beach, the new Chief Secretary, accepted and repeated the publicans' argument that, by giving encouragement to the illicit trade, Sunday closing would in fact create more problems than it would solve. He ascribed the agitation for both Sunday closing and the permissive bill to a 'number of philanthropists' and not to popular feeling. Moreover, he denied that the measure could or should be treated as a purely Irish matter as Smyth had argued. The whole British parliament had a right to deal equally with all matters brought before it. The government's uncompromising opposition put the many Ulster Conservatives, who had pledged themselves to support Sunday closing in the recent election, into a difficult position. Thomas Conolly of Donegal, who supported Sunday closing but opposed the permissive bill, warned the government that he had 'no hesitation in the line which I shall adopt; I shall be true to my constituents'. Conolly thought the government had come to a 'very precipitate determination' as regards the resolution; it was not, he said, 'graceful in them to drive their best friends away from them'. The resolution was rejected by 220 votes to 129. As the supporters of Sunday closing had feared, they were overwhelmed by English M.P.s. Of the 220 members voting against, 206 were English, 10 were Irish and 4 Scottish. Of the 129 in favour, 50 were English, 42 were Irish and 37 Scottish. Of the 42 Irish M.P.s in favour of the resolution, more than half, 25 to be exact, represented Ulster constituencies. No Ulster M.P. voted against. The 42 were composed of 20 Conservatives, 16 Home Rulers and 6 Liberals, while the 10 against comprised 3 Conservatives, 6 Home Rulers and 1 Liberal. Clearly the

Ulster Conservatives had followed Conolly in revolt against the government, for, out of 21 of them, 18 had voted for the resolution. But absenteeism continued to run at nearly fifty per cent. The temperance movement was having more success than the Irish publicans in rousing M.P.s on the issue, though it still had a long way to go to win over even half the Irish representatives. It also was relying very heavily on Ulster M.P.s, just as the Irish drink trade was relying on sympathetic English members.[24]

The government's opposition to the Sunday closing resolution and its 1874 licensing bill, which made significant concessions to the drink trade, convinced the Irish temperance movement that it was facing a 'publicans' parliament', as the I.T.L. *Journal* called it. This judgment was further strengthened in June when the permissive bill was defeated by 318 to 92. The Irish M.P.s, however, voted 30 to 18 in favour of the bill, and of the 25 Ulster M.P.s voting, 19 were for and 6 against. The I.T.L., noting that the Ulster vote was three to one in favour and formed nearly two-thirds of the Irish vote for the bill, 'heartily congratulated' the Ulster members and all their friends who had worked so hard for this result. Despite the overall defeat, the League remained doggedly optimistic. 'Temperance reformers', it said, 'will not accept this vote as decisive, even in a parliament whose councils are admittedly swayed by the great principle of beer! ... Defeat in a good cause has ever inspired men with fresh ardour.' Certainly, as far as Ireland and particularly Ulster were concerned, there was reason for optimism. The Irish vote for the bill was slowly rising, from 23 to 30 between 1873 and 1874, while the vote against was falling, from 20 to 18 over the same period. Convinced that 'truth must ultimately triumph', the *Journal* assured its readers that the victory of the bill was merely a matter of time. (**168**, 222-5; **70**, 534-8)[25]

The Irish Sunday closing movement too was campaigning assiduously in the latter part of 1874. Meetings were organised, particularly in the constituencies of hostile members, such as Athlone, Bandon, Co. Dublin, Dundalk, King's County, Kinsale and Waterford city, and numerous petitions were collected. The I.S.C.A. was determined to take up Hicks Beach's challenge and demonstrate that there was widespread public demand for Sunday closing in Ireland. By May 1875 parliament had received over 1,000 petitions from Ireland in favour of Sunday closing, bearing over 200,000 signatures. By the end of the session the number of petitions had risen to 1,500 with 225,000 signatures. Deputations from the I.S.C.A. saw Hicks Beach in December 1874 and the Lord Lieutenant in the following February. At the end of April Disraeli received a deputation including Russell and Wigham from the association, the Mayor of Belfast and ten Irish M.P.s. Colonel Taylor, who had been a Conservative chief whip for many years and was now Chancellor of the Duchy of Lancaster, presented a memorial in favour of Sunday closing signed by 2,484 clergymen, 1,413 magistrates, 774 doctors, 1,991 Poor Law Guardians, 596 town councillors, and 453 merchants and employers of labour. Smyth said that the petitions had proved that, except for the publicans, there was no substantial opposition to the bill in Ireland, and he asked for government backing. But Disraeli refused to give any undertaking, merely saying that he would consider the memorial. During this massive campaign by the I.C.S.A. the vintners had not been idle. They were certainly less active than their opponents, presumably putting their faith in the hostility of the government and most English M.P.s to the bill. Early in May, however, a deputation of publicans saw Hicks Beach in London. They told him that the 'wants and wishes of the working classes were ignored or misrepresented by the advocates of the Sunday closing bill'. According to the *Freeman's Journal*, Hicks Beach paid 'much attention' to these statements and 'occasionally verified them by reference to official returns'. (**54** [1874-5], 5-8)[26]

The second-reading debate took place on 5 May. In the preceding week a deputation from the I.S.C.A., assisted by representatives from the I.T.L. and from the English Sunday closing movement, lobbied some 200 M.P.s in last-minute efforts to ensure a majority for the bill. Smyth in his speech reiterated most of his arguments of the previous year, again warning English M.P.s not to deny Ireland its just demands. Supporters tried to appeal to the English by arguing that Sunday closing would lessen sedition and disaffection in Ireland. Edmund Dease, Home Rule M.P. for Queen's County, described it as the 'best peace preservation measure that could be given to Ireland'. But the government remained firm in its opposition. Hicks Beach claimed that Sunday closing had not lessened drunkenness in Scotland; that though the middle classes in Ireland supported it, the working classes were largely ignorant on the subject, and thus that the enforcement of Sunday closing might lead to the kind of riots that England had experienced in 1855. Moreover, the government's Licensing Act of the previous year needed more time to show what effect it would have on the situation. The I.S.C.A. was disappointed by this speech, as it had hoped for more sympathy from the government in the light of its recent campaign. Hicks Beach, however, was largely repeating the views of Commissioner Lake of the D.M.P., who informed him that the 'persons, who have signed petitions in favour of Sunday closing, do not represent the class against whom legislation on the subject is directed'. Lake considered the bill 'class legislation', which would

> greatly interfere with the privileges of the artisans and labourers, who, it must be remembered, cannot of course afford to become members of clubs, or obtain refreshments at hotels, and should the proposed bill be passed, I foresee much trouble and difficulty if not absolute danger in carrying out the provisions of it in the city of Dublin, and throughout the Metropolitan Police District.

Also he felt that the bill would do a 'serious injustice' to the publicans, who would have a strong case for demanding compensation for lost business. (**54** [1874-5], 11-14)[27]

Gladstone, who followed Hicks Beach in the debate, saw the issue in very different terms. He was not essentially concerned with where and when the Irish drank, but that the country should receive fair and equitable treatment in the British parliament:

> I have had credit and discredit — to neither of which I am entitled — for having, as was supposed, delivered myself of the sentiment that Ireland ought to be governed by Irish ideas. I never gave utterance to such a sentiment without appending to it a vital qualification which has been forgotten both by foes and friends. I said that Ireland might be properly and justly governed by Irish ideas on those matters as to which imperial interests did not call for uniform legislation. It is a fair question to put whether the particular question before us falls into the class of those subjects with respect to which the local opinion, so to call it, of one of the three kingdoms is fairly entitled to prevail. Upon that I say that parliament has already given a judgment in the case of Scotland. . . . If in that case we yielded to the judgment of Scotland, much more, in the present case, has the judgment of Ireland been clearly expressed.

Gladstone thus endorsed the principle which the supporters of the bill were urging upon English M.P.s: that in a local matter of this sort, English members should accept and follow the wishes of the majority of Irish M.P.s and not overwhelm the Irish with their votes. Towards the end of the debate Charles Lewis, M.P. for Londonderry city, who was emerging as the leader of the Ulster Conservatives, appealed strongly to English Conservative members for support:

> He appealed to them not to send them back unable to reply to the arguments of Home Rulers, who would then be able to point out that, on a social question upon which Irishmen were substantially agreed, they were overwhelmed by English votes. He was not disposed to believe the slander hurled against honourable members who sat on that side of the house, that the Conservative party was placed in power solely by the English publicans; but if they wanted to give force to that opinion — if they desired to turn a political fiction into a plausible fact, they would, upon that occasion, troop into the lobby for the purpose of imposing upon the Irish members those exceptions from which they desired to be free.

However, Murphy of Cork and Wheelhouse of Leeds, amid considerable uproar and cries for a division, were able to talk out the bill.[28]

The *Freeman's Journal*, which opposed the bill, was disturbed by Gladstone's intervention, seeing it as a step towards Sunday closing 'being sucked into the vortex of party politics'. The vintners also deplored what they saw as Gladstone's effort to 'make political capital' out of the issue. Michael Dwyer and a delegation from the Dublin vintners' association had been lobbying in London before the debate. As well as seeing Hicks Beach, they had had discussions with the 'most influential members of the trade in the metropolis' and had solicited many Home Rule M.P.s. The vintners were gratified that five Home Rulers had spoken against the bill in the debate. Certainly they were finding their most vocal Irish parliamentary supporters, like Murphy, Callan, W. H. O'Sullivan of Co. Limerick, Eugene Collins of Kinsale, Richard Power and the eccentric Major O'Gorman of Waterford city, among the ranks of the new nationalist party. But the delegation admitted that they had had 'uphill work... in canvassing the members of parliament against a measure which was supposed to be backed by a large proportion of the upper and middle classes in Ireland'. Added to this, the revolt of the Ulster Conservatives and the growing Liberal sympathy for Irish Sunday closing, shown by Gladstone's intervention, must have caused some alarm among the trade.[29]

Smyth tried to secure another day for the resumption of the debate, but, given the pressure of business and the government's lack of sympathy, this proved impossible. In June and July, however, the I.T.L. began to suspect that the government's opposition was weakening. Their task, with the approval or even the neutrality of the government, said the *Journal*, would be 'comparatively easy'. In June the League circulated a letter on the subject among its members. This claimed that if the division had taken place in May, the bill would have been carried by between fifty and sixty votes. But it was feared that if this had happened, the government would have reacted by proposing an amendment to exempt large towns from the legislation. The League instructed its supporters to write to M.P.s stressing that the bill must be passed in its entirety, without exemptions. The League felt that if the pressure could be kept up on Irish M.P.s and on the government, Sunday closing was within their grasp. Accordingly it stepped up its campaign of meetings, petitions and lobbying. All M.P.s received a letter supporting the bill, signed by, among others, the Mayors of Belfast, Derry, Limerick and Sligo, the chairmen of the Town Commissioners of Galway and Coleraine, the President of Queen's College, Belfast, and the Moderator of the Presbyterian General Assembly.[30]

In Dublin the I.S.C.A. was also extremely active. It organised meetings in Birmingham, Liverpool, Newcastle, Bolton, Leeds, Bradford, Sheffield, Exeter, Bristol and Leicester in order to put pressure on English M.P.s. In addition, it held a canvas in Dublin, Belfast, Cork, Waterford, Limerick and Derry to sample public opinion on the issue. In Dublin, for example, 28,500 were polled, of whom 25,408 were in favour of Sunday closing and 3,092 against. Among publicans the figures were 326 and 225 respectively. In

Belfast, of the 26,083 canvassed, 23,274 were for and 2,809 against. There the publicans were 229 to 138 in favour of Sunday closing. When the canvas was complete in Dublin the organisers called a meeting in order to present the results to the city's M.P.s, Brooks and Guinness. Guinness refused to attend, and Brooks was obviously discomforted and embarrassed by the proceedings. William Gernon of the I.S.C.A. told him that they did not come to handle him with 'kid gloves', but 'had assembled to tell him some plain facts, whether they were palatable to him or not'. Brooks replied by doubting the accuracy of the association's figures. At their next meeting the vintners criticised the way in which Brooks had been treated by the I.S.C.A. and reiterated his scepticism about the canvas. Dublin Castle had already looked into this question. In November 1875 Under-Secretary Burke had written to Commissioner Lake of the D.M.P. asking him to check the accuracy of the canvas. Lake replied that his men had made inquiries in the Royal Exchange ward and found 'strong reasons' for doubting the figures given. What these reasons were, beyond that 'in some instances women signed the voting papers without consulting their husbands', Lake did not specify, going on merely to repeat his objections of the previous May. He argued that the patronage given by the working classes to the public houses on Sunday demonstrated their popularity and the strength of the opposition to Sunday closing in Dublin. This remark led Hicks Beach to ask for accurate statistics on the numbers of persons visiting public houses on Sundays in the main Irish towns. As a result, on 13 February and 30 April 1876 the D.M.P. and the R.I.C. counted public-house customers in Dublin, Cork, Waterford, Limerick, Belfast and Derry. In the city of Dublin, covering six square miles within the canals, there were 765 public houses, of which 660 were open on Sunday. The police counted 122,899 persons entering these houses, which was almost exactly half the population of the city. Even allowing for some inflation in this figure due to the same people entering the public houses more than once on the day, it is still a startlingly high statistic. In the other cities and towns the percentages of the total population entering public houses were lower, but still substantial: in Cork 37 per cent, in Waterford 35 per cent, in Limerick 31 per cent, in Belfast 24 per cent, and in Derry 16 per cent. These figures illustrate why the police, particularly in Dublin, feared that Sunday closing would create widespread discontent, resulting in illicit drinking on a massive scale and public disorder. Sunday drinking in the main urban centres was simply too popular for the government to dare abolish it totally.[31]

In the 1876 session the ballot went against Smyth and he was not able to get time for a second-reading debate. So he withdrew the bill and introduced a resolution in favour of Sunday closing, as he had done in 1874. Again he attacked the discriminatory treatment Ireland appeared to be receiving with regard to this issue:

It was once suggested that the best cure for Ireland would be to put it at the bottom of the sea for a short time; but I am inclined to think that if it could only become Scotland for one session of parliament, the advantage to us would be very great, for then we should have no difficulty in carrying a remedial measure like this, which is supported by four-fifths of the people of Ireland.

The publicans of England, however, were 'to a man against it', and Smyth was very conscious, reflecting upon recent political history, of the 'formidable power' which the English trade wielded. Hicks Beach's speech clearly signalled that the government was contemplating concessions. 'If they were to alter the present law on this subject,' he said, 'they should proceed tentatively.' He then proposed that Sunday hours should be shortened to between 2 p.m. and 7 p.m. in towns and to between 2 p.m. and 5 p.m. in rural areas — shortened, in other words, by two hours. If this measure proved a success, then the government would consider introducing total Sunday closing. The Chief Secretary advised Smyth to withdraw his resolution and allow the government to legislate for shorter hours. But at the same time he attacked Conservatives who argued that Ireland should be treated separately in this matter, saying that they were in effect arguing for Home Rule. As for the Home Rulers who supported the bill, Hicks Beach accused them of seeking to impose coercive legislation on Ireland. He was undoubtedly correct in detecting curious alliances and inconsistent arguments among the advocates of the bill.[32]

In the course of the lengthy debate which followed, John Bright attacked Hicks Beach for merely proposing shorter hours, when it was known that in the previous session the government had been considering accepting the bill with the exclusion of the large towns. Bright indicated that the Liberals would have been prepared to accept this latter compromise. But he felt that the government was trapped by its commitments to the English drink trade, which wanted no compromise

It has come to this [he concluded] — government must choose this day whom ye serve. Will you serve the conspiracy of the vendors of drink in England, or will you obey the will and the eloquent voice of the whole people of Ireland.

Hicks Beach had indeed suggested Sunday closing with the exclusion of the main towns to the cabinet in 1875, but this had been rejected by his colleagues in favour of shorter trading hours. Charles Lewis followed Bright and again warned the government that it would lose support in Ulster if it continued to oppose the bill:

Every Irish Conservative member of that house felt that his position was undermined, that the interests of his constituents and party were being imperilled by the conduct, in this matter, of the government he was sent there to support.

The Chancellor of the Exchequer, Sir Stafford Northcote, repeated Hicks Beach's offer, but was answered by Gladstone in a strong speech, which concluded:

> If after giving [Sunday closing] to Scotland you withhold it from Ireland, you lay down the principle of inequality in your dealing between the three countries, the adoption of which principle, in my opinion, makes those who adopt it far more deadly enemies to the union of the two countries, both by law and by sentiment, than are any of those who recommend the dissolution of the union as a mere abstract opinion of politics, or may attempt to recommend it to any portion of the United Kingdom, provided only they are unable to support their arguments by clear evidence and demonstration that inequality governs the policy of parliament in dealing with the respective sections of the United Kingdom.

Gladstone personally was not particularly sympathetic to temperance legislation, but he obviously felt that England was only playing into the hands of the Home Rulers by ignoring the demands of the Irish middle class for such legislation. (**185**, I, 50-1; **166**, 88-9; **59**, 208-11)[33]

In the division which followed the debate the resolution was carried by 224 votes to 167, with 59 Irish M.P.s voting for and only 11 against. Of those in favour, 26 were Ulster M.P.s, comprising 18 Conservatives, 6 Liberals, and the two Ulster Home Rulers, J. G. Biggar and C. J. Fay of Co. Cavan. Of the 33 Irish M.P.s representing southern constituencies who voted for the resolution, 27 were Home Rulers, 2 Liberals, and 4 Conservatives. The recently elected M.P. for Meath, C. S. Parnell, was among this group of Home Rulers. The 11 against the Sunday closing resolution comprised 9 Home Rulers and 2 Conservatives. Most represented cities and towns with important drink industries, like Brooks and Guinness for Dublin, Murphy for Cork, Power and O'Gorman for Waterford, Callan for Dundalk, Stacpoole for Ennis, while W. H. O'Sullivan, M.P. for Co. Limerick, was himself a publican. It is striking that no Liberals and no Ulster M.P.s voted against the resolution. Of the three Ulster M.P.s who did not vote, William Johnston of Belfast was necessarily absent and paired in favour of the resolution; Viscount Crichton of Enniskillen, who was a junior member of the government, left the house rather than be compelled to vote against it; while Conolly of Donegal was suffering an illness, which would soon prove fatal. Only two Irish Conservatives, Guinness and Lord Charles Beresford, M.P. for Co. Waterford, followed their government's line and voted against the resolution. Others, such as Colonel Taylor, Chancellor of the Duchy of Lancaster, and D. R. Plunket, the Irish Solicitor-General, joined Crichton in a pointed exit prior to the division. This was indeed a substantial revolt of the government's Irish supporters. Among the Home Rule M.P.s opinion on Sunday closing was somewhat more divided, the vast majority of those voting against being members of the party. But 29 Home Rulers, almost exactly half their number, voted for Sunday closing. This was a significant increase over the 1874 figures, when only 16 Home Rulers had voted for the resolution and 6 against.[34]

The Irish M.P.s had voted 5 to 1 in favour of Sunday closing; and understandably, as a result, the Irish temperance movement was jubilant and increasingly confident. In July 1876 the I.T.L. *Journal* declared:

> The Sunday liquor traffic in Ireland we regard as doomed, and it is but a question we opine whether 1876 or 1877 is to be the great year of deliverance for our beloved country which has struggled so dauntlessly to free itself from this terrible incubus.

The *Freeman's Journal*, though it still preferred shorter Sunday trading hours to total closing, had also to admit that legislation was now inevitable. But it urged the vintners to support Hicks Beach's suggestion of shorter hours and thus try to forestall the introduction of total closing and the 'furtherance of a gloomy principle of rigid, unsocial, and objectionable sabbatarianism'. On the following day, in another leading article on the subject, the paper sourly commented on the claim by the London *Times* that the defeat of the resolution would have given an enormous fillip to the Home Rule cause:

> Are the arguments applicable to no question but that of Sunday closing? Is there no other matter which purely concerns Irish constituencies, and on which the expressed opinion of the vast majority of the representatives of Ireland has been overborne.

And it went on to mention education, land reform, union rating, railways, borough franchise, grand jury reform and fisheries as only the beginning of an 'almost interminable list' of issues on which Irish opinion had been ignored by the British parliament. Concessions made to 'objectionable sabbatarianism' were certainly not going to weaken the enthusiasm of the *Freeman's Journal* for the Home Rule cause.[35]

The Irish vintners were naturally even more troubled. The growing Liberal party support for Irish Sunday closing, together with the surprisingly high Home Rule vote, gave rise to considerable concern among them. Special meetings were held in Dublin on 16 and 18 May and plans were drawn up to raise a £1,000 defence fund, £200 of this being subscribed immediately. At the second meeting Michael Dwyer attempted to explain to members why this 'very unexpected and serious defeat' had occurred. He claimed that the Liberals were using the Irish Sunday closing issue to embarrass the Tory government. A Liberal whip had been out for the division, though the vintners had not known this until the morning of the debate. As for the Home Rulers, he claimed that Lord Francis Conyngham, Home Rule M.P. for Co. Clare, was largely responsible for persuading so many of them to vote with the Liberals, the 'bait' held out being the claim that the passing of the resolution would be a victory for Home Rule and would mean 'practically Home Rule as far as the liquor traffic is concerned'. The vintners, having already failed to win Liberal support, appeared to have lost the Home Rulers as well. Their only champions were the English Conservatives. 'It was strange, indeed,' remarked Dwyer, 'to find that it was to the British government that the people of Ireland were to look for protection against the national members.'[36]

With the success of the resolution, Smyth hoped that the government would introduce its own bill along the lines of his. However, when Disraeli made clear that the government had no intention of doing anything, Smyth reintroduced his original bill. The second-reading debate took place on 12 July. Hicks Beach announced that the government had decided to regard the vote in favour of the resolution as equivalent to a vote on the second reading. But at the same time he warned the bill's sponsors that the government did not intend the bill to become law during the current session, nor in its present form. If the bill proceeded any further, he would introduce amendments, though he declined to say what these would be. Gladstone advised Smyth to be prepared to accept such amendments, 'which might have the effect of softening and regulating what was undoubtedly an important transition', and warned him against 'any attachment to the absolute rigour of a doctrine'. Obviously the bill would only continue to receive Liberal support if its sponsors were prepared to compromise with the government. The debate dragged on for four hours as Wheelhouse, Murphy, O'Gorman and Callan denounced the measure at great length, showing that opposition to it, though small, was still very vigorous. But, with government support, the second reading was agreed to without a division.[37]

After this, however, the government took up its more customary hostile stance and refused to give time for committee debate. Here Isaac Butt came to the rescue and agreed to surrender time allotted to him on 2 August for debate on the Sunday closing bill. This forced the government to table its amendments. These proposed that public houses should be closed on Sundays, except in towns with a population of over 10,000. There the hours would be reduced to between 2 p.m. and 7 p.m. Furthermore, the act was to be limited to three years. The I.S.C.A. calculated that the exemptions would include seventeen cities and towns, with a population of around 760,000. The executive committee of the association met and rejected the proposed amendments as they compromised the principle of Sunday closing. But the bill had already been lost for the year. On 2 August ten Home Rulers, assisted by several English M.P.s, united to talk out the time allotted for debate. The next day the *Freeman's Journal*, while criticising the tactics used to kill the bill, nevertheless welcomed the time thus afforded for further consideration of the whole question. Sir Wilfrid Lawson, however, made another effort to raise the matter on 3 August. In moving the adjournment debate, he appealed to Disraeli to allow the Irish Sunday closing bill to pass. If Disraeli refused this 'almost unanimous, this earnest, this constitutional demand from the Irish people', said Lawson, then 'he is the greatest upholder of Home Rule that is to be found, and he will perpetuate Irish dissatisfaction and discontent'. Disraeli replied by stating that the bill had failed to get through simply because its promoters had refused to accept the government's proposed amendments. As for it being unanimously demanded by Ireland, he pointed out that in the debate on the previous day ten Irish M.P.s had spoken and all were opposed to the bill. Smyth was quick to explain that this had occurred because the bill's supporters, who did not wish to waste time, had deliberately refrained from speaking. But he gave no indication of a willingness to accept the amendments. The Irish temperance press was totally opposed to any compromise. 'The whole bill, and nothing but the bill, will alone satisfy the nation,' the I.T.L. *Journal* announced in August. (**54** [1875-6], 14-17)[38]

The 1877 session, despite several lengthy debates and a select committee on Sunday closing, saw only a continuation of this deadlock. The government would only drop its opposition if the major towns were exempted and a time limit placed on the operation of the measure. The temperance movement insisted on Sunday closing for the whole country, arguing that it was most needed in the large towns, where Sunday drunkenness was a major problem. There was, however, one important new element introduced. Parnell and Biggar began their campaign of systematic obstruction during this session, and the opponents of Sunday closing were quick to adopt this new and highly effective tactic. (**226**, 58-65) During the second-reading debate early in February Hicks Beach acknowledged that public expressions in favour of the bill had been far more numerous than those against it, and he was, he said, therefore prepared to take 'as settled the adoption of the principle of total Sunday closing'. But he insisted that the five major Irish towns, Dublin, Belfast, Cork, Waterford and Limerick, be exempted. In this, he said, he was following the advice of police and magistrates in these towns. If Sunday closing was attempted in these areas, he thought one of two things would occur:

> Either there would be great and widespread evasion of the law, than which I can conceive nothing more detrimental to the cause of law and order in Ireland, or else, if the law were thoroughly enforced, there would be no little danger of riotous proceedings, which I am sure we should all deplore.

Hicks Beach felt that this was particularly true in Dublin, and certainly the D.M.P., in the person of Commissioner Lake, consistently advised the

Chief Secretary against introducing Sunday closing in Dublin. Doubtless also, the pressure brought to bear on the government by the urban-based drink industry, especially that in Dublin, was an element in influencing Hicks Beach's view. As early as May 1876 he had written to Disraeli:

> Even if the question could be looked at apart from English opinion, I could not advise the government to support total Sunday closing all over Ireland. I don't think the classes who would be most affected are in the least prepared for it; and I am convinced that in the large towns, it would either be largely evaded by drinking at unlicensed houses, or an immediate agitation would arise for its repeal. Neither result would strengthen respect for parliament and the law in Ireland. But I should be very glad, so far as Ireland is concerned, if it could be either partially or gradually introduced.

Hicks Beach announced in February 1877 that the government was prepared to support the second reading of the bill, if it was then submitted to a select committee. The committee would examine, not the whole issue, but the 'applicability of the measure to the five towns'. The bill's promoters, though somewhat dissatisfied with the restricted terms of reference, nevertheless, accepted the proposal. The second reading was passed by 194 votes to 23, and the bill was accordingly referred to a select committee. (**185**, I, 50)[39]

Hicks Beach chaired the committee, which had sixteen members, the majority of them being supporters of the bill. Between 23 February and 27 April it heard evidence from thirty-seven witnesses. On 4 May, during discussion of the report, Hicks Beach moved his amendment exempting the five towns, but it was rejected by nine votes to seven. Those against were Richard Smyth, William Johnston, Charles Lewis, A. M. Sullivan, Home Rule M.P. for Co. Louth, Charles Meldon, Home Rule M.P. for Co. Kildare, Hugh Law, Liberal M.P. for Co. Londonderry, Ion Trant Hamilton, Conservative M.P. for Co. Dublin, Colonel Cole, Conservative M.P. for Fermanagh, and Charles Cameron, Liberal M.P. for Glasgow. Those in favour of the government's amendment were Maurice Brooks, N. D. Murphy, Lord Charles Beresford, Henry Bruen, Conservative M.P. for Co. Carlow, the Marquis of Hamilton, Conservative M.P. for Co. Donegal, Richard O'Shaughnessy, Home Rule M.P. for Limerick city, and Alfred Marten, Conservative M.P. for Cambridge. Here was another embarrassing defeat for the government over Sunday closing, with four Conservative M.P.s, three of them from Ulster, voting against their own party. The majority, moreover, went on to make several additions to the original bill, giving police additional powers to supervise refreshment houses and increasing penalties for unlicensed selling. On 16 May Hicks Beach was presented with a letter, signed by all the twenty-nine Ulster M.P.s, urging the government to pass the bill. (**36**, x-xiii)[40]

By exerting their power so vigorously, however, the supporters of Sunday closing had only further alienated the government and strengthened their opposition. The I.S.C.A. defended the rejection of the government's amendment, but admitted that 'Many friends of the Sunday closing movement think it would have been wiser had the committee arrived at a conclusion that would have sanctioned the exemption of the five cities and towns, and so ensured, as they suppose, the passing of the bill.' The bill's opponents were quick to point out that the committee, in tightening-up policing of licences, had exceeded its terms of reference. The government, on the advice of the Speaker, agreed and ordered the bill re-committed so that the offending sections could be removed. In the circumstances Smyth had little alternative but to submit. The government in turn, under strong pressure from Gladstone, Bright and Hartington, agreed to provide a day for another debate. The Liberals provided further assistance when Lawson offered a day set aside for the permissive bill to the supporters of Sunday closing. (**54** [1876-7], 10)

The committee stage of the bill occupied two sittings on 27 June and 3 July, but in both cases half a dozen Irish M.P.s, with assistance from several English members, managed to talk out the time available, and no progress whatsoever was made. Smyth protested strongly against such tactics:

I perceive that there is a determination that minorities shall dictate to this house, and that the will alike of the country and of this house shall be thwarted and defied by a combination of members, who, worsted in argument and in division, betake themselves to the tactics of despair and pursue a course which, if persevered in much longer, will reduce parliamentary government to an absurdity.

The majority of the opponents were Home Rulers, and A. M. Sullivan, a fellow Home Ruler, angrily accused them of trying 'to choke upon the floor of that house the voice of their own country'. On 12 July he went further and moved an adjournment motion in order to express his disgust with the government. Sullivan said that

He feared the treasury bench rejoiced and were glad that they had these thirteen members to save them from the odious work of strangling the bill, and that the thirteen had been playing the game of the government by rescuing them from a most embarrassing position, having men sitting behind them whose consciences revolted from pursuing such a course.

Sir Wilfrid Lawson also felt that the government was in sympathy with the bill's opponents, and he accused the Chancellor of the Exchequer of being the 'patron of obstruction'.[41] In truth the government was increasingly divided and embarrassed by the Sunday closing question. Public support for temperance legislation was growing, and Tory M.P.s were aware of this trend, as the actions of the Ulster M.P.s demonstrate. Yet after 1876

Disraeli was preoccupied with foreign policy issues. Lacking strong leadership over domestic affairs, the government became even more prone to the pressure of special interests like the drink trade. In 1877 a select committee of the House of Lords on intemperance was appointed to investigate the whole issue of temperance legislation, and awaiting its report provided a good excuse for inaction. But the clamour for legislation from Ireland was hard to ignore, particularly when it was strongly supported by the Irish Conservatives and when even the Chief Secretary had concluded that partial Sunday closing might be beneficial. Nevertheless, fearful of antagonising the drink industry, the government equivocated.

Although the Sunday closing bill did not become law in 1877, opposition to it was in fact weakening. Stephen Moore, Conservative M.P. for Co. Tipperary, and Richard O'Shaughnessy, Home Rule M.P. for Limerick city, who had opposed the bill, both said in the committee debates that they were planning to withdraw their opposition. Both had been impressed by the public expressions of support for the bill. The I.S.C.A. and the I.T.L. had continued petitioning parliament, collecting over 200,000 signatures in 1876-7 and over 300,000 in the following year. In December 1877 Hicks Beach was presented with a petition signed by 9,664 magistrates, clergy, Town Commissioners, Poor Law Guardians, doctors and merchants. The publicans were not able to match the temperance movement in the 'battle of the petitions', and, as the cases of Moore and O'Shaughnessy demonstrate, M.P.s were susceptible to this kind of pressure. With regard to the government, it probably did rejoice, as Sullivan claimed, over the failure of the 1877 bill, for this was Smyth's unamended bill. The government remained strongly opposed to total Sunday closing, but Hicks Beach had made clear that it was prepared to accept partial Sunday closing. In May and June 1877 Dublin Castle undertook extensive inquiries regarding the impact such a measure would have. Sub-inspectors and Resident Magistrates were sent a two-page confidential circular containing various questions on clauses of the bill. Some expressed concern as to how the bill would operate with regard to travellers, while many felt that justices were too unreliable to be trusted to handle the question of exemptions. The problems raised and doubts expressed in these replies must have made Hicks Beach acutely conscious of the difficulties that even partial Sunday closing posed. But the actions of the Castle suggest that by the middle of 1877 some form of Sunday closing in Ireland was probably inevitable. The parliamentary opponents of the measure, given their increasingly small numbers, could only stop it by obstructive tactics, but by 1878 such tactics had become counterproductive. For in opposing Parnell's use of obstruction the government had to be consistent and oppose its use by the opponents of Sunday closing as well. (54 [1877-8], 9)[42]

In the 1878 session the bill was taken charge of by The O'Conor Don, who had sat for Co. Roscommon as a Liberal from 1860 to 1874, when he had been re-elected as a Home Ruler. Smyth had relinquished his leadership because of illness, attributed by the I.S.C.A. to his great exertions on behalf of the Sunday closing bill, and in fact he died later in the year. The bill was read a second time on 21 January, but during the committee stage debate the Chancellor made it clear that the government would oppose the bill unless its sponsors accepted the amendments proposed. During the course of this debate Parnell added his voice to the growing numbers of those urging the bill's supporters to agree to the government's demand. He explained that Meath, like nearly all the Irish counties, was in favour of the bill and thus he, despite considerable personal doubts about the principle of the measure, was prepared to support it. The government had indicated that it would give facilities for the bill if its amendments were accepted. As these amendments related to the towns and not to the counties, Parnell felt himself 'absolved from any opposition' to them. He threatened to walk out of the house if the bill's promoters did not co-operate with the government. But both sides remained adamant, and so the deadlock continued. The O'Conor Don insisted that the bill be taken without amendment; its opponents used the rules of the house to stop progress; while the government would neither support the bill nor kill it. As a result, the measure made no progress at all in committee during February and March. (**54** [1877-8], 10)[43]

The opponents of Sunday closing were undoubtedly given heart at this time by the appointment of James Lowther to replace Hicks Beach as Chief Secretary. Lowther gave every indication of being far more hostile to the measure than his predecessor had been. On 2 March, for instance, he received in London a powerful delegation from the Irish drink industry. It included the Dublin distillers William Jameson and W. Talbot Power, the Cork brewer Jerome Murphy, and representatives from the Dublin, Belfast, Cork and Killarney licensed vintners' societies. Lowther informed them that he had always strongly opposed the Irish Sunday closing bill, believing that 'it partook of the most objectionable features of the two measures which he had always opposed, viz. — the permissive bill and the establishment of Home Rule'. He explained, however, that the acceptance by the house in 1876 of a resolution in favour of Sunday closing had forced a change in government policy on the issue. That policy was now to allow the bill to reach its committee stage and, if the government's amendments were accepted, not to oppose the bill's progress. But if the amendments were not accepted, Lowther warned, somewhat vaguely, that the government reserved to itself freedom of action. This policy Lowther described as 'conditional neutrality'. To the bill's supporters, who were in fact poised to accept the government's terms, this statement seemed to suggest that, even if they compromised, the government was still not going to adopt the bill and ensure that it was passed. On 28 March, speaking to a pro-Sunday closing deputation from Belfast, Lowther denied that there was any difference between his policy and Hicks Beach's, but he then turned the discussion by demanding to know if the amendments were accepted and the bill passed, would the agitation for Sunday closing cease. It was a very telling question, and the M.P.s accompanying the delegation, led by Charles Lewis, were unable to answer it.[44]

In the house matters came to a head on 1 April. Consideration of the bill began at 5 p.m., and, after five and a half hours had been consumed in speeches by N. D. Murphy, W. H. O'Sullivan and Denzil Onslow, the Conservative member for Guildford, The O'Conor Don rose to announce that 'there was no other course open to the supporters of the bill' but to accept the government's amendments, 'reserving to themselves the right of trying to modify them in some details'. He asked the obstructors to desist, as now the cities in which they were so interested would not be affected by the bill's provisions. The opposition ignored this concession, and another four hours were taken up with alternative motions to report progress and for the chairman to leave the chair. Gladstone rose at 2 a.m. to declare that, though far from being the youngest member of the house, he was prepared to sit on and support The O'Conor Don until at least some progress was made. At 3 a.m. Lowther announced that it was now too late to move the amendments, and he left the house. W. E. Forster accused him of having departed in a 'childish pet', while Gladstone rose again to deplore the fact that a handful of Irish members should defy the majority of their fellows in such an extraordinary manner. The O'Conor Don said that the government was taking a leaf out of the book of the obstructionists, Parnell, John O'Connor Power and F. H. O'Donnell. In defence Parnell rose to say that if he had behaved with regard to other bills in the way that the English and Irish opponents of Sunday closing were behaving, 'he would have been handed over by the Chancellor of the Exchequer into the custody of the Serjeant-at-Arms'. And he went on to accuse the government of behaving 'almost shabbily'. 'After promising facilities for passing the bill, which was desired by the majority of the Irish people, they had run away out of the house,' he said. It is rather ironic that the main practitioners of obstruction, Biggar, Parnell, O'Donnell and O'Connor Power, all supported the Sunday closing bill, while its opponents were mainly anti-obstructionist Home Rulers and English Conservative M.P.s. Parnell doubtless enjoyed turning the tables on the government and accusing it of conniving at obstruction. The O'Conor Don, with Liberal support, followed Gladstone's advice and refused to give up until some progress had been made. Finally at 5.30 a.m. Sir Joseph McKenna, the Home Rule member for Youghal, who was among the bill's opponents, suggested a compromise. This was that the minor amendments preceding those of the Chief Secretary be agreed to. Edward Gibson, the Irish Attorney-General, the only member of the government left in the house, agreed, and, with

Major O'Gorman still protesting furiously, this compromise was accepted and the house adjourned after more than twelve hours of continuous debate.[45]

The press was appalled by the debate. The *Freeman's Journal*, despite its reservations regarding Sunday closing, roundly condemned the actions of the bill's opponents and was especially anxious to differentiate between the obstruction that the Sunday closing bill was experiencing and that practised by Parnell and his supporters:

> There is a vital difference between a number of members who, though a minority of the whole house, are or represent a majority of the representatives of a country, opposing in the name of the people of that country legislation to which that people object, and a minority of the members of a particular country opposing not merely the opinion of the house but of the majority of the members from their own country.

The paper accused the ten or fifteen opponents of the bill of trying to defeat the 'constitutionally expressed will of the Irish people by the aid of English votes'. So even the *Freeman's Journal* had at last been convinced by the activities of the temperance movement that Sunday closing was desired by most Irish people. The fact that Dublin and the other main centres of the drink industry would not now be affected by the measure undoubtedly helped the paper to change its mind. The *Times* worried about the effect of successful obstruction on the future conduct of the house:

> If we were concerned with the fate of this particular measure only, we might view the issue with equanimity; but the spirit of the House of Commons is in danger of demoralisation, if it be not already demoralised. The knowledge of the power of stopping a bill easily spreads, and the shyness of members to use the power easily disappears.

Clearly the *Times* feared that the obstruction of the Sunday closing bill was a sign that the tactics of Parnell and Biggar were going to be taken up by other members. It joined in the widespread criticism of Lowther for leaving the house before the debate was concluded, and it generally condemned the government for equivocating in its attitude to the bill and thus allowing free rein to the obstructionists.[46]

On 4 April the government's amendments were moved and The O'Conor Don agreed to accept them because he knew the bill would never pass otherwise. W. H. O'Sullivan and Major O'Gorman, the bill's most intransigent opponents, continued to obstruct, but this brought down upon them a severe rebuke from the Chancellor. In the light of such criticism as the *Times*'s, the government seemed anxious to make clear its total opposition to obstruction. However, if the promoters of the bill now thought they were assured of vigorous government support, they were quickly disabused of this notion by Lowther. He said that the government 'had never undertaken to take charge of the bill in any way nor to support it'. The government would 'give facilities — and by facilities they, of course, meant time and nothing more', and how much time the bill received would depend on the state of government business. Given that government business was being disrupted by the obstructionists, Lowther's 'facilities' must have seemed very paltry to the Sunday closers. Moreover, acceptance of the government's amendments resulted in more criticism, from friend and foe alike. Opponents of the original bill derided the compromise. Sir Patrick O'Brien said that the amended bill would be like *Hamlet* without the prince. More seriously, some supporters now turned against the measure. F. H. O'Donnell protested against what he called this 'most immoral compromise'. He said that

> From the beginning of the agitation, the condition of the large towns in Ireland had been the main subject of complaint; and yet he now found that those who had advocated this measure readily granted to the government licence to continue all the evils of the present system, in order that those gentlemen might have the name of passing a bill.

This was certainly a valid criticism. Several supporters went so far as to vote against acceptance of the amendments. They included Sir Wilfrid Lawson, leader of the permissive bill campaign and one of the Irish temperance movement's staunchest English friends. The I.S.C.A. in its report for the year said that it had agreed reluctantly to accept the amendments on the advice of its parliamentary leaders that otherwise no bill at all would pass. But it regarded the measure as incomplete and was determined 'to secure the blessings of Sunday closing for the cities now exempted'. Yet the criticism of supporters like O'Donnell remained valid. Arrest statistics showed that drinking in towns and cities on Saturday night caused most drunkenness. But by April 1878 supporters of temperance were being asked to campaign for a bill to stop drinking in rural areas on Sunday — and then only temporarily. The chances of such legislation being effective were therefore very slight. (**54** [1877-8], 16)[47]

Debate on the committee stage was resumed at 2 a.m. on 14 May, after Parnell and his friends had spent the time since 4 p.m. obstructing the estimates for the Queen's Colleges. The opponents of the Sunday closing bill continued the obstruction, while the Chief Secretary and the Chancellor denied that the government was under any obligation to rescue the bill. Having sat continuously for ten hours, members' tempers were naturally somewhat frayed. English M.P.s fretted about the damage being done to the dignity of the house and about where the policy of obstruction would lead if, as in this case, the government did not resist it. The Home Ruler O'Connor Power joined with the Conservative Charles Lewis to condemn the government's equivocal behaviour. Lewis was, according to the *Freeman's Journal*, 'in disgrace' with the government because of his strong support for the Sunday closing bill. Parnell, obviously delighting in the government's embarrassment, rose to accuse Lowther of being an obstructionist and to demand that either the government take up the bill itself or at least provide time for a full discussion of it. Debate continued for over seven hours until 9.30 a.m., with thirteen fruitless divisions. Finally The O'Conor Don agreed to N. D. Murphy's proposal that a full debate on the amendment to exclude the five towns should take place, and the government agreed to find time for such a debate.[48]

The *Freeman's Journal* clearly reflected the irritation, frustration and growing boredom which were increasingly characterising attitudes to the Sunday closing bill among those not directly involved. Its Westminster correspondent wrote of 'weary divisions, and more wearisome speeches, repeated over and over, and with damnable iteration'. According to him,

> The one noticeable feature was the indirect support which throughout Mr Lowther gave the opposition. He went so far as to announce his personal hostility to the measure, and the self-restraint he had to exercise in not voting with its opponents. Under such circumstances progress was, of course, hopeless.

Lowther's hostility to Sunday closing in any form, coming after Hicks Beach's willingness to accept partial Sunday closing, created great confusion regarding the government's intentions. The *Freeman's Journal* correspondent saw the house 'fast sinking into demoralisation and public contempt', and he criticised the government for not providing strong enough leadership. The paper said that it was 'difficult to draw the line between Mr James Lowther and his caterwauling confreres and the Irish members whom he and they continue to render formidable'. And it speculated as to whether the government's failure to support the bill, after its amendments had been accepted, was motivated by 'pure spite', to get back at the Irish members who were obstructing government bills. The *Irish Times*, which opposed Sunday closing, also condemned the use of obstruction against the bill. However, it saw the Home Rulers rather than the government as largely responsible for the situation which had arisen:

> Among those who exclaimed most loudly against the obstruction offered to the Sunday closing bill were gentlemen who offered an equally annoying obstruction to the votes to supply. If Mr O'Sullivan, Mr Downing and Major O'Gorman maintained a vexatious opposition to the majority, most decidedly Mr Sullivan, Mr Biggar and Mr O'Connor Power did the same; so that as regards the mere blame of worrying parliament there is little to choose between the Sunday closers and their opponents.[49]

When the debate was resumed on 16 May, however, the opposition collapsed quickly and the amendments being discussed were passed. The

Irish Times claimed that the 'Sunday closers... seem to have completely cowed the treasury benches'. In fact opposition to the bill was weakening, and supporters and opponents of the measure were beginning to co-operate. The *Freeman's Journal* noted that a 'more amicable disposition seems to have grown between the two hostile camps of Sunday and anti-Sunday closers'. O'Gorman and, to a lesser extent, O'Sullivan continued to obstruct in a fairly outrageous manner, but the other opponents of the bill had changed their tactics. McKenna, Murphy and McCarthy Downing began to move amendments which would have made the bill unacceptable to the house or ineffectual in its operation. McKenna and O'Sullivan, for instance, attempted to introduce an element of local option by proposing that householders should be able to determine the hours of opening. This obviously aimed to stir up the opponents of the permissive principle against Sunday closing and so divide the bill's supporters. But such amendments were highly unlikely to be passed. Once the bill's opponents had been driven by the public outcry to drop obstruction, they had little chance of stopping the measure. Unwavering opposition was left to the eccentric O'Gorman, who told the house that the bill was 'an absolute abortion'. But his verbal excesses probably only succeeded in discrediting further opposition.[50]

When the government provided 11 July for final consideration of amendments there were only forty members in the house. But then the bill had been debated for forty-three hours during the session, and, as the *Freeman's Journal* had suggested, most members were heartily fed up with it. Its opponents continued to introduce amendments, though arguing as much with each other as with the bill's supporters. O'Gorman in frustration threatened to resign and had to be dissuaded by his colleagues. But Lowther, while stating that 'there was probably no member of the house who disliked this bill more than he did', admitted that a majority of the house was determined to proceed with it and so the government wished progress to be made as rapidly as possible. The government's more co-operative attitude was probably largely the result of a desire not to waste any more time on the bill. Government business had already fallen well behind, and, with the Congress of Berlin just ending, time was needed for foreign policy debates. The London correspondent of the *Freeman's Journal* vividly captured the atmosphere of this debate, and his report is worth quoting at length:

It is a sore trial to the patience of the government and many members of the House of Commons that another night should be devoted at this period of the session to a struggle of endurance on the question of Sunday closing in Ireland. All kinds of measures are being abandoned for want of time to discuss them, and yet the time that would save some of them has to be sacrificed on account of the opposition to this bill.... Mr

O'Sullivan... spoke during the greater part of dinner time to a house of five or six members. Twice while he was speaking attention was called to the empty benches, and twice did members come trooping in in such numbers that counting was almost a formality.

Members kept coming in, looking round, smiling at the transparent farce, exchanging a laugh with other members, a joke with the Serjeant-at-Arms, and then going out again to talk in the lobby about the burlesque to be witnessed in the first parliamentary assembly in the world.

The members who were present at a quarter to eleven o'clock enjoyed a little merriment at the expense of two occupants of the treasury bench — Mr Lowther and Sir Selwin Ibbetson — who were soundly asleep. Sir Selwin Ibbetson sat with his head resting on the top of the seat back, but Mr Lowther's head was considerably lower, and he seemed in danger of falling upon the seat towards the English Attorney-General.

The debate consumed ten hours, and not until 3 a.m. was the second reading finally passed. Even the I.S.C.A. admitted that the debate had been 'altogether unnecessary', with the 'old speeches redelivered, and the old tactics resorted to'. The English press also showed its irritation. The *Daily Telegraph* used the debate as an excuse to air its anti-Irish views. Calling the bill merely a matter for the 'parish police', the paper said it was 'scandalous' that twelve sittings had been devoted to it since January without yet having reached the third reading. If the Irish were convinced that they could not be trusted to drink on Sunday 'without prejudice to public decency and order', the paper went on, then it was not for the English to object to the measure by which they sought to 'correct their failing'. (**54** [1877-8], 14)[51]

But in fact the long struggle for Sunday closing was nearly over, for the government, despite Lowther's hostility, had at last determined to dispose of the issue. On 8 August the Chancellor told the house that, as the bill had been discussed and divided upon at every possible occasion and carried by large majorities, 'it would be unbusinesslike to allow all the time so expended to be entirely thrown away; and perhaps, to make the house appear to stultify itself'. The government, in consultation with the bill's promoters, had therefore decided to provide facilities for the bill to be read a third time and sent to the House of Lords before the end of the session. Thus, after a short debate on 10 August, the bill was passed by 63 votes to 22. Introduced into the House of Lords on 12 August, it proceeded almost without discussion, was passed on 15 August, and received the royal assent on 16 August.[52]

The campaign to win a Sunday closing act in the 1870s illustrates simultaneously the strengths and the weaknesses of the Irish temperance movement. Temperance advocates were much more successful than publicans in bringing public pressure to bear upon the government. The lists of meetings held, resolutions passed, petitions presented, delegations organised and M.P.s lobbied are very impressive indeed. In response the drink trade was forced to rely heavily on its English counterpart and the sympathy of many English Tory M.P.s. This was politically embarrassing for a group with nationalist leanings, and ultimately it proved ineffective. In Michael Dwyer the publicans had a skilful lobbyist, but he was no match for the combined talents of John Pyper and T. W. Russell and the various other paid agents of the Irish temperance societies. The emphasis on professionalism and thorough organisation, which the I.T.L. had inaugurated in the late 1850s, was fully vindicated in the long struggle for Sunday closing. The massive polls of householders in the five major towns — 74,000 in 1876 and 90,000 in 1882 — clearly revealed the sophisticated machinery that the temperance movement had developed. In this context it is interesting to note that as early as 1882, only six years after its invention, a telephone was rented by the Irish Association for the Prevention of Intemperance for its Dublin headquarters at a cost of £12 per annum. Such an improvement in communications must have been a considerable asset to a pressure group like the I.A.P.A., though the association's readiness to utilise mechanical innovations also says a lot about its imaginative tactics.

Yet despite its most strenuous endeavours during the 1870s, the temperance movement was only able to win a partial and temporary act. Divisions within its own ranks, particularly between Dublin and Belfast over the relative merits of Sunday closing and local option, certainly undermined the campaign, but as well it faced formidable opposition. The Tories were not prepared to allow the temperance movement to achieve a total victory over the drink trade. Although temperance advocates may have exaggerated the closeness of the link between Conservatism and drink, that such a link existed is undeniable. Disraeli seemed to flaunt it in 1880 when he created Sir Arthur Guinness Lord Ardilaun — 'the first direct entry of beer into the Lords', as one recent historian has put it. (**316**, 312) The temperance movement also faced determined opposition in the major Irish towns where the drink industry was principally based and where it was most effectively organised. The opposition of urban corporations, police and magistrates was another major obstacle. For example, three-quarters of the police officers and magistrates who gave evidence to the select committee of 1877 strongly opposed the introduction of Sunday closing in the towns.

In retrospect, however, the 1870s as a decade was to prove far more favourable to temperance legislation than the following two. The temperance movement found strong support in parliament among Irish and English Liberals, Ulster Conservatives and Butt's Home Rulers. This broadly based alliance faced a government headed by an ageing Prime

Minister, who was distracted by foreign policy issues as his administration increasingly lost momentum in the domestic sphere. After 1880, however, the political climate changed markedly. Put simply, with the emergence of Parnell's more militant Home Rulers and the destruction of the Irish Liberals, the temperance movement lost much of its political base. At the same time the publicans recovered theirs among the new Home Rulers. The roles of the 1870s were in fact reversed, and the Irish temperance movement found itself as heavily dependent on the goodwill of English Liberals as the publicans had been earlier on English Tories.

Temperance and the Liberal Government, 1880-85

The long parliamentary battle required to achieve even a limited and temporary Sunday closing act in Ireland did not augur well for the future of temperance legislation, and in fact no further significant Irish licensing legislation was passed before the end of the century. Little could be expected of the Conservatives, but even the Liberal governments of 1880-85, 1886 and 1892-5 produced nothing but promises as far as the Irish temperance movement was concerned. Temperance bills, particularly in the 1880s, were squeezed out of parliament by the preoccupation of government with the Irish land question and Home Rule.

At the end of 1878, however, the Irish temperance movement was supremely confident. At a meeting in Dublin on 5 November the I.S.C.A. and the I.P.B.A. were formally united as the Irish Association for the Prevention of Intemperance. The new association's president was Thomas Pim junior, its secretary was T. W. Russell, and one of its honorary secretaries was Henry Wigham. It reflected much more the outlook of the I.S.C.A. than that of the I.P.B.A., which had tended to go into decline in the late 1870s owing to the temperance movement's preoccupation with Sunday closing. Thus in the association's list of its seven main aims the extension of the Sunday closing act came first, while the introduction of local option was relegated to sixth place. The second aim of the I.A.P.I. was to limit trading hours, especially on Saturdays, and this was the first issue that it took up. Doubtless it was prompted in this by pressure from the Catholic hierarchy, who regarded Saturday drinking as the biggest problem and suspected the Sunday closers of sabbatarianism. A. M. Sullivan introduced a bill proposing Saturday closing at 6 p.m. in towns and 8 p.m. elsewhere, which was debated on 30 April 1879. Even the I.A.P.I. was not particularly optimistic about the chances of this measure, coming on top of the long Sunday closing debates, and in fact it was quickly talked out by Philip Callan. At the same time meetings supporting the measure were regularly attacked and broken up. After a riot at a meeting in the Antient Concert Rooms two spirit grocers and a grocer's assistant were prosecuted. Riots followed meetings in Limerick as well, where the publicans were described as 'bitter'. Temperance meetings had been attacked in the past, but not as frequently nor as violently as in 1879. Having failed to stop Sunday closing in parliament in 1878, the drink trade presumably decided on more forceful methods. However, they were not really necessary. (**191** [1878-9], 3-4)[53]

One problem facing the temperance movement at this time, and one which was to become increasingly serious, was the question of finance. Electioneering and parliamentary lobbying were extremely expensive activities. In 1877-8, for example, the I.S.C.A. had spent over £2,800. Voluntary subscribers from the Dublin and Belfast business communities were generous, while the United Kingdom Alliance provided an annual grant of between £100 and £200 to both the I.T.L. and the I.A.P.I.; but expenditure almost constantly exceeded income. The I.A.P.I. had taken over the liabilities of the I.S.C.A. and the I.P.B.A., which together amounted to nearly £200. The association had hoped to raise £2,000 in 1879, but because of the trade depression it was only able to raise a little over £1,200. Richard Allen of Dublin and J. G. Richardson of Bessbrook, both Quakers, were the largest contributors, each providing £100. Yet expenditure for the year was £1,300. In 1880 the association's income was £1,330, but expenditure, including £200 spent on the general election, rose to over £1,600. In 1881 for the first time the association managed to stay in the black, but it was not a particularly active year. As the decade progressed subscriptions fell markedly, from £733 in 1883-4 to £420 in 1886-7 to a mere £350 by 1890-91. In these circumstances the I.A.P.I. had no alternative but to curtail its activities drastically. In Belfast the I.T.L. faced similar problems, which became particularly acute with the two elections in 1885 and 1886. However, the League's successful cafés and coffee stands were very profitable: in the six months ending August 1892, for instance, the fifteen stands in Belfast yielded a combined profit of over £1,500. This income was vital in sustaining the organisation during the dark days of the late 1880s and early 1890s when parliamentary progress was minimal and disillusionment was reflected in declining subscriptions. (**54** [1877-8], 17; **191** [1878-9], 19, 23-7, [1879-80], 17-18, [1883-4], 19, [1886-7], 18, [1890-91], 350)[54]

The temperance movement and the drink lobby were extremely active during the general election of 1880 in Ireland, as well as in England, though in Ireland the depression, the land question and the issue of Home Rule were more urgent problems as far as most of the population was concerned. The electoral lobbying of the movement can be traced in some detail in the records of the I.T.L., which are far fuller on this subject than are those of the I.A.P.I. This, of course, restricts analysis to Ulster,though temperance as an electoral issue was undoubtedly most important there. Land reform and Disraeli's foreign policy were probably the two main issues in the province, with temperance and jury reform coming next. In the boroughs of Belfast and Carrickfergus and in the counties of Down, Armagh and Londonderry candidates referred specifically to the temperance question in their electoral addresses. Some were quite precise, like Viscount Castlereagh, the Conservative member for Down, who had been returned at a by-election in 1878 with strong support from the I.T.L. He said that he had supported the Sunday closing bill and would also support the permissive bill or a local option resolution. But most were considerably more vague, obviously not wishing to restrict their freedom of choice too narrowly. For example, Thomas Greer, the Conservative candidate in Carrickfergus, who was to defeat Dalway, said: 'I will be an advocate for such alterations in the existing laws as may afford a reasonable prospect of abating this national calamity.' Greer, like many other candidates, felt it wise to show sympathy for the temperance cause, but without pledging himself necessarily to vote for any particular piece of legislation. But the I.T.L. did work hard in order to gain specific pledges from candidates, as the minute book of the executive committee clearly illustrates. The committee met nearly every day, sometimes twice a day, throughout March and April. On 12 March the League's electoral manifesto was approved, as were three questions to be put to each candidate. These were:

(1) Will you, if elected, vote for a measure according power to the people to restrain the issue or renewal of licences for the sale of intoxicating liquors in their respective districts?

(2) Will you vote for the renewal of the Irish Sunday closing bill, and its extension to the towns now exempted?

(3) Will you vote for the early closing of public houses on Saturday evening? (**338**, 319, 305)[55]

On 15 March the executive committee organised delegations to visit each of the candidates in Ulster. In Belfast on 18 March the committee held a special meeting at which J. P. Corry and W. M. Ewart, the Conservative members for the borough, were present. Ewart, a linen merchant, had replaced Johnston after he had resigned in 1878. Both M.P.s thought 6 p.m. too early for Saturday-night closing, and Corry, while endorsing the principle of local option, was not prepared to commit himself to un-qualified support for the permissive bill. This must have disappointed the League, as Corry had been its president from 1862 to 1866. J. S. Brown, the Liberal candidate, received a League delegation and gave satisfactory answers to the three questions. But the other Conservative candidate, Dr Robert Seeds, Q.C, refused to reply to the League's invitation to a meeting and was endorsed by the vintners in a letter to the *Northern Whig*. The League decided to work actively for Seeds's defeat. On 26 March the committee ordered 2,000 handbills directed against him to be issued, and on the following day the number was raised to 10,000. It was also decided to produce posters advertising Seeds's views on temperance, the cost if possible to be covered by the other candidates. The easy return of Corry and Ewart must have pleased the League.

There were, however, more serious problems in other constituencies. In Co. Monaghan there was a close contest between the Conservative members, Sir John Leslie and S. E. Shirley, and the Liberals, John Givan and William Findlater. On 25 March the committee received reports that neither Shirley nor Findlater would endorse local option. The secretary was instructed to write to leading Liberals and Conservatives who were friends of temperance, including John Givan, and ask them to talk to the two candidates. This apparently had no effect, because on 27 March the League issued what it termed a 'whip' supporting the Conservative Leslie and the Liberal Givan. In a close vote the two Liberals were returned, with Givan topping the poll. Problems also presented themselves in Dungannon, where there was another close contest. The League received reports that the Liberal member, T. A. Dickson, and his Conservative opponent, Colonel Knox, were both offering concessions to the publicans and bidding for their support. John Pyper was dispatched immediately to interview the candidates. He reported the following day that Knox had said he supported Sunday closing but was opposed to both local option and early Saturday closing. For his part, Dickson said he supported local option and Sunday closing, but was against early Saturday closing except for towns with a population exceeding 10,000.[56] Although there is no indication in the committee's minutes which candidate they endorsed, one can only assume that it would have been Dickson, who was prepared to vote for the permissive bill. Dickson did win in a very close vote, but was subsequently unseated on petition.

The vintners, after their defeat over the Sunday closing bill, mounted a vigorous campaign to ensure the election of sympathetic candidates. The Dublin Licensed Grocers' and Vintners' Protection Society issued a circular on 10 March warning traders that the real aim of the temperance movement was 'to harass you with penal enactments, and, if possible, to crush you out of business'.

> They have struck a blow [it went on] at one of the few branches of home manufacture still permitted to survive in Ireland, and in doing so they have injured not only the manufacturer and those whom he employs, but the farmer, who in these disastrous years, has found his barley crop a drug on the market. Thus Irish trade, Irish manufacture, and Irish agriculture have been insidiously struck at by the same hostile hand.

The argument that temperance was economically injurious to Irish industry and agriculture was likely to have a strong appeal, given the existing depressed conditions, and it was especially calculated to appeal to Home Rule candidates. The vintners' society said that it was its 'duty to keep clear of party politics', but emphasised that this was a 'broad national question', affecting the 'social rights' of the Irish people as well as their economic interests. This was obviously directed at Home Rulers, and in fact the vintners were to find important allies in the emerging Parnellite party. The trade was active in Ulster as well as in the south. In Co. Cavan, for example, trade representatives saw the two Home Rule members, Biggar and Fay, and asked them to pledge themselves to vote against the early Saturday closing bill. Biggar, who was a leading champion of temperance legislation, refused, but Fay agreed and subsequently kept his promise. In Newry Henry Thomson, a wine merchant, recaptured the seat for the Conservatives, defeating P. G. H. Carvill, a Catholic barrister, in a close contest. The *Northern Whig* felt that Carvill's defeat was due to the fact that the town's Catholic publicans had withdrawn their support because of the Liberal party's connections with the temperance movement. (**338**, 321, 343)[57]

The re-election of a Liberal government and the fall of the 'publicans' parliament' was heartily welcomed by the Irish temperance movement, and great confidence was expressed in the future. Said the I.A.P.I.:

> In 1874 a parliament was elected, one of its missions being to stand by the publicans. Today we have a strong government pledged to temperance reform, and a parliament elected in spite of the publicans, that will take care the government does not escape its obligations.

But in fact the results in Ireland were decidedly mixed. There were important successes certainly, like the election of J. N. Richardson as Liberal member for Co. Armagh, the replacement of Lord Charles Beresford in Co. Waterford by the Home Ruler J. A. Blake, and Benjamin Whitworth's re-election in Drogheda. But there were also important losses: The O'Conor Don lost in Roscommon to a Parnellite; W. H. O'Shea replaced Lord Francis Conyngham in Co. Clare; Major O'Gorman was defeated in Waterford city, but was replaced by the Parnellite Edmund Leamy, who was hostile to temperance legislation; similarly in Cork city N. D. Murphy, although supported by the drink trade, was defeated by Parnell himself and by John Daly, but neither were advocates of temperance. However, perhaps A. M. Sullivan had the most unpleasant experience as a result of the election. He was re-elected in Co. Louth only to find that his fellow-member was to be Philip Callan, who had been one of the most vocal opponents of both Sunday and Saturday closing. Callan was also notorious for having appeared drunk in the House of Commons; eventually he proved such an embarrassment that Parnell contrived his defeat in Louth in 1885. But in 1880 Sullivan simply declined to sit and was replaced by A. H. Bellingham, another opponent of temperance. Sullivan eventually found a seat in Meath, vacated by Parnell, who had decided to sit for Cork city. (**39**, 423; **226**, 306-7)[58]

The defeat of many members of Butt's old Home Rule party in 1880 saw the removal from parliament of some of the leading combatants in the Sunday closing struggle of the 1870s. On the whole, however, they were replaced by opponents of temperance, or at least by those with little interest in the issue. This was particularly true of the twenty-four definite Parnellites elected: some were openly hostile to temperance, regarding it as a conservative, middle-class, Protestant movement, while others simply thought that the land and national questions were infinitely more important for Ireland. So although the election of a Liberal government seemed a victory for temperance, the appearance of a more radical Home Rule party was a definite setback in Ireland at least.

The parliament returned in 1880 was clearly more sympathetic to the temperance cause than the preceding one had been. This was demonstrated speedily and graphically with regard to the permissive bill. On 5 March a local option resolution had been rejected in the old parliament by 280 votes to 166, but on 18 June a similar resolution was carried in the new parliament by 229 votes to 203. At the first division the Irish vote had been:

	For	Against	Total
Liberals	8	2	10
Conservatives	7	5	12
Home Rulers	7	7	14
Total	22	14	36

But in June there was a significant increase in the Irish vote:

	For	Against	Total
Liberals	8	1	9
Conservatives	10	7	17
Home Rulers	18	12	30
Total	36	20	56

The I.T.L. was pleased with the Ulster vote, which in March had been 15 for and 3 against and which in June had risen to 17 for and 4 against. But the executive committee decided to write to members who had been absent or who had voted against, seeking an explanation. The increase in the Home Rule vote in favour of the resolution, from 7 in March to 18 in June, also seemed especially encouraging. However, the most striking change had occurred among English Liberals, who voted in favour of the resolution by 133 to 35. Eighteen members of the government voted with the majority, including Harcourt, Chamberlain and Bright; and although Gladstone was not among them, he announced that he had accepted the principle of the measure and promised government action as soon as the pressure of business would permit. (**167**, 223-4)[59]

In the light of these events, great hopes were held by both the Irish and English temperance movements. But as the 1880-85 government became enmeshed in the Irish land problem, in fights between Whigs and Radicals, and in a disastrous foreign policy in Egypt and the Sudan, the hopes of the temperance movement were severely dashed. As early as the middle of 1881 Sir Wilfrid Lawson began to sense that temperance legislation was slipping down the government's list of priorities. He warned Gladstone against paying too much attention to the problems of 5 million Irish, while neglecting the 35 million people 'of this island'. But in fact the problem of 'arrears of legislation' was only to become worse. If the English temperance movement did not receive the attention that it demanded from the government, this was even more so of the Irish. The government was being accused of neglecting issues like temperance to concentrate on Ireland; in such a situation the Irish temperance movement fell between the two stools. In 1881 Charles Meldon had taken over the early Saturday closing bill from Sullivan and reintroduced it. But it was opposed by the government and defeated. E. W. Forster, the Chief Secretary, argued that there was no widespread demand in Ireland for the measure and, moreover, that the Sunday closing act should be allowed to operate for a longer period before being supplemented with further legislation. Forster appealed to Meldon not to divide the house; but Meldon insisted, and the bill was lost by 49 votes to 33. The Irish members voted for, but only by a majority of three. The most interesting feature of the Irish vote, however, was the fact that the Home Rulers voted against the bill by 14 to 8, the Parnellites being 6 to 2 against. (**166**, 88-92; **136**, 85-6, 91-4; **191** [1880-81], 8-9)[60]

With the Sunday closing act due to expire on 31 December 1882, the Irish temperance movement began another substantial campaign, this time to convince the government to make the act permanent and extend it to the five exempted cities. A deputation from the I.A.P.I. saw Forster after their annual meeting in November 1881, but he would only commit the government to ensuring that the act did not lapse. The association then decided to launch another massive canvas of the five cities, even larger than the one undertaken in 1876. Householders and registered voters were polled in person or by mail in order to ascertain public opinion on the issue and hopefully pressurise the government into extending the act. Over 90,000 householders in the cities were asked: 'Are you in favour of the entire closing of public houses, beer-shops, taverns and spirit groceries on Sunday?' To this question 76,817 answered yes and 13,702 answered no. A declaration in support of the act was also drawn up and signed by 1,769 clergy, magistrates, doctors, Town Commissioners and Poor Law Guardians in the five cities. (**191** [1881-2], 5-8)

But Forster remained apparently unimpressed by these expressions of public opinion. On 28 April 1882 he told a deputation, including Corry, Richardson, Ewart, Dickson, Blake, Dean Dickinson of the Chapel Royal,

Henry Wigham and T. W. Russell, that the government was too pressed for time at present to introduce an Irish Sunday closing bill of its own. However, he suggested that if a private member introduced such a bill the government would give it all possible support. After 'considerable hesitation' the I.A.P.I. decided to take this course, and J. N. Richardson, one of the few remaining Irish Liberal M.P.s, introduced a bill that was read for the first time on 2 May. But 'the exigencies of Irish business blocked all further progress'. The new Chief Secretary, G. O. Trevelyan, however, was much more genuinely sympathetic to temperance legislation than Forster, having long been an active member of the United Kingdom Alliance. He assured an Irish delegation on 18 June that he would speak to Gladstone about the bill. But this only produced a statement in the house by Gladstone on 20 June which reiterated Forster's remarks: that the government could not commit itself at present to legislate, but that the Irish Sunday closing act would not be allowed to lapse. Richardson continued to try to secure time for a second-reading debate. He finally succeeded at nearly midnight on Saturday 22 July, after a special sitting of the house to deal with the Scottish education bill. The government continued unhelpful, trying to adjourn debate in the face of protests from J. A. Blake and Maurice Healy. But the matter was settled when, at the instigation of Philip Callan, the house was counted out. (**191** [1881-2], 12-14)[61]

The I.A.P.I. refused to be unduly pessimistic, noting that during the course of the session a Welsh Sunday closing bill had been passed and that similar bills were being promoted for English counties, including Durham, Lancashire, Yorkshire and Cornwall. Moreover, the association was convinced that the Liberal government was truly sympathetic to its cause. The only thing, concluded the I.A.P.I. report for the year, that 'stood in the way of a complete measure being carried, was the pressure of public business on the government and the House of Commons'. (**191** [1881-2], 15)

In 1883 three bills were introduced to deal with the hours of liquor trading in Ireland. Meldon, Whitworth and Blake introduced one, aimed at closing public houses on Saturday at 8 p.m. in towns and 9 p.m. elsewhere. But this bill did not proceed beyond its first reading. A private member's bill to extend and make permanent the Sunday closing act was also introduced, endorsed by Richardson, Corry, Blake, Lord Arthur Hill, Thomas Dickson, Meldon, Lewis, Ewart, Arthur O'Connor and John Redmond. But this bill was not proceeded with because a government bill was introduced in the House of Lords by Lord Carlingford, the former Chief Secretary Chichester Fortescue. The government had changed its policy of the previous year and decided to introduce its own bill. On 29 January Dublin Castle had sent a letter to Resident Magistrates requesting information about the operation of the Sunday closing act. Out of the seventy-one who replied, sixty-eight agreed that the act promoted peace in the country and sobriety among the people. Arrests for drunkenness on

Sunday had decreased by some 60 per cent in rural areas since 1878 and by some 33 per cent in the five exempted cities, where trading had been reduced by two hours. In drawing attention to these figures during the second-reading debate on 15 March, Carlingford said that the Irish government was satisfied that the act had the support of the Irish people, including that of the working class. As for the exempted cities, Carlingford considered that their exemption had been 'admitted for the sake of peace, and as a matter of precaution and prudence, and to secure the passing of the bill'. However, the recent canvas by the Sunday closing movement had convinced the government that they too now desired Sunday closing. With only halfhearted opposition from the Earl of Milltown, representing a great Irish family of brewers, the Earl of Limerick and the Marquis of Lansdowne, the bill proceeded swiftly through its stages and was sent to the Commons on 19 March.[62]

The measure received strong support from both the new Lord Lieutenant, Earl Spencer, and Chief Secretary Trevelyan. When Callan on 19 March pointed out in parliament that cases of drunkenness heard before the spring assizes that year were much more numerous than in the previous year and used this to question the government's claims that the Sunday closing act had reduced drunkenness, Trevelyan sent a circular to town and county inspectors demanding information as soon as possible. Twenty-four out of the thirty-five who replied agreed that drunkenness cases had increased, but many ascribed this to the fact that in 1882 the R.I.C. was too preoccupied with the land struggle to concern itself with arresting drunkards. On 27 April Trevelyan received a delegation in London consisting of representatives of the I.A.P.I. and the I.T.L. and thirty M.P.s. He described the Sunday closing bill as the 'first of their social bills' affecting Ireland and promised that the 'Irish government would not be satisfied without either passing this bill or being defeated over it'. These remarks 'completely reassured' the delegation. On the very day that Trevelyan said this another event occurred which could only further reassure the temperance movement as to the government's attitude. A resolution in favour of local option was again carried by a substantial majority, with Gladstone for the first time voting for the measure. Yet these events were all to prove false omens. (**191** [1882-3], 10-12)[63]

On 11 June, in response to a question from Richardson, Gladstone said that the government did want the Irish Sunday closing bill passed, but he added the significant rider that the bill would have to compete with many others for the limited amount of time available. Then on 9 July, in a speech dealing with the business of the house, Gladstone announced that eight bills would have to be dropped owing to lack of time. Expressing his regret, he named the Irish Sunday closing bill as one of them. Richardson, Corry, E. R. King-Harman and Sir Wilfrid Lawson immediately protested, Richardson in especially bitter terms:

Why [he said] the government had placed the supporters of this measure in the position of the historical donkeys which were coaxed over their journey by carrots being judiciously held to their noses. . . . The conduct of the government was a direct breach of faith with the supporters of the bill.

Richardson was careful to clear Trevelyan of any responsibility for the government's action. As early as 27 June Trevelyan had written to Richardson in apologetic terms regarding the failure to advance the bill. An 'unfortunate affair' he termed it, and he urged Richardson not 'to apportion the responsibility'. But in his speech on 9 July Richardson ignored this request and accused the government of giving way to pressure from the bill's opponents. Three days later Spencer was confronted with a large and angry delegation, including representatives of the Irish temperance movement and twenty-six M.P.s. He denied the charge that the government had, as he put it, 'knocked under to a clamorous minority' and claimed that Trevelyan's pledge in April was given 'subject to the time of parliament, over which he of course had not entire control'. It was felt, he explained, that the bill 'would take more time than could be given to it at the period of the session'. Indirectly, however, this was an admission that opposition to the bill was strong and that getting it through would be a time-consuming process. Privately Spencer wrote to Richardson on 15 July expressing his 'deep disappointment at what had occurred' and assuring Richardson that pressure of business was the only reason for the government's decision. (**191** [1882-3], 14)[64]

There seems little doubt that the Irish government genuinely desired the extension of the Sunday closing act and that Spencer and Trevelyan were both disappointed by the events of 1883. They were being inundated with petitions and resolutions in favour of the measure, while police and magistrates on the whole supported extension, believing that the closing of public houses contributed to the peace of the country during especially troubled times. Consumption of liquor in Ireland had declined during the operation of the act, and though it is doubtful that the act caused this (economic and political conditions being more likely), the temperance movement was certainly convinced that it had. Furthermore, although arrests for drunkenness had increased in 1883, they were still significantly lower than they had been immediately before the passing of the act. The Irish government had reason therefore to look upon Sunday closing as a 'peace preservation' measure. (**301**, 4; **192**, 4-5)[65]

Despite Spencer's explanation, the temperance movement was disappointed that the government did not give greater importance to anti-drink legislation. This disappointment deepened in 1884. Another government-sponsored Irish Sunday closing bill was announced in the queen's speech, and on 15 February it was introduced by Trevelyan, now

Chancellor of the Duchy of Lancaster. But because of the precedence given to the franchise reform bill and the long debates over the government's Egyptian policy, no progress was made until 20 June. On that day a long debate occurred, in which Gladstone supported the bill, saying that he had been convinced twelve or fourteen years before that the Irish people wanted Sunday closing. But the bill's opponents, in particular M. J. Kenny, the Home Rule member for Ennis, and C. N. Warton, the Conservative member for Bridport, managed to talk out the time allotted for debate. When the debate was resumed on 27 June Edmund Leamy, the Home Rule member for Waterford city, and Dr Lyons, the Liberal member for Dublin city, performed a similar task. The I.A.P.I. did not hesitate to blame the government for the bill's fate. Both 20 and 27 June were days on which, under standing orders, all debate had to cease at 6.50 p.m. In putting the Sunday closing bill down for debate on these particular days, the government was making the task of the bill's opponents comparatively easy. Nor could the I.A.P.I. have been very pleased with the remark by L. H. Courtney, representing the government, on 26 June. Agreeing with Tim Healy and W. A. Redmond that there were much more important Irish issues to consider than Sunday closing, he commented: 'We want to get rid of this bill — it is an obstacle that blocks the way.' It was obvious from the government's actions that 'getting rid' of the bill meant allowing it to be defeated rather than getting it passed. (**191** [1884-5], 5-6)[66]

Temperance and the Home Rule Party

The debate on 20 June 1884, though futile, was an interesting one, mainly in that it illustrated divisions within the Home Rule party on the subject of temperance. Tim Healy began by condemning the government for consulting temperance lobbyists like T. W. Russell, while ignoring the views of the Irish Parliamentary Party on the issue. He urged the government to bring forward 'non-contentious' measures, like the land purchase scheme, the education bill and the endowed schools bill. That temperance legislation was indeed a contentious issue within Home Rule ranks was amply demonstrated in the debate which followed Healy's remarks. Four leading Home Rulers were among those who rose to speak: two, John Redmond and J. G. Biggar, were in favour of Sunday closing, while the other two, Timothy Harrington and William O'Brien, were opposed. Even Healy's own brother, Maurice, differed from him in generally supporting temperance legislation.

William O'Brien opposed the extension of the Sunday closing act on the grounds that

> The one great effect of it would be to divide the publicans into two classes — policemen's friends and policemen's enemies — and would

result in this, that all the attention of the police would be devoted to watching the nationalist publican, while those publicans who in any way had commended themselves to the favour of the police would be allowed by them to carry on any amount of Sunday trading without interference.

Healy claimed that nationalist publicans who displayed green flags on national festivals or who closed their businesses to protest against Parnell's arrest in 1881 found that renewal of their licences was opposed by the police.[67] Doubtless there is truth in this, and it certainly was a claim frequently made by critics of temperance legislation. Many publicans were supporters of the Land League, and they were vastly over-represented among those arrested under the Protection of Person and Property Act of 1881. Of 845 arrested, 68 or 8.1 per cent were innkeepers or publicans, though, according to the 1881 census, this group only composed 0.4 per cent of the labour force. Public houses were commonly used for Land League meetings and for the posting of League placards, with the result that over 40 per cent of publicans arrested were accused of holding illegal meetings or displaying threatening notices. The publicans had become important leaders of the national movement at the local level. In such circumstances many Home Rulers felt obliged to defend their interests in parliament against the temperance movement, which was hardly noted for its nationalist sympathies. (**102**, 455, 467; **104**)

To many Home Rule nationalists, temperance advocates were, to quote O'Brien again, a

sect of puritans, who wished to impose their own opinions forcibly on the Irish people, and who really desired to treat the Irish people as though they were dipsomaniacs, and needed to be put under restraint.

Their aim, O'Brien maintained, was to restrict legitimate recreation, which the vast majority of Irishmen indulged in moderately. Moreover, their proposed restriction would fall most heavily upon the working classes, who did not have access to private cellars and clubs. O'Brien argued that the

lives of the Irish people were sufficiently joyless already; and he thought the legislators of that house would be far better employed in doing something which would substantially improve the condition of the Irish people than by assisting in debarring them of one of the few enjoyments they had.

O'Brien rejected the temperance argument that drunkenness created poverty and said he believed instead that misery and poverty drove people into the public house. He also repeated the publicans' view that temperance legislation would seriously damage one of the very few successful industries in Ireland.[68]

That the 1878 act had been administered discriminately against nationalist publicans and that positive action should be taken to improve socio-economic conditions in Ireland, rather than negative measures like Sunday closing, were the two main arguments used by Home Rule M.P.s against the bill to extend Sunday closing. Some also thought that issues like temperance distracted and divided the party, which should have been devoting its attention solely to gaining Home Rule. Perhaps the clearest expression of this view came from T. P. O'Connor, who told the annual convention of the Irish National League in September 1890 that nationalism must take precedence over teetotalism and that an Irish nationalist teetotaller must vote for Gladstonian candidates at all elections. The temperance policy of voting for candidates who pledged themselves to support temperance legislation, irrespective of their party affiliations, was, of course, quite contrary to Home Rule policy. O'Connor went on:

> The settlement of the Irish question is the first and most necessary preliminary to a real advance of teetotal or labour principles.... The great cause of intemperance in Ireland, as the great and fundamental cause of every other evil in Ireland, is the absence of self-government among the Irish people, and until we have given to the Irish nation the dignity and self-respect of a self-governed people we shall not lay the real foundations of temperance principles.[69]

But there were strong feelings on both sides in the party. Among Home Rulers who sponsored Irish temperance bills in the 1880s were J. A. Blake, Maurice Healy, John Redmond, Arthur O'Connor, J. G. Biggar and, after the 1885 and 1886 elections, Jeremiah Jordan of Clare, Pierce Mahony of Meath, and Alexander Blaine of Armagh. It was because of these differences of opinion within the party that Parnell, who in the 1870s had at times supported and voted for the Sunday closing bill, attempted in the 1880s to tread a more neutral path.

In 1886, for instance, he informed the mover of a bill dealing with the sale of liquor to children that a majority of his colleagues wanted Ireland excluded from the scope of the measure, because they were not able to reach agreement as a party whether to support it or not. And he went on to inform the house that he 'had always attempted to keep clear of these temperance questions' and 'had never voted on any of them', because he believed that the 'question of temperance and of the control of the liquor trade is one which, of all others, could most suitably and properly be left to an Irish legislature to deal with'. His claim that he had never voted on temperance questions was, of course, not true. But the argument that the drink question should be left to an Irish legislature was common currency in the Home Rule party, particularly during the latter part of the 1880s, when it was given added impetus by the prospect of the establishment of local government authorities in Ireland in the foreseeable future. Parnell supported plans to give councils licensing powers and argued strongly in 1886 for control of excise to be included among the powers of the proposed Home Rule parliament. It was left to Maurice Healy, however, to point out the glaring inconsistency in arguing that the drink question be left to Irish local or national governing bodies while at the same time demanding that the parliament at Westminster legislate on 'all kinds of topics, social and political, covering the whole field of social life'. But Healy, although he personally supported temperance legislation, said that he could see one strong reason for deferring it. This was that the

> question of closing public houses was of so angering and embittering a nature that it was inexpedient to raise it at the present time because of the effect it would have on the party ... destroying amongst them the union which then existed.

He told the house that he understood that this was Parnell's own view. Certainly it is consistent with Parnell's statement in 1886, when in effect he admitted that his party was so divided over the question of licensing legislation that he preferred to have Ireland excluded from the proposed act and so avoid a damaging intra-party confrontation. (**226**, 343-4)[70]

In 1888, in a debate on early Saturday closing for Ireland, Parnell made his most extended statement to date on the subject of temperance legislation. He said that he had watched, with the 'utmost interest', the parliamentary struggle over Irish Sunday closing for ten or twelve years. Originally he had supported the measure, but since 1878 he had come to the conclusion that it was not likely to serve the true interests of temperance, that in fact 'it was attended with greater evils than those which it sought to cure'. Parnell proclaimed himself a supporter of temperance:

> I am [he said], with perhaps a single exception, the largest employer of labour among the Irish members of all parties, and it has been brought constantly to my notice that the question of intemperance is undoubtedly a very great impediment to the progress of the industries of Ireland, and to the success of manufacturing and other operations, as well as to the welfare and well-being of the people.

But at the same time he was 'firmly convinced' that measures proceeding from Westminster for the promotion of temperance would 'not have any chance of fair play in Ireland'. The 'backs of the people would be put up against them in advance', while there would be 'defects in administration', which would increase public hostility and 'largely nullify the good intention of the legislature in passing such measures'. Parnell felt the Irish would regard such legislation, coming from the British parliament, as coercive, and particularly so if it was administered in a discriminatory fashion, as the Sunday closing act had been. He therefore advised delay, 'postponement, but not abandonment', and looked to the proposed local government bill, supporting moves to vest licensing powers in the new local authorities:

> I believe [he concluded] that Irishmen acting at home, discussing this question amongst themselves, free from your interference, will decide this question much more advantageously and much more suitably and justly than you can ever hope to decide it here, and their decisio will be attended with much better and happier results for the people.

While declaring himself in favour of temperance, Parnell, as a nationalist, was careful to introduce a disclaimer as to the seriousness of the drink problem in Ireland. He could not admit, he said, for a 'single moment' that the Irish were a less temperate people than the English or the Scots, and, though remarking upon the odiousness of comparisons, he went on to observe that 'Certainly the balance is not against us, and may be in our favour.' Like other Home Rule nationalists, Parnell did not like to see Liberal and Conservative Irish M.P.s portraying the Irish people before the British parliament as peculiarly prone to drunkenness.[71]

Basically it would seem that Parnell was not greatly interested in the issue of temperance for its own sake, beyond a general desire to prevent drunkenness from seriously damaging the economic life of the country. But some members of his party were passionately committed, both for and against. He also doubtless had to consider the influence of the drink trade. Publicans were important supporters of his party, as had been demonstrated by the numbers arrested during the land war. In rural areas they acted as local leaders, while in the cities they formed a powerful element in many corporations. Moreover, they had contributed generously to the 'Parnell tribute'. Like the Catholic church, the drink industry was an important element in Irish political and social life, an element that Parnell could not afford to alienate. Home Rule support for temperance legislation would certainly have alienated the publicans, just as Liberal support for such measures had driven them in the early 1870s into the arms of the Conservative party. Parnell's attitude to temperance is further illustrated by a remark he made in 1888 to Elizabeth Mathew, a collateral descendant of Father Mathew's, who was later to marry John Dillon. In her diary for 11 May of that year she recorded Parnell as having wished that there would be another apostle of temperance, since a crusade against whiskey 'would put the government in a difficulty, besides being good for the people, by diminishing an enormous source of revenue'. This remark clearly reflects Parnell's pragmatic approach to the issue. Temperance was a matter to be exploited or ignored, depending on the political advantages to be gained, and throughout the 1880s the balance was generally in favour of ignoring it. (**39**, 418; **266,** 143-4; **226**, 385-6)

Temperance in Decline from 1885

In the 1880s and 1890s the campaign for Irish temperance legislation faced a rather bleak outlook. Its strongest parliamentary support came from Ulster Conservative and Liberal Unionists, but Salisbury's government showed itself unsympathetic to the demand for legislation except of a very moderate variety. On the other hand, the Liberals, though increasingly attached to the temperance movement in England, found their Irish Home Rule allies divided on the issue, though with the most influential members of the party opposed to legislation emanating from Westminster. This frustration, however, was not alone felt by the Irish temperance movement. The Liberals' failure to introduce major temperance legislation caused severe discontent within the party and among English temperance advocates as well. Many felt that Gladstone's obsession with justice for Ireland was preventing social reform in England, which should have been the party's main preoccupation. Members of his governments, notably John Morley and Sir William Harcourt, repeatedly urged upon him the wisdom of substituting temperance reform for Home Rule as the party's main political banner. But such pressure was unsuccessful: Gladstone was never able to summon up much enthusiasm for the temperance cause, while some feared that it might prove even more divisive within the party than Home Rule. (**59,** 208-11; **166,** 131-2, 170-1, 204-7)

Disillusionment with the Liberals was evident in the Irish temperance movement's response to the 1885 and 1886 general elections. On 29 May 1885 the executive committee of the I.T.L. passed a resolution approving the proposed increases in taxes on spirits and beer which were contained in the budget. But at the same time the League noted that the government had not been prompted in its action by considerations of temperance. The government was defeated on this point on 9 June, when some 41 Home Rule M.P.s voted with the Conservatives and many Liberals abstained. Of the 15 Irish Liberals, 7 voted for the government and one, William Findlater of Co. Monaghan, against, while the rest abstained. Among the abstainers was J. N. Richardson, who had been so disappointed with the government's failure to pass the Irish Sunday closing bill in 1883. In the debate preceding the division W. H. O'Sullivan, or 'Whiskey' O'Sullivan, as he was called for his devotion to the drink cause, referred to the frequent attempts made during the previous thirty years by the Liberal party to destroy the Irish drink trade, which, with linen manufacturing, was Ireland's most vital industry. Even Arthur O'Connor, one of the most consistent supporters of temperance legislation among the Home Rulers, attacked the proposed increases on economic grounds. He claimed that they would not only damage Irish industry and increase foreign imports, but that they would also adversely affect Irish agriculture, because Irish farmers produced substantial amounts of grain for distilling. The fall of the government was not, however, essentially due to its policies with regard to the drink industry, nor was the issue a prominent one in the election campaigns of 1885 and 1886.[72]

The I.T.L. was considerably less active in 1885 than it had been in 1880. The Home Rule issue predominated, and moreover the League was experiencing financial problems, which curtailed its activities. But a manifesto was again issued, and some 5,000 posters and 300,000 handbills were circulated. Candidates were canvassed and asked two questions:

(1) Will you, if elected to parliament, vote for, and use all reasonable efforts to obtain, a measure giving ratepayers a direct veto over the issue and renewal of licences for the common sale of intoxicating liquors in their respective districts?

(2) Will you, if elected to parliament, vote for, and use all reasonable efforts to obtain, an immediate extension of the provisions of the Irish Sunday closing act to the whole of Ireland?

Throughout the campaign the I.T.L. *Journal* condemned the Liberal government. In August, for instance, it asserted that

The subject of local option [has] been kept dangling before the temperance party for the last five years, and all they have got from a parliament which they did so much to elect has been empty promises, hopes deferred, hollow excuses, vain regrets, and downright trifling.

This only begged the question of what the temperance movement could do to ensure that the new parliament would take the issue more seriously. At an executive committee meeting on 14 August it was suggested that the League should find a constituency and provide its own candidate to stand on a temperance platform. This suggestion was not proceeded with, but it reflects the temperance movement's frustration with the existing parties. Mainly the *Journal* counselled a 'more determined spirit' on the part of temperance advocates, though it failed to spell out how this determination could be translated into political advantage.[73]

In Dublin the I.A.P.I. responded to temperance's failures at the national level by turning its attention to municipal politics and to the courts. While disavowing 'any desire to interfere in political matters as such', the association said that it 'felt that if the large number of persons engaged in the liquor trade and cognate interests then seeking admission to the corporation were successful, the result would not be creditable or beneficial to the city'. In 1883, therefore, T. W. Russell, the I.A.P.I. secretary, stood in the Royal Exchange ward as a temperance candidate against Edward O'Leary, a publican. But Russell was defeated by fourteen votes, and the I.A.P.I. annual report regretted that the 'result of the election as a whole, was to largely increase the already powerful influence of the drink trade in the corporation'. However, the campaign experience was doubtless of use to Russell, who stood unsuccessfully as a Liberal in Preston in 1885 and then beat William O'Brien in Tyrone South in 1886, standing as a Liberal Unionist. Russell's defection from the Liberals over the Home Rule issue created problems with some of his temperance affiliations. Thus, when the United Kingdom Alliance continued to endorse the Liberal party, he resigned as a vice-president of the organisation. Many Liberal Unionists were in effect forced to chose between temperance and Home Rule. But during his thirty years in parliament Russell continued to work for temperance legislation, though his increasingly moderate stance was to· alienate some of his former prohibitionist allies in the I.T.L. (**191** [1883-4], 12; **136**, 99-100)

If the I.A.P.I.'s venture into local politics had failed, its legal activities were to be even more disastrous. In 1885 it was involved in an extremely expensive legal action aimed at upsetting the decision in the case of *The Recorder of Dublin v. Clitheroe*. This decision made in 1878 allowed a licence, once granted, to be transferred in perpetuity and only suppressed on account of misconduct on the part of the licencee: in other words, it gave the publican a vested interest in his or her licence. Not only did the I.A.P.I. lose the case, but its legal expenses amounted to £190 and it finished the year £100 in the red. This doubtless is why it informed its members, with regard to the election, that it had 'not deemed it necessary to do more than keep a watchful attitude upon the progress of political affairs'. But the I.A.P.I. was as outspoken as the I.T.L. in its condemnation of the Liberal government. It too felt that the Liberals had largely been elected by temperance votes and that therefore the temperance movement had 'just reason to feel aggrieved':

> The strongest hopes were held out by Liberal candidates during the general election of 1880 [complained the 1884-5 report] that legislation upon this important and pressing social question should be one of their chief aims. Yet despite these promises and hopes, six years have passed away and we stand on the threshold of a new election practically where we stood when the last parliament commenced its labours. It is true that the House of Commons thrice affirmed the principle of local option; it is true that on two occasions the government held out expectations in the speech from the throne that Irish Sunday closing would be settled in a permanent and satisfactory way; but it is equally true that no fruit has been gathered of these promises and expectations. On the subject of Sunday closing for our own country we have just reason to feel aggrieved, and your committee cannot help saying that if the members of the government had been as much in earnest when in power as they were when in opposition in the year 1877 and '78, Sunday closing in Ireland would have been long since accomplished.

Like the I.T.L., the I.A.P.I. looked to individual enthusiasts rather than to parties to further the cause. It noted approvingly that Michael Davitt, 'one of the most representative public men in Ireland', 'is in thorough sympathy with our aims and objects'. What was really needed in the next parliament, it said, was the 'presence of a few uncompromising temperance reformers who will insist that the question shall no longer be pushed aside'. (**191** [1884-5], 6-8, 13, 16)

The election in Ireland, however, failed to produce even these few. The Irish Liberals, who had generally supported temperance legislation, were totally wiped out, while the Conservatives were reduced to 18: 16 in Ulster and 2 for Dublin University. Friends of temperance, such as the Liberals T. A. Dickson, Thomas Lea, J. S. Brown and the former Tory M. R. Dalway and the Conservatives Sir J. P. Corry, I. T. Hamilton and Sir John Leslie, were all defeated Nationalists elected in Ulster included well-known opponents of temperance legislation, such as T. M. Healy and M. J. Kenny. Perhaps the only consolation for the temperance movement was the defeat of Philip Callan in Louth. W. H. O'Sullivan had not stood, but in Peter McDonald, the new member for Sligo North, the drink industry was to find another important champion at Westminster. (**337**, 130-6)

Neither the I.A.P.I. not the I.T.L. appears to have been very active in the 1886 general election: the minute book of the I.T.L. does not even mention it. In August the *Journal* described the election as 'singularly disappointing':

> The issue [it said], the one formal issue, before the country was Home Rule or no Home Rule, and upon this issue the contest was nearly everywhere carried on. In many constituencies something like civil war went on, and the temperance organisations hardly found it possible to take any very prominent part in the proceedings.

C. E. Lewis was unseated on petition in Londonderry city, but Corry was elected in Mid-Armagh, and T. W. Russell in Tyrone South. The League said that it looked to Russell and William Johnston in Belfast for 'a decided temperance policy'. Johnston had earlier in the year introduced a local option bill for Ulster. The bill made no progress, but it reflected the growing desperation of the I.T.L. The chances of winning local option for England or the south of Ireland seemed slight in the face of Tory and Home Rule opposition and Liberal equivocation. So the League was forced to look to its own stronghold, hoping that the small band of Ulster Conservatives could persuade the government to grant local option to Ulster. Johnston's bill, however, was blocked by southern Home Rulers, who saw it merely as the thin end of the wedge opening the way to the introduction of prohibition throughout the country.[74]

The Conservative government elected in 1886 proved predictably suspicious of temperance legislation. Hicks Beach as Chief Secretary refused even to receive an I.A.P.I. delegation in November, and he subsequently informed the association by letter that the government had no intention of introducing temperance legislation in the coming session. But Ireland's two Liberal Unionist M.P.s, T. W. Russell and Thomas Lea of Londonderry South, introduced bills on behalf of the I.A.P.I. to extend Sunday closing and also to curtail Saturday trading hours. No progress was made in 1887, but in 1888 the government acquiesced in the second reading of both bills on the understanding that they be submitted to a select committee. The I.A.P.I. was not very happy about the committee, as the suggestion had originated with Thomas Sexton, Home Rule M.P. for Belfast West, one of the bill's opponents. The committee when selected consisted of fourteen members, with D. H. Madden, the Irish Solicitor-General, as chairman. Only seven of the members were Irish M.P.s, and only four were Home Rulers. In fact the majority were pro-temperance. John O'Connor, Home Rule M.P. for Tipperary South, and Peter McDonald of Sligo North, who were both on the committee, opposed the addition of Russell, whom they considered 'biased', and of William Johnston, regarded by O'Connor as a 'fanatic'. When this failed they tried to have Sexton and Harrington added as well, but were successfully opposed by Biggar, who said that the publicans were exerting excessive pressure to get their nominees onto the committee. Madden was also relatively sympathetic to the bills and in his draft report recommended that the Sunday closing act be made perpetual, that the *bona fide* traveller limit be extended to six miles, and that Saturday closing be set at 9 p.m. However, he rejected total Sunday closing for the five exempted cities, recommending that in them trading hours be reduced to between 2 p.m. and 5 p.m. This seemed a reasonable compromise. It would have ended the need to continue the Sunday closing act from year to year, made abuse of the act by pseudo-travellers less easy, and struck a blow at the real problem of Saturday-night drinking. At the same time the powerful urban drink trade would have been permitted to continue operating on Sundays, though during reduced hours. On the whole, Madden's report seemed to offer more to the temperance movement than to the drink trade. But what happened was largely a repeat of what had occurred with regard to the 1877 select committee. The pro-temperance majority on the committee accepted the chairman's report, but substituted total Sunday closing for shorter hours in the five cities. Again, as in 1877, by refusing to compromise, the temperance movement only succeeded in alienating the government, which refused to take up the bill produced by the select committee. Thus it made no progress. In 1890, in commenting on the failure of another Sunday closing bill, the I.T.L. *Journal* observed: 'So the lifeless thing stands, a monument to the apathy of some, the hostility of others, and the impotence of others still.' Perhaps it should have added a further reason: the refusal of yet others to compromise. (**191** [1886-7], 5-7; **39**, xii-xxiii)[75]

At the same time opinions within the Home Rule party were hardening against temperance legislation. Doubtless the uncompromising stance of the temperance movement contributed to this development, though it was to be further strengthened by the split in 1890-91. This hardening can be seen in the votes cast by Home Rulers in divisions on temperance legislation. In 1888, for instance, when the second reading of Russell's early Saturday closing bill was passed by 178 votes to 102, the Irish M.P.s voted against by 23 to 18. All the 23 opposed to the bill were Home Rulers. In 1890 a local option bill for Ireland, again sponsored by Russell, was defeated by 131 votes to 124. The Irish voted in favour, but the turnout was very poor, the vote being 16 to 9. But 8 of the 9 against the bill were Home Rulers.[76]

Parnell, who had voted for temperance legislation in the 1870s and tried in the 1880s not to commit himself to either side, was by 1891 definitely opposed. In a speech opposing the second reading of the Intoxicating Liquors (Ireland) Bill, which combined both the Sunday and Saturday closing bills, he asserted that Sunday closing had 'not in the slightest degree' diminished intemperance or the consumption of alcohol in Ireland, and that in fact it had increased drunkenness. But he failed to provide any evidence to support these contentions. Instead he went on to claim that neither the people of Ireland nor their representatives had sought this measure. Rather was it the result of Liberal hypocrisy:

> No one would dare to propose such a measure as this for any English city, and surely English Liberals and Radicals, who have pledged themselves to the principle of Home Rule, and who denounce all English legislation for Ireland on the ground that it comes in a foreign garb, might have waited for some cases to be set up of exceptional intemperance before they support this coercion bill, for it is one. ... No attempt has ever been made to show in the case of these Irish towns that there is any exceptional drunkenness or crime arising out of intemperance.

The bill would come to Ireland, he said, 'as a patronising attempt on the part of the majority of English members in the House of Commons to make the Irish people sober'. But Irishmen declined to 'believe in our excessive drunkenness in comparison with our kind English friends'. Again, as he had done in 1888, though in even stronger terms, Parnell argued that the issue of licensing should be left to an Irish parliament, and he spurned English 'meddlesome interference and bungling attempts to legislate in reference to the wants of people whom they cannot possibly understand'. The second reading was carried by 250 votes to 96, with the Irish voting 27 to 21 in favour. The 2 Liberal Unionists and 12 Conservatives voted for the bill, as did 13 Anti-Parnellite Home Rulers. Those against were all Home Rulers, 15 being Anti-Parnellites and 6 Parnellites. The Parnellites were especially hostile to the bill, and of the ten Irish M.P.s who spoke against it in the debate, half were Parnellites. It is obvious from Parnell's speech that his hostility to the measure reflected his personal anger at the Liberals for their part in the split over the party leadership. The Liberals were identified with temperance, and so it provided a handy stick with which to beat them. But in addition he was attempting, as the I.T.L. *Journal* put it, to reassure 'the publicans that he was their friend'. In the scramble to win support in Ireland in 1891 both sections of the party sought to woo the publicans. This was particularly true of the Parnellites. One temperance advocate later remarked that they had

> bodily gone over to the licensed vintners. Money is scarce, and there is no body in Ireland gets the money so easily, and of course to get votes they are prepared to subscribe to party funds.

Parnell received most support from cities like Dublin, Waterford, Kilkenny and Cork, which had important drink industries. Bishop O'Callaghan of Cork thought that his main supporters in the city were either Fenians or publicans. In such circumstances opposition to the introduction of Sunday closing in these cities was calculated to increase Parnell's popularity among the drink trade. (**40**, 297; **226**, 576; **39**, 423)[77]

For the temperance movement only the return of a Liberal government seemed to hold out any hope of success in parliament. Although the Liberals had failed conspicuously in 1880-85 to pass temperance legislation, since their return to the opposition benches they had moved even closer to the English temperance movement. In 1891, for instance, they had incorporated local option into their Newcastle programme. In 1893 the new Liberal government did indeed introduce an Irish Sunday closing bill. As in 1883, the bill was first introduced into the House of Lords. It was moved by Lord O'Neill and strongly supported by Spencer, who was then First Lord of the Admiralty. But the opposition to the bill in the Lords proved much stronger than it had been ten years before. Lord Rockwood and Lord Wemyss argued that there was no demand in the five exempted cities for Sunday closing and moved that the hours of trading instead be reduced to between 2 p.m. and 5 p.m. O'Neill in reply moved that total Sunday closing be at least applied to Belfast, where he argued there was a real demand for it. But his amendment was defeated and Rockwood's accepted. The Earl of Meath, supported by Archbishop Plunket of Dublin, then sought to have the boundary of Dublin defined as the municipal boundary rather than the metropolitan police district boundary. This would have brought the six townships of Rathmines, Pembroke, Blackrock, Kingstown, Dalkey and Killiney under total Sunday closing. Spencer, for the government, supported this proposal, saying that majorities in the townships were in favour of Sunday closing. The amendment was accepted, and on 30 June the amended bill was passed and sent to the Commons. The bill, of course, was now no longer acceptable to the temperance movement, and moreover the Commons were totally absorbed in debating Gladstone's second Home Rule bill. The Sunday closing bill therefore made no further progress. The bill was unsuccessful in the ballot in 1894 and did not reach a second reading, while in 1895, although the second reading was passed by 170 to 71, the dissolution of parliament prevented further progress. So the slim hope that a Liberal government would see to the passing of further Irish temperance legislation was proved false again. And again Gladstone's preoccupation with Home Rule was the major cause. The anger with which the Irish temperance movement viewed the blocking of temperance legislation by Home Rule was perhaps most clearly expressed by the I.T.L. *Journal* in May 1891 after Parnell had vigorously opposed the second reading of the Sunday and Saturday closing bill. The Irish people, it said,

> are well nigh sick of the 'Irish question' ... and disgusted with the 'Irish leaders'; and they are resolving, whatever either Mr Gladstone or Lord Salisbury may say, that Ireland shall no longer be allowed to 'block the way' to urgently needed reform or be made the pretext for the indefinite postponement of social legislation. It is one of the most disgraceful scandals of the time (and that is saying much!) that the people have been compelled to groan and sweat under greedy taskmasters, to starve while 'making many rich', to pine and die in helpless sight of luxury, to drink and be damned for national revenue, and to have to wait for relief from all their cruel wrongs until it suit the convenience and the pleasures of a man like C. S. Parnell! It is a dishonour to the country of Cromwell that eighty-six men, or three times that number, should be able to reduce its legislature to ignominious impotence.

The Unionist sympathies of the temperance movement, combined with Protestant disgust with Parnell over the O'Shea divorce revelations, are clearly evident in this extract. (**136**, 132-3; **191** [1892-3], 3-5, [1894-5], 3-5)[78]

In the latter part of the 1890s the Irish temperance movement continued to sponsor bills to make Sunday closing permanent, to extend it to the five exempted cities, to curtail the hours of Saturday trading, to establish local option, and to place a limit on the numbers of licences issued. But the Conservative government was not very sympathetic to such measures, while the two sections of the Nationalist party continued to vie with each other for the support of the publicans. In these circumstances even John Redmond, who had sponsored the Sunday closing bill for ten years, found himself unable to vote for it. Local option was never obtained for Ireland, but finally, in 1906 after twenty-eight years, the Sunday closing act was made permanent. But it was not extended to the five exempted cities. There hours were merely shortened on both Sunday and Saturday, as the

Conservative government had recommended in 1888, while the *bona fide* traveller limit was raised from three to five miles. The second reading of the bill was carried in May by 244 votes to 50. But the Irish vote was much closer, being 37 to 32 in favour. All the 32 voting against were Nationalists, and they included John Redmond. The main supporter of this compromise was, ironically, T. W. Russell, and his stance on the bill brought him the hostility not only of the Nationalist party but of the Irish temperance movement as well. The I.A.P.I. endorsed the compromise, but the I.T.L. refused to do. The latter was represented in parliament by T. H. Sloan, Johnston's successor in Belfast South, who fought to have the *bona fide* traveller limit set at seven rather than five miles. In answer to these attacks, Russell observed, somewhat world-wearily perhaps, that

> None who had spent twenty years in this house could fail to learn one lesson, namely, that he could not get everything that he liked. It was one of the finest places for smashing or destroying ideals to be found in the whole world.

This comment could probably stand as an epitaph for the whole legislative campaign, from O'Reilly's first Sunday closing bill in 1867 up until the act making partial Sunday closing permanent nearly forty years later. With regard to the frustration of the I.T.L., it is perhaps interesting to note that in 1920 temperance advocates were among the first to support the idea of a separate northern parliament, hoping 'that their special interests might receive a friendlier hearing in a Belfast parliament than at Westminster'. As we have seen, they had very good grounds for expecting little from Westminster; and despite the fact that James Craig came from a well-known family of distillers, Stormont did prove more amenable to temperance lobbying. (**191** [1906], 4-7; **79**; **253**, 124; **343**, 125-6)[79]

The long struggle by the Irish temperance movement, which had commenced in the 1860s and continued beyond the turn of the century, for coercive legislation against the drink industry is essentially a story of disappointed hopes, smashed ideals and ultimate frustration. The hostility of important sections of the Home Rule party and of Conservative governments generally, and the preoccupation of all parties with more pressing Irish issues, such as the land question and Home Rule, left little room in the political arena for temperance. Nor did the Irish movement derive any great benefit from the championship of temperance by many English Liberals. The Liberals' involvement in other Irish issues and later their alliance with the Irish Parliamentary Party largely neutralised their sympathetic attitude. In these circumstances the unwillingness to compromise demonstrated by the Irish temperance movement, and particularly by the Ulster section of it, meant that most of the few opportunities that arose for getting legislation through were lost. The Sunday closing act of 1878 was the main exception to this. But the act was passed before Butt's conservative Home Rulers had been replaced by Parnell's more demanding militants, and its passage was only ensured after the temperance movement, in an uncharacteristic gesture, agreed to compromise with the government. The fact that the temperance campaign for legislation was strongest among Ulster Protestants and Unionists also had the effect of giving it an increasingly sectional character as time passed. Nationalists and Catholic clergy were very suspicious of its motives, even though they may have personally sympathised with its aims. Furthermore, despite its efforts to prove to government that it had the support of the working classes, the legislative campaign remained essentially a middle-class movement. The land question and Home Rule, although the I.T.L. considered these 'minor' issues, were far more successful in stirring the enthusiasm of the rural and urban masses. Put beside the chance of self-government or of a better deal from the landlords and later even ownership of the land, temperance legislation must have seemed to offer but little to the ordinary Irish man or woman. As the 1880s progressed the temperance movement therefore became increasingly isolated from the mainstream of Irish social and political life.

Another factor militating against political action to promote temperance was that the trend of drink consumption in Ireland was going in directions which the government largely approved. Spirit drinking had, on the whole, been declining since the 1850s, while beer drinking was on the increase. Both industries had prosperous export trades, which afforded the government substantial tax revenue. Illicit distillation had been brought under control, and the 1872 and 1874 Licensing Acts cleared up many of the problems associated with the issuing and regulation of retail licences. Given this state of affairs, government felt no great pressure to embark on a scheme of major change. The timing of the 1878 act is interesting in this context, for the mid-1870s were years of unusually high alcohol consumption in Ireland. A decline set in in 1879, caused not by the Sunday closing act as temperance advocates claimed, but by the economic depression which affected Ireland in that year. This decline, with some variations, generally continued to the end of the century and was more than a mere function of falling population. The demand for local option and Sunday closing under these circumstances must have seemed, as it largely was, the demand of a relatively small number of religious enthusiasts. While the Conservative party did not wish to alienate its Ulster supporters nor the Liberal party its English pro-temperance members, neither felt that this entailed conceding the demands of the Irish temperance movement. As a result, well before the turn of the century the initiative in temperance affairs had passed out of the hands of groups like the I.T.L. and the I.A.P.I. and into very different hands indeed.

6

Temperance and the Churches after 1870

WHILE the Irish Temperance League and the Irish Association for the Prevention of Intemperance concentrated on the campaign for temperance legislation in the last quarter of the nineteenth century, the Irish churches, both Protestant and Catholic, were also grappling with the issue. Some church-sponsored societies were active in the legislative campaign, but to many churchmen temperance seemed a religious rather than a political matter, a question to be determined by the clergy or by the individual's conscience rather than by the state.

Temperance and the Protestant Churches

We have already noted that from the 1830s the Presbyterian church in Ulster was particularly active in the Irish temperance movement. By the early 1870s, however, temperance enthusiasts were distinctly dissatisfied with the progress of total abstinence within the church. In 1874 an anonymous correspondent wrote in the I.T.L. *Journal*:

> Look at the Presbyterian church.... Her ministers are, many of them, zealous workers in the total abstinence cause. In her roll of church membership are found the names of some of the most active members of the varied temperance organisations; but, as a church, what is her position in this respect?... She is not altogether silent, it is true, but her utterances are measured and temporising. She is not entirely out of the field, but she is far from leading the van, far from taking the position which would rightfully be hers, were she consistent with her principles and faithful to her duty.

The temperance movement wanted the Presbyterian church, as a church, to speak out in favour of total abstinence. The *Journal* correspondent felt she was inhibited in this regard by the numbers of drink sellers who sat on church committees and by the financial support she received from the drink industry. The church reasoned, he said, that 'the trade is bad, no doubt,... but — the money! Oh, the money builds churches, aids the "sustentation fund".' Certainly drink manufacturers like Alexander Findlater and the Guinness family did make substantial donations to the Presbyterian church. (**291**, 248-9) The temperance movement sought what the *Journal* termed the 'absolute separation of the church from the liquor traffic'.[1] In 1875, with drinking and drunkenness obviously on the increase, the church finally faced up to the issue of total abstinence. Referring to this increase and fearing 'that this state of matters will continue as long as drinking customs are encouraged and patronised', the General Assembly declared it 'incumbent upon our ministers and people seriously to consider what may be their duty in regard to the use of intoxicating liquors as beverages'. Presbyteries were instructed to consider the issue and report to the temperance committee before April 1876. Of the thirty-six presbyteries in the church, twenty-one reported in favour of total abstinence. Accordingly in 1876 the General Assembly passed the following resolution:

> That as the Assembly has already given instruction to train up the young in the habit of abstaining from intoxicating drinks, by enrolling them in Bands of Hope, we cannot but commend the action of those who would lead them to continue in after-life in the practice in which they have been trained: and as no less than twenty-one presbyteries have declared in favour of abstinence from drinking customs, or from intoxicating drinks as ordinary beverages, we feel constrained to commend such abstinence to the consideration and adoption of our people. (**310**, 63)

The temperance movement rightly saw this as an important victory. Here was the Presbyterian church, as a church, recommending total abstinence to its members. The acceptance of total abstinence by the church within ten years of John Edgar's death was undoubtedly speeded by the work of the society of abstaining clergy. Since being established in 1850 it had grown steadily, working to convert ministers through the circulation of tracts and pamphlets. By 1879, of 644 Irish Presbyterian ministers, 260 were members, though I. N. Harkness, the secretary, claimed that the great majority, perhaps two-thirds, of the clergy were in practice abstainers. But the impact of the Presbyterian church's increasingly hostile attitude to drink can probably best be seen in the decline in the numbers of Presbyterian publicans. In Belfast, for example, Presbyterians fell from being a quarter of the trade in 1871 to being a mere 7 per cent in 1911. Members of the Church of Ireland, though not quite as numerous, fell almost as drastically over the same period, while Catholics increased from a little over 50 per cent to 86 per cent. There seems no other explanation for this marked decline in Protestant involvement in Belfast's retail drink trade but the impact of temperance propaganda. (**179**, 39-41)

As in Edgar's time, however, the temperance cause continued to generate fierce scriptural debate within the Presbyterian church. Whereas the issue of the 1830s and 1840s had been the biblical basis of total abstinence, by the latter part of the century the controversy centred on the question of the nature of the wine referred to in the Bible. Many temperance advocates, led by John Pyper, the former agent of the I.T.L. and the driving force in the Good Templar movement, insisted that the wine used by the Jews and by Jesus was unfermented. It therefore followed that the communion wine should also be unfermented. The year 1875, which saw the total abstinence issue before the General Assembly in Derry, also saw the Bible wine issue debated at length. But, whereas the teetotallers had emerged victorious in the debate over the former, they were soundly defeated over the latter. Pyper spoke at the Assembly, but later complained: 'I addressed a most impatient and unwilling audience, for nearly an hour at midnight, in the midst of frequent and most disorderly interruptions, by the Moderator... by Dr Watts, our chief opponent, and by others.' Dr Robert Watts was professor of systematic theology at Assembly's College in Belfast, an influential and orthodox theologian and a formidable opponent of novel biblical interpretations. He in fact had initiated the debate by proposing four resolutions: affirming that the wine referred to in the Bible was 'the ordinary wine of the country, that is fermented juice of the grape'; recommending that churches use a 'mild, natural wine'; advising all members of the church 'to adhere to the simple and significant usage of scripture' and 'to avoid divisive courses'; and finally ordering the production of a pastoral letter setting out the Assembly's views. The Assembly accepted these resolutions and rejected Pyper's efforts to amend them by a vote of 301 to 20. The I.T.L. *Journal* thought that the vote reflected a desire by the anti-teetotal faction in the Assembly 'to strike a deadly blow against the cause of total abstinence... through the subject of sacramental wine'. It so, they failed, for Pyper was not deterred by the Assembly vote, and in the same year he formed an Irish Sacramental Wine Association, later called the Bible Temperance Association. The association's declared object was 'the promotion of the divine glory, through the removal of the intoxicating cup from the table of the Lord and the entire separation of the church from the liquor traffic'. Pyper and his friends, through the columns of the *Bible Temperance Educator*, begun in 1881, bitterly assailed what they claimed was the church's support for drunkenness. 'A.J.C. of Londonderry' claimed in March 1881 that it was

> at the door of the church that the great sin of our national intemperance lies... that in her skirts is to be found the blood of thousands who annually sink into drunkards' graves.

And in the same issue, referring to the Bible wine question, Pyper declared that the church 'on this question is about as anti-Christian as it is possible to be', the only redeeming feature he found being that 'she is not unanimous: her members, thank God, do not all bow the knee to her drink-idol'. Only 'uncompromising hostility to the vile drink-system' would, in Pyper's view, deliver the church 'from her present degraded position'. Given that Presbyterians had been in the forefront of the Irish temperance movement since its inception, these charges were clearly unjustified and not a little hysterical. In their zeal to purify both the church and the Bible from the taint of alcohol the teetotallers were justifying some of the concerns expressed by John Edgar fifty years before, in particular that such a perfectionistic doctrine was inconsistent with scripture and that the two would inevitably clash.[2]

The Bible wine issue was to prove divisive, and not only in the Presbyterian church. The Church of Ireland stood out against the trend to introduce unfermented wine into the communion service. In 1888 the *Irish Ecclesiastical Gazette* declared:

> We desire to raise our voice against a practice which has begun, and may probably grow, in the Church of Ireland, of using a concoction which is not 'the fruit of the vine', in the administration of the Lord's Supper. We have no hesitation in saying that these artificial 'wines' destroy the truth of the sacrament, which might as well be administered in milk or water as in a non-fermented ingredient compounded probably in a chemist's or apothecary's establishment.

The Church of Ireland resisted the extremist trend, arguing that the drinking of wine was lawful according to the scriptures, as was abstinence, but that 'to say that a thing is lawful is not to say that it ought to be done'. But the Bible wine campaign achieved a considerable degree of success among Presbyterians and other Nonconformists. By 1888 the General Assembly had come round to ruling that the use of unfermented grape juice should be optional in churches. (**250**, 133; **100**, 7)

The fierceness of the controversy in the Presbyterian church is seen in the case of St Enoch's, Hugh Hanna's Belfast church. The issue was first raised in 1876 and reached a crisis twenty years later. According to the church's historian,

> Those who desired the use of 'unfermented' wine, finding it impossible to get the whole congregation to agree, asked the session that they should be allowed to have a second 'table', at which unfermented wine would be used, and to which any who wished might come instead of going to the first table, at which fermented wine was used. Many solutions were put forward and rejected; but in the end, by the narrowest of majorities, the compromise of the two 'tables' was carried through . . . the first table being taken before and the second after the sermon. This solution, while it had neither historical nor liturgical justification and was theologically indefensible, was adopted as a compromise in the interests of peace.

The opponents of the compromise appealed to the presbytery of Belfast and, when defeated there, to the General Assembly. But their appeal was dismissed, and the congregation was urged to end its disputes. Finally in 1905 the Assembly's 1875 decision rejecting the use of unfermented wine was repealed. Probably by the mid-1890s the majority of Nonconformist churches were using non-alcoholic wine for their communion services. (**60**, 84-5; **86**, 106)

That the Bible wine controversy could generate such protracted and bitter debate within the Presbyterian church is a measure of the importance of the issue of temperance within the church. The I.T.L., the largest and most active of the Irish temperance societies from the 1850s to 1900, drew much of its support from the northern Presbyterian community. Similarly, many of the staunchest supporters of temperance legislation in parliament from the 1860s were Presbyterians representing Ulster constituencies: Richard Smyth, Charles Lewis and J. P. Corry are three examples. Thomas McClure and, at a later date, T. H. Sloan suffered electorally when they compromised their temperance principles.

In the mid-1870s, with drink consumption increasing and temperance legislation figuring prominently in parliament, there was an upsurge of interest within the Irish churches. The Presbyterians, as we have seen, debated the Bible wine question in 1875 and in 1876 endorsed total abstinence. In the latter year the Church of Ireland Temperance Society was established. The Methodist church was also influenced by this trend. Wesley himself had condemned drunkenness and recognised the virtues of total abstinence. He criticised spirit drinking and forbade Methodists to buy, sell or drink spirits. But, like many at the time, he believed in the health-giving properties of beer. Thus, while he counselled total abstinence with regard to spirits, he advised moderation for beer and wine drinkers. In line with these views, the Methodist Conference meeting in Dublin in 1787 had advised preachers against drinking brandy and spirits and had ordered them to discourage whiskey drinking at wakes, but on wine and beer it made no comment. However, the more fundamentalist Methodist sects were quick to support the temperance movement when it first appeared. In England the Primitive Methodists recommended temperance societies in 1832, and in 1841 they directed that unfermented wine be used at communion. But the Wesleyans were hostile to total abstinence: in 1841 their Conference at Manchester forbade preachers to advocate teetotalism, to allow chapels to be used for temperance meetings, and to employ unfermented wine in the sacrament. In Ireland one of the first signatories to Edgar's temperance pledge in 1829 had been the Wesleyan Matthew Tobias, whose chapel in Donegall Square was the venue for Edgar's first temperance lecture. But with the advent of total abstinence, Wesleyan support for the temperance movement waned. (**330**, 33; **173**, 180; **206**, 42-3; **251**, 38) In England in 1873, however, the Wesleyan Conference established a committee to investigate intemperance. This led the church in 1875 to endorse the Band of Hope movement, which sought to impose the total abstinence pledge on children. In 1877 adult societies, containing both total abstainers and non-abstainers, were recommended, though not until 1892 were pure total abstinence societies permitted in the church. The Irish church followed this general development. In 1877 the Irish Wesleyan Conference, 'feeling that there was a necessity for some further connexional action to promote the spread of true temperance principles, and to influence the cause of imperial legislation affecting the liquor traffic', sanctioned the establishment of a connexional temperance association. The association aimed to suppress intemperance and to promote five major objects: the establishment of refreshment rooms and reading-rooms; the discouragement of drinking on social occasions, at funerals and during commercial transactions; the removal of working men's benefit societies from public houses and the discontinuance of the payment of wages in public houses; the reclamation of the drunkard; and the training of the young in total abstinence. Total abstinence was only imposed upon the young, and the church embarked on the vigorous promotion of Bands of Hope: membership jumped from 8,000 in 1877 to over 17,000 in 1879. But the step from juvenile to adult total abstinence was a logical one, and the Irish church followed the English in this regard. At a meeting of Wesleyan total abstainers in connection with the 1875 Conference in Belfast one speaker said:

> The founder of Methodism did not object to the use of wine in moderation; and those rules, as observed by the societies, he was sorry to say had been a failure in effecting the putting down of the use of intoxicating drinks, and the putting down of drunkenness. They were required now, such are the drinking customs of the country and the usages of the country, to go further than these rules. They must go the length of entire abstinence from the use of intoxicating drinks.[3]

That Wesley's rules had been formulated under different circumstances, and that the present problem required more extreme measures, was to prove a persuasive argument. The Methodists had also to face up to the Bible wine issue. In 1875 some churches asked the Conference for permission to replace the port wine they had been using with grape juice. The Conference refused, saying that it could not condemn what God had not condemned. But the Methodists changed their minds far more quickly than the Presbyterians. Whereas the Presbyterians did not permit the use of both fermented and unfermented grape juice until 1888, the Methodist Conference sanctioned this compromise in 1878. (**330**, 42; **310**, 66-8; **108**, 35-6)

Perhaps the most consistently active supporter of the temperance cause in Ireland, among religious groups, was the Society of Friends. As early as 1815 and 1818 the Quakers' Dublin Tract Association had published two pamphlets advocating temperance. This involvement was to continue at a relatively high level until the end of the century. The I.T.L., the I.S.C.A. and later the I.A.P.I. all received substantial financial support from the Quaker business community. For example, Richard Allen, the Dublin draper, made contributions of between £50 and £100 per annum to the I.S.C.A. and then to the I.A.P.I. until his death in 1886. J. G. Richardson, the Bessbrook linen merchant, until his death in 1890 made similar annual contributions to both the I.T.L., of which he was president in the 1880s, and to the I.A.P.I. Pim Brothers and J. Edmundson & Co., both Dublin Quaker firms, also contributed to the I.S.C.A. and the I.A.P.I. Edmundsons went a step further in their support for the temperance cause and refused to do any work for publicans, brewers and distillers. Large subscribers to these organisations sometimes expected material benefits in return. Thus in 1886 J. N. Richardson reduced his subscription to the I.T.L. to a mere 11 guineas, complaining that the League was not buying his butter for its Belfast cafés as it had promised. With or without strings attached, however, Quaker financial support was vital to the major Irish temperance societies. The Friends were also active on the committees of many temperance groups. As mentioned, J. G. Richardson was president of the I.T.L. in the 1880s; Henry J. Allen was chairman of the I.A.P.I. in the 1880s and 1890s; while various members of the Webb, Wigham, Pim and Shackleton families were on the committees of both and of other smaller societies. (**39**, 296)[4]

A good example of a Quaker temperance enthusiast is provided by Henry Wigham (1822-97). Born in Edinburgh, Wigham, while still in his twenties, had been active in the anti-slavery and peace movements. He came to Dublin in 1856 and worked for forty years with Edmundson & Co., the electrical engineers. On his arrival he became involved almost immediately in the temperance work of Haughton, Spratt, Richard Allen and R. D. Webb. He was president of the Dublin Total Abstinence Society, honorary secretary of the I.S.C.A. throughout its existence, and continued in that capacity with the I.A.P.I. from its inception in 1878 until his death twenty years later. He was president of the Hibernian Band of Hope Union, founded in Dublin in 1873 to unite the juvenile temperance work of the various Protestant churches, and of the Dublin United Temperance Council, established in 1889 to co-ordinate the activities of the city's main temperance societies. At his death in 1897 the *Alliance News* commented that he 'was connected in one way or another with almost every temperance association in Ireland'. A resolution passed at a special meeting of the I.A.P.I. described him as 'the leader of the movement in Ireland'. He was a tireless lobbyist on behalf of Irish temperance legislation, and the I.T.L. *Journal* said that 'No one was so well known as he in the lobby of the House of Commons.' Perhaps only Haughton, Pyper and Russell could match Wigham in terms of commitment to the temperance cause. He was less articulate and less of a striking personality than these others; he did not use his pen to the extent that they did, nor take such an active political role; but he epitomised the convinced, hard-working temperance advocate of the period. (**310**, 84-6; **191** [1888-9] 11-12)[5]

Some of the most interesting comments on Quaker temperance work, especially in Dublin, come from the unpublished autobiography of Alfred Webb, Home Rule M.P. for Waterford West from 1890 to 1895 and treasurer of the party. Webb, born in 1834, was the son of R. D. Webb, the Dublin printer, who printed most of the early tracts of the Dublin and Hibernian Temperance Societies. Like his friend James Haughton, R. D. Webb was active in many of the reformist movements of the day, most notably the anti-slavery campaign. He wrote a life of John Brown and contributed regularly to both American and British abolitionist periodicals. 'He was better known in America than here,' his son said of him. But R. D. Webb also threw himself 'with ardour' into the temperance movement from its beginnings in Dublin. 'Father Mathew was often at our house,' Alfred remembered, and he also recalled seeing the Capuchin administer the pledge from the steps of the Custom House. The movement won strong support from the Dublin Quaker community generally. 'In our Quaker circle, with the exception of a very few of the elder generation, the use of intoxicants gradually died out.' But R. D. Webb was among those who strongly disapproved of Father Mathew's behaviour in the United States. 'My father lost respect for him in consequence of his pandering to the slave power,' wrote Alfred, and he conceded that James Haughton 'clung more hopefully to the temperance cause than did my father'.[6] Hannah Maria Wigham in her life of Richard Allen, published in 1886, quoted Alfred Webb describing the Dublin group of Quaker philan-thropists in the 1830s and 1840s:

> From about 1834 until the Irish famine of 1845, and the political events that followed, my father, Richard Allen, James Haughton, uncles James and Thomas Webb, and others in Dublin were the centre of a general movement for reform, and the amelioration of the ills of humanity in every direction.... Slavery, temperance, British India, anti-opium, anti-capital punishment, anti-Corn Law, mesmerism, cold-water cure — everything was taken up. I remember they were called by a jocose newspaper editor 'anti-everythingarians'. But temperance and slavery were the central interests. At one time Richard Allen gave up so much of his time to these reforms that his business was almost going to ruin. I suppose it was about 1844 that he 'eased off' in his attention to them, and devoted himself more to the development of his business.... I remember in those times we children playing with our dolls, and saying: 'Now thee's going to a slavery meeting; now thee's going to a temperance meeting.' (**341**, 13-14)

Alfred Webb, however, noted with regret that as the Friends prospered in their business enterprises they were inclined to move out of the city centre to the more prosperous suburban townships. Recalling the 1840s, he wrote:

> Friends were our principal society. None of them lived out of town. They lived over or by their places of business, and most of our circle then kept shops in which they themselves served behind the counter. Friends thus lived in Thomas Street, Meath Street and the contiguous streets, in Townsend Street and on the quays. Scores of houses at present foul as tenement lodgings let in rooms, where pale and ragged children play at battered doorways or look out of the broken windows, were then pure, sweet and well-ordered. Friends have 'risen' out of the station in society they then occupied, and they were then much above their position in education and feeling and enlightenment. Our class have gained in many ways by suburban residence. The poor, amongst whom we formerly lived, have lost. The children of our class lose in many respects. It was an advantage to live near the shop or workrooms in which the parent made his money, and it was a pleasure to him to be near his family.[7]

It is interesting to note here that James Haughton, despite his prosperity, never moved out into the suburbs. He lived for some forty years in Eccles Street. Richard Allen did make the move described by Webb, but regretted it. From High Street Allen moved to De Vesci Lodge in Monkstown in 1836, and then in 1847 to Brooklawn in Blackrock, which remained his home until his death. But in 1854, after visiting the poor during a severe winter, he wrote:

> Surely, if we went more amongst the poor it would be good for us; we would learn to sympathise with them, yes, and to respect them. . . . True, they are low and clamorous many of them, and imprudent and drunken; but while we blame surely we ought to make allowance. What do we know of their temptations, pressed as they are by want and often by hunger itself; and should we wonder, if, wet, cold, and weary, they run into the public house and avail themselves of the temporary stimulus which strong drink affords? (**341**, 94-5)

From their comfortable suburban villas, however, the Quakers were prone to adopt a much more censorious attitude towards the poor, or to sink into indifference.

The deaths of many of the leaders of the Quaker temperance movement, combined with the frustration of the parliamentary campaign to which most of them were committed, produced, towards the end of the century, a decline in temperance activity among the Quaker community. Perhaps also, as Alfred Webb and Richard Allen indicated, the growing affluence of the Friends was tending to cut them off from direct contact with the social problems of Dublin, and thus produce a certain amount of apathy. James Haughton and R. D. Webb both died in 1872, Jonathan Pim in 1885, Richard Allen in 1886, J. G. Richardson in 1890, and Henry Wigham in 1897. Haughton's daughters and his brother William continued to contribute money to the temperance cause, though without taking an active role. Thomas Pim junior, the brother of Jonathan, worked for various Dublin temperance societies in the 1870s and 1880s. Thomas Webb, the brother of R. D. Webb, and J. R. Wigham, the brother of Henry Wigham, were both energetic committee members of the I.A.P.I. The Shackletons, another prominent Quaker family, also contributed a number of workers to the temperance cause, most notably Abraham Shackleton, Richard Allen's son-in-law, who was treasurer of the I.A.P.I. in the 1890s.

But the children of the Allens, Haughtons, Wighams, Webbs and Pims, who had grown up in the second half of the century, generally did not take up the temperance cause with the same enthusiasm that their parents had displayed. Many did not take it up at all. Richard Allen's son, Henry J. Allen, was an exception, being chairman of the I.A.P.I. in the 1890s. More typical were Alfred Webb and J. N. Richardson, the son of J. G. Richardson. Though both were teetotallers and supporters of temperance legislation, both were more involved in the issues of land and Home Rule, which dominated Irish politics in the 1880s and 1890s. Alfred Webb in his autobiography sought to explain the reasons for his failure to follow in his father's footsteps with regard to the cause of temperance:

> Drink though perhaps the worst of all evils in these countries never roused my enthusiasm against it in proportion to its enormity. For this reason. That its use is deliberately held to by those fully informed and who are free agents. They have a right to drink if they wish. Even the Irish people if they really desired could scotch the traffic in Ireland. I can feel no enthusiasm in trying to persuade people to do their duty by themselves.

What really aroused his enthusiasm, wrote Webb, were 'people oppressed who could not help themselves', like slaves, women denied the vote, Indians without a say in their government, and Chinese forced to accept the trade in opium. An aversion to coercive legislation was obviously a factor in Alfred's thinking, and certainly it was hard to reconcile support for coercive temperance legislation with opposition to other coercive measures passed at Westminster. Also, with illicit distillation well under control and spirit consumption in Ireland generally falling from the mid-1870s, temperance must have seemed a less pressing issue to Alfred in the 1880s and 1890s than it had seemed to his father in the 1830s and 1840s. The children of other leaders of the Dublin movement were even less enthusiastic than Webb. Of Samuel Haughton, James's only son, who wrote a useful biography of his father, Alfred Webb commented: 'He had not much belief in any cause or any movement — the direct antithesis of his father.' After making a substantial amount of money with his father in the corn trade, Samuel abandoned business altogether and spent the rest of his life wandering around Europe, occasionally turning up in Dublin, where 'he spent much of his time in reading-rooms always ready for a gossip'. As we have seen, James's daughters continued to contribute financially to the temperance cause, but when one of them bequeathed £1,000 to the Home Rule organisation the rest of the family contested the will. This move may have been inspired by Samuel, who was no friend of Home Rule. The family succeeded, but only at considerable financial cost. One cannot doubt that James Haughton would have been bitterly disappointed by his son's neglect of both his temperance and nationalist principles.[8]

The Church of Ireland had been slow to take up the temperance cause, as had the Established Church in England. Both had been alarmed by some of the excesses of total abstinence and especially its identification with radical political movements in the 1840s: Chartism in England and Repeal in Ireland. But in 1862 both churches established total abstinence societies. Evangelicals within the churches had been impressed by the links between teetotalism and religious recruitment evident during the Ulster revival. In Ireland the Evangelicals gained greater influence, along with the laity, after Disestablishment and found in temperance a congenial cause. (**174**; **173**, 182; **44**; 302; **232**, 58) In this connection it is interesting to note that the Church of Ireland Total Abstinence Association, established in 1862, had an unusually large number of women on its executive and its council; for many years its honorary secretary and most active agent was a Miss J. E. Moses of Leeson Park, Dublin. This probably reflects the fact that the association had grown out of the Dublin Ladies' Total Abstinence Association, which was encouraged by Evangelical clerics like John Gregg, Bishop of Cork, and Baron Plunket, later Archbishop of Dublin. In its report for 1871-2 the C.I.T.A.A. explained that, before its establishment, churchmen as a rule 'kept aloof from the movement, and spoke of it as fanatical and absurd'. But the association attributed the absurdities, which it conceded had arisen, to the fact that 'men of sense and education for the most part refused to join'. In the 'past few years', however, the urgency of the problem had been brought home to churchmen. The growing interest of other churches in temperance in fact acted as a spur to the Episcopalians. The report continued:

> Of this we may be certain that sooner or later the evils of intemperance must be vigorously grappled with, and it will not be to the credit of the Church of Ireland, foremost as she is in social influence and purity of doctrine, if she holds back in this crisis, and is content to see the work

done by Roman Catholics and Nonconformists. . . . While so many held back, your society stood forward as the exponent of moderate views, avoiding all absurd and vexatious arguments, and content to rest their cause, and to advocate temperance on this one great principle, which they maintain has never yet been answered — the necessity of Christian expediency. (**101** [1871-2], 7-8)

The Church of Ireland clearly wished to avoid the theological controversies that had arisen, particularly in the Presbyterian and Catholic churches, over total abstinence and the pledge, and thus it based its advocacy on expediency rather than on doctrinal grounds. Flexibility was to be the keynote.

The church's total abstinence society was not a success in the 1860s. By 1873 it had only twenty-two affiliated societies, most being in Dublin city, Co. Wicklow and Ulster, all centres of Episcopalian strength in Ireland. Its income in the same year was only £32. In 1872 the Church of England Total Abstinence Association had reformed itself into the Church of England Temperance Society, established on a 'dual basis', combining in one society both abstainers and non-abstainers. Here was an example of expediency, and the Church of Ireland followed suit. The General Synod in 1875 appointed a committee to examine and consider 'what measures ought to be taken to repress intemperance'. After consultation with various diocesan committees and councils, the committee reported recommending the establishment of a Church of Ireland temperance society on 'nearly the same lines' as the C.E.T.S. The already existing total abstinence association indicated that it was willing to merge with a 'wider society', which it hoped would 'draw into membership very many persons who have not joined the abstinence association'. Most churches, as we have seen, started off with mixed societies and only later accepted pure total abstinence societies. The Church of Ireland was peculiar in having gone in the opposite direction. Total abstinence obviously had greater appeal among Nonconformists than it had among Episcopalians. (**101** [1872-3], 12-13; **98**, III, 151-2)

The objectives of the new society were the 'reformation of the intemperate' and the 'promotion of habits of temperance', and its *modus operandi* was 'union and co-operation between abstainers and non-abstainers, on the broad principle of Christian liberty, for the promotion of the above objects, by moral, social and legislative means'. (**99** [1879], 3) The Church of Ireland Temperance Society cast its net widely. Total abstinence was essentially envisaged as being necessary to achieve its first objective, the reclamation of the drunkard. But those who had never indulged in alcohol to excess were merely urged to continue their moderation and recommend it to others. Writing in the society's journal, the *Temperance Visitor*, in March 1889, an anonymous correspondent advised:

> The teetotallers ought not to judge the man who feels it needful for his health to take a little wine. The man who is not a total abstainer must not abuse total abstainers as despising God's gifts. Both are agreed about the awful evil; both wish to check it.

But it was not at all easy to maintain equal and harmonious relations between the two groups. Many of the leading and most active members of the society were total abstainers, who were likely to be sceptical of the value of temperance. While urging co-operation, the correspondent quoted above also remarked that the 'C.I.T.S. is a temperance, not a total abstinence society, though the most important and ordinary means it employs is total abstinence'. And he went on:

> The practical working of the section of our society called the temperance section is a more difficult matter; in country places it seldom succeeds. The promise is too indefinite to be of any use as a help to a man who is tempted. He cannot resist a treat, or two or three treats, in a fair. A total abstainer is a safer man.

This rather tortuous reasoning concerning the merits of total abstinence as opposed to temperance illustrates some of the problems faced by the Church of Ireland in its efforts to provide as wide a basis as possible for its temperance work. In practice what tended to happen was that the C.I.T.S. advocated total abstinence for the drunkard and the working classes, while reserving temperance for the middle classes. Drunkenness was regarded as a much more widespread and serious problem among the poor. It was a drastic problem, requiring a drastic solution. An article in the C.I.T.S. journal in July 1889 warned that if the working classes 'choose to become a class of sots they must inevitably succumb to the law of the survival of the fittest. They will disappear, and their place will be taken by automata and machinery.' These remarks suggest little understanding of the relationship between drink and poverty, and even less sympathy. The views of the C.I.T.S. resembled those of the anti-spirits movement of the 1830s.[9]

The report to the General Synod in 1876, which had led to the establishment of the C.I.T.S., had, however, stressed the importance of social reform and the need for counter-attractions. Mention was made of improvements in housing and sanitary conditions and the provision of 'healthful and attractive substitutes for the allurements of the public house'. (98, III, 153) But this kind of work remained low on the society's list of priorities. When in 1891 the journal published a list of the principal means employed by the C.I.T.S., the provision of counter-attractions came second last, after prayer, teaching and publicity, the formation of new branches, legislation, and memorials to local and national authorities. As its last method, the C.I.T.S. committed itself to reforming social and commercial customs that necessitated drinking, such as wakes, fairs, harvest festivals and apprenticeship rituals. The C.I.T.S., like most Irish temperance organisations, drew its main support from the middle class. Its attitude to the working and poorer classes was at best paternalistic; at worst, as we have seen, it could calmly contemplate their disappearance. It believed that the middle class could be convinced by argument and reason to drink moderately. But the working class was not generally amenable to reason, and thus more extreme measures were needed: total abstinence in the case of the individual, and legislative coercion in the case of the group.[10]

The C.I.T.S., however, really 'existed in name only' until the appointment of a permanent secretary. In August 1878 William Jones, who had worked for the United Kingdom Alliance for fifteen years, was invited by the Dublin diocesan committee of the society to take up this job. He agreed and immediately issued 500 circulars to parishes announcing that he was ready to visit them and form branches of the society. But only five or six favourable replies were received. This did not deter Jones. In February 1879 he began the publication of the *Temperance Visitor*. A thousand copies of the first issue were printed, but by the end of the year circulation had jumped to 2,000. In March a council was organised, composed of twenty clergymen and seventeen lay delegates. There were already diocesan committees in Dublin, Glendalough and Kildare and in Down, Connor and Dromore, representing about 130 branches and 16,000 members. At the General Synod in April the constitution of the C.I.T.S. was amended so as to make it compulsory for each diocese or united diocese to appoint a diocesan temperance committee annually. Thus did Jones seek to extend and strengthen the organisation of the C.I.T.S. By the end of the year the society had 293 branches and 37,000 members. Doubtless Jones's endeavours were assisted by the recent success of the Irish Sunday closing movement in parliament and the promise of further such progress. Growth continued to be rapid: by the end of 1880 there were 373 branches and 48,610 members. Of these branches, 160 were in Ulster, 111 in Leinster, but only 55 in Munster and 47 in Connacht. This expansion was achieved at the cost of considerable financial difficulties: in 1879, after only three years of operation, the society had a deficit of £230, which had to be cleared by the establishment of a special fund. The Dublin, Glendalough and Kildare committee had raised most of the money for the organisation. Jones estimated that at least £450 per annum was needed to finance their operations, and he recommended that every diocesan committee should collect 5s per annum from every branch. In January 1880 it was decided to institute a special temperance sermon to be preached on the first Sunday of Lent, with the offertory, or at least part of it, going to the C.I.T.S. In the first year some 200 parishes co-operated and £137 was raised. By 1889 300 parishes were involved and the society was chiefly dependent on the money thus raised to finance its work. (**99**[1879], 9-11, [1880], 3; **98**, III, 23)[11]

In 1882 Earl Spencer, a supporter of the Irish Sunday closing act, agreed to become patron of the C.I.T.S. But although laity were well represented on the general council, the clergy effectively dominated the organisation. Apart from Jones, who resigned to take up a curacy in Armagh in 1892, the most active members were Dean Dickinson of the Chapel Royal, Dean Chadwick of Armagh, and Gilbert Mahaffy, rector of St Paul's, Dublin. Dickinson had been a stalwart of the society from its inception, and his services to the temperance cause were recognised in 1896 when he was appointed to the royal commission investigating the liquor licensing laws. Mahaffy was especially concerned about the effects of drink on the Dublin poor and made great efforts to publicise the problem. Dickinson's membership of the 1896 royal commission and the participation of the Archbishop of Dublin, who was one of the C.I.T.S.'s presidents, in debates dealing with the Irish Sunday closing bill in the House of Lords reflect the society's involvement in the campaign for restrictive legislation. It worked in close co-operation with the I.A.P.I., especially in support of the Sunday closing bill. The *Temperance Visitor* contained regular and detailed reports of the progress of Irish temperance bills, and members of the organisation frequently joined deputations to the Chief Secretary on the subject. In February 1889, for instance, the Archbishop of Dublin, at such a meeting, told the Chief Secretary that all the Church of Ireland bishops supported the Sunday closing bill then before parliament. William Johnston, M.P. for Belfast South and a frequent sponsor of temperance legislation, was a member of the C.I.T.S. council and doubtless kept his fellow-members in close touch with developments in the House of Commons. Like Johnston, the leaders of the society were generally conservative in their political outlook. The *Temperance Visitor*'s comments on the Conservative government's failure to introduce temperance legislation in the 1880s and 1890s were far from harsh. The lack of progress of the Sunday closing bill in 1889, for instance, was blamed on the 'waste of time, caused by factious opposition'. 'The government', said the journal, 'were obliged to drop a number of their own cherished measures, surely they ought to be believed when they say that for the same reason they were unable to pass the Sunday closing bill.' In January 1891, while addressing a Dublin public meeting sponsored by the C.I.T.S., Dean Chadwick, in the wake of the Parnell split, left no doubt in his listeners' minds as to where he thought the responsibility for the failure of Irish temperance legislation lay:

When I reckon up the misdeeds of the party which professes to monopolise [the] affection [of Ireland], when I ask is it possible, even in the face of the witness which its leaders have recently borne to one another's merits, that they may have some real, though misguided, affection for our common country, my heart grows hard towards them again as I remember our increasing drink bill with our dwindling population, and the stubborn resistance by which the great majority of the patriots have obstructed every effort to purify this pollution at least one day in seven. Be it ours to show a nobler patriotism.[12]

As well as playing an active part in the political campaign, the C.I.T.S. was also involved in the legal side of temperance work. The Dublin diocesan committee had a licensing laws sub-committee, which co-operated with the I.A.P.I. in employing solicitors to oppose applications for licences before the magistrates' courts. Justifying its participation, the C.I.T.S. explained in 1891:

> For many generations the granting of licences has been the special privilege of the magistrates, and not a few of them seem to have grown into the belief that when an application is made it ought, in the absence of any opposition, to be granted. And who can blame them? If the inhabitants of a parish are so indifferent as not to take the trouble to oppose, why should not their silence be taken to mean consent? When pressure is put on the magistrates on one side without a counter-balancing pressure on the other, what is to be expected?

The C.I.T.S. thus saw itself as providing a necessary counter-balance to the power of the publicans, who dominated so much of Dublin economic and political life. Though restrained in its criticism of magistrates, perhaps because such people were among its members, the C.I.T.S. was far more severe in its censorship of the police:

> What then are we to think of the police [asked the *Temperance Visitor* in September 1889] except that they are absolutely afraid of the publicans or have been bribed to inaction? ... Every night that passes the members of G division lounge about the city placidly smoking cigars. We shall, as convenient, keep this disgraceful state of things before the public. Neither threats nor foolish names can frighten us. We consider the publicans as enemies of civilisation, and the besotted hirelings of the public house organs are, if anything, a more degraded class.

The society's language in fact frequently belied the moderation which it upheld. For example, in commenting upon the dirt and decay of Killarney, despite its tourist revenue, the *Temperance Visitor* observed that the only thriving buildings were those of the priest and the publican. 'And of these two preponderating influences,' it said, 'either the one *will not* exert himself to raise the people from dirt, dissipation and idleness, or *the other,* as seems highly probable, will not let him.' Such sectarian remarks were unusual for the temperance literature of the period. Generally the various churches refrained, in public at least, from criticism of each other's temperance work. If mention was made of another denomination by Protestant temperance men, it was usually to suggest co-operation. Fairly typical were the remarks of the Bishop of Cork at the C.I.T.S.'s annual general meeting in

April 1889. He spoke of his profound admiration for the work of the League of the Cross in Cork and urged co-operation between different religious and political groups in the struggle against intemperance. But in fact co-operation between the churches during this period was minimal. Episcopalians, Presbyterians and other Nonconformists differed in their attitudes to total abstinence, the pledge, the Bible wine controversy and the effectiveness of legislation. The Catholics, as we shall soon see, were striving principally to create an exclusively Catholic temperance movement. One of the major criticisms levelled at Father Mathew by Catholic writers on temperance was that he had encouraged Protestants to join his crusade. The Catholic temperance organisations of the 1880s and 1890s were determined not to make the same mistake.[13]

By 1889 the C.I.T.S. had nearly 800 branches and over 100,000 members, though a chronic shortage of funds continued to be a major problem. However, in the 1890s the failure to secure further temperance legislation began to produce discouragement within the society. In 1892 the Dublin, Glendalough and Kildare branch, which had long been the most active, issued a circular urging the establishment of branches in all parishes and noting that interest in some already existing branches needed rekindling. The committee ventured to remind these branches that 'Incomplete success is not failure, whether in temperance work or in the work of the church at large.' The circular recognised that discouragement was to some extent inevitable, for the 'charm of novelty' had gone, and the

> enthusiasm of those who from childhood have been members of the society (and these form a large proportion nowadays in many branches) is not so warm or so constantly aggressive as the enthusiasm of those who have joined its ranks against opposition from within or without.

This succinctly describes the problem that the Quaker temperance movement was also facing at the time. To combat this waning enthusiasm the circular advised that more attention be given to the education of members: 'Our members young and old, need to be supplied with *reasons* for their membership, if they are to be faithful to their promise and useful as workers.' To ease financial difficulties co-operation between neighbouring branches in organising meetings and supplying speakers was suggested. Local branches were also encouraged to try to keep down the numbers of public houses in their districts by opposing applications for new licences. But the minute book of the C.I.T.S. general council shows that lack of money and declining enthusiasm continued to be problems up until the end of the century and beyond.[14]

In all the main Irish Protestant churches there was an upsurge in temperance work dating from the mid-1870s. The increasing consumption of drink and the publicity given to temperance legislation in parliament both doubtless contributed to this trend, as did the renewed interest among the sister churches in England. But the organisation of church-based temperance societies posed many problems. Finance was frequently a limiting factor, particularly if a society wished to undertake expensive parliamentary lobbying in support of temperance legislation or legal action to stop the issuing of new licences. The scriptural basis of total abstinence and the practical effectiveness of temperance continued, as they had done since the 1830s, to cause dispute and division. On the whole, the Nonconformist churches tended to come down in favour of total abstinence, while the Church of Ireland tried, albeit with difficulty, to encompass both equally. However, once the total abstainers were in the ascendancy, they usually sought to eliminate any connection whatsoever between their church and drink. The acceptance of money from the drink industry for church and school building was condemned, and efforts were made to root out drink dealers from church bodies. The most dramatic manifestation of this drive was the replacement in many Protestant churches of the communion wine by fruit juice. The Church of Ireland seemed to remain relatively immune from this obsession to purify the churches. It never gave itself up wholly to total abstinence, regarding this as something for zealots and for those most in danger of abusing drink. Its two Dublin cathedrals were renovated and maintained with money largely provided by drink manufacturers, the Roe distillery contributing to Christ Church and Guinness's brewery to St Patrick's. Nor was the church willing to abandon wine in its communion service. By the turn of the century, however, much of the initial enthusiasm with which the churches had embarked on temperance work had been dissipated. We have seen that among Quakers and Episcopalians the converts of the early years proved far more zealous than their children. The failure of temperance in parliament and the emergence of more pressing political issues discouraged and distracted the church organisations as well as the secular temperance societies. Even in Ulster. which had largely dominated the Irish temperance movement since the 1830s, decline was evident. In an effort to rectify this situation, a new temperance revival was proclaimed in 1909 by the Rev. Robert Patterson of Armagh in the form of the Catch-my-pal Protestant Total Abstinence Union. But its work lies outside the scope of this study. It is sufficient for the moment merely to note the decline of Protestant temperance societies in the 1890s. (**291**, 247-8; **195**, 210-24)

Temperance and the Catholic Church

After the death of Father Mathew, as we have seen, the Catholic church remained ambivalent in its attitude to the temperance cause. Some individual bishops were enthusiastic and instituted regulations within their own dioceses to promote temperance. Many also lent their names to established temperance societies and to the campaign for restrictive legislation. But it was not until the late 1860s that a resurgence of largely Catholic temperance societies became evident. This trend, appearing almost simultaneously in England and the United States, culminated in 1872 with the establishment of both the English League of the Cross and the Catholic Total Abstinence Union of America. (**72; 217**) In 1867 Cardinal Manning had appeared on the platform at the annual meeting of the United Kingdom Alliance, marking a notable departure in Catholic policy towards the temperance movement. Manning was anxious to improve the image of Catholicism in England and to promote greater Catholic participation in public life. As some eighty per cent of Catholics in England were Irish, feared and hated by many Englishmen, Manning came to concentrate particularly on promoting sobriety, thrift, a respect for order and better education among his Irish flock. He feared the revolutionary potential latent in such an alienated section of society and saw temperance as part of a campaign to integrate Irish Catholics into English society. Drink, wrote Manning, is the cause of

> crime, of madness, of poverty; of ruined reputations, of strife, of murder; it empties churches, keeps souls from the sacraments; it leads to immorality, loss of faith, apostasy; it ruins homes, desolates families, brings scandal upon the church; it makes bad husbands, bad wives, immoral children. Drink ruins body and soul. It is the stumbling-block of the laity, the source of grief and care to the priest.

The problem, he thought, was most severe among the working and poorer classes, where Catholics were disproportionately numerous. While opposing prohibition, Manning told the U.K.A. in 1868 that he fully supported Sunday closing and the permissive bill. But as well as legislative measures to curb the drink trade, Manning also saw the need for an exclusively Catholic temperance society. He wanted both to prevent the Catholic faith being undermined in non-Catholic organisations and to avoid Father Mathew's mistake by establishing structures that would ensure the continuation of the work after his own departure from the scene. He aimed, he said, to create an organisation 'as strictly Catholic as is the church from which it springs'. Thus the rules of the League of the Cross, drawn up by Manning, stipulated that only Catholics could be members, that all members after they had joined the League must 'live as good practical Catholics', and that only a 'practical Catholic' could hold any office in the League. The aim of the League, according to its constitution, was to unite Catholics, both clergy and laity, in a 'holy war against intemperance' and thereby to raise the 'religious, social and domestic stature of our Catholic people, especially the working classes'. (**138**, 495; **216**, 39-40; **215; 165**)[15]

As well as being intensely Catholic, the movement initiated by Manning was also inclined to be sympathetic to Irish nationalist aspirations. The link between Catholic temperance and Irish nationalism had been forged in the 1840s when many of Father Mathew's teetotallers joined the Repeal movement; it was renewed in the 1860s among the Irish in Liverpool. John Denvir, a Fenian agent in Liverpool and later the first general secretary of the Home Rule Confederation of Great Britain, as a boy of nine had taken the pledge three times from Father Mathew, inspired by his mother's superstitious faith in the Capuchin's miraculous powers. But, unlike many others, Denvir maintained his total abstinence from drink and also his faith in the temperance cause beyond the 1840s. He worked closely with Father James Nugent, a nationalist priest, who ran the Liverpool *Catholic Times* and various Catholic temperance and charitable societies in the city. When Manning founded the League of the Cross, Nugent amalgamated his existing organisations with it. (**133**, 250-1; **134**, 117-18, 137)

If the link between Irish nationalism and the Catholic temperance movement could be seen in England, in people like Denvir and Nugent, it was even more apparent in America. In 1882 Bishop John Ireland of St Paul, Minnesota, told the Catholic Total Abstinence Union of America that

> The time is propitious; it is an era of Irish patriotism. The virtues and the sufferings of the Irish people have awakened universal interest. The day in the designs of providence is manifestly dawning, when the tears of centuries shall be dried, and their hearts throb at last under the influence of unalloyed joy. To hasten their deliverance, friends and patriots are on hand in numbers, each with his remedy for the ills of the Irish people. I HAVE MY REMEDY, AND I WILL PUBLISH IT TO THE WORLD — TOTAL ABSTINENCE.

Bishop Ireland argued that though the Irish did not drink more alcohol than the English or the Scots, alcohol did more harm among the Irish people 'because the warm nature of the Irish people yields more readily to its flames, and, in the wreck which follows, they have more virtues to sacrifice'. And he went on to dwell upon these virtues:

> The picture of their virtues entrances. They are the most liberty-loving people on the earth. Eight hundred years of oppression have left no mark in their freemen hearts. Generous — the will is ever beyond the means; selfishness melts and vanishes beneath their soft skies. Brave and spirited — battle-fields tell their valour, as the counsels of nations speak their wisdom. Pure in morals — the gem of purity nothing can snatch away from the coronet of the isle of virgins and martyrs. Such are the children of Erin. But in an evil hour, hell — whoever may have been its agents — distilled alcohol through their plains and over their mountains, and, despite their grand qualities, a sad story of misery has to be told. ... This has been Ireland's curse, and he who still loves alcohol joins hands with Ireland's most bitter foe.

If nationalists in the past had found it difficult to accept the seriousness of the Irish drink problem, as this would have offended their nationalist principles, Bishop Ireland's solution was to attribute the problem to Satan himself, he being the only agent powerful enough to overcome this virtuous people. One could hardly wish for a clearer expression of temperance nationalism. For Bishop Ireland the Irish people were superior to other nations, and although they were corrupted by drink and oppressed by British rule, he was confident that their liberation from both forms of tyranny was near at hand. Their liberators were to be the Home Rule party and the Catholic total abstinence movement. (**190**, 7-8)

While temperance organisations with a strong Irish and Catholic identity were appearing in England and in the United States in the 1870s, a similar trend was apparent in Ireland itself, though temperance continued to create problems within the Irish church. We have seen that Bishop Furlong and Archbishop Leahy championed the cause in the 1860s, and their successors, Bishop Warren and Archbishop Croke, followed in this course; and by the 1880s temperance was finding more widespread support among the clergy. To some extent this was a result of the developments in England and America. While Manning was encouraged to join the movement by clerical efforts in Ferns and Cashel to enforce Sunday closing, the League of the Cross in turn extended its work to Ireland. Under the name of St Patrick's League of the Cross, it made Cork the centre of its operations. Similarly, Bishop Ireland and other leaders of the American movement visited the home country in the 1880s, seeking to promote the Catholic temperance cause. Of considerable importance in this regard was a letter sent to Bishop Ireland by the pope in 1887, in which he endorsed the controversial total abstinence pledge as the 'proper and the truly efficacious remedy for this very great evil' and generally gave papal blessing to the new movement. But despite these developments, in the 1880s and 1890s the Irish church remained deeply divided in its attitude to the anti-drink movement. (**138**, 488; **218**; **111**; **216**, 40-2)

Temperance was endorsed by the church as one of the basic Christian virtues, but total abstinence was a different matter. It continued to be identified with Protestantism, an identification which was doubtless reinforced by the support given by Ulster Protestants to measures like Sunday closing and the permissive bill. Writing in 1888 in the influential *Irish Ecclesiastical Record*, Father James Halpin sought to explain this connection:

[In] modern Protestantism... there must be some substitute for any fixed or certain body of doctrine, which we know is becoming gradually less and less. The substitute is generally something like the temperance rage; a social panacea or high project of philanthropy. Dogma yields its place to moral teaching; then the supernatural will soon have to disappear before the national or rational; and the end is reached with, what we find to be practically the sum total of the teaching of some of our modern so-called Christian sects, some new phase of deism or merely natural religion.

This was exactly the basis on which J. H. Newman criticised Manning's temperance work: that it was substituting social welfare for Christian doctrine. Newman felt that temperance and similar lay reformist movements were campaigning for moral improvement on purely secular grounds. 'We are having a wedge thrust into us which tends to the destruction of religion altogether,' he warned, and when Manning sought his support for temperance reform Newman loftily replied: 'As for me, I do not know whether we have too many public houses or too few.' These reservations were in fact not restricted to Catholics; many Protestant, particularly Episcopal, clerics shared them. Total abstinence also continued to evoke fears of Manicheism. In 1875 Manning endeavoured to clear himself of this charge by saying:

> I will go to my grave without tasting intoxicating drinks; but I repeat distinctly that any man that would say that the use of wine or any like thing is sinful, when it does not lead to drunkenness, *that man is a heretic* condemned by the church. With that man I will never work.

But this was not always an easy distinction to maintain. By endorsing the total abstinence pledge as 'efficacious', the pope had considerably strengthened the hand of the teetotallers within the church. But as one priest warned,

> Like most good things, it is liable to be abused.... A pledge of itself does not work a sudden, moral or physical change;... it is not a sacrament.... A pledge... is not an oath, nor a vow, but at most a solemn resolution, or a promise made to man.

That such careful explanations of teetotalism and the pledge were still required was a measure of the continuing problems that the anti-drink movement posed for the church. (**165**, 1118; **228**, 22; **138**, 503-4)[16]

There were more practical problems posed as well. Drink and the public house played a vital role in Irish society, especially in rural areas. Priests, who were both products of this society and its natural leaders, were understandably loath to create dissension by insisting on total abstinence for all. Dr Patrick Coffey in a lecture to a teetotal society at Maynooth in 1903 warned the students that they should not alienate the publicans:

> The total abstaining priest, therefore, need not, and ought not be the declared enemy of all publicans as such.... He need not, for instance, pass public judgment on the publican's claims to respectability.... Neither will the priest serve any good purpose by denouncing the 'trade' generally as dishonest, unprincipled, insincere. There are good, bad and indifferent people in it as in every other trade.

With the spread of temperance principles the publicans would inevitably suffer severely, Coffey acknowledged, but he warned the students that the priest 'ought not give unnecessary offence by uncharitably rejoicing in their loss or suffering'. Coffey implicitly recognised that the publican was another important figure in rural Ireland, often the most important after the priest. Frequently a shopkeeper as well as a drink seller, he was a vital source of credit for farmers, and his house afforded an essential meeting and socialising centre. Moreover, from the 1870s the publican was usually a supporter of the Home Rule party, providing money, facilities and valuable local knowledge and influence, especially during elections. Given these considerations, the reluctance of the church to attack the publicans is understandable. Yet the close relationship that frequently existed between priest and publican had its critics, none more vitriolic perhaps than F. H. O'Donnell, M.P. for Dungarvan from 1877 to 1885. In a pamphlet entitled *Political Priests and Irish Ruin* O'Donnell claimed that 'It is the drink money from the publican's till which supplies the richest contribution to the collecting plate,' and he went on to call the publicans the clergy's 'principal paymasters, who are at the same time the principal paymasters of the political agitations which the clergy maintain throughout Ireland'. O'Donnell was a bitter and vindictive man, and yet there is certainly truth in his claim that there was an alliance between 'whiskey and holy water' and that this alliance was vital to the Home Rule party. But the Irish church was in a very different position from the immigrant churches in England or the United States. It did not share their need to prove Catholic sobriety and respectability in a Protestant-dominated state. In Ireland the teetotallers' demand that church and trade be totally separated was simply impractical. (**244**, 110; **267**, 72-3) Thus the Irish church was slower than the churches in England and America to take up the total abstinence banner, and in fact it never took it up wholeheartedly.

In this period, nevertheless, two important factors emerged which helped create, among some clergy at least, a more sympathetic attitude to total abstinence. The first was the growth of new devotional practices and the emphasis on piety and asceticism that went with them. Total abstinence in this context could be seen as a sacrifice made by the especially devout on behalf of their less zealous brethren. The second factor was the appearance, after the death of Parnell, of new nationalist organisations. These movements, unlike Home Rule, put considerable emphasis on the personal habits and behaviour of the individual. Like Thomas Davis, they saw individual moral reform as a necessary forerunner of political reform. In the 1890s both sections of the Home Rule party were closely identified with the drink trade, but the new nationalism of the Gaelic Athletic Association and the Gaelic League proved much more amenable to total abstinence. (**212**, 644-5)

The issue of total abstinence was debated at length in the Irish church during the years 1889-91. The centenary of Father Mathew's birth was celebrated in 1890, and many of the bishops were moved to use the occasion to establish temperance societies. But this brought them face to face with the problem of whether such societies should only cater for total abstainers, and, if for moderationists as well, how they were to be organised. It was the same problem that had faced many Protestant churches in the 1870s. Disagreements on this issue occurred not only within the Irish church but between the Irish and English churches. Criticism of total abstainers was frequently severe. In 1889, for example, Father John S. Vaughan, an Irish priest working in London, regretted the 'rhapsodies of certain self-righteous water-nymphs, whose speeches seem to presuppose and imply something intrinsically evil in the very nature of spirits, wine, and beer'. Such an implication was, of course, heretical.

> Some excellently good men [Vaughan went on] may be found who speak and act just as though a bottle of Guinness's stout were the very incarnation of evil; and who look upon a glass of whiskey and water as suspiciously as though it held a dozen mortal sins in solution. If, indeed, the devil himself were to appear *in propria persona* from out of the mystic wreath of encircling vapour arising from the mimic caldron to hurry off the drinker's soul to perdition, I don't think it would add much to their present horror and consternation.

But while he chose to ridicule the extreme teetotallers, Vaughan did not deny the seriousness of the drink problem. He rejected the defence 'set up by certain rubicund worshippers of wine and wassail' that all things created by God are good. Anyone,

> unless his brain be of the texture of brown paper and sawdust . . . will see that the truth of the premises can give no countenance to such a conclusion. Of course everything is good. . . . Prussic acid is good, and so are salts of lemon, yes, very good, for destroying rats; but because they are good, is that any reason why we should make our dinner of them?

While drink was not intrinsically evil, Vaughan acknowledged that it did frequently lead to evil. He was prepared to accept moderation: 'So long as a man does not exceed the due bounds, he is acting entirely within his own rights.' He thought that total abstainers often acted as a 'mutual admiration society', replacing the sin of gluttony by that of pride. But he was ready to recommend total abstinence in two instances: for the drunkard, who could not control his drinking, and, interestingly, for the priest. The pastor, he thought, 'cannot influence his people to sign the pledge half as easily if he be not an abstainer himself'. (**333**, 869-73)

Vaughan represented the views of a significant group of priests, including many members of the hierarchy. The total abstainers realised that their opponents were numerous. In the same volume of the *Irish*

Ecclesiastical Record in which Vaughan's article appeared there was another by Father Walter J. P. O'Brien, a staunch teetotaller. But O'Brien recognised that many priests did not share his views and referred specifically to their laxity in enforcing the church's ban on drinking at funerals. (**263**) This particular issue of drinking at funerals, and the more general question of priests interfering with local customs by opposing drinking, is illustrated vividly by Canon Sheehan in his novel *Luke Delmege*, published in 1901. Sheehan personally supported the temperance movement, but in his novel he explores the problems of a young priest who has worked in England and returns to impose the practices he has learned there upon his Irish flock. When his kindly old parish priest offers Luke a tumbler of whiskey punch after dinner, 'following a time-honoured custom of thirty years', Luke abruptly refuses it and demands coffee instead. When the offer is renewed on another occasion Luke is offended and throws the drink out the window. But worse is to come when Luke refuses to conduct a funeral because he finds that the mourners have been drinking. In this he is adhering to church statutes, but at the same time grossly offending community feelings. The old priest warns him: 'You'll have a nice row over this, young man. They may forgive all your abuse of the country, and your comparisons with England; but they'll never forgive you for turning your back on the dead. And Myles McLoughlin was the decentest man in the parish.' In retaliation the people refuse to attend church when Luke is officiating, and the bishop is forced to transfer him to another parish. According to Sheehan, Luke 'knew well that, although he had maintained a great principle, it had left a stain on his character forever'. Sheehan fully appreciated that a rigorous enforcement of anti-drink regulations, such as teetotallers desired, was simply unrealistic in rural Ireland and would probably do more harm than good. We have seen that although traditional festivals declined during the nineteenth century, drink still remained an important ingredient at weddings, wakes and fairs. Many priests therefore opposed total abstinence societies and prohibitionist legislation, believing that they would cause great disruption and hardship in rural Ireland. (**307, 241-2, 355-6**)

In 1890 Father Geoghegan, writing in the *Irish Ecclesiastical Record*, acknowledged that

> The inducements to break the pledge in the country, while not as frequent as in the towns, are in many cases far more dangerous and deep-rooted ... the greatest danger of all — and that which is the most general — when friends meet at fair or market, race or pattern; and when the treat of friendship is offered and accepted.

Unlike the teetotallers, Geoghegan recommended a pragmatic approach to the problem:

> Do not those act more comprehensively who go to work not subjectively

but objectively? Not subjectively, i.e. not setting to work with a pre-conceived plan in their minds, to which all would be called on to comply, no matter what their own inclinations or wants might be; but objectively, i.e. working according to the material to be found in the parish.

In each parish, Geoghegan felt, there would be a certain number who could not drink without getting drunk, and clearly these needed to be induced to take a total abstinence pledge. But there would be others who were moderate in their drinking and simply did not need to become total abstainers: 'To go on urging them to become such would be for the priest a task of much labour and little fruit.' For children and the young, who had not tasted alcohol, again total abstinence would be feasible. Geoghegan therefore advocated the establishment of both total abstinence and temperance societies: 'Each association to have its own banners and guilds quite distinct, but their meetings to be held together in the church, to save the overworked priest the labour of separate addresses.' Geoghegan was in general agreement with Vaughan, and their flexible view was embodied in the 1890 pastoral on temperance issued by Archbishop Walsh and the bishops of Leinster. (**158**, 214)

Divisions over the church's attitude to total abstinence were apparent in the hierarchy as well as among the lower clergy. Thus, when Archbishop Walsh decided to inaugurate a temperance crusade to mark the Father Mathew centenary in 1890, he found himself under attack from within the church. In 1889, in order to publicise the issue, Walsh preached a series of sermons on intemperance and the best methods to deal with it. Speaking at the blessing of a new bell at St Michan's in North Anne Street on 10 November, he criticised total abstinence, reiterating the old argument that it partook of Manicheism. He said that the total abstinence pledge, approved by the pope, was in some cases the best way in which drinking could be curbed, but he did not consider it by any means the only method.

> I desire [he concluded] to promote total abstinence in every way I can. I will encourage all societies of total abstainers. But the moment I see men not charitable, attempting to trample down those who do not belong to the total abstainers, from that moment I will cease to work with those men.

This statement brought down upon Walsh the criticism of the *Catholic Times*, Father Nugent's Liverpool newspaper, which was committed to total abstinence. The paper quoted Manning in favour of teetotalism and the impossibility of abstainers and non-abstainers working together. 'We cannot conceive', it said, 'how any organisation other than a total abstinence society pure and simple could be considered a suitable memorial to the Apostle of Temperance.' It had little faith, it concluded, in the 'mixed method of working'. Walsh replied with an angry letter accusing the paper of inaccurately reporting Irish ecclesiastical affairs. And he made his displeasure public in Ireland by informing a meeting at Dolphin's Barn that the *Catholic Times* opposed his temperance work. 'No Irish Catholic newspaper would criticise an English Catholic bishop,' he said, 'so why should any English paper do the reverse? The *Catholic Times* is a bit too independent and the Bishop of Liverpool has little control over it.' The *Catholic Times* in turn expressed itself 'amazed' at the vehemence of Walsh's reaction, saying that it had no desire whatsoever to obstruct his work. Moreover, the leader-writer objected to Walsh's inference that English Catholics should not involve themselves in Irish affairs: 'The blood that flows in the veins of the writer of the articles to which Archbishop Walsh directs attention is, he is proud to confess, as Irish as His Grace's.' There was criticism of Walsh from within Ireland as well. Father Walter O'Brien, curate at Midleton, Co. Cork, who in 1896 was to establish the Father Mathew Union, a total abstinence society for priests, set forth his views very clearly in the *Freeman's Journal*:

> As well might you suggest a union... between Home Rulers and separatists, or between Conservatives and Liberal Unionists, as between men who drink... and men who don't.... To suggest any movement short of a total abstinence association as a memorial to Father Mathew is, in my humble opinion, to misinterpret his life and work.... Let us then, in God's name, have total abstinence or nothing.[17]

It was hardly an auspicious start to Walsh's temperance crusade to become involved in a bitter exchange with one of the leading organs of the English Catholic temperance movement. Both sides had quoted Manning's views, though to opposite effect: Walsh against fanatical tee-totalism, and the *Catholic Times* leader-writer against moderation. Walsh had sought Manning's advice on the issue, and on 12 November Manning wrote saying that he thought a 'dual system' was 'inevitable' at first. 'There are many', he said, 'who have never been drunk in the days of their life, but have often not been sober — that is they have been in a state, in which they ought not to say their prayers, in which they would be sorry to die.' Manning thought that there were many such 'free livers', who would claim to be moderationists, and a dual system would probably attract them. Walsh hoped to combine the two groups into one society and also to introduce a class of probationers, who would be preparing themselves to take the total abstinence pledge. Manning objected to these plans, particularly as Walsh wanted to draw St Patrick's League of the Cross into his scheme. On 14 March 1890 Manning informed Walsh that he considered it 'morally impossible' to combine 'baptismal temperance' with the 'counsel of total abstinence'. He was, he said, afraid of two things, 'the one a divergence and friction; the other a relaxation, and undermining of total abstinence'. He advised Walsh to treat moderate drinkers and total abstainers separately:

Let St Patrick's League of the Cross work unchanged and independently as it is. The addition of a temperance organisation with the wise and useful rules you have already printed, will do an immeasurable good. All are bound to temperance: none to total abstinence. Let each follow his own liberty.

On 17 March he wrote again opposing Walsh's plans for a probationary group:

I am afraid of anything which touches the simplicity and solidity of the League of the Cross. It is well and I would let well alone.[18]

Manning was anxious that the League of the Cross should not be tampered with, and particularly that its commitment to total abstinence should not be compromised. Yet Walsh's desire to reform it was understandable in that the organisation had not been a great success in Ireland. It had begun among inmates of the Cork workhouse late in 1884 and was spread by Catholic women visiting the homes of the poor. In May 1885 the first branch was established in St Finbar's parish, with a lay committee and a priest as president. By the end of the year there were thirty branches scattered through the city and county, and though clergy headed all of these, laity were prominent. In 1886 a central council was formed composed of the clerical presidents together with two lay representatives from each branch; in other words, though a specially Catholic organisation, the League was dominated by the laity. Father O'Brien of Midleton objected to it as 'parochially speaking... a one-man movement', depending on individual enthusiasm and not properly integrated into the body of the church. Father Michael Kelly agreed, calling it a 'false start' and characterising its conventions in Ireland as 'unhappy failures'. (**218**, 5-10; **263**, 719; **202**, 1114; **201**, 259-60) Kelly elaborated on his views in a letter written to a fellow-priest in November 1889, which was passed on to Walsh. He criticised the English organisation and found it inappropriate to Irish circumstances. Of English Catholics, Kelly wrote:

Their people are mostly labourers and tradesmen with their families; they have no pretence to anything like general reform, and nothing short of total abstinence will save *the few* whom they seek to save. The very Sundays are unsanctified by very many, and the sacraments are neglected by the majority. As to sermons, there is no mind for them at all. So halls and lay-speakers etc. cannot be dispensed with beyond the channel in the support of temperance.

The Irish situation, according to Kelly, was the reverse of this. 'Parochial organisation effectively worked by the parish priest and his clergy is what

Catholic Ireland wants,' he insisted. 'Our halls must be the churches, and our speakers must be our preachers.' Kelly spoke approvingly of Manning's championship of total abstinence, but condemned the independent nature of the League of the Cross and its use of lay agencies. In Ireland, however, even the organisation's commitment to total abstinence was to be compromised. At the Thurles convention in 1889 Nugent and his supporters had asked Archbishop Croke to become president of the Irish branch. Croke was a strong supporter of the temperance movement, but was not personally an advocate of total abstinence. (**323**, 189) Admitting that total abstinence was 'disliked and sometimes unfairly contradicted in many clerical circles', Kelly in his letter went on to claim that the 'actions of the managers of the Thurles convention' had had the effect of discrediting total abstinence further:

> Irish total abstainers were required to acquiesce in the unjustified pre-arrangements of Father Nugent and, amongst other things, accept as head of their body one not of uniform mind and practice with its members. Their alternative was to act uncivilly towards their revered and more than kind host. . . . It would have been all right to ask Dr Croke to become patron of the Irish branch of the League of the Cross, but it was suicidal to ask and petition him to be its president.

Convinced total abstainers like Kelly considered it absurd that Archbishop Croke, as president of a total abstinence society, should still establish and support temperance societies, which is exactly what happened. In a circular to his clergy in February 1890 Croke ordered that at confirmation all children should be enrolled in the League of the Cross until the age of twenty-one, but his instructions as regards adults were that 'a temperance society, or, better still, a branch of St Patrick's League of the Cross, or both if deemed advisable, be established in every parish in the archdiocese of Cashel and Emly'. Croke, like Walsh, remained committed to the dual approach. The League of the Cross thus failed to satisfy extreme tee-totallers, like Kelly, on the one hand, while at the same time it did not win the wholehearted support of moderates, like Archbishop Walsh, on the other. In these circumstances it had little, if any, hope of success. In 1890 the *Freeman's Journal* noted that of 150 delegates attending the League's annual convention, the majority were English, and the Irish contingent was 'remarkably small'. Yet this convention was in Cork, the League's Irish headquarters.[19]

The controversies between moderationists and teetotallers, between supporters of the League of the Cross and those of an indigenous organisation, were very discouraging for Walsh. In February 1890 he laid the foundation stone of the Father Mathew Hall in Church Street, Dublin, which was to be used by total abstinence societies associated with the Capuchins. In his speech he sounded very dispirited:

It would, indeed, be anything but honest of me if I were to conceal from you that I am by no means as hopeful in this matter as I was some few months ago . . . I have come to learn — and learned it with amazement as well as with sorrow — how widespread is the feeling of indifference that exists as to the success or failure of the project of a national movement for the rooting out of the vice of drunkenness from Ireland. I must not shrink from saying that, as the result of this, the conclusion has been all but forced upon me that the hopes which recently were raised to so high a pitch of sanguine expectations are doomed to end in a deplorable, if not disastrous disappointment.

Croke wrote immediately expressing sorrow at Walsh's remarks and hoping that he was not intending to 'throw up the sponge'. Walsh, however, was probably right in identifying apathy as the major barrier to a successful temperance crusade, more important even than divisions within temperance ranks. The parliamentary campaign and the Protestant temperance societies were facing the same problem. Walsh had also suffered a public rebuff from the Dublin corporation over the centenary, which could only have contributed to his gloom. He opposed the corporation's plans to erect a statue of Father Mathew. He preferred 'some vigorous effort to perpetuate his work' and felt that 'until this has been done . . . a statue of Father Mathew erected in any public place in Dublin would serve only as a standing public record of reproach to us all'. But the publican-dominated corporation decided that a statue would be a 'suitable mode' of spreading the principles of Father Mathew, and accordingly it rejected the archbishop's objection. The celebrations were marred by other clashes between the supporters of temperance and the upholders of the drink interest. At a public meeting to mark the centenary the Lord Mayor of Dublin attacked T. W. Russell as a hypocrite who preached morality but who 'would shoot and hang the people'. In Cork a priest, Dr Kearne, in a centenary sermon created a stir by condemning the Home Rule party for its championing of the drink interest. The *Freeman's Journal* felt that such things 'had much better be left unsaid'. But at the same time it recognised the hollowness of the celebrations, for it asked: 'How can it be said that [ceremonials and processions] are not a pretence and a dishonest mockery so long as the principles of him in whose honour it is all done are generally ignored?' Walsh's pessimism may also have arisen from other non-related issues. The O'Shea divorce petition had been filed in December 1889, and in February Walsh was receiving very bleak reports about the possible outcome. The fall and death of Parnell in 1890-91 were certainly to put temperance out of most people's minds. (**226**, 465, 468-9)[20]

A year later, however, in his speech opening the Father Mathew Hall in January 1891, Walsh was rather more optimistic, though no less moderate. Admitting that there had been 'a sort of disappointment at the start' and that 'no sooner had the project of organisation begun to take shape, when difficulties arose, difficulties that I could not but feel were of the very gravest character', he nevertheless thought that things now looked rather brighter. The diocese had 62,000 members of temperance societies and 61,000 who had taken the total abstinence pledge, 38,000 of the latter being children. Despite pressure from the teetotallers, Walsh was pursuing his moderate approach. He hoped that an effort would be made to induce the licensing authorities to reduce the numbers of public houses in Dublin. But he was quick to add: 'Mind, I am not disclaiming against the existence of public houses.' He was, he said, 'no advocate of sensational extreme measures in this or any other branch of temperance work':

> I say nothing of the Main liquor law, or of local option or even of Sunday closing. There are aspects of this question as to which I candidly confess myself unable to form a judgment with anything like the confidence that would enable me to feel justified in giving public utterance to my views.[21]

The efforts of Walsh and Croke to mark the Mathew centenary with a renewed temperance crusade, organised by the hierarchy from within the church, had shown that the church was still divided on the issue of total abstinence, as it had been in Father Mathew's day. Despite the support given to teetotalism by Manning and American leaders like Bishop Ireland, many Irish bishops and clergy considered it at best impractical and at worst heretical. In rural society especially drink formed too basic a part of the socio-economic system to be condemned outright without the church incurring grave risks to its authority and status. But there were zealous advocates of total abstinence among the Irish clergy who were by no means satisfied with the hierarchy's essentially moderate position. The problem they faced in the 1880s and 1890s was how to promote total abstinence from within the church, but without at the same time alienating their superiors.

Father James Cullen and the Pioneers

The diocese of Ferns in the south-east part of Ireland was an important stronghold of the temperance movement from the 1850s into the 1880s, under Bishops Furlong and Warren. It provided a training ground for several of the leaders of the Catholic temperance movement, most notably Father Michael Kelly and Father James Cullen, who both spent many years at the House of Missions in Enniscorthy. We have already examined some of Kelly's writings on the subject of Catholic temperance. Now it is time to look closely at his fellow temperance priest, James Cullen, whose establishment of the Pioneer Total Abstinence Association marks the climax of the temperance movement in nineteenth-century Ireland.

Father James Cullen was the antithesis of Father Mathew in many respects. An extremely devout but rather gloomy man, he was a born organiser, who worked with great energy over many years to perfect the institutions he had created. (**107**) Unlike Father Mathew, Cullen was not converted dramatically to the temperance cause, but developed his views over a long period; in fact the formation of the Pioneer Association was preceded by nearly thirty years' experience of temperance work. Nor did Cullen allow his own personality to become the focus of his movement. He certainly dominated the organisation until his death in 1921, but the association was far more widely known than its founder and was structured so as to be self-perpetuating. His death therefore by no means spelt the end of it. Even today Father Mathew's name is far better known in Ireland, and there are many who assume that he established the Pioneer Association. That Cullen deliberately courted obscurity is shown by his response to a request for biographical information from the editors of the massive American *Standard Encyclopedia of the Alcohol Problem*. In their short entry on Cullen the editors remarked:

> Father Cullen was one of the most modest of men: he absolutely declined to furnish any biographical data for the *Standard Encyclopedia*, on the ground that only his work, and not his life was worthy of record. (**92**, II, 742)

We are fortunate therefore in having a substantial biography of Cullen, written shortly after his death by his fellow-Jesuit, Father Lambert McKenna. McKenna had access to personal diaries and letters which appear no longer to survive. Of these he made good use. While fulfilling the role of hagiographer and devoting a large section of the book to the spiritual life of his subject, he also fulfilled the role of historian, devoting some two-thirds of the work to a detailed account of Cullen's life and work. An examination of Cullen's life provides a valuable insight into both the development of his own thinking on the subject of temperance and into the growth of the more extreme sections of the Catholic temperance movement in the last quarter of the nineteenth century.

Cullen was born in New Ross in 1841 into the family of a prosperous Catholic merchant. The family was pious, especially his mother, whose own family had provided many priests. His father's politics appear to have been nationalist, though more in line with O'Connell's than the Young Irelanders'. James, however, was certainly a nationalist. McKenna tells us that his initial aversion to the Jesuits was partially due to their conservative political views, which he had experienced as a student at Clongowes Wood College. Cullen when still young became familiar with stories of the rising in Wexford in 1798. Later in life he was to express sympathy and support for the rebels, largely attributing their failure to drunkenness.[22] After four years with the Christian Brothers, Cullen was sent to Clongowes in 1856, as his parents had been impressed by Jesuit missions in New Ross. According to McKenna, even at this young age Cullen exhibited a strong missionary impulse, establishing confraternities in the school. After Clongowes came three years at Carlow College, from 1861 to 1864, where Cullen gained a reputation for being 'very exact and pious', characteristics which he never lost. He was ordained in Carlow cathedral in October 1864 and took up a curacy in Wexford town. In his two years at Wexford he developed something of a reputation as a preacher. Though not naturally eloquent, Cullen prepared his sermons carefully, and McKenna thought that his 'power came from his intense earnestness, his absolute singleness of purpose'. He also introduced new devotional practices and organisations in Wexford, especially sodalities for women and children. So, right from the commencement of his priestly career, Cullen used devotional rituals as a means of strengthening piety among the more enthusiastic of his flock. He did not, however, during the period of his curacy show any particular interest in the temperance cause. McKenna aptly sums up the church's attitude to teetotalism at this time:

> For a considerable time before Father Mathew's death, and for many years after it, the general body of the clergy disapproved of total abstinence except as a desperate remedy for confirmed drunkards. The few priests here and there who adopted it as a practice were generally considered either to be faddists or to be guided by mistaken zeal.

One of Ireland's first temperance societies had been established in New Ross in 1829 by the Rev. G. W. Carr, and Father Mathew had visited the town in 1840, but all signs of total abstinence had apparently disappeared. When the Redemptorists held a major mission in 1854, which Cullen attended, there was no reference to pledge renewal or even to pledge-taking. McKenna says that Cullen, while at home on holidays from Carlow in 1862, was shocked by a visit from a drunken priest. This experience inspired him to take a pledge against drinking whiskey punch, but he continued to drink wine with his meals. As a curate in Wexford he administered pledges against drunkenness, but not total abstinence pledges. Similarly, McKenna found in Cullen's diaries notes for sermons against drunkenness which he had delivered in the late 1860s, but these contained no commitment to total abstinence. What brought the seriousness of the drink problem home to him was probably his work among the boatmen of Enniscorthy. (**235**, 19-20, 36, 308-10)

In the 1850s the Jesuits and Redemptorists had begun conducting parish missions in Ireland. At the same time Cardinal Wiseman was encouraging similar missions among the Irish in London. One of the leading priests involved in England was the convert George Spencer, who as Father Ignatius Spencer, a Passionist, conducted numerous missions in Ireland in the 1850s. Spencer called on the Irish to contribute both money and prayer for the conversion of England. In addition, he preached the benefits of total abstinence; his so-called 'little missions' of three to four days in each parish usually involved the administering of the total abstinence pledge to children. Bishop Furlong was very impressed by this work and decided that every parish in his diocese should have a regular mission. The great obstacle, however, was the lack of trained priests to undertake the work. Furlong decided therefore to establish a mission institute in his diocese, like those found on the continent. In 1866 his House of Missions was set up in Enniscorthy, staffed initially by four of his younger and more active priests. These were Father Warren, subsequently Furlong's successor, Father Brownrigg, later Bishop of Ossory, Father Cloney and Father James Cullen. Cullen, who had already shown an inclination for mission work, was an ideal choice for the new venture. The priests, after instruction from the Jesuits in Dublin, held their first mission at Rathnure in May 1867. This was the beginning of an almost continuous series of missions. In the 1870s, for instance, Cullen held retreats in all the towns and most of the villages of Co. Wexford. (**154**, 133-4; **160**; **272**; **235**, 50-2)

The mission house was on the east bank of the Slaney, in a district called the Shannon, at the foot of Vinegar Hill. Surrounding it were the homes of the river boatmen and the many public houses which catered for them. The boatmen, who were relatively well paid for transporting crops and merchandise along the river between Enniscorthy and Wexford town, were notorious for their drunkenness. Cullen took the lead in organising a temperance mission for this group. He was at first not particularly impressed with the effectiveness of the pledge, whether temporary or lifelong, in changing the habits of the Slaney boatmen. Instead he felt that their religious life needed to be revitalised and that alternative forms of recreation needed to be supplied. Accordingly he established a sodality of the Sacred Heart for them and a similar organisation for their wives, believing that 'by their tippling they were directly responsible, not merely for their own sins, but for those of their husbands as well'. He also formed a brass band, found a teacher, instruments and uniforms, and tried to promote music as an alternative activity to drinking. Presumably Father Mathew's temperance bands acted as the model here. The emphasis on devotional organisation, the influence of women and alternative activities were all features that are found throughout Cullen's temperance work. He was also conscious of the social problems that often lay behind heavy drinking. McKenna described his attitude thus:

There is a minimum of comfort without which the observance of the Christian precepts becomes normally impossible. The ordinary man, therefore, will fail in his duties as a Christian if he is placed in cir- cumstances of extraordinary difficulty. . . . Slumdom means not merely suffering, but sin. A zealous priest, even if his heart be untouched by the sight of misery, cannot view it with indifference when it threatens to render fruitless all his zeal. Father Cullen was always alive to this truth. He was never tired of insisting, in season and out of season, that the spiritual evils, and especially drink, which were working havoc among the people, could never be exorcised by merely spiritual influences as long as men had not houses capable of becoming decent homes.

This belief led Cullen to begin a co-operative building society, supported financially by Furlong and businessmen of the town, with the aim of rebuilding the slum districts of Enniscorthy. This work seems to have influenced Cullen in the direction of the total abstinence pledge. Presumably, like many priests, he found that partial and temporary pledges were not very effective. Not until October 1874, however, while on a mission at Glynn, did he himself take the full pledge. Later he wrote: 'At this time, this step was very unusual. I knew its prudence would be challenged, and its utility denied.' Thus did he acknowledge the considerable opposition to total abstinence which existed in the Catholic church. (**235**, 58, 64-5, 311)

This important step initially produced no noticeable results as far as Cullen was concerned. McKenna notes that he did not establish his first total abstinence society till 1876 and attributes this to Furlong's opposition to teetotalism. With Furlong's death in 1875 and his replacement by Warren early in 1876, the whole situation as regards the temperance campaign in the diocese was transformed. In February 1876, three months after Furlong's death, Cullen established a total abstinence society for the staff and students of St Peter's College, Wexford, and in March another among the students of the Christian Brothers in the town. Moreover, Bishop Warren, his former fellow-priest from Enniscorthy, proved an enthusiastic temperance advocate. In November 1876, some six months after his consecration, Warren publicly took the total abstinence pledge in Enniscorthy cathedral and announced the establishment of a diocesan total abstinence society. The society, the Catholic Total Abstinence Society of the Sacred Thirst and Agony and the Compassionate Heart of Mary, was, as its title proclaims, a Catholic devotional society. It aimed to unite 'all Catholics in a warfare against the drinking habits of society', to prevent intemperance in the young and to reform those already addicted. The pledge taken by a member required him to 'abstain during my life from all intoxicating liquors, and to discountenance their use by others as far as possible'. Alcohol, however, could be taken by a member under doctor's orders. Attendance at meetings of the society, membership of confraternities, prayer and frequent participation in the sacraments were the members' main obligations. Cullen was made secretary of the society and was in fact its chief organiser. It is perhaps possible to detect his rigorous hand in the procedure established to police members. The diocese was to be divided into districts, over each of which were to be two super-intendents. 'These, being supplied with pocket-registers containing the names and addresses of members', were to 'exercise a supervision over them, and report to the rev. president any deviation from the rules'. Such a policing procedure was an innovation in temperance organisation and certainly underlines the determination of Warren and Cullen to make their society a success. By 1879 it had seventeen clerical members and 25,000 lay members. Cullen, characteristically, worked hard to establish the organisation. He set up many branches personally and organised large temperance processions in order to arouse enthusiasm. McKenna, however, speculates that his drive may partly have been the result of sub-limation: McKenna's study of Cullen's diaries showed that from at least 1870 he had been contemplating entry into the Society of Jesus. In 1873 he definitely decided to seek entry. But Warren, when he became bishop, apparently opposed Cullen's wish because he wanted him to establish the diocesan total abstinence society. Not until late in 1881, when the society was firmly established, did Warren withdraw his veto. (**235**, 314-17, 79-81, 320)

So after five years of intensive temperance work under the guidance of Bishop Warren, Cullen withdrew completely from the movement. He spent two years in Belgium, at Arlon and Louvain, undergoing what, for a man of forty, must have been a very demanding period of instruction. Having been received into the Society of Jesus, he returned to Ireland late in 1883 to work at Milltown Park in Dublin. His superiors in the order, recognising his ability and experience in mission work, set him to conduct missions and retreats in schools, colleges and religious houses. As part of this work, Cullen regularly administered the total abstinence pledge and encouraged the establishment of total abstinence societies. He organised such societies at All Hallows' College, at Belvedere, to where he was transferred in 1884, at Thurles College, at Carlow College, at St Finbar's in Cork and at Belfast College, to name only some. But these 'Catholic total abstinence societies', as he called them, were quite independent of each other and cannot be regarded as one organisation. (**235**, 100)

In November 1887 Cullen's career took an important turn when he was appointed director of the Apostelship of Prayer in Ireland. This was a devotional movement, begun in France in 1844, which emphasised prayer and was particularly associated with veneration of the Sacred Heart. The Apostleship had a highly structured organisation, being divided into what were termed 'three degrees'. Members of the first degree were required to make a 'morning offering'; those of the second degree a 'morning offering' plus the 'papal decade' (one Our Father and ten Hail Marys); and in the third degree was added the 'communion of reparation'. Prayers and devotions took place both in the home and church. Members were divided into guilds of fifteen, headed by a 'promoter' who ensured that practices were properly conducted and that members were supplied with literature. Promoters reported each month to local directors, normally parish priests or curates, who were in turn responsible to a diocesan director. The director-general of the Apostleship was the father-general of the Society of Jesus. Cullen was undoubtedly impressed by the well-developed structure of the Apostleship, for he was later to adopt a similar one for his teetotal society. In 1898 he claimed that the Apostleship had 20 million members worldwide and described it as 'one of the principal institutions raised up by divine providence for the succour of the church in these days of coldness and infidelity'. Earlier he likened it to the 'huge primary wheel in a factory, to which any number of bands may be attached, and which turns them all with equal facility'. Certainly under its aegis Cullen was to find plenty of scope for promoting his many pious causes, including total abstinence. In 1861 the Apostleship had established its own journal, the *Messenger of the Sacred Heart*, and by the 1890s various versions of the paper were appearing in seventeen languages in twenty-eight countries. Cullen, who felt that 'in our century no cause is fully equipped that has not a special organ', was quick to begin publishing an *Irish Messenger of the Sacred Heart*, and from 1889 he used the periodical to promote the teetotal cause. His exploitation of his new position in favour of special causes did not, however, proceed without criticism. McKenna remarks that

> A full year elapsed before he began — as from the beginning he had secretly intended — to use the *Messenger* for the furthering of his temperance campaign. He had to go warily. His critics — and they were many — were to have no opportunity of saying that the journal was merely a temperance magazine camouflaged as a *Messenger*. Besides, his whole conception of temperance as a positive thing, an act of love — and not a negative thing, an act of fear and flight — dictated the necessity of first establishing firmly among the people devotion to the Sacred Heart before calling on them to practise temperance as a part of that devotion.

Cullen had come to regard total abstinence as an essential element in the devotions of a pious Catholic. But, as McKenna indicates, he had to proceed cautiously. During the controversies surrounding the centenary of Father Mathew's birth Archbishop Walsh's suspicious attitude to teetotalism became well known. In publishing his *Temperance Catechism* in 1891, Cullen sent copies of the proofs to Walsh in order to gain his imprimatur. But the archbishop's letter of acknowledgment, while it praised the work, at the same time clearly revealed Walsh's reservations regarding teetotalism. He commended Cullen for not 'exaggerating' the importance of total abstinence. 'It is no small merit', he wrote, 'that your catechism is free from every trace of that aggressiveness which unfortunately so often forms a prominent feature in the writings of would-be temperance reformers.' Only by moderating his essentially hardline teetotal views could Cullen hope to retain the approval of the hierarchy. (**124**, 514-19; **121**, 131; **120**, 932; **235**, 101; **122**, v)

In 1889 another important development occurred in his thinking with regard to the tactics of the teetotal movement. Doubtless the opportunities that his new position had opened up made him devote more thought to the question of how best the cause of total abstinence could be pursued. He, like other priests, had administered total abstinence pledges, both lifelong and for shorter periods, to whole congregations at once. The temperance societies he had established were, as we have seen, independent of each other, and they were composed of both temporary and lifelong abstainers. Pledges, though based on religious motives, were not expressly connected with particular forms of devotion. By March 1889 Cullen was extremely unhappy with this whole system. To quote McKenna again:

> This dissatisfaction became so acute, that when on March 17, 1889, he was asked by the parish priest of St Peter's Church, in Belfast, where he was conducting a temperance mission, to give the collective pledge, he refused to do so. He said he was willing to give a total abstinence pledge, but only to those men and women who had proved themselves already temperate, and who, for the sake of the Sacred Heart and by way of example to others, were ready to make a promise of total abstinence for life. This determination to concentrate on the forming of an elite, who would make an 'heroic offering' for love of the Sacred Heart and from a desire of giving good example, never was departed from by him during the rest of his life.

Typically Cullen immediately sought to institutionalise this innovation. He established the Total Abstinence League of the Sacred Heart as a branch of the Apostleship of Prayer in June 1889. He divided the members into three classes: firstly, those who, having been strictly temperate for a long period, made the 'heroic offering', or who, after a lifetime of intemperance, resolved to abstain altogether from drink, with a view to making the 'heroic offering' when they felt confident of their abstinence; secondly, those who had taken a temporary pledge in honour of the Sacred Heart; and thirdly, those who, without abstaining from drink, offered their prayers and alms for the suppression of intemperance. Cullen may have thought it unwise at this stage to attempt to impose a pure total abstinence society on the Apostleship. The first two groups, however, grew rapidly and by July 1891 there were 10,103 'heroic offerings' and 261,890 temporary total abstinence pledges. But Cullen's keenness for organisation did not stop there. For those who made the 'heroic offering', which was the group he was essentially interested in, he set up an organisation similar to the Apostleship of Prayer. Members were divided into what Cullen called 'pioneer bands' of thirty-three. Each band included a 'promoter', whose duties were, firstly, to procure members for the band, taking care that these, had they ever been intemperate, should put in a probationary period of three years' total abstinence; secondly, to see that the members of the band were faithful to their promise; and thirdly, to enlist the more enthusiastic of them in the work of organising other similar bands. Tiny pieces of green ribbon were worn by those who had made the 'heroic offering'. The League of the Cross had used a similar means to identify its members in Ireland. (**235**, 103, 324-5)[23]

With this total abstinence league and its disciplined bands of 'pioneers', Cullen was well on the way to establishing a permanent organisation for his elite of devout Catholics. In 1891 he published his very successful *Temperance Catechism*, which sold 60,000 copies in twelve months. But temperance was by no means the only cause to which Cullen directed his considerable organisational abilities. His 'pioneers' were expected to demonstrate their piety and asceticism in many areas, and in each Cullen provided the necessary structures, all geared to the great wheel of the Apostleship of Prayer. In 1890 he established an Apostleship of Cleanliness and Home Comfort. The emphasis was on 'domestic cleanliness' for, according to Cullen, 'A dirty home, a dirty wife and dirty children, are direct incentives to excessive drinking.' In 1892 he began an Apostleship of Study for children. It again was characterised by complex grades and devotions. Later came leagues against gambling and against 'immodesty in dress'. The sodalities and confraternities of the Sacred Heart, Blessed Sacrament and Blessed Virgin Mary that Cullen established are far too numerous even to attempt to list them. Yet other groups he set up to encourage daily mass, frequent communion, early communion, and the nine first Fridays devotion. A survey of his many societies leaves one with the feeling that Father Cullen was almost a one-man 'devotional revolution'. Cullen remained anxious, as he had been in Enniscorthy in the 1860s, to provide healthy and morally uplifting recreation for the working classes. McKenna says that

> Warmly embracing the idea of the Gaelic League, he would argue that the degenerate tastes and mental stagnation of the people came, not merely from their oppression in penal times, but from their having been deprived of their Gaelic culture and habits of life.

The movements to restore the Irish language and sports thus found a staunch supporter in Cullen. Later at St Francis Xavier Hall, which he erected in Gardiner Street, Dublin, in 1908, Cullen would organise classes in Irish and in Gaelic games. (**235**, 364, 371-6, 356, 360)

Perhaps if Cullen had continued to work intensively in the total abstinence cause, he would have established a new national organisation in the early 1890s. But his mind and his person were distracted from temperance work by the call of foreign missions, just as they had been distracted from the Wexford temperance crusade in 1881 by the call of the

Jesuits. He had long hoped to work as an overseas missionary and was therefore glad to accept an invitation in 1892 to undertake a mission in the Cape Colony. Cullen was anxious as to how his new total abstinence league would fare during his six months' absence, but he was determined to create an organisation that could function without him, and therefore perhaps he regarded his trip as a useful test. In the five years that followed his return from southern Africa in 1893 he took no new initiatives in the field of teetotalism but was mainly engaged in spreading the Apostleship of Prayer and its associated societies throughout the country. But, given Cullen's tendency towards what McKenna calls 'ruthless self-examination', it was perhaps predictable that he would soon become dissatisfied with his total abstinence league and seek to improve its structure. Cullen himself said: 'I felt instinctively that the last word had not been spoken, nor the last blow struck.' (**123**, 500)

The league was spreading, but Cullen was distressed by the number of lapses which were occurring, both among those who had taken the temporary pledge and those who had made the 'heroic offering'. The membership needed to be purged and a more committed and tightly-knit organisation created. He aimed, says McKenna, to weld those who had made the 'heroic offering' into

> a compact *corps d'élite* on whose perseverance he could confidently rely. They would be known everywhere as people who had not needed to take any pledge, but who had taken it for the love of the Sacred Heart and to give a good example. The old-time stigma of the pledge would thus be destroyed; little by little, abstinence from drink would come to be considered a virtue, because an act of sacrifice for God's sake.

He decided therefore to keep the system of bands and promoters, but to insist on stricter conditions of admission, stricter regulation of members, and, above all, on the obligation of members to wear the external token of their 'heroic offering'. Only those who were truly genuine in their commitment, Cullen reasoned, would be prepared to exhibit it in such a public manner. Initially he decided that this new society would be restricted to women only. Explaining the reasoning behind this, Cullen said:

> On the wives, mothers, and daughters of a nation, all confess, a nation's weal or woe largely depends. As the mother moulds the children, so as a rule will the children grow up. All men agree, that, it is worse than folly to attempt any great social reform, or furnish a remedy for any great social evil, without counting on female energetic co-operation as the most important element of success.

Accordingly on 27 December 1898 Cullen met four women who were zealous promoters of pioneer bands in the parlour of the presbytery of St Francis Xavier's Church in Upper Gardiner Street. They agreed to form a new organisation, to be called the Total Abstinence League of the Sacred Heart for Females Exclusively. Only those who had made the 'heroic offering' were to be admitted, and a brooch signifying membership was to be worn at all times. Perhaps because of its ungainly title, the society was simply known as the Brooch League. Its business affairs were put into the hands of the Sisters of Charity in North William Street, and the committee began immediately to establish branches in parishes, schools and convents. It is worth quoting the instructions that Cullen gave to his four-woman committee:

> Band together in death-grip unity of purpose, through the length and breadth of Ireland, souls capable of heroic self-sacrifice and good example for the sake of weaker brethren. Then, bind them by a voluntary promise of total abstinence for life. Next, give them some external emblem by which they may recognise each other when they meet, and thus gather strength from sympathy of purpose and numbers. Thus united, prepare them to face fearlessly for God's cause, the idiotic banter, sneers, ridicule, coaxing, importunities, threats, or apprehensions held out by those who believe in the omnipotence of alcohol for food, medicine or sociability, and the enterprise would be in great measure effected. Finally, let their motto be, deeds rather than words; precept, but precept backed up by example.

Cullen at this stage obviously envisaged his pioneers as a small band of dedicated enthusiasts operating in a largely hostile environment. (**235**, 123; **123**, 502)

Early in 1899, just before he left for another year at the Cape, Cullen was conducting a mission in Cork. There a number of young male teetotallers asked to join his Brooch League. As a result, he sanctioned the formation of the first male branch in Cork. When he returned from Africa in 1900 he also began to give thought to the establishment of a juvenile section. Cullen strongly approved the practice, which Bishop Furlong had initiated, of giving the total abstinence pledge to children at confirmation. But here too he thought there should be an organisation to give support and prevent lapses. 'The impression made on the children's minds, at a time of religious fervour,' he wrote, 'speedily evaporated in presence of the rooted belief and universal custom they had to encounter on their return to their homes.' Early in 1901 he therefore began a juvenile section. Child members were obliged to wear a badge acknowledging their total abstinence, to repeat the pledge each morning and evening, to promise not to enter a public house, nor to associate with drinkers.

Cullen completed the process he had begun in December 1989 when, in September 1901, he called his new temperance league the Pioneer Branch of the Total Abstinence Association of the Sacred Heart. The formation of the Pioneer Association during these three years was in retrospect to prove

Cullen's most lasting contribution to the total abstinence cause. The pioneers were, of course, the vanguard of the old total abstinence league that he had established in connection with the Apostleship of Prayer in 1889. He retained the concept in his new organisation, which was also based on bands of thirty-three supervised by promoters. But he purged the organisation of ex-drunkards, temporary abstainers and moderationists. All members now had to make the 'heroic offering' for life and to repeat it each morning and evening. The very first rule of the association made it clear that it did 'not aim directly at the reclamation of victims of excessive drinking'. The Pioneers were primarily a Catholic devotional society. McKenna repeatedly uses the word 'elite' to describe Cullen's view of them. He did not expect the association to attract vast numbers of members in the way Father Mathew's mass crusade had done. On one occasion he described them as a 'special regiment in the great temperance army. . . . Necessarily they will be few, for the conditions of their enlistment are strenuous, almost drastic.' In accordance with this elitist view, one of his constant themes in later years was the need to keep the organisation pure, free of 'wobblers', as he called those whose commitment did not satisfy him:

> For chronic drunkards and periodic boozers, jovial tipplers, 'weary wobblers', or even moderate drinkers, we keep no ordinary or reserved seats. They must travel by other trains — ours is a special.

This implied that the work of the association would be slow, and its growth not particularly spectacular. Cullen was perfectly willing to accept this implication. He told the Pioneers that

> The demoralisation of Ireland has been brought about slowly, but with deadly certainty, and its cure must be, at least comparatively, slow if it is to make Ireland permanently sober and Ireland permanently free! Rome was not built in a day, and a thoroughly sober Ireland will take some years to construct. There is a question of putting brick after brick in the walls we build. . . . We want no jerry-building in our work! It must be lasting.

Perhaps what distinguishes Cullen most from his predecessors in the Irish temperance movement is not just his obsession with organisation and commitment, but his patience. He certainly built slowly and with a view to producing a lasting monument. (**123**, 503-9; **235**, 333)[24]

In October 1901 the first annual general meeting of the Pioneer Association was held at the Ignatian Chapel in Gardiner Street, with some 900 people in attendance. As this substantial turnout suggests, membership was growing rapidly, more rapidly than Cullen had anticipated. By 1909 there were 150,000 members, and by 1914 the figure was 270,000. Membership had been boosted by the introduction in 1904 by Cullen of a probationary period of two years. Probationers, in preparing themselves to make the 'heroic offering', would take a total abstinence pledge for two years. Cullen directed that probationers were to be carefully policed, and any who broke the pledge had to begin the probationary period over again. The movement, however, was not without its setbacks. In 1904 Cullen lost control of the *Messenger* and was moved from Belvedere to Gardiner Street. His use of the journal as an organ for his total abstinence movement had caused discontent, and McKenna notes that after his departure the amount of temperance propaganda published in the *Messenger* declined. But Cullen, ever conscious of the need for a public organ, persuaded the editor of the *Irish Catholic* to give him a weekly column in that paper. From February 1912 until October 1921, just five weeks before his death, Cullen produced the column, with 'barely a single omission'. Despite the evidence of hostility from within the church, Cullen devoted much effort to recruiting priests for his Pioneer Association. He established branches in theological colleges and won over an important supporter in the person of Dr Daniel Mannix, the President of Maynooth. In 1909 Cullen told the annual general meeting that one-third of the priests in Ireland were either Pioneers or total abstainers. Cullen saw priests and children as two groups that would ensure the transmission of total abstinence principles. Priests who were members of the Pioneer Association would encourage their congregations to join; and as for children, he said:

> If 'the child is father to the man', then what the child learns, assimilates and believes will constitute the motive power of the man, when he is called to take his place in the battle against evil, especially against drink. . . . Given a generation or two of children thoroughly instructed in the unvarying effects of alcohol . . . there will soon arise a generation of men who will not only be personal abstainers, but men who will use every legitimate influence to have the temptation to drink and opportunities for indulgence in alcoholic beverages curtailed, and finally completely abolished.

Like the Protestants with their Bands of Hope, Cullen saw that children raised on total abstinence principles would ultimately lead to the triumph of the movement. So while he saw his adult Pioneers as an elite, in his child Pioneers he saw the foundations of whole generations of total abstainers. (**235**, 334, 127, 129)[25]

We have already remarked upon Cullen's nationalism. He followed Drennan and Davis in detecting a deliberate attempt on the part of the English to keep Ireland submissive through drink:

> A drunken Ireland, England knew, could never be a free Ireland — then or now! [he said, referring to the 1840s] And let us say it, during the last fifty years, since Father Mathew's time, England could never have

withheld self-government from Ireland if, by her shameful licensing opportunities and laws, she had not first stupefied, paralysed, degraded and disgraced the people she feared and hated. The rebellion of '98, with its terrible disasters, brought about by drink at Ross, Vinegar Hill and Arklow, disclosed the fatal secret of success to the English commanders. Let the wild Irish drink, they thought, and, despite all their military skill and valour, we shall easily conquer them — let the Irish drink and their slavery is secured — make Ireland and keep Ireland a nation of drunkards — then hold its people up to the scorn of the world and our object is gained!

For Cullen temperance was an essential element in the nationalist struggle. The motto 'Ireland sober, Ireland free', first used by the I.A.P.I. in the 1880s, succinctly expressed his attitude. The Pioneer Association, he said, would grow and prosper side by side 'with the vigorous life of Irish Ireland in the coming parliament of our own legislative and domestic independence'. While he talked of Home Rule, Cullen clearly had little time for the Home Rule politicians and their allies in the drink trade. He looked more to the new cultural movements. He urged Pioneers to throw themselves 'heart and soul' into the Irish language movement: 'into the music, the songs, the games and dances of Irish Ireland, and into all the approved associations for the betterment of our country'. He acknowledged that members of the Gaelic League were frequently the most active and committed Pioneers. And, echoing Sinn Féin, he urged in 1905 that Pioneers should give preference to goods manufactured in Ireland as a means of promoting Irish industry and ending emigration. Gaelic organisations regularly participated in temperance processions, and in 1906 the *Irish Independent* described the Dublin Catholic temperance societies as 'acting as propagandists for the Gaelic League'.[26]

The new nationalism in turn found much to admire in the temperance cause. The Gaelic Athletic Association, at the urging of Archbishop Croke, was quick to exclude drink from its meetings and to refuse sponsorship by publicans. Arthur Griffith in *The Resurrection of Hungary* showed how the Austrians foisted a reputation for drunkenness upon the Hungarians in an effort to discredit them as a nation and implied that the English had done the same to the Irish. Moreover, Sinn Féin found itself battling the drink interests, the so-called 'whiskey ring' which had dominated the Dublin corporation for many years. Jim Larkin, a lifelong teetotaller, was anxious to encourage his union members to take the pledge, telling them on one occasion that it was 'the duty of everyone who had at heart the welfare of Ireland to call upon the national representatives to put in the forefront of their programme legislation to crush the curse of intemperance'. In the north Bulmer Hobson and Denis McCullough reformed the Belfast section of the Irish Republican Brotherhood and decided in future only to accept members who did not drink. But perhaps the most striking combination of nationalism and teetotalism was to be found in the person of Patrick Pearse. Pearse was a dedicated non-drinker from a very early age. 'He abhorred pubs,' says his most recent biographer. In the prospectus for St Enda's, produced in 1908, he vowed to teach his students, among other virtues, temperance. But his own preference was obviously for total abstinence, as both he and his brother Willie were Pioneers. (**276**, 63, 78, 87; **162**, 79-80; **131**, 51; **213**, 6,48-9, 126-7, **186**, 35, 98; **145**, 24, 116, 129)

The establishment of the Pioneer Association in 1898-1901 marked the beginning of the most successful Catholic temperance movement in Ireland since the 1840s. But Father Cullen's organisation was vastly different from Father Mathew's crusade. Firstly, it *was* an organisation: carefully thought out, highly structured, and integrated within the body of the church. Its members were an elite, noted for their discipline and commitment. The association was a world away from the hysteria and chaos which characterised Father Mathew's crusade. A comparison of the two in fact further highlights the superstitious and messianic aspects of the earlier movement. The Pioneer Association was also more truly Catholic than the 1840s crusade. Cullen worked from within the church. As with Father Mathew, his status as a religious gave him considerable independence and the ability to travel and to establish contacts throughout the country. But he believed that only through the organs of the church could any lasting impact be made. He learned well the lesson of Father Mathew's crusade: that the achievements of an individual or a society operating outside the church could not endure once the initial enthusiasm had dissipated. Father Michael Kelly had stressed the need for 'perpetuity and Catholicity', and Cullen clearly felt that the latter was essential in guaranteeing the former. There was certainly still much suspicion within the church regarding teetotalism, as the controversy over the Mathew centenary in 1890 demonstrated. But Cullen was far more successful than Father Mathew had been in handling such opposition. He repeatedly emphasised that his Pioneers were a small band of dedicated Catholics who took the total abstinence pledge as a sacrifice and a sign of their piety. It was hard for critics of teetotalism, either within the church or in the drink trade, to condemn such devotion. No one could accuse Cullen of flouting the authority of his superiors, of allying himself with Protestants, or of seeking to destroy the drink industry, in the way Father Mathew had done. But the very name 'Pioneer', of course, implied that the elite were preparing the way for far greater numbers in the future. Unlike Father Mathew, Father Cullen expected the conversion of Ireland to teetotalism to be a slow process, stretching over generations. An enduring organisation was thus required.

The Pioneers also drew great strength from their alliance with the Gaelic revival. Repeal and teetotalism had been closely allied in the 1840s, but this had proved problematical for Father Mathew, creating much hostility among his Protestant sympathisers. The growing links between the Home Rule party and the drink trade from the 1880s alienated many temperance advocates who found the cultural nationalism of the 1890s far more congenial. Revivalists and teetotallers could agree on the glorification of Gaelic society. Michael Kelly was reflecting widely held views within temperance circles when he claimed that traditional Irish society had been temperate and that it had been the English conquest and its accompanying penal laws which had driven the Irish to drink. Gaelic sports, music and dancing, to say nothing of language classes, provided exactly the sort of sober, uplifting recreation that the temperance movement had been promoting for decades.

So Cullen succeeded where Mathew had failed: he established an enduring total abstinence movement allied to the two most powerful forces in Irish society, Catholicism and nationalism.

Conclusion

THIS study has charted the course of the Irish temperance movement during the nineteenth century and has shown that the movement went through a number of phases during which its aims, methods and supporters varied significantly. At different times the banner of temperance was carried by middle-class Protestants, by impoverished peasants, by fundamentalist Presbyterian clergy, by radical Quakers, by nationalist priests and by Gaelic revivalists. The aims of the movement also changed markedly: from merely moderating consumption to banning it totally. Methods too showed considerable variety. Some temperance advocates sought to persuade by sophisticated analysis and argument, some by an emotional popular crusade, others by coercive legislation, and yet others by an appeal to religious piety and devotion. Supporters expected numerous, though rather different, benefits from the restriction of alcohol consumption: to the middle class it offered the prospect of a docile and law-abiding lower class; to the poor it held out the chance of economic and social advancement; to the clergy, whether Catholic or Protestant, it seemed a means of promoting more restrained social behaviour and better religious observance; while to nationalists it promised to create a sober, disciplined and determined population bent on securing greater political independence. But, in the end, the question arises: how successful was this movement (in whatever form and with whatever means)? Did drink consumption and drunkenness decline?; and, if so, was the temperance movement to any degree responsible for this change? Underlying this question is the even more difficult issue of the level of drink consumption in nineteenth-century Ireland and how it is to be assessed. Did the Irish drink excessively during this period; or, in other words, is the almost universal stereotype of the drunken 'Paddy' an accurate one?

Even acknowledging the unsatisfactory nature of many of the statistics at our disposal, it is still possible to discern general trends in the pattern of drink consumption in Ireland during the nineteenth century. These trends can be summarised briefly as follows. With regard to spirits, the middle to late 1820s and the middle to late 1830s appear to have been periods of record consumption, with annual legal consumption reaching over 9 million gallons during the first period and over 12 million during the second. Other, though less dramatic, peaks were reached in the early 1850s and mid-1870s when annual consumption reached nearly 8 million gallons and over 6 million respectively. Contemporary informed opinion and the statistics for detections of illicit distilling suggest that the 1820s and 1830s were years in which the illegal industry was also booming, to the extent that it was probably at times even larger in terms of output than the legal industry. This means that the consumption peaks of the pre-famine period may be underestimated by anything up to 100 per cent. Consumption plummeted in the late 1830s and early 1840s and again in the late 1850s and early 1860s. It recovered somewhat in the early to middle 1870s, but then appears to have stagnated for the remainder of the century. Production, however, actually increased significantly during the last quarter of the century as Coffey's patent still came into widespread use, the system of bonding whiskey was improved and the export market expanded rapidly. So the Irish distilling industry was still able to prosper, despite a shrinking home market. (**234**, 297-300)

The pattern of spirit consumption cannot, however, be treated in isolation; it has to be interpreted in conjunction with changes in the pattern of beer consumption. The wine market was so small at this time that it can be disregarded for the present purposes. Brewing, after stagnating, if not declining, during the pre-famine period, began a slow but steady growth from the mid-1850s, so that by the end of the century annual production was nearly five times what it had been in 1850. The growth of Guinness's brewery was, however, much more spectacular: between 1850 and 1875 its sales increased a massive 600 per cent. One of the most interesting features of Guinness's expansion was that from the mid-1850s the Irish rural market became the most dynamic part of Guinness's business. From taking a 21 per cent share of business in 1855 it rose to 30 per cent in the early 1870s and reached 40 per cent by 1880. While overall rural beer consumption almost certainly did not grow as rapidly as that of Guinness's stout, as Professor Lee has demonstrated, nevertheless there was a significant increase from the 1850s. The greater prosperity of rural Ireland after the famine was an important factor promoting beer consumption; but the turn away from spirits due to the massive tax increases of the late 1850s was also important, as were better transportation and distribution facilities. Beer was thus becoming an increasingly popular drink in Ireland in the second half of the century, with Guinness taking the lead in penetrating the former bastions of spirit drinking in the countryside. (**225**, 201, 211; **219**, 184-6)

Efforts to assess changes in the level of alcohol consumption cannot ignore the dramatic fall in population that occurred in Ireland from the 1840s onwards. Perhaps the most useful statistic, though admittedly even it is not without problems, is a *per capita* consumption measure, as it allows population changes to be taken into account. Annual *per capita* spirit consumption fluctuated considerably between 1821 and 1861: from 0.49 gallons per head in 1821 it jumped to 1.12 gallons in 1831, fell back to 0.79 gallons in 1841, jumped again to 1.15 gallons in 1851, and declined substantially again to 0.72 gallons by 1861. Thereafter, until the end of the century, it hovered around 1.0 gallon per head per annum. The changes in *per capita* beer consumption, particularly after 1850, were rather more dramatic. In 1831 *per capita* annual consumption was 3.5 gallons; it declined to 2.3 gallons in 1841, recovered to 3.5 gallons again in 1851, and then began a marked rise to 6.6 gallons in 1861 and 10.8 gallons in 1871. The rise levelled off slightly in 1881 at 13.4 gallons, but then surged ahead to 19.8 gallons in 1891 and 26 gallons in 1901. On their own these figures are not very informative, but a sense of their significance can be gained if we compare them with figures for the United Kingdom and the United States during the same period and with twentieth-century consumption statistics. Taking the census years from 1821 to 1901, only twice, in 1831 and 1851, did Irish *per capita* spirit consumption exceed that prevailing in the United Kingdom as a whole. From 1861 onwards Irish consumption was consistently slightly below that for the United Kingdom. Given that Scotland rather than England was the other major spirit-consuming nation in the United Kingdom, these figures would suggest that Scottish consumption, certainly after 1850, was considerably in excess of Irish. The Irish figures for the pre-famine period are, of course, incomplete owing to the existence of a large illegal industry. As for the United States, a recent study of American drink consumption in the nineteenth century would suggest that *per capita* consumption of spirits was at least double that prevailing in Ireland up to 1860, and only in the 1890s did American consumption come down to approach Irish levels. As for beer consumption, Irish *per capita* figures were always exceeded, often two to four times, by figures from the United Kingdom as a whole, while Irish consumption generally exceeded that of the United States by a substantial amount. Generally these figures would suggest that after 1850 Irish spirit consumption was exceeded by that of Scotland and the United States and that perhaps even before 1850 the Americans drank more spirits per head than the Irish. Beer consumption in Ireland was well behind that prevailing in the United Kingdom as a whole, though it was significantly greater than American consumption. If we turn to more recent times, we find that in Ireland in 1975, during a period of rising alcohol consumption, *per capita* consumption of spirits was 0.42 gallons and of beer 19.1 gallons. In a list ranking consumption figures during the same year for twenty-nine Western countries Ireland came twentieth in spirit consumption, with Poland at the top consuming 0.88 gallons of spirits per head per annum, and tenth in beer consumption, with Czechoslovakia at the top consuming 33.6 gallons of beer per head per annum. These modern comparative figures suggest that spirit consumption in Ireland throughout the nine-teenth century was high, being generally in excess of the peak international level of the 1970s. Beer consumption, on the other hand, only reached current Irish levels in the 1880s, and even then was not unduly high by modern world standards. But Irish spirit consumption, while it was high by modern standards, was not in excess of comparable countries during the nineteenth century. (**343**, 331-9; **296**, 10-11; **109**, 112)

In considering the factors that brought about changes in alcohol con-sumption, economic forces are immediately obvious. The levels of excise duty, the size of grain harvests and general economic prosperity were all crucial. Thus, as K. H. Connell has shown in his lively essay on illicit dis-tillation, the expansion of the illegal industry between the 1780s and 1840s was largely a response to the high cost and poor quality of legal whiskey and a reflection of the desperate need in the countryside to supplement income in order to pay rents and tithes. Economic forces, this time in the shape of the famine, can also be seen as largely responsible for decimating the illicit market in the 1840s. (**112**, 1-50)

Legislation and policing obviously had a part to play in these changes as well. The abolition of the old inefficient revenue police and the transferring of its responsibilities to the Irish Constabulary in the late 1850s was an important factor further contributing to the decline in illicit distilling. But perhaps here a note of warning should be sounded regarding the statistics for arrests and prosecutions. J. J. Tobias in his study of nineteenth-century crime has demonstrated that arrest figures were very much a function of the zeal of the police rather than a measure of the actual level of crime. This argument is clearly applicable to Ireland in the case of drunkenness. For instance, arrests for drunkenness fell markedly in the middle to late 1860s and again in the early 1880s. Consumption was certainly down in the latter years as a result of economic difficulties, but in the former period it was on the rise. In both instances, however, the police were preoccupied with political crime. Arresting Fenians and Land Leaguers obviously took precedence over arresting drunkards. Police actions were also influenced by the nature of the laws that policemen were called upon to enforce. From the 1830s a large number of statutes were passed aimed at suppressing illegal trading and at regulating the legal industry. Trading hours were shortened, and efforts were made to ensure the good character of licence-holders. As we have seen, the provisions in some of these statutes created rather than solved problems, and the licensing laws remained complex and confusing. Nevertheless, on the whole the drink trade was brought under stricter supervision, and this undoubtedly contributed to the more law-abiding nature of the retail industry after 1850. The number of publicans' licences did not increase markedly during this period, varying from 15,000 to 17,500, though, owing to the fall in population, the number of persons per public house did fall considerably, from 463 in 1851 to 252 in

1901. The decline in illegal trading, combined with the reluctance of licensing authorities in many areas to grant new licences, had the effect of making publicans more prosperous and ultimately more respectable. Those unable to obtain a publican's licence usually opted to become spirit grocers, and these licences increased substantially in number, from 200 in 1860 to over 1,200 by 1900. Despite some criticism of the behaviour of spirit grocers, particularly in Dublin, by the end of the century the trade was generally wealthier, more respectable and more politically powerful than it had been in 1850. Traders were selling a more expensive drink to fewer customers and in more pleasant surroundings, for as publicans became more prosperous and customers became fewer so public houses were made more attractive and comfortable. (**324**, 14-21; **343**, 404-5)

Brian Harrison in his major study of the English temperance movement has listed a large number of factors which contributed to diminished alcohol consumption between the 1820s and 1870s. These include improved water supplies; the provision of cheaper alternative beverages, like tea, coffee and cordials; the establishment of cafés, restaurants, clubs and halls which competed with the facilities offered by the public house; the ending of job recruitment and wage payment in public houses; the increasing hostility to drink among doctors and their growing reluctance to prescribe it as medicine; the standardisation of holidays and regularising of working hours which limited drinking opportunities; the opposition of the churches to drinking at family and religious festivals; improvements in working-class housing; the restriction of opening hours; the imposition of fines for drunkenness; the decline in wakes and fairs and the growth of organised spectator sports; faster and more comfortable travel due to the railway, and the resulting decline in the numbers of inns. (**173**, 298-347)

Most of these changes would have had an impact on Ireland as well, though Harrison is thinking particularly in terms of urbanised and industrialised English society. Ireland, however, was still largely rural. Harrison refers to changes in traditional recreational habits as tending to diminish alcohol consumption, and this factor was of prime importance in rural Ireland. We have seen that the countryside was characterised by a circumstantial drinking pattern which had been remarked upon from at least the seventeenth century. From the late eighteenth century this pattern came under increasing attack from clergy, magistrates and land-lords. Even before the famine many patterns, wake-games, sports and fairs had been either totally suppressed or drastically reformed. Temperance advocates were active in this campaign, and both Father Mathew and Dr Spratt attacked the famous Donnybrook fair in Dublin, which was finally suppressed in the 1850s. Other temperance men concentrated on trying to promote sober and restrained alternative recreations. Father Mathew and Father Cullen encouraged bands and music, while James Haughton campaigned tirelessly to have parks, gardens and museums opened to working people, particularly on Sunday. The growing popularity of English spectator sports like rugby, soccer and cricket in the second half of the century caused concern among Gaelic revivalists and contributed to the formation of the Gaelic Athletic Association in 1884. Under Archbishop Croke's leadership it sought to separate drink from sport by banning alcohol from meetings. In rural Ireland therefore opportunities for heavy recreational drinking were diminished. Fewer marriages and an older population, which characterised post-famine society, meant less courting or marriage bargaining and fewer weddings. New sober devotions replaced the old drunken festivities associated with saints' days and holydays. Although the Catholic church may have remained suspicious of total abstinence, it was nevertheless to the fore in efforts to curb drunken and riotous behaviour at weddings, wakes, patterns, dances and sports. By the end of the century the prolonged drinking, extending over several days, which had once characterised festivals and fairs was very much a thing of the past. (**243**)

Economic, legal, social and recreational changes had a significant impact on drink consumption, all tending in the direction of diminishing it. But before returning to our initial question concerning the role of the temperance movement, there are rather less tangible explanations of changes in drink consumption put forward by sociologists and psychologists which might reward examination. It has been common to portray heavy drinking as something that people are driven to by despair and as a means of escape from intolerable socio-economic circumstances. Nationalist temperance advocates from Thomas Davis to Father James Cullen expressed this view regarding Ireland, and more recently Donald Horton's classic 1943 study of seventy-seven traditional societies suggested that drunkenness was highly correlated with the general anxiety level of the population. This interpretation, however, begs many questions: how can anxiety levels be accurately measured?; what causes such anxiety?; and, perhaps most importantly, does alcohol consumption really relieve anxiety? Subsequent studies have been rather inconclusive, some appearing to confirm and some to contradict Horton's findings. In 1961 Peter Field noted that most of the societies Horton identified as high-consumption ones had suffered social disintegration after contact with Western culture. He went on to argue that social instability caused anxiety, which was relieved in turn by drinking. Other, more recent, studies have interpreted drinking patterns in terms of changing power relationships between groups and classes within society: put simply, drinking can lead to a sense of power, particularly for weak or threatened groups. (**296**, 241-5; **302**, 78-100)

With regard to Ireland, it is tempting to interpret the exceptionally high consumption figures of the 1820s and 1830s as a function of the growing economic crisis and to argue that the impoverished peasants of the pre-famine era drowned their sorrows in drink. This is certainly the view that Thomas Davis expressed at the time:

> [The Irishman] drank nothing for some 350 days in the year; but once or maybe oftener in the month, he got roaring drunk. This occasional debauch was the Lethe-moment of all his sorrows. He then forgot all his wrongs. His cabin was warm, his belly full, his back covered — for an afternoon; but he woke in the morning penniless, broken-headed, guilty, conscience-sore.... Still the very greatness of his suffering was his excuse — his natural excuse for making it greater, in order to achieve liberty and luxury for an hour by the magic of intoxication.[1]

While not denying that there is validity in Davis's picture, the truth is that the increase in spirit consumption during the pre-famine period can be quite adequately explained solely in terms of economic and social factors: the development of illicit distilling as a cottage industry after the misguided reforms of 1780; the abolition of the still-licence system in 1823 which boosted the legal industry; the popular taste for cheap whiskey and the lack of alternative beverages; the involvement of drink with numerous social practices and customs. Moreover, what Davis is describing is the circumstantial drinking pattern which had characterised Irish rural society for centuries and was not merely the product of the pre-famine crisis. If we look only at economic stresses, then in fact the evidence would appear to contradict the anxiety thesis, suggesting that people drank less during times of depression and more during times of prosperity. This is clear in the post-famine period, when Irish spirit consumption rose in the late 1860s and early 1870s and fell in the early 1880s. A similar conclusion has been reached in recent studies of late nineteenth-century England and France by A. E. Dingle and Michael Marrus in which a positive correlation between wages and drink consumption was observed. This same pattern is discernible even in the pre-famine period, though the existence of a huge, if largely unquantifiable, illegal industry makes it difficult to arrive at definite conclusions. However, apparent falls in the levels of consumption in the early 1820s, early 1830s and late 1840s all coincided with economic difficulties and famines. Obviously some degree of prosperity beyond basic subsistence level was essential in order to sustain a fairly high level of alcohol consumption. In other words, alcohol consumption, like the consumption of tea, coffee or tobacco, can be seen as a measure of affluence rather than as a sign of economic crisis. While there is doubtless truth in the anxiety thesis, few if any scholars these days would regard it as a complete explanation of heavy drinking, and the Irish example would certainly support this scepticism. (**137**; **245**)

As for the power relations hypothesis, the Irish situation provides some evidence to confirm it, but again suggests that at best it can only be a partial explanation. The decline in drinking among the upper and middle classes, noted by visitors from about the 1780s, and the support among these same classes for temperance can be viewed as an effort on the part of the Portestant ascendancy to bolster their status during troubled times by proving their moral superiority to their economic inferiors. By labelling the masses as drunkards — or rebels or papists for that matter — the ascendancy both defined itself and justified its dominance. This approach is clear in the anti-spirits movement, though with the advent of teetotalism the ascendancy were faced with millions of Irish people claiming the right to advancement through sobriety. No wonder it was necessary to discredit Father Mathew's crusade by portraying it as a front for Repeal or even Ribbonism. Temperance, through economic betterment and greater respectability, offered power to its followers. But it is less clear in this context how power could be seen as deriving from heavy drinking, as the power relations hypothesis would suggest. This might be so in a society that condoned heavy drinking, which seems to have been the case in eighteenth-century Ireland, but as a more censorious attitude to heavy drinking developed after 1800 so drinkers became less acceptable and more marginal figures.

It would appear that patterns of drink consumption are determined by a complex interplay of forces, with the state of the economy, licensing laws, government policy regarding the drink industry, popular attitudes to drunkenness and the prevailing definition of respectable behaviour all being significant factors. What role, then, did the temperance movement play in this rather confusing drama?

There seems little evidence that the anti-spirits movement of the 1830s had any noticeable impact on drink consumption, and in fact consumption of spirits reached record levels in the middle to late 1830s. The anti-spirits movement did, however, mark the beginning of reasonably well-organised temperance societies and of the production of a carefully argued anti-drink literature. Many of the medical, religious and economic arguments against drink had been aired in the previous century by people like William Henry, but on nothing like the scale of the pamphlets and periodicals produced in the early 1830s. That these publications had an impact in Dublin Quaker and medical circles and among Ulster Protestants is clear. But this impact was obviously a sectional one, for the anti-spirits movement, being largely Protestant, middle-class and conservative, had little to offer the mass of the people.

Only with the coming of Father Mathew's crusade after 1838 is it possible to detect a significant impact on drink consumption itself. While economic factors, such as excise duty and grain prices, had some influence on the dramatic falls in consumption that occurred around 1840, there seems little doubt that the teetotal crusade was the major factor involved. It has been commonly assumed, however, that the effects of Father Mathew's crusade were temporary and that it had virtually no lasting significance.

The crusade certainly declined rapidly and was on the wane even before the famine. But it is striking to see how many later temperance sympathisers admitted to having taken the pledge from Father Mathew or at least to having been influenced by his teaching. Dr John Forbes's tour of the country in the early 1850s showed that remnants of the movement did survive and provided the basis for co-operative societies, if not for new ventures in the field of temperance. Both Bishop Furlong and Archbishop Leahy in attempting to rekindle a Catholic temperance movement in the late 1850s were directly influenced by Father Mathew, and they in turn inspired Archbishop Croke, Cardinal Manning and Father James Cullen. How many of the millions who took the pledge from Father Mathew actually kept it or at least moderated their drinking? It is simply impossible to say. Yet it stands to reason that even if only a tiny fraction remained faithful, this would have amounted to a substantial minority of abstainers in the population. It is interesting to note that among Fenian leaders, although the movement had no coherent temperance policy, there were a number of teetotallers who as boys or young men had taken the pledge from Father Mathew. Figures as diverse as John Denvir, Charles Kickham and Jeremiah O'Donovan Rossa were total abstainers for some, if not all, of their lives. Apart from the actual numbers who kept their pledge, Father Mathew's crusade had more subtle long-lasting effects. Although the Catholic church may have been deeply suspicious of the crusade, Father Mathew nevertheless established in the popular mind a connection between teetotalism and Catholicism. Temperance could no longer be identified solely with English or Irish Protestants and seen as merely a cloak for proselytism. Father Mathew had made temperance fully Irish and fully Catholic, while O'Connell and the Young Irelanders, by linking temperance with Repeal, had shown that the anti-drink movement was not necessarily inconsistent with nationalism. Although later Catholic teetotallers may have been severe in their condemnation of Father Mathew's shortcomings, he had in fact provided them with a basis from which to work by rescuing temperance from the domination of Protestant Unionists. (**244**, 84-90)

While Father Mathew's crusade was the most dramatic manifestation of temperance in Ireland and probably had the most marked impact on drink consumption, the societies that flourished after 1850 were not without importance. Perhaps their most notable successes before 1900 were among Ulster Protestants. Spurred by the Evangelical revival of the 1850s and the parliamentary advances of the 1870s, the Presbyterian, Methodist and smaller Protestant churches all spoke out strongly against drunkenness and in most cases in favour of total abstinence. By the end of the century a significant percentage of Ulster's Protestant population were teetotallers; Protestants had largely abandoned the retail drink trade, though they remained prominent in the brewing and distilling industries. The Church of Ireland did not go quite as far in championing teetotalism as the other Protestant churches, but it produced an active temperance society in the 1870s, and its hierarchy supported the campaign for reforming the licensing laws. In the Catholic church, however, it was not until after the turn of the century with the dramatic growth of the Pioneer Total Abstinence Association that another major teetotal surge was apparent. By 1914 the Pioneers were claiming over a quarter of a million members out of a total Catholic population of less than three and a half million. But again, as with Father Mathew's crusade, it was not just in recruiting members that the temperance societies had an impact on drink consumption. Temperance men were often the driving force in efforts to tighten licensing laws and ensure greater police vigilance; they campaigned against traditional recreations and in favour of opening parks, museums and libraries; some supported the Gaelic Athletic Association and efforts to revive Gaelic culture; temperance advocates were to be found lobbying magistrates to restrict retail licences and to penalise offending publicans; they were active in campaigns to improve working-class housing and supported bodies like the Dublin Artisans' Dwelling Company; temperance societies established cafés, coffee stalls, drinking fountains, hotels and working men's institutes; they publicised the evils of drink among doctors, lawyers, magistrates, clergy, businessmen and M.P.s. Temperance was at the heart of a much wider late nineteenth-century movement for social amelioration. It is impossible to measure exactly how influential all these activities were, but after 1850 they certainly contributed to a more censorious attitude towards drunkenness, to the restriction of opportunities for heavy drinking, and to the increase in facilities for sober recreation and entertainment.

While admitting the shortcomings of the temperance movement (the sectional nature of the anti-spirits societies, the swift decline of Father Mathew's crusade, the failure to secure major temperance legislation after 1878, and the Catholic church's hostility to teetotalism), the fact remains that in the nineteenth and early twentieth centuries Irish people, both Catholic and Protestant, subscribed to teetotalism in remarkably large numbers. In fact, in terms of the proportion of the population joining, the temperance movement had a far greater impact on Ireland than on either the United States or Britain. Nor was this to prove a temporary phenomenon. A study published in 1976 of drinking habits among adult males in Co. Monaghan found that 25.5 per cent of the sample were total abstainers; among Protestants the figure was as high as 31 per cent. Another survey carried out in 1978, this time of Northern Ireland, found that 34 per cent of the population — 20 per cent of males and 46 per cent of females — were total abstainers. These are remarkably high percentages for a Western country: in Britain the comparable figure is 9 per cent and in Australia about 12 per cent. While we may not know the numbers of teetotallers in 1850 or in 1900, the existence of such a large number during the 1970s — a period of high alcohol consumption and low temperance activity — points to a strong and continuing influence among both Catholics and Protestants of temperance ideologies originating in the nineteenth century. (**279**; **130**, 244)

The popular successes of teetotalism in Ireland since the 1830s need to be kept in mind when considering the reputation that the Irish have gained as a heavy-drinking people. Although nationalist claims that Irish drinking was deliberately encouraged by the British in order to demoralise the population are an exaggeration, nevertheless the Irish reputation for drunkenness has certainly been publicised by English observers, from seventeenth-century soldiers to nineteenth-century caricaturists and the twentieth-century popular press. Like most colonial peoples, the Irish have had to suffer not just conquest and foreign rule but also the denigration made essential by the need to justify conquest and foreign rule. So, in English eyes, the Irish became violent, cruel and drunken to a degree that was scarcely human. While it is easy to detect and dismiss the excesses of this stereotype, it still remains remarkably persistent. In academic circles the Irish reputation for drunkenness has apparently been confirmed by the work of a number of American sociologists. Robert Bales in the 1940s and Richard Stivers in the 1970s both examined the high incidence of alcoholism among Irish immigrants in the United States and sought explanations for this phenomenon in post-famine Irish society. Such studies have, however, approached Ireland with the unspoken assumption that the heavy drinking characteristic of a struggling immigrant community is also characteristic of the home country. A recent article along these lines, though dealing with the pre-famine period, is entitled 'Why Paddy Drank'. The assumption is that 'Paddy' did drink excessively (though this is in no way proved) and that it is merely a matter of uncovering the reasons for this. But a more valid approach would be to set aside the immigrant experience and ask 'Did Paddy Drink?': in other words, to find out if alcohol consumption in nineteenth-century Ireland was really unusually high, and only then to set about seeking explanations. A comparison of consumption statistics would suggest that Irish spirit drinking, while high by modern standards, was not in fact unusual by nineteenth-century standards — Americans at the time drank much more heavily. The dangers of drawing wide-ranging conclusions from an immigrant group experience are well illustrated in Joyce O'Connor's study, published in 1978, of drinking patterns among Irish immigrants in England. She took three sample groups: one Irish, one English, and one immigrant Irish. Of her sample of Irish males, 13.1 per cent were abstainers and 34.7 per cent were classed as very heavy drinkers. But among Irish immigrants the figures for these categories were 1.1 per cent and 57.0 per cent respectively, suggesting that immigrants were far heavier drinkers than the Irish at home. Interestingly, for her English sample the figures were 2.5 per cent abstainers and 43 per cent very heavy drinkers. So the Irish at home were much more likely to be abstainers and less likely to be very heavy drinkers than either the English or Irish immigrants. Among women the picture was even more clear-cut, with 25.6 per cent of the Irish being abstainers and only 2.6 per cent very heavy drinkers, compared with 5.9 per cent abstainers and 9.3 per cent very heavy drinkers among Irish immigrants. Clearly no judgements about Irish drinking habits in Ireland can be drawn from studies of Irish drinking habits in England or America. The immigrant community is significantly different in its social behaviour from the community left in the home country. (**57**; **318**; **62**; **265**, 81, 172)

The present study would suggest that the answer to the question 'Did Paddy Drink?' is a complex one, being both yes and no. In fact the question might most helpfully be worded 'Which Paddy Drank?' For during the last hundred years, and perhaps since Father Mathew's crusade of the 1830s and 1840s, a significant proportion, as high even as one-third, of the Irish population have been total abstainers. This is why some reservations were expressed about the use of a *per capita* measure of alcohol consumption, as such a large number of teetotallers would distort *per capita* figures, producing a marked underestimate. The truth seems to be that at certain times during the nineteenth century and among certain groups drink consumption was heavy, but that it would be a gross oversimplification to characterise the whole society during the whole century as a heavy-drinking one. On the contrary, nineteenth-century Ireland experienced several very influential temperance movements, and that influence remains apparent to this day. Large numbers of women, of northern Protestants and of devout Catholics were and are teetotallers. From the 1840s onwards Irish society seems to have become increasingly polarised as regards drink consumption. On one hand there was a growing number of teetotallers, while on the other beer consumption was increasing substantially and spirit consumption, though much lower than during the pre-famine period, was still high by modern standards. Certain groups in the society were obviously drinking heavily. Sociologists have pointed to the low marriage rate prevailing after the famine and to the growing sexual puritanism and have suggested that heavy drinking was most characteristic of middle-aged bachelor farmers and that the all-male drinking group offered an emotional substitute for marriage and family. Such an interpretation is speculative, being largely based on twentieth-century fieldwork. If it is unacceptable to project the immigrant experience onto the home country, it is equally unacceptable to project the twentieth-century experience back into the nineteenth century. The temperance movement did not single out bachelor farmers as the major drink consumers. It tended to direct its propaganda to tradesmen and labourers in the cities, to children and to women, though these groups may simply have

been easier to reach, particularly for urban-based societies, than a scattered rural population. The fact that corporations and trades councils from
the major towns lobbied successfully to have themselves exempted from
Sunday closing and that police and magistrates felt that Sunday closing
was impractical in these areas would suggest that urban drinkers were a
formidable group and certainly wielded more political power than rural
drinkers. Because some sociologists noted heavy drinking among
unmarried farmers in the 1930s, but did not examine urban drinking
patterns, we cannot conclude that farmers were the main drinking group in
the 1870s or 1880s. Contemporary comments suggested that rural drinking
was still irregular, being mainly confined to Sunday and special occasions,
while urban drinking was far more likely to occur daily. It would seem that
if farmers were drinking heavily, so were tradesmen and urban labourers.
(**318**, 75-100)

The temperance movement had important successes in Ireland, though
admittedly these successes were confined to sections of the population.
Much attention, both serious and frivolous, has been devoted to the heavy-
drinking Irishman, to the drunken 'Paddy', beloved of the popular press
and music hall. But the drunken 'Paddy' is only one side of the coin; the
other side is the teetotal 'Paddy'. The vast numbers of non-drinking
Irishmen and Irishwomen have been largely ignored. They and the successes of the temperance movement are hard to reconcile with the national
stereotype. But perhaps it is time to stop seeing men like John Edgar,
Theobald Mathew, James Haughton, T. W. Russell and James Cullen as
marginal and unrepresentative figures and to acknowledge their substantial contribution to contemporary Irish social mores.

Notes to Manuscript and Periodical Sources

The following abbreviations are used in the references.

A.N.	*Alliance News*
B.N.L.	*Belfast Newsletter*
B.T.A.	*Belfast Temperance Advocate*
C.E.	*Cork Examiner*
C.S.O., R.P.	Chief Secretary's Office, Registered Papers
C.T.	*Catholic Times*
D.D.A.	Dublin Diocesan Archives
D.E.M.	*Dublin Evening Mail*
D.E.P.	*Dublin Evening Post*
D.W.H.	*Dublin Weekly Herald*
F.J.	*Freeman's Journal*
I.C.	*Irish Catholic*
I.I.	*Irish Independent*
I.P.	*Irish Presbyterian*
I.T.	*Irish Times*
I.T.L.G.	*Irish Temperance and Literary Gazette*
I.T.L.J.	*Irish Temperance League Journal*
I.T.S.	*Irish Temperance Star*
L.R.	*Limerick Reporter*
N.L.I.	National Library of Ireland
P.R.O.N.I.	Public Record Office of Northern Ireland
S.M.P.	*Strabane Morning Post*
S.P.O.	State Paper Office of Ireland
S.R.	*Southern Reporter*
T.V.	*Temperance Visitor*

Chapter 1
Drink and Temperance in Ireland before 1830
(pp. 1-55)
1. Matthews to Downshire, 9 May 1796, 16 Jan. 1797 (P.R.O.N.I., Downshire Papers, D607/D/58, D607/E/35).

Chapter 2
Moderation *versus* Teetotalism
(pp. 56-100)
 1. *B.N.L.*, 14 Aug. 1829.
 2. *I.T.L.G.*, 12 Nov. 1836.
 3. *S.R.*, 23 Jan. 1841.
 4. *I.T.L.G.*, 12 Nov. 1836.
 5. *C.E.*, 4 Oct. 1841.
 6. *B.T.A.*, Feb. 1833, 129.
 7. *I.T.L.G.*, 13 May 1837, 18 Nov. 1837, 3 Mar. 1838.
 8. *B.T.A.*, Aug. 1833, 55, Feb. 1833, 129-30.
 9. *I.T.L.G.*, 10 Mar. 1838.
10. Ibid., 18 Feb. 1837.
11. Ibid., 19 Nov. 1836, 12 Nov. 1836.
12. *D.W.H.*, 4 Jan. 1840.
13. *I.T.L.G.*, 12 Nov. 1836, 8 Apr. 1837, 3 June 1837, 24 Feb. 1838, 31 Mar. 1838.
14. *D.E.P.*, 7 Dec. 1839; *S.M.P.*, 29 Mar. 1836, 28 June 1836; *I.T.L.G.*, 11 Nov. 1837, 28
     Apr. 1838, 14 July 1838.
15. *I.T.L.G.*, 12 Nov. 1836.
16. *S.M.P.*, 28 June 1836, 29 Mar. 1836, 5 July 1836.
17. *I.T.L.G.*, 31 Mar. 1838, 3 Feb. 1838, 22 July 1837.
18. Ibid., 7 Jan. 1837, 18 Feb. 1837, 16 Sept. 1837, 16 Dec. 1837, 20 Jan. 1838; *D.W.H.*, 17
     Nov. 1838, 1 Dec. 1838, 15 Dec. 1838.
19. *D.W.H.*, 22 Dec. 1838; *I.T.L.G.*, 25 Feb. 1837.
20. *D.W.H.*, 4 May 1839; *I.T.L.G.*, 13 Jan. 1838.
21. *I.T.L.G.*, 24 Feb. 1838, 12 May 1838, 23 June 1838, 9 June 1838; *D.W.H.*, 1 Dec. 1838.
22. *I.T.L.G.*, 5 May 1838.
23. *D.W.H.*, 4 May 1939, 12 Dec. 1838.
24. Ibid., 22 Jan. 1842.
25. Ibid, 16 Feb. 1839, 30 Mar. 1839, 12 Apr. 1839.
26. *I.T.L.G.*, 18 Mar. 1837, 9 Sept. 1837; *D.W.H.*, 24 Nov. 1838, 8 Dec. 1838.
27. *I.T.L.G.*, 1 Apr. 1837.
28. Ibid., 12 Nov. 1836, 19 Nov. 1836.
29. *D.W.H.*, 11 May 1839, 23 Mar. 1839.
30. Ibid., 23 Mar. 1839, 13 Feb. 1841; Mahony to Lord Lieutenant, 6 Feb. 1841 (S.P.O.,
     C.S.O., R.P., Outrage Papers, 1841/9/1429); Haughton to Eliot, 22 Oct. 1844 (ibid.,
     1844/014836).
31. *B.T.A.*, Apr. 1832, 12; *I.T.L.G.*, 12 Nov. 1836, 22 Sept. 1838, 31 Mar. 1838; *D.W.H.*, 11
     May 1839, 30 Mar. 1839.
32. *D.W.H.*, 23 Feb. 1839, 16 Feb. 1839, 30 Mar. 1839; *I.T.L.G.*, 3 Feb. 1838.

Chapter 3
'Mathew the Martyr'
(pp. 101-150)
 1. Information on the political careers of the Mathews was kindly provided by Dr Peter
     Jupp.
 2. *S.R.*, 4 Mar. 1841.
 3. *D.E.P.*, 19 Oct. 1839.
 4. Ibid.
 5. Typed extract from KcKenna's MS Histroy of the Temperance Crusade, 73 (Capuchin
     Friary, Church Street, Dublin, Mathew Papers, uncatalogued); *L.R.*, 12 Nov. 1839.
 6. McKenna MS, 76.
 7. *I.T.L.G.*, 21 July 1838, 8 Sept. 1838.

8. Ibid., 4 May 1839; *D.E.P.*, 24 Sept. 1839, 12 Oct. 1839, 19 Oct. 1839, 29 Oct. 1839, 5 Nov. 1839; *D.W.H.*, 21 Dec. 1839.

9. *D.E.P.*, 7 Nov. 1839; Report of Inquiry into the Progress of Temperance, Mar. 1840 (S.P.O., C.S.O., Misc. Papers, IA/76/3).

10. *D.E.P.*, 29 Oct. 1839, 7 Nov. 1839.

11. *D.W.H.*, 9 Feb. 1839; *D.E.P.*, 19 Oct. 1839.

12. *D.W.H.*, 4 May 1839, 28 Dec. 1839; *D.E.P.*, 28 Nov. 1839.

13. *D.W.H.*, 7 Dec. 1839; *C.E.*, 18 Oct. 1841.

14. *D.W.H.*, 21 Dec. 1839.

15. *D.E.P.*, 5 Dec. 1839, 12 Dec. 1839; *D.E.M.*, 24 Jan. 1840, 27 Mar. 1840; *Limerick Standard*, 19 Mar. 1840.

16. *D.W.H.*, 7 Dec. 1839.

17. Ibid., 21 Nov. 1840, 22 May 1841, 8 Feb. 1840, 12 Sept. 1840; *S.R.* 20 Feb. 1841.

18. Father Mathew Temperance Cards (N.L.I., Mathew Papers, MS 10731(17)).

19. *F.J.*, 30 Apr. 1842; *C.E.*, 31 Jan. 1842; *D.E.M.*, 9 Mar. 1840.

20. *D.W.H.*, 20 Nov. 1841.

21. *C.E.*, 4 Oct. 1841.

22. *S.R.*, 20 Feb. 1841.

23. *F.J.*, 15 Mar. 1842, 30 Mar. 1842.

24. Davys to Mathew, 12 Aug. 1840 (Capuchin Friary, Mathew Papers, Letters, 1:36).

25. *D.E.P.*, 9 Nov. 1839.

26. *F.J.*, 30 Apr. 1842; *D.W.H.*, 29 May 1841, 5 June 1841.

27. Parkinson to Mathew, 21 July 1840 (Capuchin Friary, Mathew Papers, Letters, 4:305).

28. Father Mathew Temperance Cards (N.L.I., Mathew Papers, MS 10731(17)).

29. Report of Inquiry into the Progress of Temperance, Mar. 1840 (S.P.O., C.S.O., Misc. Papers, 1A/76/3); Mathew to Bullen, n.d. (Capuchin Friary, Mathew Papers, Letters, 1:33).

30. *D.W.H.*, 14 Aug. 1841.

31. 3 & 4 Will, IV, c. 68; 6 & 7 Will. IV, c. 38; 2 & 3 Vict. c. 79.

32. *D.E.P.*, 10 Dec. 1839, 17 Dec. 1839.

33. *D.W.H.*, 20 Mar. 1841.

34. Mathew to Bullen, n.d. (Capuchin Friary, Mathew Papers, Letters, 1:33); *D.W.H.*, 22 May 1841, 8 Jan. 1842.

35. *D.W.H.*, 14 Aug. 1841; *Nation*, 28 Jan. 1843.

36. Report of Inquiry into the Progress of Temperance, Mar. 1840 (S.P.O., C.S.O., Misc. Papers, IA/76/3).

37. Cantillon to Ray, 30 May 1843 (N.L.I., O'Connell Papers, MS 13625).

38. *Nation*, 28 Jan. 1843.

39. *C.E.*, 25 Oct. 1841.

40. *D.E.M.*, 1 Apr. 1840, 11 Mar. 1842, 19 Oct. 1842; *C.E.*, 28 Mar. 1842.

41. *D.W.H.*, 20 Mar. 1841, 3 Aug. 1841, 19 Sept. 1840; Mathew to Chapman, 1 Apr. 1847 (N.L.I., Mathew Papers, MS 5055).

42. Alfred Webb, MS Autobiography, I, 58-9 (Friends' Library, Eustace Street, Dublin, Webb Papers, R.4, Sh.P., 33/Q).

43. *D.W.H.*, 8 Jan. 1840; *S.R.*, 4 Mar. 1841.

44. Burke to Mathew, 4 Sept. 1840 (Capuchin Friary, Mathew Papers, Letters, 2:196).

45. Haughton to Mathew, 26 Nov. 1845 (ibid., 4:331); Mathew to Haughton, n.d. (ibid., 17:1622).

46. *D.E.M.*, 5 Feb. 1840.

47. Mathew to Purcell, 23 Feb. 1844 (Capuchin Friary, Mathew Papers, Letters, 13:1247).

48. Browne to Mathew, 31 Aug. 1841 (ibid., 4:316).

49. Mathew to Kellehan, 3 Sept. 1847, 29 Sept. 1846 (ibid., 21:2008, 18:1709).

50. Mathew to Feeny, 25 Aug. 1846 (ibid., 22:2101).

51. Mathew to Magill, n.d. (ibid., 19:1893).
52. MS Notes by William Pike of Thomastown on Mathew Family, n.d. (ibid., uncatalogued).
53. Mathew to Dowden, n.d. (ibid., Letters, 12:1104); Mathew to Spratt, 8 Nov. 1844 (ibid., 19: 1889); Mathew to Duffy, n.d., (ibid, 18:1755); Mathew to Haughton, n.d. (ibid., 17:1602).
54. Mathew to Simpson, 10 Aug. 1846 (ibid., 12:1139).
55. Mathew to Hurley, n.d. (ibid., 12:1128).
56. Mathew to Lenihan, 8 July 1847 (ibid., 12:1169).

Chapter 4
Realignments: the 1850s and 1860s
(pp. 151-205)

1. *I.P.,* I (June 1853), 165, II (June 1854), 161.
2. Ibid., I (June 1853), 192-3.
3. *B.N.L.,* 5 July 1854, 29 Jan. 1856; *I.P.,* III (May 1855), 135.
4. *I.P.,* IV (Dec. 1856), 326.
5. *B.N.L.,* 26 July 1854.
6. Ibid., 15 July 1857.
7. *I.P.,* V (Sept. 1857), 246, IV (Dec. 1856), 326-8, V (July 1857), 179, V (Feb. 1857), 49.
8. Ibid., IV (Mar. 1856), 78, III (June 1855), 161.
9. *B.N.L.,* 18 June 1850.
10. Ibid., 26 Jan. 1856.
11. Ibid., 16 Mar. 1857, 18 July 1857; *I.P.,* V (Apr. 1857), 107.
12. *B.N.L.,* 1 July 1856, 21 Oct. 1858.
13. *I.T.L.J.,* IV, 5 (May 1866), 47-8, XXXIII, 10 (Oct. 1896), 147.
14. *B.N.L.,* 7 July 1859, 16 July 1859.
15. *I.T.L.J.,* IV, 10 (Oct. 1866), 107-9, I, 1 (Feb. 1863), 20.
16. Ibid., I, 8 (Sept. 1863), 143.
17. Ibid., I, 1 (Feb. 1863), 17.
18. Ibid., I, 2 (Mar. 1863), 36.
19. Minute Book of the Executive Committee of the I.T.L., 24 May 1872 (P.R.O.N.I., I.T.L. Papers, D2663/A1/1); *I.T.L.J.,* I, 3 (Apr. 1863), 58, I, 7 (Aug. 1863), 128-9.
20. *I.T.L.J.,* I, 7 (Aug. 1863), 128.
21. Ibid., I, 4 (May 1863), 78-9, I, 3 (Apr. 1863), 59, II, 10 (Oct. 1864), 176, III, 10 (Oct. 1865), 148.
22. Ibid., I, 3 (Apr. 1863), 59, I, 8 (Sept. 1863), 145, II, 10 (Oct. 1864), 176.
23. Ibid., III, 2 (Feb. 1865), 17-18, III, 3 (Mar. 1865), 34, III, 9 (Sept. 1865), 134.
24. *I.T.S.,* I, 10 (Oct. 1866), 145, 147-8; *I.T.L.J.,* III, 9 (Sept. 1865), 134.
25. *I.T.S.,* I, 11 (Nov. 1866), 166-7.
26. Ibid., I, 10 (Oct. 1866), 148, I, 11 (Nov. 1866), 168.
27. Ibid., I, 2 (Feb. 1866), 30-1, I, 12 (Dec. 1866), 186.
28. Ibid., I, 1 (Jan. 1866), 17, I, 12 (Dec. 1866), 186-7, I, 4 (Apr. 1866), 64, I, 6 (June 1866), 108.
29. *I.T.L.J.,* I, 1 (Feb. 1863), 18; *C.E.,* 17 Oct. 1856, 31 Dec. 1856, 14 Oct. 1857.
30. *I.T.S.,* I, 1 (Jan. 1866), 15, I, 3 (Mar. 1866), 48.
31. *F.J.,* 5 May 1875, 17 Sept. 1875.
32. *I.T.L.J.,* I, 6 (July 1863), 112, I, 9 (Oct. 1863), 160.
33. *F.J.,* 10 Dec. 1873.
34. Ibid., 14 Feb. 1882; Notebook of Father D. A. Mitchell, n.d. (Capuchin Friary, Church Street, Dublin, uncatalogued); *Hansard 3,* CCLXXXIX, 1599.
35. *F.J.,* 20 Mar. 1868; MacNally to priests of Clogher, 28 Oct. 1862 (P.R.O.N.I., Clogher

Diocesan Papers, DIO(RC) 1/10C/8); Furlong Pastoral Letters, 1865, 1867, 1871 (St Mary's Cathedral Archives, Sydney, Kelly Papers, uncatalogued).

36. *L.R.*, 24 Apr. 1863.
37. O'Kearney to Leahy, 20 Mar. 1868, 19 Apr. 1868 (N.L.I., Leahy Papers, Microfilm P6009, nos 30, 37).
38. Spratt to Under-Secretary, 20 Feb. 1841 (S.P.O., C.S.O., R.P., 1841/9/5701).
39. *A.N.*, 20 July 1867.
40. *F.J.*, 24 Nov. 1873; Cullen to Leahy, 7 Apr. 1869 (N.L.I., Leahy Papers, Microfilm P6009, no. 20).
41. *I.T.L.J.*, I, 6 (July 1863), 112.
42. Ibid., II, 10 (Oct. 1864), 158, 172-4, I, 7 (Aug. 1863), 127.
43. Ibid., III, 8 (Aug. 1865), 117-21, 128.
44. Ibid., V, 2 (Feb. 1867), 13-14; *F.J.*, 30 Nov. 1866, 20 Dec. 1866; *I.T.*, 20 Dec. 1866.
45. *I.T.L.J.*, V, 2 (Feb. 1867), 14, V, 3 (Mar. 1867), 26.
46. Ibid., V, 8 (Aug. 1867), 85-6, V, 12 (Dec. 1867), 134.
47. *F.J.*, 13 June 1867, 27 June 1867.
48. *I.T.L.J.*, V, 8 (Aug. 1867), 86; *Hansard 3*, CLXXXVII, 1645-8, CLXXXVII, 918-22.
49. *I.T.*, 25 May 1868.
50. *F.J.*, 10 Mar. 1868, 16 Mar. 1868, 26 May 1868; *I.T.L.J.*, VI, 8 (Aug. 1868), 113.
51. *Hansard 3*, CXCIV, 989-95, CXCVI, 1451-7.
52. *F.J.*, 11 Mar. 1869, 12 Mar. 1869, 10 June 1869; *I.T.*, 4 Mar. 1868.
53. *I.T.L.J.*, V, 8 (Aug. 1867), 86.
54. Ibid., VI, 12 (Dec. 1868), 196.
55. *F.J.*, 26 May 1869; *I.T.L.J.*, VII, 6 (June 1869), 81-2.

Chapter 5
Temperance in Parliament, 1870-1900
(pp. 206-275)
1. *F.J.*, 18 May 1878.
2. Return of Spirit Grocers in the D.M.P. District, 28 Feb. 1877 (S.P.O., C.S.O., R.P., 1878/3243).
3. *F.J.*, 6 Apr. 1876.
4. Return of Beerhouse Licences, Jan. 1877 (S.P.O., C.S.A., R.P., 1871/3070).
5. *F.J.*, 21 May 1872.
6. Licensing Laws: Case of the I.P.B.A. Deputation, 15 Nov. 1876; Statement of the Commissioner of Police in Reply, n.d. (S.P.O., C.S.O., R.P., 1878/3243).
7. Sunday Closing Resolutions, 1870, 1871 (ibid., 1870/4043, 1871/2229, 1871/7506, 1871/8773).
8. *F.J.*, 24 Nov. 1871, 3 Jan. 1872.
9. Ibid., 31 Jan. 1872.
10. Ibid., 11 Dec. 1871, 13 Jan. 1872, 15 Jan. 1872, 17 Jan. 1872.
11. *Hansard 3*, CCXII, 258; *Times*, 1 Apr. 1872; *F.J.*, 6 Mar. 1872, 16 Mar. 1872.
12. *F.J.*, 16 Mar. 1872, 22 Mar. 1872.
13. Ibid., 20 Apr. 1872.
14. Ibid., 20 June 1872.
15. Minute by Lake, 7 Sept. 1872 (S.P.O., C.S.O., R.P., 1874/9655); I.T.L. to Hartington, 3 Sept. 1872, Lake to Burke, 31 July 1873 (ibid., 1873/10450 (1914/13590); Dwyer to Hartington, 5 May 1873 (ibid., 1873/6572).
16. *Hansard 3*, CCXVII, 97-119; *F.J.*, 10 Dec. 1873.
17. *F.J.*, 24 Jan. 1874, 27 Jan. 1874; *I.T.*, 27 Jan. 1874, 29 Jan. 1874.
18. *F.J.*, 28 Jan. 1874, 6 Feb. 1874, 7 Feb. 1874, 9 Feb. 1874, 21 Feb. 1874.
19. Ibid., 5 Mar. 1874.

20. Minute Book of the Executive Committee of the I.T.L., 28 June 1872, 26 July 1872, 9 Aug. 1872, 8 Nov. 1872 (P.R.O.N.I., I.T.L. Papers, D2663/A1/1) (hereafter cited as I.T.L. Minute Book).

21. *I.T.L.J.*, XIII, 1 (Jan. 1874), 11.

22. I.T.L. Minute Book, 29 Jan. 1874, 2 Feb. 1874.

23. *I.T.L.J.*, XIII, 3 (Mar. 1874), 49-51, XIII, 4 (Apr. 1874), 56.

24. *Hansard 3*, CCXVIII, 1992-2020; *I.T.L.J.*, XIII, 6 (June 1874), 89-91.

25. *I.T.L.J.*, XIII, 7 (July 1874), 119, 105-7.

26. *F.J.*, 1 May 1875, 5 May 1875, 10 May 1875; *I.T.L.J.*, XIV, 6 (June 1875), 89.

27. *Hansard 3*, CCXXIV, 137-43; Lake to Burke, 21 May 1875 (S.P.O., C.S.O., R.P., 1876/6443).

28. *Hansard 3*, CCXXIV, 146-7, 150

29. *F.J.*, 6 May 1875, 13 May 1875.

30. *I.T.L.J.*, XIV, 7 (July 1875), 117, XIV, 6 (June 1875), 102-3.

31. Ibid, XV, 2 (Feb. 1876), 22 *F.J.*, 1 Feb. 1876, 2 Feb. 1876; *Hansard 3*, CCXXIX, 318-20; Lake to Burke, 15 Apr. 1876, Return of Number of Persons Entering Public Houses, 1 May 1876 (S.P.O., C.S.O., R.P. 1876/6443).

32. *Hansard 3*, CCXXIX, 496, 521-2, 526.

33. Ibid., 562, 564, 577.

34. *I.T.L.J.*, XV, 6 (June 1876), 90-2, 102; *Hansard 3*, CCXXXI, 426.

35. *I.T.L.J.*, XV, 7 (July 1876), 118; *F.J.*, 15 May 1876, 16 May 1876; *I.T.*, 13 May 1876, 15 May 1876, 16 May 1876.

36. *F.J.*, 17 May 1876, 19 May 1876.

37. *Hansard 3*, CCXXIX, 920-1, 1275, CCXXX, 1335-6, 1341-2; *I.T.L.J.*, XV, 8 (Aug. 1876), 121-3.

38. *Hansard 3*, CCXXXI, 330-65, 429-33, *F.J.*, 3 Aug. 1876; *I.T.*, 3 Aug. 1876; *I.T.L.J.*, XV, 8 (Aug. 1876), 123.

39. *Hansard 3*, CCXXXII, 194-6; Lake to Burke, 21 May 1875 (S.P.O., C.S.O., R.P., 1876/6443).

40. *I.T.L.J.*, XVI, 6 (June 1877), 99-100.

41. *Hansard 3*, CCXXXIV, 1949, 1769-77, CCXXXC, 322-82, 689-732, 1184, 1193.

42. Ibid., CCXXXV, 703-6; Sale of Intoxicating Liquors on Sunday (Ireland) Bill: Circular to Magistrates and Sub-Inspectors, June 1877 (S.P.O., C.S.O., R.P., 1877/9953).

43. *Hansard 3*, CCXXXVII, 277-302, 1692-1721.

44. *F.J.*, 4 Mar. 1878, 5 Mar. 1878, 29 Mar. 1878; *I.T.*, 4 Mar. 1878, *Hansard 3*, CCXXXVIII, 756-7.

45. *Hansard 3*, CCXXXIX, 339, 369-84, 392; *I.T.*, 15 May 1878.

46. *F.J.*, 3 Apr. 1878; *Times*, 3 Apr. 1878.

47. *Hansard 3*, CCXXXIX, 623-45; *F.J.*, 6 Apr. 1878.

48. *F.J.*, 20 May 1878; *Hansard 3*, CCXXXIX, 1819-29, 1842, 1853.

49. *F.J.*, 15 May 1878; *I.T.*, 15 May 1878.

50. *Hansard 3*, CCXL, 95-122, 821-2, 1024-5; *F.J.* 17 May 1878, 22 May 1878; I.T., 17 May 1878.

51. *Hansard 3*, CCXL, 1309; *F.J.*, 12 July 1878; *Daily Telegraph*, 15 July 1878.

52. *Hansard 3*, CCXLII, 1618, 1721-48.

53. *Times*, 25 Jan. 1879, 28 Jan. 1879, 4 Apr. 1879, 23 Apr. 1879; *Hansard 3*, CCXLV, 1434-79.

54. I.T.L. Minute Book, 5 Mar. 1886, 28 Oct. 1892.

55. Ibid., 10 May 1878; *I.T.L.J.*, XVII, 4 (Apr. 1880), 39-40.

56. I.T.L. Minute Book, 18 Mar. 1880, 23-27 Mar. 1880.

57. *I.T.L.J.*, XVII, 4 (Apr. 1880), 40; *Northern Whig*, 5 Apr. 1880.

58. *I.T.L.J.*, XVII, 12 (Dec. 1880), 140.

59. Ibid., XVII, 4 (Apr. 1880), 42, XVII, 6 (July 1880), 84; I.T.L. Minute Book, 25 June 1880.
60. *Hansard 3*, CCLXVII, 524-5.
61. Ibid., CCLXXII, 1483.
62. Reports of Resident Magistrates on Sunday Closing Act, Jan.-Mar. 1883 (S.P.O., C.S.O.,C.S.O., R.P., 1885/20644); *Hansard 3*, CCLXXVII, 520-2.
63. Reports of R.I.C. Inspectors on Drunkenness, Mar.-Apr. 1883 (S.P.O., C.S.O., R.P., 1885/29644); *Hansard 3*, CCLXXVIII, 1280-1379.
64. *Hansard 3*, CCLXXX, 228, CCLXXXI, 810, 826; Trevelyan to Richardson, 27 June 1883 (P.R.O.N.I., Richardson Papers, D1006/3/1/17); Spencer to Richardson, 15 July 1883 (ibid., D1006/3/1/19).
65. See, for example, Report of Captain Stokes, R.M., Blarney, Co. Cork, 1 Feb. 1883 (S.P.O., C.S.O., R.P., 1885/20644).
66. *Hansard 3*, CCLXXXIX, 1039-41, 1583-1604, 1513-14.
67. Ibid., 1021-2, 1031.
68. Ibid., 1032.
69. *F.J.*, 29 Sept. 1890.
70. *Hansard 3*, CCCIV, 694, CCCXXV, 1772-3; *I.T.L.J.*, XXV, 4 (Apr. 1888), 78.
71. *Hansard 3*, CCCXXV, 1786-7.
72. I.T.L. Minute Book, 29 May 1885; *Hansard 3*, CCXCVIII, 1450-1, 1470-8.
73. I.T.L. Minute Book, 11 Dec. 1885, 27 Nov. 1885, 14 Aug. 1885, 24 July 1885; *I.T.L.J.*, XXII, 8 (Aug. 1885), 180-2, XXII, 2 (Feb. 1885), 23.
74. *I.T.L.J.*, XXIII, 8 (Aug. 1886), 169, XXIII, 3 (Mar. 1886), 49.
75. *Hansard 3*, CCCXXI, 173-5, CCCXXIII, 1702-9, CCCXXIV, 911-15; *I.T.L.J.*, XXVII, 8 (Aug. 1890), 178.
76. *Hansard 3*, CCCXXV, 1794-5; *I.T.L.J.*, XXVII, 5 (May 1890), 104-5.
77. *Hansard 3*, CCCLIII, 585-640; *I.T.L.J.*, XXVIII, 5 (May 1891), 72-3.
78. *Hansard 4*, XII, 177-89, XIII, 741-52, 303-9, 536; *Times*, 16 Dec. 1892; *I.T.L.J.*, XXVIII, 5 (May 1891), 72.
79. *I.T.L.J.*, XXXIV, 6 (June 1897), 87; *Hansard 4*, CLVII, 1622-3, CLXII, 594; *I.I.*, 28 June 1906.

Chapter 6
Temperance and the Churches after 1870
(pp. 276-321)

1. *I.T.L.J.*, XIII, 1 (Jan. 1874), 7, XXVI, 7 (July 1889), 150.
2. *Bible Temperance Educator*, II, 3 (July 1882), 111-12, I, 2 (Mar. 1881), 50-8; *I.T.L.J.*, XIV, 7 (July 1875), 107.
3. *I.T.L.J.*, XIV, 7 (July 1875), 119.
4. I.T.L. Minute Book, 20 Aug. 1886.
5. A.N., 26 Nov. 1879; Album of W. R. Wigham, n.d. (Friends' Library, Wigham Papers, R.4, Sh.LD, p. 9, no. 87); *I.T.L.J.*, XXXIV, 12 (Dec. 1897), 17.
6. Notes on R. D. Webb by Alfred Webb, c. 1900 (Friends' Library, Webb Papers, R.4, P.5B/6-7); Webb MS Autobiography, I, 58-9, 70 (ibid., R.4, Sh.P., 33/Q).
7. Webb MS Autobiography, I, 27.
8. Ibid., II, 394-5, 375.
9. *T.V.*, XI, 3 (Mar. 1889), 38, XI, 7 (July 1889), 141.
10. Ibid., XIII, 8 (Aug. 1891), 120.
11. Ibid., XI, 8 (Aug. 1889), 113, XI, 2 (Feb. 1889), 17.
12. Ibid., XI, 1 (Jan. 1889), 4, XI, 3 (Mar. 1889), 36-7, XI, 10 (Oct. 1889), 145-6, XIII, 2 (Feb. 1891), 22.
13. Ibid., XIII, 3 (Mar. 1891), 34, XI, 9 (Sept. 1889), 141, 130, XI, 6 (June 1889), 81.

14. Ibid., XI, 4)Apr. 1889), 49, XIV, 3 (Mar. 1982), 44-5? C.I.T.S. General Council Minute Book, 1896-1904 (Representative Church Body Library, Braemor Park, Dublin, uncatalogued).
15. *A.N.*, 17 Oct. 1868; *C.T.*, 18 Sept. 1885.
16. *F.J.*, 22 June 1902.
17. Ibid., 11 Nov. 1889, 13 Mar. 1890; *C.T.*, 22 Nov. 1889.
18. Manning to Walsh, 12 Nov. 1889, 14 Mar. 1890, 17 Mar. 1890 (D. D. A., Walsh Papers, 404/2/12A, 404/4/40A, 404/4/44A).
19. Kelly to Pettit, 26 Nov. 1889 (ibid., 404/2/15); Croke to Walsh, 17 July 1889, 11 Mar. 1890 (ibid., 404/2/16, 404/4/35); *F.J.*, 17 Feb. 1890, 9 Oct. 1890.
20. *I.C.*, 2 Feb. 1890; Croke to Walsh, 3 Feb. 1890 (D.D.A., Walsh Papers, 404/4/1); *Times*, 10 Oct. 1890, 11 Oct, 1890; *F.J.*, 9 Oct. 1890, 10 Oct. 1890, 11 Oct. 1890.
21. *F.J.*, 26 Jan. 1891.
22. *Father Mathew Record*, VI 7 (July 1911), 178-9.
23. *League of the Cross Magazine*, II, 2 (Feb. 1885), 143.
24. *I.C.*, 31 Jan. 1914, 9 Dec. 1905, 7 Feb. 1914.
25. Ibid., 4 Dec. 1909, 7 Feb. 1914, 10 Dec. 1904, 24 Nov. 1906, 14 Feb. 1914.
26. Ibid., 10 Jan. 1913, 9 Dec. 1905; *I.I.*, 20 Oct. 1906.

Conclusion
(pp. 322-334)
1. *Nation*, 28 Jan. 1843.

Bibliography

1. MANUSCRIPT SOURCES

BELFAST
Public Record Office of Northern Ireland
   Clogher Diocesan Papers
   Downshire Papers
   Irish Temperance League Papers
   Richardson Papers

DUBLIN
Capuchin Friary, Church Street
   Mathew Papers
Church of Ireland Library, Braemor Park
   Church of Ireland Temperance Society Papers
Dublin Diocesan Archives, Holy Cross College, Clonliffe
   Walsh Papers
National Library of Ireland
   Leahy Papers (microfilm)
   Mathew Papers
   O'Connell Papers
Friends' Library, Eustace Street
   Webb Papers
   Wigham Papers
State Paper Office, Dublin Castle
   Chief Secretary's Office, Registered Papers

SYDNEY
St Mary's Cathedral Archives
   Kelly Papers

2. NEWSPAPERS AND PERIODICALS

Alliance News (Manchester)
Belfast Newsletter
Belfast Temperance Advocate
Bible Temperance Educator (Belfast)
Catholic Times (Liverpool)
Cork Examiner
Daily Telegraph (London)

Dublin Evening Mail
Dublin Evening Post
Dublin Weekly Herald
Father Mathew Record (Dublin)
Freeman's Journal (Dublin)
Good Templar (Belfast)
Hansard (London)
Irish Catholic (Dublin)
Irish Independent (Dublin)
Irish Messenger of the Sacred Heart (Dublin)
Irish People (Dublin)
Irish Presbyterian (Belfast)
Irish Temperance League Journal (Belfast)
Irish Temperance and Literary Gazette (Dublin)
Irish Temperance Standard (Belfast)
Irish Temperance Star (Dublin)
Irish Times (Dublin)
League of the Cross Magazine (London)
Limerick Reporter
Limerick Standard
The Nation (Dublin)
Northern Whig (Belfast)
Southern Reporter (Cork)
Strabane Morning Post
Temperance Visitor (Dublin)
The Times (London)
Waterford Chronicle

3. OFFICIAL SOURCES

1 Morrin, James (ed.), *Calendar of Patent and Close Rolls of Chancery . . . 18th to 45th Queen Elizabeth*, II, Dublin 1862

2 *Calendar of State Papers Relating to Ireland, 1509-73* [hereafter *C.S.P.I.*], London, 1860.

3 *C.S.P.I., 1600,* London 1903

4 *C.S.P.I., 1601-3,* London 1912

5 *C.S.P.I., 1611-15,* London 1877

6 *C.S.P.I., 1615-25,* London 1880

7 *C.S.P.I., 1625-32,* London 1900

8 *C.S.P.I., 1633-47,* London 1901

9 *C.S.P.I., 1647-60,* London 1903

10 *C.S.P.I., 1660-62,* London 1905

11 *C.S.P.I., 1663-5,* London 1907

12 *C.S.P.I., 1666-9,* London 1908

13 *C.S.P.I., 1669-70,* London 1910

14 *Calendar of State Papers, Domestic Series, Nov. 1673-Feb. 1675* [hereaferr *C.S.P.D.*], London 1904

15 *C.S.P.D., Mar. 1675-Feb. 1676, London 1907*

16 *C.S.P.D., Jan.-June 1683,* London 1933.

17 *The Statutes at Large, Passed in the Parliaments Held in Ireland: from . . . 1310 to . . . 1786*, 13 vols, Dublin 1786

18 *The Journals of the House of Commons of the Kingdom of Ireland [1613-1800]*, 19 vols, Dublin 1796-1800

19 *The Parliamentary Register; or, History of the Proceedings and Debates of the House of Commons of Ireland* [*1781-97*], 17 vols, Dublin 1782-1801

20 *Report from the Committee on the Distilleries in Ireland* H.C. 1813 (269), VI

21 *An Account of All Wines Imported into Ireland in the Years 1816, 1817 and 1818* . . . H.C. 1819 (66), XVI

22 *Accounts Relating to Still Fines and Convictions for Illicit Distillation* H.C. 1819 (252), XV

23 *Fifth Report of the Commissioners of Inquiry into the Collection and Management of the Revenue Arising in Ireland; Distilleries* H.C. 1823 (405), VII

24 *Minutes of Evidence taken before the Select Committee of the House of Lords, Appointed to Inquire into the State of Ireland* H.L. 1825 (181), IX

25 *An Account of the Quantities of the Following Articles which have Paid the Duties . . . Similar Accounts of Spirits Made in Ireland and Scotland, since the Year 1820* H.C. 1829 (340), XV

26 *Report from the Select Committee on Inquiry into Drunkenness* H.C. 1834 (559), VIII

27 *Seventh Report of the Commissioners of Inquiry into the Excise Establishment . . . British Spirits: Pt I* H.C. 1834 (7), XXV

28 *Seventh Report of the Commissioners of Inquiry into the Excise Extablishment . . . British Spirits: Pt I* H.C. 1834 (7), XXV

29 *Seventh Report of the Commissioners of Inquiry into the Excsie Establishment . . . British Spirits: Pt II* H.C. 1835 (8), XXX

30 *Third Report from the Select Committee Appointed to Inquire into . . . Orange Lodges . . .* H.C. 1835 (476), XVI

31 *Return of . . . Spirits Distilled and Charged with Duty in Ireland . . . from 1800 to 1852 . . . and Number of Persons Prosecuted for Illicit Distillation . . .* H.C. 1852-3 (547), XCIX

32 *Report of the Select Committee . . . Appointed to Consider . . . Extending the Functions of the Constabulary in Ireland to the Suppression or Prevention of Illicit Distillation . . .* H.L. 1854 (53), X

33 *Report from the Select Committee on the Sale of Liquors on Sunday (Ireland) Bill* H.C. 1867-8 (280), XIV

34 *Report of the Commissioners of Inland Revenue on the Duties under their Management . . . 1856 to 1869 . . . Vol. II* H.C. 1870 [C 82-I], XX

35 Historical Manuscripts Commission *Second Report of the Royal Commission on Historical Manuscripts* [C 441], London 1874

36 *Report from the Select Committee on Sale of Intoxicating Liquors on Sunday (Ireland) Bill* H.C. 1877 (198), XVI

37 *Fourth Report . . . from the Select Committee of the House of Lords on Intemperance* H.L. 1878 (338), XIV

38 Historical Manuscripts Commission, *Tenth Report, Appendix, Pt V: The Manuscripts of the Marquis of Ormonde, the Earl of Fingall, the Corporations of Waterford, Galway, etc.* [C 4576-I], London, 1885

39 *Report from the Select Committee on Sunday Closing Acts (Ireland)* H.C. 1888 (255), XIX

40 *Royal Commission on Liquor Licensing Laws . . . Vol. VII* [*Ireland*] H.C. 1898 [C 8980], XXXVII

41 Historical Manuscripts Commission, *Report on the Manuscripts of the Earl of Egmont, Vol. I, Pt II* [Cd 2318], London 1905

4. BOOKS, ARTICLES, PAMPHLETS, REPORTS, THESES

42 *Agricola's Letters to the Right Hon. the Chancellor of the Exchequer, Demonstrating the Pernicious Effects of the Cheapness of SPirituous Liquors . . .*, Dublin 1791

43 Ainsworth, John (ed.), *The Inchiquin Manuscripts*, Dublin 1961

44 Akenson, D. H., *The Church of Ireland: Ecclesiastical Reform and Revolution, 1800-85*, New Haven, Conn./London 1971

45 d'Alton, Ian, *Protestant Society and Politics in Cork 1812-44*, Cork 1980

46 Anon., *An Accurate Report of the Proceedings of the Very Rev. Theobald Mathew, in Dublin, in the Cause op Temperance . . .*, Dublin 1840

47 Anon., *The Complete Brewer, or, The Art and Mystery of Brewing Explained . . . by a Brewer of Extensive Practice*, Dublin 1766

48 Anon., *The Importance of Sobriety, Illustrated by the Evils of Intemperance, in Extracts from Several Authors*, Dublin 1818

49 Anon., *Local Option at Bessbrook, the Temperance Colony in Ireland*, London 1884

50 Anon., *Observations on the Brewing Trade of Ireland, Submitted to the Public, by an Officer of the Revenue*, Dublin [1778]

51 Anon., *Report of the Total Temperance Society, Founded at Mount Sion, in the City of Waterford . . . by the Right Rev. Dr Nicholas Foran*, Cork 1840

52 Anon., *Thoughts on the Present State of the Cottiers and Day Labourers of this Kingdom . . .*, Dublin, 1794

53 Armstrong, John, *The Art of Preserving Health: A Poem*, Dublin 1744

54 Association for Stopping the Sale of Intoxicating Liquors on Sunday in Ireland, *Annual Reports, 1873-8*, Dublin 1874-8

55 [Association for Stopping the Sale of Intoxicating Liquors on Sunday in Ireland], *Report of the National Conference for Closing Public Houses on Sundays, Held in Dublin, 9 December 1873*, Dublin 1874

56 Augustine, Fr, *Footprints of Father Mathew, O.F.M.Cap., Apostle of Temperance*, Dublin 1947

57 Bales, Robert F., *'Attitudes towards Drinking in the Irish Culture'* in D. J. Pittman and C. R. Snyder (ed), *Society Culture and Drinking Patterns*, New York/London 1962, 157-87.

58 Bardon, Jonathan, *Belfast: An Illustrated History*, Belfast 1982

59 Barker, Michael, *Gladstone and Radicalism*, Hassocks 1975

60 Barkley, J. M., *St Enoch's Congregation, 1872-1972*, Belfast 1972

61 Barnard, T. C., *Cromwellian Ireland*, London 1975

62 Barrett, James R., 'Why Paddy Drank: The Social Importance of Whiskey in Pre-Famine Ireland', *Journal of Popular Culture*, XI, 1 (Summer 1977), 155-66

63 Barrington, Jonah, *Personal Sketches of His Own Times*, 3rd ed., 2 vols, London 1869

64 Beames, M. R., 'The Ribbon Societies: Lower-Class Nationalism in Pre-Famine Ireland', *Past and Present*, 97 (Nov. 1982), 128-43

65 Beddoes, Thomas, *Hints to Husbandmen*, new ed., Dublin 1813

66 *Belfast Directories*, 1835-6, 1840-41, 1846-7, 1856

67 [Berkeley, George], *The Querist*, 3 pts, Dublin 1735-7

68 Berman, David, 'Bishop Berkeley and the fountains of living waters', *Hermathena*, 128 (summer 1980), 21-31

69 Birmingham, James, *A Memoir of the Very Rev. Theobald Mathew*, 2nd ed., Dublin 1840

70 Blake, Robert, *Disraeli*, London 1966

71 Bland, F. E., *How the Church Missionary Society Came to Ireland*, Dublin 1935

72 Bland, Joan, *Hibernian Crusade: The Story of the Catholic Total Abstinence Union of America*, Washington, D.C. 1951

73 Blaney, Roger, 'Alcoholism in Ireland: Medical and Social Aspects', *Journal of the Statistical and Social Inquiry Society of Ireland*, XXIII, 1 (1975), 108-24

74 Blaney, Roger, 'The Prevalence of Alcoholism in Northern Ireland,' *Ulster Medical Journal*, XXXVI (winter 1967), 33-43

75 Blaney, Roger and Mackenzie, Gilbert 'The Prevalence of Problem Drinking in Northern Ireland: A Population Study', *International Journal of Epidemiology*, IX, 2 (1980), 159-66

76 Bowen, Desmond, *Paul Cardinal Cullen and the Shaping of Modern Irish Catholicism*, Dublin 1983

77 Bowen, Desmond, *The Protestant Crusade in Ireland, 1800-70*, Dublin 1978

78 Boyd, Andrew, *Holy War in Belfast*, 2nd ed., Tralee 1969

79 Boyle, John, 'The Belfast Protestant Association and the Independent Orange Order, 1901-10', *Irish Historical Studies*, XIII, 50 (Sept. 1962), 117-52

80 Bretherton, George, 'The Irish Temperance Movement, 1829-47' (Ph.D. thesis, Columbia University, New York, 1978)

81 Brewer, J. S., and Bullen, William (ed.), *Calendar of the Carew Manuscripts*, 6 vols, London 1867-73

82 Budge, Ian, and O'Leary, Cornelius, *Belfast: Approach to Crisis. A Study of Belfast Politics, 1613-1970*, London 1973.

83 *Burke's Irish Family Records*, London 1976

84 Burke, Bernard, *A Genealogical History of the Dormant, Abeyant, Forfeited, and Extinct Peerages of the British Empire*, new ed., London 1866

85 Burns, Dawson, *Temperance History*, 2 vols, London [1889]

86 Burns, Dawson, *Temperance in the Victorian Age*, London 1897

87 Campbell, T. J., *Fifty Years of Ulster, 1890-1940*, Belfast 1941

88 Carr, Sir John, *The Stranger in Ireland*, London 1806

89 Carroll, W. G., *A Memoir of the Right Rev. James Thomas O'Brien, D.D., (Late Lord Bishop of Ossory, Ferns and Leighlin)* . . . , Dublin/London 1875

90 Caulfield, Richard (ed.), *The Council Book of the Corporation of Youghal, 1610-59, 1666-87, 1690-1800*, Guildford 1878

91 Chart, D. A. (ed.), *The Drennan Letters*, Belfast 1931

92 Cherrington, E. H. et al. (ed.), *Standard Encyclopedia of the Alcohol Problem*, 6 vols, Westerville, Ohio 1925-30

93 Cheyne, George, *A Treatise on Health and Long Life*, 10th ed., Mullingar 1787

94 [Cheyne, John], *A Letter from the Late Eminent Physician Dr Cheyne, of Dublin, to Dr Joshua Harvey* . . . , Ipswich Temperance Tract No. 311, London n.d.

95 [Cheyne, John], *A Letter on the Effects of Wine and Spirits, by a Physician*, H.T.S. Tract No. 1, Dublin 1829.

96 [Cheyne, John], *A Second Letter on the Effects of Wine and Spirits, by a Physician*, H.T.S. Tract No. 2, Dublin 1829

97 Chichester, Edward, *Oppressions and Cruelties of Irish Revenue Officers*, London 1818

98 [Church of Ireland], *Journal of the Session of the General Synod of the Church of Ireland*, Dublin 1876

99 Church of Ireland Temperance Society, *Annual Reports Presented to the Synod of the Church of Ireland, 1879-92, 1899, Nos 2-15, 23*, Dublin 1880-93, 1900

100 Church of Ireland Temperance Society, *Temperance Facts: Twelve Chapters on Temperance*, Dublin 1884

101 Church of Ireland Total Abstinence Association, *Annual Reports Presented to the Synod of the Church of Ireland, 1871-2, 1872-3, Nos 10, 11*, Dublin 1872, 1873

102 Clark, Samuel, 'The Social Composition of the Land League', *Irish Historical Studies*, XVII, 68 (Sept. 1971), 447-69

103 Clark, Samuel, *Social Origins of the Irish Land War*, Princeton, N.J. 1979

104 Clark, Samuel, 'The Political Mobilisation of Irish Farmers', *Canadian Review of Sociology and Anthropology*, XII, 4, 2 (1975), 483-99

105 Clarke, Aidan, *The Old English in Ireland, 1625-42*, London 1966

106 Coffey, Aeneas, *Observations on the Rev. Edward Chichester's Pamphlet, Entitled 'Oppressions and Cruelties of Irish Revenue Officers'*, London 1818

107 Coffey, Patrick 'A Modern Apostle: Fr James Cullen, S.J. (1841-1921)', *Irish Ecclesiastical Record*, 5th ser., XXIV, 3 (Sept. 1924), 233-42

108 Cole, R. L., *History of Methodism in Ireland: One Methodist Church*, IV, Belfast 1960

109 Commonwealth Department of Health, *Alcohol in Australia: A Summary of Related Statistics*, Canberra 1979

110 *The Complete Peerage*, VII, London 1929.

111 Conaty, Thomas J., *An Address to the Father Mathew, O.S.F.C., Total Abstinence League of the Sacred Thirst...*, Liverpool 1889

112 Connell, K. H., *Irish Peasant Society: Four Historical Essays*, Oxford 1968

113 Connell, K. H., *The Population of Ireland, 1750-1845*, Oxford 1950

114 Connolly, S. J., 'The "Blessed Turf": Cholera and Popular Panic in Ireland, June 1832', *Irish Historical Studies*, XXIII, 91 (May 1983), 214-32

115 Connolly. S. J., *Priests and People in Pre-Famine Ireland*, Dublin/New York 1982

116 Cooke, William, *The Principles of Total Abstinence Exhibited and Defended...in a Lecture*, Belfast 1838

117 Coombes, James, 'Europe's First Total Abstinence Society', *Journal of the Cork Historical and Archaeological Society*, LXXII, 215 (Jan.-June 1967), 52-7

118 Coombes, James, *Utopia in Glandore: James Redmond Barry and Willian Thompson, Socialist*, Butlerstown, Co. Cork 1970

119 Craig, E. T., *An Irish Commune: The History of Ralahine*, ed. Diarmuid Ó Cobhthaigh, Dublin n.d.

120 Cullen, James, 'The Apostleship of Prayer: Its Origins, Progress and Organisation', *Irish Ecclesiastical Record*, 3rd ser., XII, 10 (Oct. 1891), 928-33

121 Cullen, James, 'The Apostleship of Prayer: Various Works Included under the Apostleship of Prayer', *Irish Ecclesiastical Record*, 3rd ser., XIII, 2 (Feb. 1892), 131-8

122 Cullen, James, *Temperance Catechism*, Dublin 1891

123 Cullen, James, 'Total Abstinence League of the Sacred Heart', *Irish Ecclesiastical Record*, 4th ser., IX, 6 (June 1901), 498-509

124 Cullen, James, 'Two Great Spiritual Associations', *Irish Ecclesiastical Record*, 4th ser., III, 6 (June 1898), 513-25

125 Cullen, L. M., *Anglo-Irish Trade, 1660-1800*, Manchester 1968

126 Cullen, L. M., *An Economic History of Ireland since 1660*, London 1972

127 Cullen, L. M., 'Economic Trends, 1660-91' in T. W. Moody et al. (ed.), *A New History of Ireland, III: Early Modern Ireland, 1534-1691*, Oxford 1976, 387-407

128 Cullen, L. M., *The Emergence of Modern Ireland*, London 1981
d'Alton, *see* Alton

129 Daly, Mary E, *Dublin: the Deposed Capital: A Social and Economic History, 1860-1914*, Cork 1984

130 Davies, Phil, and Walsh, Dermot, *Alcohol Problems and Alcohol Control in Europe*, London/Canberra/New York 1983

131 Davis Richard, *Arthur Griffith and Non-Violent Sinn Féin*, Dublin 1974

132 Dawson, N. M., 'Illicit Distillation and the Revenue Police', *Irish Jurist*, XII, 2 (1977), 282-94

133 Denvir, John, *The Irish in Britain from the Earliest Times to the Fall and Death of Parnell*, London 1892

134 Denivr, John, *The Life Story of an Old Rebel*, ed. Leon Ó Broin, reprint, Shannon 1972

135 *Dictionary of National Biography*, 63 vols, London 1885-1900

136 Dingle, A. E., *The Campaign for Prohibition in Victorian England*, London 1980

137 Dingle, A. E., 'Drink and Working-Class Living Standards in Britain, 1870-1914', *Economic History Review*, 2nd ser., XXV, 4 (Nov. 1972), 608-22

138 Dingle, A. E., and Harrison, B. H., 'Cardinal Manning as Temperance Reformer', *Historical Journal*, XII, 3 (1969), 485-510

139 Dinneen, Patrick S., and O'Donoghue, Tadhg (ed.), *The Poems of Egan O'Rahilly*, 2nd ed., London 1911

140 Downes, George, *Darby and Paddy; in Two Dialogues...*, Dublin [1832]

141 Doyle, James, *Two Letters from the Right Rev. Doctor Doyle...on Temperance Societies*, Dublin [1830]

142 *The Dublin Almanac and General Register of Ireland*, 1840

143 *Dublin Directory*, 1832

144 Dublin Temperance Society, *Address of the D. T.S. to their Fellow-Citizens*, H.T.S. Tract No. 7, Dublin 1830

145 Dudley Edwards, Ruth, *Patrick Pearse: The Triumph of Failure*, London 1977

146 Dunlop, Robert, *Ireland under the Commonwealth*, 2 vols, Manchester 1913

147 Dunton, John, *The Dublin Scuffle: Being a Challenge Sent by John Dunton, Citizen of London, to Patrick Campbell, Bookseller in Dublin...*, London 1699

148 Edgar, John, *Temperance and Revival in Ulster*, 2nd ed., Belfast 1861

149 Edgeworth, Maria, *Castle Rackrent*, London 1800

150 [Edgeworth, Richard, and Edgeworth, Maria], *Memoirs of Richard Lovell Edgeworth, Esq., begun by himself and concluded by his daughter, Maria Edgeworth*, 2 vols, London 1820

151 Falkiner, C. Litton, *Illustrations of Irish History and Topography, Mainly of the Seventeenth Century*, London 1904

152 Fitzpatrick, W. J. (ed.), *Correspondence of Daniel O'Connell, the Liberator*, 2 vols, London 1888

153 Forbes, John, *Memorandums of a Tour in Ireland*, 2 vols, London 1853

154 Fothergill, Brian, *Nicholas Wiseman*, London 1963

155 G.B., 'On the Early Use of Aqua-Vitae in Ireland', *Ulster Journal of Archaeology*, VI (1858), 283-93

156 Garner, M. A. K., *Robert Workman of Newtownbreda, 1835-1921*, Belfast 1969

157 Garvin, Tom, 'Defenders, Ribbonmen and Others: Underground Political Networks in Pre-Famine Ireland', *Past and Present*, 96 (Aug. 1982), 133-55

158 Geoghegan, Michael, 'The Pledge in Practice — the Difficulties that Beset it — the Helps to Keep it', *Irish Ecclesiastical Record*, 3rd ser., XI, 3 (Mar. 1890), 207-19

159 Gibson, William, *The Year of Grace*, Jubilee ed., Edinburgh/London 1909

160 Gilley, Sheridan, 'Catholic Faith of the Irish Slums: London, 1840-70' in H. J. Dyos and Michael Wolff (ed.), *The Victorian City*, II, London/Boston 1973, 837-53

161 Girouard, Mark, *Life in the English Country House*, London 1979

162 Griffith, Arthur, *The Resurrection of Hungary: A Parellel for Ireland*, Dublin 1904

163 Hales, Stephen, *A New-Years-Gift to Dram-Drinkers...*, 2rrd ed., Dublin 1762

164 Hall, S. C., and Hall, A. M., *Ireland, Its Scenery, Character, &c.*, 3 vols, London 1841-3

165 Halpin, James, 'The League of the Cross', *Irish Ecclesiastical Record*, 3rd ser., IX, 12 (Dec. 1888), 1113-22

166 Hamer, D. A., *Liberal Politics in the Age of Gladstone and Rosebery*, Oxford 1972

167 Hamer, D. A., *The Politics of Electoral Pressure: A Study in the History of Victorian Reform Agitations*, Hassocks 1977

168 Hanham, H. J., *Elections and Party Management: Politics in the Time of Disraeli and Gladstone*, repr., Hassocks 1978

169 Hanly, John (ed.), *The Letters of Saint Oliver Plunkett, 1625-81, Archbishop of Armagh and Primate of All Ireland*, Dublin 1979

170 Harbinson, J. F., *The Ulster Unionist Party, 1882-1973*, Belfast 1973

171 Harpur, Singleton, *A Sermon Against the Excessive Use of Spirituous Liquors...*, 2nd ed., Dublin 1788

172 Harrison, Brian, *Dictionary of Temperance Biography*, Coventry 1973

173 Harrison, Brian, *Drink and the Victorians: The Temperance Question in England, 1815-72*, London 1971

174 Harrison, Brian, 'Teetotal Chartism', *History*, LVIII, 193 (June 1973), 193-217

175 [Harvey, Joshua], *Political Evils of Intemperance... by J.H.*, H.T.S. Tract No. 4, Dublin 1829

176 [Harvey, Joshua], *Some Observations and Advice, Addressed to the Mechanic and Industrious Classes, on the Use of Ardent Spirits...*, Dublin 1830

177 Henry, William, *An Earnest Address to the People of Ireland, Against the Drinking of Spirituous Liquors*, Dublin 1753

178 Henry William, *A Letter to Arthur Gore, Esq.; Relating to the Present Abuse of Spirituous Liquors; and a Method to Remedy the Evil*, Dublin 1755

179 Hepburn, A. C., 'Belfast 1871-1911: Work, Class and Religion', *Irish Economic and Social History*, X (1983), 33-50

180 Hewitt, Esther (ed.), *Lord Shannon's Letters to his Son*, Belfast 1983

181 Hibernian Temperance Society, *Address of the H.T.S. to their Countrymen*, H.T.S. Tract No. 8, Dublin 1830

182 Hibernian Temperance Society, *Paper A: Sketch of the Rise and Progress of Temperance Societies*, Dublin 1830

183 Hibernian Temperance Society, *Paper D: Auxiliary Societies: Observations and Anecdotes Respecting Temperance*, Dublin 1830

184 Hibernian Temperance Society, *Proceedings of the First Annual Meeting Held at the Rotunda on the 7th of April, 1830*, Dublin 1830

185 Hicks Beach, Victoria, *Life of Sir Michael Hicks Beach (Earl of St Aldwyn)*, 2 vols, London 1932

186 Hobson, Bulmer, *Ireland Yesterday and Tomorrow*, Tralee 1968

187 Holinshed, Raphael, *The First and Second Volumes of Chronicles, Comprising 1. The Description and History of England; 2. The Description and History of Ireland; 3. The Description and History of Scotland*, [London 1586]

188 Holmes, Finlay R., *Henry Cooke*, Belfast/Ottawa 1981

189 Hurst, Michael, *Maria Edgeworth and the Public Scene*, London 1969

190 Ireland, John, *How Fare the Irish People?*, Dublin 1882

191 Irish Association for the Prevention of Intemperance, *Annual Reports, 1878-1916, Nos 1-38*, Dublin 1879-1916

192 Irish Association for the Prevention of Intemperance, *Sunday Closing in Ireland: What Are the Facts?*, Dublin 1884

193 Jackson, K. H., *Celtic Miscellany*, Harmondsworth 1971

194 James, F. G., 'Irish Smuggling in the Eighteenth Century', *Irish Historical Studies*, XII, 48 (Sept. 1961), 299-317

195 Johnstone, Thomas M., *The Vintage of Memory*, Belfast 1942

196 Justamond, J. O. (ed.), *Miscellaneous Works of the Late Philip Dormer Stanhope, Earl of Chesterfield...*, 3 vols, Dublin 1777

197 Kavanagh, M. B., and Quill, A. W., *The Licensing Acts, 1872-74...*, Dublin 1875

198 Kearney, H. F., 'Father Mathew: Apostle of Modernisation' in Art Cosgrove and Donal McCartney (ed.), *Studies in Irish History*, Dublin 1979, 164-75

199 Kearney, H. F., 'Select Documents, XVI: The Irish Wine Trade, 1614-15', *Irish Historical Studies*, IX, 36 (Sept. 1955), 400-42

200 Keefe, Joan (ed.), *Irish Poems, from Cromwell to the Famine: A miscellany*, Lewisburg, Pa./London 1977

201 Kelly, Michael, 'The Catholic Temperance Movement: The Surest Way to its Success, I, II, III', *Irish Ecclesiastical Record*, 3rd ser., XII, 1 (Jan. 1891), 15-28; 2 (Feb. 1892), 158-70; 3 (Mar. 1891), 242-61

202 Kelly, Michael, 'The Suppression of Intemperance, I, II, III', *Irish Ecclesiastical Record*, 3rd ser., X, 3 (Mar. 1889), 237-45; 7 (July 1889), 623-43; 12 (Dec. 1889), 1104-19

203 Kennedy, K. A., et al., 'The Demand for Beer and Spirits in Ireland', *Proceedings of the Royal Irish Academy*, LXXIII, sect. C, 13 (1973), 669-711

204 Kerr, Donal A., *Peel, Priests and Politics*, Oxford 1982

205 Kertland, William, *The Woe of Whiskey, or The Sorrowful History of Patrick and Kathleen, an Irish Tale; 'Too True!'*, Dublin 1823

206 Killen, W. D., *Memoir of John Edgar, D.D., LL.D.*, Belfast 1867

207 [Killen, W. D. (ed.)], *Select Works of John Edgar, D.D., LL.D.*, Belfast 1868

208 Kinsella, Thomas (trans.), *The Táin*, Oxford/Dublin 1970

209 Kirkham, Graeme, 'Economic Diversification in a Marginal Economy: A Case Study' in Peter Roebuck (ed.), *Plantation to Partition*, Belfast 1981, 64-81

210 Knowler, William (ed.), *The Earl of Strafforde's Letters and Despatches* . . . , 2 vols, Dublin 1740

211 Kohl, J. G., *Travels in Ireland*, London 1844

212 Larkin, Emmet, 'The Devotional Revolution in Ireland, 1850-75', *American Historical Review*, LXXVII, 3 (June 1972), 625-52

213 Larkin, Emmet, *James Larkin, Irish Labour Leader, 1876-1947*, London 1968

214 Lawrence, Richard, *The Interest of Ireland in its Trade and Wealth Stated in Two Parts*, Dublin 1682

215 The League of the Cross, *Constitution and Rules*, London 1888

216 The League of the Cross, *For Private Circulation: The League of the Cross*, Market Weighton 1890

217 The League of the Cross, *Official Report of the Conventions of 1875 and 1876*, Manchester n.d.

218 The League of the Cross, *A Year's Work in Cork*, Cork 1886

219 Lee, Joseph, 'Money and Beer in Ireland, 1790-1875, I', *Economic History Review*, 2nd ser., XIX, 1 (1966), 183-90

220 Lender, M. E., and Martin, J. K., *Drinking in America: A History*, New York/London 1982

221 Leslie, J. B., *Ferns Clergy and Parishes*, Dublin 1936

222 Lockhart, J. G., *Memoirs of the Life of Sir Walter Scott, Bart*, VI, Edinburgh/London 1837

223 Longfield, A. K. (ed.), *The Shapland Carew Papers*, Dublin 1946

224 [Luckombe, Philip], *A Tour through Ireland wherein the Present State of the Kingdom is Considered* . . . , Dublin 1780

225 Lynch, Patrick, and Vaizey, John, *Guinness's Brewery in the Irish Economy, 1759-1876*, Cambridge 1960

226 Lyons, F. S. L., *Charles Stewart Parnell*, London 1977

227 McCaffrey, Lawrence J., *Daniel O'Connell and the Repeal Year*, Lexington, Ky. 1966

228 McClelland, V. A., *Cardinal Manning: His Public Life and Influence, 1865-92*, London 1962

229 M'Connell, James, *Presbyterianism in Belfast*, Belfast 1912

230 McCutcheon, Alan, *Wheel and Spindle: Aspects of Irish Industrial History*, Belfast 1977

231 MacDonagh, Oliver, 'The Politicisation of the Irish Catholic Bishops, 1800-50', *Historical Journal*, XVIII, 1 (1975), 37-53

232 McDowell, R. B., *The Church of Ireland, 1869-1969*, London/Boston 1975

233 MacErlean, John C. (ed.), *The Poems of David Ó Bruadair*, 3 vols, London 1910-17

234 McGuire, E. G., *Irish Whiskey: A History of Distilling in Ireland*, Dublin/New York 1973

235 McKenna, Lambert, *Life and Work of Rev. James Aloysius Cullen, S. J.*, London 1924

236 MacKnight, Thomas *Ulster As It Is, or Twenty-Eight Years' Experience as an Irish Editor*, 2 vols, London 1896

237 MacLysaght, Edward, *Irish Life in the Seventeenth Century*, 2nd ed., Cork/Oxford 1950

238 MacLysaght, Edward (ed.), *The Kenmare Manuscripts*, repr., Dublin 1970

239 [Madden, Samuel], *Reflections and Resolutions Proper for the Gentlemen of Ireland* . . . , Dublin 1738

240 Maguire, J. F., *Father Mathew: A Biography*, London 1863

241 Malcolm, Elizabeth, 'The Catholic Church and the Irish Temperance Movement, 1838-1901', *Irish Historical Studies*, XXIII, 89 (May 1982), 1-16

242 Malcolm, Elizabeth, 'The Drink Question in Ireland, 1856-1901' (Ph.D. thesis, Trinity College, Dublin, 1980)

243 Malcolm, Elizabeth, 'Popular Recreation in Nineteenth-Century Ireland' in Oliver

MacDonagh et al. (ed.), *Irish Culture and Nationalism, 1750-1950*, London/Canberra 1983, 40-55

244 Malcolm, Elizabeth, 'Temperance and Irish Nationalsim' in F.S.L. Lyons and R. A. J. Hawkins (ed.), *Ireland under the Union: Varieties of Tension: Essays in Honour of T. W. Moody*, Oxford 1980, 69-114

245 Marrus, Michael R., 'Social Drinking in the "Belle Epoque" ', *Journal of Social History*, XII, 2 (Dec. 1974), 115-41

246 Mathew, A. H., *Genealogy of the Earls of Llandaff, of Thomastown, County Tipperary, Ireland*, London n.d.

247 Mathew, Frank J., *Father Mathew: His Life and Times*, London 1890

248 Mathias, Peter, *The Brewing Industry in England, 1700-1830*, Cambridge 1959

249 Maxwell, W. H., *History of the Irish Rebellion in 1798*, London 1845

250 Megahey, A. J., 'Irish Protestant Churches and Social and Political Issues, 1870-1914' (Ph.D. thesis, Queen's University, Belfast, 1969)

251 [Methodist Church], *Minutes of the Methodist Conference in Ireland, I: 1752-1819*, Dublin 1864

252 Miller, David W., 'Presbyterianism and "Modernisation" in Ulster', *Past and Present*, 80 (1978), 67-90

253 Miller, David W., *Queen's Rebels: Ulster Loyalism in Historical Perspective*, Dublin/New York 1978.

254 Morewood, Samuel, *A Philosophical and Statistical History of . . . the Manufacture and Use of Inebriating Liquors . . .*, Dublin 1838

255 Morgan, James, *Recollections of My Life and Times: An Autobiography . . . with Selections from his Journal edited by his son*, Belfast 1874.

256 Murphy, Denis (ed.), *The Annals of Clonmacnoise*, Dublin 1896

257 Nelson, Isaac, *The Year of Delusion*, Belfast 1861

258 Newenham, Thomas, *A Statistical and Historical Inquiry into the Progress and Magnitude of the Population of Ireland*, London 1805

259 O'Brien, Eoin, *Conscience and Conflict: A Biography of Sir Dominic Corrigan, 1802-80*, Dublin 1983

260 O'Brien, George (ed.), *Advertisements for Ireland, Being a Description of the State of Ireland in the Reign of James I*, Dublin 1923

261 O'Brien, George, *The Economic History of Ireland in the Seventeenth Century*, Dublin/London 1919

262 O'Brien, George, *The Economic History of Ireland from the Union to the Famine*, London 1921

263 O'Brien, W. J. P., 'The League of the Cross', *Irish Ecclesiastical Record*, 3rd ser., X, 8 (Aug. 1889), 710-21

264 O'Connor, Frank, *Kings, Lords and Commons*, London 1961

265 O'Connor, Joyce, *The Young Drinkers: A Cross-National Study of Social and Cultural Influences*, London 1978

266 O'Day, Alan, *The English Face of Irish Nationalism*, Dublin/Toronto 1977

267 O'Donnell, F. H., *Political Priests and Irish Ruin*, London 1912

268 O'Donovan, John (ed.), *Annals of the Kingdom of Ireland, by the Four Masters*, IV, Dublin 1851

269 O'Faolain, Seán, *An Irish Journey*, London 1940

270 O'Farrell, Patrick, 'Millennialism, Messianism, and Utopianism in Irish History', *Anglo-Irish Studies*, II (1976), 45-68

271 O'Grady, Hugh, *Strafford and Irelnad: The History of his Vice-Royalty with an Account of his Trial*, 2 vols, Dublin 1923

272 Ó Murchadha, Pádraig, 'Fr Ignatius Spencer and Ireland', *Catholic Bulletin*, V, 9 (Sept. 1915), 677-88

273 Orr, J. E., *The Second Evangelical Awakening in Britain*, London/Edinburgh 1949

274 Orrery and Cork, Countess of (ed.), *The Orrery Papers*, 2 vols, London 1903

275 Ó Súilleabháin, Seán, *Irish Wake Amusements*, Cork 1967

276 O'Sullivan, T. F., *Story of the G.A.A.*, Dublin 1916

277 Ó Tuathaigh, Gearóid, 'The Folk-Hero and Tradition' in Donal McCartney (ed.), *The World of Daniel O'Connell*, Dublin 1980, 30-42

278 Oulton, Richard, *A Review of the Ulster Revival in the Year 1859*, Dublin 1859

279 Owens, J. M., et al., 'Drinking Patterns in an Irish County', *Irish Medical Journal*, LXIX, 6 (Mar. 1976), 134-9

280 Pakenham, Thomas, *The Year of Liberty: The Story of the Great Irish Rebellion of 1798*, repr., London 1972

281 Pankhurst, R. K. P., *William Thompson (1775-1833): Britain's Pioneer Socialist, Feminist and Co-operator*, London 1954

282 Pender, Séamus (ed.), *Council Books of the Corporation of Waterford, 1662-1700*, Dublin 1964

283 Petty, Sir William, *Political Survey of Ireland...*, 2nd ed., London 1719

284 Pius, Fr, *Life of Father Ignatius...(the Hon. and Rev. George Spencer)*, Dublin 1866

285 Porter, J. L., *The Life and Times of Henry Cooke, D.D., LL.D.*, 2nd ed., London 1871

286 [Presbyterian Church], *First Report of the Home and Foreign Missions of the General Assembly of the Presbyterian Church in Ireland*, Belfast 1841

287 [Presbyterian Church], *Minutes of the Proceedings of the General Assembly of the Presbyterian Church in Ireland, 1840-60*, 2 vols, Belfast 1851-61

288 Réamonn, Seán, *History of the Revenue Commissioners*, Dublin 1981

289 Reed, Sir Andrew, *Irish Constable's Guide*, 3rd ed., Dublin 1895

290 Reed, Sir Andrew, *The Liquor Licensing Laws of Ireland*, Dublin 1889

291 Rentoul, J. A., *Stray Thoughts and Memories*, Dublin 1921

292 Riach, Douglas C., 'O'Connell and Slavery' in Donal McCartney (ed.), *The World of Daniel O'Connell*, Dublin 1980, 175-85

293 Rich, Barnaby, *A New Description of Ireland...*, London 1610

294 Rogers, Patrick, *Father Theobald Mathew, Apostle of Temperance*, London 1945

295 Ronan, Myles V., *An Apostle of Catholic Dublin: Father Henry Young*, Dublin 1944

296 Rorabaugh, W. J., *The Alcoholic Republic: An American Tradition*, New York/Oxford 1979

297 Rose, R. B., 'John Finch, 1784-1857', *Transactions of the Historic Society of Lancashire and Cheshire*, CIX (1957), 159-84

298 Ross, Anne, *Everyday Life of the Pagan Celts*, London/New York 1970

299 Rothery, E. J., 'Aeneas Coffey, 1780-1852', *Chemistry and Industry* (1969), 1824-6

300 Russell, T. W., *Ireland and the Empire: A Review, 1800-1900*, London 1900

301 Russell, T. W., *A Social Experiment; or Five Years Before and After Sunday Closing in Ireland*, Dublin 1884

302 Sargent, Margaret, *Drinking and Alcoholism in Australia: A Power Relations Theory*, Melbourne 1979

303 Scheper-Hughes, Nancy, *Saints, Scholars, and Schizophrenics: Mental Illness in Rural Ireland*, Berkeley/Los Angeles/London 1979

304 Scott, A. R., 'The Ulster Revival of 1859' (Ph.D. thesis, Trinity College, Dublin, 1962)

305 Scott, Benjamin, *The Revival in Ulster*, London 1860

306 [Shackleton, Betsy], *Dialogues on Whiskey, between John Sheppard, the Millwright, and Peter Carroll, the Cooper; by a Lady*, Dublin 1832

307 Sheehan, P. A., *Luke Delmege*, London [1901]

308 Sheehy, Jeanne, *The Rediscovery of Ireland's Past: The Celtic Revival, 1830-1930*, London 1980

309 Sheil, J. B., *History of the Temperance Movement in Ireland*

310 Sherlock, Frederick (ed.), *Fifty Years Ago; or, Erin's Temperance Jubilee*, Belfast 1879

311 Shipkey, Robert, 'Problems of Alcohol Production and Controls in Early Nineteenth-Century Ireland', *Historical Journal*, XVI, 2 (1973), 291-302

312 Simms, J. G., 'The Restoration' in T. W. Moody et al. (ed.), *A New History of Ireland, III: Early Modern Ireland, 1534-1691*, Oxford 1976, 420-53

313 Simon, André L., *Bottlescrew Days: Wine Drinking in England during the Eighteenth Century*, London 1926

314 Simpson, Jonathan, *Annals of My Life, Labours, and Travels*, Belfast 1895

315 Smith, Joseph (ed.), *A Descriptive Catalogue of Friends' Books...*, 2 vols, London 1867

316 Smith, Paul, *Disraelian Conservatism and Social Reform*, London 1967

317 Stewart, David, *The Seceders in Ireland with Annals of their Congregations*, Belfast 1950

318 Stivers, Richard, *A Hair of the Dog: Irish Drinking and American Stereotype*, University Park, Pa./London 1976

319 Street, J. C., et al. (ed.), *Proceedings of the International Temperance and Prohibition Convention...*, London 1862

320 Swift, Jonathan, *The Journal to Stella, 1710-13*, ed. Frederick Ryland, London 1908

321 *Thom's Directory*, Dublin 1846

322 Thornley, David, *Isaac Butt and Home Rule*, London 1974

323 Tierney, Mark, *Croke of Cashel*, Dublin 1976

324 Tobias, J. J., *Crime and Industrial Society in the 19th Century*, London 1967
Tone, *see* Wolfe Tone

325 Treadwell, Victor, 'The Establishment of the Farm of the Irish Customs, 1603-13', *English Historical Review*, XCIII, 368 (July 1978), 580-602

326 Treadwell, Victor, 'The Irish Customs Administration in the Sixteenth Century', *Irish Historical Studies*, XX, 80 (Sept. 1977), 384-417

327 Tuke, Henry, *Temperance and Chastity Inculcated*, Dublin 1815

328 [Twiss, Richard], *A Tour in Ireland in 1775*, London 1776

329 Tyrrell, Ian R., *Sobering Up: From Temperance to Prohibition in Antebellum America, 1800-60*, Westport, Conn./London 1979

330 Unwin, E. C., *Methodism and Sobriety*, London 1943

331 Urwick, William, *The Life and Times of William Urwick, D.D., of Dublin*, London/Dublin 1871

332 [Urwick, William], *Remarks on the Evils, Occasions, and Cure of Intemperance; by W.U.*, H.T.S. Tract No. 4, Dublin 1829

333 Vaughan, J. S., 'Drunkenness v. Teetotalism', *Irish Ecclesiastical Record*, 3rd ser., X, 10 (Oct. 1889)), 865-74

334 Vaughan, W. E., and Fitzpatrick, A. J. (ed.), *Irish Historical Statistics: Population, 1821-1971*, Dublin 1978

335 Vossen, A. F. (ed.), *Two Bokes of the Histories of Ireland, Compiled by Edmunde Campion*, Assen 1963

336 Wakefield, Edward, *An Account of Ireland, Statistical and Political*, 2 vols, London 1812

337 Walker, Brian M. (ed.), *Parliamentary Election Results in Ireland, 1801-1922*, Dublin 1978

338 Walker, Brian M., 'Parliamentary Representation in Ulster, 1868-86' (Ph.D. thesis, Trinity College, Dublin, 1976)

339 Walsh, Dermot, 'Alcoholism in the Republic of Ireland', *British Journal of Psychiatry*, CXV (1969), 1021-5

340 Weir, John, *Irish Revivals: The Ulster Awakening*, London 1860

341 Wigham, H. M., *A Christian Philanthropist of Dublin: A Memoir of Richard Allen*, London 1886

342 Wilson, Anne C., *Food and Drink in Britain*, Harmondsworth 1973

343 Wilson, George B., *Alcohol and the Nation*, London 1940

344 Winskill, P T., *The Temperance Movement and its Workers*, 4 vols, London/Glasgow 1892

345 [Wolfe Tone, Theobald], *Life of Theobald Wolfe Tone...edited by his son William Theobald Wolfe Tone*, 2 vols, Washington, D.C. 1826

346 Wright, Thomas, *Account of James Gillray*, repr., New York 1968

347 Young, Arthur, *A Tour in Ireland...*, 2 vols, Dublin 1780

348 [Young, Henry], *Short Essay on the Grievous Crime of Drunkenness, in Prose and Verse, by a Roman Catholic Clergyman*, Dublin 1823

Index

The following abbreviations have been
used in the index:

C.I.T.S.   Church of Ireland Temperance Society
D.T.S.   Dublin Temperance Society
H.T.S.   Hibernian Temperance Society
I.A.P.I.   Irish Association for the Prevention of Intemperance
I.T.L.   Irish Temperance League
I.T.U.   Irish Temperance Union
M.T.S.   Markethill Temperance Society
U.T.S.   Ulster Temperance Society

Abercromby, Sir Ralph, 54
abstinence *see* teetotalism
Achill, temperance society in, 78,79
Adams, Dr Neason, 75
alehouses
    condemnation of, 211-12
    licensing of, 5, 11-12, 15-17, 206-8
Allen, Richard, 93, 94, 134, 195, 224, 282, 284
American Temperance Society, 56, 61-2, 63
anti-spirits societies, 21, 43, 148-9
    aims of, 99
    decline in, 86-7
    effects of, 329
Antrim, County
    conversions in, 164
    lectures on prohibition in, 156, 162
    temperance movement in, 153
Apostleship of Prayer, 311-12, 314
Armagh County, temperance in, 21, 79, 153
Armagh County Temperance Association, 78, 80
Armstrong, Dr John, 41-2
army, drunkenness in, 54
Athlone, temperance movement in, 152

Ballitore Temperance Society, 75
Ballina, 36
Ballycastle, temperance movement in, 152
Ballymena, teetotal lectures in, 162
Bands of Hope, 161, 162, 169, 176, 281
Barrington, Sir Jonah, 46-7
Barry, James Redmond, and the H.T.S., 77, 91
Beddoes, Dr Thomas, 48
Beecher, Rev. Lyman, and *Six sermons on intem-
    perance*, 61
beer, 5, 6, 10, 19
    compared with whiskey, 44, 72

consumption of in 18th century, 22
consumption of in 19th century, 275, 323, 324
duties on, 14-15, 27
quality of, 24-5
see also brewing industry
beer drinking, references to in Irish sagas, 1
beerhouses *see* alehouses
Beerhouses Act, 211
Begley, Anthony, 88
Belfast
    abstinence societies in, 91, 133
    anti-spirit society in, 21, 165
    as a centre of temperance movement, 57-9, 72,
    157
    enforcement of licensing laws in, 215-16
    increase in drunkenness in, 166
    spirit consumption in, 55
    and Sunday closing, 233-4, 239
Belfast Temperance Advocate, 80, 82, 161
Belfast Total Abstinence Association, 160, 168
Benson, Benjamin, 163, 177, 178, 204
Beresford, John, 24, 28
Berkeley, George, Bishop of Cloyne, 38-9
Bessbrook, public houses banned in, 175
Bible Temperance Association, 278
Bible wine, 278-80
Biggar, J.G., 244, 247, 255, 261, 270
Blacker, Rev. James, 79
Blacker, William, and the M.T.S., 79-81 *passim*
Blake, Dr Michael, 68, 69
Bodley, Sir Josias, 3-4
brandy, 8, 18, 23, 30
Bray, temperance society in, 79
Brereton, Sir William, 4, 5, 36-7
brewing industry, 22, 24-8, 84, 127, 323
Bright, John, 235

Brooch League, 316
Brooks, Maurice, 225
Bruce, H.A. (Home Secretary), 217, 219
Bruce, Sir Hervey, 223
Bruen, Henry, 223
Burns, Dr Dawson, historian of the temperance movement, 77, 85
Butt, Isaac, 238, 275
Byrne, Laurence, 221, 225

Cairns, Sir Hugh, 193-4
Callan, Philip, 223, 233, 251, 255, 258, 259
Carey, James, 197-8, 200
Carlisle, Anne Jane, 161, 162
Carlow County, temperance societies in, 78, 82, 177
Carr, Rev. G. W., 64-5, 74, 82-4, 86
Carvill, P. G. H., 255
Cashel, temperance missions in, 186-8 *passim*
Castlebar, temperance movement in, 152
Catholic Church
  campaigns against drink, 68, 69
  and Pioneer Association, 318
  and teetotalism, 89, 299-301, 303-4
  and temperance, 181-91, 296, 298
Catholic temperance societies and Irish nationalism, 294, 295-6
Catholic Times, 302
Catholic Total Abstinence Society of the Sacred Thirst and Agony and the Compassionate Heart of Mary, 310-11
Catholics
  and abstinence, 92
  support of for temperance movement, 84
Cavan County, temperance movement in, 78, 80
Chadwick, Rt. Rev. George Alexander, Dean of Armagh, 290
Chalmers, Thomas, 155
Chesterfield, Philip Stanhope, 4th Earl of, 39-41
Cheyne, Dr George, 41
Cheyne, Dr John, 65, 69, 70, 76, 86
Chichester, Rev. Edward, 37
children, temperance work among, 162, 263, 316, 318
cholera 43, 85-6
Church of Ireland
  and Bible wine issue, 279
  and temperance, 286-93
Church of Ireland Temperance Society, 280, 287-92 *passim*
Church of Ireland Total Abstinence Association, 286
clergy
  associated with U.T.S., 81
  attitude to abstinence of, 122-5, 126, 188
  attitude to Sunday closing of, 188
  drinking habits of, 20-1, 59-60
  and temperance movement, 84-5
clerical temperance association, 157-8, 159, 277

Cloncurry, Lord, 76
Coates, John, President of the I.T.L., 163
coffee houses, as centres for abstinence, 97, 178, 180
Coffey, Aeneas, 32, 36, 37
Coffey, Dr Patrick, 297-8
Coleraine, temperance movement in, 152
Connacht
  beer drinking in, 26
  branches of C.I.T.S. in, 289
  illicit spirit consumption in, 55
  teetotal missions in, 119
Connolly, Daniel, 95
Conservative Party (in Great Britain), attitude of to temperance legislation, 218, 227, 229-30, 233, 238, 269-70, 273
consumption of drink
  dangers of, 43, 71
  decline of in later 17th century, 11
  in 18th century, 22-3
  in 19th century, 203, 260, 275, 322
  reasons for changing patterns in, 325, 326-31
  see also beer; spirits; whiskey
Conyngham, Lord Francis, 237-8, 255
Cooke, Henry, 58, 60-1
Coppinger, Father, 83, 85
Cork
  brewing in, 22
  as a centre of distilling, 33
  enforcement of licensing laws in, 215
  publicans in, 213
  sale of beer banned in, 13
  spirit consumption in, 55
  and Sunday closing in, 233-4 239
  teetotalism in, 89-90, 97, 105, 109, 111, 119, 145
  temperance societies in, 78, 83, 133
  and the wine trade, 8
Cork Refreshment Rooms Company Ltd., 178-9
Cork and South of Ireland Temperance League, 178
Cork Total Abstainer, 122
Cork Total Abstinence Society, 111
Corkran, Charles, 91, 94
Corrigan, Sir DOminic, 219, 220-1, 222-3
Corry, J. P., 163, 193, 197, 227, 253, 257, 269
Cox, George, 94, 110
Crampton, Sir Philip (Surgeon-General), 74, 155
Crampton, Philip Cecil, 86
  and the D.T.S., 69, 70
  and the H.T.S., 73, 74, 76, 83
Crean, Eugene, 213
Cremorne, Lord, 198
Croke, Rt. Rev. Thomas, Archbishop of Cashel, 189, 191, 304, 305, 330
Cromwell, Henry, 14
Cullen, Father James, 306-21, 326, 330
Cullen, Rt. Rev. Paul, Archbishop of Armagh, 183-4, 222

Dalway, M. R., President of the I.T.L., 163, 202, 269
Daly, Rev. Robert, 79
Darwin, Dr Erasmus, 47-8
Davis, Thomas, of Young Ireland, 131, 328
Dease, Edmund, 231
Derry
  revival in, 165
  teetotal society in, 85, 88, 90, 153
De Vesci, Lord, 78, 79
Dickinson, Rt. Rev. H. H., Dean of the Chapel Royal and the C.I.T.S., 257, 290
Dickson, T. A., 171, 254, 257, 269
Dingle, temperance society in, 78, 79
Disraeli, Benjamin, 238, 239
distilling, 2, 21, 23-4,
  see also illicit distilling
doctors, advising against spirits, 74
Donegal, illicit distilling in, 34, 35
Donovan, Father Daniel, 104
Douglas, Gen. Sir James, 76
Dowden, Richard, 94, 109, 122, 134
Down County, temperance in, 78, 80
Downes, George, 75
Downing, McCarthy, 223
Doyle, Rt Rev. James, Bishop of Kildare, 65, 76, 84, 86, 122
Drennan, Dr William, 49
drink, consumption of, *see* consumption of drink
drinking habits
  criticism of, 38-42
  in the 18th century, 40-50
  in the 19th century, 145
drinks trade, opposed to permissive bill, 201
  drinks trade, illegal, 212-15
drunkenness
  arrests for, 165, 187, 325
  criticisms of, 11, 13, 68-9, 182, 191
  decline in, 165-6
  and economic crises, 327-8, 332
  effects of, 52-4, 66-7, 294
  figures on, in 17th century, 19
  public opinion of, 214
  on Sundays after 1878, 258-9
Dublin
  anti-spirits society in, 21, 94
  as a centre for brewing, 22, 25, 127
  C.I.T.S. in, 292
  enforcement of licensing laws in, 216
  spirit consumption in, 50-1, 55, 72
  and Sunday closing, 233-4, 239-40
  temperance societies in, 65, 67, 69, 83, 119, 133, 176, *see also* Dublin Temperance Society
  and the wine trade, 8
Dublin Evening Mail, 132
Dublin Evening Post, 111, 113, 124
Dublin Juvenile Temperance Society, 90, 91, 97
Dublin Licensed Grocers' and Vintners' Protection Society, 254

Dublin Metropolitan Police, enforcement of licensing laws by, 215-17
Dublin Temperance Society, 69, 71-3
Dublin Temperance Tract and Visiting Association, 176
Dublin Total Abstinence Society, 94, 133, 176, 190
Dublin Weekly Herald, 117, 118
Dunscombe, Rev. Nicholas, 90, 94, 109, 110
Dwyer, Michael, of Licensed Grocers' and Vintners' Association, 202, 208, 210, 220, 233, 237-8, 250

Eger, Father, 83, 85
Edgar, Dr John
  against abstinence, 72-4, 82, 91
  on Belfast Assembly's temperance committee, 158
  gives evidence to committee on drunkenness, 34
  leader of the temperance cause, 57-60, 62, 63, 86, 154, 161
  on revivalism, 167
  and the U.T.S., 81-2
Edgeworth, Maria, 47-9
Edgeworth, Richard, 47, 58
Enniscorthy, temperance campaign in, 185, 308-10 *passim*
Enniskillen, temperance movement in, 153
evangelicalism
  attacked by Catholics, 164
  and temperance, 56, 71, 79, 87, 154, 286
Ewart, W. M., 253, 257
  excise duty, 13-15, 32
excisemen, 35-7

Falkiner, E. R., 213-14
Farnham, Lord, 78-81 *passim*, 87
Fenians, 193
  teetotallers among, 330
Fermanagh County, temperance movement in, 36, 78
Finch, John, 77, 88, 89
Foley, J. H., 178
Foran, Rt Rev. Nicholas, Bishop of Waterford, 116, 117, 122
Forbes, Sir John, 152-3
Forster, W. W., 257
Fortescue, Chichester, 200, 201, 259
Freeman's Journal
  on beerhouses, 211
  on Father Mathew, 121, 305
  on licensing, 219
  on Sunday closing, 220, 222, 225, 232, 237, 246
Furlong, Rt Rev. Thomas, Bishop of Ferns, 306, 309, 310, 330

Gaelic Athletic Association, 319, 331
  bans alcohol from meetings, 327
Gaelic League, 314, 319
Galway, 17
  teetotal society in, 85, 89, 90, 119, 123, 152, 177
  and the wine trade, 8
Garrett, Rev. Dr John, 195, 196-7
Gayer, A.E., 77, 83
General Election, 1868, results of in Ireland, 202
General Election, 1874
  significance of result to temperance movement,
  225-8
General Election, 1880
  results of in Ireland, 255-6
  and temperance movement, 252-4
gentry
  criticism of, 39, 40
  decline in heavy drinking by, 48-9
  drinking by, at feasts, 10, 29
  temperance movement aimed at, 76-7
Geoghegan, Father Michael, 300-1
Getty, S. G., 194
Gibbs, George, 94, 110
Gibson, Rev. William, 165, 166
gin, 23
Gladstone, William Ewart
  on Sunday closing legislation, 232, 236
  and temperance, 266
Glandore, temperance in, 77
Glendalough, C.I.T.S. branch in, 292
Good Templars, 226, 278
Gosford, Earl of, 78, 79, 80
Gough, J. B., 177-8
Grant, Rev. John, 79, 94
Grattan, Henry, 26-7
Gray, Sir John, 197, 198, 221
Greer, Thomas, 253
Grocers' Assistants' Association, 200
Guinness, Arthur, 26, 202, 225, 234, 250
Guinness, Benjamin Lee, 194-5, 197
Guinness's Brewery, 323

Hanna, Hugh, 164-8 *passim*
Harkness, I.N., 159, 160
Harrington, Timothy, 261, 270
Hartington,, Lord, 219, 222
Harvey, Dr Joshua
  and teetotalism, 70-1
  and the temperance movement, 65-6, 67, 69,
  72, 75, 86
Haughton, James, 92, 177, 190, 191, 203, 283,
  284
  appeals to clergy for support, 125
  and Dublin Juvenile Society, 94, 128
  and Father Mathew, 134, 135, 140-1, 149
  and the I.T.L., 168, 194-5
  promotes alternative recreations, 179, 326
Haughton, Samuel, son of J. H., 286
Hay, James, Earl of Carlisle, 7, 11, 12

Healy, Maurice, 207-8, 258, 264
Healy, Tim, 261
Henry, Dr William, 42-4
Herberton, Lord, 78
Hibernian Temperance Society, 73-7 *passim*
Hicks Beach, Sir Michael, 229, 231, 235, 238,
  239, 240, 242
Hincks, Thomas, 63
Hockings, John, 90-3
Home Rule Party
  and Sunday Closing Bills, 233, 236-7, 247, 251,
  273
  and temperance, 256, 261-5, 271
Houston, Thomas, 63, 168
Hunter, Hugh, 63

illicit distilling, 24, 31, 33-4, 37-8, 55, 98-9
  decline in, 325
  fines imposed for, 35, 37
Inishowen, illicit distilling in, 34
Ireland, Rt Rev. John, Bishop of St John,
  Minnesota, 295-6
Irish Association for the Prevention of
  Intemperance
  financial problems of, 252
  formation of, 251
  in local politics, 267-8
  organises poll on Sunday closing, 257-8
  and Saturday night drinking, 270
Irish Messenger of the Sacred Heart, 312, 318
Irish MPs, voting statistics of in Sunday closing
  bills, 229, 236, 240
Irish Permissive Bill Association, 177, 203, 216,
  218-19
Irish Sunday Closing Association, 182-3, 196,
  217, 241
  formation of, 177, 195
  and 1874 bill, 230-1, 233-4, 246
  national conference of, 224
Irish Sunday Closing Bill, 1872, 220
Irish Sunday Closing Bill, 1873, 223
Irish Sunday Closing Bill, 1876/77, 238-42
  obstruction of, 243-5
  becomes law, 249
Irish Sunday Closing Bill, 1893, 272-3
Irish Temperance League, 152, 163, 168-71, 180
  canvasses in 1874 election, 226-7
  canvasses in 1880 election, 252-5, 256
  canvasses in 1885 election, 267
  financial problems of, 252, 267
  sets up branch in Dublin, 171, 175-6
  and Sunday closing, 192-7, 202, 230, 233, 237,
  250
Irish Temperance and Literary Gazette, 82, 83, 87, 92,
  93, 113
Irish Temperance Star, 176
Irish Temperance Union, 93-4, 97, 98
Irish Times, 199

Jesuits, 308
Johnston, William, 157, 158, 159, 163, 202, 269, 270 290
Jones, William, 289

Kavanagh, Thomas, 78
Kelly, Father Michael, 181-2, 190, 191, 303-4
Kenmare, temperance in, 152
Kenyon, Father John, 85, 87, 124
Kerry County, teetotal mission in, 177
Kertland, William, 67-8
Kildare County, temperance societies in, 50, 78, 95, 292
Kilkenny County, 104, 131, 177
temperance societies in, 78
Killarney, 291
temperance movement in, 152
King's County, temperance societies in, 78, 82
Kingstown, Rev. Thomas, 79
Kirkpatrick, W. B., 157, 159
Knight, H. C., 193, 197
Knox, Robert, 160
Knox, Stuart, 223

Ladies Metropolitan Temperance Union, 176
Lake, Col. Henry, 217, 222, 231, 234, 239
Larne, temperance movement in, 152, 153, 165
La Touche, David, 26, 27, 51, 79
Lawrence, Col. Richard, 18-19
Lawson, Sir Wilfrid, 246, 257
permissive bill of, 169, 217
and Sunday closing bill, 239, 241
Lea, Sir Thomas, 269, 270
League of the Cross *see* St Patrick's League of the Cross
Leahy, Rt Rev. Patrick, Archbishop of Cashel, 185, 186-7, 188-9, 224, 330
Lees, Dr F. R., 170, 171
Le Hunte, Sir Francis, 78
Leighton, Sir Ellis, 5
Leinster
C.I.T.S. branches in, 289
drinking patterns in, 22, 26
Leitrim, County, 36
Lewis, Charles, 226, 232, 235, 247
Lewis, Thomas Frankland, 56-7
Liberal Party (of Great Britain)
attitude to temperance legislation of, 203, 218, 227-8, 233, 237, 266, 268, 272-3
licences, beer, 27, 211-12
licences, public-house *see* alehouses, licensing of
licences, spirit grocer *see* spirit grocers, licensing of
Licensed Grocers' and Vintners' Association, 197, 201, 208, 219-20
licensing laws, 12-13, 16, 206-12, 222
attacked by Russell, 174-5, 177
enforcement of, 213-17

licensing monopolies, 11-12, 14
licensing reform, 15, 27, 127, 202-3
Limavady, temperance movement in, 153, 165
Limerick, 85
enforcement of licensing laws in, 215
and Sunday closing, 233-4, 239
teetotalism in, 89, 115-16, 145
temperance movement in, 83, 85, 152
wine trade in, 8
Lisburn, 60
local government
controls on drink in 17th century, 17
Lockhart, J. G., 34-5
Logue, Daniel, 36
Londonderry County, temperance work in, 162
Lowther, James, 243, 245, 248, 249
Lucas, Frederick, 137-8

McCabe, Rt Rev. Edward, Archbishop of Dublin, 184-5
McClure, Thomas, 226, 227
McCraith, Aindrias, *Small beer*, 25
MacHale, Rt Rev. John, Archbishop of Tuam, 89, 135-7
Mackay, John, 71
McKenna, James, 90, 92, 110, 111, 125
McKenna, Sir Joseph, 244
Madden, D. H., 270
Madden, Rev. Samuel, 39
Maguire, J. F., biographer of Father Mathew, 101-50 *passim*, 178, 189, 199
Mahaffy, Gilbert, 290
Maine Law *see* prohibition
Mandeville, Lord, 78, 79
Manning, Henry, 294, 296, 297, 302-3, 330
Marchant, Charles, 75
Markethill Temperance Society, 79, 80
Martin, William, 89, 94, 109, 110, 122, 134
Maryborough, 21
Mathew, Father Theobald, 48, 79, 91-4 *passim*, 101-50, 326
centenary celebrations for, 299, 301, 305, 306
erection of statue to, 178, 305
and the sick, 155
Matthews, Major George, 54
Mayne, A. S., 161-2, 163
Maynooth, temperance procession at, 95
Meath County
and Sunday closing, 243
teetotal mission in, 177
Mechanics' Temperance Association, 75
Meldon, Charles, 240, 257
Methodist church
and abstinence, 280-1
Moore, S. J., 157, 160
Morgan, James, 55-60, 643, 168
Morpeth, George Howard, Lord, 127
Morton, Samuel, 89
Moryson, Fynes, 3, 6, 10-11, 49

Mowatt, J. A., 173, 174, 200
Munster
  beer drinking in, 26
  C.I.T.S. branches in, 289
  suppression of alehouses in, 17
Murphy, Rt Rev. John, Bishop of Cork, 122, 142
  Murray, Rt Rev. Daniel, Archbishop of Dublin, 104, 122, 123
museums as an alternative recreation, 179, 326
music as an alternative recreation, 96, 326

Nass, 21
National Total Abstinence Association, 95-6
nationalism *see under* teetotalism; temperance movement
Neilson, Samuel, 53
Nelson, Rev. Isaac, 166
New Ross
  anti-spirits society in, 21
  mission in, in 1854, 308
New Ross Temperance Society, 64-5
Newenham, W. H. W., 77, 109
Newman, J. H., 297
Newry, temperance movement in, 153

O'Brien, Lucius, 26, 31, 51
O'Brien, Patrick, 223, 246
O'Brien, Father Walter, 300
O'Brien, William, 261, 262
Ó Bruadair, Dáibhí, 5, 9-10
O'Carroll, Father, 188
O'Connell, Daniel
  connections with drink industry, 127
  support for teetotalism, 130-1
  and the temperance movement, 128-9
O'Connor, Arthur, 266
O'Connor, T. P., 263
O'Connor Power, John, 244, 246
O'Conor Don, The, 242-3, 244
O'Donel, Sir Richard, 78, 79, 87
O'Donnell, F. H., 298
O'Ferrall, J. L., 214
O'Gorman, Major Purcell, 233, 238
  and Sunday closing, 245, 248
Oliver, R. D., 76
Orange Order, 60
  and temperance societies, 79-80
Ó Rathaille, Aodhágan, 9
O'Reilly, Myles, 199, 209
  introduces Sunday closing bill, 197-201 *passim*
Ormond, James, Duke of, 15-16
Orrery, John Boyle, Earl of, 39
O'Sullivan, Michael, 85
O'Sullivan, W. H., 233, 266
  and Sunday closing, 245, 248
Oulton, Rev. Richard, 165-6
Oxmantown, Lord, 78

parks as an alternative recreation, 179, 326
Parnell, C. S.
  and Sunday closing, 239, 243, 244
  and temperance legislation, 263-5, 271-2, 273
Parsonstown Temperance Society, 85
Patton, Dr, 79
Pearse, Patrick, 320
Pelham, Sir William, 7
Penney, Rev. Joseph, 61-2
permissive bill, 194, 197, 203
Petty, Sir William, 11
Pim, Jonathan, 198, 200, 202, 219, 224, 225
Pim, Thomas jnr., 251, 285
Pioneer Total Abstinence Association of the Sacred Heart, 306, 316-18, 320, 331
Pious Society for the Conversion of Poor Sinners Given to Drinking, 186-7
Plunkett, Oliver, 20
police, and enforcement of licensing laws, 213-16
Pope, Dr James, 75
Portrush, mission work in, 155
poteen, attraction of, 34
Presbyterian church
  and abstinence, 276-7
  in Belfast, 59
  and Bible wine, 278-80
  missions of, 154, 161
  and the temperance movement, 154, 157, 160, 164
prohibition, 156, 159, 169, 174, 175
Protestants, 330
  decline in support of for anti-drink movement, 132-3
  and the temperance movement, 86-7, 136
publicans, 207-9, 325-6
  and the Catholic Church, 298
  and the nationalist movement, 262, 265
  and Sunday closing, 234-5, 250
Purgatorian Society of St John, 68
Pyper, John, 204, 254
  and the I.T.L., 170-1, 202, 250, 279

Quakers
  importance of in temperance movement, 65, 66-7, 75, 281-6
  and the I.T.U., 94
  promote alternative recreations, 179
  support abolition of slavery, 72, 134
  and teetotalism, 98
Queen's County, temperance societies in, 78, 82

Ralph, Michael, 209, 211
rebellion of 1798, 52-3, 54, 95, 319
Redmond, John, 261, 273
Reed, Sir Andrew, 214
Religious Tract Society, 59
Rentoul, J. L., 168
Repeal Association, 125-9 *passim*, 131
Revenue Act, 1863, 211

Revenue Commissioners, 15, 23, 24, 35, 36, 167
revenue officers *see* excisemen
Rich, Barnaby, 6
Richardson, J. G., 282, 285
Richardson, J. N., son of J. G. R. 255, 257, 266
    and I.T.L., 282
    introduces Sunday closing bill, 258, 260
Robinson, Rev. Archibald, 165
Roper, Sir Thomas, 5
rum, 23
rural Irish, drinking habits of, 10-11, 49-50, 326, 333-4
Russell, T. W., 171-7, 258
    and the I.A.P.I., 252, 267-8
    on licensing laws, 213, 224
    and Sunday closing, 183, 195, 250, 274
    and the temperance movement, 204, 305

Sabbath observance, 157-8, 185
St George's District Temperance Association, 75
St Kevin's District Temperance Association, 75
St Patrick's League of the Cross, 294, 296, 302-3, 304
St Peter's District Temperance Association, 75
Saturday-night closing, 183-4, 270, 271
Scott, Benjamin, 165
Scott, William M., 163
Sedwards, Jeffrey, 78
Seeds, Robert, 253-4
Sexton, Thomas, 270
Shaw, Frederick, 74
Sheehan, Canon P. A., *Luke Delmege*, 300
Sheil, J. B., historian of the temperance movement, 85, 86
Shuldam, W. L., 77, 109
Simpson, Jonathan, 154-7, 163-4
Sinclair, Thomas, 157, 158
Sinn Féin, 319
Sirr, Henry Charles, 74
Skibbereen Temperance Society, 77-8, 83, 152
Slattery, Rt Rev. Michael, Archbishop of Cashel, 124 142-3
slavery, abolition of, 134-5, 162-3, 283
Sligo
    revenue police in, 36
    temperance society in, 78
Smith, John, teetotal lecturer, 94-5
smuggling, 30-1
Smyth, Richard, 228-9, 231, 233, 235, 238-9, 241, 242
Society of Friends *see* Quakers
Spencer, John, 5th Earl of, 259, 260, 289-90
spirit grocers, licensing of, 52, 209-11, 220
Spirit Grocers' Association, 201
spirits
    consumption of, 22-3, 85, 98-9, 166-7, 275, 322-5
    duty on, 14-15, 23, 27, 32, 33, 166
    evasion of duty on, 31

medicinal qualities of, 2, 4, 41-2
Spratt, Dr John
    and Father Mathew, 136
    and Sunday closing, 182, 195
    supports total abstinence, 189-90
    temperance work of, 84-5, 87, 122, 124, 133, 176-7
Strabane
    as a centre for distilling, 21
    teetotal society in, 85, 88-9
Sullivan, A. M., 240, 241, 255
Sunday closing, 157, 158, 169, 183-90
    campaigns for legislation, 192-202, 217-51, 257-60, 270-3
    see also Irish Sunday Closing Bills
Sunday Closing Association, 193, 195
    see also Irish Sunday Closing Association
Sweetman, John, 53
Synod of Ardpatrick, 1678, 20

Talbot, Capt. George, Commissioner of D.M.P., 210, 213, 215
teetotal pledges, 137, 310, 313
teetotalism
    arguments for, 98
    beginnings of, 87-8
    criticisms of, 89
    effects of, 329-30, 331-2
    growth of, 90-1, 93
    and nationalism, 95, 96-7, 131, 295-6, 319-21
    and religion, 88-9, 148, 296, 297-304, 312
temperance hotels, 178-9
temperance medals, 91, 96, 111, 125-6
    sale of, 138
temperance meetings, riots at, 251-2
temperance movement
    influenced by England, 88, 90, 99, 151, 294
    and nationalism, 128, 129, 130, 132
    sectarian aspect of, 150
temperance processions, 95-7
temperance societies, 56-7, 63
    beginnings of, 85
    finances of, 252
    see also under names of individual societies
Temperance Visitor, 289, 290, 291
Thompson, William, 88
Tighe, William, 78
Tipperary County, 131, 187
    temperance society in, 82, 85
Tobias, Matthew, 63
Tone, Theobald Wolfe, 53-4
Total Abstinence League of the Sacred Heart, 313-14, 315
Townsend, Henry, 77
Trevelyan, G. O., 258, 259, 260
Tuke, Henry, 66
Twiss, Richard, 45
Tynan, Dr P. J., 183, 184
Tyrone County, temperance societies in, 80-1

Ulster
  C.I.T.S. branches in, 289
  1874 election results in, 227
  revival in, 160-8
  support of its MPs for temperance legislation, 230
  teetotal missions in, 119
  teetotalism among Protestants in, 330-1
  temperance societies in, 76-81 *passim*, 85, 152-3
  whiskey popular in, 22
Ulster Temperance Society, 8
  formation of, 63
  support for, 81-3 *passim*
Ulster Tract Society, 161
United Irishmen, 52-3
United Kingdom Alliance, 159, 169, 170, 192, 294
Urwick, Dr William, 79, 168, 195
  and the D.T.S., 69, 71
  and Father Mathew, 133

Vaughan, Father John, 299
Ventry, Lord, 78, 79, 87
vintners
  canvass in 1874 election, 224-5
  canvass in 1880 election, 254-5
  and Sunday closing, 220-2, 231, 233, 237

Wakefield, Edward, 49
wakes, drinking at, 21, 60-1
Walsh, Rt Rev. William, Archbishop of Dublin, 301-6 *passim*
Warren, Rt Rev. Michael, Bishop of Ferns, 310, 311
Waterford
  enforcement of licensing laws in, 215
  and Sunday closing, 233-4, 239
  teetotalism in, 145
  temperance movement in, 83, 116-17
  and wine trade, 8, 17
Waterford Chronicle, 114, 117
Watts, Dr Robert, 278
Webb, Alfred, son of R. D. W., 283-4, 285
Webb, R. D., 66, 224, 284

and abolition of slavery, 134, 283
and D.T.S., 69, 70, 75
and I.T.U., 94
Wentworth, Sir Thomas, Earl of Strafford, 12-13
Westport
  teetotalism in, 89
  temperance work in, 78, 152
Wexford County, 131, 308
  temperance societies in, 78, 82, 92
whiskey
  compared with beer, 44, 72
  consumption of, 23, 26, 50-2, 55, 143-5
  dangers of, 2-3, 26
  first reference to consumption of in Irish annals, 2
  legislative controls on, 2
  medicinal properties of, 4, 5
  production of, 23-4
White, R. G., 89
Wicklow County, temperance missions in, 69
Wigham, Henry, 258
  and I.A.P.I., 251, 282-3
  and Sunday closing, 182, 183, 195, 224
wine, 6-7, 8
  condemned in the Bible, 73
  consumption of, 29
  drunk by urban middle class, 10
  duties on, 14-15, 28
  smuggling of, 30-1
wine trade, 7-8, 11, 22
  disrupted by wars, 8, 28, 29
women, role of in temperance movement, 176, 286
working class
  aims to reform drinking habits of, 75, 78
  and Sunday closing, 234
  support for abstinence among, 92, 93, 95
Workman, Robert, 81

Yore, Dr, 69, 122
Youghal, teetotal meetings in, 92, 93
Young, Arthur, 46
Young, Father Henry, 68-9, 85
Young Ireland, 131, 147, 330